D0857381

CCVP Self-Study
Cisco QOS
Exam Certification Guide,
Second Edition

Wendell Odom, CCIE No. 1624
Michael J. Cavanaugh, CCIE No. 4516

Cisco Press

800 East 96th Street
Indianapolis, IN 46240 USA

Cisco QOS Exam Certification Guide,
Second Edition

Wendell Odom, Michael J. Cavanaugh

Copyright© 2005 Cisco Systems, Inc.

Published by:
Cisco Press
800 East 96th Street
Indianapolis, IN 46240 USA

Printed in the United States of America   8 9 0

Eighth Printing September 2007

Library of Congress Cataloging-in-Publication Number: 2004103871

ISBN: 1-58720-124-0

Warning and Disclaimer

This book is designed to provide information about the Cisco QOS exam #642-642. Every effort has been made to make this book as complete and as accurate as possible, but no warranty or fitness is implied.

The information is provided on an "as is" basis. The authors, Cisco Press, and Cisco Systems, Inc. shall have neither liability nor responsibility to any person or entity with respect to any loss or damages arising from the information contained in this book or from the use of the discs or programs that may accompany it.

The opinions expressed in this book belong to the author and are not necessarily those of Cisco Systems, Inc.

Trademark Acknowledgments

All terms mentioned in this book that are known to be trademarks or service marks have been appropriately capitalized. Cisco Press or Cisco Systems, Inc. cannot attest to the accuracy of this information. Use of a term in this book should not be regarded as affecting the validity of any trademark or service mark.

Corporate and Government Sales

Cisco Press offers excellent discounts on this book when ordered in quantity for bulk purchases or special sales. For more information, please contact: **U.S. Corporate and Government Sales**   1-800-382-3419   corpsales@pearsontechgroup.com

For sales outside of the U.S. please contact: **International Sales**   international@pearsoned.com

Feedback Information

At Cisco Press, our goal is to create in-depth technical books of the highest quality and value. Each book is crafted with care and precision, undergoing rigorous development that involves the unique expertise of members from the professional technical community.

Readers' feedback is a natural continuation of this process. If you have any comments regarding how we could improve the quality of this book, or otherwise alter it to better suit your needs, you can contact us through email at feedback@ciscopress.com. Please make sure to include the book title and ISBN in your message.

We greatly appreciate your assistance.

Publisher: John Wait

Editor-in-Chief: John Kane

Executive Editor: Brett Bartow

Production Manager: Patrick Kanouse

Senior Development Editor: Christopher Cleveland

Project Editor: Sheila Schroeder

Copy Editor: Bill McManus

Editorial Assistant: Tammi Barnett

Cisco Representative: Anthony Wolfenden

Cisco Press Program Manager: Nannette M. Noble

Technical Editors: Paul Negron, Drew Rosen

Cover and Interior Designer: Louisa Adair

Compositor: Mark Shirar

Indexer: Tim Wright

CISCO SYSTEMS

Corporate Headquarters	European Headquarters	Americas Headquarters	Asia Pacific Headquarters
Cisco Systems, Inc.	Cisco Systems International BV	Cisco Systems, Inc.	Cisco Systems, Inc.
170 West Tasman Drive	Haarlerbergpark	170 West Tasman Drive	Capital Tower
San Jose, CA 95134-1706	Haarlerbergweg 13-19	San Jose, CA 95134-1706	168 Robinson Road
USA	1101 CH Amsterdam	USA	#22-01 to #29-01
www.cisco.com	The Netherlands	www.cisco.com	Singapore 068912
Tel: 408 526-4000	www-europe.cisco.com	Tel: 408 526-7660	www.cisco.com
800 553-NETS (6387)	Tel: 31 0 20 357 1000	Fax: 408 527-0883	Tel: +65 6317 7777
Fax: 408 526-4100	Fax: 31 0 20 357 1100		Fax: +65 6317 7799

Cisco Systems has more than 200 offices in the following countries and regions. Addresses, phone numbers, and fax numbers are listed on the
Cisco.com Web site at www.cisco.com/go/offices.

Argentina • Australia • Austria • Belgium • Brazil • Bulgaria • Canada • Chile • China PRC • Colombia • Costa Rica • Croatia • Czech Republic
Denmark • Dubai, UAE • Finland • France • Germany • Greece • Hong Kong SAR • Hungary • India • Indonesia • Ireland • Israel • Italy
Japan • Korea • Luxembourg • Malaysia • Mexico • The Netherlands • New Zealand • Norway • Peru • Philippines • Poland • Portugal
Puerto Rico • Romania • Russia • Saudi Arabia • Scotland • Singapore • Slovakia • Slovenia • South Africa • Spain • Sweden
Switzerland • Taiwan • Thailand • Turkey • Ukraine • United Kingdom • United States • Venezuela • Vietnam • Zimbabwe

About the Authors

Wendell Odom, certified Cisco Systems instructor No. 1624, is a senior instructor with Skyline Advanced Technology Services, where he teaches the QOS, CCIE, and SAN courses. Wendell has worked in the networking arena for 20 years, with jobs in pre- and post-sales technical consulting, teaching, and course development. He has authored several books with Cisco Press, including *Cisco ICND Exam Certification Guide, Cisco INTRO Exam Certification Guide,* and *Computer Networking First-Step,* and he coauthored the first edition of this book.

Michael J. Cavanaugh, certified Cisco Systems instructor No. 4516, has been in the networking industry for more than 18 years. His employment with such companies as General Electric, Cisco Systems, Inc., and Bell South Communications Systems has allowed him to stay at the forefront of technology and hold leading-edge certifications. His current focus is on AVVID implementations, providing convergence consulting, professional services, and technical support. Michael's passion is learning the practical applications of new technologies and sharing knowledge with fellow engineers.

About the Technical Reviewers

Paul Negron, **CCSI No. 22752**, **CCIP**, has been a senior instructor for Skyline Computer Corporation for the past four years. He currently instructs all the CCIP level courses to include Advanced BGP, MPLS, and the QOS course. Paul has six years experience with Satellite Communications as well as six years with Cisco platforms.

Drew Rosen, **CCIE No. 4365**, **CCSI No. 22045**, is a product marketing manager in the Cisco Internet Learning Solutions Group and has been with Cisco for eight years. In his present role, Drew manages a team of technical consultants focusing on educational products in the advanced technology areas of security, optical, storage networking, and IP telephony and mobility. Previously, Drew spent four years as a systems engineer working on large-named accounts in the enterprise space. He was involved in the production and launch of numerous ILSG learning products including Building Scalable Cisco Internetworks (BSCI), Configuring BGP on Cisco Routers (BGP), Configuring Cisco Routers for IS-IS (CCRI), and Implementing Cisco QOS (IQOS). Drew was the lead developer of the new Implementing Cisco Quality of Service (QOS) v2.0 course upon which this text is based. Drew lives in Florida with his wife, Meredith, and their two children, Chelsea and Chandler.

Dedications

Wendell Odom: For Dr. Lawrence Lesser, who has dedicated his life to helping countless heart patients enjoy a much better and longer quality of life. It was the NBA's loss that he chose medicine over basketball, but like the young doctor in the movie "A Field of Dreams", who also chose medicine over professional sports, his true value has been in how he has touched the lives of so many patients – including me and my Granny. Thanks so much for making a difference for us!

Michael J. Cavanaugh: I would like to dedicate this book to my lovely wife KC and beautiful daughter Caitlin, for their patience and understanding through the years. Without their love and support, this endeavor would not be possible.

Acknowledgments

Wendell Odom: Michael J. Cavanaugh, my coauthor, worked tirelessly to finish several key components of the book. His vast practical skills have improved the book tremendously. Michael created some of the more challenging parts of the book, and under duress – Michael, thanks so much for making the difference!

Chris Cleveland, the development editor for this book did his usual wonderful job and proved he's still the best in the business. Chris's great work at juggling the schedule and keeping his eye on every detail, after we authors are tired from the long process, has helped improve this book greatly. Thanks again for the wonderful work, Chris!

Brett Bartow, executive editor for this project, managed the business end of the project with his usual steady and insightful direction. Brett helped us stay on track in spite of all the distractions this year - thanks Brett for the continued support.

Finally, the production side of the business does not get as much notice, because the author (me) who writes these acknowledgments seldom works directly with them. Over the last few years, I've gotten to see more of their work, and believe me, I really do have the easy part of the job. I deliver Word documents and Powerpoint (rough) drawings—and all production does is somehow make this wonderfully polished book appear. Thanks for making me look good again, and again, and again!

As usual, the technical editors deserve most of the credit for making the content of this book robust and complete. For this edition, Drew Rosen and Paul Negron did the technical editing. Drew's job at Cisco made him the perfect candidate to help ensure that the scope of topics in the book matched the new QoS exam. Besides that, Drew's technical expertise and attention to detail improved the quality of the book tremendously. Paul helped the book a lot as well, particularly with helping us refine how to approach some of the topics and what to emphasize. His experience teaching QoS to hundreds of students helped him interpret the text from the viewpoint of the readers. Drew and Paul, thanks much!

Ultimately, Michael and I are most responsible for the contents of the book, so any errors you find are certainly our fault. However, if you do think you found an error, the best way to get in touch to report the error is to go to ciscopress.com, click the **Contact Us** tab and fill in the form. When it's something that needs a look from the authors, the information gets to us expediently. If it's a problem that can be handled by the publisher, they can get to it even more quickly!

Finally, no section called acknowledgments could be complete without acknowledging a few others. My wife Kris, as usual, helped me keep my balance on life, especially without moving to another state during the same time as the final work on this book was completed. Thanks for being there, Kris! And most of all for my savior, Jesus Christ, thanks for ordering my steps with this project.

Michael J. Cavanaugh: I would like to thank Wendell Odom for giving me the opportunity to once again coauthor a book. It has been an exciting, challenging, and rewarding experience. I would also like to thank Chris Cleveland, Brett Bartow, all the people at Cisco Press, and the technical editors that made this book a reality.

Contents at a Glance

Contents

Icons Used in This Book

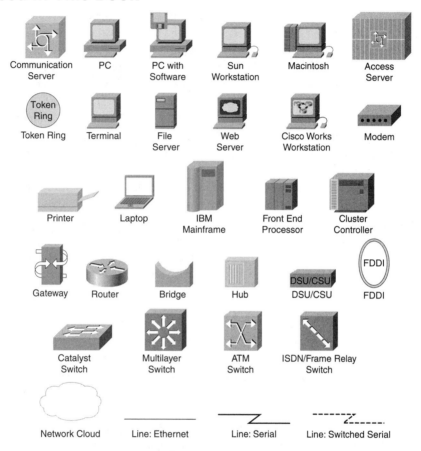

Command Syntax Conventions

The conventions used to present command syntax in this book are the same conventoins used in the IOS Command Reference. The Command Reference describes these conventions as follows:

- **Boldface** indicates commands and keywords that are entered literally as shown. In actual configuration examples and output (not general command syntax), boldface indicates commands that are manually input by the user (such as a **show** command).

- *Italics* indicate arguments for which you supply actual values.

- Vertical bars (|) separate alternative, mutually exclusive elements.

- Square brackets [ ] indicate optional elements.

- Braces { } indicate a required choice.

- Braces within brackets [{ }] indicate a required choice within an optional element.

Introduction

Computing in general, and networking in particular, must deal with the issues relating to constrained resources. For computers, operating systems must find a way to equitably distribute the CPU time and memory among the various programs running on the computer. When the need for memory exceeds the available memory, the CPU spends more time performing memory management, moving data from memory to permanent storage, typically on a hard disk. Of course, the computer might be low on CPU resources at the same time, meaning the CPU has less available time to devote to overhead tasks like memory management. With only a small load on the computer, all is well. When the load exceeds the capacity of the CPU, memory, and other resources, a lower volume of useful work is accomplished, and the users get worse response time from the computer.

The competition for bandwidth is the classic battle for resources in networking. If the offered load sent into the network exceeds the available bandwidth, the network must react by either discarding packets, or queuing them in memory waiting for the bandwidth to become available. The packets that are queued experience more delay in the network than do packets that happen to be sent when the network is not congested. When consecutive packets experience different amounts of delay, variable delay, or jitter, has occurred. So, although bandwidth might be the constrained resource for which many network attached devices compete, other side effects—delay, jitter, and loss—occur as a result.

Cisco calls the general topic of how to manipulate bandwidth, delay, jitter, and loss characteristics in a network *quality of service*, or QoS. The Cisco QOS exam 642-642 tests your knowledge of QoS features and configurations covered in the course "Implementing Cisco Quality of Service (QOS)." This book covers the topics on the QOS exam, with some additional detailed explanations beyond what you find in the QOS course. By going deeper, you can approach the exam with more confidence, while learning valuable information that will help you deploy QoS in real networks. This book also attempts to cover the same breadth of topics found in the QOS course and exam, so it will keep you focused on what's on the exam.

In years past, Cisco actually had two QoS courses, and exams based on each course. With the availability of the QOS 642-642 exam, and the course of the same name, Cisco converged the two courses into a single course.

This introduction discusses the QOS exam, including the exam topics covered, and some reasons why you might be interested in the exam.

Why Should I Take the QOS Exam?

Most people that take the QOS exam do so for one of three reasons:

- The Cisco Channel Partner Specialization Program
- The Cisco Qualified Specialist Program
- The Cisco Career Certification Program

The next few sections provide an explanation for each of these programs and how the QOS 642-642 exam relates.

The Cisco Channel Partner Specialization Program

The most popular reason for taking the QOS exam relates to the Cisco Channel Partner Specialization Program. Cisco calls their resellers and services partners Channel Partners. The way the program works is that Cisco moves more than 90 percent of its product sales, in dollar volumes, through its Channel Partners. So, Cisco is motivated to help themselves by working well with its Channel Partner community.

Cisco also focuses heavily on customer satisfaction. So, Cisco uses both a carrot and a stick to motivate Channel Partners to certify their employees with different technology specializations, which helps ensure that the Channel Partner engineers know what they are doing for the Cisco customers. For instance, to become a Gold partner, you need a certain number of points. To get the points, you need a certain number of technology specializations. To get the specializations, you need a particular mix of employees to certify in different roles—for instance, one role might be as a presales engineer, and another as a help desk customer service representative. To certify for a particular role, that employee must pass one or more certification exams, depending on the role.

Can the different Cisco Channel Partner roles, specializations, exams, and so on, become confusing? Sure. Suffice it to say that Channel Partners want to get the points needed to reach the next level of partnership with Cisco (Premier, Silver, and Gold, in order). Even if a Channel Partner does not want to make the next level of partnership with Cisco, it can use the fact that it has additional Channel Partner Technology Specializations when trying to win business.

At press time, Cisco had two active partner specializations that required the QOS exam. The two specializations are "Cisco IP Telephony Services" and "Cisco IP Communications Express." The first is related to a wide range of skills with Cisco IP Telephony, and the latter is related more specifically to Cisco CallManager Express.

In order for a company to achieve a particular specialization, it must have a specified number of individuals who have passed a set of exams. A person who has passed one of the sets of exams is considered to be able to serve in a particular *job role*. For instance, for the Cisco IP Telephony Services Specialization, one of the job roles is "Cisco IP Telephony Design Specialist." In order for a Cisco partner to qualify for this specialization, at least one employee must meet the job role. To meet the job role, that employee must have passed three exams, one of which is the QOS exam.

To see the larger picture, imagine a partner wanted to sell and service the Cisco IP Telephony products. By getting the Cisco IP Telephony Services Specialization, the Cisco partners can work more closely with Cisco and provide reassurance of their credential legitimacy to their customers.

In order to get the Specialization, a Cisco Channel Partner must meet the job role requirements in Table I-1.

Table I-1 *IP Telephony Services Specialization: Roles and Requirements*

Role	Exams/Certifications Required
Design Engineer (Data) (2 required)	CCDA* Telephony Fundamentals Exam (#9E0-400) Enterprise Voice over Data Design (#9E0-412 EVODD) Cisco IP Communications Exam (#9E0-441 CIPT) **Implementing Cisco QOS Exam (#642-642 QOS)** Cisco Unity Engineer Exam (#9E0-805 UNITY) One employee must be CCIE, and another Microsoft MCSE (Win2K and Exchange 2K)
Field Engineer (2 required)	CCNA Telephony Fundamentals Exam (#9E0-400) Cisco Voice Over Frame Relay, ATM and IP Exam (#9E0-431 CVOICE) Cisco IP Communications Exam (#9E0-441 CIPT) Cisco Unity Engineer Exam (#9E0-805 UNITY) **Implementing Cisco QOS Exam (#642-642 QOS)**
Design Engineer (Voice)	Does not require the QOS exam; other exam details not listed
Project Manager	Does not require the QOS exam; other exam details not listed
Engagement Manager	Does not require the QOS exam; other exam details not listed

* More advanced certifications can be subsituted. For instance, the person can be CCNP instead of CCDA, or CCIE instead of CCNP.

As you can see from Table I-1, a Partner must have two employees each meet the "Design Engineer (Data)" and "Field Engineer" job roles as part of meeting the requirements for the specialization. As part of meeting those job roles, the Partner would need four different employees to pass the QoS exam, as well as several others listed in the table.

Cisco also has a "Cisco IP Communications Express" Specialization, which focuses more on issues relating to the Cisco CallManager Express product. Table I-2 lists the job roles and requirements.

Table I-2 *IP Communications Express Specialization: Roles and Requirements*

Role	Exams/Certifications Required
Systems Engineer	CCDA* Meet Cisco IPT Express Specialist Requirements, which are the following: Cisco Voice Over Frame Relay, ATM and IP Exam (#9E0-431 CVOICE) **Implementing Cisco QOS Exam (#642-642 QOS)** Cisco Call Manager Express (#644-141 CME)
Field Engineer	CCNA* Meet Cisco IPT Express Specialist Requirements, which are the followinf: Cisco Voice Over Frame Relay, ATM and IP Exam (#9E0-431 CVOICE) **Implementing Cisco QOS Exam (#642-642 QOS)** Cisco Call Manager Express (#644-141 CME)
Account Manager	Does not require the QOS exam; other exam details not listed

* More advanced certifications can be subsituted. For instance, the person can be CCNP instead of CCDA, or CCIE instead of CCNP.

In short, if you work for a Channel Partner, and you design, sell, or implement IP Telephony solutions, you will most likely be asked to certify in one of the job roles listed in the table. And because several job roles for the IP Telephony Specializations require the QOS exam, the chances are you will need to pass this exam.

Cisco Focused Certification

For any networker in any networking job, it helps to have knowledge and skills. Networkers can benefit from having "proof" that they know a set of technologies. Having the right certification on your resume can help you land a job, both at another firm and inside the same company. For those networkers who work with customers and clients, having the right credentials, in the form of certifications, can help convince the salesman to convince the customer to hire your company for the consulting job.

Cisco offers a wide range of certifications, including a series of certifications in the Cisco Focused Certification program. Cisco focused certifications focus on one particular technology area, requiring multiple exams from that technology area to obtain a particular certification credential. The goal of the CQS certifications is to let people prove their knowledge and skill about a particular technology, as compared to the Cisco Career Certifications, which cover a broad range of topics.

Four different Cisco focused certifications require the QOS exam. Unsurprisingly, these four Cisco Focused Certifications all focus on IP telephony. Table I-3 lists the certifications, along with the required exams.

Table I-3   *Cisco Qualified Specialist Certifications Requiring the QoS Exam*

Role	Exams/Certifications Required
Cisco IP Telephony Design Specialist	CCDA* Enterprise Voice over Data Design (#9E0-412 EVODD) **Implementing Cisco QOS Exam (#642-642 QOS)**
Cisco IP Telephony Support Specialist	CCNP* Cisco Voice Over Frame Relay, ATM and IP Exam (#9E0-431 CVOICE) Cisco IP Communications Exam (#9E0-441 CIPT) **Implementing Cisco QOS Exam (#642-642 QOS)**
Cisco IP Telephony Operations Specialist	CCNA* **Deploying QOS in the Enterprise Exam (#9E0-601 DQOS)** Cisco IP Telephony Troubleshooting Exam (#9E0-422 IPTT)
Cisco IP Telephony Express Specialist	Cisco Voice Over Frame Relay, ATM and IP Exam (#9E0-431 CVOICE) **Implementing Cisco QOS Exam (#642-642 QOS)** Cisco Call Manager Express (#644-141 CME)

* More advanced certifications can be subsituted. For instance, the person can be CCNP instead of CCDA, or CCIE instead of CCNP.

The QOS exam is the only exam required for all four of Cisco's IP Telephony-related CQS certifications. With the requirement for the QOS exam for the technical roles in the Cisco Channel Partner IP Telephony Technology Specialization, pretty much anyone working with IP Telephony or voice over IP (VoIP) will need to take the exam, assuming that they want to be certified.

You might have noticed that the Cisco focused certifications exam requirements are very similar to the Channel Partner roles. In fact, the Cisco focused certifications requirements from Table I-3 are a subset of the requirements for a comparable Channel Partner certifications listed in Tables I-1 and I-2. Cisco has stated that, over time, the Partner Specialization job role requirements will meld with the Cisco focused certifications requirements, so that the requirements for a job role are essentially defined by a Cisco focused certifications specialization.

For more information on the Cisco Channel Partner Technology Specializations, and the Cisco Focused Certification program, refer to http://www.cisco.com/go/partner.

Cisco Certified Internetwork Professional (CCIP)

The Cisco primary certifcations fall under a program called the Cisco Career Certifications Program. That's the Cisco program that implements its most popular certifications, including Cisco Certified Network Associate (CCNA), Cisco Certified Network Professional (CCNP), and Cisco Certified Internetwork Expert (CCIE).

Over the years, Cisco has added several additional Professional level certifications. Originally, Cisco offered CCNP, which required a skill level between the basic CCNA and the advanced CCIE Routing/Switching certification. Now, Cisco offers the Cisco Certified Design Professional (CCDP), Cisco Certified Security Professional (CCSP), and Cisco Certified Internetwork Professional (CCIP) certifications.

The QOS exam is part of the CCIP certification. The exams required for the CCIP certificataion (at press time) are as follows:

- Building Scalable Cisco Internetworks (BSCI) - 642-801 BSCI
- Implementing Cisco Quality of Service (QOS) - 642-642 QOS
- Configuring BGP on Cisco Routers (BGP) - 642-661 BGP
- Implementing Cisco MPLS (MPLS) - 642-611 MPLS

So what are the main motivations to get the CCIP certification? Well, the most obvious reason is to build your resume. Also, Cisco occasionally permits you to substitute CCIP instead of CCNP as the prerequisite for some certifications. Also, the Cisco Partner Specializataions sometimes require CCIP or allow CCIP to be substituted for another certification.

The overwhelming number of people who take the QOS exam do so in order to meet a job role requirement when working for a Cisco Partner. However, individuals also benefit with a more well-rounded resume, even if no job requirements exist.

Implementing the Cisco QOS Exam 642-642

The QOS exam consists of a 90 minute exam administered at a proctored exam facility affiliated either with VUE (http://www.vue.com) or Prometric (http://www.2test.com). The exam typically includes approximately 45-55 questions. (And of course, the time and the number of questions can certainly change at a later date, so do check cisco.com for the latest information.)

Cisco lists the topics covered in the QOS exam on its website; the list is repeated here. Like many Cisco exams, the QOS exam covers the topics in the Cisco QOS course, so those of you taking the QOS course from a Cisco Learning Partner, or a Cisco sponsered organization, will get some direct help in passing the exam.

> **NOTE** The time allowed for the exam, the number of questions, and even the exam topics covered can change, without a change to the exam number. So, do check cisco.com for the latest information.

The exam topics are as follows:

IP QoS Fundamentals

- Given a description of a converged network, identify problems that could lead to poor quality of service and explain how the problems might be resolved
- Define the term Quality of Service (QoS) and identify and explain the key steps to implementing QoS on a converged network

IP QoS Components

- List and explain the models for providing Quality of Service on a network
- Explain the purpose and function of the DiffServ model
- Describe the basic format of and explain the purpose of the DSCP field in the IP header
- Define and explain the different per hop behaviors used in DSCP
- Explain the interoperability between DSCP-based and IP-precedence-based devices in a network
- Given a list of QoS actions, correctly match the QoS actions to mechanisms for implementing QoS and identify where in a network the different QoS mechanisms are commonly used

Modular QoS CLI and Auto-QoS

- Given a network requiring QoS, explain how to implement a QoS policy using MQC
- Explain how AutoQoS is used to implement QoS policy

Classification and Marking

- Explain how link layer and network layer markings are used to define service classes and the different applications represented by each of these service classes
- Given a network and a description of QoS issues, use MQC CLI commands to classify packets
- Given a network and a description of QoS issues, use class-based marking to assign packets to a specific service class
- Describe the function of Network Based Application Recognition
- Describe the purpose of pre-classification to support QoS in various VPN (IPSEC, GRE, L2TP) configurations
- Describe QoS trust boundaries and their significance in LAN based classification and marking
- Identify the different classification and marking options available on Cisco L2 and L3 switching platforms

Congestion Management Methods

- List and explain the different queuing algorithms
- Explain the components of hardware and software queuing systems on Cisco routers and how they are effected by tuning and congestion
- Describe the benefits and drawbacks of using WFQ to implement QoS
- Explain the purpose and features of Class-Based WFQ (CBWFQ)
- Explain the purpose and features of Low Latency Queuing (LLQ)
- Identify the Cisco IOS commands required to configure and monitor LLQ on a Cisco router
- Describe and explain the different queuing capabilities available on the Cisco Catalyst 2950 Switch

Congestion Avoidance Methods

- Describe the drawbacks of tail drop as a congestion control mechanism
- Describe the elements of a RED traffic profile
- Describe Weighted Random Early Detection and how it can be used to prevent congestion
- Identify the Cisco IOS commands required to configure and monitor DSCP-based CB-WRED
- Explain how ECN interacts with WRED in Cisco IOS

Traffic Policing and Shaping

- Describe the purpose of traffic conditioning using traffic policing and traffic shaping and differentiate between the features of each
- Explain how network devices measure traffic rates using single rate or dual rate, single or dual token bucket mathematical models
- Identify the Cisco IOS commands required to configure and monitor single rate and dual rate CB-Policing
- Identify the Cisco IOS commands required to configure and monitor percentage based CB-Policing
- Explain how the two rate limits, average rate and peak rate, can be used to rate limit traffic
- Identify the Cisco IOS commands required to configure and monitor CB-Shaping
- Identify the Cisco IOS commands required to configure and monitor Frame Relay adaptive CB-Shaping on Frame Relay interfaces

Link Efficiency Mechanisms

- Explain the various link efficiency mechanisms and their function
- Identify the Cisco IOS commands required to configure and monitor CB header compression
- Given a list of link speeds and a specific delay requirement, determine the proper fragment size to use at each link speed and identify the typical delay requirement for VoIP packets
- Identify the Cisco IOS commands required to configure and monitor Multilink PPP with Interleaving
- Identify the Cisco IOS commands required to configure and monitor FRF.12

QoS Best Practices

- Explain the QoS requirements of the different application types
- List typical enterprise traffic classes then identify the delay, jitter, packet loss and bandwidth requirements of each traffic class
- Explain the best practice QoS implementations and configurations within the campus LAN
- Explain the best practice QoS implementations and configurations on the WAN customer edge (CE) and provider edge (PE) routers

NOTE The list of objectives was taken from the Cisco website at http://www.cisco.com/warp/public/10/wwtraining/certprog/testing/current_exams/642-642.html.

Interpreting the QOS Exam Topics

The exam topics, like most exam topics listed by Cisco for other exams, use action words that follow a quasistandard called "Bloom's Taxonomy of the Cognitive Domain." Bloom's taxonomy defines a standard for word usage for when educators create objectives for courses. Objectives written according to Bloom's Taxonomy define what the learner should be able to accomplish after taking the class.

So, when you look at an exam topic, look for the action word. If you want to see a description of Bloom's Taxonomy, search the Internet, and you will find a lot of matches. My favorite quick list of terms is at http://chiron.valdosta.edu/whuitt/col/cogsys/bloom.html. The action word in the exam topic gives you a good hint about the level of knowledge and skill you need to have before taking the exam. For instance, a course objective that uses the word "list" as the action word means that you should be able to list the features, but an action word such as "configure" means you should know all the related configuration commands, and how to use them. "Troubleshoot" might mean that you need to know what all the **show** and **debug** commands do for a particular topic.

For a specific example, under the section about Traffic Policing and Shaping, the last exam topic says "Identify the Cisco IOS commands required to configure and monitor Frame Relay adaptive CB-Shaping on Frame Relay interfaces." So, you had better know the configuration for adaptive CB-Shaping, and not just the concepts.

What does Bloom's Taxonomy mean in terms of how you study for the exam? It means that you should focus on the action words in the exam topics, and make sure you can do those things for the stated topics. In a perfect world, the exam questions would also follow the same convention. However, some questions will slip through. However, when you are trying to determine your strategy for studying, and you are choosing the topics to focus on, or the basic topics, you should definitely interpret the meaning of the exam topics.

In addition, Cisco states that the posted exam topics for all its certification exams are guidelines. Cisco makes the effort to store their questions in an exam databases within the confines of the stated exam objectives, but doing this for every question and every exam is difficult. Thus, you could see questions that both fall outside the scope, and the depth, implied by the exam topics. However, if you follow the Cisco exam topic "guidelines," you should have a good understanding of the breadth and depth of topics on the exam.

About the QOS 642-642 Exam Certification Guide

This section provides a brief insight into the contents of the book and the major goals, as well as some of the book features that you will encounter when using this book.

Goals of This Book

Unquestionably, the primary goal for this book is to help you pass the QOS certification exam. However, the means by which that goal is accomplished follows the Cisco Press Exam Certification Guide philosophy, which makes a statement about helping a reader pass the test through a deeper understanding of the material, as opposed to simply helping the reader memorize the answers to multiple-choice questions.

To accomplish this goal, the book's main chapters cover all the topics on the QOS exam, plus an occasional mention of topics outside the scope of the exam just to make a key point. The depth of the conceptual coverage exceeds the depth of coverage in the QOS course. By doing so, you should be able to pass the exam with greater confidence.

A secondary goal for this book is to help you prepare for the CCIE Routing/Switching and CCIE Voice exams. Although this goal wasn't actually intended when we wrote the first edition of this book, it turns out that a lot of people found the book useful for CCIE preparation as well. However, this second edition actually covers a narrower range of topics. Because CCIE covers a broad range of QoS topics, we kept some materials from earlier editions of the book and placed them in appendixes on the CD-ROM so that people working toward CCIE can still have the materials available.

The third goal is not so obvious. While written to help you pass the exams, it is our hope that this book will also be useful to anyone who needs to deploy QoS tools using Cisco gear. We hope that if you take the exam, you will keep this book as a desk reference, and for those of you who don't take the exam, we hope you find this book a useful tool for delving into the details and really understanding QoS.

After teaching the DQOS course for the last couple of years, and after hearing students continually ask where they could read more on QoS topics, it became apparent that there were few good options available. This book fills that gap and provides a comprehensive reference for Cisco QoS.

Book Organization

This book contains 10 core chapters with titles that are comparable to the major headings listed in the QOS exam topics. For QOS exam candidates, you can simply dive into Chapter 1 and read through Chapter 10.

Chapters 1–3 cover most of the core background information needed to understand the different classes of Cisco QoS tools.

Chapters 4–8 each cover a different major type of QoS tool, covering the concepts, as well as the configuration of the tools.

Chapter 9 specifically addresses QoS issues on LAN switches to a depth and breadth appropriate to the exam.

Finally, Chapter 10 covers information about QoS best practices as described in the QoS course materials. As always, make sure you check www.cisco.com for the latest news about any future changes to the exam.

Appendix A provides the answers to the "Do I Know This Already?" Quizzes and Q&A sections found in Chapters 1–10.

Additionally, you can find Appendix B, "Additional QoS Reference Materials," Appendix C, "Voice Call Admission Control Reference," and Appendix D, "LAN QoS Reference" on the CD-ROM accompanying this book. These CD-only appendixes are designed to supplement what you definitely need to know for the QOS exam with some topic area coverage that you should know as a CCIP candidate.

Following is a description of each chapter's coverage:

■ Chapter 1, "QoS Overview"

   QoS affects the characteristics of network traffic. To understand the QoS concepts and configurations discussed in other chapters, you must know what can be manipulated – namely, bandwidth, delay, jitter, and packet loss. Also, different types of traffic have different needs for bandwidth, delay, jitter and loss. Chapter 1 defines QoS terms, explains the concepts relating to bandwidth, delay, jitter, and packet loss, and identifies the traffic characteristcs of data, voice, and video traffic.

■ Chapter 2, "QoS Tools and Architectures"

   Cisco provides a large number of QoS tools inside the router IOS. One of the biggest challenges when preparing for either exam is remembering all the tools and keeping track of which tools provide what features. Chapter 2 begins by listing and describing the classes of tools, and then also listing the tools themselves. The remaining chapters delve into more depth on each particular class of tool.

   QoS tools typically either follow one of two QoS architectural philosophies. The two archtectures are called Differentiated Services and Integrated Services. The second part of this chapter explains the two architectures.

- Chapter 3, "MQC, QPM, and AutoQoS"

  Many of the best QoS tools in IOS today use a set of CLI commands called the Modular QoS CLI, or MQC. This chapter begins by explaining MQC and showing how MQC commands can be used to configure QOS.

  The other major topic in this chapter is AutoQoS, which automatically configures QoS features according to the Cisco best practices for QoS in a network with VoIP traffic. Along the way, a few related, minor topics are covered, such as QPM.

- Chapter 4, "Classification and Marking"

  Classification and Marking defines how a networking device can identify a particular packet and change some bits in the frame or packet header. The changed bits "mark" the packet, so other QoS tools can react to the marked field. This chapter covers the concepts, as well as five different classification and marking tools.

- Chapter 5, "Congestion Management"

  Queuing tools on routers manage packets while they are waiting to exit an interface. This chapter discusses the general concepts of queuing in Cisco routers, and then covers the concepts and configuration behind a large variety of queuing tools. The Cisco DQOS exam topics refer to Queuing as "Congestion Management."

- Chapter 6, "Traffic Shaping and Policing"

  Policing tools discard traffic that exceeds a particular rate. Shaping tools delay traffic so that, over time, the traffic rate does not exceed a particular rate. Both classes of tools use a concept of measuring the rate of sending or receiving bits. This chapter covers the general concepts of policing and shaping in Cisco routers, followed by the detailed concepts and configuration for two policing tools and four shaping tools.

- Chapter 7, "Congestion Avoidance Through Drop Policies"

  Interestingly, statistics show that the biggest reason that packets are lost in networks is because a queue fills, leaving no room to hold another packet, forcing the device to discard the packet. Congestion Avoidance tools monitor queue depths, discarding some packets before the queue fills. The early discards cause the computers that sent the dropped packets to slow down the rate of sending packets, abating the congestion. As usual, this chapter covers the concepts and then the configuration behind two congestion avoidance tools.

- Chapter 8, "Link Efficiency Tools"

  Link Efficiency tools deal with how to best use the bandwidth on a link between two routers. Compression, which is one class of link efficiency tool, reduces the required bandwidth. Fragmentation tools reduce delay for small, delay-sensitive packets by breaking large packets into smaller packets. The smaller delay-sensitive packets can be sent before the fragments of the original larger packet. This chapter covers the base concepts as well as the configuration details.

- Chapter 9, "LAN QoS"

  The QoS exam covers some specific tools for QoS on Cisco LAN switches. These topics are collected into a single chapter, with examples using 2950 Series switches.

- Chapter 10, "Cisco QoS Best Practices"

  The Cisco QoS course covers a set of recommendations for QoS in the Enterprise, as well as for service providers. This chapter covers those details.

- Appendix A, "Answers to the 'Do I Know This Already?' Quizzes and Q&A Sections"

  This appendix lists the questions covered at the beginning and end of each chapter, as well as their answers.

- Appendix B, "Additional QoS Reference Materials" (found on the book's accompanying CD-ROM)

  This appendix contains material from earlier editions of this book. A few topics might be useful as background information for your preparation for the exam, but the main purpose of the appendix is to list coverage of topics that could be on the CCIE exams. (These topics were not updated for this edition of the book and are available for reference with that caveat in mind.)

- Appendix C, "Voice Call Admission Control Reference" (found on the book's accompanying CD-ROM)

  This appendix is a reprint of the DQOS Exam Certification Guide's chapter on Voice Call Admission Control. Voice CAC is no longer on the QoS exam; it is included on the CD-ROM for reference for anyone interested in Voice CAC. (These topics were not updated for this edition of the book and are available for reference with that caveat in mind.)

- Appendix D, "LAN QoS Reference" (found on the book's accompanying CD-ROM)

  This appendix is a reprint of the DQOS Exam Certification Guide's chapter on LAN QoS. The current QoS exam covers different topics on LAN QoS, with specific focus on the QoS commands on the 2950 Series switches. This appendix contains a broader coverage of LAN QoS, and some samples and comparisons of QoS on different Cisco switches. (These topics were not updated for this edition of the book and are available for reference with that caveat in mind.)

Book Features

The core chapters of this book have several features that help you make the best use of your time:

- **"Do I Know This Already?" Quizes**—Each chapter begins with a quiz that helps you determine the amount of time you need to spend studying that chapter. If you follow the directions at the beginning of the chapter, the "Do I Know This Already?" quiz directs you to study all or particular parts of the chapter.

- **Foundation Topics**—These are the core sections of each chapter. They explain the protocols, concepts, and configuration for the topics in that chapter.

- **Foundation Summary**—Near the end of each chapter, a summary collects the most important tables and figures from the chapter. The "Foundation Summary" section is designed to help you review the key concepts in the chapter if you scored well on the "Do I Know This Already?" quiz. This section is also an excellent tool for last-minute reviews before you take the exam.

- **Q&A**—Each chapter ends with a Q&A section that forces you to exercise your recall of the facts and processes described in the chapter's foundation topics. The questions are generally harder than the actual exam, partly because the questions are in "short answer" format, instead of multiple choice format. These questions are a great way to increase the accuracy of your recollection of the facts and to practice for taking the exam.

- **Examples**—Located inside the Foundation Topics of most chapters, the text includes screen captures from lab scenarios that show how each tool works. The examples include a topology, the configuration, and show command output that matches the examples.

- **CD-based practice exam**—The companion CD contains multiple-choice questions and a testing engine. As part of your final preparation, you should practice with these questions to help you get used to the exam-taking process, as well as help refine and prove your knowledge of the exam topics.

This chapter covers the following exam topics specific to the QoS exam:

QoS Exam Topics

- Given a description of a converged network, identify problems that could lead to poor quality of service, and explain how the problems might be resolved

- Define the term Quality of Service (QoS) and identify and explain the key steps to implementing QoS on a converged network

- Explain the QoS requirements of the different application types

CHAPTER 1

QoS Overview

Cisco provides a large number of quality of service (QoS) features inside Cisco IOS Software. When most of us think about QoS, we immediately think of the various queuing mechanisms, such as Weighted Fair Queuing, or Custom Queuing. QoS features include many more categories, however — fragmentation and interleaving features, compression, policing and shaping, selective packet-drop features, and a few others. And inside each of these categories of different QoS tools, there are several competing options—each with varying degrees of similarities both in concept and configuration.

To remember all the details about QoS tools, you need a firm foundation in the core concepts of QoS. This chapter, as well as Chapter 2, "QoS Tools and Architectures," provides the foundation that you need to organize the concepts and memorize the details in other chapters.

"Do I Know This Already?" Quiz

The purpose of the "Do I Know This Already?" quiz is to help you decide whether you really need to read the entire chapter. If you already intend to read the entire chapter, you do not necessarily need to answer these questions now.

The 10-question quiz, derived from the major sections in the "Foundation Topics" portion of the chapter, helps you determine how to spend your limited study time.

Table 1-1 outlines the major topics discussed in this chapter and the "Do I Know This Already?" quiz questions that correspond to those topics.

Table 1-1   *"Do I Know This Already?" Foundation Topics Section-to-Question Mapping*

Foundation Topics Section Covering These Questions	Questions	Score
QoS: Tuning Bandwidth, Delay, Jitter, and Loss	1–5	
Traffic Characteristics of Voice, Video, and Data	6–8	
Planning and Implementing QoS Policies	9–10	

CAUTION The goal of self-assessment is to gauge your mastery of the topics in this chapter. If you do not know the answer to a question or are only partially sure of the answer, mark this question wrong for purposes of the self-assessment. Giving yourself credit for an answer you correctly guess skews your self-assessment results and might provide you with a false sense of security.

You can find the answers to the "Do I Know This Already?" quiz in Appendix A, "Answers to the 'Do I Know This Already?' Quizzes and Q&A Sections." The suggested choices for your next step are as follows:

- **8 or less overall score**—Read the entire chapter. This includes the "Foundation Topics," the "Foundation Summary," and the "Q&A" section.

- **9 or 10 overall score**—If you want more review on these topics, skip to the "Foundation Summary" section and then go to the "Q&A" section. Otherwise, proceed to the next chapter.

QoS: Tuning Bandwidth, Delay, Jitter, and Loss Questions

1. Which of the following are not traffic characteristics that can be affected by QoS tools?

   a. Bandwidth

   b. Delay

   c. Reliability

   d. MTU

2. Which of the following characterize problems that could occur with voice traffic when QoS is not applied in a network?

   a. Voice sounds choppy.

   b. Calls are disconnected.

   c. Voice call requires more bandwidth as lost packets are retransmitted.

   d. VoIP broadcasts increase as Queuing delay increases, causing delay and caller interaction problems.

3. What does a router base its opinion of how much bandwidth is available to a queuing tool on a serial interface?

   a. The automatically-sensed physical transmission rate on the serial interface.

   b. The **clock rate** command is required before a queuing tool knows how much bandwidth is available.

   c. The **bandwidth** command is required before a queuing tool knows how much bandwidth is available.

    d. Defaults to T1 speed, unless the **clock rate** command has been configured.

    e. Defaults to T1 speed, unless the **bandwidth** command has been configured.

4. Which of the following components of delay varies based on the varying sizes of packets sent through the network?

    a. Propagation delay

    b. Serialization delay

    c. Codec delay

    d. Queuing delay

5. Which of the following is the most likely reason for packet loss in a typical network?

    a. Bit errors during transmission

    b. Jitter thresholds being exceeded

    c. Tail drops when queues fill

    d. TCP flush messages as a result of Round-Trip Times varying wildly

Traffic Characteristics of Voice, Video, and Data Questions

6. Ignoring Layer 2 overhead, how much bandwidth is required for a VoIP call using a G.729 coded? (Link: Voice Bandwidth Considerations)

    a. 8 kbps

    b. 16 kbps

    c. 24 kbps

    d. 32 kbps

    e. 64 kbps

    f. 80 kbps

7. Which of the following are components of delay for a VoIP call, but not for a data application?

    a. Packetization delay

    b. Queuing delay

    c. Serialization delay

    d. Filling the De-jitter buffer

8. Which of the following are true statements of both Voice and Video conferencing traffic?

    a. Traffic is isochronous

    b. All packets in a single call or conference are a of single size

    c. Sensitive to delay

    d. Sensitive to jitter

Planning and Implementing QoS Policies

9. Which of the following are not one of the major planning steps when implementing QoS Policies?

    a. Divide traffic into classes

    b. Define QoS policies for each class

    c. Mark traffic as close to the source as possible

    d. Identify traffic and its requirements

10. When planning QoS policies, which of the following are important actions to take when trying to identify traffic and its requirements?

    a. Network audit

    b. Business audit

    c. Testing by changing current QoS settings to use all defaults

    d. Enabling shaping, and continually reducing the shaping rate, until users start complaining

Foundation Topics

When I was a young lad in Barnesville, Georgia, I used to go to the bank with my dad. Each bank teller had his or her own line of people waiting to talk to the teller and transact their business. Invariably, we would always get behind someone who was really slow. (We called that Bubba's law — you always get behind some large, disagreeable guy named "Bubba" in line.) So, someone who came to the bank after we did would get served before we would, because he or she didn't get behind a "Bubba." But, it was the rural South, so no one was in that much of a hurry, and no one really worried about it.

Later we moved to the big city of Snellville, just outside Atlanta. At the bank in Snellville, people were in a bigger hurry. So, there was one line and many tellers. As it turns out, and as queuing theory proves, the average time in the queue is decreased with one queue served by many tellers, rather than one queue for each teller. Therefore, if one slow person (Bubba) was talking to teller 1, when teller 2 became available, my dad and I could go next, rather than the person who showed up at the bank after we did. Figure 1-1 depicts the two competing queuing methods at a typical bank or fast-food chain—multiple queues, multiple servers versus single queue, multiple servers. The single queue/multiple servers method improves average wait time, but also eliminates the possibility of your good luck in choosing a fast line—the one with no Bubbas in it.

Figure 1-1 *Comparing Multiple Server/Multiple Queue to Multiple Server/Single Queue*

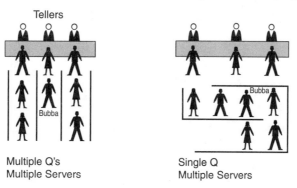

The bank in Snellville just chose a different queuing method, and that positively affected everyone, right? Well, the choice of using a single queue did have one negative effect — because there was only one queue, you could never show up, pick one of the many queues, and happen to get in the one with only fast people in it. In this scenario, on average everyone gets better service, but you miss out on the chance to get in and out of the bank really fast. In short, most customers' experience is improved, and some customers' experience is degraded.

In networking, QoS describes a large array of concepts and tools that can be used to affect the packet's access to some service. Most of us think of queuing features when we think of QoS—reordering the output queue so that one packet gets better service than another. But many other QoS features affect the quality—compression, drop policy, shaping, policing, and signaling, to name a few. In the end, whichever mechanism you use, you improve the behavior for one type of packet over another. Just like at the bank, implementing QoS is "managed fairness," and at the same time it is "managed unfairness"—you purposefully choose to favor one packet over another. In fact, quoting Cisco's QoS course, QoS can be defined as follows:

> The ability of the network to provide better or "special" service to a set of users/applications to the detriment of other users/applications

All of us can relate to the frustration of waiting in lines (queues) for things in our daily lives. It would be great if there were never any people in line ahead of us at the tollbooths, or waiting to get on a ride at Disneyland (or any other place). For that to be possible, however, there would need to be a lot more tollbooths, Disneyland would need to be 20 times larger, and banks would need to hire a lot more tellers. Even so, adding more capacity would not always solve the problem—the tollbooth would still be crowded at rush hour, Disneyland would still be crowded when schools are not in session, and banks would still be crowded on Friday afternoons when everyone is trying to cash his or her weekly paycheck (at least where I live!). Making Disneyland 20 times larger, so that there are no queues, is financially ridiculous—likewise, the addition of 20 times more bandwidth to an existing link is probably also financially unreasonable. After all, you can afford only so much capacity, or bandwidth in the case of networking.

This chapter begins by taking a close look at the four traffic characteristics that QoS tools can affect:

- Bandwidth

- Delay

- Jitter

- Packet loss

Whereas QoS tools improve these characteristics for some flows, the same tools might degrade service for other flows. Therefore, before you can intelligently decide to reduce one packet's delay by increasing another packet's delay, you should understand what each type of application needs. The second part of this "Foundation Topics" section examines voice, video, and data flows in light of their needs for bandwidth, delay, jitter, and loss.

QoS: Tuning Bandwidth, Delay, Jitter, and Loss

Different types of end-user traffic require different performance characteristics on a network. A file-transfer application might just need throughput, but the delay a single packet experiences might not matter. Interactive applications might need consistent response time. Voice calls need low, consistent delay, and video conferencing needs low, consistent delay as well as high throughput.

Users might legitimately complain about the performance of their applications, and the performance issues may be related to the network. Of course, most end users will believe the network is responsible for performance problems, whether it is or not! Reasonable complaints include the following:

- My application is slow.

- My file takes too long to transfer now.

- The video freezes.

- The phone call has so much delay we keep talking at the same time, not knowing whether the other person has paused.

- I keep losing calls.

In some cases, the root problem can be removed, or at least its impact lessened, by implementing QoS features.

So, how do voice, video, and data traffic behave in networks that do not use QoS? Well, certainly the performance varies. Table 1-2 outlines some of the behaviors in a network without QoS.

Table 1-2   *Traffic Behavior with No QoS*

Type of Traffic	Behavior Without QoS
Voice	Voice is hard to understand.
	Voice breaks up, sounds choppy.
	Delays make interacting difficult; callers do not know when other party has finished talking.
	Calls are disconnected.
Video	Picture displays erratically; jerky movements.
	Audio not in sync with video.
	Movement slows down.
Data	Data arrives after it is no longer useful.
	Customer waiting for customer care agent, who waits for a screen to display.
	Erratic response times frustrate users, who may give up or try later.

QoS attempts to solve network traffic performance issues, although QoS is not a cure-all. To improve network performance, QoS features affect a network by manipulating the following network characteristics:

- Bandwidth

- Delay

- Jitter (delay variation)

- Packet loss

Unfortunately, improving one QoS characteristic might degrade another. Bandwidth defines the capacity of the transmission media. Compression tools reduce the amount of bandwidth needed to send all packets, but the compression process adds some delay per packet and also consumes CPU cycles. Jitter is the variation in delay between consecutive packets, so it is sometimes called "delay variation." A router can reduce jitter for some traffic, but that usually increases delay and jitter for other traffic flows. QoS features can address jitter problems, particularly the queuing features that have priority queuing for packets that need low jitter. Packet loss can occur because of transmission errors, and QoS mechanisms cannot do much about that. However, more packets might be lost due to queues filling up rather than transmission errors— and QoS features can affect which packets are dropped.

You can think of QoS as "managed fairness" and, conversely, as "managed unfairness." The real key to QoS success requires you to improve a QoS characteristic for a flow that needs that characteristic, while degrading that same characteristic for a flow that does not need that characteristic. For instance, QoS designs should decrease delay for delay-sensitive traffic, while increasing delay for delay-insensitive traffic.

The next four short sections take a closer look at each of these four traffic characteristics.

Bandwidth

The term *bandwidth* refers to the number of bits per second that can reasonably be expected to be successfully delivered across some medium. In some cases, bandwidth equals the physical link speed, or the clock rate, of the interface. In other cases, bandwidth is smaller than the actual speed of the link. Consider, for example, Figure 1-2, which shows two typical networks, one with a point-to-point serial link, and the other using Frame Relay.

Figure 1-2 *Two Similar Networks, One with Point-to-Point, One with Frame Relay*

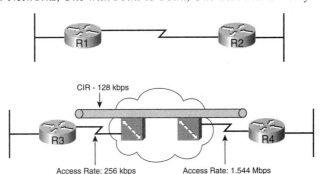

In the point-to-point network, WAN bandwidth equals the physical link speed, or clock rate, on the physical medium. Suppose, for instance, that the link is a 64-kbps link—you could reasonably expect to send 64 kbps worth of traffic, and expect it to get to the other side of the link. You would never expect to send more than that, because you cannot send the bits any faster than the clock rate of the interface. Bandwidth, in this case, is indeed rather obvious; you get 64 kbps in both directions.

The Frame Relay network provides a contracted amount of bandwidth. In practice, however, many installations expect more than that! The committed information rate (CIR) defines how much bandwidth the provider guarantees will pass through their network between the data terminal equipment (DTE) at each end of a virtual circuit (VC). That guarantee is a business proposition—a Layer 8 issue using the OSI reference model. On some occasions, you might not actually even get CIR worth of bandwidth. However, the Frame Relay provider commits to engineering a network so that they can support at least the CIRs of their collective VCs. In effect, bandwidth per VC equals the CIR of each VC, respectively.

Unfortunately, bandwidth on multiaccess networks is not that simple. Consider the fact that R3 has a 256-kbps access rate, and R4 has a T1 access rate. When R3 sends, it must send the bits at access rate—otherwise, Layer 1 functions would not work at all. Similarly, R4 must send at T1 speed. One of Frame Relay's big selling points throughout its large growth years was that you "get something for nothing"—you pay for CIR of x, and you get more than x worth of bandwidth. In fact, many data network engineers design networks assuming that you will get an average of one and a half to two times CIR over each VC. If R3 and R4 send too much, and the provider's switches have full queues, the frames are discarded, and the data has to be re-sent. If you pay for 128-kbps CIR between R3 and R4, and over time actually send at 192 kbps, or 256 kbps, and it works, how much bandwidth do you really have? Well, on a multiaccess network, such as Frame Relay or ATM, the actual amount of bandwidth is certainly open to argument.

Frame Relay bandwidth might even be less than CIR in practice. Suppose that R4 is the main site, and there are 15 remote sites identical to R3 (including R3). Can you reasonably expect to send at 128 kbps (CIR) to all 15 sites, at the same time, when R4 has a 1.544-Mbps access rate? No! All 15 sites sending at 128 kbps requires 1.920 Mbps, and R4 can only send and receive at 1.544 Mbps. Would an engineer design a network like this? Yes! The idea being that if data is being sent to all VCs simultaneously, or the Frame Relay switch will queue the data (for packets going left to right). If data is not being sent to all 15 remote sites at the same time, you get (at least) 128 kbps to each site that needs the bandwidth at that time. The negative effect is that a larger percentage of packets are dropped due to full queues; however, for data networks that is typically a reasonable tradeoff. For traffic that is not tolerant to loss, such as voice and video, this type of design may not be reasonable.

Throughout this book, when multiaccess network bandwidth is important, the discussion covers some of the implications of using the more conservative bandwidth of CIR, versus the more liberal measurements that are typically a multiple of CIR.

The clock rate Command Versus the bandwidth Command

When you are using a Cisco router, two common interface commands relate to bandwidth. First, the **clock rate** command defines the actual Layer 1 bit rate. The command is used when the router is providing clocking, typically when connecting the router using a serial interface to some other nearby device (another router, for instance). The **bandwidth** command tells a variety of Cisco IOS Software functions how much bandwidth is assumed to be available on the interface. For instance, Enhanced Interior Gateway Routing Protocol (EIGRP) chooses metrics for interfaces based on the **bandwidth** command, not based on a **clock rate** command. In short, bandwidth only changes the behavior of other tools on an interface, and it affects the results of some statistics, but it never changes the actual rate of sending bits out an interface.

Some QoS tools refer to interface bandwidth, which is defined with the **bandwidth** command. Engineers should consider bandwidth defaults when enabling QoS features. On serial interfaces on Cisco routers, the default bandwidth setting is T1 speed—regardless of the actual bandwidth. If subinterfaces are used, they inherit the bandwidth setting of the corresponding physical interface. In Figure 1-2, for example, R3 would have a default bandwidth setting of 1544 (the units are in kbps), as opposed to a more accurate 128, 192, or 256 kbps, depending on how conservative or liberal the engineer can afford to be in this network.

QoS Tools That Affect Bandwidth

Several QoS features can help with bandwidth issues. You'll find more detail about each of these tools in various chapters throughout this book. For now, however, knowing what each class of QoS tool accomplishes will help you sift through some of the details.

The best QoS tool for bandwidth issues is more bandwidth! However, more bandwidth does not solve all problems. In fact, in converged networks (networks with voice, video, and data), adding more bandwidth might be masking delay problems that are best solved through other QoS tools or through better QoS design. To quote Arno Penzias, former head of Bell Labs and a Nobel Prize winner: "Money and sex, storage and bandwidth: Only too much is ever enough." If you can afford it, more bandwidth certainly helps improve traffic quality.

Some link-efficiency QoS tools improve bandwidth by reducing the number of bits required to transmit the data. Figure 1-3 shows a rather simplistic view of the effect of compression, assuming the compression ratio is 2:1. Without compression, with 80 kbps of offered traffic, and only a 64-kbps point-to-point link, a queue will form. The queue will eventually fill, and packets will be dropped off the end of the queue—an action called tail drop. With compression, if a ratio of 2:1 is achieved, the 80 kbps will require only 40 kbps in order to be sent across the link— effectively doubling the bandwidth capacity of the link.

This book covers several options for compression, some of which happen before the queuing process (as shown in Figure 1-3), and some that happen after the queuing process.

The other QoS tool that directly affects bandwidth is call admission control (CAC). CAC tools decide whether the network can accept new voice and video calls. That permission might be based on a large number of factors, but several of those factors involve either a measurement of bandwidth. For example, the design might expect only three concurrent G.729A VoIP calls over a particular path; CAC would be used for each new call, and when three calls already exist, the next call would be rejected. (If CAC did not prevent the fourth call, and a link became oversubscribed as a result, all the quality of all four calls would degrade!) When CAC rejects a call, the call might be rerouted based on the VoIP dial plan, for instance, through the Public Switched Telephone Network (PSTN). (As it turns out, CAC tools are not covered in the current version of the QOS exam, 642-642.)

Queuing tools can affect the amount of bandwidth that certain types of traffic receive. Queuing tools create multiple queues, and then packets are taken from the queues based on some scheduling algorithm. The scheduling algorithm might include a feature that guarantees a minimum amount of bandwidth to a particular queue. Figure 1-4, for example, shows a two- queue system. The first queue gets 25 percent of the bandwidth on the link, and the second queue gets 75 percent of the bandwidth.

Figure 1-3 *With a 2:1 Compression Ratio Versus No Compression*

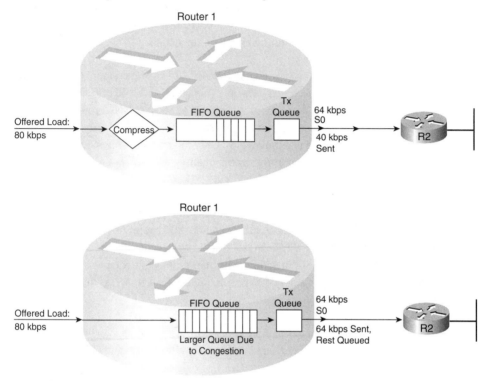

Figure 1-4 *Bandwidth Reservation Using Queuing*

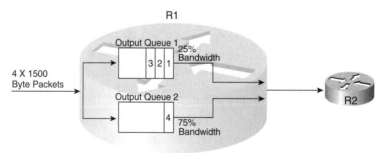

With regard to Cisco IOS Software queuing tools that reserve bandwidth, if both queues have packets waiting, the algorithm takes packets such that, over time, each queue gets its configured percentage of the link bandwidth. If only one queue has packets waiting, that queue gets more than its configured amount of bandwidth for that short period.

Although adding more bandwidth always helps, the tools summarized in Table 1-3 do help to improve the efficient utilization of bandwidth in a network.

Table 1-3 *QoS Tools That Affect Bandwidth*

Type of QoS Tool	How It Affects Bandwidth
Compression	Compresses either payload or headers, reducing overall number of bits required to transmit the data
CAC	Reduces overall load introduced into the network by rejecting new voice and video calls
Queuing	Can be used to reserve minimum amounts of bandwidth for particular types of packets

Delay

All packets in a network experience some delay between when the packet is first sent and when it arrives at its destination. Most of the concepts behind QoS mechanisms relate in some way to delay. Therefore, a deeper look into delay is useful. Take a look at Figure 1-5; this sample network is used often in this book.

Figure 1-5 *Sample Network for Discussion of Delay*

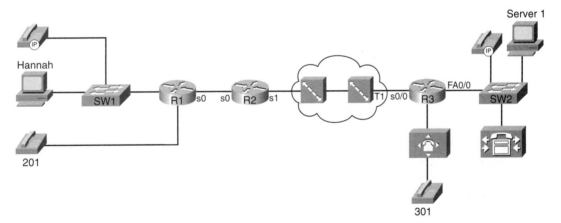

At what points will delay occur in this network? Well, at all points, in actuality. At some points in the network, the delay is so small that it can just be ignored for practical purposes. In other cases, the delay is significant, but there is nothing you can do about it! For a fuller understanding, consider the following types of delay:

■ Serialization delay (fixed)

■ Propagation delay (fixed)

- Queuing delay (variable)

- Forwarding/processing delay (variable)

- Shaping delay (variable)

- Network delay (variable)

- Codec delay (fixed)

- Compression delay (variable)

Each of these types of delay is explained over the next several pages. Together, the types of delay make up the components of the end-to-end delay experienced by a packet.

Serialization Delay

Imagine you are standing at a train station. A train comes by but doesn't stop; it just keeps going. Because the train cars are connected serially one to another, a time lag occurs between when the engine car at the front of the train first gets to this station and when the last car passes by. If the train is long, it takes more time until the train fully passes. If the train is moving slowly, it takes longer for all the cars to pass. In networking, serialization delay is similar to the delay between the first and last cars in a train.

Serialization delay defines the time it takes to encode the bits of a packet onto the physical interface. If the link is fast, the bits can be encoded onto the link more quickly; if the link is slow, it takes longer to encode the bits on the link. Likewise, if the packet is short, it does not take as long to put the bits on the link as compared with a long packet.

Use the following formula to calculate serialization delay for a packet:

$$\frac{\#bits\ sent}{Link\ speed}$$

Suppose, for instance, that Hannah in Figure 1-5 sends a 125-byte packet to Server1. Hannah sends the packet over the Fast Ethernet to the switch. The 125 bytes equal 1000 bits, so at Fast Ethernet speeds, it takes 1000 bits/100,000,000 bits per second (bps), or .01 ms, to serialize the packet onto the Fast Ethernet. Another .01 ms of serialization delay is experienced when the switch sends the frame to R1. (I ignored the data-link header lengths to keep the math obvious.)

Next, when that same packet leaves R1 over a 56 kbps link to R2, serialization takes 1000 bits/56,000 bps, or 17.85 ms. The serialization component over Fast Ethernet is insignificant, whereas serialization becomes a more significant number on lower-speed serial links. Figure 1-6 shows the various locations where the packet from Hannah to Server1 experiences serialization delay.

Figure 1-6 *Serialization Delay*

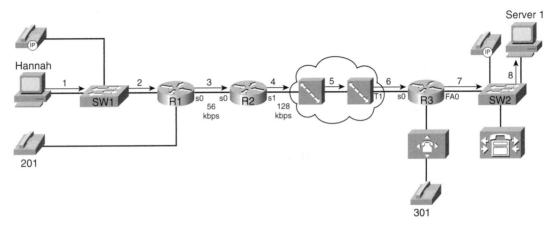

As Figure 1-6 shows, serialization delay occurs any time a frame is sent. On LAN links, the delay is insignificant for most applications. At steps 3 through 6 in the figure, the serialization delay is 17.85 ms, 7.8 ms, .02 ms, and .65 ms for the 125-byte packet, respectively. Also note that serialization delays do occur inside the Frame Relay cloud. (You can read more about delays inside the cloud in the "Network Delay" section later in this chapter.)

Table 1-4 lists the serialization delay for a couple of frame sizes and link speeds.

Table 1-4 *Example Serialization Delay Values*

Clock Rate of Link	Serialization Delay (125-Byte Frame; Milliseconds)	Serialization Delay (1500-Byte Frame; Milliseconds)
100 Mbps	.01	.12
1.544 Mbps	.65	8
512 kbps	2	24
128 kbps	7.8	93
56 kbps	17.85	214

Propagation Delay

Imagine you are watching a train again, this time from a helicopter high in the air over the tracks. You see the train leaving one station, and then arriving at the second station. Using a stopwatch, you measure the amount of time it takes from the first car leaving the first station until the first car arrives at the second station. Of course, all the other cars take the same amount of time to get there as well. This delay is similar to propagation delay in networking.

Propagation delay defines the time it takes a single bit to get from one end of the link to the other. When an electrical or optical signal is placed onto the cable, the energy does not propagate to the other end of the cable instantaneously—some delay occurs. The speed of energy on electrical and optical interfaces approaches the speed of light, and the network engineer cannot override the laws of physics! The only variable that affects the propagation delay is the length of the link. Use the following formula to calculate propagation delay:

$$\frac{\text{Length of Link (meters)}}{3.0 \times 10^8 \text{ meters/second}}$$

or

$$\frac{\text{Length of Link (meters)}}{2.1 \times 10^8 \text{ meters/second}}$$

where $3.0 * 10^8$ is the speed of light in a vacuum. Many people use $2.1 * 10^8$ for the speed of light over copper and optical media when a more exact measurement is needed. (Seventy percent of the speed of light is the generally accepted rule for the speed of energy over electrical cabling.)

Propagation delay occurs as the bits traverse the physical link. Suppose, for instance, that the point-to-point link between R1 and R2 is 1000 kilometers (1,000,000 meters) long. The propagation delay would be as follows:

$$\frac{1,000,000}{2.1 * 10^8} = 004.8 \text{ ms}$$

Figure 1-7 shows two contrasting examples of serialization and propagation delay.

Figure 1-7 *Serialization and Propagation Delay for Selected Packet and Link Lengths*

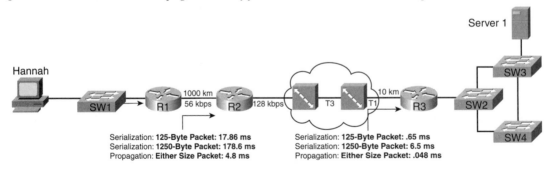

As you can see in Figure 1-7, the length of the link affects propagation delay, whereas the size of the packet and link speed affect serialization delay. The serialization delay is larger for larger packets, but the propagation delay is equal for different-sized packets, on the same link. One common misconception is that the link speed, or clock rate, affects propagation delay—it does not! Table 1-5 lists the various propagation delays and serialization delays for parts of Figure 1-6.

Table 1-5 *Example Serialization and Propagation Delays with Figure 1-7*

Step Number from Figure	Length of Link	Clock Rate of Link	Propagation Delay (Milliseconds)	Serialization delay (125-Byte Packet; Milliseconds)	Serialization Delay (1500-Byte Packet; Milliseconds)
1	50 m	100 Mbps	.002	.01	.12
2	10 m	100 Mbps	.0004	.01	.12
3	1000 km	56 kbps	4.8	17.85	214
4	5 km	128 kbps	.024	7.8	94
5	1000 km	44.232 Mbps	4.8	.02	.24
6	10 km	1.544 Mbps	.048	.65	7.8

If the link from Hannah to SW1 is 100 meters, for example, propagation is $100/(2.1 * 10^8)$, or .48 microseconds. If the T3 between the two Frame Relay switches is 1000 kilometers, the delay is $1,000,000/(2.1 * 10^8)$, or 4.8 ms. Notice that propagation delay is not affected by clock rate on the link—even on the 56-kbps Frame Relay access link, at 1000 km (a long Frame Relay access link!), the propagation delay would only be 4.8 ms.

Queuing Delay

Packets experience *queuing delay* when they must wait for other packets to be sent. Most people think of queuing delay when they think of QoS, and most people think of queuing strategies and tools when they think of QoS tools—but queuing tools are just one category of QoS tool. Queuing delay consists of the time spent in the queues inside the device—typically just in output queues in a router, because input queuing is typically negligible in a router. However, the queuing time can be relatively large—hundreds of milliseconds, or maybe even more. Consider Figure 1-8, where R1 queues four 1500-byte packets that Hannah sent to Server1.

Figure 1-8 *R1 Queues Four 1500-Byte Packets for Transmission*

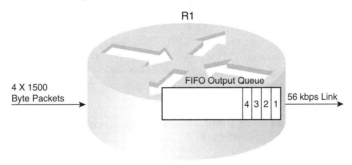

Because it takes 1500 * 8 / 56,000, or 214 ms, to serialize each 1500-byte packet, the other packets need to either be stored in memory or discarded. Therefore, the router uses some memory to hold the packets. The simplest form of queuing is to use a single queue, serviced with first-in, first-out (FIFO) logic—as is shown in the figure. After 856 ms, all four packets would have been sent out the serial link. Assuming that the link was not busy when Hannah sent these four packets, how much queuing delay did each packet experience? Well, the first packet experienced no queuing delay. The second packet waited on the first, or 214 ms. The third packet waited on the first two—or 428 ms. And the fourth packet waited on the first three, for a total of 642 ms.

Queuing provides a useful function, because the second, third, and fourth packets would have had to have been discarded without queuing. However, too much of a good thing is not always good! Imagine that Hannah sends 100 * 1500-byte packets all at once. If the queue in R1 is large enough, R1 could queue all 100 packets. What would the delay be for the one-hundredth packet? Well, 99 * 214 ms per packet, or roughly 21 seconds! If Hannah uses TCP, then TCP has probably timed out, and re-sent the packets—causing more congestion and queuing delay. And what about another user's packet that showed up right after Hannah's 100 packets? Still more delay. So, some queuing helps prevent packet drops, but large queues can cause too much delay.

Figure 1-9 combines all the delay components covered so far into one small diagram. Consider the delay for the fourth of the four 1500-byte packets sent by Hannah. The figure lists the queuing, serialization, and propagation delays.

Figure 1-9 *Delay Components: Three Components, Single Router (R1)*

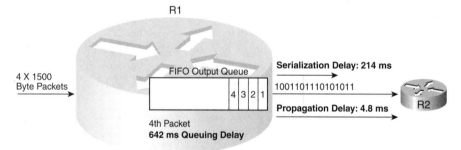

The overall delay for a packet is the sum of all these delays from end to end. At R1, when all four packets have been received, the fourth packet experiences a total of about 860 ms of delay before it has been fully received at R2. And this example just shows the queuing delay in a single router (R1), and the serialization and propagation delay over a single link—end-to-end delay includes these delays at each router (queuing) and link (serialization and propagation) in the network.

Forwarding Delay

The term *forwarding delay* refers the processing time between when a frame is fully-received, and when the packet has been placed in an output queue. So, forwarding delay does not include the time the packet sits in the output queue waiting to leave the router. It does include the time required for the router to process the route, or forward, the packet.

Cisco does not normally quote statistics about forwarding delay numbers for different models of routers with different types of internal processing. However, the higher volume of packets that a router can forward, and the higher volume of packets forwarded using a particular processing method, presumably the lower the forwarding delay.

Most delay components in LAN switches are small enough not to matter. However, switches incur forwarding delay, just like routers—most of the time. Some LAN switches use a "store- and-forward" forwarding logic, when the entire frame must be received before forwarding any part of the frame. However, some switches use cut-through or fragment-free forwarding, which means that the first bits of a frame are forwarded before the final bits are fully received. Technically, if you define forwarding delay as the time between receipt of the entire frame until that frame is queued for transmission, some LAN switches might actually have negative forwarding delay! It just depends on how you decide to define what parts of the overall delay end up being attributed. Forwarding delay is typically a small enough component to ignore in overall delay budget calculations, so this book does not punish you with further discussion about these details!

For more information on internal processing methods such as Cisco Express Forwarding (CEF), you can review the Cisco Press book *Inside Cisco IOS Software Architecture*.

Shaping Delay

Traffic shaping causes additional delays by serving queues more slowly than if traffic shaping were not used. Why should a router slow down sending packets if it does not have to? Well, traffic shaping helps match the overall forwarding rate of traffic when a carrier might discard traffic if the rates exceed the contracted rate. So, which is better?

■ Sending packets really fast and having them be dropped

■ Sending packets more slowly, but not having them be dropped

The right answer is—it depends! If you want to send more slowly, hoping that packets are not dropped, however, traffic shaping is the solution.

Carriers can drop frames and packets inside their network for a variety of reasons. One of the most typical reasons is that most central-site routers use a fast access link, with remote sites using much slower links. If the central site uses a T1, and the remote site uses a 56-kbps link, frames may fill the queue inside the service provider's network, waiting to go across the 56-kbps access link. Many other events can cause the carrier to drop packets; these reasons events explained more fully in Chapter 6, "Traffic Policing and Shaping."

To understand the basic ideas behind shaping in a single router, consider Figure 1-10, where R2 has a 128-kbps access rate and a 64-kbps CIR on its VC to R3.

Figure 1-10   *Traffic Shaping over the Frame Relay Network*

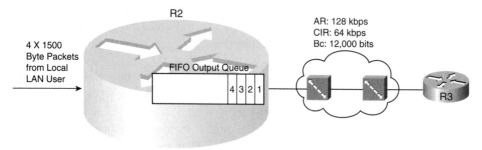

Suppose that the Frame Relay provider agrees to the 64-kbps CIR on the VC from R2 to R3, but the carrier tells you that they aggressively discard frames when you send more than 64 kbps. The access rate is 128 kbps. Therefore, you decide to shape, which means that R2 will want to average sending at 64 kbps, because sending faster than 64 kbps hurts more than it helps. In fact, in this particular instance, if R2 sends packets for this VC only half the time, the rate averages out to 64 kbps. Remember, bits can only be sent at the physical link speed, which is also called the access rate in Frame Relay. In effect, the router sends all packets at access rate, but the router purposefully delays sending packets, possibly even leaving the link idle, so that the rate over time averages to be about 64 kbps.

Chapter 6 will clear up the details. The key concept to keep in mind when reading other sections of this book is that traffic shaping introduces additional delay. Like many QoS features, shaping attempts to enhance one particular traffic characteristic (drops), but must sacrifice another traffic characteristic (delay) to do so.

Network Delay

Most people draw a big cloud for a Frame Relay or ATM network, because the details are not typically divulged to the customer. However, the same types of delay components seen outside the cloud also exist inside the cloud—and the engineer that owns the routers and switches outside the cloud cannot exercise as much QoS control over the behavior of the devices in the cloud.

So how much delay should a packet experience in the cloud? Well, it will vary. The carrier might commit to a maximum delay value as well. However, with a little insight, you can get a solid understanding of the minimum delay a packet should experience through a Frame Relay cloud. Consider Figure 1-11, focusing on the Frame Relay components.

Figure 1-11   *Frame Relay Network: Propagation and Serialization Delay Components*

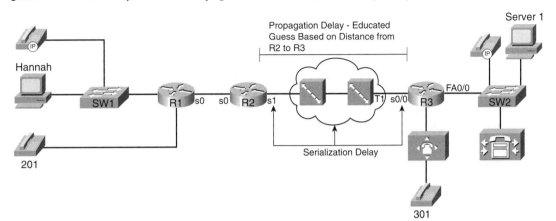

The propagation delay and serialization delay can be guessed pretty closely. No matter how many switches exist between R2 and R3, the cumulative propagation delays on all the links between R2 and R3 will be at least as much as the propagation delay on a point-to-point circuit. And with most large providers, because they have many points of presence (PoPs), the Frame Relay VC probably takes the same physical route as a point-to-point circuit would anyway. As for serialization delay, the two slowest links, by far, will be the two access links (in most cases). Therefore, the following account for most of the serialization delay in the cloud:

■   The serialization delay to send the packet into the cloud

■   The serialization delay at the egress Frame Relay switch, sending the packet to R3

Suppose, for example, that R2 and R3 are 1000 km apart, and a 1500-byte packet is sent. The network delay will at least be the propagation delay plus both serialization delays on the two access links:

Propagation = 1000 km / 2.1 * 10^8 = 4.8 ms

Serialization (ingress R2) = 1500 bytes * 8 / 128,000 bps = 94 ms

Serialization (egress R3) = 1500 bytes * 8 / 1,544,000 = 7.8 ms

For a total of 106.6 ms delay

Of course, the delay will vary—and will depend on the provider, the status of the network's links, and overall network congestion. In some cases, the provider will include delay limits in the contracted service-level agreement (SLA).

Queuing delay inside the cloud creates the most variability in network delay, just as it does outside the cloud. These delays are traffic dependent, and hard to predict.

Delay Summary

Of the types of delay covered so far in this chapter, all except shaping delay occur in every network. Shaping delay occurs only when shaping is enabled.

Two other delay components may or may not be found in a typical network. First, codec delay will be experienced by voice and video traffic. Codec delay is covered in more depth in the section titled "Voice Delay Considerations" later in this chapter. Compression requires processing, and the time taken to process a packet to compress or decompress the packet introduces delay. Chapter 8, "Link-Efficiency Tools," covers compression delay.

Table 1-6 summarizes the delay components listed in this section.

Table 1-6 *Components of Delay Not Specific to One Type of Traffic*

Delay Component	Definition	Where It Occurs
Serialization delay (fixed)	Time taken to place all bits of a frame onto the physical medium. Function of frame size and physical link speed.	Outbound on every physical interface; typically negligible on T3 and faster links.
Propagation delay (fixed)	Time taken for a single bit to traverse the physical medium from one end to the other. Based on the speed of light over that medium, and the length of the link.	Every physical link. Typically negligible on LAN links and shorter WAN links.
Queuing delay (variable)	Time spent in a queue awaiting the opportunity to be forwarded (output queuing), or awaiting a chance to cross the switch fabric (input queuing).	Possible on every output interface. Input queuing unlikely in routers, more likely in LAN switches.
Forwarding or processing delay (variable)	Time required from receipt of the incoming frame, until the frame/packet has been queued for transmission.	On every piece of switching equipment, including routers, LAN switches, Frame Relay switches, and ATM switches.
Shaping delay (variable)	Shaping (if configured) delays transmission of packets to avoid packet loss in the middle of a Frame Relay or ATM network.	Anywhere that shaping is configured, which is most likely on a router, when sending packets to a Frame Relay or ATM network.
Network delay (variable)	Delays created by the components of the carrier's network when using a service. For instance, the delay of a Frame Relay frame as it traverses the Frame Relay network.	Inside the service provider's network.

QoS Tools That Affect Delay

Several QoS features can help with delay issues. You'll find more detail about each of these tools in various chapters throughout this book. For now, however, knowing what each class of QoS tool accomplishes will help you sift through some of the details.

The best QoS tool for delay issues is . . . more bandwidth—again! More bandwidth helps bandwidth-related problems, and it also helps delay-related problems. Faster bandwidth decreases serialization delay. Because packets exit more quickly, queuing delay decreases. Higher CIR on your VCs reduces shaping delay. In short, faster bandwidth reduces delay!

Unfortunately, more bandwidth does not solve all delay problems, even if you could afford more bandwidth! In fact, in converged networks (networks with voice, video, and data), adding more bandwidth might mask delay problems that are best solved through other QoS tools or through better QoS design. The sections that follow address the QoS tools can affect the delay a particular packet receives.

Queuing (Scheduling)

The most popular QoS tool, queuing, involves choosing the packets to be sent based on something other than arrival time. In other words, instead of FIFO queuing with one queue, other queuing mechanisms create multiple queues, place packets into these different queues, and then pick packets from the various queues. As a result, some packets leave the router more quickly, with other packets having to wait longer. Although queuing does not decrease delay for all packets, it can decrease delay for delay-sensitive packets, and increase delay for delay-insensitive packets—and enabling a queuing mechanism on a router does not cost any cash, whereas adding more bandwidth does.

Each queuing method defines some number of different queues, with different methods of scheduling the queues—in other words, different rules for how to choose from which queue the next packet to be sent will be chosen. Figure 1-12 depicts a queuing mechanism with two queues. Suppose Hannah sent four packets, but the fourth packet was sent by a video- conferencing package she was running, whereas the other three packets were for a web application she was using while bored with the video conference.

Figure 1-12 *Sample Queuing Method: Two Queues*

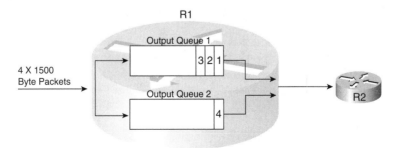

R1 could notice that packet 4 has different characteristics, and place it into a different queue. Packet 4 could exit R1 before some or all of the first three packets.

Link Fragmentation and Interleaving

The time required to serialize a packet on a link is a function of the speed of the link, and the size of the packet. When the router decides to start sending the first bit of a packet, the router continues until the whole packet is sent. Therefore, if a delay-sensitive packet shows up just after a long packet has begun to be sent out an interface, the delay-sensitive packet must wait until the longer packet has been sent.

Suppose, for example, that two packets have arrived at R1. Packet 1 is 1500 bytes, and packet 2 is 200 bytes. The smaller packet is delay sensitive. Because packet 2 arrived just after the first bit of packet 1 was sent, packet 2 must wait 214 ms for packet 1 to be serialized onto the link. With link fragmentation and interleaving (LFI), packet 1 could be broken into three 500-byte fragments, and packet 2 could be interleaved (inserted) and sent on the link after the first of the three fragments of packet 1. Figure 1-13 depicts LFI operation.

Figure 1-13 *Link Fragmentation and Interleaving*

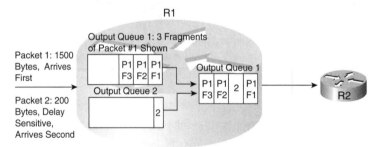

Legend: Px Fy Means Packet Number x, Fragment Number y

Note that packet 1 was fragmented into three pieces. Because packet 2 arrived after packet 1 had begun to be sent, packet 2 had to wait. With LFI, packet 2 does not have to wait for the entire original packet, but rather it waits for just 1 fragment to be sent.

Compression

Compression takes a packet, or packet header, and compresses the data so that it uses fewer bits. Therefore, a 1500-byte packet, compressed to 750 bytes, takes half as much serialization time as does an uncompressed 1500-byte packet.

Compression reduces serialization delay, because the number of bits used to send a packet is decreased. However, delay may also be increased because of the processing time required to compress and decompress the packets. Chapter 8, "Link Efficiency Tools," covers the pros and cons of each type of compression.

Traffic Shaping

Traffic shaping actually increases delay, in an effort to reduce the chance of packet loss. Shaping is mentioned here just because of its negative impact on delay.

Although adding more bandwidth always helps, the tools summarized in Table 1-7 do help to improve the effects of delay in a network.

Table 1-7 *QoS Tools That Affect Delay*

Type of QoS Tool	How It Affects Delay
Queuing	Enables you to order packets so that delay-sensitive packets leave their queues more quickly than delay-insensitive packets.
Link fragmentation and interleaving	Because routers do not preempt a packet that is currently being transmitted, LFI breaks larger packets into smaller fragments before sending them. Smaller delay-sensitive packets can be sent after a single smaller fragment, instead of having to wait for the larger original packet to be serialized.
Compression	Compresses either payload or headers, reducing overall number of bits required to transmit the data. By requiring less bandwidth, queues shrink, which reduces delay. Also serialization delays shrink, because fewer bits are required. Compression also adds some processing delay.
Traffic shaping	Artificially increases delay to reduce drops inside a Frame Relay or ATM network.

Jitter

Consecutive packets that experience different amounts of delay have experienced jitter. In a packet network, with variable delay components, jitter always occurs—the question is whether the jitter impacts the application enough to degrade the service. Typically, data applications expect some jitter, and do not degrade. However, some traffic, such as digitized voice, requires that the packets be transmitted in a consistent, uniform manner (for instance, every 20 ms). The packets should also arrive at the destination with the same spacing between them. (This type of traffic is called *isochronous traffic*.)

Jitter is defined as a variation in the arrival rate (that is, variation in delay through the network) of packets that were transmitted in a uniform manner. Figure 1-14, for example, shows three packets as part of a voice call between phones at extension 301 and 201.

Figure 1-14 *Jitter Example*

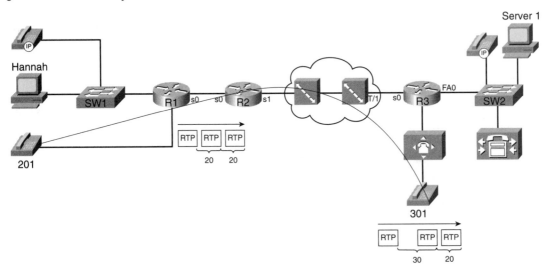

The phone sends the packets every 20 ms. Notice that the second packet arrived 20 ms after the first, so no jitter occurred. However, the third packet arrived 30 ms after the second packet, so 10 ms of jitter occurred.

Voice and video degrade quickly when jitter occurs. Data applications tend to be much more tolerant of jitter, although large variations in jitter affect interactive applications.

QoS Tools That Affect Jitter

Several QoS features can help with jitter issues. You'll find more detail about each of these tools in various chapters throughout this book. For now, however, knowing what each class of QoS tool accomplishes will help you sift through some of the details.

The best QoS tool for jitter issues is . . . more bandwidth—again! More bandwidth helps bandwidth-related problems, and it also helps delay-related problems. If it helps to reduce delay, and because jitter is the variation of delay, jitter will be smaller. Faster bandwidth decreases serialization delay, which will decrease jitter. For instance, if delay has been averaging between 100 ms and 200 ms, jitter would typically be up to 100 ms. If delay is reduced to between 50 ms and 100 ms by adding more bandwidth, the typical jitter can be reduced to 50 ms. Because packets exit more quickly, queuing delay decreases. If queuing delays had been between 50 and 100 ms, and now they are between 10 and 20 ms, jitter will shrink as well. In short, faster is better for bandwidth, delay, and jitter issues!

Unfortunately, more bandwidth does not solve all jitter problems, even if you could afford more bandwidth! Several classes of QoS tools improve jitter; as usual, decreasing jitter for one set of packets increases jitter for others.

The same set of tools that affect delay also affect jitter; refer to Table 1-8 for a brief list of these QoS tools.

Table 1-8 *QoS Tools That Affect Jitter*

Type of QoS Tool	How It Affects Jitter
Queuing	Enables you to order packets so that delay-sensitive packets leave their queues more quickly than delay-insensitive packets.
Link fragmentation and interleaving	Because routers do not preempt a packet that is currently being transmitted, LFI breaks larger packets into smaller fragments before sending them. Smaller delay-sensitive packets can be sent after a single smaller fragment, instead of having to wait for the larger original packet to be serialized.
Compression	Compresses either payload or headers, reducing overall number of bits required to transmit the data. By requiring less bandwidth, queues shrink, which reduces delay. Also serialization delays shrink, because fewer bits are required. Compression also adds some processing delay.
Traffic shaping	Artificially increases delay to reduce drops inside a Frame Relay or ATM network.

Loss

The last QoS traffic characteristic is *packet loss*, or just *loss*. Routers lose/drop/discard packets for many reasons, most of which QoS tools can do nothing about. For instance, frames that fail the incoming frame check sequence (FCS) are discarded—period. However, QoS tools can be used to minimize the impact of packets lost due to full queues.

In most networks today, the number of packets lost due to bit errors is small, typically less than one in one billion (bit error rate [BER] of 10^{-9} or better). Therefore, the larger concern for packet loss is loss due to full buffers and queues. Consider Figure 1-15, with Hannah sending 50 consecutive 1500-byte packets, and R1 having a queue of size 40.

The term "tail drop" refers to when a router drops a packet when it wants to put the packet at the end or the tail of the queue. As Figure 1-15 shows, when all 40 queue slots are filled, the rest of the 50 packets are dropped. In a real network, a few of the packets might be sent out the serial link before all 50 packets are received, so maybe not all 10 packets are lost, but certainly a large number of packets would be lost.

Figure 1-15   *50 Packets Sent, Only 40 Slots in the Queue*

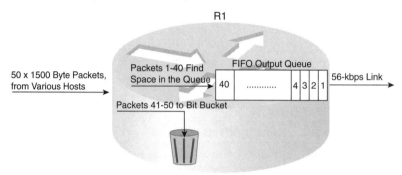

Some flows tolerate loss better than others do. For instance, the human ear can detect loss of only 10 ms of voice, but the listener can generally understand speech with such small loss. Cisco digital signal processors (DSPs) can predict the contents of lost voice packets, up to 30 ms when using the G.729 codec. By default, each voice packet contains 20 ms of voice; so if two consecutive voice packets are lost, the DSP cannot re-create the voice, and the receiver can actually perceive the silence. Conversely, web traffic tolerates loss well, using TCP to recover the data.

QoS Tools That Affect Loss

Only a few QoS features can help with packet loss issues. You'll find more detail about each of these tools in various chapters throughout this book. For now, however, knowing what each class of QoS tool accomplishes will help you sift through some of the details.

By now, you should guess that bandwidth will help prevent lost packets. More bandwidth helps—it just does not solve all problems. And frankly, if all you do is add more bandwidth, and you have a converged voice/video/data network, you will still have quality issues.

How does more bandwidth reduce loss? More bandwidth allows packets to be transmitted faster, which reduces the length of queues. With shorter queues, the queues are less likely to fill. Unless queues fill, packets are not tail dropped.

You can use one class of tool to help reduce the impacts of loss. This class is called *Random Early Detection*.

Random Early Detection (RED)

TCP uses a windowing protocol, which restricts the amount of data a TCP sender can send without an acknowledgment. Each TCP window for each different TCP connection grows and shrinks based on many factors. RED works under the assumption that if some of the TCP connections can be made to shrink their windows before output queues fill, the collective number of packets sent into the network will be smaller, and the queue will not fill. During times when the queues are not getting very full, RED does not bother telling the TCP senders to slow down, because there is no need to slow down.

RED just discards some packets before a queue gets full and starts to tail drop. You can almost think of RED tools as managing the end of a queue, while the queuing tool manages the front of the queue! Because most traffic is TCP based and TCP slows down sending packets after a earlier packet is lost, RED reduces the load of packets that are entering the network before the queues fill. RED requires a fairly detailed explanation for a true understanding of what it does, and how it works. However, the general idea can be easily understood, as long as you know that TCP will slow down sending, by reducing its window size, when packets are lost.

TCP uses a window, which defines how much data can be sent before an acknowledgment is received. The window changes size dynamically, based on several factors, including lost packets. When packets are lost, depending on other conditions, a TCP window shrinks to 50 percent of the previous window size. With most data traffic being TCP in a typical network, when a large amount of tail drop occurs, almost all, if not all TCP connections sending packets across that link have their TCP windows shrunk by 50 percent at least once.

Consider the example in Figure 1-15. As that figure shows, 50 packets were sent, and the queue filled, and 10 of those packets were lost. If those 50 packets were part of 10 different TCP connections, and all 10 connections lost packets in the big tail drop, the next time the hosts send, only 25 total packets would be sent (windows all cut in half).

With RED, before tail drop occurs, RED discards some packets, forcing only a few of the TCP connections to slow down. By allowing only a few of the TCP windows to be reduced, tail drops can be avoided, and most users get better response time. The collective TCP sending rate stabilizes to a level for which tail drops seldom if ever occur. For those TCP connections for which RED dropped packets, response time is temporarily slow. However, that is much better than all users experiencing slow response time!

Queuing accomplishes a lot of tasks—including reducing loss. Because loss occurs when queues fill, and because the queuing methods typically provide the ability to configure the maximum queue size, you can just make the queue longer. With a longer maximum queue size, likelihood of loss decreases. However, queuing delay increases. Consider, for instance, Figure 1-16.

Figure 1-16 *Queuing Affects on Packet Loss*

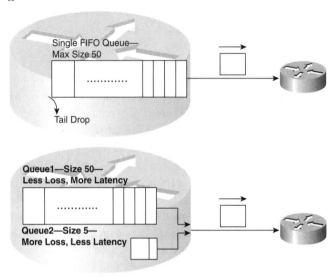

In the top example, a single FIFO queue is used. For delay-sensitive traffic, waiting behind 49 other packets might not work well. For applications that are loss sensitive, but not as delay sensitive, however, a long queue might work better. One goal might be to put delay-sensitive traffic into a different queue from loss-sensitive traffic, with an extra-long queue length for the loss-sensitive traffic, as shown in the bottom part of the figure. As usual, a tradeoff occurs—in this case, between low loss and low delay.

Table 1-9 summarizes the points concerning the two types of QoS tools that affect loss.

Table 1-9 *QoS Tools That Affect Loss*

Type of QoS Tool	Brief Description
Queuing	Implementing longer queues increases delay, but avoids loss.
RED	Implementing RED drops packets randomly as queues approach the point of being full, slowing some TCP connections. This reduces overall load, shortening the congested queue, while affecting only some user's response times.

Summary: QoS Characteristics: Bandwidth, Delay, Jitter, and Loss

This book covers a wide variety of QoS tools, and every tool either directly or indirectly affects bandwidth, delay, jitter, or loss. Some tools improve a QoS characteristic for one packet, but degrade it for others. For example, queuing tools might let one packet go earlier, reducing delay, while increasing delay for other packets. Some QoS tools directly impact one characteristic, but indirectly affect others. For instance, RED manages loss directly, but it indirectly reduces delay for some flows because RED generally causes queue sizes to decrease.

As this book explains each new feature in detail, you will also find a summary of how the feature manages bandwidth, delay, jitter, and loss.

Traffic Characteristics of Voice, Video, and Data

So why do you need QoS? QoS can affect a network's bandwidth, delay, jitter, and packet loss properties. Applications have different requirements for bandwidth, delay, jitter, and packet loss. With QoS, a network can better provide the right amounts of QoS resources for each application.

The next three sections cover voice, video, and data flows. Earlier versions of the QOS exam included more coverage of the QoS characteristics of voice, video, and data; however, the current QoS exam does not cover these topics in as much depth. Many readers of the previous edition of this book let us know that the following sections provided a lot of good background information, so, it's probably worth reading through the details in the rest of this chapter, but more of the focus on the QOS exam will come from the remaining chapters in this book. If you choose to skip over this section, make sure to catch the short section titled "Planning and Implementing QoS Policies" near the end of this chapter's "Foundation Topics" Section.

Voice Traffic Characteristics

Voice traffic can degrade quickly in networks without QoS tools. This section explains enough about voice traffic flows to enable the typical reader to understand how each of the QoS tools applies to voice.

> **NOTE**   This book does not cover voice in depth because the details are not directly related to QoS. For additional information, refer to the following sources:
>
> *Deploying Cisco Voice over IP Solutions*, Cisco Press, Davidson and Fox
>
> *IP Telephony*, Hewlett-Packard Professional Books, Douskalis
>
> *Voice over IP Fundamentals*, Cisco Press, Davidson and Peters
>
> *IP Telephony*, McGraw Hill, Goralski and Kolon
>
> www.cisco.com/warp/public/788/voip/delay-details.html

Without QoS, the listener experiences a bad call. The voice becomes choppy or unintelligible. Delays can cause poor interactivity—for instance, the two callers keep starting to talk at the same time, because the delays sound like the other person speaking has finished what he or she had to say. Speech is lost, so that there is a gap in the sound that is heard. Calls might even be disconnected.

Most QoS issues can be broken into an analysis of the four QoS characteristics: bandwidth, delay, jitter, and loss. The basics of voice over data networks is covered first, followed by QoS details unique to voice in terms of the four QoS characteristics.

Voice Basics

Voice over data includes Voice over IP (VoIP), Voice over Frame Relay (VoFR), and Voice over ATM (VoATM). Each of these three voice over data technologies transports voice, and each is slightly different. Most of the questions you should see on an exam will be related to VoIP, and not VoFR or VoATM, because of the three options, VoIP is the most pervasive. Also calls between Cisco IP Phones use VoIP, not VoFR or VoATM.

Imagine a call between the two analog phones in Figure 1-17, extensions 201 and 301.

Figure 1-17 *Call Between Analog Phones at Extensions 301 and 201*

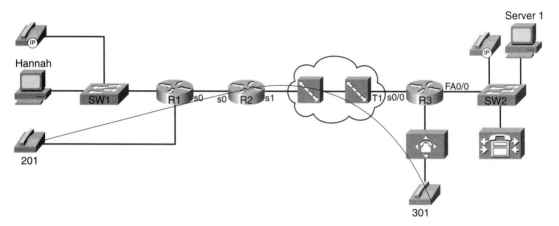

Before the voice can be heard at the other end of the call, several things must happen. Either user must pick up the phone and dial the digits. The router connected to the phone interprets the digits and uses signaling to set up the VoIP call. (Because both phones are plugged into FXS analog ports on R1 and R3, the routers use H.323 signaling.) At various points in the signaling process, the caller hears ringing, and the called party hears the phone ringing. The called party picks up the phone, and call setup is complete.

The actual voice call (as opposed to signaling) uses Real-Time Transport Protocol (RTP). Figure 1-18 outlines the format of an IP packet using RTP.

Figure 1-18 *IP Packet for Voice Call: RTP*

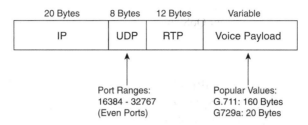

In the call between the two analog phones, the router collects the analog voice, digitizes the voice, encodes the voice using a voice codec, and places the encoded voice into the payload field shown in Figure 1-18. For instance, R1 would create an IP packet as shown in Figure 1-18, place the encoded voice bits into the voice payload field, and send the packet. The source IP address would be an IP address on R1, and the destination IP address would be an IP address on R3. When R3 receives the packet, it reverses the process, eventually playing the analog waveform for the voice out to the analog phone.

The IP Phones would experience a similar process in concept, although the details differ. The signaling process includes the use of Skinny Station Control Protocol (SSCP), with flows between each phone and the Cisco CallManager server. After signaling has completed, an RTP flow has been completed between the two phones. CallManager does not participate directly in the actual call, but only in call setup and teardown. (CallManager does maintain a TCP connection to each phone for control function support.) R1 and R3 do not play a role in the creation of the RTP packets on behalf of the IP Phone, because the IP Phones themselves create the packets. As far as R1 and R3 are concerned, the packets sent by the IP Phones are just IP packets.

Finally, the network administrator can choose from various coders/decoders (codecs) for the VoIP calls. Codecs process the incoming analog signal and convert the signal into a digital (binary) signal. The actual binary values used to represent the voice vary based on which codec is used. Each codec has various features, the most significant feature being the amount of bandwidth required to send the voice payload created by the codec. Table 1-10 lists the most popular codecs, and the bandwidth required for each.

Table 1-10 *Popular Voice Codecs and Payload Bandwidth Requirements*

Codec	Bit Rate for Payload* (in kbps)	Size of payload (20-ms Default in Cisco IOS Software)
G.711 Pulse Code Modulation (PCM)	64	160 bytes
G.726 ADPCM	32	80 bytes
G.729	8	20 bytes
G.723.1 ACELP	5.3	20 bytes

* The payload contains the digitized voice, but does not include headers and trailers used to forward the voice traffic.

This short section on voice basics (and yes, it is very basic!) can be summarized as follows:

- Various voice signaling protocols establish an RTP stream between the two phones, in response to the caller pressing digits on the phone.

- RTP streams transmit voice between the two phones (or between their VoIP gateways).

Why the relatively simple description of voice? All voice payload flows need the same QoS characteristics, and all voice signaling flows collectively need another set of QoS characteristics. While covering each QoS tool, this book suggests how to apply the tool to "voice"—for two subcategories, namely voice payload (RTP packets) and voice signaling. Table 1-11 contrasts the QoS requirements of voice payload and signaling flows.

Table 1-11 *Comparing Voice Payload to Voice Signaling: QoS Requirements*

	Bandwidth	**Delay**	**Jitter**	**Loss**
Voice Payload	Low	Low	Low	Low
Voice Signaling	Low	Low	Medium	Medium

QoS tools can treat voice payload differently than they treat voice signaling. To do so, each QoS tool first classifies voice packets into one of these two categories. To classify, the QoS tool needs to be able to refer to a field in the packet that signifies that the packet is voice payload, voice signaling, or some other type of packet. Table 1-12 lists the various protocols used for signaling and for voice payload, defining documents, and identifying information.

Table 1-12 *Voice Signaling and Payload Protocols*

Protocol	**Documented By**	**Useful Classification Fields**
H.323/H.225	ITU	Uses TCP port 1720
H.323/H.245	ITU	TCP ports 11xxx
H.323/H.245	ITU	TCP port 1720 (Fast Connect)
H.323/H.225 RAS	ITU	TCP port 1719
Skinny	Cisco	TCP ports 2000-2002
Simple Gateway Control Protocol (SGCP)		TCP ports 2000-2002
Media Gateway Control Protocol (MGCP)	RFC 2705	UDP port 2427, TCP port 2428
Intra-Cluster Communications Protocols (ICCP)	Cisco	TCP ports 8001–8002

Table 1-12 *Voice Signaling and Payload Protocols*

Real-Time Transport Protocol (RTP)	RFC 1889	UDP ports 16384–32767, even ports only
Real-Time Control Protocol (RTCP)	RFC 1889	UDP ports 16385–32767, odd ports only; uses RTP port + 1

The next few sections of this book examine voice more closely in relation to the four QoS characteristics: bandwidth, delay, jitter, and loss.

Voice Bandwidth Considerations

Voice calls create a flow with a fixed data rate, with equally spaced packets. Voice flows can be described as isochronous, which, according to Dictionary.com, means "characterized by or occurring at equal intervals of time." Consider Figure 1-19, where a call has been placed between analog phones at extensions 201 and 301.

Figure 1-19 *Isochronous Packet Flow for Voice Call*

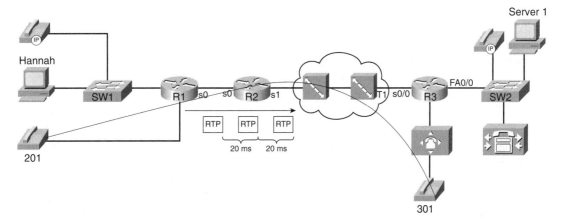

R1 creates the IP/UDP/RTP voice payload packets and sends them, by default, every 20 ms. Because Cisco IOS Software places 20 ms of encoded voice into each packet, a packet must be sent every 20 ms. So, how much bandwidth is really needed for the voice payload call? Well, actual bandwidth depends on several factors:

■ Codec

■ Packet overhead (IP/UDP/RTP)

■ Data-link framing (depends on data links used)

■ Compression

Most people quote a G.711 call as taking 64 kbps, and a G.729 call as taking 8 kbps. Those bandwidth numbers consider the payload only—ignoring data-link, IP, UDP, and RTP headers.

The bandwidth requirements vary dramatically based on the codec and the compression effect if RTP header compression is used. Compressed RTP (cRTP) actually compresses the IP/UDP/ RTP headers, with dramatic reduction in bandwidth when used with lower bit-rate codecs. With G.711, because a large percentage of the bandwidth carries the payload, cRTP helps, but the percentage decrease in bandwidth is not as dramatic. In either case, cRTP can increase delay caused while the processor compresses and decompresses the headers.

> **NOTE**   Although other codecs are available, this book compares G.711 and G.729 in most examples, noting any conditions where a different specific codec may need different treatment with QoS.

ATM can add a significant amount of data-link overhead to voice packets. Each ATM cell has 5 bytes of overhead; in addition, the last cell holding parts of the voice packet may have a lot of wasted space. For instance, a voice call using G.729 will have a packet size of 60 bytes. ATM adds about 8 bytes of framing overhead, and then segments the 68-byte frame into two cells— one using the full 48 bytes of ATM cell payload, and the other only using 20 bytes of the cell payload area—with 28 bytes "wasted." Therefore, to send one voice "packet" of 60 bytes, two cells, in total 106 bytes, must be sent over ATM. One option to lessen the overhead is to change the payload size to contain 30 ms of voice with a G.729 codec—which interestingly also only takes two ATM cells.

Voice Activity Detection (VAD) also affects the actual bandwidth used for a voice payload call. VAD causes the sender of the voice packets to not send packets when the speaker is silent. Because human speech is typically interactive (I know there are some exceptions to that rule that come to mind right now!), VAD can decrease the actual bandwidth by about 60 percent. The actual amount of bandwidth savings for each call cannot be predicted—simple things such as calling from a noisy environment defeats VAD. Also VAD can be irritating to listeners. After a period of not speaking, the speaker starts to talk. The VAD logic may perform front-end speech clipping, which means that the first few milliseconds of voice are not sent.

Table 1-13 shows a side-by-side comparison of the actual bit rates used for two codecs and a variety of data link protocols. This table also shows rows when using the most popular codec's default of 20 ms of voice payload (50 packets per second) for a voice call, versus 30 ms of voice payload per packet (33.3 packets per second).

Table 1-13 *Updated Bandwidth Requirements for Various Types of Voice Calls*

Bandwidth Consumption, Including L2 Overhead	Layer 3 Bandwidth Consumption*	802.1Q Ethernet (32 Bytes of L2 Overhead)	PPP (9 Bytes of L2 Overhead)	MLP (13 Bytes of L2 Overhead)	Frame-Relay (8 Bytes of L2 Overhead)	ATM (Variable Bytes of L2 Overhead, Depending on Cell-Padding Requirements)
G.711 at 50 pps	80 kbps	93 kbps	84 kbps	86 kbps	84 kbps	106 kbps
G.711 at 33 pps	75 kbps	83 kbps	77 kbps	78 kbps	77 kbps	84 kbps
G.729A at 50 pps	24 kbps	37 kbps	28 kbps	30 kbps	28 kbps	43 kbps
G.729A at 33 pps	19 kbps	27 kbps	21 kbps	22 kbps	21 kbps	28 kbps

*Layer 3 bandwidth consumption refers to the amount of bandwidth consumed by the Layer 3 header through the data (payload) portion of the packet.

One of the more interesting facts about the numbers in this table is that G.729 over ATM has a significant advantage when changing from 50 pps (20 ms of payload per packet) to 33 pps (30 ms of payload per packet). That's because you need 2 ATM cells to forward a 60-byte VoIP packet (20 ms payload of G.729), and you also need two cells to forward an 80-byte VoIP packet (30 ms payload of G.729).

Voice Delay Considerations

Voice call quality suffers when too much delay occurs. The symptoms include choppy voice, and even dropped calls. Interactivity also becomes difficult—ever had a call on a wireless phone, when you felt like you were talking on a radio? "Hey Fred, let's go bowling—OVER"— "Okay, Barney, let's go while Betty and Wilma are out shopping—OVER." With large delays, it sometimes becomes difficult to know when it is your turn to talk.

Voice traffic experiences delays just like any other packet, and that delay originates from several other sources. For a quick review on delay components covered so far, consider the delay components listed in Table 1-14.

Table 1-14   *Components of Delay Not Specific to One Type of Traffic*

Delay Component	Definition	Where It Occurs
Serialization delay	Time taken to place all bits of a frame onto the physical medium. Function of frame size and physical link speed.	Outbound on every physical interface; typically negligible on T3 and faster links.
Propagation delay	Time taken for a single bit to traverse the physical medium from one end to the other. Based on the speed of light over that medium, and the length of the link.	Every physical link. Typically negligible on LAN links and shorter WAN links.
Queuing delay	Time spent in a queue awaiting the opportunity to be forwarded (output queuing), or awaiting a chance to cross the switch fabric (input queuing).	Possible on every output interface. Input queuing unlikely in routers, more likely in LAN switches.
Forwarding or processing delay	Time required from receipt of the incoming frame until the frame/packet has been queued for transmission.	On every piece of switching equipment, including routers, LAN switches, Frame Relay switches, and ATM switches.
Shaping delay	Shaping (if configured) delays trans mission of packets to avoid packet loss in the middle of a Frame Relay or ATM network.	Anywhere that shaping is configured, which is most likely on a router, when sending packets to a Frame Relay or ATM network.
Network delay	Delays created by the components of the carrier's network when using a service. For instance, the delay of a Frame Relay frame as it traverses the Frame Relay network.	Inside the service provider's network.

Figure 1-20 shows an example of delay concepts, with sample delay values shown. When the delay is negligible, the delay is just listed as zero. The figure lists sample delay values. The values were all made up, but with some basis in reality. Forwarding delays are typically measured in microseconds, and become negligible. The propagation delay from R1 to R2 is calculated based on a 100-km link. The serialization delays shown were calculated for a G.729 call's packet, no compression, assuming PPP as the data- link protocol. The queuing delay varies greatly; the example value of 15 ms on R1's 56-kbps link was based on assuming a single 105-byte frame was enqueued ahead of the packet whose delay we are tracking—which is not a lot of queuing delay. The network delay of 50 ms was made up—but that is a very reasonable number. The total delay is only 94 ms—to data network engineers, the delay seems pretty good.

Figure 1-20 *Example Network with Various Delay Components Shown: Left-to-Right Directional Flow*

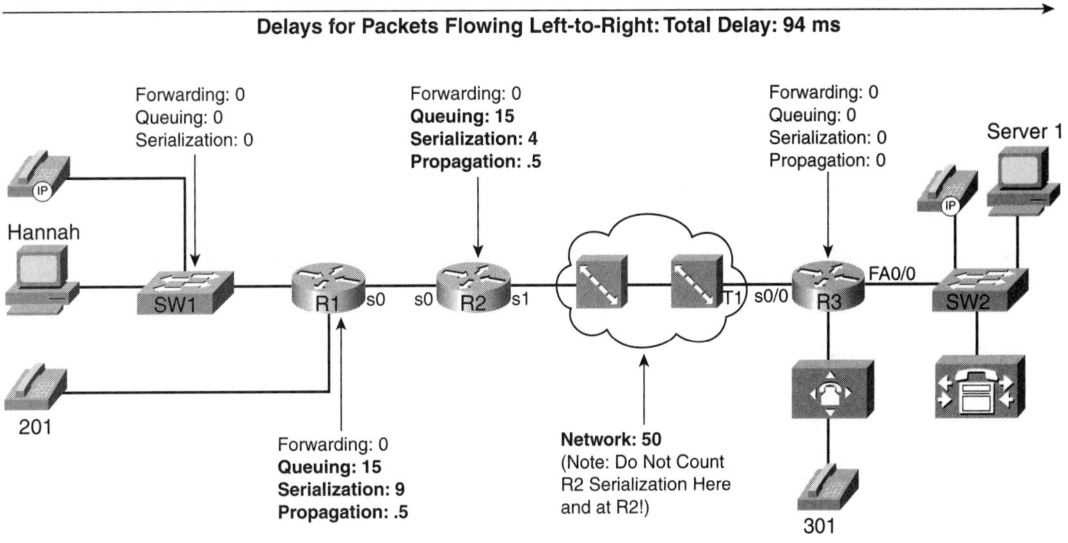

Delays for Packets Flowing Left-to-Right: Total Delay: 94 ms

So is this good enough? How little delay does the voice call tolerate? The ITU defines what it claims to be a reasonable one-way delay budget. Cisco has a slightly different opinion. You also may have applications where the user tolerates large delays to save cash. Instead of paying $3 per minute for a quality call to a foreign country, for instance, you might be willing to tolerate poor quality if the call is free. Table 1-15 outlines the suggested delay budgets.

Table 1-15 *One-Way Delay Budget Guidelines*

1-Way Delay (in ms)	Description
0–150	ITU G.114's recommended acceptable range
0–200	Cisco's recommended acceptable range
150–400	ITU G.114's recommended range for degraded service
400+	ITU G.114's range of unacceptable delay in all cases

With the example in Figure 1-20, the voice call's delay fits inside the G.114 recommended delay budget. However, voice traffic introduces a few additional delay components, in addition to the delay factors that all data packets experience:

■ Codec delay

■ Packetization delay

■ De-jitter buffer delay (initial playout delay)

Be warned—many books and websites use different terms to refer to the component parts of these three voice-specific types of delay. The terms used in this book are consistent with the Cisco courses, and therefore with the exams.

Codec delay and packetization delay coincide with each other. To get the key concepts of both, consider Figure 1-21, which asks the question, "How much delay happens between when the human speaks, and when the IP packets are sent?"

Figure 1-21 *Codec and Packetization Delays Between the Instant the Speaker Speaks and When the Packet Holding the Speech Is Sent*

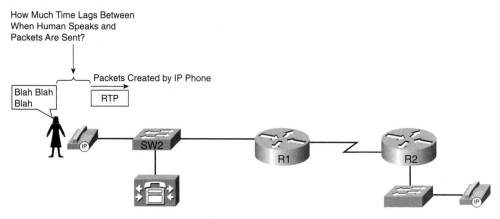

Consider what has to happen at the IP Phones before a packet can be sent. The caller dials digits, and the call is set up. When the call is set up, the IP Phone starts sending RTP packets. When these packets begin, they are sent every 20 ms (default)—in other words, each packet has 20 ms of voice inside the voice payload part of the packet. But how much time passes between when the speaker makes some sound and when the voice packet containing that sound is first sent?

Consider sounds waves for an instant. If you and I sit in the same room and talk, the delay from when you speak and when I hear it is very small, because your voice travels at the speed of sound, which is roughly 1000 km per hour. With packet telephony, the device that converts from sound to analog electrical signals, then to digital electrical signals, and then puts that digital signal (payload) into a packet, needs time to do the work. So there will be some delay between when the speaker speaks and when the IP/UDP/RTP payload packet is sent. In between when the speaker talks and when a packet is sent, the following delays are experienced:

- Packetization delay

- Codec delay

Packetization Delay

The IP Phone or voice gateway must collect 20 ms of voice before it can put 20 ms worth of voice payload into a packet. (The defaults for G.711 and G.729 on IP Phones and Cisco IOS Software gateways are to put 20 ms of voice into an RTP packet; the value can be changed.) Therefore, for the sake of discussion in this book, we consistently consider packet delay always to be 20 ms in examples. That is, the speaker must talk for 20 ms before a packet containing 20 ms of voice can be created.

Codec Delay

Codec delay has two components:

- The time required to process an incoming analog signal and convert it to the correct digital equivalent

- A feature called *look-ahead*

With the first component of codec delay, which is true for all codecs, the IP Phone or gateway must process the incoming analog voice signal and encode the digital equivalent based on the codec in use. For instance, G.729 processes 10 ms of analog voice at a time. That processing does take time—in fact, the actual conversion into G.729 CS-ACELP (Conjugate Structure Algebraic Code Excited Linear Predictive) takes around 5 ms. Some documents from Cisco cite numbers between 2.5 and 10 ms, based on codec load.

The codec algorithm may cause additional delays due to a feature called *look-ahead*. Look-ahead occurs when the codec is predictive—in other words, one method of using fewer bits to encode voice takes advantage of the fact that the human vocal cords cannot instantaneously change from one sound to a very different sound. By examining the voice speech, and knowing that the next few ms of sound cannot be significantly different, the algorithm can use fewer bits to encode the voice—which is one way to improve from 64-kbps G.711 to an 8-kbps G.729 call. However, a predictive algorithm typically requires the codec to process some voice signal that will be encoded, plus the next several milliseconds of voice. With G.729, for example, to process a 10-ms voice sample, the codec must have all of that 10 ms of voice, plus the next 5 ms, in order to process the predictive part of the codec algorithm.

So, the G.729a codec delays the voice as follows, for each 10-ms sample, starting with the time that the 10 ms to be encoded has arrived:

5 ms look-ahead + 5 ms processing (average) = 10 ms

Remember, codec delay is variable based on codec load. The white paper, "Understanding Delay in Packet Voice Networks," at Cisco.com provides more information about this topic (www.cisco.com/warp/public/788/voip/delay-details.html).

Considering the Effects of Packetization and Codec Delay

You need to consider packetization delay and codec delay together, because they do overlap. For instance, packetization delay consumes 20 ms while waiting on 20 ms of voice to occur. But what else happens in the first 20 ms? Consider Table 1-16, with a timeline of what happens, beginning with the first uttered sound in the voice call.

Table 1-16 *Typical Packetization and Codec Delay Timeline—G.729*

Timeline	Action	Codec Delay	Packetization Delay
T=0	Begin collecting voice samples for A/D conversion, encoding	Not begun yet (by this book's definition)	Begins
T=10	Collected complete 10-ms sample, which will be encoded with G.729	Codec delay begins	10 ms so far; packetization delay continues
T=15	Collected first 5 ms of second 10-ms sample	5 ms so far; G.729 now has the 5-ms look-ahead that the algorithm needs to encode first 10 ms sample	15 ms so far; packetization delay continues
T=20	Finished collecting second 10-ms sample	10 ms so far; codec delay finished for first 10-ms sample; second 10-ms sample in memory; codec delay for second sample begins	Packetization delay complete at 20 ms, because 20 ms of voice has been collected
T=25	Collected first 5 ms of third 10-ms sample	5-ms delay so far on second 10-ms sample; 15 ms total; G.729 now has the 5-ms look-ahead that the algorithm needs to encode second 10-ms sample	Finished with packetization delay; 20 ms voice has been received
T=30	Finished collecting third 10-ms sample	20 ms total codec delay; RTP and payload ready to be sent	Finished. 20 ms total
Total delays for first packet		20 ms	20 ms

Notice that the packetization and codec delays overlap. Although each takes 20 ms, because there is overlap, the packet actually experiences about 30 ms of total delay instead of a total of 40 ms.

De-Jitter Buffer Delay

De-jitter buffer delay is the third voice delay component. Jitter happens in data networks. You can control it, and minimize it for jitter-sensitive traffic, but you cannot eliminate it. Buy why talk about jitter in the section on delay? Because a key tool in defeating the effects of jitter, the de-jitter buffer (sometimes called the *jitter buffer*) actually increases delay.

The de-jitter buffer collects voice packets and delays playing out the voice to the listener, to have several ms of voice waiting to be played. By doing so, if the next packet experiences jitter and shows up late, the de-jitter buffer's packets can be played out isochronously, so the voice sounds good. This is the same tool used in your CD player in your car—the CD reads ahead several seconds, knowing that your car will hit bumps, knowing that the CD temporarily will not be readable—but having some of the music in solid-state memory lets the player continue to play the music. Similarly, the de-jitter buffers "reads ahead" by collecting some voice before beginning playout, so that delayed packets are less likely to cause a break in the voice.

The de-jitter buffer must be filled before playout can begin. That delay is called the *initial playout delay* and is depicted in Figure 1-22.

Figure 1-22 *De-Jitter Buffer Initial Playout Delay, No Jitter in First Three Packets*

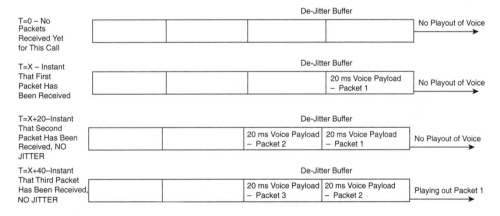

In this figure, the de-jitter buffer shows the initial playout delay. The time difference between when the initial packet arrives, and when the third packet arrives, in this particular case, is 40 ms. (Cisco IOS gateways default to 40 ms of initial playout delay.) In fact, if the initial playout delay were configured for 40 ms, this delay would be 40 ms, regardless of when the next several packets arrive. Consider, for instance, Figure 1-23, which gives a little insight into the operation of the de-jitter buffer.

In Figure 1-23, the playout begins at the statically set playout delay interval—40 ms in this case—regardless of the arrival time of other packets. A 40-ms de-jitter playout delay allows jitter to occur—because we all know that jitter happens—so that the played-out voice can continue at a constant rate.

Figure 1-23 *De-Jitter Buffer Initial Playout Delay, 10 ms Jitter for Third Packet*

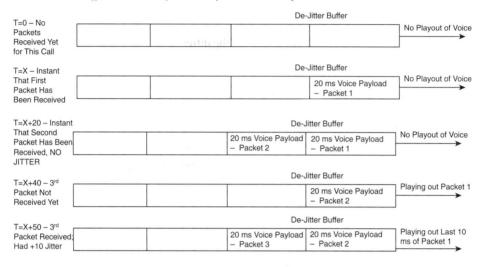

Figure 1-24 summarizes all the delay components for a voice call. This figure repeats the same example delay values as did Figure 1-20, but with voice-specific delays added for codec, packetization, and de-jitter delays shown.

Figure 1-24 *Complete End-to-End Voice Delay Example*

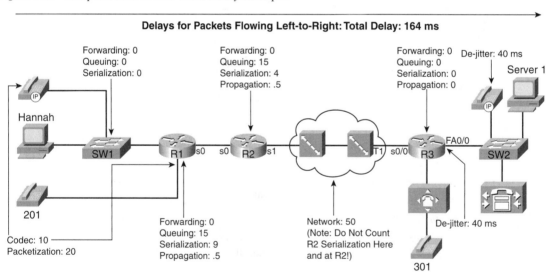

The delay has crept beyond the acceptable limits of one-way delay, according to G.114, but slightly under the limit of 200 ms suggested by Cisco. Without the additional voice delays, the 150-ms delay budget seemed attainable. With 30 ms of codec and packetization delay, however, and a (reasonable) default of 40-ms de-jitter delay (actually, de-jitter initial playout delay), 70 ms of that 150/200-ms delay is consumed. So, what can you do to stay within the desired delay budget? You attack the variable components of delay. Table 1-17 lists the different delay components, and whether they are variable.

Table 1-17   *Delay Components, Variable and Fixed*

Delay Component	Fixed or Variable	Comments	QoS Tools That Can Help
Codec	Fixed	Varies slightly based on codec and processing load; considered fixed in course books (and probably on exams). Typically around 10 ms.	None.
Packetization	Fixed	Some codecs require a 30-ms payload, but packetization delay does not vary for a single codec. Typically 20 ms, including when using G.711 and G.729.	None.
Propagation	Variable	Varies based on length of circuit. About 5 ms/1000 km	Move your facilities to the same town.
Queuing	Variable	This is the most controllable delay component for packet voice	Queuing features, particularly those with a priority-queuing feature.
Serialization	Fixed	It is fixed for voice packets, because all voice packets are of equal length. It is variable based on packet size for all packets.	Fragmentation and compression.
Network	Variable	Least controllable variable component.	Shaping, fragmentation, designs mindful of reducing delay.
De-jitter buffer (initial playout delay)	Variable	This component is variable because it can be configured for a different value. However, that value, once configured, remains fixed for all calls until another value is configured. In other words, the initial playout delay does not dynamically vary.	Configurable playout delay in IOS gateways; not configurable in IP Phones.

Voice Jitter Considerations

The previous section about delay explained most of the technical details of voice flows relating to jitter. If jitter were to cause no degradation in voice call performance, it would not be a problem. However, jitter causes hesitation in the received speech pattern and lost sounds, both when the jitter increases quickly and when it decreases quickly. For instance, consider Figure 1-25, where packets 3 and 4 experience jitter.

Figure 1-25 *De-Jitter Buffer Underrun Due to Jitter*

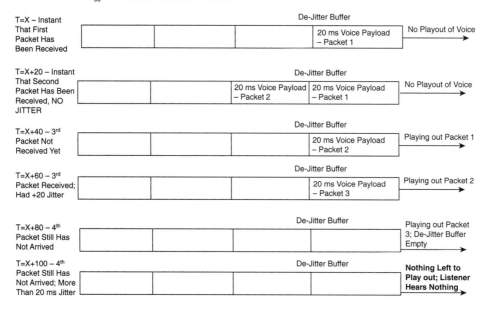

In Figure 1-25, the second packet experiences the same delay as the first packet. How can you tell? The IP Phone or Cisco IOS gateway sends the packets every 20 ms; if they arrive 20 ms apart, the delay for each packet is the same, meaning no jitter. However, packet 3 arrives 40 ms after packet 2, which means packet 3 experienced 20 ms of jitter. Packet 4 does not arrive until 45 milliseconds later than packet 3; because packet 4 was sent 20 ms after packet 3, packet 4 experienced 25 ms of jitter. As a result, the de-jitter buffer empties, and there is a period of silence. In fact, after packet 4 shows up, the receiver discards the packet, because playing the voice late would be worse than a short period of silence.

Another way to visualize the current size of the de-jitter buffer is to consider the graph in Figure 1-26. The packet arrivals in the figure match Figure 1-25, with the size of the de-jitter buffer shown on the y-axis.

Figure 1-26   *De-Jitter Buffer Underrun Graph*

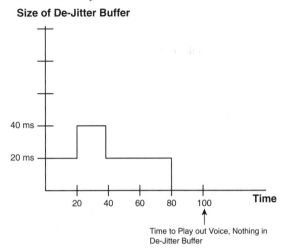

What caused the jitter? Variable delay components. The two most notorious variable delay components are *queuing delay* and *network delay*. Queuing delay can be reduced and stabilized for voice payload packets by using a queuing method that services voice packets as soon as possible. You also can use LFI to break large data packets into smaller pieces, allowing voice to be interleaved between the smaller packets. And finally, Frame Relay and ATM networks that were purposefully oversubscribed need to be redesigned to reduce delay. Jitter concepts relating to voice, and QoS, can be summarized as follows:

- Jitter happens in packet networks.

- De-jitter buffers on the receiving side compensate for some jitter.

- QoS tools, particularly queuing and fragmentation tools, can reduce jitter to low enough values such that the de-jitter buffer works effectively.

- Frame Relay and ATM networks can be designed to reduce network delay and jitter.

NOTE   IP Phones display statistics for jitter if you press the information ("i") button on the phone.

Voice Loss Considerations

Routers discard packets for a variety of reasons. The two biggest reasons for packet loss in routers are

- Bit errors

- Lack of space in a queue

QoS cannot help much with bit errors. However, QoS can help a great deal with loss due to queue space. Figure 1-27 contrasts FIFO queuing (one queue) with a simple queuing method with one queue for voice payload, and another for everything else.

Suppose, for instance, that four packets arrive almost instantaneously, numbered 1 through 4, with packet 1 being the first to arrive. In the FIFO scheme, the router places the packets into the FIFO output queue, in the same order as arrival. What happens, however, if the output queue only has space for three packets, as shown in the figure? Well, the fourth packet is tail dropped.

Now suppose that the fourth packet is a voice packet, and the two-queue system is used. Each queue has space for three packets. In this case, the router does not drop the voice packet (packet 4). In fact, assuming the router serves the voice queue so that any packets always get to be sent next, this router reduces the delay for the voice packet.

Figure 1-27 *FIFO Queuing Versus Imaginary Two-Queue System (One Queue for Voice, One for Everything Else)*

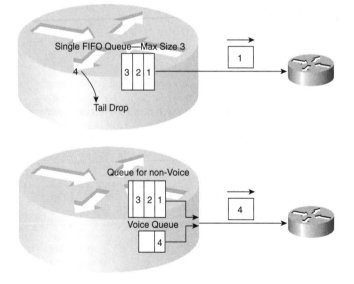

> **NOTE**   A queue of size 3 is too small; however, showing a queue of size 40 just seemed to be a little clumsy in the figure!

With the simple example in Figure 1-27, the router does not drop the voice packet. However, the real power of this two-queue system shines through with a little closer examination. Suppose that CAC allows only two concurrent G.729a calls to run through this router, and suppose the router does not use cRTP. The bandwidth required would be 26.4 kbps for each call, or a total of 52.8 kbps. Now imagine that the queuing method always sends the voice packets at next opportunity when a voice packet arrives, only waiting for the "currently being sent" packet to finish. Also imagine that the queuing method guarantees at least 60 kbps of this 128-kbps link for the voice queue. With all these features, the voice queue should never get very long (assuming the following parameters):

- Queuing that always takes voice packets at first opportunity.

- Call admission control that prevents too many voice calls.

- LFI, which allows voice packets to be interleaved between fragments of large data packets.

- The voice queue would never fill and voice packets would not be tail dropped on this interface.

Another type of QoS tool, call admission control (CAC), provides a very important component of a strategy to avoid packet loss, and thereby improve voice quality. The best router-based queuing tools for voice include a setting for the maximum amount of bandwidth used by the voice queue. If exceeded, when the interface has other packets waiting, the excess voice packets are discarded. Literally, adding one call too many can make what was a large number of quality voice calls all degrade to poor quality. Some form of CAC must be considered to avoid loss for all calls.

Finally, one additional feature helps when a single voice payload packet is lost. G.729 codecs compress the voice payload in part by predicting what the next few milliseconds of voice will look like. G.729 uses this same logic to perform a function called *autofill* when converting from digital to analog at the receiving side of the call. G.729 autofill makes an educated guess at what the next few milliseconds of sound would have been if the next packet in sequence has been lost. Autofill makes this educated guess, filling in up to 30 ms of "lost" voice. Because IP Phone and IOS gateways default to sending 20 ms of voice per packet, with G.729, a single packet can be lost, and the G.729 autofill algorithm will play out a best guess as to what was in the missing voice packet.

Loss considerations for voice can be summarized as follows:

■ Routers drop packets because of many reasons; the most controllable reason is tail drop due to full queues.

■ Queuing methods that place (isochronous) voice into a different queue than bursty data reduce the chance that voice packets will be tail dropped.

■ The QoS tools that help voice already, particularly queuing and LFI, reduce the chance of the voice queue being full, thereby avoiding tail drop.

■ Whereas other QoS tools protect voice from other types of packets, CAC protects voice from voice.

■ Single voice packet loss, when using G.729, can be compensated for by the autofill algorithm.

Video Traffic Characteristics

Without QoS, video flows typically degrade. The pictures become unclear. Movement is jerky. Movement appears to be in slow motion. Often, the audio becomes unsynchronized with the video. The video can be completely gone, but the audio still works. In short, unless the network has significantly more bandwidth than is needed for all traffic, video quality degrades.

Just like the coverage of voice in this chapter, this section breaks down an analysis of video traffic as it relates to the four QoS characteristics: bandwidth, delay, jitter, and loss. First, the basics of packet video are explained, followed by QoS details unique to video in terms of the four QoS characteristics.

Video Basics

IP packet video can be categorized into two main categories:

■ **Interactive video**—Includes H.323-compliant video conferencing systems, such as Cisco's IP/VC 3500 series of products, and Microsoft's NetMeeting desktop video- conferencing product. H.323-compliant video-conferencing tools use the familiar RTP protocol for transmission of the voice and audio payload, typically sending the audio in a separate RTP stream than the video.

■ **Noninteractive video**—Includes typical e-learning video services and streaming media, and includes products such as Cisco's IP/TV, Microsoft Windows Media Technologies products, and RealNetworks products. Some noninteractive video uses H.323 standards for video call setup and teardown, and some do not—for instance, RealNetworks most recent servers use Real-Time Streaming Protocol (RTSP) for call setup/teardown, and either the proprietary RealNetworks Data Transport (RDT) or RTP for video payload, depending on the video player used.

Like voice, video codecs convert the analog audio and video to packetized form. Codec delay, packetization delay, and de-jitter initial playout delay are all included in video delay, just like with voice. Familiar voice codecs, including G.711 and G.729, convert the audio stream, which is typically sent as a separate flow from the video signal. The video signals use a large variety of codecs, including ITU H.261, and the popular Moving Pictures Experts Group (MPEG) codecs. Figure 1-28 depicts a typical video conference between two H.323-compliant video- conference systems.

Figure 1-28 *H.323 Video Conference*

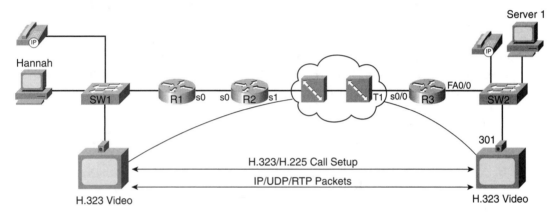

Before the video conference can be begin, several things must happen:

■ A user must point/click the correct application settings to ask for a conference, typically something as simple as telling the H.323 application that you want a conference with a particular host name.

■ The VC units must perform the H.323/H.225 call setup messages.

■ Two RTP streams must be established—one for audio, and one for video.

So far, the similarities between voice and video outstrip the differences. The biggest difference is the bandwidth required for video. (Bandwidth requirements are covered in the upcoming section "Video Bandwidth Considerations.") Table 1-18 summarizes the type of QoS characteristics that video requires, as well as voice.

Table 1-18 *Comparing Voice and Video QoS Requirements*

	Bandwidth	Delay	Jitter	Loss
Voice Payload	Low	Low	Low	Low
Video Payload	High	Low	Low	Low
Voice Signaling	Low	Low	Medium	Medium
Video Signaling	Low	Low	Medium	Medium

Just like with voice, most QoS effort goes toward giving the video payload flows the QoS characteristics it needs. However, you might still want to treat video signaling traffic differently than other data traffic, and treat the video payload traffic differently. To classify, the QoS tool needs to be able to refer to a field in the packet that signifies that the packet is video payload, video signaling, or some other type of packet. Table 1-19 lists the various protocols used for signaling and for voice payload, defining documents, and identifying information.

Table 1-19 *Video Signaling and Payload Protocols*

Protocol	Documented By	Useful Classification Fields
H.323/H.225	ITU	Uses TCP port 1720
H.323/H.245	ITU	TCP ports 11xxx
H.323/H.225 RAS	ITU	TCP port 1719
RTSP	IETF RFC 2326	TCP or UDP port 554
Real-Time Transport Protocol (RTP)	RFC 1889	UDP ports 16384–32767, even ports only

The next few sections of this book examine video more closely in relation to the four QoS characteristics:

- Bandwidth

- Delay

- Jitter

- Loss

Video Bandwidth Considerations

Unlike voice, video uses a variety of packet sizes and packet rates to support a single video stream. Most video codecs take advantage of what can loosely be called "prediction," by sending an encoded video frame (large packet), followed by a series of vectors describing changes to the previous frame (small packet). Although this type of algorithm greatly reduces the required bandwidth, it does cause video streams to use a dynamic packet rate, with a range of packet sizes. Also the actual average bandwidth required for a section of video depends on the complexity and amount of movement in the video. Table 1-20 lists four popular video codecs and the required bandwidth ranges for each:

Table 1-20   *Video Codecs and Required Bandwidth*

Video Codec	Required Range
MPEG-1	500 to 1500 kbps
MPEG-2	1.5 to 10 Mbps
MPEG-4	28.8 to 400 kbps
H.261	100 to 400 kbps

Different codecs simply provide different tradeoffs for quality and bandwidth, and many different codecs are needed to support applications of all types. For instance, MPEG includes several standards that were created for different types of applications. ITU H.261 provides a video standard for video conferencing, which works well when the callers do not move around too much! If you have ever been on a video conference and watched someone who used their hands a lot to talk, for instance, you might have seen jerky arm movements. All these codecs operate with dynamic bandwidth, and with different-sized packets. Figure 1-29 shows a packet distribution for percentages of packets at various sizes in an H.261 conference call.

Figure 1-29   *Packet Size Distributions in a Video Conference Using H.261*

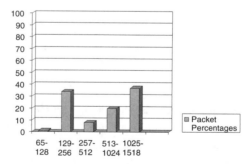

As mentioned earlier, video flows vary both the size of packets sent and the packet rate. In a high-quality video conference that might average 768 kbps of bandwidth, for example, the packet rates might vary from as low as 35 pps to as many as 120 pps. Also, some overhead will be needed for ongoing video signaling traffic. Some QoS tool configuration options might be affected by not only the bandwidth required (kbps), but also by the packet rate (pps). Remember, queue sizes are measured in packets; so to avoid tail drop, a queue holding video traffic may need a much larger queue size than a queue holding voice. Also, Cisco now recommends that when configuring queuing tools for video, you should allow for 20 percent more than the average bandwidth to deal with this small amount of variability in video traffic flows. Cisco also recommends that no more than 33 percent of the link be reserved for video traffic. Table 1-21 summarizes some of the key bandwidth differences between voice and video traffic.

Table 1-21 *Voice and Video Bandwidth Contrasted*

Feature	Voice	Video
Number of flows in each direction	1	2 (1 audio, 1 video)
Packet sizes	Static, based on codec	Variable
Packet rate	Constant (isochronous)	Variable

Video Delay Considerations

Two-way or interactive packet video experiences the same delay components as does a voice call. However, one-way or streaming packet video tolerates a fairly large amount of delay. Consider Figure 1-30, which shows a packet video device receiving a one-way streaming video stream.

Figure 1-30 *Large Playout Buffers for One-Way Video*

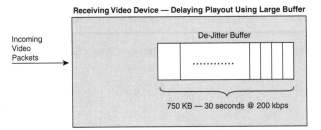

The initial playout delay takes 30 seconds—not 30 ms, but 30 seconds—in the example of Figure 1-30. No interaction occurs, and no video flows back to the video server; by far, the most important feature is that, when the video does play, it has high quality. With a 30-second de- jitter buffer, a cumulative jitter of 30 seconds (not milliseconds) can occur without having playout problems due to delay or jitter.

For two-way interactive packet video, delay of course does impact quality. The previous section about voice and voice delay explains most of what you need to know about video delay. Video experiences codec delay, packetization delay, and de-jitter (initial playout) delay. Of particular note, video delay budgets typically run from 0 to 200 ms for high-quality video conferencing, and de-jitter initial playout delays typically range from 20 to 70 ms.

Video Jitter Considerations

Just like for delay, one-way video tolerates jitter much more so than two-way, interactive video. When planning for QoS, two-way video should be treated just like voice in terms of minimizing delay. Furthermore, proper and accurate bandwidth allocation/provisioning is recommended. One-way, streaming video should be given enough bandwidth, but extra delay and jitter can be tolerated.

Jitter concerns for video networks can be summarized as follows:

- Jitter still happens in packet networks.

- De-jitter buffers on the receiving side compensate for some jitter.

- De-jitter buffers for interactive video typically run in the tens of milliseconds, allowing even small amounts of jitter to affect video quality.

- De-jitter buffers for streaming video typically run into the tens of seconds, allowing significant jitter to occur without affecting video quality

- QoS tools, particularly queuing and fragmentation tools, can reduce jitter to low enough values such that the de-jitter buffer for interactive video works effectively.

Video Loss Considerations

Video flows degrade when packets are lost. The picture becomes jerky due to missing frames, the images freeze, and the audio may cut in and out. In short, video does not tolerate loss very well.

Routers drop packets for many reasons; packet loss due to full queues can be addressed with several types of QoS tools. Remember, tail drop describes the situation when a queue fills, another packet needs to be added to the queue, so the router throws away the packet that needs to be added to the tail of the queue. You can use four general QoS strategies to reduce the chance of lost (dropped) video packets:

- Enable queuing and putting video in a different queue than bursty data traffic.

- Configure the video queue to be longer.

- Enable CAC to protect the video queue from having too many concurrent video flows in it—in other words, CAC can protect video from other video streams.

- Use a Random Early Detect (RED) tool on the loss-tolerant flows (typically data, not video!), which causes those flows to slow down, which in turn reduces overall interface congestion.

Comparing Voice and Video: Summary

Table 1-22 summarizes the QoS requirements of video in comparison to voice.

Table 1-22 *Comparing Voice and Video QoS Requirements*

	Bandwidth	Delay	Jitter	Loss
Voice Payload	Low	Low	Low	Low
Video Payload Interactive (2Way)	High	Low	Low	Low
Video Payload Streaming (1Way)	High	High	High	Low
Video Signaling	Low	Low	Medium	Medium
Voice Signaling	Low	Low	Medium	Medium

Data Traffic Characteristics

This book, as well as the exams about which this book prepares you, assumes you have a fairly high level of knowledge about data traffic before using this book. In fact, the QoS course assumes that you have been to the ICND and BSCI courses at least, and hopefully the BGP course. In fact, when the Cisco QoS course first came out, the expectation was that students should be CCNPs before attending the course.

QoS has always been important, but QoS has become vitally important with the convergence of data, voice, and video into a single network. As with any convergence of technologies, professionals working in the networking arena come from many different backgrounds. This section about data is intended for those who do not come from a data background.

> **NOTE** If you want to read more on TCP/IP protocols, take a look at the latest Douglas Comer's *Internetworking with TCP/IP* books. Volume 1 is most appropriate for networking engineers. A good alternative is Richard Stevens's *TCP/IP Illustrated*, Volume I.

Just like the coverage of voice and video in this chapter, this section breaks down an analysis of data traffic as it relates to the four QoS characteristics: bandwidth, delay, jitter, and loss. The discussion begins with the basics of data application flows, followed by QoS details as they relate to data in terms of the four QoS characteristics.

IP Data Basics

With voice and video, signaling occurred first in order to create the voice or video call. Although it is not called signaling in the data world, something similar does occur—for instance, when you open a web browser, and browse www.cisco.com, several things happen before the first parts of the web page appear. For our purposes for QoS, this book focuses on the actual payload flows—the actual data—rather than the data equivalent of signaling.

Most applications use one of two TCP/IP transport layer protocols: User Datagram Protocol (UDP) or Transmission Control Protocol (TCP). The person writing the application chooses which transport layer protocol to use. Most of the time the application programmer uses standard protocols, which tell them whether to use TCP or UDP. For instance, web servers use TCP, so if writing a web application, TCP is used.

TCP performs error recovery, but UDP does not. To perform error recovery, TCP sends some initialization messages to create a TCP connection, which coincidentally initializes some counters used to perform the error recovery. Figure 1-31 shows an example of connection establishment.

Figure 1-31 *TCP Connection Establishment*

TCP signals connection establishment using 2 bits inside flags field of the TCP header. Called the SYN and ACK flags, these bits have a particularly interesting meaning. SYN means "synchronize the sequence numbers," which is one necessary component in initialization for TCP. The ACK field means "the acknowledgment field is valid in this header."

When the three-way TCP handshake is complete, the TCP connection is up, and error recovery can be performed. Figure 1-32 shows how the sequence and acknowledgment fields are used, after the connection has been established.

Figure 1-32 *TCP Acknowledgments*

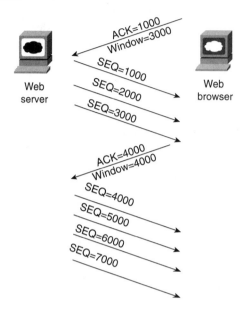

In the figure, the server sends data and labels it with the sequence number. The acknowledgment field in the TCP header sent back to the server by the web client (4,000) implies the next byte to be received; this is called *forward acknowledgment*. In essence, the browser acknowledged the receipt of all three packets, with sequence numbers 1000, 2000, and 3000. (Each packet contains 1000 bytes of data in this example.) The sequence number reflects the number of the first byte in the segment. Keep in mind that on the packet whose sequence number is 3000, with 1000 bytes, that bytes 3000 to 3999 are in the packet—so the browser should expect to get byte 4000 next.

TCP also controls the rate of sending data using windowing. This window field implies the maximum number of unacknowledged bytes allowed outstanding at any instant in time. Figure 1-34 shows windowing with a current window size of 3000, which increases to a window of 4000 by the end of the example. (Remember, each TCP segment has 1000 bytes of data in this example.) The window then "slides" up and down based on network performance, so it is sometimes called a *sliding window*. When the sender sends enough bytes to consume the current window, the sender must wait for an acknowledgment, which controls the flow of data. Effectively, the available window decreases as bytes are sent and increases as acknowledgment for those bytes are received.

The biggest difference between TCP and UDP is that TCP performs error recovery. Therefore, some people refer to TCP as reliable, and UDP as unreliable. And remember, voice and video flows that use RTP also use UDP—so why would voice and video use a protocol that is unreliable? The answer is simple: By the time a voice or video packet was sent, and TCP noticed that the packet was lost, and caused a retransmission, far too much delay would have already occurred. Therefore, resending the voice or video packet would be pointless. For data applications, however, where all the data really does need to make it to the other side of the connection, even if it takes additional time, TCP can be very useful. Figure 1-33 outlines the basic error-recovery logic of TCP.

Figure 1-33   *TCP Error Recovery*

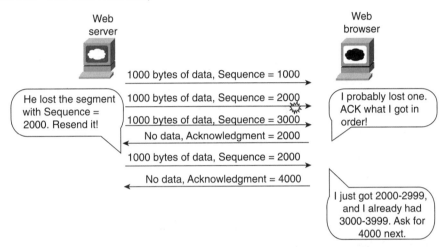

Figure 1-33 depicts a flow where the second TCP segment was lost or was in error. The web client's reply has an ACK field equal to 2000, implying that the web client is expecting byte number 2000 next. The TCP function at the web server then could recover lost data by resending the second TCP segment. The TCP protocol allows for resending just that segment and then waiting, hoping that the web client will reply with an acknowledgment that equals 4000.

Finally, you should understand one additional feature of TCP and UDP before continuing with your examination of QoS. That feature concerns a part of the TCP and UDP headers called the *source and destination port numbers*. The main purpose for port numbers can be seen with a simple example; for QoS, port numbers can be used to classify a packet, which in turn allows a router or switch to choose a different QoS action. In this case, Hannah is using three applications, and server Jessie is the server for all three applications. This particular company wrote an Advertising application and a wire-transfer application, both in use. In addition, Hannah is using a web-based application, as shown in Figure 1-34.

Figure 1-34 *Hannah Sending Packets to Jessie, with Three Applications*

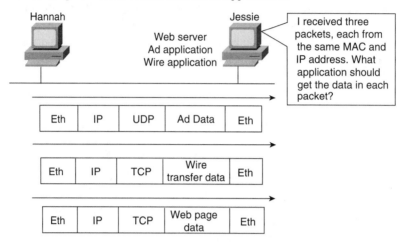

After receiving a packet, Jessie needs to know which application to give the data to, but all three packets are from the same Ethernet and IP address. You might think that Jessie could look at whether the packet contains a UDP or a TCP header, but, as you see in the figure, two applications (wire transfer and web) both are using TCP. Well, UDP and TCP designers purposefully included a port number field in the TCP and UDP headers to allow multiplexing. "Multiplexing" is the term generally used to describe the capability to determine which application gets the data for each packet. Each of the applications uses a different port number, so Jessie knows which application to give the data to, as seen in Figure 1-35.

Figure 1-35 *Hannah Sending Packets to Jessie, with Three Applications Using Port Numbers to Multiplex*

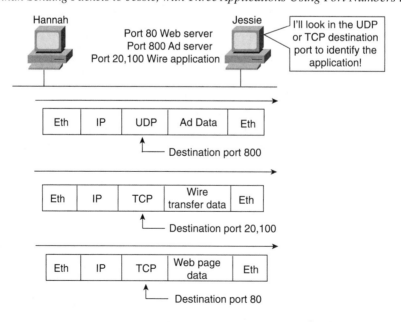

Most well-known applications, such as web, FTP, TFTP, Telnet, SMTP, POP3, and so on, use a well-known port. Using an application would be cumbersome if before you used it you had to call someone to find out what port number it uses. With well-known ports, you can assume that web servers use port 80, for instance. For QoS tools, if you want to classify web traffic, you can just look for packets that use port 80.

Certainly, you could spend a career just learning about, and working with, all the protocols inside the realm of TCP/IP. This brief introduction provides a little background that will help with some of the things you will read about in later sections. Table 1-23 lists the key points to remember about TCP and UDP.

Table 1-23   *TCP and UDP Comparison Chart*

Feature	TCP	UDP
Error recovery	Yes	No
Uses port number	Yes	Yes
Uses windowing for flow control	Yes	No

The next few sections of this book examine data more closely in relation to the four QoS characteristics: bandwidth, delay, jitter, and loss.

Data Bandwidth Considerations

Unlike voice, which consumes a constant amount of bandwidth, and unlike video, which consumes a range of bandwidth, data bandwidth requirements range wildly. Some applications might literally need less than 1 kbps, whereas others would take literally as much bandwidth as they can get.

The bigger question with data bandwidth revolves around OSI Layer 8—the business layer. For instance, how much bandwidth should web traffic get? Well, in many shops, web traffic consumes 80 percent of the network bandwidth used. However, a better question might be "How much bandwidth does important business web traffic get?" A financial-planning web application ought not to have to compete too hard with my surfing the ESPN.com website to check out the latest scores. A stockbroker might prefer that stock quotes get the lowest latency, for instance, and I would just have to wait a little longer to see the latest sports scores.

The other legitimate question with data application flows concerns whether the application is interactive or not. An interactive application needs less bandwidth typically (not always!) than do the typical noninteractive applications. The traditional comparison between Telnet (very low bandwidth) and FTP (takes as much bandwidth as it can get) implies that interactive implies low bandwidth. Well, many interactive applications today are web based, and if the web pages contain large amounts of graphics, the bandwidth required can also be pretty large.

Bandwidth, delay, jitter, and loss characteristics of data traffic vary based on these factors and others. In fact, one data application's QoS characteristics might be different at two different companies! Because so many factors must be considered, and because it varies from network to network, no one set of requirements really works.

However, do not despair! You should at least consider one perspective on bandwidth, based on business reasons. Simply put, some applications are business critical, and some are not. At a minimum, a QoS strategy should include identifying the critical applications, and giving these application flows the QoS characteristics they need. The rest of the data traffic can take the crumbs that have fallen off the table—or, in QoS terms, be treated as "best-effort" traffic. Table 1-24 summarizes some of the key bandwidth differences between all three types of traffic.

Table 1-24 *Voice, Video, and Data Bandwidth Contrasted*

Feature	Voice	2-Way Video	Data
Number of flows	2 (1 in each direction)	4 (1 audio and 1 video in each direction)	1 bidirectional flow
Packet sizes	Fixed, based on codec	Variable	Varies greatly
Packet rate	Constant (isochronous)	Variable	Varies greatly
Traffic load in opposite directions	Asymmetric	Symmetric	Asymmetric

Data Delay Considerations

Unlike voice and video, the perceived quality of the data application does not degrade quickly when delay increases by mere hundreds of milliseconds. In fact, relative to voice and interactive video, data applications tolerate delay very well. Also unlike voice and video, data applications tend to have round-trip delay requirements.

Two factors affect the delay requirements of a data application, as summarized in Table 1-25.

Table 1-25 *Factors to Consider for Data Delay*

Factor	Mission Critical	Not Mission Critical
Interactive	Should get the lowest delay of all data applications. Most shops strive for 1–2-second application response time— per-packet delay must be shorter.	Applications could benefit from lower delay. Also differentiating between mission critical and not mission critical can be difficult.
Not interactive	While mission-critical, noninteractive applications typically need particular bandwidth requirements met, delay can vary greatly as long as bandwidth is supplied.	Best candidate for getting any leftover bandwidth, with all other voice, video, and data applications getting better QoS treatment.

Because data QoS requirements vary greatly, more communication happens among the staff when deciding how to treat different applications with QoS. With more communication, the chances of miscommunication increase. If you talk to someone who does not just focus on the network, for instance, he might say "we need consistent 1- to 3-second response time on this mission-critical application!" What he means is that all packets, in both directions, that need to flow, in order for the user to see the complete response from the application, must occur in 1 to 3 seconds. Do not be fooled into thinking that a one-way delay for one packet of 1 to 3 seconds is what the user meant when he asked for 1- to 3-second application response time!

Data applications do not suffer from all the same causes of delay as do voice and video traffic. Earlier in the chapter you learned about the core delay components—queuing, serialization, propagation, network, processing, and shaping. Data does not suffer from the additional delay caused by codec, packetization, and de-jitter buffer delays.

Data Jitter Considerations

Just like for delay, data application tolerate jitter much more so than voice and video. Interactive applications are much less tolerant of jitter. I learned networking at a large SNA network inside IBM, and the adage when adjusting routes and QoS (built-in to SNA from the early days, but that's another story!) was that it was okay to have longer response times, as long as the response times were consistent. Human nature for some reason made consistency more important than net response time to most human interactive users, and that fact remains true today.

Interactive data applications cannot tolerate as much jitter or delay as noninteractive applications can. Voice and video applications can tolerate even less jitter or delay than interactive data applications. Because voice and video cannot tolerate any significant delay and jitter, engineers might choose to use QoS tools to decrease jitter for voice and video—which in turn increases delay and jitter for data applications! If a router sends a voice packet next rather than a data packet, for instance, the voice packet has a better chance of meeting its delay budget—but the data packet experiences more delay. Knowing that data can tolerate delay and jitter more than voice enables the engineer to make this tradeoff.

Jitter concerns for data networks can be summarized as follows:

- Jitter still happens in packet networks.

- Data applications do not have a de-jitter buffer—instead, the user always experiences some jitter, perceived simply as variable response times.

- Interactive applications are less tolerant of jitter, but jitter into the hundreds of milliseconds can be tolerated even for interactive traffic.

- In a converged network, QoS tools that improve (lower) jitter are best applied to voice and video traffic; the penalty is longer delays and more jitter for data applications.

Data Loss Considerations

Unlike voice and video, data does not always suffer when packets are lost. For most applications, the application needs to get all the data; if the lost packets are re-sent, however, no real damage occurs. Some applications do not even care whether a packet is lost. For perspective, consider applications to fall into one of three categories: those that use UDP and the applications perform error recovery, those that use UDP and the applications do not perform error recovery, and applications that use TCP.

UDP Applications That Perform Error Recovery

Some applications need error recovery but choose instead to implement the error recovery with application code. For instance, Network File System (NFS) and Trivial File Transfer Protocol (TFTP) both use UDP, and both perform error recovery inside the application. NFS provides the capability to read from and write to remote file servers—certainly guaranteeing that data is not lost would be important to NFS! Likewise, TFTP transfers files, so ensuring that the file was not missing parts would also be important. So, UDP applications that provide application layer recovery tolerate loss.

UDP Applications That Do Not Perform Error Recovery

Some applications simply do not need error recovery. The most popular of these protocols is Simple Network Management Protocol (SNMP), which allows management software to interrogate managed devices for information. Network management stations retrieve huge amounts of individual data, and often times a missed statistic occasionally does not impact the worker using the management software. SNMP designers purposefully avoided TCP and application layer error recovery to keep SNMP simple, and therefore more scalable, knowing that SNMP would be used in large volumes. Because the application does not care whether a packet is lost, these applications tolerate lost packets.

TCP-Based Applications

Because TCP-based applications expect TCP to recover lost packets, higher loss rates are acceptable. Although the lost packets may be transparent to the user, the added load on the network caused by retransmission of the packets can actually increase the congestion in the network.

Comparing Voice, Video, and Data: Summary

Table 1-26 summarizes the QoS requirements of data, in comparison to voice and video.

Table 1-26 *Comparing Voice, Video, and Data QoS Requirements*

	Bandwidth	Delay	Jitter	Loss
Voice Payload	Low to Medium	Low	Low	Low
Video Payload Interactive (2Way)	Medium	Low	Low	Low
Video Payload Streaming (1Way)	Medium to High	High	High	Low
Video Signaling	Low	Low	Medium	Medium
Voice Signaling	Low	Low	Medium	Medium
Data: Interactive, Mission Critical	Low to Medium	Low to Medium	Low to Medium	Medium to high
Data: Not Interactive, Mission Critical	Variable, typically high	High	High	Medium
Data: Interactive, Not Critical	Variable, typical medium	High	High	Medium
Data: Not Interactive, Not Critical	Variable, typically high	High	High	High

Planning and Implementing QoS Policies

Now you understand bandwidth, delay, jitter, and packet loss, as well as how those things impact voice, video, and data traffic. However, before you can go further with applying these concepts to a real network, you need to step back for a moment and consider a process by which you could examine a network, and then make good choices about how to proceed in implementing QoS.

To that end, the QoS course from Cisco suggests a three-step process for planning and implementing QoS. This is not the only possible process you could use, but it is the one from the QoS course, and the process is directly referenced by one of the exam objectives, so it's a good one to read through here. While the concepts might be somewhat intuitive, the steps are important. This short section takes a look at that particular process, which runs as follows:

Step 1   Identify traffic and its requirements

Step 2   Divide traffic into classes

Step 3   Define QoS policies for each class

The next few pages examines each step in succession.

Step 1: Identify Traffic and Its Requirements

When I teach QoS courses, I sometimes jokingly ask if everyone in the room knows all the types of traffic running through their networks. Seldom does anyone confidently say that they really do know what's running through their network. Do they have a good idea of the main applications, and the protocols they use? Sure. But seldom do people have a real sense for how much bandwidth is being used, or is needed, by a certain set of applications.

Step 1 in this 3-step process suggests that you should identify the traffic, which really boils down to a technical step (Step 1a), and a business step (Step 1b):

Step 1a   Perform a network audit by using trace analysis tools, management tools, Network-Based Application Recognition (NBAR), or any other tool to identify protocols and traffic volume

Step 1b   Perform a business audit to determine the importance of the discovered traffic types to the business

Step 1b might actually end up being the more difficult of the two because the network audit tends to be a very objective task, whereas the business audit can be a bit subjective.

In Step 1, you need to decide for each type of traffic what "its requirements" are, to quote the actual verbiage. Well, you've already read a lot about what different types of traffic need—but that's not what this step means. Instead, it boils down to service levels. What level of service does each type of traffic need to have in order to meet business goals? That's a hard question to answer. The concepts you've read about in this chapter will certainly be useful in making these choices, but you will also need to look at how much of each type of traffic will go to each site, find out current performance levels, and other analysis before deciding on an appropriate set of service levels for each traffic class.

Step 2: Divide Traffic into Classes

After completing Step 1, you should have a pretty good idea about the specific different types of traffic in your network. However, there might be lots of different types of traffic. This step suggests that you make decisions about which types of traffic end up in the same traffic class or service class.

The term *service class* refers to a set of one or more types of traffic that will be treated the same in terms of QoS. For instance, at Step 1 you might have examined five different mission critical applications, and defined service levels for each. However, if all five applications require the same QoS characteristics, then you can place all packets from all five applications into the same service class. You will define service classes in your router and switch configurations so that the router and switch QoS tools can attempt to provide the right levels of bandwidth, delay, jitter, and loss.

So, an expanded definition of this step might be to place each known type of traffic into a service class, with the intent to provide each service class with a unique quality of service.

The number of service classes will vary from site to site. However, for voice and video, you will likely end up with 3 classes:

- **One for voice payload**—The reason that most sites end up with all voice payload in one service class is that the voice calls have the same QoS requirements.

- **One for video payload**—Video differs from voice slightly, with variable packet rates, and a slightly variable bit rate, as compared to constant packet and bit rates for a voice call. As a result, it makes sense to separate voice and video into separate service classes

- **One for both voice and video signaling traffic**— Voice and video signaling traffic is actually more like a data application than voice or video, at least in terms of QoS. The signaling protocols tolerate delay and jitter very well, making them good candidates to be in a separate service class from voice and video.

For data, you might end up with only one or two service classes, or a lot. Cisco tends to highlight the following general classes in the QoS course:

- **Mission Critical**—typically interactive, with significant importance to the business

- **Transactional**—typically interactive, important to the business

- **Best-Effort**—General web browsing, e-mail, other unspecified traffic

- **Scavenger (Less-than-best-effort)**—Known types of insignificant or troublesome traffic, for instance, Napster or KaZaa

At the end of this step, you should have a written record of exactly what types of traffic end up in each class. The only exception is the best effort class, which by definition catches all the traffic that was not otherwise specified to be in some other service class.

Step 3: Define Policies for Each Traffic Class

A QoS policy is a written document that defines the QoS-related service levels for each service class. Essentially, the QoS policy includes the documentation of the work performed in the first two steps, plus the definitions of the QoS actions that should be taken in the routers and switches in order to reach the service levels defined in the QoS policy document.

In order for a QoS policy to actually provide a particular level of service, the policy defines actions to be taken on the packets inside a service class. These actions cause some change in the bandwidth, delay, jitter, and/or loss characteristics of those packets. For instance, a QoS policy might call for a queuing tool to give a guaranteed amount of bandwidth to a class of traffic. Another example might be to more aggressively discard one service class's packets, in order to reduce packet loss for another service class. A QoS policy might set a limit to the amount of bandwidth allowed for a service class, in order to prevent that service class from taking more bandwidth than it should.

While these steps may seem somewhat intuitive, once you read more about the QoS tools themselves, particular those that use the Modular QoS CLI (MQC), you will see that this 3-step process does provide a good basic framework with which to attack QoS efforts.

Foundation Summary

The "Foundation Summary" is a collection of tables and figures that provide a convenient review of many key concepts in this chapter. For those of you already comfortable with the topics in this chapter, this summary could help you recall a few details. For those of you who just read this chapter, this review will help solidify some key facts. For any of you doing your final prep before the exam, these tables and figures will be a convenient way to review the day before the exam.

Table 1-27 outlines some of the behaviors seen when no QoS is applied in a network.

Table 1-27 *Traffic Behavior with No QoS*

Type of Traffic	Behavior Without QoS
Voice	Voice is hard to understand.
	Voice breaks up, sounds choppy.
	Delays make interacting difficult; callers do not know when other party has finished talking.
	Calls are disconnected.
Video	Picture displays erratically; jerky movements.
	Audio not in sync with video.
	Movement slows down.
Data	Data arrives after it is no longer useful.
	Customer waiting for customer care agent, who waits for a screen to display.
	Erratic response times frustrate users, who may give up or try later.

As shown in Figure 1-36, with compression, if a ratio of 2:1 is achieved, the 80-kbps flow will only require 40 kbps in order to be sent across the link—effectively doubling the bandwidth capacity of the link.

Figure 1-36 *With a 2:1 Compression Ratio Versus No Compression*

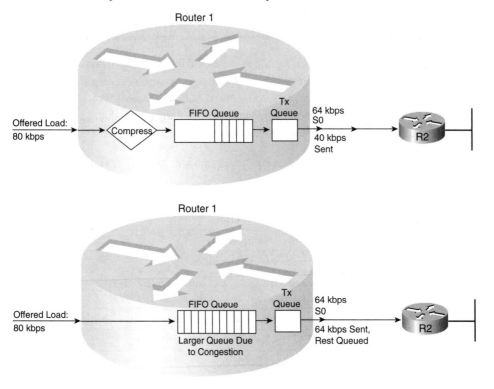

Figure 1-37 shows a two-queue system where the first queue gets 25 percent of the bandwidth on the link, and the second queue gets 75 percent of the bandwidth.

Figure 1-37 *Bandwidth Reservation Using Queuing*

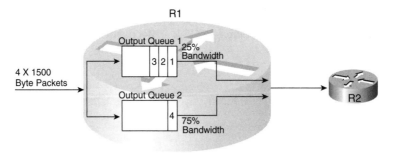

Figure 1-38 shows two contrasting examples of serialization and propagation delay.

Figure 1-38 *Serialization and Propagation Delay for Selected Packet and Link Lengths*

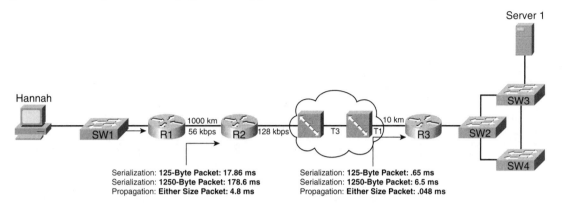

Serialization: **125-Byte Packet: 17.86 ms**
Serialization: **1250-Byte Packet: 178.6 ms**
Propagation: **Either Size Packet: 4.8 ms**

Serialization: **125-Byte Packet: .65 ms**
Serialization: **1250-Byte Packet: 6.5 ms**
Propagation: **Either Size Packet: .048 ms**

Figure 1-39 lists the queuing, serialization, and propagation delays experienced by data, voice, and video traffic.

Figure 1-39 *Delay Components: Three Components, Single Router (R1)*

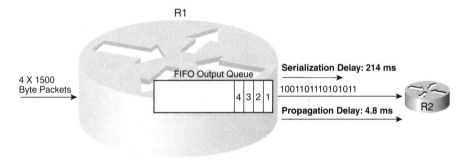

Figure 1-40 depicts LFI operation.

Figure 1-40 *Link Fragmentation and Interleaving*

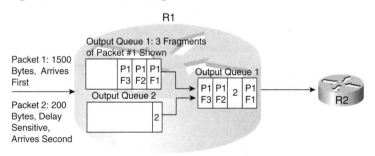

Legend: Px Fy Means Packet Number x, Fragment Number y

Figure 1-41 shows the jitter experienced by three packets as part of a voice call between phones at extension 301 and 201.

Figure 1-41 *Jitter Example*

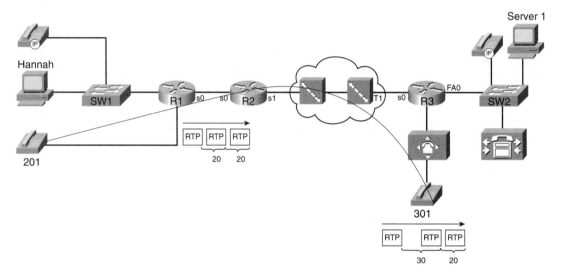

Figure 1-42 outlines the format of an IP packet using RTP.

Figure 1-42 *IP Packet for Voice Call—RTP*

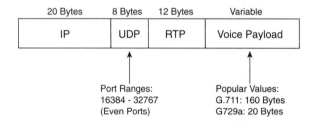

Table 1-28 lists the bandwidth requirements when using one of two codecs, with varying types of data link protocols.

Table 1-28 *Updated Bandwidth Requirements for Various Types of Voice Calls*

Bandwidth Consumption, Including L2 Overhead	Layer 3 Bandwidth Consumption *	802.1Q Ethernet (32 Bytes of L2 Overhead)	PPP (9 Bytes of L2 Overhead)	MLP (13 Bytes of L2 Overhead)	Frame-Relay (8 Bytes of L2 Overhead)	ATM (Variable Bytes of L2 Overhead, Depending on Cell-Padding Requirements)
G.711 at 50 pps	80 kbps	93 kbps	84 kbps	86 kbps	84 kbps	106 kbps
G.711 at 33 pps	75 kbps	83 kbps	77 kbps	78 kbps	77 kbps	84 kbps
G.729A at 50 pps	24 kbps	37 kbps	28 kbps	30 kbps	28 kbps	43 kbps
G.729A at 33 pps	19 kbps	27 kbps	21 kbps	22 kbps	21 kbps	28 kbps

*Layer 3 bandwidth consumption refers to the amount of bandwidth consumed by the Layer 3 header through the data (payload) portion of the packet.

Figure 1-43 shows an example of delay concepts, with sample delay values shown. When the delay is negligible, the delay is just listed as zero.

Figure 1-43 *Example Network with Various Delay Components shown: Left-to-Right Direction*

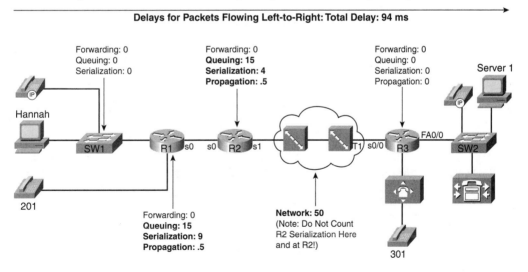

Table 1-29 outlines the suggested delay budgets.

Table 1-29 *One-Way Delay Budget Guidelines*

1-Way Delay (in ms)	Description
0–150	ITU G.114 recommended acceptable range
0–200	Cisco's recommended acceptable range
150–400	ITU G.114's recommended range for degraded service
400+	ITU G.114's range of unacceptable delay in all cases

All the delay components for a voice call are summarized in the example in Figure 1-44.

Figure 1-44 *Complete End-to-End Voice Delay Example*

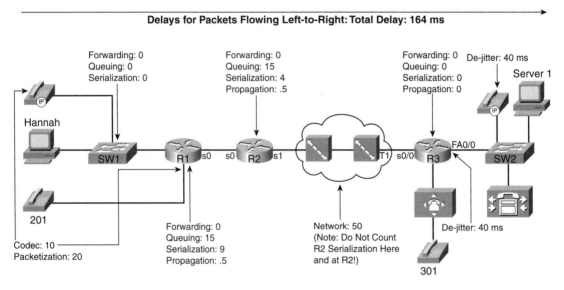

Table 1-30 lists the different delay components and whether they are variable.

Table 1-30 *Delay Components, Variable and Fixed*

Delay Component	Fixed or Variable	Comments	QoS Tools That Can Help
Codec	Fixed	Varies slightly based on codec and processing load; considered fixed in course books (and probably on exams). Typically around 10 ms.	None.

Table 1-30   *Delay Components, Variable and Fixed (Continued)*

Delay Component	Fixed or Variable	Comments	QoS Tools That Can Help
Packetization	Fixed	Some codecs require a 30-ms payload, but packetization delay does not vary for a single codec. Typically 20 ms, including when using G.711 and G.729.	None.
Propagation	Variable	Varies based on length of circuit. About 5 ms/1000 km	Move your facilities to the same town.
Queuing	Variable	This is the most controllable delay component for packet voice	Queuing features, particularly those with a priority-queuing feature.
Serialization	Fixed	It is fixed for voice packets, because all voice packets are of equal length. It is variable based on packet size for all packets.	Fragmentation and compression.
Network	Variable	Least controllable variable component.	Shaping, fragmentation, designs mindful of reducing delay.
De-jitter buffer (initial playout delay)	Variable	This component is variable because it can be configured for a different value. However, that value, once configured, remains fixed for all calls until another value is configured. In other words, the initial playout delay does not dynamically vary.	Configurable playout delay in IOS gateways; not configurable in IP Phones.

Table 1-31 summarizes the QoS requirements of data, in comparison to voice and video.

Table 1-31   *Comparing Voice, Video, and Data QoS Requirements*

	Bandwidth	Delay	Jitter	Loss
Voice Payload	Low to Medium	Low	Low	Low
Video Payload Interactive (2Way)	Medium	Low	Low	Low
Video Payload Streaming (1Way)	Medium to High	High	High	Low
Video Signaling	Low	Low	Medium	Medium
Voice Signaling	Low	Low	Medium	Medium

continues

Table 1-31 *Comparing Voice, Video, and Data QoS Requirements (Continued)*

	Bandwidth	Delay	Jitter	Loss
Data: Interactive, Mission Critical	Low to Medium	Low to Medium	Low to Medium	Medium to high
Data: Not Interactive, Mission Critical	Variable, typically high	High	High	Medium
Data: Interactive, Not Critical	Variable, typical medium	High	High	Medium
Data: Not Interactive, Not Critical	Variable, typically high	High	High	High

Q&A

As mentioned in the Introduction, you have two choices for review questions. The questions that follow next give you a more difficult challenge than the exam itself by using an open-ended question format. By reviewing now with this more difficult question format, you can exercise your memory better, and prove your conceptual and factual knowledge of this chapter. You can find the answers to these questions in Appendix A.

The second option for practice questions is to use the CD-ROM included with this book. It includes a testing engine and more than 200 multiple-choice questions. You should use this CD-ROM nearer to the end of your preparation, for practice with the actual exam format.

1. List the four traffic characteristics that QoS tools can affect.

2. Describe some of the characteristics of voice traffic when no QoS is applied in a network.

3. Describe some of the characteristics of video traffic when no QoS is applied in a network.

4. Describe some of the characteristics of data traffic when no QoS is applied in a network.

5. Interpret the meaning of the phrase, "QoS is both 'managed fairness,' and at the same time 'managed unfairness'."

6. Define bandwidth. Compare and contrast bandwidth concepts over point-to-point links versus Frame Relay.

7. Compare and contrast bandwidth and clock rate in relation to usage for QoS.

8. List the QoS tool types that affect bandwidth, and give a brief explanation of why each tool can affect bandwidth.

9. Define delay, compare/contrast one-way and round-trip delay, and characterize the types of packets for which one-way delay is important.

10. List the categories of delay that could be experienced by all three types of traffic: data, voice, and video.

11. Define, compare, and contrast serialization and propagation delay.

12. Define network delay.

13. List the QoS tool types that affect delay and give a brief explanation of why each tool can affect delay.

14. Define jitter. Give an example that shows a packet without jitter, followed by a packet with jitter.

15. List the QoS tool types that affect jitter and give a brief explanation of why each tool can affect jitter.

16.   Define packet loss and describe the primary reason for loss for which QoS tools can help.

17.   List the QoS tool types that affect loss and give a brief explanation of why each tool can affect loss.

18.   Describe the contents of an IP packet carrying the payload for a G.729 VoIP call.

19.   Describe the amount of bandwidth required for G.711 and G.729 VoIP calls, ignoring data-link header/trailer overhead.

20.   List the delay components that voice calls experience, but which data-only flows do not experience.

21.   Define the meaning of the term "packetization delay" in relation to a voice call.

22.   List the different one-way delay budgets as suggested by Cisco and the ITU.

23.   Define the term "codec delay" and discuss the two components when using a G.729 codec.

24.   Describe the affects of a single lost packet versus two consecutive lost packets, for a G.729 voice call.

25.   Describe a typical video payload flow in terms of packet sizes and packet rates.

26.   Discuss the delay requirements of video traffic.

27.   List the basic differences between TCP and UDP traffic.

28.   Contrast the QoS characteristics needed by interactive data applications, as compared to the QoS needs of voice payload flows.

29.   What are the three steps suggested in this chapter for planning QoS policy implementation?

30.   The chapter provides a suggested process for planning and implementing QoS policies. The first step involves identifying traffic classes and requirements. That step lists two specific types of audits that should be performed in this step. List and give a brief description of the two audit steps.

31.   Early in the chapter, a couple of different definitions of QoS were supplied. Paraphrase your own general definition of the term "QoS".

32.   What is the purpose of service classes when implementing a QoS policy?

33.   What are the three steps suggested in this chapter for planning QoS policy implementation?

34.   The chapter provides a suggested process for planning and implementing QoS policies. The first step involves identifying traffic classes and requirements. That step lists two specific types of audits that should be performed in this step. List and give a brief description of the two audit steps.

35.   Early in the chapter, a couple of different definitions of QoS were supplied. Paraphrase your own general definition of the term "QoS".

36.   What is the purpose of service classes when implementing a QoS policy?

QoS Exam Topics

This chapter covers the following exam topics specific to the QOS exam:

- List and explain the models for providing Quality of Service on a network

- Explain the purpose and function of the DiffServ model

- Describe the basic format of and explain the purpose of the DSCP field in the IP header

- Define and explain the different per hop behaviors used in DSCP

- Explain the interoperability between DSCP-based and IP-precedence-based devices in a network

- Given a list of QoS actions, correctly match the QoS actions to mechanisms for implementing QoS and identify where in a network the different QoS mechanisms are commonly used

CHAPTER 2

QoS Tools and Architectures

To build a house, you need tools, you need materials, you need labor, and you need architectural plans. To build a network using quality of service (QoS), you need tools, labor, and an architecture. This chapter lists the various IOS QoS tools and explains the two predominant QoS architectures: integrated services (IntServ) and differentiated services (DiffServ).

Chapter 1, "QoS Overview," covered various types of QoS tools. There are several different categories of QoS tools in Cisco IOS Software. This chapter begins by listing the tools in each category—at least the ones covered on the QOS exam. This first section also includes a brief introduction to concepts behind each type of tool. All the tools listed here get further treatment in later chapters of the book.

As a tool for learning, the second section of this chapter explains the basics of flow-based QoS tools and Class-Based QoS tools. Taking a few minutes to think about these concepts, and why they make sense, is useful before looking at the two formalized QoS models — namely DiffServ and IntServ.

Next, this chapter then examines the DiffServ architecture in detail. DiffServ attempts to provide Internet-scale QoS, which is a lofty goal indeed! DiffServ uses a Class-Based approach to differentiate between packets, which scales somewhat better than its predecessor, IntServ. Whether DiffServ succeeds in this goal remains to be seen; however, many of the concepts can be helpful with any QoS implementation.

Finally, the chapter ends with a short discussion on IntServ and Best Effort architectures. IntServ uses the Resource Reservation Protocol (RSVP) to reserve bandwidth for individual flows in the network. Best Effort is actually just a plan in which the network makes no real effort to give one type of packet better service than any other.

This chapter concludes the introductory materials in this book; the remainder of this book delves into the details of the various QoS tools.

"Do I Know This Already?" Quiz

The purpose of the "Do I Know This Already?" quiz is to help you decide whether you need to read the entire chapter. If you already intend to read the entire chapter, you do not necessarily need to answer these questions now.

The 12-question quiz, derived from the major sections in the "Foundation Topics" section of this chapter, helps you determine how to spend your limited study time.

Table 2-1 outlines the major topics discussed in this chapter and the "Do I Know This Already?" quiz questions that correspond to those topics.

Table 2-1 *"Do I Know This Already?" Foundation Topics Section-to-Question Mapping*

Foundation Topics Section Covering These Questions	Questions	Score
QoS Tools	1–4	
Classifying Using Flows or Service Classes	5–6	
The Differentiated Services QoS Model	7–11	
The Integrated Services QoS Model	12	
Total		

CAUTION   The goal of self-assessment is to gauge your mastery of the topics in this chapter. If you do not know the answer to a question or are only partially sure of the answer, mark this question wrong for purposes of the self-assessment. Giving yourself credit for an answer you correctly guess skews your self-assessment results and might provide you with a false sense of security.

You can find the answers to the "Do I Know This Already?" quiz in Appendix A, "Answers to the 'Do I Know This Already?' Quizzes and Q&A Sections." The suggested choices for your next step are as follows:

- **10 or less overall score**—Read the entire chapter. This includes the "Foundation Topics," the "Foundation Summary," and the "Q&A" sections.

- **11 or 12 overall score**—If you want more review on these topics, skip to the "Foundation Summary" section and then go to the "Q&A" section. Otherwise, proceed to the next chapter.

QoS Tools Questions

1. Which of the following are not Queuing tools?

   a. LLQ

   b. CBPQ

   c. CBWFQ

   d. CBCQ

   e. WRR

2. Which of the following tools monitors the rate at which bits are sent out an interface?

   a. LLQ

   b. CB Shaping

   c. WRED

   d. CB Policing

   e. MLP LFI

3. Which of the following tools can mark IP packet's DSCP field?

   a. CB Marking

   b. WRED

   c. CB Policing

   d. MLP LFI

   e. NBAR

4. Which of the following tools chooses to discard packets even though the router either has memory to queue the packets, or available physical bandwidth to send the packets?

   a. CB Marking

   b. WRED

   c. CB Policing

   d. MLP LFI

   e. NBAR

   f. ECN

Classifying Using Flows or Service Classes Questions

5. Which of the following are not used to identify a flow?

    a. ECN bits

    b. Source port

    c. Layer 4 protocol type

    d. Destination IP address

    e. TCP acknowledgment number

6. Which of the following are likely places at which to mark packets in a network using good QoS design practices?

    a. In client PCs

    b. As close to the client as possible without allowing end users to mark packets

    c. As packets enter an SP from a customer network

    d. As packets enter the LAN switch to which the destination host is attached

The Differentiated Services QoS Model Questions

7. What does DSCP stand for?

    a. Diffserv Static Code Point

    b. Diffserv Standardized Configuration Process

    c. Differentiated Services Code Point

    d. Differentiated Services Configuration Point

8. According to the DiffServ, which PHB defines a set of three DSCPs in each service class, with different drop characteristics for each of the three DSCP values?

    a. Expedited Forwarding

    b. Class Selector

    c. Assured Forwarding

    d. Multi-class-multi-drop

9. Which of the following is true about the location of DSCP?

    a. High order 6 bits of ToS byte

    b. Low order 6 bits of ToS byte

    c. Middle 6 bits of ToS byte

    d. High order 5 bits in ToS byte

10. Imagine a packet is marked with DSCP CS3. Later, a QoS tool classifies the packet. Which of the following classification criteria would match the packet, assuming the marking had not been changed from the original CS3 marking?

    a. Match of DSCP CS3

    b. Match of precedence 3

    c. Match on DSCP AF32

    d. Match on DSCP AF31

    e. Match on DSCP decimal 24

11. Imagine a packet is marked with AF31. Later, a QoS tool classifies the packet. Which of the following classification criteria would match the packet, assuming the marking had not been changed from the original AF31 marking?

    a. Match of DSCP CS3

    b. Match of precedence 3

    c. Match on DSCP AF32

    d. Match on DSCP AF31

    e. Match on DSCP 24

The Integrated Services QoS Model Questions

12. Which of the following are reasons why IntServ does not scale as well as DiffServ?

    a. Keeps flow state on each node

    b. Flow-based architecture

    c. Requires complex configuration for matching criteria for each possible flow

    d. Continuous signaling to maintain QoS reservation

Foundation Topics

This chapter introduces the long list of QoS tools and two important QoS architectures—differentiated services (DiffServ) and integrated services (IntServ). You can think of QoS implementation as building a house. To properly build a house, you certainly need (and use) a large variety of tools. An experienced builder might be able to use the tools to build a house without an architectural plan. With the architectural plans, however, an experienced house builder can build a better house! Similarly, an experienced network engineer can use QoS tools with good results, without considering the DiffServ and IntServ architectures. By considering these architectures, however, a network engineer can use the tools to implement the QoS policies more consistently and efficiently, and thereby guarantee better QoS.

This chapter begins with an introduction to the various QoS tools in Cisco IOS Software. The next section covers some basic concepts about flows, service classes, and where you might use a tool in a network. Following coverage of these topics, the chapter examines the three major QoS models, with particular emphasis on DiffServ.

Introduction to IOS QoS Tools

The next few pages introduce each class of QoS tool in a Cisco router as well as list the specific tools in each class. The specific classes of tools are as follows:

- Classification and marking

- Congestion Management (Queuing)

- Shaping and policing

- Congestion Avoidance

- Link-efficiency

- Call admission control (CAC)

Ultimately, this book focuses on topics covered on the Cisco QOS exam. To that end, this section introduces the specific QoS tools covered on the exam, with specific focus on router-based QoS tools. Chapters 3 through 8 provide much more detail about each tool. Also, if there's a QoS tool in router IOS that's not listed here, and you want more information, you might look at the introduction to this book, which lists the contents of a CD-ROM-only appendix. That appendix, found on the CD-ROM in the back of this book, contains coverage from previous editions of this book for QoS tools that are no longer covered on the Cisco QOS exam.

Chapter 9, "LAN QoS," covers the details of QoS tools on LAN switches.

Classification and Marking

Almost every QoS tool uses classification to some degree. To put one packet into a different queue than another packet, the IOS must somehow differentiate between the two packets. To perform header compression on RTP packets, but not on other packets, the IOS must determine which packets have Real Time Protocol (RTP) headers. To shape data traffic going into a Frame Relay network, so that the voice traffic gets enough bandwidth, the IOS must differentiate between Voice over IP (VoIP) and data packets. If an IOS QoS feature needs to treat two packets differently, you must use classification.

Classification involves differentiating one packet from another, typically by examining fields inside the headers. After classification, a QoS tool can treat packets in one class differently than others. To just give all VoIP traffic preference over all other traffic, the queuing tool would need to classify traffic into one of two categories: VoIP or not-VoIP.

Because most QoS tools need to differentiate between packets, most QoS tools have classification features. In fact, you may already know something about several of the QoS tools described in this book. You may realize that you already know how to perform classification using some of those tools. Many QoS tools enable you to classify using access-control lists (ACLs) — for instance, if ACL 101 "permits" a packet, the packet falls into one queue; if ACL 102 permits a packet, it is placed in a second queue; and so on. In one way of thinking, queuing could instead be called "classification and queuing," because the queuing feature must somehow decide which packets end up in which queue. Similarly, traffic shaping could be called "classification and traffic shaping," policing could be called "classification and policing," and so on. Because most QoS tools classify traffic, however, the names of most QoS tools never evolved to mention the classification function of the tool.

Only one category of QoS tool, called *classification and marking*, highlights the classification feature in the name of the tool. For other tools, the classification function is just part of the story; with classification and marking tools, classification is the whole point of the tool. To appreciate the need for classification and marking tools, consider Figure 2-1. The figure shows the QoS policies for traffic flowing right to left. R3 performs queuing and shaping, and R2 performs queuing only. However, for both sets of queues, and for the shaping function, classification must occur. The classification part of the effort seems to be a simple task, but it may cause many comparisons to be made. For instance, each packet exiting R3's S0 and R2's S0 interfaces might be compared for the following:

■ From source address 10.1.1.1, TCP source port 80 (Server1 web traffic)

■ Using User Datagram Protocol (UDP), port number range 16384 to 32767 (voice payload) — may also want to check IP address ranges to match IP Phones' voice subnets, or voice gateway IP addresses

- Using TCP port 1720 (H.323 voice signaling)

- Using TCP port range 11000 to 11999 (Voice signaling)

- Using TCP port 1719 (Voice signaling)

- Using TCP port 2000 to 2002 (Skinny voice signaling)

- Using UDP port 2427 and 2428 (MGCP voice signaling)

Figure 2-1 *Sample Network, with Queuing and Shaping Tools Enabled*

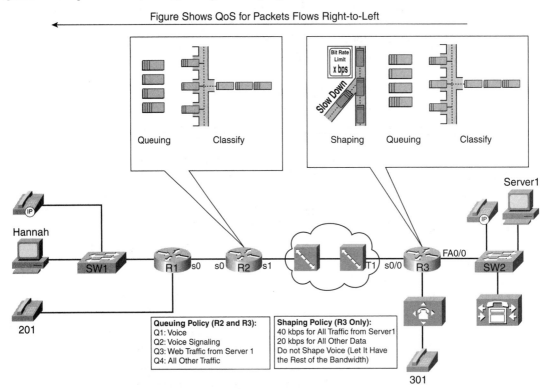

Classification and marking tools simplify the classification process of the other QoS tools. Even with seemingly simple requirements, the classification functions can require many comparisons to every packet. Rather than have each tool do extensive packet matching, classification and marking tools do the extensive classification once, and mark a field in a packet header. The remaining QoS tools just need to look for this marked field, simplifying the repetitive classification work.

The two most commonly used marking fields in the IP header are the IP Precedence field, and the Differentiated Services Code Point (DSCP) field. You will see the details of these two fields, along with the other fields that can be used for marking, later in this chapter. Consider Figure 2-2, where classification and marking is performed on input of R3.

Figure 2-2 *Sample Network, with Simplified Classification as a Result of Classification and Marking*

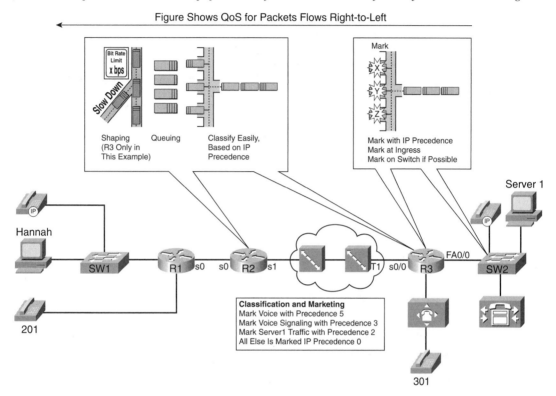

The queuing and shaping features can now classify more efficiently. Queuing is still performed on R3 and R2, and shaping is still performed on R3. However, the extensive matching logic for each packet done for all incoming traffic can be performed once on R3's FA0/0 interface, or once on one of the LAN switches, such as SW3. Once marked, the other QoS tools can react to the marked value, which each QoS tool can efficiently match in the end-to-end path through the network.

Classification and Marking Tools

A variety of classification and marking tools exist. Classification and marking tools first classify by looking at something inside each packet; you can compare these tools by listing the fields the tool can examine. Classification and marking tools mark the frame or packet based on the earlier comparisons; you can compare these tools by listing the fields that can be marked. Some classification and marking tools also perform other functions, as noted in Table 2-2.

Chapter 4, "Classification and Marking," explains the details of each of the tools, all the marked fields, and the configuration of each tool.

Table 2-2 *Comparison of Classification and Marking Tools*

Tool	Other Functions Besides Class and Mark	Fields That Can Be Examined for Classification	Fields That Can Be Marked*
Class-Based marking (CB marking)	None	IP ACLs Any markable fields Input interface MAC addresses All NBAR-enabled fields	IP precedence DSCP 802.1P CoS ISL Priority ATM CLP Frame Relay DE MPLS Experimental QoS Group
Network based application recognition (NBAR)	Statistical information about traffic mix; recognition of applications that use the dynamic port	Extensive list (see Chapter 3, "Classification and Marking")	None; used in conjunction with CB marking

* All claims about features/functions that may be affected by IOS versions assume version 12.2T, unless otherwise noted.

Queuing

Queuing, frequently called Congestion Management in Cisco documents, and also occasionally called "scheduling," provides the ability to reorder packets when congestion occurs. Whereas queuing sometimes occurs at the ingress interface, called "input queuing," most queuing methods implement only output queuing. The general idea is simple, but the details can be a little overwhelming. Consider Figure 2-3, with a simple two-queue output queue system.

Figure 2-3 *Simple Output Queuing, Two Queues*

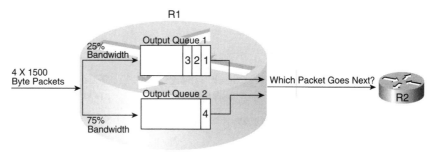

In the figure, four packets arrived in order, at about the same time. The queuing tool's classification feature classified packets 1 through 3 as belonging in Queue 1, and packet 4 as belonging in Queue 2. The figure implies that Queue 2 should receive 75 percent of the bandwidth. But which packet is sent next? In what order do these four packets leave the router? If packet 5 shows up a little later, could it be sent before some of packets 1 through 4? Could the tool support more than two queues? Well, the answers to these questions define the key comparison points between the various queuing tools. You should look for the following when comparing queuing tools:

■ Classification capabilities, particularly the packet header fields that can be matched to classify a packet into a particular queue. In some cases, the queuing tool automatically classifies traffic, whereas other tools require you to configure the values to be matched in the packets explicitly.

■ The maximum number of queues (sometimes called the maximum number of classes). If you need to distinguish between x different types of traffic for queuing, you need at least x queues.

■ The scheduling algorithm. For some queuing tools, Cisco publishes the algorithms used to decide what packet is taken from which queue next; for other tools, Cisco publishes the net effect of the algorithm. In either case, you can still make a good choice as to which tool to use.

Ultimately, you use these queuing features, and other less-obvious features, when choosing the right queuing tool for a particular need in a particular network.

Queuing Tools

QoS queuing tools provide you with a variety of queuing methods. Queuing tools define a number of queues. Cisco publishes the queue service algorithm in some cases; in others, Cisco publishes only the end result (the "what"), but not the algorithm (the "how"). Table 2-3 outlines the key features of IOS queuing methods.

Table 2-3 *Comparison of Queuing Tools*

Tool	Maximum Number of Queues	Classification Capabilities	Queue Service Algorithm/ End Result of Algorithm
Priority Queuing (PQ)	4	IP ACL Input interface Fragments	Strict service; always serves higher-priority queue over lower queue.
Custom Queuing (CQ)	16	IP ACL Input interface Fragments	Serves a configured number of bytes per queue, per round-robin pass through the queues. Result: Rough percentage of the bandwidth given to each queue under load.
Weighted Fair Queuing (WFQ)	4096	Automatic, based on flows. (Flow identified by source/destination address and port numbers, plus protocol type.)	Each flow uses a different queue. Queues with lower volume and higher IP precedence get more service; high volume, low precedence flows get less service.
Class-Based Weighted Fair Queuing (CBWFQ)	64	IP ACL NBAR Same as CB marking	Service algorithm not published; results in set percentage bandwidth for each queue under load.
Low Latency Queuing	N/A	Same as CBWFQ	LLQ is a variant of CBWFQ, which makes some queues "priority" queues, always getting served next if a packet is waiting in that queue. It also polices traffic.
Modified Deficit Round-Robin (MDRR)	8	IP precedence	Similar to CQ, but each queue gets an exact percentage of bandwidth. Supports LLQ mechanism as well.

Chapter 5, "Congestion Management," covers each of the queuing tools in detail.

Shaping and Policing

Because shaping and policing provide two different functions, you may wonder why shaping and policing are covered here at the same time. The simple answer is this: Networks that use policing typically need shaping as well. Also both shaping and policing measure the rates at which traffic is sent and received in a network, so some of the underlying features are similar. Both can be described using similar metaphors of "token buckets." Finally, from a business perspective, shaping and policing are typically implemented at or near the edge between an enterprise and a service provider. Therefore, when considering whether you need to use one type of tool, you need to be thinking about the other type.

Traffic shaping, or shaping, delays packets by putting packets in a queue, even when real bandwidth is available. It's like being at the bank. A teller finishes with a customer, and you're next in line. You have to wait another minute or two, however, while the teller finishes doing some paperwork for the preceding customer. Why would a router ever want to delay packets? Well, the short answer is "because delaying these packets is better than what happens if you don't delay them." Figure 2-4 shows just one example where shaping is useful.

Figure 2-4   *Sample Network, Speed Mismatch (T/1 and 128 kbps)*

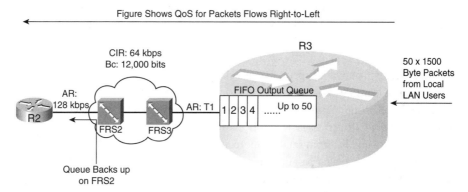

This example results in a large queue forming at Frame Relay Switch 2 (FRS2) due to the speed mismatch between the access links at R2 and R3. In this example, 50 1500-byte packets arrive over R3's Ethernet during a 500-ms span, needing to be delivered to R2. If all 50 packets were to arrive one after the other, with no gaps, a queue would form on R3's S0 interface. Because it takes a little less than 10 ms to send a 1500-byte packet over T/1, however, all 50 packets would drain from the queue within that 500 ms.

However, because the access link between FRS2 and R2 clocks at 128 kbps, it takes almost 100 ms to serialize a 1500-byte packet. So, although some queuing happens at R3, FRS2's egress queue on the link to R2 fills — in this case, it needs to be 45 packets long. (Five packets could be sent over this link during the 500 ms that the rest of the packets are arriving.)

What happens if FRS2's maximum egress queue size is only 20 frames? In such a scenario, around half of the frames are discarded. What is the impact? The quality of voice and video streams degrades. Most data applications resend their data — which may well cause the same phenomena all over again. Both results, of course, are bad.

Traffic shaping solves this particular problem. If R3 had just waited and sent one 1500-byte packet every 100 ms, because FRS2 can send one 1500-byte packet in a little less than 100 ms, no queue would have formed on FRS2's egress interface. Even if R3 were to send one 1500-byte packet every 50 ms, FRS2's egress queue would grow, but only a few packets would be lost.

Whenever a speed mismatch occurs, shaping may be able to reduce the chance that packets get dropped. In the previous example, a speed mismatch occurred on the access rates of two Frame Relay-connected routers. In other cases, it may be that many VCs terminate at one router, and the collective VC committed information rates (CIRs) far exceed the access rate (oversubscription). In either case, queues may form, and they may form in a place where the engineer cannot control the queue—inside the Frame Relay cloud.

Shaping may help in one other specific case: when the Frame Relay service provider uses policing. The service provider may need to limit a VC to use just the CIR amount of bandwidth. Most providers, as well as their customers, expect the Frame Relay data terminal equipment (DTE) to send more than the CIR across each VC. However, the provider may decide that in this case, they need to prevent R3 and R2 from sending more than CIR. Why? For many reasons, but one common reason may be that a particular part of their network may have enough capacity to support the CIRs of all VCs for all customers, but not much bandwidth beyond that. To protect customers from each other, the provider may limit each VC to CIR, or some percentage over CIR, and discard the excess traffic.

The QoS tool used to monitor the rate, and discard the excess traffic, is called traffic policing, or just policing. Because the provider is monitoring traffic sent by the customer, traffic policers typically monitor ingress traffic, although they can monitor egress traffic as well. Figure 2-5 shows the same network, but with policing and shaping enabled for traffic entering FRS3 from R3.

Figure 2-5 *Traffic Policing and Shaping*

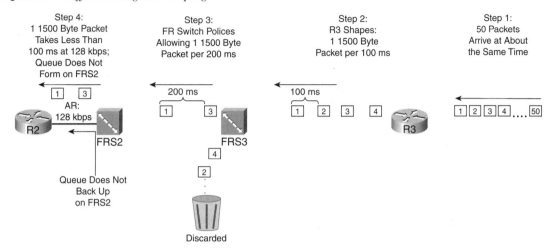

In the shaping discussion, one solution involved sending only one 1500-byte packet every 100 ms, which prevented an egress queue from forming on FRS2. As seen in this figure, however, the ingress policer on FRS3 monitors incoming traffic on the VC from R3 to R2, allowing only one 1500-byte packet per *200* ms. Policers discard the excess traffic, which in this case, even with shaping enabled on R3, half of the packets will be discarded when the network is busy! The solution, when the provider enables policing, is to configure shaping such that R3 only sends traffic at a rate that the policer function allows. In summary, some of the reasons behind shaping and policing are as follows:

■   Packets might be lost in a multiaccess WAN due to access rate speed mismatch, oversubscription of CIRs over an access link, or by policing performed by the provider.

■   Traffic shaping queues packets when configured traffic rates are exceeded, delaying those packets, to avoid likely packet loss.

■   Traffic policing discards packets when configured traffic rates are exceeded, protecting other flows from being overrun by a particular customer.

Shaping and Policing Tools

Cisco IOS provides several options for shaping and policing tools. As usual, you may consider many factors when comparing these tools. (Table 2-4 lists a few of these factors.) First, not all shaping and policing tools support every data-link protocol. Second, some tools can be enabled on a subinterface, but not on a per data-link connection identifier (DLCI); therefore, in cases where a network uses multipoint subinterfaces, one tool may give more granularity for shaping/policing. With regard to policers, some categorize packets as either conforming to or exceeding a traffic contract (called a two-headed policer), and some categorize packets as either conforming to, exceeding, or violating a traffic contract (a three-headed policer).

Table 2-4 *Comparison of Shaping and Policing Tools*

Tool	Policer or Shaper	Interfaces Supported	Per Subinterface, and Per VC, Support
Class-Based policing (CB policing; sometimes just called policer)	Policer	All that are supported by Cisco Express Forwarding (CEF)	Per subinterface
Class-Based shaping	Shaper	All that are supported by CEF	Per subinterface
Frame Relay traffic shaping (FRTS)	Shaper	Frame Relay	Per DLCI

Chapter 6, "Traffic Policing and Shaping," covers each of the policing and shaping tools in detail.

Congestion Avoidance

When networks become congested, output queues begin to fill. When new packets need to be added to a full queue, the packet is dropped—a process called *tail drop*. Tail drop happens in most networks every day—but to what effect? Packet loss degrades voice and video flows significantly; for data flows, packet loss causes higher-layer retransmissions for TCP-based applications, which probably increases network congestion.

Two solutions to the tail-drop problem exist. One solution is to lengthen queues, and thereby lessen the likelihood of tail drop. With longer queues, fewer packets are tail dropped, but the average queuing delay is increased. The other solution requires the network to ask the devices sending the packets into the network to slow down before the queues fill — which is exactly what the Congestion Avoidance QoS tools do.

Congestion Avoidance tools operate under the assumption that a dropped TCP segment causes the sender of the TCP segment to reduce its congestion window to 50 percent of the previous window. If a router experiences congestion, before its queues fill completely, it can purposefully discard several TCP segments, making a few of the TCP senders reduce their window sizes. By reducing these TCP windows, these particular senders send less traffic into the network, allowing the congested router's queues time to recover. If the queues continue to grow, more TCP segments are purposefully dropped, to make more TCP senders slow down. If the queues become less congested, the router can stop discarding packets.

Congestion Avoidance Tools

This book covers three Congestion Avoidance tools. One of the tools was never implemented in IOS (Random Early Detection, or RED) — but because the other two features are based on RED concepts, Chapter 7, "Congestion Avoidance Through Drop Policies," covers the basics of RED as well.

All Congestion Avoidance tools consider the queue depth—the number of packets in a queue—when deciding whether to drop a packet. Some tools weigh the likelihood of dropping a packet based on the IP precedence or IP DSCP value. One Congestion Avoidance tool doesn't actually discard packets but instead uses bits in the IP and TCP header to signal to the TCP sender asking it to slow down. Table 2-5 lists the tools and the various points for comparison.

Table 2-5 *Comparison of Congestion Avoidance Tools*

Tool	Can Be Enabled in IOS?	Weights Based On IP Precedence Or DSCP?	Doesn't Drop Packets, But Instead Signals Sender To Slow Down
Random Early Detection (RED)	No	No	No
Weighted Random Early Detection (WRED)	Yes	Yes	No
Explicit Congestion Notification (ECN)	Yes	Yes	Yes

Chapter 7 covers each of the Congestion Avoidance tools in detail.

Link Efficiency

The category of link efficiency encompasses two related topics: compression and fragmentation. Rather than treat these topics in two separate chapters, I have included them in one chapter (Chapter 8, "Link Efficiency Tools") to match the organization of the Cisco QOS courses (and the IOS documentation to some degree).

Compression reduces bandwidth utilization by making packets smaller before transmission. Two general types of compression tools exist in IOS—payload compression and header compression. Payload compression compresses the "packet" — the portion of the data link frame between the frame header and trailer. Header compression compresses just particular headers. Figure 2-6 shows the typical scope of the compressed portions of a frame over a PPP link.

Figure 2-6   *Scope of Compression for Payload and Header Compression Types*

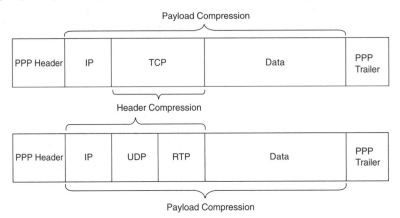

Compression tools differ in how much CPU load they create and which parts of the frame they compress. Based on the CPU load and what is compressed, you can make good decisions about when to use each tool.

Payload compression can be applied to all packets, with some good results. Suppose that the compression algorithm manages to compress x bytes of payload into half that size — a reasonable 2:1 compression ratio. The router saves a lot of bandwidth with the compression a 1500-byte packet into a 750-byte packet. Given the variation and unpredictable nature of the contents of the packets, compression ratios between 2:1 and 4:1 are reasonable with payload compression.

Header compression takes advantage of the fact that the headers being compressed are predictable. Much larger compression ratios can be achieved, many times with less CPU load than payload compression. However, header compression only operates on headers. For instance, compressed RTP compresses packets with IP/UDP/RTP headers, as shown in Figure 2-6. The 40 bytes of the IP/UDP/RTP headers compress to between 2 and 4 bytes. For a minimum packet size of 60 bytes, typical of G.729 VoIP calls, cRTP reduces the packet from 60 bytes to between 22 to 24 bytes, a significant improvement. However, head compression does not provide much benefit for larger packets, because the headers make up such a small percentage of the packets.

The other major category of link-efficiency tools is link fragmentation and interleaving (LFI), also just called fragmentation. The concept is simple: When a router starts sending a packet, it never just stops sending that packet in order to send a higher-priority packet — it finishes sending the first packet, and then sends the higher-priority packet. On slow links, the time it takes for one large packet to be serialized may cause too much delay, particularly for VoIP and video traffic. LFI tools fragment large packets into smaller packets, and then interleave the high-priority packet between the fragments. For instance, it takes 214 ms to serialize one 1500-byte packet over a 56-kbps link, which blows the VoIP one-way delay budget. (As described in Chapter 8, Cisco recommends that you considered LFI when the link speed is 768 kbps or less.) Figure 2-7 shows the process of fragmentation.

Figure 2-7 *Link Fragmentation and Interleaving*

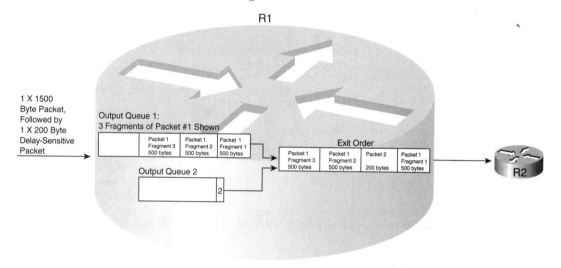

Without LFI, packet 2 has to wait 214 ms on the 1500-byte packet. With LFI fragmenting packet 1 into three parts, the serialization delay is reduced to about 72 ms.

Link-Efficiency Tools: Summary

Most link-efficiency tools have a specific application that becomes obvious when you discover what each tool can and cannot do. Not all compression and LFI tools support every type of data link. Both compression and LFI tools may operate on a subset of the packets that exit an interface. For instance, TCP header compression just compresses IP packets that also have TCP headers. Frame Relay fragmentation only operates on a subset of the packets, based on which of two styles of fragmentation is configured. So depending on what you want to accomplish with link efficiency, you can typically use a single tool. Table 2-6 lists the link- efficiency tools and some of the pertinent comparison points.

Chapter 8 covers each of the link-efficiency tools in detail.

Table 2-6 *Comparison of Link-Efficiency Tools*

Tool	Data Links Supported	Types of Packets to Which Tool Can Be Applied
Payload compression	All; recommended on serial links (T/1, E/1, and slower)	All IP packets
Class-Based RTP header compression (cRTP)	All; recommended on serial links (T/1, E/1, and slower)	All packets with IP/UDP/RTP headers
Class-Based TCP header compression	All; recommended on serial links (T/1, E/1, and slower)	All IP packets with TCP headers
Multilink PPP fragmentation and interleaving (MLPPP LFI)	Multilink PPP	All packets larger than a configured length
Frame Relay fragmentation (FRF*)	Frame Relay	All packets larger than a configured length (FRF.12) or all non-VoFR frames (FRF.11c)
Link fragmentation and interleaving for Frame Relay and ATM VCs	Frame Relay and ATM	All IP packets

*The Frame Relay Forum is often referred to as FRF; their document names tend to begin with the letters FRF as well. The QoS feature called Frame Relay Fragmentation is also referred to as FRF.

Call Admission Control

Call admission control (CAC) protects network bandwidth by preventing more concurrent voice and video flows than the network can support. By doing so, it not only protects data traffic, but it also protects the quality of voice and video calls that are already set up. If a network engineer designs a network to support 3 concurrent G.729 calls, for instance, which take roughly 85 kbps, depending on the data links used, but if 10 concurrent calls occur, taking roughly 285 kbps, many bad things happen. Data applications may not get enough bandwidth. Also all the voice calls tend to degrade quickly—not just the "extra" calls.

The current Cisco QOS exam does not cover CAC tools; however, if you want more information, Appendix C, "Voice Call Admission Control Reference," (found on the book's accompanying CD-ROM) contains the CAC chapter from the previous edition of this book. Also, you will want to search for information at cisco.com, particularly about a Cisco CallManager feature called "locations," which is an effective CAC tool when deploying Cisco IP Telephony.

If you do not work with QoS tools every day, and you are reading this book to pass one of the Cisco QOS exams, you might be feeling overwhelmed after reading the first section of this chapter! However, do not be dismayed—the remaining chapters in this book are devoted to a deeper description of the tools introduced here. Even if most of the tools listed in this chapter so far are new to you, by the time you read the detail, you'll probably have memorized the names of the tools.

Next, you'll read about a few background concepts before diving into the detail of how DiffServ works.

Classifying Using Flows or Service Classes

Before covering the depth and details in the upcoming chapters, you should consider some basic terms, concepts, and strategies for applying QoS in a network. The next few pages covers a few more concepts and terms that can help you better appreciate the two major QoS architectural models, namely DiffServ and IntServ. In particular, you should have a good understanding of the difference between flow-based QoS tools and Class-Based QoS tools. This short section takes a closer look at both.

Flow-Based QoS

A flow consists of all the packets about which the following are true:

■ All packets use the same transport layer protocol (for instance, UDP or TCP).

■ All packets have the same source IP address.

■ All packets have the same source port number.

■ All packets have the same destination IP address.

■ All packets have the same destination port number.

The slightly different, but just as exact definition, is that a flow consists of the packets between two IP sockets. For instance, a web browser on a PC, connecting to a server, creates a flow. (Actually, in the case of HTTP, it may create multiple TCP connections, which would actually be multiple flows.) Regardless, consider Figure 2-8. In this network, one flow exists from Hannah to Server1's web server.

Figure 2-8   *Flow-Based Approach to QoS for a Single Flow*

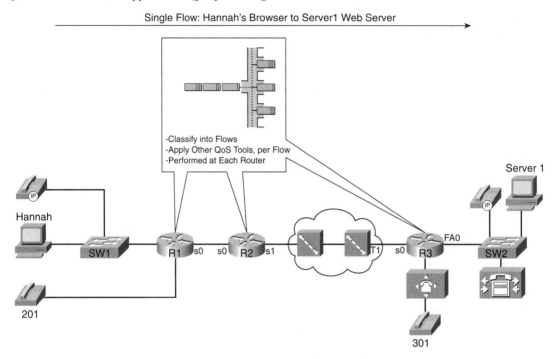

The single flow shown in the figure consists of the packets sent by Hannah to Server1. Note that flows are unidirectional — in effect, two flows, one in each direction, would exist. To reduce the complexity, the samples in this section show flows going left to right only.

Flow-based QoS tools behave like the logic shown in the figure. These QoS tools recognize flows and treat packets in one flow differently than another flow. So, common sense may imply that the QoS tools must first identify the packets that belong to this single flow, and then take some QoS action — such as queuing, LFI, shaping, and so on — for the packets in that flow. The tools may be applied for packets entering an interface, and other QoS tools may be applied for packets exiting an interface. Some tools may even be applied on the LAN switches. Some QoS tools may be applied in the Frame Relay cloud — but those are not typically under your control.

Real networks will have a widely varying number of flows, but the general ideas behind flow-based QoS tools do not change when more flows exist. Take a look at Figure 2-9, which shows a fairly small network with only four flows at this point.

Figure 2-9   *Flow-Based Approach to QoS for Multiple Flows*

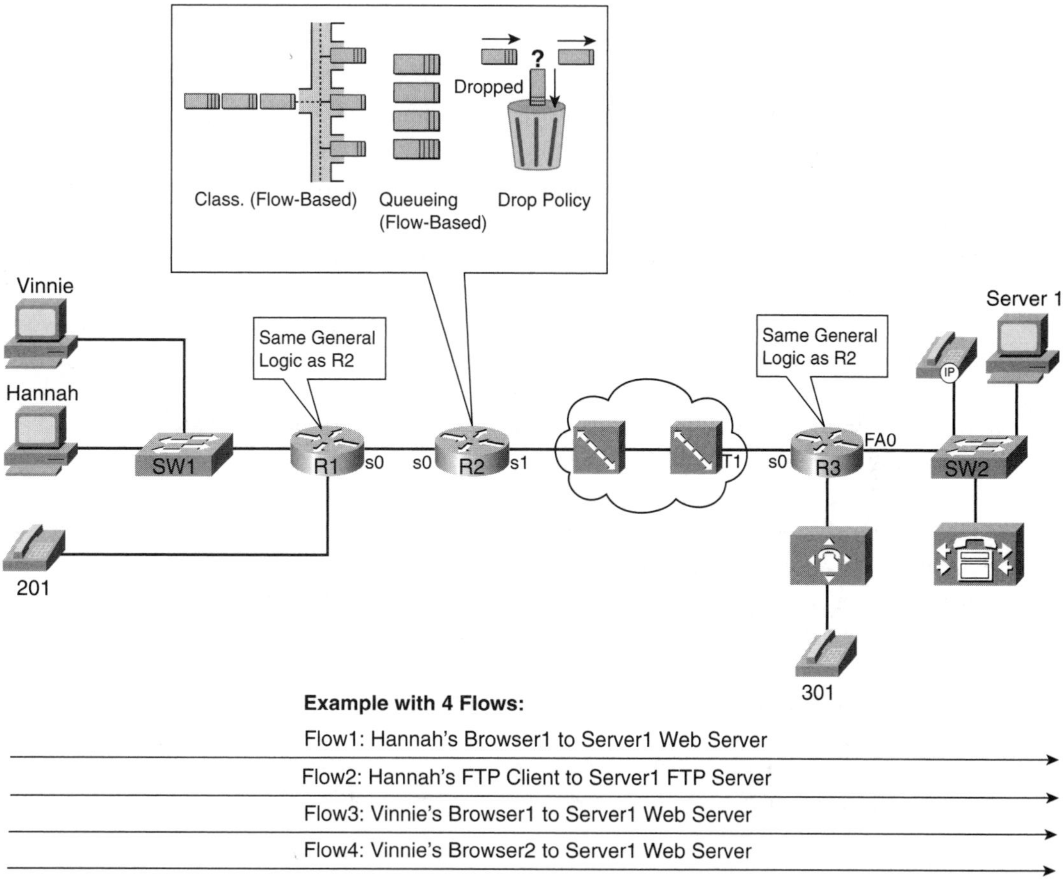

Example with 4 Flows:

Flow1: Hannah's Browser1 to Server1 Web Server

Flow2: Hannah's FTP Client to Server1 FTP Server

Flow3: Vinnie's Browser1 to Server1 Web Server

Flow4: Vinnie's Browser2 to Server1 Web Server

This figure shows four flows. Even though Vinnie sends all packets for both flows to Server1, they are in two different flows, because each of the two browser windows would open separate TCP connections, with different source TCP port numbers. (Note: HTTP 1.1 could cause multiple connections to be opened; FTP uses a control and data connection, which would result in two flows.) However, assume that only four flows exist at this point.

Flow-based QoS tools identify each and every flow based on its unique source/destination address/ port values. The QoS actions at each router may be different for each flow—for instance, maybe FTP just gets leftover bandwidth, or maybe Hannah gets better treatment for her web flow than does Vinnie. The reasons and rationale behind deciding what traffic gets what QoS treatment will change from network to network, but the basic process works the same:

■   Identify each packet, *determining which flow* it belongs to.

■   Apply some QoS action to the packets in each *flow.*

- The QoS actions on a single router may be different for each *flow*.

- The QoS actions among all routers may be different for each *flow*.

Flow-based QoS tools provide some advantages and some disadvantages. Because each separate flow is identified, the QoS tools can literally provide different levels of service to every flow. A single queue could be used for each flow, for instance, giving each a different reserved bandwidth. With a large number of flows, however, the overhead associated with keeping state information about each flow can be a lot of work. Imagine a router with 1000, or even 10,000, concurrent flows, which would not be surprising in the Internet — and then imagine the overhead in trying to perform queuing with 1000 or 10,000 queues! So, flow-based QoS tools provide a great deal of granularity, but they do not scale as well as some other QoS tools that do not consider flows (particularly with very large networks or the Internet).

Engineers gain another advantage and disadvantage when configuring flow-based QoS tools. Suppose that your job is to explicitly configure the routers in Figure 2-9 as to which source and destination IP addresses and ports to use to find each flow. And instead of 4 flows, there are 1000 concurrent flows. Over the course of a day, there may be hundreds of thousands of flows. Your job is to find the details that make each flow unique and configure it! Well, that would be rather ridiculous, a lot of work, and mostly impractical. Therefore, flow-based tools typically require no configuration to match and classify packets into a flow. However, some configuration control is lost.

The following list summarizes the key points about flow-based QoS tools:

- Flow-based QoS tools automatically recognize flows based on the source and destination IP address and port numbers, and the transport layer protocol.

- Flow-based tools automatically identify flows, because it would be impractical to configure parameters statically to match the large number of dynamically created flows in a network.

- Flow-based tools provide a great amount of granularity, because each flow can be treated differently.

- The granularity may create scaling problems when the number of flows becomes large.

Class-Based QoS

Most QoS tools do not need to differentiate between each flow; instead, they characterize packets into one or more service classes. In Figure 2-9, for instance, flows to web Server1 were identified. Most network engineers would want to treat those collective web flows the exact same way with their QoS tools. Therefore, most QoS tools tend to operate on the idea of a category, or service class, of flows and packets. Consider Figure 2-10, for example, which has thousands of flows, all of which are classified into four types of traffic.

Figure 2-10 *Class-Based Approach to QoS*

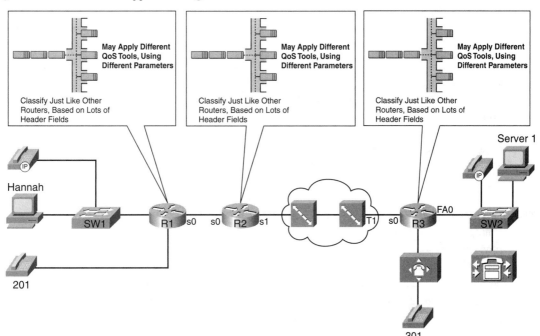

Class-Based QoS tools do not have to identify each flow. However, they do need to identify packets based on something in the packet header — such as TCP destination port 80 for web traffic — and consider that traffic to be in one category or class for QoS treatment. Once again, the reasons and rationale behind deciding what traffic gets what QoS treatment changes from network to network, but the basic process works the same, but per class rather than per flow:

- Identify each packet, determining which class it belongs to.

- Apply some QoS action to the packets in each class.

- The QoS actions on a single router may be different for each class.

- The QoS actions among all routers may be different for each class.

Unlike flow-based QoS tools, Class-Based QoS tools typically require the engineer to specify exactly what must be seen in the packet header to classify a packet. If this network currently has 4 flows to the web server, or 400, or 4000, if the classification criteria just states "all TCP port 80 traffic," no additional configuration is required as the network scales. Both flow-based and Class-Based tools need to examine every packet to classify the packet into the appropriate flow or class. Because Class-Based tools typically only need a small number of classifications, however, the tool can reasonably be configured to specify the types of traffic that get added to each class.

Class-Based QoS tools can use more complex rules to classify packets than do flow-based tools. For instance, a Class-Based tool can examine subsets of the IP addresses (matching a subnet, for example), the incoming interface, the URL for web traffic, and anything that an IP ACL can match. For flow-based tools, the router always look at five fields, all in the IP header—Source and Destination Address, Source and Destination Port, and the Protocol Type field (which identifies the transport layer protocol). In short, classification options for Class-Based tools tend to be much more varied and functional, but they require more configuration work to take advantage of the different options.

Flow-based and Class-Based QoS tools both have a useful place in a QoS strategy for a network. Most QoS tools tend to be based on general classes, as opposed to looking at each individual flow.

Proper Planning and Marking for Enterprises and Service Providers

Enterprise networks can take advantage that all routers and switches resident at the Enterprise's physical locations. Through good QoS design, you can solve the problem of having every router in the network examining a lot of fields in every packet header. This design choice reduces the complexity of the configurations as well. Packets can be classified and marked near the ingress points of traffic into the network; the QoS tools in the center of the network can look for the marked field in the packet header, as shown in Figure 2-11.

One of the most important design goals for Enterprise QoS is to enable Classification and marking near the edge of the network. Doing so simplifies the classification logic and configuration at the rest of the routers in the network. For instance, the figure shows the same classes as Figure 2-10, but with classification and marking performed near the ingress edge of the network. Ideally, packets should be marked even before they reach the first router, typically by a LAN switch. If not, packets entering R1's E0 interface can be classified and marked. R1, R2, and R3 all still need to classify packets, but now the classification details just look for a single well-known field inside the IP header. (Note: The two IP header fields used are the IP Precedence and IP DSCP fields.) This design choice simplifies the QoS configuration and reduces the processing effort for the intermediate routers. (Note: Classification and marking can happen in the switches, IP Phones, and end-user computers — all of which are discussed in detail in Chapter 4, "Classification and Marking.")

It is possible to plan QoS classes for an enterprise network. However, planning service classes for all networks in the Internet is a bit more challenging. For instance, although everyone may agree that VoIP and video may need different treatment than data, they probably do not agree about differentiation between different types of data traffic. Also, a company paying a premium to a service provider may expect better service — translated, better QoS treatment — so the classification may be based on the source IP addresses, and may be different for different ISPs.

Figure 2-11 *Good QoS Design: Mark Packets near the Edge of the Network*

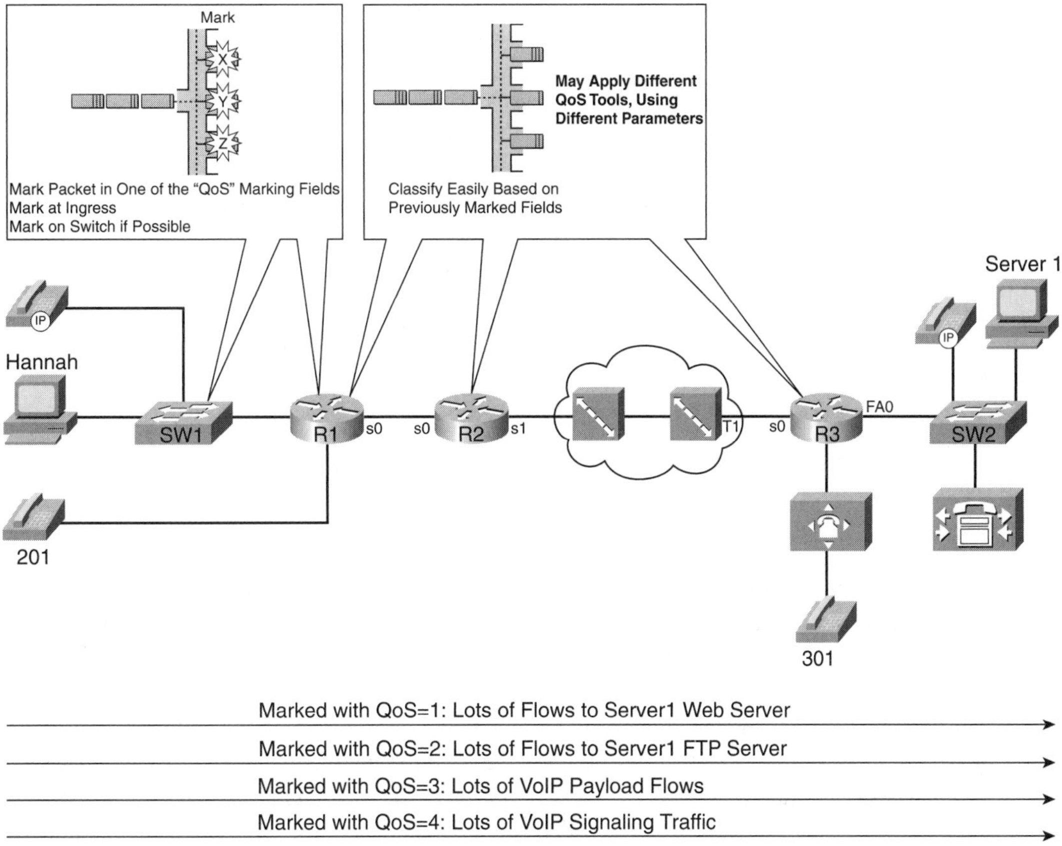
Mark
Mark Packet in One of the "QoS" Marking Fields
Mark at Ingress
Mark on Switch if Possible
May Apply Different QoS Tools, Using Different Parameters
Classify Easily Based on Previously Marked Fields
Hannah
SW1
R1
s0
s0
R2
s1
T1
s0
R3
FA0
SW2
Server 1
201
301
Marked with QoS=1: Lots of Flows to Server1 Web Server
Marked with QoS=2: Lots of Flows to Server1 FTP Server
Marked with QoS=3: Lots of VoIP Payload Flows
Marked with QoS=4: Lots of VoIP Signaling Traffic

Therefore, although the political and business challenges of Internet-scale QoS might be difficult, cases will still exist where QoS can be implemented over the Internet. Many ISPs today provide service differentiation for customers, allowing the customer to specify what types of traffic get better QoS service. Consider Figure 2-12, which shows two companies, each connected to two different ISPs.

Figure 2-12 *QoS Between Different Companies over the Internet*

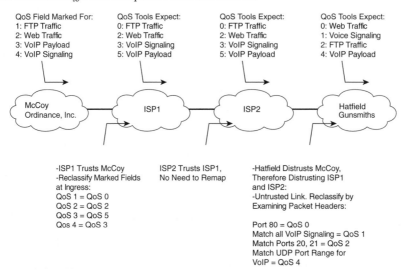

Two key QoS issues exist in this case. First, the parties must agree to the different classifications of packets. In this example, all four networks agree to the need for four classes. (Agreement will not always occur with multiple ISPs!) For instance, McCoy Enterprises may want a different class for customer web traffic versus supplier web traffic, but other companies might want to treat all web traffic equally. Even if all companies want these same general categories, it is difficult to effectively match the correct traffic for all companies connected to the Internet, because every company has different customers and suppliers. Therefore, QoS across the Internet may well end up using general categories — categories such as voice, video, voice/video signaling, important data, and not-so-important data.

Even with general categories agreed upon, not every network chooses to mark the IP packets with the same value to denote the same service class. Figure 2-12 shows just such a case, where ISP1 and ISP2 agree to the values to use when marking packets, but McCoy Ordinance and Hatfield Gunsmiths, two long-time competitors, do not agree on what marked values to use.

Three commonsense QoS design choices help overcome common Internet QoS issues:

■ If neighboring autonomous systems do not agree about what traffic should be in each class, each autonomous system should reclassify ingress traffic based on more complex matching of packets based on the large variety of packet header fields.

■ If neighboring autonomous systems do agree about the classes, but not the marked values, each autonomous system should reclassify ingress traffic based on simple matching of packets based on the previously marked fields in the IP header, as shown in Figure 2-13.

■   If an autonomous system does not trust its neighbor regarding QoS, neighboring autonomous systems should also reclassify traffic at ingress, based on detailed matching of packets.

The section that follows disusses Differentiated Services, also known as DiffServ, the first of two QoS architectures that you will read about. DiffServ formally defines the concept of service classes and re-marking packets as packets pass between autonomous systems.

The Differentiated Services QoS Model

Differentiated Services, also known as DiffServ, takes many of the common sense concepts you've already read about, and formalizes them into a cohesive architecture for applying QoS. The RFCs that define DiffServ go into a lot more depth than you will read here, but the core concepts of DiffServ can be summarized as follows:

■   Takes advantage of the scaling properties of Class-Based QoS tools to differentiate between types of packets, with the goal of "scalable service differentiation in the Internet."

■   In a single network, packets should be marked at the ingress point into a network, with other devices making QoS choices based on the marked field.

■   The marked field will be in the IP header, not a data-link header, because the IP header is retained throughout the network.

■   Between networks, packets can be reclassified and re-marked at ingress into another network.

■   To facilitate marking, the IP header has been redefined to include a 6-bit Differentiated Services Code Point (DSCP) field, which allows for 64 different classifications.

To some extent, DiffServ formally defines a QoS architecture using common sense, or "best practices," for QoS design today. Along with the formal definitions comes a lot of terminology — terminology that is purposefully vendor neutral. So, after learning the DiffServ terms, you need to relate them to Cisco tools and terms. But DiffServ is more than just recording some good ideas about QoS — DiffServ defines another useful field in the IP header (DSCP), as well as some conventions for usage of the new DSCP field. Finally, DiffServ defines general categories of QoS functions and the purpose of the tools in each category. This book has already covered those same concepts and terms from the Cisco perspective, so in this section, you will read about the DiffServ terms for categories or types of QoS tools and how they relate to Cisco terms.

DiffServ Specifications and Terminology

DiffServ is defined by the RFCs listed in Table 2-7.

Table 2-7 *DiffServ RFCs*

RFC	Title	Comments
2474	Definition of the Differentiated Services Field (DS Field) in the IPv4 and IPv6 Headers	Contains the details of the 6-bit DSCP field in IP header.
2475	An Architecture for Differentiated Service	This is the core DiffServ conceptual document.
2597	Assured Forwarding PHB Group	Defines a set of 12 DSCP values and a convention for their use.
2598	An Expedited Forwarding PHB	Defines a single DSCP value as a convention for use as a low-latency class.
3260	New Terminology and Clarifications for DiffServ	Clarifies, but does not supercede, existing DiffServ RFCs.

The RFCs introduce many new terms. Table 2-8 lists the terms and their definitions. This table provides a reference for study for the Cisco QOS exam; the rest of this section relates the terms to some network diagrams.

Table 2-8 *DiffServ Terminology and Their Definitions*

Term	Definition
Behavior aggregate (BA)	A DS behavior aggregate.
BA classifier	A classifier that selects packets based only on the contents of the DS field.
Classifier	An entity that selects packets based on the content of packet headers according to defined rules.
DS behavior aggregate	A collection of packets with the same DS code point crossing a link in a particular direction.
DS boundary node	A DS node that connects one DS domain to a node either in another DS domain or in a domain that is not DS capable.
DS code point	A specific value of the DSCP portion of the DS field, used to select a PHB.
DS compliant	Enabled to support differentiated services functions and behaviors as defined in [DSFIELD], this document, and other differentiated services documents; usually used in reference to a node or device.

Table 2-8 *DiffServ Terminology and Their Definitions (Continued)*

Term	Definition
DS ingress node	A DS boundary node in its role in handling traffic as it enters a DS domain.
DS field	The IPv4 header ToS octet or the IPv6 traffic class octet when interpreted in conformance with the definition given in [DSFIELD]. The bits of the DSCP field encode the DS code point, whereas the remaining bits are currently unused.
Dropper	A device that performs dropping.
Marker	A device that performs marking.
Meter	A device that performs metering.
MF classifier	A multifield (MF) classifier that selects packets based on the content of some arbitrary number of header fields; typically some combination of source address, destination address, DS field, protocol ID, source port and destination port.
Per-hop behavior (PHB)	The externally observable forwarding behavior applied at a DS-compliant node to a DS BA.
Policing	The process of discarding packets (by a dropper) within a traffic stream in accordance with the state of a corresponding meter enforcing a traffic profile.
Re-mark	To change the DS code point of a packet, usually performed by a marker in accordance with a TCA.
Shaper	A device that performs shaping.
Traffic conditioner	An entity that performs traffic-conditioning functions and which may contain meters, markers, droppers, and shapers. Traffic conditioners are typically deployed in DS boundary nodes only. A traffic conditioner may re-mark a traffic stream or may discard or shape packets to alter the temporal characteristics of the stream and bring it into compliance with a traffic profile.

*Table 2-8 material reprinted from RFC 2475

DiffServ terminology overwhelms most people when first learning the architecture. Not all the DiffServ terms are even listed in the table. In fact, I wouldn't be surprised if you are already wondering which of these terms you really need to know when using QoS and which of these terms you need to know for the Cisco QOS exam. The exam does not focus on DiffServ as an end to itself. If you glance over the table, and read this section, you should become familiar enough with the terms to do well on those questions on the exams. It certainly isn't worth the effort to memorize all the terms in Table 2-8; the table is just included for reference.

The rest of this section explores some examples of usage of DiffServ terminology. The first two terms are "behavior aggregate" and "per-hop behavior." If you read the previous section you already know the concepts behind the terms. Figure 2-13 shows the terms in a figure that is a duplicate of Figure 2-11.

Figure 2-13 *Behavior Aggregates and Per-Hop Behavior*

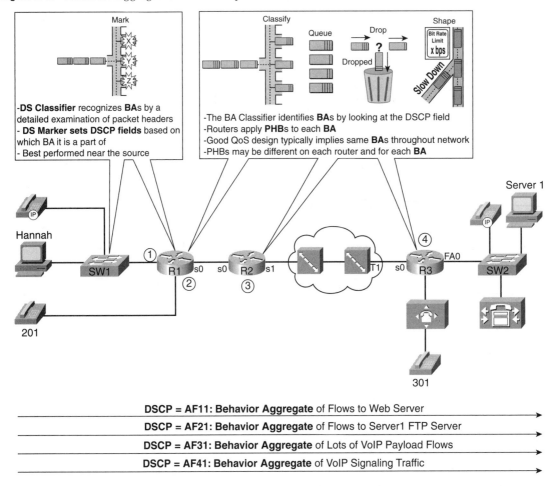

DSCP = AF11: **Behavior Aggregate** of Flows to Web Server

DSCP = AF21: **Behavior Aggregate** of Flows to Server1 FTP Server

DSCP = AF31: **Behavior Aggregate** of Lots of VoIP Payload Flows

DSCP = AF41: **Behavior Aggregate** of VoIP Signaling Traffic

Consider the flow of packets from left to right in this network. The following list numbers correspond to the steps in the figure:

1.   The packets are classified or categorized by matching fields in the header. For instance, packets with Server1's destination IP address, and destination port 80, would be in the first class. The process of classifying the packets is performed by the DS classifier, MF classifier, or just classifier. The classifier marks the DSCP field inside the IP header; DSCP is a 6-bit field inside

the DS field (byte) inside the IP header. Classification and marking are considered to be two different steps — the DiffServ marker actually performs the process of marking the packets. DiffServ defines each class or category of packets as a BA.

2. Router R1 determines which packets are part of which BA by using a BA classifier. A BA classifier only examines the DSCP field, so technically it differs from an MF classifier, as described in step 1, because the MF classifier can look at many fields besides the DSCP field. When R1 decides to apply a QoS tool to a BA (for example, queuing), the action is called a per-hop behavior. The term PHB makes sense to most people, particularly if you think of it as a per-hop QoS behavior.

3. Router R2 performs the same types of tasks as R1; these tasks are described with the same terms as in step 2. Also note that the PHBs can be, and often are, different on one router to the next. In this case, R2 may want to use a shaping PHB — DiffServ would call the shaping tool a shaper — but because all implemented shaping tools need to calculate the rate at which packets are sent, DiffServ would consider both a meter and shaper to be used.

4. Likewise, no new terminology is required to describe step 4, as compared with the two preceding steps. However, the terms "AF11," "AF21," "AF31," and "AF41" have not yet been defined. DiffServ defines several suggested values to be used in the DSCP field. Most installations do not need all 64 values possible in DSCP. The next section in this chapter covers the details, but in this case, AF11, AF21, AF31, and AF41 represent four different DSCP values.

DiffServ models good QoS design specifically to support Internet-scale QoS. Reading through the RFCs, you will notice that DiffServ focuses on issues between different networks. Figure 2-14 shows the same two enterprise networks and the same two ISPs shown in Figure 2-12 earlier in this chapter. The figure shows examples of several of the DiffServ terms that relate to interconnecting networks.

Figure 2-14 *DiffServ Domains, Regions, and Nodes*

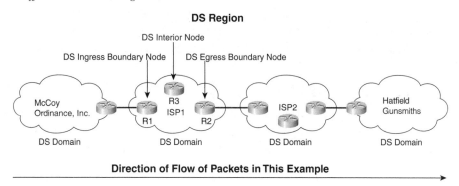

The terms in this figure only apply in cases where multiple organizations' networks are interconnected. The entire figure comprises one DS region, which includes connected networks that are providing differentiated services. Each individual network, typically an autonomous system, is a single DiffServ domain.

The remaining terms in the figure relate to the particular direction of flow of the packets. In this figure, packets flow left to right. Therefore, R1 is a DS ingress boundary node, because it is on the boundary between two domains, and packets first enter the DS domain through R1. Similarly, R2 is a DS egress boundary node. R3 is a DS interior node, because it is not on the boundary of the network. Ingress and egress DS boundary nodes typically perform reclassification and re-marking work.

By this point, you might be wondering about all this new jargon with DiffServ. So far, this section has introduced you to many of the specific formal terms used with DiffServ. The next two sections examine two important aspects of DiffServ more closely, namely the DSCP field and the different types of PHBs. These two topics are certainly the most important DiffServ topics for the exam. As described so far, DiffServ operation can be summarized as follows:

1. Good planning must be performed to define the BAs needed for a network.

2. To mark packets to signify what BA they belong to, DiffServ suggests using MF classifiers, which can look at all fields in the packet header.

3. The classifier should be used near the ingress point of the network to assign unique DSCP values to packets inside each BA.

4. After marking has occurred, interior DS nodes use BA classifiers. BA classifiers only look at the DSCP field. When the BA is identified, that node's PHBs can take action on that packet.

5. The ingress DS boundary node in a neighboring downstream DS domain network may not trust the neighboring upstream DS domain at all, requiring an MF classifier and marker at the DS ingress boundary node to reclassify and re-mark all traffic.

6. If the ingress DS boundary node trusts the neighboring DS domain, but the domains use different DSCP values for the same BA, a BA classifier function can be used to reclassify and re-mark the ingress traffic.

DiffServ Per-Hop Behaviors

Other than the general QoS strategies described in this chapter, DiffServ really provides two additional key features: the DSCP field, and some good suggestions on how to use the DSCP field. In fact, two of the DiffServ RFCs, 2597 and 2598, are devoted to describing a set of DSCP values, and some suggested PHBs that should be associated with each DSCP value.

IP defined a type of service (ToS) byte in RFC 791, which came out in September 1981. The IP protocol creators intended the ToS byte to be used as a field to mark a packet for treatment with QoS tools. Inside the ToS byte, the first 3 bits were defined as a field called IP Precedence, which can be marked for the purposes of implying a particular class of service. The Precedence field values imply that the larger the value, the more important the traffic. In fact, names were given to each value 0 from routine (precedence 0) to critical (precedence 5) and network control (precedence 7). The complete list of values from the ToS byte's original IP Precedence 3-bit field, and the corresponding names, are listed in Table 2-9.

Table 2-9 *IP Precedence Values and Names*

Field and Value (Decimal)	Binary Value	Name
Precedence 0	**000**	Routine
Precedence 1	**001**	Priority
Precedence 2	**010**	Immediate
Precedence 3	**011**	Flash
Precedence 4	**100**	Flash Override
Precedence 5	**101**	Critic/ECP (occasionally called *critical* as well)
Precedence 6	**110**	Internetwork Control
Precedence 7	**111**	Network Control

In addition to the Precedence field, the ToS byte included other flag fields that were toggled on or off to imply a particular QoS service — for instance, low or high delay would be signaled by a 1 or a 0 in the delay bit. Bits 3 through 5 (RFC 795) comprised the ToS field inside the ToS byte, with flags for throughput, delay, and reliability. RFC 1349 expanded the ToS field to bits 3 through 6, adding a cost flag. For instance, the original ToS byte creators envisioned the ability to choose a different route, using a more reliable link, for packets with the reliability flag set.

The DS field redefines the ToS byte in the IP header. It removes the definition of the 4 ToS bits (bits 3 through 6). DiffServ creates a replacement for the Precedence field with a new 6-bit field called the Differentiated Services (DS) field. (The last 2 bits of the ToS bytes are used as flow control bits with the Explicit Congestion Notification (ECN) feature, as specified by RFC 3168.) Figure 2-16 shows the fields inside the ToS byte (per RFC 1349) and the DS field (per RFC 2474).

Figure 2-15 *IP ToS Byte and DS Field*

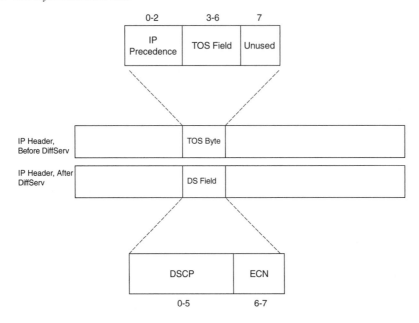

Changing a protocol that is used in production may result in compatibility issues. If the protocol has available unused fields in the header, and those can be added to the protocol specifications, then all is well. When changing the meaning of an already defined field, however, problems can occur. In this case, DiffServ took advantage of the fact that the ToS field (not ToS byte, but just bits 3 through 6 of the ToS byte) were seldom used. Therefore, DiffServ only had to build compatibility with the Precedence field.

The Class Selector PHB and DSCP Values

RFC 2475, which defines DiffServ, became an RFC in December 1998. Even today, some QoS features in IOS do not support DiffServ! Some QoS features will never support DiffServ, because newer, better tools that can do the same thing may have been introduced. All tools that support the Cisco strategic direction for QoS configuration, using the Modular QoS command-line interface (MQC), support DSCP. However, depending on the tools you need to use, and the IOS revisions you use in your network, you may not be able to use only tools that support DiffServ.

So how does the lack of DiffServ support affect a network based on the DiffServ model? With a well-chosen binary value in the DSCP field, PHBs performed by QoS tools can react to the whole DSCP, or just the first 3 bits, with good effect. Consider Figure 2-16. The DSCP values are marked near the edge. R1 performs PHBs based on the DSCP value, and R2 performs PHBs based on what it thinks is IP precedence, but is really just the first 3 bits of the DSCP.

Figure 2-16 *Supporting IP Precedence in a DiffServ Domain*

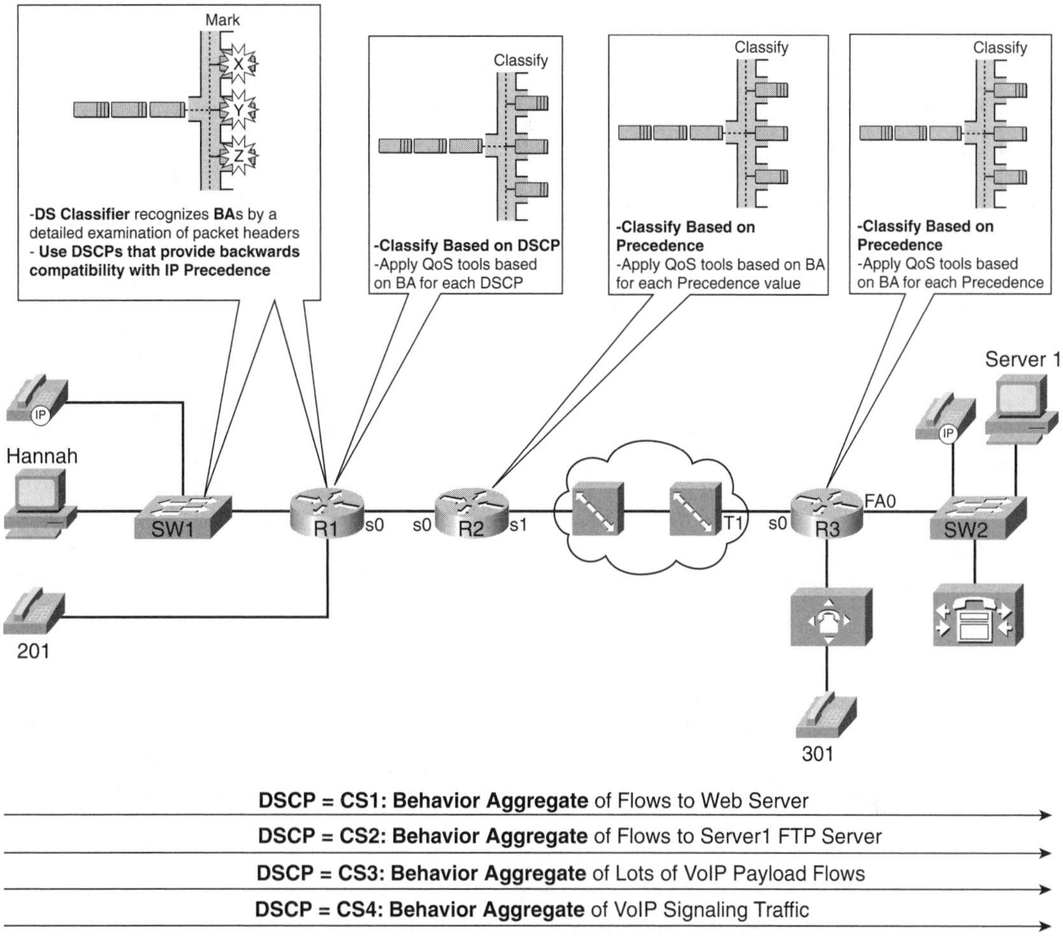

DSCP = CS1: **Behavior Aggregate** of Flows to Web Server

DSCP = CS2: **Behavior Aggregate** of Flows to Server1 FTP Server

DSCP = CS3: **Behavior Aggregate** of Lots of VoIP Payload Flows

DSCP = CS4: **Behavior Aggregate** of VoIP Signaling Traffic

The figure lists text telling us that R1 only reacts to DSCP, R2 only reacts to precedence, and R3 has tools that react to both. A QoS tool without DS support may just look at precedence, whereas other QoS tools can look at the DSCP field. The DSCP values marked in this figure were designed to provide backward-compatability with the IP Precedence field. Table 2-14 lists the DSCP values specifically designed for backwards-compatability. (Note: DiffServ calls DSCP values used for backward-compatibility with IP Precedence "class selectors.")

Table 2-10 *Default and Class Selector DSCP Values*

Name of DSCP Class Selector Values Used by IOS	Binary Values of DSCP	Equivalent Precedence Value (Decimal)
Default	**000**000	0
CS1	**001**000	1
CS2	**010**000	2
CS3	**011**000	3
CS4	**100**000	4
CS5	**101**000	5
CS6	**110**000	6
CS7	**111**000	7

The names of the code points in Table 2-14 match parameters found on IOS DiffServ-compliant classi-fication commands. Because an "all-zeros" DSCP called "default" was already defined, there was no need to create a CS0 DSCP name.

The class selector PHB and DSCP values defined by DiffServ are listed in Table 2-10. These DSCP values provide backward compatibility with precedence. By examining the first 3 bits in each binary DSCP value in the table, you can see that these 8 DSCP values match the 8 different values that can be encoded in the 3-bit Precedence field. Any router looking instead for the Precedence field will just find the first 3 bits of the DSCP field. And just like with IP precedence, the CS DSCP values all imply that the bigger the binary number, the better the PHB.

Although DiffServ supplies the eight CS DSCP values for backward compatibility with IP precedence, many DSCP values actually provide backward compatibility. For instance, DSCP values decimal 8 through 15 all begin with the binary string 001 in the 6-bit DSCP field, making each of these 8 DSCP values compatible with IP precedence 1 (binary 001). In fact, there are 8 DSCP values that provide backward compatibility with every IP precedence value. Table 2-11 lists the values.

Table 2-11 *Range of DSCP Values Compatible with IP Precedence*

Range of DSCP Values, in Decimal	Binary Value	Compatible with These IP Precedence Values
0–7	**000**xxx	0
8–15	**001**xxx	1
16–23	**010**xxx	2

Table 2-11 *Range of DSCP Values Compatible with IP Precedence (Continued)*

Range of DSCP Values, in Decimal	Binary Value	Compatible with These IP Precedence Values
24–31	**011**xxx	3
32–39	**100**xxx	4
40–47	**101**xxx	5
48–55	**110**xxx	6
56–63	**111**xxx	7

As you will read in the upcoming sections, the DSCP values suggested for use by DiffServ include the consideration of making the values meaningful to devices that do not understand DSCP, but only understand IP precedence.

NOTE   It is important to distinguish between what the values of the precedence and DSCP fields *can* mean and what they *should* mean if following suggested QoS design practices. IP precedence value 0 should imply the lowest QoS service possible, with precedence 7 implying the best QoS service. The class selector PHB values follow that same logic. However, most QoS tools can be configured to do just the opposite — for instance, giving precedence 0 traffic the best service, and precedence 7 the worst. Conversely, some other QoS tools are not as flexible and assume a bigger precedence is better. For instance, Weighted Fair Queuing (WFQ) always gives more queuing preference to higher-precedence value flows, all other facts being equal.

NOTE   As seen later with the assured forwarding (AF) PHB and DSCP values, the actual binary values for DSCP do not conform to the "bigger-is-better" logic for the actual values.

DiffServ suggests two other sets of PHBs and DSCP values besides the class selector values, namely assured forwarding (AF) and expedited forwarding (EF). Can you just decide to make up random 6-bit values to associate with each BA? Yes. Can you configure most QoS tools to give each BA the PHB that you desire? Sure. If you take the time to learn and follow DiffServ's suggestions, such as CS, AF, and EF, however, then you can take advantage of some good defaults in IOS, increase the odds of compatibility between your DS domain and others, and avoid a lot of extra configuration.

Table 2-12 summarizes some of the key points about choosing to follow DiffServ's suggestions.

Table 2-12 *Comparing Choices: Making Up DSCP Values, or Using Suggested Values from the RFCs*

Using Suggested DSCP Values	Making Up DSCP Values
More likely to be using the same values as neighboring DS domains; still dependent on whether BAs match	Unlikely to be using the same values as neighboring DS domains
Can configure all QoS tools to create the needed PHBs	Can configure most, but not all, QoS tools to create the needed PHBs
Defaults for some QoS tools already set to good values	Must create more configuration to override defaults that Cisco chose based on DSCP suggestions
Can use well-known names for DSCP values, ignoring actual value; IOS stores values as names in configuration file	Must configure DSCP values as decimal numbers

The next two sections cover the DiffServ RFCs' main suggestions for DSCP values to be assigned.

The Assured Forwarding PHB and DSCP Values

RFC 2597 defines something called "the assured forwarding per-hop behaviors." This RFC suggests that one good DiffServ design choice would be to allow for four different classes for queuing purposes. Within each queue, three levels of drop probability could be implied. The RFC title rightfully suggests that the focus is on the QoS behavior —the PHB — at each node. Most engineers also think of the RFC as defining the 12 DSCPs that are used in conjunction with the AF PHBs.

An individual PHB describes what happen in a single hop, most typically a router. In the case of AF, each PHB contains two separate QoS function, typically performed by two different QoS tools. The first function is queuing. Each router classifies the packets into four different classes, and packets from each class are placed in a separate queue. AF does also specify that the queuing method support the ability to reserve a minimum configured bandwidth for each class.

The AF PHB defines Congestion Avoidance as the second behavior that comprises the AF PHB. Routers drop packets when a queue is full and the router needs to place the packet in the queue; this action is called tail drop. Congestion Avoidance tools discard packets before tail drop is required, hoping that fewer packets are dropped, as described earlier in this chapter. In Cisco routers, this part of the AF PHB is implemented using some form of RED.

The AF PHB does not define that it wants a guarantee that each packet will be delivered, nor does it imply any form of error recovery. The name *assured forwarding* sometimes evokes visions that the bandwidth throughout the network is guaranteed, but it is not. The real objective can be seen with a short read of RFC 2597, which reveals a view of an enterprise and an ISP. The ISP wants to assure the customer that his traffic will get through the network, so long as the customer does not send more data than is contracted. For instance, maybe the enterprise has three classes (BAs) of traffic, for which they contract 300 kbps for the first, 200 kbps for the second, and 100 kbps for the third. The ISP would like to assure that these levels are met. Because many queuing tools effectively guarantee bandwidth over time, the ISP can give these BAs the appropriate amount of bandwidth. Because packet arrival times and rates vary, however, the queues inside the ISP's network will grow and shrink. Congestion will occur; the ISP knows it, and the enterprise customer knows it. So, when temporary congestion occurs in the ISP network, it would be nice to know which type of packets to throw away under limited congestion, and which type to throw away under moderate congestion, and which ones to throw away under heavy congestion. Letting the customer define which traffic is discarded most aggressively also lets the customer achieve some control of how its traffic is treated by the ISP. Therefore, assured forwarding does not mean that an individual packet is assured of making it across the network; it does mean that attempts will be made to assure that queuing tools provide enough bandwidth, and when congestion does occur, less important traffic will be discarded first.

RFC 2597, and the AF PHB concepts, can be summarized as follows:

■ Use up to four different queues, one for each BA.

■ Use three different congestion thresholds inside each queue to determine when to begin discarding different types of packets.

■ To mark these packets, 12 DSCP values are needed; the names of these values as start with "AF" (assured forwarding).

> **NOTE**   RFC 3260 clarifies some of the meaning and terminology used with DiffServ. Technically, the AF PHB, according to RFC 3260, is actually four different PHBs —one for each class. Frankly, for purposes of passing the Cisco QOS exam, I do not think that will ever matter; I only mention it here to be fully correct.

Table 2-13 lists the names of the DSCP values, the queuing classes, and the implied drop likelihood.

Table 2-13 *Assured Forwarding DSCP Values and Meaning*

	Low Drop Probability Within Class	Medium Drop Probability Within Class	High Drop Probability Within Class
Class 1	AF11	AF12	AF13
Class 2	AF21	AF22	AF23
Class 3	AF31	AF32	AF33
Class 4	AF41	AF42	AF43

Pay particular attention to the explanation of Table 2-13 inside this paragraph, because the values in the chart can be counterintuitive. Unlike the CS PHB, AF does not follow the "bigger-is- better" logic for the AF DSCPs. First, AF11, AF12, and so on are names for DSCP values, not the binary or decimal equivalent. (Those values are listed momentarily.) Given the names, at least you can think of the first "digit" after the AF to be the queuing classification — for example, all AF4x code points are in the same class for queuing. No specific queuing parameters are implied for any of these classes, so there is no inherent advantage to being in class 4 versus class 1.

Similarly, the second numeric digit in the AF DSCP names imply the drop preference—with 3 meaning highest likelihood of being dropped, and 1 meaning the least likelihood. In other words, inside a single class, an AFx3 DSCP would mean that these packets would be dropped more quickly (more aggressively) than AFx2, which would be dropped more aggressively than AFx1 packets. In the actual DSCP names, a bigger number for the second numeric digit actually implies a less-desirable QoS behavior. (This convention is also true of the actual binary values.)

You can read about DiffServ AF PHBs, configure DiffServ-compliant IOS tools, and never really have to know the underlying binary values and their decimal equivalents. For reference, however, Table 2-14 includes them. As noted earlier, the numeric parts of the AF code points did not follow the same bigger-is-better scheme that IP precedence did in the past. Likewise, the actual underlying binary values do *not* follow a bigger-is-better scheme, either.

Table 2-14   *Assured Forwarding DSCP Values — Names, Binary, and Decimal*

	Low Drop Probability Within Class	Medium Drop Probability Within Class	High Drop Probability Within Class
	Name/Decimal/Binary	Name/Decimal/Binary	Name/Decimal/Binary
Class 1	AF11 / 10 / 001010	AF12 / 12 / 001100	AF13 / 14 / 001110
Class 2	AF21 / 18 / 010010	AF22 / 20 / 010100	AF23 / 22 / 010110
Class 3	AF31 / 26 / 011010	AF32 / 28 / 011100	AF33 / 30 / 011110
Class 4	AF41 / 34 / 100010	AF42 / 36 / 100100	AF43 / 38 / 100110

The binary DSCP values imply the queuing class with the first 3 bits (bits 0 through 2), and the drop preference in the next two bits (bits 3 and 4). Queuing tools that operate only on IP precedence can still react to the AF DSCP values, essentially making the AF DSCPs backward compatible with non-DiffServ nodes for queuing, at least. Note that the "bigger-is-not-always- better" attitude continues with the actual binary values—the smaller the value of bits 3 and 4, the lower the probability of being discarded.

> **NOTE**   To convert from the AF name to the decimal equivalent, you can use a simple formula. If you think of the AF values as AFxy, the formula is
>
> $8x + 2y$ = decimal value.
>
> For example, AF41 gives you a formula of $(8 * 4) + (2 * 1) = 34$.

In summary, DiffServ AF PHB provides the following:

- An overriding goal to provide PHBs that provide enough bandwidth for each class, with the ability to drop less important traffic, hoping to avoid dropping more important traffic, if congestion does occur.

- A convention that provides 4 classes for queuing.

- The convention includes three drop preferences inside each class.

- Twelve code point names and values to use to create the four classes with three drop levels each.

The Expedited Forwarding PHB and DSCP Values

RFC 2598 defines the expedited forwarding per-hop behaviors. This RFC defines a very simple PHB (low latency, with a cap on bandwidth), and a single DSCP (EF) to represent it. Expedited forwarding simply states that a packet with the EF DSCP should minimize delay, jitter, and loss, up to a guaranteed bandwidth level for the class.

Like AF, the EF RFC suggests two QoS actions be performed to achieve the PHB. First, queuing must be used to minimize the time that EF packets spend in a queue. To reduce delay, the queuing tool should always service packets in this queue next. Anything that reduces delay reduces jitter. Always servicing the EF queue first greatly reduces the queue length, which in turn greatly reduces the chance of tail drop due to the queue being full. Therefore, EF's goal of reducing delay, jitter, and loss can be achieved with a queuing method such as Priority Queuing, with EF traffic in the most important queue.

The second component of the EF PHB is policing. If the input load of EF packets exceeds a configured rate, the excess packets are discarded. If 100 kbps is reserved for the EF BA, and 200 kbps enters the network, for example, supporting the extra traffic may be unreasonable. Why not just accept the extra traffic? The queuing method used to achieve low delay, low jitter, and low loss, would prevent other types of traffic from getting any bandwidth, because the queuing method always gives preference to EF traffic. Thus, EF protects the other traffic by capping the amount of bandwidth for the class. In other words, EF suggests a great level of service, but just up to the contracted amount of bandwidth.

The expedited forwarding PHB uses a DSCP name of EF, whose binary value is 101110, with a decimal value of 46.

Table 2-15 summarizes many of the key points about the various DiffServ PHBs.

Table 2-15 *Comparison of DiffServ PHBs*

PHB	Key Components	Names of DSCPs
Best effort (BE)	PHB for getting no specific QoS treatment	DSCP BE (default)
Class selector (CS)	Uses 8 DSCPs, all with binary 0s for the last 3 bits. Used for backward compatibility with IP precedence. Uses "bigger-is-better" logic—the bigger the DSCP, the better the QoS treatment.	CS1, CS2, CS3, CS4, CS5, CS6, CS7
Assured forwarding (AF)	PHB consists of 2 components: queuing to provide a minimum bandwidth to each for 4 different queues, and 3 drop thresholds inside each queue. DSCPs do not always follow the "bigger-is-better" logic.	AF11, AF12, AF13, AF21, AF22, AF23, AF31, AF32, AF33, AF41, AF42, AF43
Expedited forwarding (EF)	PHB also has 2 components: queuing to provide low delay/jitter/loss plus a guaranteed amount of bandwidth, and policing to prevent EF from preventing other types of traffic from getting enough bandwidth.	EF

DiffServ provides a formalized but sensible approach to QoS over the Internet. By using classes that aggregate the packets of many flows, DiffServ can scale well in the Internet. The next section covers the other specification for an Internet QoS model: IntServ.

The Integrated Services QoS Model

Integrated services (IntServ) defines a different model for QoS than does DiffServ. IntServ defines a signaling process by which an individual flow can request that the network reserve the bandwidth and delay needed for the flow. The original work grew out of the experiences of the IETF in multicasting the audio and video for IETF meetings in the early to mid-1990s.

To provide guarantees per flow, IntServ RFC 1633 describes two components: resource reservation and admission control. Resource reservation signals the network elements about how much bandwidth and delay a particular flow needs. If the signaling completes successfully, the various network components have reserved the needed bandwidth. The collective IntServ nodes (typically routers) reserve the appropriate amount of bandwidth and delay in response to the signaling messages.

IntServ admission control decides when a reservation request should be rejected. If all requests were accepted, eventually too much traffic would perhaps be introduced into the network, and none of the flows would get the requested service.

Figure 2-17 shows the general idea behind the IntServ reservation requests.

Figure 2-17   *Integrated Services Reservation Requests*

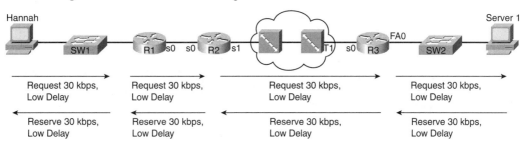

IntServ uses Resource Reservation Protocol (RSVP, RFCs 2205 through 2215) for signaling to reserve the bandwidth. With a full IntServ implementation (more on that later), the originator of the flow (Hannah) begins signaling. At each router along the route, the router asks itself, "Can I support this request?" If the answer is yes, it forwards the request to the next router. Each router holds the bandwidth temporarily, waiting on the confirmation to flow back to the originator (Hannah). When each router sees the reserve RSVP command flow back to the originator, each router completes the reservation.

What does it mean for the router to "reserve" something? In effect, the router reserves the correct queuing preferences for the flow, such that the appropriate amount of bandwidth is allocated to the flow by the queuing tool. RSVP can also request a certain (low) amount of delay, but implementing a guarantee for delay is a little more difficult; IOS, for instance, just reserves the queuing preference. In fact, IntServ RFCs actually define the term "guarantee" as a relatively loose goal, and it is up to the actual implementation to decide how rigorous or general to make the guarantees.

RSVP continues signaling for the entire duration of the flow. If the network changes, or links fail and routing convergence occurs, the network may no longer be able to support the reservation. Therefore, RSVP reserves the bandwidth when the flow initializes and continues to ensure that the flow can receive the necessary amount of bandwidth.

IntServ has some obvious disadvantages, and it has several advantages. IntServ actually predates DiffServ; DiffServ, to some degree, was developed to provide an Internet-scale QoS model, because IntServ scales poorly. IntServ expects the hosts to signal for service guarantees, which brings up two issues—whether the hosts can be trusted by the network and whether the hosts actually support RSVP. Alternatively, routers can be configured to reserve bandwidth on behalf of hosts, but the configuration can quickly become an administrative problem because additional configuration would need to be added for each reserved flow. Also IntServ works best when all intermediate networks support IntServ. Take a look at Figure 2-18, for example. Whereas McCoy, Hatfield, and ISP2 support IntServ, ISP1 does not.

Figure 2-18 *IntServ Through the Internet, with Partial Support*

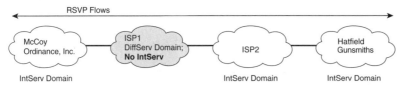

IntServ, with RSVP signaling, can work in this network. However, for ISP1, one of two things must be done to support IntServ:

- ISP1 must pass the RSVP messages through; the ISP1 router just treats the traffic as best effort.

- ISP1 passes the RSVP messages; RSVP flows are mapped to DiffServ classes inside the ISP1 DiffServ domain.

Another problem with IntServ in large networks and in the Internet relates to the fact the RSVP reserves bandwidth per flow. With DiffServ, for instance, all web traffic might be marked with DSCP AF21 and placed into a single class—even if there are hundreds, thousands, or tens of thousands of flows. With IntServ, each flow causes a separate reservation. In fact, DiffServ created an "Internet-scale" QoS model in part because the earlier IntServ specification did not scale well for the Internet, even if you could get most or all ISPs to implement IntServ and RSVP.

Are there advantages to IntServ? Of course. It can reserve specific amounts of bandwidth for a particular flow, which can be very useful. However, IntServ may never be pervasively deployed in an enterprise, or throughout the Internet. For instance, reserving bandwidth for flows between key video-conferencing stations may be useful. Allowing voice gateways to request reservations for VoIP calls can also help. The DiffServ model can be used to place all VoIP into a class, and give the class better treatment, but IntServ can guarantee the QoS behavior and reject new calls if the network is currently not ready to accept more traffic.

The QOS exams cover IntServ-related concepts and features, although DiffServ-related features certainly get much more coverage. The following list summarizes some of the key points about IntServ that you will want to remember for the QOS exams:

- Integrated services defines the need, and suggests mechanisms, to provide bandwidth and delay guarantees to flows that request it. RFC 1633 defines it.

- IntServ contains two components: resource reservation and admission control.

- RSVP, as defined in RFCs 2205 through 2215, provides the IntServ resource reservation function. RFC 2210 specifically discusses RSVP's usage for IntServ.

- With end-to-end RSVP, each intermediate router reserves the needed bandwidth when receiving a reservation request and confirms the request with RSVP reserve messages. If a router in the path does not speak RSVP, it just transparently passes the flow.

- When IntServ has not been implemented end to end, the RSVP messages can be forwarded in the non-IntServ part of the networks. In that case, the non-IntServ networks can either provide best-effort (BE) service, or provide IntServ-DSCP mapping if the intermediate network is a DiffServ domain.

- A router can offload the admission control function to a COPS server.

Comparison of the Three QoS Models

So far, you've read about the two actual QoS models, DiffServ and IntServ. Arguably, there is a third QoS model called Best Effort, which simply means that no QoS is applied to any of the traffic. Although that might seem to be a bad idea, remember that most Enterprise networks began using Best Effort, and the Internet was originally established as a Best Effort service, and it continues to be so today to a large degree. And by having more bandwidth available in the network than the network traffic requires, Best Effort can be a reasonable strategy in some networks.

Although all three QoS models are important, the QOS exam focuses on DiffServ. It is important, however, to note the advantages and disadvantages of all three QoS models, as listed in Table 2-16.

Table 2-16 *Comparison of QoS Architectural Models*

Model	Advantage	Disadvantage
Best effort (BE)	Scales well No QoS tools required	No guaranteed service No difference in service for different traffic classes
DiffServ	Highly scalable Large number of service classes possible	No guaranteed service level Complicated tools
IntServ	Performs admission control for each request Supports signaling for dynamic ports, e.g. H.323	Scales poorly because of: • Flow-based architecture • Repetitive signaling for each flow • Keeps flow state on each node

Foundation Summary

The "Foundation Summary" is a collection of tables and figures that provide a convenient review of many key concepts in this chapter. For those of you already comfortable with the topics in this chapter, this summary could help you recall a few details. For those of you who just read this chapter, this review should help solidify some key facts. For any of you doing your final prep before the exam, these tables and figures are a convenient way to review the day before the exam.

Table 2-17 lists the IOS classification and marking tools, along with a few key features that differentiate the tools.

Table 2-17 *Comparison of Classification and Marking Tools*

Tool	Other Functions Besides Class and Mark	Fields That Can Be Examined for Classification	Fields That Can Be Marked*
Class-Based marking (CB marking)	None	IP ACLs Any markable fields Input interface MAC addresses All NBAR-enabled fields	IP precedence DSCP 802.1P CoS ISL Priority ATM CLP Frame Relay DE MPLS Experimental QoS Group
Network based application recognition (NBAR)	Statistical information about traffic mix; recognition of applications that use the dynamic port	Extensive list (see Chapter 3, "Classification and Marking")	None; used in conjunction with CB marking

* All Claims about features/functions that may be affected by IOS versions assume version 12.2T, unless otherwise noted.

Table 2-18 outlines the key features of IOS queuing methods.

Table 2-18   *Comparison of Queuing Tools*

Tool	Maximum Number of Queues	Classification Capabilities	Queue Service Algorithm/ End Result of Algorithm
Priority Queuing (PQ)	4	IP ACL* Input interface Fragments	Strict service; always serves higher-priority queue over lower queue.
Custom Queuing (CQ)	16	IP ACL* Input interface Fragments	Serves a configured number of bytes per queue, per round-robin pass through the queues. Result: Rough percentage of the bandwidth given to each queue under load.
Weighted Fair Queuing (WFQ)	4096	Automatic, based on flows. (Flow identified by source/destination address and port numbers, plus protocol type.)	Each flow uses a different queue. Queues with lower volume and higher IP precedence get more service; high volume, low precedence flows get less service.
Class-Based Weighted Fair Queuing (CBWFQ)	64	IP ACL* NBAR Same as CB marking	Service algorithm not published; results in set percentage bandwidth for each queue under load.
Low Latency Queuing	N/A	Same as CBWFQ	LLQ is a variant of CBWFQ, which makes some queues "priority" queues, always getting served next if a packet is waiting in that queue. It also polices traffic.
Modified Deficit Round-Robin (MDRR)	8	IP precedence	Similar to CQ, but each queue gets an exact percentage of bandwidth. Supports LLQ mechanism as well.

Figure 2-19 depicts the typical points in a network where policing and shaping are typically deployed.

Figure 2-19 *Traffic Policing and Shaping*

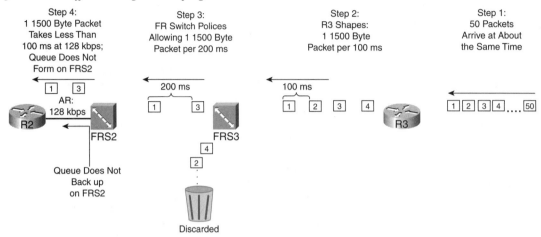

Table 2-19 outlines the key features of IOS policing and shaping tools.

Table 2-19 *Comparison of Shaping and Policing Tools*

Tool	Policer or Shaper	Interfaces Supported	Per Subinterface, and Per VC, Support
Class-Based policing (CB policing; sometimes just called policer)	Policer	All that are supported by Cisco Express Forwarding (CEF)	Per subinterface
Class-Based shaping	Shaper	All that are supported by CEF	Per subinterface
Frame Relay traffic shaping (FRTS)	Shaper	Frame	Per DLCI

Table 2-20 lists the tools, and the various points for comparison, for Congestion Avoidance tools.

Table 2-20 *Comparison of Congestion Avoidance Tools*

Tool	Can Be Enabled in IOS?	Weights Based on IP Precedence or DSCP?	Doesn't Drop Packets, but Instead Signals Sender to Slow Down
Random Early Detection (RED)	No	No	No
Weighted Random Early Detection (WRED)	Yes	Yes	No
Explicit Congestion Notification (ECN)	Yes	Yes	Yes

Table 2-21 lists the link-efficiency tools and some of the pertinent comparison points.

Table 2-21 *Comparison of Link-Efficiency Tools*

Tool	Data Links Supported	Types of Packets to Which Tool Can Be Applied
Payload compression	All; recommended on serial links (T/1, E/1, and slower)	All IP packets
Class-Based RTP header compression (cRTP)	All; recommended on serial links (T/1, E/1, and slower)	All packets with IP/UDP/RTP headers
Class-Based TCP header compression	All; recommended on serial links (T/1, E/1, and slower)	All IP packets with TCP headers
Multilink PPP fragmentation and interleaving (MLPPP LFI)	Multilink PPP	All packets larger than a configured length
Frame Relay fragmentation (FRF*)	Frame Relay	All packets larger than a configured length (FRF.12) or all non-VoFR frames (FRF.11c)
Link fragmentation and interleaving for Frame Relay and ATM VCs	Frame Relay and ATM	All IP packets

*The Frame Relay Forum is often referred to as FRF; their document names tend to begin with the letters FRF as well. The QoS feature called Frame Relay Fragmentation is also referred to as FRF.

Table 2-22 lists the RFCs that define DiffServ.

Table 2-22 *DiffServ RFCs*

RFC	Title	Comments
2474	Definition of the Differentiated Services Field (DS Field) in the IPv4 and IPv6 Headers	Contains the details of the 6-bit DSCP field in IP header.
2475	An Architecture for Differentiated Service	This is the core DiffServ conceptual document.
2597	Assured Forwarding PHB Group	Defines a set of 12 DSCP values and a convention for their use.
2598	An Expedited Forwarding PHB	Defines a single DSCP value as a convention for use as a low-latency class.
3260	New Terminology and Clarifications for DiffServ	Clarifies, but does not supercede, existing DiffServ RFCs.

Figure 2-20 puts some of the DiffServ terminology in context.

Figure 2-20 *Behavior Aggregates and Per-Hop Behavior*

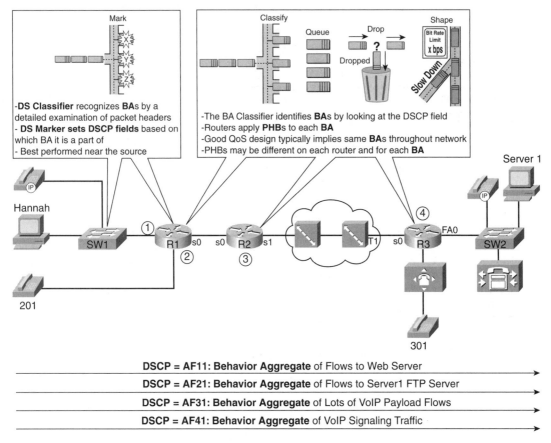

Figure 2-21 shows two enterprise networks and two ISPs, with examples of several of the DiffServ terms relating to interconnecting networks.

Figure 2-21 *DiffServ Domains, Regions, and Nodes*

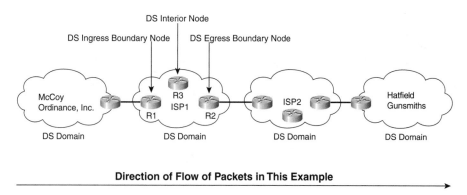

DS Region

DS Interior Node

DS Ingress Boundary Node   DS Egress Boundary Node

R3
ISP1
R1   R2

McCoy
Ordinance, Inc.

ISP2

Hatfield
Gunsmiths

DS Domain   DS Domain   DS Domain   DS Domain

Direction of Flow of Packets in This Example

Figure 2-22 shows the fields inside the ToS byte (per RFC 1349) and the DS field (per RFC 2474).

Figure 2-22 *IP ToS Byte and DS Field*

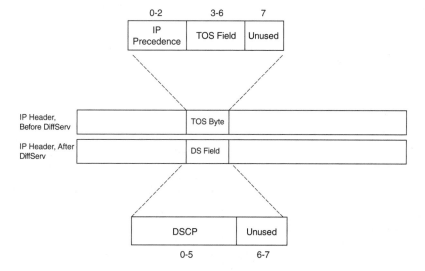

0-2   3-6   7

IP
Precedence   TOS Field   Unused

IP Header,
Before DiffServ   TOS Byte

IP Header, After
DiffServ   DS Field

DSCP   Unused

0-5   6-7

Table 2-23 lists DSCP values useful for QoS tools that only use precedence, and for those that also use DSCP.

Table 2-23   *Default and Class Selector DSCP Values*

Name of DSCP Class Selector Values Used by IOS	Binary Value	Equivalent Precedence Value (Decimal)
Default	**000**000	0
CS1	**001**000	1
CS2	**010**000	2
CS3	**011**000	3
CS4	**100**000	4
CS5	**101**000	5
CS6	**110**000	6
CS7	**111**000	7

The names of the code points in Table 2-14 match parameters found on IOS DiffServ-compliant classification commands. Because an "all-zeros" DSCP called "default" was already defined, there was no need to create a CS0 DSCP name.

Table 2-24 lists the DiffServ AF DSCPs.

Table 2-24   *Assured Forwarding DSCP Values—Names, Binary, and Decimal*

	Low Drop Probability Within Class	Medium Drop Probability Within Class	High Drop Probability Within Class
	Name/Decimal/Binary	Name/Decimal/Binary	Name/Decimal/Binary
Class 1	AF11 / 10 / 001010	AF12 / 12 / 001100	AF13 / 14 / 001110
Class 2	AF21 / 18 / 010010	AF22 / 20 / 010100	AF23 / 22 / 010110
Class 3	AF31 / 26 / 011010	AF32 / 28 / 011100	AF33 / 30 / 011110
Class 4	AF41 / 34 / 100010	AF42 / 36 / 100100	AF43 / 38 / 100110

Table 2-25 summarizes many of the key points about the various DiffServ PHBs.

Table 2-25 *Comparison of DiffServ PHBs*

PHB	Key Components	Names of DSCPs
Best effort (BE)	PHB for getting no specific QoS treatment	DSCP BE (default)
Class selector (CS)	Uses 8 DSCPs, all with binary 0s for the last 3 bits. Used for backward compatibility with IP precedence. Uses "bigger-is-better" logic—the bigger the DSCP, the better the QoS treatment.	CS1, CS2, CS3, CS4, CS5, CS6, CS7
Assured forwarding (AF)	PHB consists of 2 components: queuing to provide a minimum bandwidth to each for 4 different queues, and 3 drop thresholds inside each queue. DSCPs do not always follow the "bigger-is-better" logic.	AF11, AF12, AF13, AF21, AF22, AF23, AF31, AF32, AF33, AF41, AF42, AF43
Expedited forwarding (EF)	PHB also has 2 components: queuing to provide low delay/jitter/loss and a guaranteed amount of bandwidth, and policing to prevent EF from preventing other types of traffic from getting enough bandwidth.	EF

Q&A

As mentioned in the Introduction, you have two choices for review questions. The questions that follow next give you a more difficult challenge than the exam itself by using an open-ended question format. By reviewing now with this more difficult question format, you can exercise your memory better, and prove your conceptual and factual knowledge of this chapter. You can find the answers to these questions in Appendix A.

The second option for practice questions is to use the CD-ROM included with this book. It includes a testing engine and more than 200 multiple-choice questions. You should use this CD-ROM nearer to the end of your preparation, for practice with the actual exam format. You can even customize the CD-ROM exam to include, or not include, the topics that are only on the CCIP QoS.

1. List the two classification and marking tools mentioned in this chapter, including the full names and popular acronyms.

2. List four queuing tools, including the full names and popular acronyms.

3. List the two shaping tools mentioned in this chapter, including the full names and popular acronyms.

4. List three Congestion Avoidance tools, including the full names and popular acronyms.

5. List four link efficiency tools, including the full names and popular acronyms.

6. List the QoS tools that perform some classification function.

7. Which of the following tools can be used for classification and marking? CB marking, PQ, CB shaping, WFQ, WRED, FRTS, LLQ, MLPPP LFI, NBAR, QPM, cRTP

8. Which of the following tools can be used for queuing? CB marking, PQ, CB shaping, WFQ, WRED, FRTS, LLQ, MLPPP LFI, NBAR, QPM, cRTP

9. Which of the following tools can be used for shaping? CB marking, PQ, CB shaping, WFQ, WRED, FRTS, LLQ, MLPPP LFI, NBAR, QPM, cRTP

10. Which of the following tools can be used for link efficiency? CB marking, PQ, CB shaping, WFQ, WRED, FRTS, LLQ, MLPPP LFI, NBAR, QPM, cRTP

11. Define the DiffServ term "behavior aggregate."

12. Define the DiffServ term "DSCP," including what the acronym stands for.

13. Define the DiffServ term "PHB," including what the acronym stands for.

14. Define the DiffServ term "MF classifier," including what the acronym stands for.

15.   Define the DiffServ term "DS ingress node," including what the acronym stands for.

16.   Compare and contrast the terms "BA classifier" and "MF classifier," according to DiffServ specifications. Suggest typical points in the network where each is used.

17.   Compare and contrast the contents of the IP ToS byte before and after the advent of DiffServ.

18.   Describe the QoS behavior at a single DS node when using the AF PHB. Also explain what the acronym "AF PHB" represents and identify the RFC that defines it.

19.   Explain (by comparing and contrasting) whether AF and CS PHB DSCPs conform to the concept that "bigger DSCP values are better than smaller values."

20.   Describe the QoS behavior at a single DS node when using the EF PHB. Also explain what the acronym "EF PHB" represents and identify the RFC that defines it.

21.   Describe the process used by RSVP to reserve bandwidth in a network.

22.   Compare and contrast DiffServ and IntServ in terms of using classes, flows, and scalability.

23.   List and describe the two key advantages of the Best Effort model for QoS.

24.   List and describe the two key advantages of the DiffServ model for QoS.

25.   List and describe the two key disadvantages of the DiffServ model for QoS.

26.   List and describe the two key disadvantages of the IntServ model for QoS.

QoS Exam Topics

This chapter covers the following exam topics specific to the QoS exam:

■ Given a network requiring QoS, explain how to implement a QoS policy using MQC

■ Explain how AutoQoS is used to implement QoS policy

CHAPTER 3

MQC, QPM, and AutoQoS

Most of the topics covered in Chapters 1, "QoS Overview," and 2, "QoS Tools and Architectures," can apply to a network that uses equipment from most any manufacturer. Sure, there were some specifics about Cisco IOS QoS tools and about Cisco IP Phones, but all the concepts about QoS architectures and traffic characteristics of voice, video, and data apply to any network, regardless of manufacturer.

This chapter is specific about discussing several tools available only for Cisco products. Most of the more modern QoS tools from Cisco use configuration commands that conform to a convention called the Modular QoS CLI (MQC), which significantly reduces the complexity of QoS configuration as compared to QoS tools that don't use MQC commands. Frankly, before MQC, QoS configuration was one of the more challenging things to configure in Cisco IOS Software. With MQC, most of the complexity has been removed.

Although easier configuration of a router or switch using MQC is indeed wonderful, MQC enables a couple of other important Cisco QoS tools. Cisco offers a management application called QoS Policy Manager (QPM), which provides a web browser interface to network engineers, allowing them to easily define QoS policies for a network, all with intuitive pointing and clicking. QPM can baseline the network's QoS performance, configure the routers and switches based on the policy, measure the ensuing performance, and monitor the configurations to make sure no one changes the QoS configuration.

Compared to the old days, MQC makes it easier to configure each device, and QPM makes it easier to configure and monitor QoS for an entire network.

In addition, Cisco offers a tool called AutoQoS in Cisco IOS Release 12.3 mainline router and Cisco IOS Release 12.1EA 2950 switch. (Go to http://www.cisco.com/go/fn to use the Cisco Feature Navigator to find more specific information about AutoQoS support on different platforms.) AutoQoS allows a network engineer to configure a single device with just a few generic commands, and the device automatically configures all the appropriate QoS tools. So, even without QPM, a network engineer can configure QoS with confidence. Also, the automatically generated configuration can be changed, if the default settings are not quite what the engineer wants.

MQC, QPM, and AutoQoS provide some fantastic advantages. In this chapter, you'll read about all three. After that, Chapters 4 through 9 take a closer look at six categories of QoS tools available in Cisco routers.

"Do I Know This Already?" Quiz Questions

The purpose of the "Do I Know This Already?" quiz is to help you decide whether you need to read the entire chapter. If you already intend to read the entire chapter, you do not necessarily need to answer these questions now.

The 12-question quiz, derived from the major sections in the "Foundation Topics" portion of the chapter, helps you determine how to spend your limited study time.

Table 3-1 outlines the major topics discussed in this chapter and the "Do I Know This Already?" quiz questions that correspond to those topics.

Table 3-1 *"Do I Know This Already?" Foundation Topics Section-to-Question Mapping*

Foundation Topics Section Covering These Questions	Questions	Score
Cisco Modular QoS CLI	1–5	
Cisco QoS Policy Manager	6	
Cisco AutoQoS Feature	7–11	
Comparisons of CLI, MQC, and AutoQoS	12	
Total Score		

> **CAUTION** The goal of self-assessment is to gauge your mastery of the topics in this chapter. If you do not know the answer to a question or are only partially sure of the answer, mark this question wrong for purposes of the self-assessment. Giving yourself credit for an answer you correctly guess skews your self-assessment results and might provide you with a false sense of security.

You can find the answers to the "Do I Know This Already?" quiz in Appendix A, "Answers to the 'Do I Know This Already?' Quizzes and Q&A Sections." The suggested choices for your next step are as follows:

- **10 or less overall score**—Read the entire chapter. This includes the "Foundation Topics," the "Foundation Summary," and the "Q&A" sections.

- **11 or 12 overall score**—If you want more review on these topics, skip to the "Foundation Summary" section and then go to the "Q&A" section. Otherwise, move to the next chapter.

Cisco Modular QoS CLI

1. What does MQC stand for?

   a. Multiprotocol QoS Commands

   b. Multiprotocol QoS CLI

   c. Modular QoS Commands

   d. Modular QoS CLI

   e. Modular QoS Convention

2. Which of the following MQC commands is most related to the process of classifying packets into service classes?

   a. **service-policy**

   b. **route-map**

   c. **map-policy**

   d. **policy-map**

   e. **map-class**

   f. **class-map**

3. Which of the following is *not* a benefit of MQC?

   a. Reduces configuration time

   b. Provides Modular QoS Call-Admission-Control

   c. Same set of commands on all Cisco IOS platforms

   d. Separates classification from per-hop behavior (PHB) actions

4. Which of the following is not true about the mechanics of MQC?

   a. Packets are classified inside a class map.

   b. PHBs are defined inside a service policy.

   c. Matching multiple DSCPs requires multiple **match** commands.

   d. One command is used to enable a QoS policy on an interface for packets both entering and exiting an interface.

5. Examine the configuration snippet that follows. Which of the following statements is true about the configuration?

   ```
   Router(config)#class-map fred
   Router(config-cmap)#match dscp EF
   Router(config-cmap)#match access-group 101
   ```

   a. Packets with DSCP EF and that also match ACL 101 will match the class.

   b. Packets that either have DSCP EF or that match ACL 101 will match the class.

    c. Packets that match ACL 101 will match the class because the second **match** command replaces the first.

    d. Packets will match only DSCP EF because the first match exits the class map.

The Cisco QoS Policy Manager

6. Which of the following is false about QPM?

    a. Provides a standard set of commands for configuring QoS

    b. Allows a user to specify QoS policies without knowing the MQC command syntax

    c. Graphs QoS performance

    d. Takes advantage of Cisco QoS MIBs

The Cisco AutoQoS Feature

7. Which option on a 2950 switch **auto qos voip** command tells the switch to trust the CoS only if a Cisco IP Phone is attached to the port?

    a. trust cos

    b. ciscophone

    c. cisco-phone

    d. ciscoipphone

8. Which option on a 6500 switch **set port qos** command tells the switch to trust the CoS only if a Cisco IP Phone is attached to the port?

    a. trust cos

    b. ciscophone

    c. cisco-phone

    d. ciscoipphone

9. Which of the following PHBs cannot be enabled using the AutoQoS VoIP feature on a router?

    a. Low Latency Queuing

    b. CB Marking

    c. Shaping

    d. MLP LFI

    e. Policing

10. Which router commands display the configuration that results from enabling AutoQoS VoIP on a router's S0/0 interface, including the details of any class maps or policy maps?

   a. **show autoqos**

   b. **show auto qos**

   c. **show auto qos interface s0/0**

   d. **show running-config**

11. Which of the following statements are true about requirements before AutoQoS can be enabled on a router interface?

   a. CEF must be enabled unless trust is to be configured.

   b. No **service-policy** commands can be on the interfaces.

   c. WFQ must be disabled using the **no fair-queue** command.

   d. HDLC encapsulation must be changed to PPP.

   e. For proper operation, bandwidth should be set to the correct value.

Comparisons of CLI, MQC, and AutoQoS

12. Comparing CLI, MQC, and AutoQoS, which is considered to require the least amount of time to implement?

   a. CLI

   b. MQC

   c. AutoQoS

   d. All take equal time

Foundation Topics

All the tools covered in this chapter provide some important advantages for companies that choose to use Cisco products. Together, these tools improve accuracy of QoS configurations, make the configurations easier to understand to everyone working on the network, and help make converged multiservice traffic run more smoothly through the network. Ultimately, these tools take advantage of the native QoS tools described in Chapters 4 through 9.

This chapter starts with MQC, then covers QPM, and ends with AutoQoS.

Cisco Modular QoS CLI

Back in the mid 1980s, Cisco Systems got its start by building and selling routers. As time went on, Cisco kept adding more and more features to its router software, called Cisco IOS Software, including some QoS features.

Each feature could be configured using the Cisco command-line interface (CLI), but in most cases, each QoS tool used a totally different set of commands than the other tools. At the same time, the networks in which the routers and switches were installed started to have more stringent QoS requirements, causing Cisco customers to need to use multiple QoS tools. As a result, the task of figuring out what to do with the various QoS tools, how to configure them, and how to monitor the success of those tools in the network was a bit daunting.

The Cisco Modular QoS CLI (MQC) helped resolve these problems by defining a common set of configuration commands to configure most QoS features in a router or switch. After hearing the term MQC for the first time, many people think that Cisco has created a totally new CLI, different from IOS configuration mode, to configure QoS. In reality, MQC defines a new set of configuration commands—commands that are typed in using the same IOS CLI, in configuration mode.

As time goes on, and as Cisco creates new IOS releases for both routers and switches, all QoS tools will use MQC. In fact, almost all the tools covered by the current QoS exam use MQC.

You can identify an MQC-based tool because the name of the tool starts with the phrase "class-based" (commonly noted as "CB"). These tools include CB Marking, CB Weighted Fair Queuing (CBWFQ), CB Policing, CB Shaping, and CB Header Compression. Most QoS tools need to perform classification functions; all MQC supporting tools use the same commands for classification. The person configuring the router needs to learn only one set of commands for classification for all these MQC-based tools, which reduces effort and reduces mistakes.

The Mechanics of MQC

MQC separates the classification function of a QoS tool from the action (the per-hop behavior, or PHB) that the QoS tool wants to perform. To do so, there are three major commands with MQC, with several subordinate commands:

- The **class-map** command defines the matching parameters for classifying packets into service classes.

- Because different tools create different PHBs, the PHB actions (marking, queuing, and so on) are configured under a **policy-map** command.

- Because MQC operates on packets that either enter or exit an interface, the policy map needs to be enabled on an interface by using a **service-policy** command.

Figure 3-1 shows the general flow of commands.

Figure 3-1 *MQC Commands and Their Correlation*

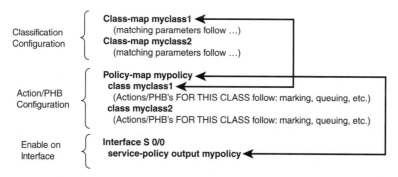

In Figure 3-1, the network's QoS policy calls for two service classes. (The actual types of packets that are placed into each class are not shown, just to keep the focus on the general flow of how the main commands work together.) Classifying packets into two classes calls for the use of two **class-map** commands. Each **class-map** command would be followed by a **match** subcommand, which defines the actual parameters that are compared to packet header contents to match packets for classification.

For each class, some QoS action (PHB) needs to be applied—the configuration for these actions is made under the **policy-map** command. Under a single policy map, multiple classes are referenced, in this case, the two classes myclass1 and myclass2. Inside the single policy called mypolicy, under each of the two classes myclass1 and myclass2, you can configure separate QoS actions. For instance, you could apply different marking to packets in class myclass1 and myclass2 at this point. Finally, when the **service-policy** command is applied to an interface, the QoS features are enabled.

Classification Using Class Maps

Almost every QoS tool uses classification to some degree. To put one packet into a different queue than another packet, IOS must somehow differentiate between the two packets. To perform header compression on Real-Time Transport Protocol (RTP) packets, but not on other packets, IOS must determine which packets have RTP headers. To shape data traffic going into a Frame Relay network so that the voice traffic gets enough bandwidth, IOS must differentiate between Voice over IP (VoIP) and data packets. If an IOS QoS feature needs to treat two packets differently, it must use classification.

MQC-based tools classify packets using the **match** subcommand inside an MQC class map. Several examples in this section point out some of the key features of class maps. Table 3-2 lists the **match** command options available for Cisco IOS Software Release 12.2(15)T, which is covered by the current QoS exam.

Table 3-2 **match** *Configuration Command Reference for MQC Tools*

Command	Function
match [ip] precedence *precedence-value* [*precedence-value precedence-value precedence-value*]	Matches precedence in IPv4 packets when the **ip** parameter is included; matches IPv4 and IPv6 packets when the **ip** parameter is missing.
match access-group {*access-group* | **name** *access-group-name*}	Matches an ACL by number or name.
match any	Matches all packets.
match class-map *class-map-name*	Matches based on another class map.
match cos *cos-value* [*cos-value cos-value cos-value*]	Matches a CoS value.

Table 3-2 **match** *Configuration Command Reference for MQC Tools (Continued)*

Command	Function
match destination-address mac *address*	Matches a destination MAC address.
match fr-dlci *dlci-number*	Matches a particular Frame Relay DLCI.
match input-interface *interface-name*	Matches an input interface.
match [ip] dscp *ip-dscp-value* [*ip-dscp-value ip-dscp- value ip-dscp-value ip-dscp-value ip-dscp-value ip- dscp-value ip-dscp-value*]	Matches DSCP in IPv4 packets when the **ip** parameter is included; matches IPv4 and IPv6 packets when the **ip** parameter is missing.
match ip rtp *starting-port-number port-range*	Matches the RTP's UDP port-number range, even values only.
match mpls experimental *number*	Matches an MPLS Experimental value.
match mpls experimental topmost *value*	Matches the MPLS EXP field in the topmost label when multiple labels are in use.
match not *match-criteria*	Reverses the matching logic; in other words, things matched by the matching criteria do not match the class map.
match packet length {**max** *maximum-length-value* [**min** *minimum-length-value*] | **min** *minimum-length-value* [**max** *maximum-length-value*]}	Matches packets based on the minimum length, maximum length, or both.
match protocol citrix app *application-name-string*	Matches Network Based Application Recognition (NBAR) Citrix applications.
match protocol http [**url** *url-string* | **host** *hostname-string* | **mime** *MIME-type*]	Matches a host name and URL string.
match protocol *protocol-name*	Matches NBAR protocol types.
match protocol rtp [**audio** | **video** | **payload-type** *payload-string*]	Matches RTP audio or video payload, based on the payload type. Also allows explicitly specified payload types.
match qos-group *qos-group-value*	Matches a QoS group.
match source-address mac *address-destination*	Matches a source MAC address.

MQC Example 1: Voice and Everything Else

The first example (Example 3-1) shows the basic flow of the commands. Two class maps are used—one that matches voice packets, and one that matches everything else. Note that class map names are case sensitive, as are policy maps.

Example 3-1   *Basic Classification with Two Class Maps*

```
R3#conf t
Enter configuration commands, one per line.  End with CNTL/Z.
R3(config)#!
R3(config)#class-map voip-rtp
R3(config-cmap)#match ip rtp 16384 16383
R3(config-cmap)#class-map all-else
R3(config-cmap)#match any
R3(config-cmap)#policy-map voip-and-be
R3(config-pmap)#class voip-rtp
R3(config-pmap-c)#! Several options in here; CB Marking shown with the set command
R3(config-pmap-c)#set ip DSCP EF
R3(config-pmap-c)#class all-else
R3(config-pmap-c)#set ip dscp default
R3(config-pmap-c)#interface fa 0/0
R3(config-if)#service-policy input voip-and-be
R3(config-if)#end
R3#
R3#show running-config
Building configuration...
!Portions removed to save space…
ip cef
!
class-map match-all voip-rtp
  match ip rtp 16384 16383
class-map match-all all-else
  match any
!
!
policy-map voip-and-be
  class voip-rtp
   set dscp EF
  class all-else
   set dscp default
!
interface Fastethernet0/0
 description connected to SW2, where Server1 is connected
 ip address 192.168.3.253 255.255.255.0
 service-policy input voip-and-be
```

First, focus on the command prompts in Example 3-1. Note that the **class-map** command moves the CLI into class map configuration mode, with the prompt **R3(config-cmap)**. The **policy-map** command moves the CLI into policy map configuration mode, and the **class** command that follows (not **class-map**, but just **class**) moves the CLI into an additional subconfiguration mode that has no specific name.

NOTE   Class map names are case-sensitive.

Next, examine the **match** commands. The **match ip rtp** command matches only the even-numbered ports in this same UDP port range and does not match the odd-numbered ports used by the Real-Time Control Protocol (RTCP) voice-signaling protocol. (VoIP payload uses only the even port numbers.) Therefore, the **match ip rtp** command matches all VoIP payload. The other **match** command in **class-map all-else**, **match any** does exactly that—it matches anything. So, one class map matches VoIP payload, and the other matches any traffic.

A little later in this chapter, you will read more about the actions (PHBs) that can be taken inside a policy map. For this example, CB Marking, using the **set** command, is shown. Continuing down the configuration, examine the **policy-map set** commands. The first command sets a Differentiated Services Code Point (DSCP) of EF (expedited forwarding) for all traffic that matches **class-map voip-rtp**. The other **set** command, which follows the **class all-else** command, sets a DSCP of Default for traffic that matches the **class-default class-map**. In other words, the policy map sets DSCP EF for packets that match one class, and DSCP Default, using the keyword **default**, for the other class.

Finally, the **service-policy** command enables CB Marking for ingress packets with the **service-policy input voip-and-be** interface subcommand. When enabled, IOS applies the policy map classes in the order they appear in the **policy-map** command. In this example, for instance, the **voip-rtp** class is used to examine the packet first; if a match appears, the packet is marked with DSCP EF. After the packet has been matched and marked, it exits the policy map. If no match occurs, only then is the next class, **all-else**, used to examine the packet.

MQC Example 2: Matching ACLs and Using class-default

Example 3-1 could have been done more efficiently using the **class-default** class, which is a class inside every policy map, at the end of the policy map. If a packet is examined by a policy map and it does not match any of the explicitly defined classes, the packet is considered to match **class-default**. Example 3-2 shows another configuration, this time with **class-default** in use.

Example 3-2 *Class Maps Matching Voice, ACL 101, and Using* **class-default**

```
R3#show running-config
Building configuration...
!Portions removed to save space…
ip cef
!
class-map match-all voip-rtp
  match ip rtp 16384 16383
class-map match-all class2
  match access-group 101
!
!
policy-map voip-101-be
  class voip-rtp
   set dscp EF
  class class2
   set dscp AF11
  class class-default
   description this class matches everything else by default
   set dscp BE
!
interface Fastethernet0/0
 description connected to SW2, where Server1 is connected
 ip address 192.168.3.253 255.255.255.0
 service-policy input voip-101-be
!
access-list 101 permit tcp any any eq 23
access-list 101 permit tcp any eq 23 any
```

This example uses the same **class-map voip-rtp** command, which matches voice payload packets. A new **class-map class2** command defines a new class, matching packets that are permitted by ACL 101. In this case, ACL 101 matches Telnet packets.

policy-map voice-101-be refers to the two explicitly defined class maps, as well as the default class map called **class-default**. The router processes the policy map logic in the order shown in the configuration, always placing class **class-default** at the end of the policy map. With an implied **match any** included in the **class-default** class, all packets that have not already matched classes **voip-rtp** or **class2** will end up matching **class-default**.

Example 3: Matching Opposites with match not

MQC includes a feature to enable you to match packets that do not meet the specified criteria. For instance, Example 3-2 included a class (**class2**) that matched packets permitted by ACL 101. If you wanted instead to match all packets that did not match ACL 101 with a **permit** action, you could use the **match not** command. Example 3-3 duplicates Example 3-2, but with the **match not** command in use.

Example 3-3 *Class Maps Matching Voice, ACL 101, and Using* **class-default**

```
R3#show running-config
Building configuration...
!Portions removed to save space…
ip cef
!
class-map match-all voip-rtp
  match ip rtp 16384 16383
class-map match-all not-class2
  description all packets denied by ACL 101 match
  match not access-group 101
!
!
policy-map voip-101-be
  class voip-rtp
    set dscp EF
  class not-class2
    set dscp BE
  class class-default
    description this class matches everything else by default
    set dscp AF11
!
interface Fastethernet0/0
 description connected to SW2, where Server1 is connected
 ip address 192.168.3.253 255.255.255.0
 service-policy input voip-101-be
!
access-list 101 permit tcp any any eq 23
access-list 101 permit tcp any eq 23 any
```

Both Examples 3-2 and 3-3 end up doing the same thing in this case. With some MQC-based QoS tools, the **class-default** class has some special characteristics, so you might prefer to explicitly match the Telnet (ACL 101) traffic as in Example 3-2, or you might prefer to explicitly match all other traffic using **match not**, as in Example 3-3.

Example 4: Matching More Than One Thing

You might have noticed that the **class-map** commands in the **show running-config** output all have a parameter called **match-all**. The syntax of the **class-map** command is actually **class-map [match-all | match-any]** *class-name*, with **match-all** being the default setting if you do not choose either option.

The **match-all** and **match-any** commands tell the router or switch how to process the class map if multiple **match** commands are used. So far in this chapter, only one **match** command has been used in each class map. However, IOS allows you to refer to multiple fields inside each packet to match it, and to do so, you simply use multiple **match** commands.

The **match-all** and **match-any** parameters tell IOS whether to match packets that match all the **match** commands (**match-all**) or to match packets that match one or more of the **match** commands (**match-any**). If you prefer Boolean logic, **match-all** means that there is a logical AND between each **match** command with **match-all**, and a logical OR between each **match** command with **match-any**. Example 3-4 shows an example of class maps with **match-all** and **match-any**. Note that because the focus of this example is on how the matching logic works, the example does not bother showing a **policy-map** or a **service-policy** command.

Example 3-4 *Class Maps with* **match-all** *and* **match-any**

```
class-map match-all ex4-1
  match ip rtp 16384 16383
  match precedence 5
!
class-map match-any ex4-2
  match access-group 102
  match dscp AF21
!
class-map match-all ex4-3
  match dscp 0
  match dscp 1
!
class-map match-any ex4-4
  match dscp 0
  match dscp 1
!
class-map match-any ex4-5
  match dscp 0 1
!
```

First, examine **class-map match-all ex4-1**. The packet must be an RTP packet within the stated UDP port number range, plus it must also already have been marked as precedence 5. If either match condition is not true about a particular packet, the packet is not considered to match the class map. So, in this case, voice packets that had not been marked yet would not be part of this class.

Next, examine **class-map match-any ex4-2**. With match-any logic, packets match this class if they are permitted by ACL 102 (not shown), or if they are marked with DSCP AF21. If your QoS policy defined that packets matching ACL 102 should be treated as if they were marked with AF21, this class map makes sure that any packets that were not correctly marked already are still treated as AF21 traffic.

You can use multiple **match** commands to match multiple criteria; however, there might be cases in which you want to match multiple marked values, for instance, multiple DSCP values in one class map. The **class-map ex4-3**, **class-map ex4-4**, and **class-map ex4-5** commands show some of the dangers and possibilities with matching multiple DSCP values; **class-map match-all ex4-3** uses match-all logic and lists **match** commands for two DSCP values (0 and 1). No one single packet can be marked with both DSCP 0 and 1, so no packets could possibly match **class-map match-all ex4-3**. To correctly match packets that have either DSCP 0 or 1, **class-map match-any ex4-4** could be used, because it matches if only one of the **match** commands conditions are met.

You can, however, use a more convenient method for matching packets based on multiple DSCP, precedence, or CoS values. The **class-map ex4-5** command shows how a single **match** command can be used to match multiple DSCPs. Note the syntax of the **match dscp**, **match precedence**, and **match cos** commands in Table 3-2. With precedence and CoS, you can supply four different values in a single **match** command; with DSCP, you can supply eight different values. When you supply more than one DSCP, precedence, or CoS value in one **match** command, IOS uses logic such as **match-any**, meaning that a packet with any of the stated values matches the condition.

> **NOTE**   The earliest Cisco IOS releases that supported MQC commands used a syntax such as **match ip dscp af11** to match a DSCP value. Later releases support that syntax, as well as syntax that does not include the **ip** keyword—for instance, **match dscp af11** is also valid. Similarly, the **match ip precedence 1** command was originally specified, and now the **match precedence 1** command can also be used.

Example 5: Complex Matching with match-class

In most networks, you already have seen enough examples so that you can configure **class-map** commands effectively. This final example in this section points out one less-obvious way to use class maps by referring to other class maps using the **match class-map** command.

Imagine that you want to match based on several things in the headers of a packet; however, the logic you want to use runs something like this:

If condition A and B are true, or if condition C is true, then place packet in this class.

The **match-all** and **match-any** keywords do not allow you to just code three **match** commands and achieve this logic. With the **match class** *class-map-name* command, you can achieve this logic, as shown in Example 3-5.

Example 3-5 *Complex Matching with* **match class** *Command*

```
class-map match-all ex5-1
  match ip rtp 16384 16383
  match precedence 5
!
class-map match-any ex5-2
  match class ex5-1
  match cos 5
```

In **class-map match-all ex5-1**, the class map looks for VoIP RTP traffic that has been marked with precedence 5. Both the RTP designation and precedence 5 must be true to match the conditions in this class map. The **class-map match-any ex5-2** command uses match-any logic, so either **match** command's conditions can be met to classify a packet into **class-map ex5-2**. Interestingly, **class-map ex5-2** uses the **match class ex5-1** command, which of course refers to the first class map, which uses match-all logic. In effect, the logic is the following:

> Match packets with RTP protocol, even-numbered UDP ports between 16384 and 32767, AND marked with precedence 5

> or

> Packets with CoS 5

You will see many more examples of how to use the MQC **class-map** and **match** commands in later chapters. Next, you will read a little more about the **policy-map** and **service-policy** commands.

Performing QoS Actions (PHBs) Using policy-map Commands

MQC uses a three-step approach:

1. **class-map** commands classify packets into service classes.

2. **policy-map** commands define PHB actions.

3. **service-policy** interface subcommands enable the logic of a policy map on an interface.

As shown in Example 3-1, the **policy-map** command refers to class maps using the **class** command. Example 3-6 repeats an excerpt from Example 3-1, with specific commands highlighted.

Example 3-6 *Basic Flow of* **policy-map** *Commands*

```
class-map match-all voip-rtp
  match ip rtp 16384 16383
class-map match-all all-else
  match any
!
!
policy-map voip-and-be
  class voip-rtp
! (any action can be configured here; CB Marking is shown)
  set dscp EF
  class all-else
! (any action can be configured here; CB Marking is shown)
  set dscp default
!
interface Fastethernet0/0
 description connected to SW2, where Server1 is connected
 ip address 192.168.3.253 255.255.255.0
 service-policy input voip-and-be
```

Policy maps rely on the classification logic in **class-map** commands to treat packets differently. In Example 3-6, the **policy-map voip-and-be** command includes two **class** subcommands—**class voip-rtp** and **class all-else**. Underneath the **class** commands, you can configure many different commands that define a PHB or action to be taken against packets in that class. (Upcoming Table 3-3 lists the action or PHB subcommands available underneath a **class** command.) In this example, the **set** command is used, which means that marking is the action taken on packets in each class.

The **service-policy input voip-and-be** interface subcommand enables the policy map on the Fastethernet0/0 interface for incoming packets.

> **NOTE** Policy map names are case-sensitive. Because class map names are also case-sensitive, be careful when configuring **class** commands that refer to class map names.

Table 3-3 lists the various MQC subcommands available in Cisco IOS Software for defining actions to be taken. Chapters 4 through 9 describe each of these options in more detail, including the meaning of the parameters of the commands.

Table 3-3 *Action (PHB) Subcommands Inside a Policy Map*

Command	Function
set	CB Marking action, with options to mark several fields inside headers
bandwidth	Reserves bandwidth for the class for CBWFQ
priority	Reserves bandwidth and provides Low Latency Queuing (LLQ) with CBWFQ
shape	Shapes traffic in the class with a defined bandwidth and burst sizes
police	Polices traffic in the class with a defined bandwidth and burst sizes
compress	Performs TCP and RTP header compression on packets in the class

Enabling a Policy Map Using service-policy

You have already seen the **service-policy** command in use in several examples. This short section points out a few of the important features of the **service-policy** command.

The full syntax of the command is **service-policy** {**input** | **output**} *policy-map-name*. Note that the curly brackets mean that you must choose either input or output—you cannot leave that parameter off the command. In effect, **service-policy** tells the router or switch to perform the logic in the policy map for packets either entering (input) or exiting (output) the interface.

Some actions might not be supported in both the input and output directions. For instance, in a router, CBWFQ can be performed only on packets exiting the interface. So, you can configure the policy map with **bandwidth** subcommands, with no problems. When you try to enable the policy map with the **service-policy input** command, the router will give you an error message and not add the **service-policy** command to the configuration.

Finally, some features require that Cisco Express Forwarding (CEF) switching be enabled before the action can work. If CEF has not been enabled with the **ip cef** global command, you can still configure a policy map for an action. However, when you try to enable it with the **service-policy** command, the router will tell you that CEF switching is required.

Each interface can have at most two **service-policy** commands—one for input packets and one for output.

show Commands for MQC

MQC configuration commands provide the wonderful advantage of a set of standard commands for configuring QoS. Cisco also standardized **show** commands for MQC-based tools as well, with three commands providing all the information for any MQC configuration.

The **show class-map** *class-map-name* command lists configuration information about the class map listed in the command, and the **show class-map** command lists information about all class maps. Similarly, the **show policy-map** *policy-map-name* command lists configuration information about a specific policy map, and the **show policy-map** command lists information about all policy maps. The same general information can be seen with a **show running-config** command.

The one command that shows counters and performance information is the **show policy-map interface** *interface-name* [**input** I **output**] command. The output differs based on the PHBs that have been configured; for instance, it shows queuing statistics when CBWFQ has been configured, shows marking statistics when CB Marking has been configured, and so on. In some of the examples in this chapter, a policy map was enabled on interface Fastethernet 0/0. So, the **show policy-map interface fastethernet0/0** command shows statistics for any policy maps enabled with the **service-policy** command in either direction. Alternatively, the **show policy-map interface fastethernet0/0 input** command lists statistics only for any policy maps enabled for input packets on interface Fastethernet0/0.

MQC helps Cisco router and switch engineers easily configure and monitor QoS features and with better results. Next, you will read about QoS Policy Manager, which is a network management tool that also helps engineers configure and monitor QoS tools.

QoS Policy Manager (QPM)

QPM provides many of the features that you need when you get serious about deploying QoS across an enterprise. The following list summarizes some of the more important features:

- Enables you to define a QoS policy based on business rules.

- Automatically configures some or all network devices with QoS features, based on the QoS policy described to QPM. The features that QPM enables include marking, queuing, shaping, policing, and Link Fragmentation and Interleaving (LFI) tools.

- Loads the correct configurations automatically.

- Enables you to monitor the device configurations to make sure no one has made changes to them. If the configurations have been changed, you can use QPM to restore the original configuration.

To get a sense of how QPM eases QoS configuration, imagine that you want to create a policy to mark all VoIP traffic with DSCP EF as near to the edge of the network as possible. You simply point and click to tell QPM what fields to look for in the packet or frame header. QPM creates the CB Marking configuration and loads it into all the appropriate devices. So, to use QPM, you still need to know what the base QoS tools can do, but you do not have to know the configuration syntax of all the different QoS tools, and you do not have to repeat the configuration task on all the devices—QPM takes care of that for you.

QPM runs on Microsoft Windows 2000 Professional or Server with Service Packs 3 or 4, or with Microsoft Windows Advanced Server (without terminal services). (See http://www.cisco.com/en/US/partner/products/sw/cscowork/ps2064/products_user_guide_chapter09186a0080080808.html#4048 for the hardware and software requirements of the latest release of QPM, version 3.2, as of press time.)

To configure a common QoS policy and push this policy to the network devices, QPM needs to be able to learn which devices are present in the network and communicate with those devices. QPM can use the CiscoWorks database to discover the location of the devices in the network.

Figure 3-2 outlines the overall location and functions between the QPM server and the rest of the network.

Figure 3-2   *QPM Server and Communication with Other Devices*

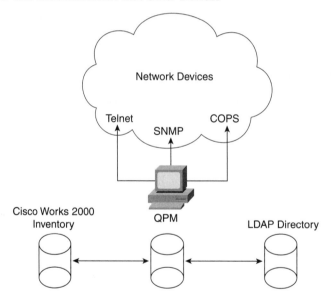

For QPM to create configurations, load the configurations, and monitor the configurations for changes, QPM must know which devices it should manage. The most convenient way to define the devices for QPM to manage is to use the device list from the CiscoWorks2000 database. Cisco requires that QPM be installed on a machine that also has CiscoWorks Common Services 2.2, with Service Pack 2, which allows QPM to automatically discover the network devices; however, you can statically define devices to QPM as well.

QPM is an important tool for networks that deploy QoS extensively. The following list outlines some of the more popular features:

- Supports a wide variety of routers and switches

- Allows network-wide QoS policy definition, followed by automatic deployment of appropriate configurations

- Creates graphs of real-time performance

- Creates graphs of historical performance

- Allows end-user viewing of reports and configuration using a web browser

- Manages only a single device from the browser

- Manages the entire network from one browser window

- Implements the actual probes and responses when necessary for measuring network performance

SNMP Support for QoS

QPM uses Telnet and the Simple Network Management Protocol (SNMP) to configure and monitor devices. Cisco IOS includes a couple of important proprietary SNMP Management Information Bases (MIBs) that provide a lot of good information about QoS performance in a router. When QPM displays performance data for MQC-based QoS tools in a router, the performance data comes mostly from these specialized QoS MIBs.

First, the Class-Based QoS MIB (CBQoSMIB) contains variables that describe the MQC configuration commands in a router. This MIB also includes statistical variables, which are essentially the same kinds of stats seen with the **show policy-map** interface command.

More interestingly, CBQoSMIB goes beyond those statistics, providing statistics for packets before a policy map has been processed, and afterward. In other words, you can see statistics about packets before the PHBs have been applied and after they are applied. QPM, of course, knows about this MIB, so it is ready to show graphs of packet statistics comparing the pre- and post-policy map.

Network Based Application Recognition (NBAR) can be used by MQC **class-map** commands to help classify traffic. NBAR can also be used to simply recognize and count traffic based on different protocol types. Of particular interest, NBAR can recognize hard-to-recognize protocols that do not use well-known ports, or that use dynamically allocated port numbers, by looking past the TCP and UDP headers into the application layer protocol. So, NBAR provides some interesting statistics about what protocols might be running through a network. (Chapter 4, "Classification and Marking," covers NBAR in much more detail.)

You can look at NBAR statistics for different protocols with the **show nbar protocol-discovery** command from a router; however, IOS includes the Cisco NBAR Protocol Discovery (CNPD) MIB, making the same statistics available from CiscoWorks and QPM. In particular, when planning a QoS implementation, NBAR can be a useful tool for figuring out what protocols are actually being sent through the network. The CNPD MIB can be used to easily graph and track the counters to decide how much bandwidth is needed for each particular type of application.

An engineer has a great set of tools for configuring and managing QoS with MQC at the command line, and QPM and these specialized MIBs from the management station. However, Cisco has one other significant tool that aids in QoS implementations, called AutoQoS, which will be covered in the last section of this chapter.

Cisco AutoQoS Feature

AutoQoS is a feature on some Cisco routers and switches that enables you to configure QoS on a device with only a few **auto qos** commands. By following some restrictions, and using the **auto qos** command, you can cause the router or switch to have a valid, working QoS configuration. Best of all, you do not have to know anything about how the QoS features work to use AutoQoS!

Because routers and switches do different tasks, QoS differs slightly between them. To get an idea about what AutoQoS does, consider that AutoQoS on routers works to classify packets into three service classes:

- Voice payload
- Voice signaling
- All other traffic

If you look in the router IOS documentation, AutoQoS is actually called AutoQoS VoIP, in reference to the design goal behind AutoQoS that is to provide good performance for voice traffic. That is true on both routers and switches.

> **NOTE** This section covers AutoQoS VoIP, which is supported in IOS 12.3 mainline. Note that Cisco has also announced AutoQoS Enterprise, which is part of IOS 12.3T.

AutoQoS provides some great advantages. AutoQoS automatically classifies traffic, generating the MQC QoS commands, as well as QoS commands for a couple of other QoS features. The configurations are indeed consistent if AutoQoS is used throughout the network. You can modify the automatically generated configurations as well, so you can have AutoQoS do the hard work, and then come behind it and tweak the configuration. AutoQoS also re-marks all non-voice traffic that has DSCP EF, AF31, or CS3 to DSCP 0, which helps prevent data applications from attempting to get the same treatment as voice. And AutoQoS conforms to the Cisco current *Best Practices for Voice QoS*, so you can be confident the voice traffic will be treated well.

AutoQoS is supported on routers, on IOS-based switches, and in Cat-OS on 6500 switches. The next three sections take a look at AutoQoS in each of these three contexts.

AutoQoS VoIP for Routers

The beauty of AutoQoS is that you need to configure only a simple command or two, and AutoQoS does the rest. This section starts with some explanation of how to configure AutoQoS on a router, followed by an explanation of what AutoQoS automatically configured on the router.

AutoQoS VoIP Default Configuration

Before configuring AutoQoS VoIP, you should refer to the *IOS 12.3 QoS Configuration Guide,* which lists several considerations and conditions for the right environment for enabling this feature. For QOS exam purposes, repeating the full list here is not helpful; however, considering a couple of the most common considerations can help. For instance

■ AutoQoS VoIP requires that CEF be enabled first.

■ AutoQoS VoIP cannot be used if the interface already has a **service-policy** command configured.

■ Because AutoQoS VoIP relies on the bandwidth settings configured in the **bandwidth** command, the routers should be configured with correct bandwidth settings on each interface before enabling AutoQoS VoIP. (If you change the bandwidth after enabling AutoQoS VoIP, AutoQoS VoIP does not react and does not change the QoS configuration.)

■ Supports only point-to-point subinterfaces on Frame Relay interfaces.

■ Supports HDLC, PPP, Frame Relay, and ATM data link protocols.

None of these considerations poses a big problem in most networks. Having met those requirements, configuring AutoQoS VoIP is quite easy. For reference, Table 3-4 lists the commands related to AutoQoS VoIP, followed by an example configuration.

Table 3-4 *Command Reference for AutoQoS VoIP (for Routers)*

Command	Function
auto qos voip [**trust**] [**fr-atm**]	Configuration command that enables AutoQoS VoIP on an interface (PPP or HDLC) or VC (FR and ATM)
no auto qos	Disables AutoQoS VoIP on an interface (PPP or HDLC) or VC (FR and ATM)
show auto qos [**interface** *interface-type*]	Displays what AutoQoS actually created
show policy-map interface *interface-name* [**input** | **output**]	Displays actual configuration of MQC-based parts of the configuration, including any later changes made by an engineer

To begin, look at Figure 3-3 and Example 3-7. Figure 3-3 shows R1 and R3 connected over a serial link, with 2950 switches attached to each router. As noted earlier, AutoQoS VoIP on routers supports serial link protocols (such as PPP), but it does not support LAN interfaces. This example begins with the pertinent configuration before enabling AutoQoS VoIP and then shows the configuration command.

Figure 3-3 *AutoQoS VoIP: Example Network with PPP*

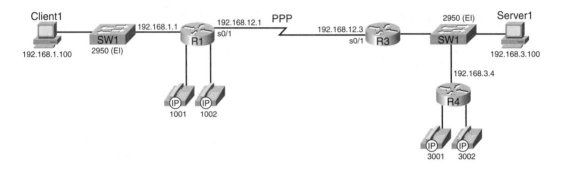

Example 3-7 *AutoQoS Configuration with PPP*

```
R3#show running-config
! portions omitted for brevity
ip cef
!
interface Serial0/1
 ip address 192.168.12.3 255.255.255.0
 encapsulation ppp
!
r3#configure terminal
Enter configuration commands, one per line.  End with CNTL/Z.
R3(config)#int s 0/1
R3(config-if)#auto qos voip
R3(config-if)#end
R3#
R3#show int s 0/1
Serial0/1 is up, line protocol is up
  Hardware is PowerQUICC Serial
  Internet address is 192.168.12.3/24
  MTU 1500 bytes, BW 1544 Kbit, DLY 20000 usec,
      reliability 255/255, txload 1/255, rxload 1/255
```

In this example, the configuration already uses CEF, as shown in the **ip cef** command. Also, interface Serial0/1 does not have a **service-policy** command. Next, the **auto qos voip** command enables AutoQoS VoIP on the interface. AutoQoS VoIP is supposed to be easy to configure—and it is. That is all there is to the typical configuration.

Of course, if you are willing to dig into QoS enough to pass the QOS exam, you are probably curious as to what the router just did for you (or to you, depending on your perspective). Example 3-8 lists the output of two **show** commands that list the new configuration generated by AutoQoS VoIP.

Example 3-8   **show auto qos** *Commands*

```
R3#show auto qos
!
! First ACL matches Voice payload, second match Voice signaling
!
  ip access-list extended AutoQoS-VoIP-RTCP
   permit udp any any range 16384 32767
  ip access-list extended AutoQoS-VoIP-Control
   permit tcp any any eq 1720
   permit tcp any any range 11000 11999
   permit udp any any eq 2427
   permit tcp any any eq 2428
   permit tcp any any range 2000 2002
   permit udp any any eq 1719
   permit udp any any eq 5060
!
! Next class-map matches voice payload
!
  class-map match-any AutoQoS-VoIP-RTP-UnTrust
   match protocol rtp audio
   match access-group name AutoQoS-VoIP-RTCP
!
! Next class-map matches voice control traffic
!
  class-map match-any AutoQoS-VoIP-Control-UnTrust
   match access-group name AutoQoS-VoIP-Control
!
! This one matches all non-voice that was already marked like voice
!
  class-map match-any AutoQoS-VoIP-Remark
   match ip dscp ef
   match ip dscp cs3
   match ip dscp af31
!
! Policy-map performs low latency queuing for voice payload, CBWFQ for
! Voice signaling, re-marks non-voice packets that are marked like voice,
! and queues all non-voice in class-default.
!
```

continues

Example 3-8 **show auto qos** *Commands (Continued)*

```
   policy-map AutoQoS-Policy-UnTrust
    class AutoQoS-VoIP-RTP-UnTrust
     priority percent 70
     set dscp ef
    class AutoQoS-VoIP-Control-UnTrust
     bandwidth percent 5
     set dscp af31
    class AutoQoS-VoIP-Remark
     set dscp default
    class class-default
     fair-queue

 Serial0/1 -
 !
  interface Serial0/1
   service-policy output AutoQoS-Policy-UnTrust
 !
 ! Sends rmon events for packet drops for voice to the SNMP manager
 !
  rmon event 33333 log trap AutoQoS description "AutoQoS SNMP traps for Voice Dr
ops" owner AutoQoS
  rmon alarm 33333 cbQosCMDropBitRate.1161.1163 30 absolute rising-threshold 1 3
3333 falling-threshold 0 owner AutoQoS
R3#show auto qos int s 0/1

 Serial0/1 -
 !
  interface Serial0/1
   service-policy output AutoQoS-Policy-UnTrust
```

Of the two commands shown, **show auto qos** shows all the configuration generated by AutoQoS VoIP. Had any changes been made to the configuration, they would not be shown in the output of this command—a **show running-config** command would be required to see those changes. The **show auto qos interface serial0/1** command simply shows the policy map enabled on the interface with the **service-policy** command.

You have not read enough of the book to appreciate the details of the configuration, but by the end of the book, you should be able to easily understand the configuration shown in Example 3-8.

More AutoQoS Configuration Options

To remove the AutoQoS configuration, you simply use the **no** form of the command—in other words, **no auto qos voip**. However, if you happened to change the QoS configuration manually, this command will not necessarily remove all the configuration. In that case, you have to remove the configuration manually.

The **auto qos voip** command comes with two optional parameters, **trust** and **fr-atm**. The **trust** parameter tells AutoQoS VoIP to trust the incoming DSCP markings. So, the automatically configured QoS commands will not look for voice payload and voice signaling. Instead, following best practices, the commands look for packets with DSCP EF as voice payload, and DSCPs AF31 and CS3 as voice signaling. This option makes sense if you know that the packets have already been marked close to the edge of the network. By leaving off the **trust** option, you are essentially telling the router that you do not trust the markings, so AutoQoS VoIP generates configurations that classify based on other packet headers besides DSCP.

The **fr-atm** option is used with Frame Relay permanent virtual circuits (PVCs) when the PVC is using ATM service interworking. *Service interworking* means that one end of the VC is Frame Relay and the other end is ATM. AutoQoS VoIP configures Frame Relay Fragmentation by default, which is not supported with service interworking VCs. The **fr-atm** parameter makes AutoQoS VoIP use another fragmentation tool, called Multilink Point-to-Point Protocol (MLP) over Frame Relay and ATM, to perform fragmentation.

Ignoring the details of the configuration that AutoQoS VoIP generates, it is easy to choose the right parameters. If all packets have not been marked by the time they arrive at the router, do not use the **trust** option; if they have already been marked, use the **trust** option. If using Frame Relay and the VC uses service interworking, use the **fr-atm** option. Make sure you configure bandwidth correctly and look at the list of considerations in the QoS configuration guide.

Although making AutoQoS VoIP work is easy, it is important to understand what it is trying to do. The next section takes a closer look at what AutoQoS is actually trying to accomplish on a router.

AutoQoS VoIP for Router PHBs

The key to appreciating what AutoQoS VoIP configures is to focus on two facts:

- It is oriented toward making VoIP traffic work well.

- It follows Cisco best practices for the various QoS tools in regard to VoIP.

By reading the rest of the chapters in this book, including the material in Chapter 10, "Cisco QoS Best Practices," you will learn more about what is best to use for QoS. However, any time someone suggests the best way to do something with technology, there can always be some points of disagreement. Table 3-5 shows the PHBs that can be configured by AutoQoS VoIP on a router and some comments about its choices.

Table 3-5 *PHBs Generated by AutoQoS VoIP Configuration (for Routers)*

PHB	Comments
Class and Mark	If the **trust** option is omitted, AutoQoS VoIP configures CB Marking, using NBAR, to classify traffic into voice payload (marked DSCP EF), voice signaling (marked DSCP AF31), and all else (marked DSCP BE).
Queuing	Voice payload is placed into an LLQ. Voice signaling is in another queue with a low-bandwidth CBWFQ queue. All other traffic defaults into the **class-default** queue, which by default gets 25 percent of link bandwidth.
Compression	If the link has a bandwidth of 768 kbps or less, cRTP is enabled.
LFI	If the link has a bandwidth of 768 kbps or less, AutoQoS enables LFI. For interfaces originally configured for HDLC or PPP, AutoQoS reconfigures MLP with LFI on those interfaces. For Frame Relay, AutoQoS configures FR Fragmentation, unless the **fr-atm** option is configured on the **auto qos** command. In that case, AutoQoS configures MLP over Frame Relay LFI. In each case, the fragment size is tuned for a 10-ms fragment.
Shaping	On Frame Relay interfaces, Frame Relay Traffic Shaping (FRTS) is configured, tuned for a Shaping interval of 10 ms.

This table actually summarizes a lot of the best practices for QoS in an enterprise network. It is difficult to appreciate the details until you read the remaining chapters, so as a suggestion, go ahead and read through the rest of the chapters of the book. Chapter 10 reminds you to come back to this section of Chapter 3 and review what AutoQoS VoIP thinks of as best practices. You will have a much better appreciation for what it does for you at that point.

If you do take this suggestion, you might enjoy looking through a Frame Relay configuration as well. Example 3-9 shows how to configure AutoQoS VoIP on a Frame Relay interface, along with the resulting QoS configuration. After reading the rest of the book, working through this configuration can be an interesting exercise, both for reviewing what you learned and for solidifying your understanding of the PHBs created by AutoQoS VoIP.

Example 3-9 *Low-Bandwidth (256 kbps) Frame Relay AutoQoS Configuration*

```
R3#conf t
Enter configuration commands, one per line.  End with CNTL/Z.
R3(config)#int s 0/0.1
R3(config-subif)#bandwidth 256
R3(config-subif)#frame-relay interface-dlci 143
R3(config-fr-dlci)#auto qos voip
R3(config-fr-dlci)#^Z
R3#
R3#sh auto qos
 !
  ip access-list extended AutoQoS-VoIP-RTCP
   permit udp any any range 16384 32767
 !
  ip access-list extended AutoQoS-VoIP-Control
   ended IP access list AutoQoS-VoIP-Control
   permit tcp any any eq 1720
   permit tcp any any range 11000 11999
   permit udp any any eq 2427
   permit tcp any any eq 2428
   permit tcp any any range 2000 2002
   permit udp any any eq 1719
   permit udp any any eq 5060
 !
  class-map match-any AutoQoS-VoIP-RTP-UnTrust
   match protocol rtp audio
   match access-group name AutoQoS-VoIP-RTCP
 !
  class-map match-any AutoQoS-VoIP-Control-UnTrust
   match access-group name AutoQoS-VoIP-Control
 !
  class-map match-any AutoQoS-VoIP-Remark
   match ip dscp ef
   match ip dscp cs3
   match ip dscp af31
 !
   policy-map AutoQoS-Policy-UnTrust
    class AutoQoS-VoIP-RTP-UnTrust
     priority percent 70
     set dscp ef
    class AutoQoS-VoIP-Control-UnTrust
     bandwidth percent 5
     set dscp af31
    class AutoQoS-VoIP-Remark
```

continues

Example 3-9   *Low-Bandwidth (256 kbps) Frame Relay AutoQoS Configuration (Continued)*

```
      set dscp default
     class class-default
      fair-queue

!  Serial0/0.1: DLCI 143 -
 !
  interface Serial0/0
   frame-relay traffic-shaping
  !
  interface Serial0/0.1 point-to-point
   frame-relay interface-dlci 143
     class AutoQoS-VoIP-FR-Serial0/0-143
   frame-relay ip rtp header-compression
 !
 map-class frame-relay AutoQoS-VoIP-FR-Serial0/0-143
  frame-relay cir 256000
  frame-relay bc 2560
  frame-relay be 0
  frame-relay mincir 256000
  service-policy output AutoQoS-Policy-UnTrust
  frame-relay fragment 320
  !
  rmon event 33333 log trap AutoQoS description "AutoQoS SNMP traps for Voice Dr
ops" owner AutoQoS
  rmon alarm 33338 cbQosCMDropBitRate.1619.1621 30 absolute rising-threshold 1 3
3333 falling-threshold 0 owner AutoQoS
```

> **NOTE**   The current QOS exam does not cover FRTS as a topic unto itself. Chapter 7,
> "Congestion Avoidance Through Drop Policies," covers some basics of FRTS so that you
> understand some of the Frame Relay Fragmentation coverage. However, AutoQoS creates FRTS
> configuration in some cases. Appendix B, "Additional QoS Reference Materials" (found on the
> book's accompanying CD-ROM), includes coverage of FRTS from the previous edition of this
> book, if you want more background information.

AutoQoS VoIP for Cisco IOS Switches

Cisco supports AutoQoS VoIP on 2950 (Enhanced Image), 3550, 4500, and 6500 Series switches.
It is similar to AutoQoS VoIP for routers in philosophy but different in the details. For instance, for
both switches and routers, AutoQoS VoIP does the following:

- Automatically configures QoS settings based on simple configuration commands

- Classifies based on voice payload, voice signaling, and other traffic

- Follows Cisco Best Practices for QoS

AutoQoS VoIP for Cisco IOS switches differs from routers in terms of both what PHBs are configured and the configuration commands created by AutoQoS. Even though IOS-based Cisco switches support MQC-style commands, many of the core QoS features are not configured with MQC commands. Also, different QoS tools are used on the switches (as compared to routers) but the ultimate goal is still the same—to ensure VoIP traffic works well, with minimal configuration.

As with AutoQoS VoIP for routers, this section begins with some discussion of the configuration and then moves on to discuss the PHBs created by the automatically configured QOS commands.

AutoQoS VoIP Configuration for IOS Switches

IOS switches use the same basic interface subcommand as routers, but with a couple of different options. The full syntax is as follows:

```
auto qos voip {cisco-phone | trust}
```

Note that you must choose either **cisco-phone** or **trust**. To appreciate which one to use, consider a typical campus switch design, as shown in Figure 3-4.

Figure 3-4 *Typical Campus Switch Design*

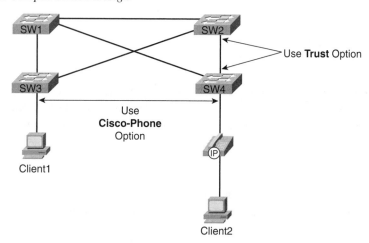

Figure 3-4 shows that for switch ports connected to end-user devices, the **cisco-phone** option is suggested. Alternatively, for trunks between two switches, the **trust** option is suggested. But why? Figure 3-5 shows the explanation against the same diagram, with the explanation following.

Figure 3-5 *Two Settings, Three Actions, for Classification and Marking*

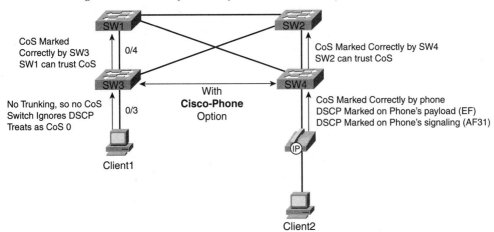

The **cisco-phone** parameter tells the switch to use CDP version 2 to recognize whether a phone is currently attached to the port. If a Cisco IP Phone is there, the switch can trust the QoS markings from the phone. If a phone is not there, the switch simply does not trust the QoS markings on the frames entering that interface and treats all traffic as BE traffic.

In effect, the **cisco-phone** option tells the switch to extend the *trust boundary* down to the Cisco IP Phone.

As a result of the actions at SW3 and SW4, SW1 and SW2 can simply trust the CoS values of the incoming frames. For frames that come in from an untrusted device or port, as with Client1 and SW3, SW3 forwards the frame to SW1 with a CoS of 0, because SW3 did not trust the device off that port. However, SW4 trusted the IP Phone to mark the CoS value correctly, so frames forwarded by SW4 to SW2 have CoS 5 (voice payload), CoS 3 (voice signaling), or CoS 0 (traffic from PC Client2).

To summarize, configure the **cisco-phone** setting on ports connected to end users, and the **trust** setting when connecting to other switches, assuming the CoS values will be marked correctly.

Example 3-10 shows a configuration for SW3, with both **cisco-phone** and **trust** configured.

Example 3-10 *2950 (EI) Configuration for AutoQoS VoIP*

```
SW3#conf t
Enter configuration commands, one per line.  End with CNTL/Z.
SW3(config)#int fa 0/3
SW3(config-if)#auto qos voip cisco-phone
SW3(config-if)#int fa 0/4
SW3(config-if)#auto qos voip trust
SW3(config-if)#^Z
SW3#show auto qos
```

Example 3-10 *2950 (EI) Configuration for AutoQoS VoIP (Continued)*

```
Initial configuration applied by AutoQoS:
wrr-queue bandwidth 20 1 80 0
no wrr-queue cos-map
wrr-queue cos-map 1 0 1 2 4
wrr-queue cos-map 3 3 6 7
wrr-queue cos-map 4 5
mls qos map cos-dscp 0 8 16 26 32 46 48 56
!
interface FastEthernet0/3
 mls qos trust device cisco-phone
 mls qos trust cos
!
interface FastEthernet0/4
 mls qos trust cos
SW3#
```

The configuration itself is easy. On ports known to be end-user ports, such as FastEthernet0/3, the **auto qos voip cisco-phone** interface subcommand is used. On trunk ports, assuming the frames will be marked with correct CoS values, the **auto qos voip trust** interface subcommand is used.

The resulting configuration shown in the **show auto qos voip** command is difficult to understand until you have learned more about QoS configuration on a 2950 switch. You might want to return to this section of Chapter 3 after reading Chapter 9, "LAN QoS," after which the output of the **show auto qos voip** command should be more meaningful.

AutoQoS VoIP for IOS Switch PHBs

It is important to understand what the AutoQoS VoIP configured, at least in terms of the meaning behind the commands. As with routers, two key points help in understanding the PHBs created on the switches:

■ It is oriented toward making VoIP traffic work well.

■ It follows Cisco Best Practices for the various QoS tools in regard to VoIP.

The list of PHBs created by AutoQoS VoIP on a 2950 switch differs from routers and is summarized in Table 3-6.

Table 3-6   *PHBs Generated by AutoQoS VoIP Configuration (for 2950 EI Switches)*

PHB	Comments
Class and Mark	Classifies based on CoS on trusted ports, or on cisco-phone ports on which an actual phone is attached. Assumes CoS 0 on ports with **cisco-phone** configured when no phone is detected with CDP 2.0. Re-marks DSCP of packets based on CoS (CoS 5 – DSCP EF, CoS 3 – DSCP AF31, CoS 0 – DSCP BE).
Queuing	Creates an LLQ for voice payload (CoS 5) and assigns 20 percent of remaining bandwidth to voice signaling (CoS 3) and 80 percent to all other (CoS 0) traffic.

Chapter 9 provides details of the underlying QoS commands created by AutoQoS.

Next, this chapter ends with a short description of AutoQoS for Cat-OS on the 6500 Series switches.

AutoQoS VoIP for 6500 Cat-OS

The Cisco 6500 series switches support Cat-OS when running the Catalyst Operating System (Cat-OS). Like AutoQoS on routers and IOS-based switches, AutoQoS uses simple commands to initiate the automatic configuration of QoS commands, with settings that help ensure good performance of VoIP traffic.

The Cisco QoS course and exam tend to focus on switch examples using IOS-based switches and mostly ignores commands on Cat-OS. The one exception to that rule in the Cisco QoS course is the coverage of the AutoQoS commands in Cat-OS. So, for the purposes of this book, this short section explains the commands and their meaning.

Table 3-7 lists the Cat-OS commands related to AutoQoS VoIP.

Table 3-7   *Command Reference for AutoQoS VoIP (for 6500 Cat-OS)*

Command	Function
set qos autoqos	Sets global settings, such as for a CoS-DSCP map
set port qos autoqos *mod/port* **trust** [**cos** | **dscp**]	For the specified ports, tells the switch to trust the DSCP or CoS setting of incoming frames
set port qos autoqos *mod/port* **voip** [**ciscosoftphone** | **ciscoipphone**]	For the specified ports, tells the switch to use CDP V2 to sense the presence of a phone and to trust CoS if a phone is found (**ciscoipphone**), or to trust DSCP but police traffic so a PC running Cisco SoftPhone does not abuse the privilege of having its DSCP trusted (**ciscosoftphone**)

To configure AutoQoS on a 6500 switch, you first need to use the **set qos autoqos** command. Afterward, you need to use a **set port qos autoqos** command covering each port, choosing either **trust cos**, **trust dscp**, **voip ciscoipphone**, or **voip ciscosoftphone** as options. To appreciate each of the four options, consider Figure 3-6, which demonstrates the implementation of all four options.

Figure 3-6 *AutoQoS Options on 6500 Cat-OS*

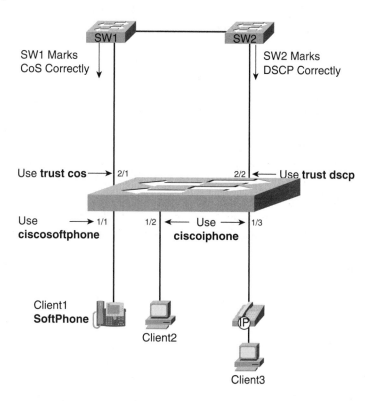

Some of the options for the 6500 switch are the same as for IOS-based switches such as the 2950. For instance, if frames have already been marked with the correct CoS value on a trunk, as is the case on port 2/1 in Figure 3-6, the command **set port qos autoqos 2/1 trust cos** tells the switch to trust CoS on that port. That is the same action as with the switch IOS command **auto qos voip trust**.

Another option that works like AutoQoS on an IOS switch is the **ciscoipphone** option. If a port might have an IP Phone, or it might not, such as on ports 1/2 and 1/3 in Figure 3-6, the command **set port qos autoqos 1/2 voip ciscoipphone** is the correct setting. As with the switch IOS command

auto qos voip cisco-phone, this **set** command tells the switch to use CDP V2 to discover if a Cisco IP Phone is on the port. If a Cisco IP Phone is on the port, trust CoS and extend the trust boundary down to the Cisco IP Phone, marking CoS 0 for all traffic sent by the PC attached to the phone. If no Cisco IP Phone is on the port, treat all traffic as CoS 0.

Of the other two options, using the command **set port qos autoqos 2/2 trust dscp** is the most obvious. If the DSCP has already been set correctly, you should use this command to tell the switch to trust the incoming DSCP setting.

Finally, the command **set port qos autoqos 1/1 voip ciscosoftphone** is recommended on port 1/2 in Figure 3-6. The PC attached to that port is running the Cisco SoftPhone application, which in effect creates an IP Phone via software running on the PC. However, the Cisco SoftPhone marks DSCP correctly (EF for payload, AF31 for signaling), but it does not mark CoS—in fact, trunking is not even needed on this port. You could just trust DSCP on this port, but the danger is that the PC could set DSCP EF or AF31 for other IP packets, hoping to get good performance from the network. To prevent such abuse, the **set port qos autoqos 1/1 voip ciscosoftphone** command also enables policing at a rate of 320 kbps for DSCP EF traffic and 32 kbps for DSCP AF31 traffic. Cisco SoftPhone can use up to 256 kbps for a single call, although it typically uses less. So, rather than just trusting DSCP, the **ciscoipphone** option lets you trust DSCP, but it reduces the impact if the end user is marking other packets as DSCP EF or AF31.

Table 3-8 lists the four competing options for AutoQoS settings on each port.

Table 3-8 *Comparing Options for* **set port** *Command with AutoQoS*

Command	Function
trust cos	Accept the CoS of incoming frames.
trust dscp	Accept the DSCP of incoming packets.
voip ciscoipphone	Use CDPv2 to discover the absence or presence of an IP Phone. If one is there, trust CoS and extend the trust boundary to the IP Phone, causing the PC's frames to be marked CoS 0. If no phone is there, treat all incoming frames as CoS 0.
voip ciscosoftphone	Trust DSCP, but police DSCP EF at 320 kbps and DSCP AF31 at 32 kbps.

Comparisons of CLI, MQC, and AutoQoS

In the past, QoS tools each had a different set of CLI configuration commands. Over time, with the addition of more and more tools, configuring QoS became a challenge. With the advent of MQC, and with the more recently developed and most useful QoS tools using MQC commands, the configuration complexity was reduced tremendously. Going a step further, by creating AutoQoS VoIP, Cisco provided an even simpler way to configure QoS for VoIP traffic, with no requirement to understand QoS to make the network work well.

The QoS course includes a wonderful table comparing these three options, included here as Table 3-9, summarizing the comparison points between the three options.

Table 3-9 *Comparisons of CLI, MQC, and AutoQoS*

	CLI	MQC	AutoQoS
Ease of Use	Poor	Easier	Simple
Ability to Fine Tune	OK	Very Good	Very Good
Time to Implement	Longest	Average	Shortest
Modularity	Poor	Excellent	Excellent

Foundation Summary

The "Foundation Summary" is a collection of tables and figures that provide a convenient review of many key concepts in this chapter. For those of you already comfortable with the topics in this chapter, this summary can help you recall a few details. For those of you who just read this chapter, this review should help solidify some key facts. For any of you doing your final preparation before the exam, these tables and figures are a convenient way to review the day before the exam.

Figure 3-7 shows the general flow of MQC commands.

Figure 3-7 *MQC Commands and Their Correlation*

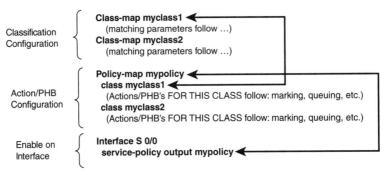

Table 3-10 lists the **match** command options available for the IOS revision covered by the current QOS exam, 12.2(15)T.

Table 3-10 **match** *Configuration Command Reference for MQC Tools*

Command	Function
match [ip] precedence *precedence-value* [*precedence-value precedence-value precedence-value*]	Matches precedence in IPv4 packets when the **ip** parameter is included; matches IPv4 and IPv6 packets when the **ip** parameter is missing.
match access-group {*access-group* | **name** *access- group-name*}	Matches an ACL by number or name.
match any	Matches all packets.
match class-map *class-map-name*	Matches based on another class map.
match cos *cos-value* [*cos-value cos-value cos-value*]	Matches a CoS value.
match destination-address mac *address*	Matches a destination MAC address.

Table 3-10   **match** *Configuration Command Reference for MQC Tools (Continued)*

Command	Function
match fr-dlci *dlci-number*	Matches a particular Frame Relay DLCI.
match input-interface *interface-name*	Matches an input interface.
match [ip] dscp *ip-dscp-value [ip-dscp-value ip-dscp- value ip-dscp-value ip-dscp-value ip-dscp-value ip- dscp-value ip-dscp-value]*	Matches DSCP in IPv4 packets when the **ip** parameter is included; matches IPv4 and IPv6 packets when the **ip** parameter is missing.
match ip rtp *starting-port-number port-range*	Matches the RTP's UDP port-number range, even values only.
match mpls experimental *number*	Matches an MPLS Experimental value.
match mpls experimental topmost *value*	When multiple labels are in use, this command matches the MPLS EXP field in the topmost label.
match not *match-criteria*	Reverses the matching logic; in other words, things matched by the matching criteria do not match the class map.
match packet length {**max** *maximum-length-value* [**min** *minimum-length-value*] | **min** *minimum-length-value* [**max** *maximum-length-value*]}	Matches packets based on the minimum length, maximum length, or both.
match protocol citrix app *application-name-string*	Matches NBAR Citrix applications.
match protocol http [**url** *url-string* | **host** *hostname- string* | **mime** *MIME-type*]	Matches a host name and URL string.
match protocol *protocol-name*	Matches NBAR protocol types.
match protocol rtp [**audio** | **video** | **payload-type** *payload-string*]	Matches RTP audio or video payload, based on the payload type. Also allows explicitly specified payload types.
match qos-group *qos-group-value*	Matches a QoS group.
match source-address mac *address-destination*	Matches a source MAC address.

Table 3-11 lists the various MQC subcommands available in Cisco IOS Software for defining actions to be taken.

Table 3-11 *Action (PHB) Subcommands Inside a Policy Map*

Command	Function
set	CB Marking action, with options to mark several fields inside headers
bandwidth	Reserves bandwidth for the class for CBWFQ
priority	Reserves bandwidth, and provides LLQ with CBWFQ
shape	Shapes traffic in the class with a defined bandwidth and burst sizes
police	Polices traffic in the class with a defined bandwidth and burst sizes
compress	Performs TCP and RTP header compression on packets in the class

Because routers and switches do different tasks, QoS differs slightly between them, but to get an idea about what AutoQoS does, consider that AutoQoS on routers works to classify packets into three service classes:

■ Voice payload

■ Voice signaling

■ All other traffic

Table 3-12 lists the commands related to AutoQoS VoIP, followed by an example configuration.

Table 3-12 *Command Reference for AutoQoS VoIP (for Routers)*

Command	Function
auto qos voip [trust] [fr-atm]	Configuration command that enables AutoQoS VoIP on an interface (PPP or HDLC) or VC (FR and ATM)
no auto qos	Disables AutoQoS VoIP on an interface (PPP or HDLC) or VC (FR and ATM)
show auto qos [interface *interface-type*]	Displays what AutoQoS actually created
show policy-map interface *interface-name* [input | output]	Displays actual configuration of MQC-based parts of the configuration, including any later changes made by an engineer

Table 3-13 shows the PHBs that can be configured by AutoQoS VoIP on a router and some comments about its choices.

Table 3-13   *PHBs Generated by AutoQoS VoIP Configuration (for Routers)*

PHB	Comments
Class and Mark	If the **trust** parameter is omitted, AutoQoS VoIP configures CB Marking, using NBAR, to classify traffic into voice payload (marked DSCP EF), voice signaling (marked DSCP AF31), and all else (marked DSCP BE).
Queuing	Voice payload is placed into an LLQ. Voice signaling is in another queue with a low-bandwidth CBWFQ queue. All other traffic defaults into the **class-default** queue, which by default gets 25 percent of link bandwidth.
Compression	If the link has a bandwidth of 768 kbps or less, cRTP is enabled.
LFI	If the link has a bandwidth of 768 kbps or less, AutoQoS enables LFI. For interfaces originally configured for HDLC or PPP, AutoQoS reconfigures MLP with LFI on those interfaces. For Frame Relay, AutoQoS configures FR Fragmentation, unless the **fr-atm** option is configured on the **auto qos** command. In that case, AutoQoS configures MLP over Frame Relay LFI. In each case, the fragment size is tuned for a 10-ms fragment.
Shaping	On Frame Relay interfaces, FRTS is configured, tuned for a Shaping interval of 10 ms.

Cisco IOS switches use the same interface subcommand as routers, but with a couple of different options. The full syntax is as follows:

```
auto qos voip {cisco-phone | trust}
```

Figure 3-8 shows the locations where the **cisco-phone** and **trust** options should be used, along with some notes about how the **cisco-phone** option works.

Figure 3-8   *Two Settings, Three Actions, for Classification and Marking*

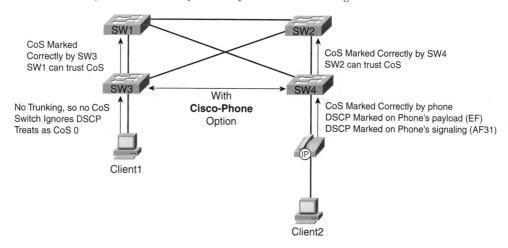

The list of PHBs created by AutoQoS VoIP differs from routers and is summarized in Table 3-14.

Table 3-14 *PHBs Generated by AutoQoS VoIP Configuration (for 2950 EI Switches)*

PHB	Comments
Class and Mark	Classifies based on CoS on trusted ports, or on cisco-phone ports on which an actual phone is attached. Assumes CoS 0 on ports with **cisco-phone** configured when no phone is detected with CDP 2.0. Re-marks DSCP of packets based on CoS (CoS 5 – DSCP EF, CoS 3 – DSCP AF31, CoS 0 – DSCP BE).
Queuing	Creates an LLQ for voice payload (CoS 5), and assigns 20 percent of remaining bandwidth to voice signaling (CoS 3), and 80 percent to all other (CoS 0) traffic.

Table 3-15 lists the four competing options for AutoQoS settings on each port when configuring AutoQoS on Cat-OS. The QoS course includes a wonderful table comparing these three options, included here as Table 3-16, summarizing the comparison points between the three options.

Table 3-15 *Comparing Options for* **set port** *Command with AutoQoS*

Command	Function
trust cos	Accept the CoS of incoming frames.
trust dscp	Accept the DSCP of incoming packets.
voip ciscoipphone	Use CDPv2 to discover the absence or presence of an IP Phone. If one is there, trust CoS, and extend the trust boundary to the IP Phone, causing the PC's frames to be marked CoS 0. If no phone is there, treat all incoming frames as CoS 0.
voip ciscosoftphone	Trust DSCP, but police DSCP EF at 320 kbps and DSCP AF31 at 32 kbps.

Table 3-16 *Comparisons of CLI, MQC, and AutoQoS*

	CLI	MQC	AutoQoS
Ease of Use	Poor	Easier	Simple
Ability to Fine Tune	OK	Very Good	Very Good
Time to Implement	Longest	Average	Shortest
Modularity	Poor	Excellent	Excellent

For Further Reading

This book attempts to cover the breadth and depth of QoS as covered on the QOS exam (642-642). However, you might want to read more about topics in this chapter, or other classification and marking topics.

For more on the topics in this chapter:

■   Cisco IOS 12.2(15)T AutoQoS Configuration Guide (http://www.cisco.com/univercd/cc/td/doc/product/software/ios122/122newft/122t/122t15/ftautoq1.htm)

■   Cisco 2950 QoS Configuration Guide (http://www.cisco.com/univercd/cc/td/doc/product/lan/cat2950/12119ea1/2950scg/swqos.htm)

■   6500 Catalyst OS Auto QoS Configuration Guide (http://www.cisco.com/univercd/cc/td/doc/product/lan/cat6000/sw_8_2/confg_gd/autoqos.htm)

■   "Cisco AutoQoS White Paper" (http://cisco.com/en/US/tech/tk543/tk759/technologies_white_paper09186a00801348bc.shtml)

For design-related guidance:

■   "Cisco AVVID Network Infrastructure Enterprise Quality of Service Design" (http://cisco.com/application/pdf/en/us/guest/netsol/ns17/c649/ccmigration_09186a00800d67ed.pdf)

Q&A

As mentioned in the Introduction, you have two choices for review questions. The following questions give you a more difficult challenge than the exam itself by using an open-ended question format. By reviewing now with this more difficult question format, you can exercise your memory better, and prove your conceptual and factual knowledge of this chapter. You can find the answers to these questions in Appendix A.

The second option for practice questions is to use the CD-ROM included with this book. It includes a testing engine and more than 200 multiple-choice questions. You should use this CD-ROM nearer to the end of your preparation for practice with the actual exam format:

1.   Configure two class maps, one that matches the packets permitted by ACL 101, and one that matches packets denied by ACL 101. Do not use **class-default**, and do not bother configuring a policy map.

2. Configure a policy map that refers to predefined classes c1, C2, and c3, with the action for each class map being to set the DSCP value to AF11, AF21, and AF22, respectively. Assume that the class maps are already defined.

3. List the three major configuration steps and the main command used in each step for the configuration of a QoS feature using MQC.

4. Describe two different ways with which you could classify packets with DSCP AF31, AF32, and AF33 into a single class using MQC commands.

5. List three benefits of MQC as compared with non-MQC-based QoS features.

6. Consider the configuration snippet that follows. What commands would list statistics for the QoS policy implemented on fastethernet 0/0?

```
class-map fred
 match dscp ef
policy-map barney
 class fred
  set dscp af11
 class class-default
  set dscp be
interface fastethernet0/0
 service-policy input barney
```

7. List the two SNMP MIBs included in Cisco router IOS that can be used by QPM to improve the statistics presented to a QPM user. List the long version of the names and the acronyms.

8. What information can be seen by using the CBQoSMIB that cannot be seen with **show** commands on the device being managed?

9. How many classes can be associated with a single policy map in Cisco IOS Software Release 12.2(15)T?

10. On a router using AutoQoS, what command enables the feature for Frame Relay VCs that use Frame Relay-to-ATM service interworking?

11. On a router using AutoQoS, what command enables the feature on a serial interface when the router can trust the DSCP settings of incoming packets?

12. Describe the classification configuration created by a router when enabling AutoQoS on a serial interface, with all default values chosen on the **auto qos** command.

13. Describe the marking actions created by a router when enabling AutoQoS on a serial interface, with all default values chosen on the **auto qos** command.

14. List three of the requirements on router AutoQoS that need to be true before actually configuring AutoQoS.

15. List the data link protocols on a router that support AutoQoS.

16. List the PHBs created by a router when the **auto qos voip** command is used on a PPP serial interface with the default bandwidth setting.

17. List the PHBs created by a router when the **auto qos voip** command is used on a PPP serial interface with **bandwidth 768** configured.

18. List the PHBs created by a router when the **auto qos voip** command is used on a Frame Relay PVC with **bandwidth 832** configured.

19. When configuring AutoQoS on a router, with a Frame Relay interface, what configuration mode must you be in before using the **auto qos** command? What command gets you into that configuration mode?

20. When configuring a 2950 switch with the **auto qos voip trust** command, what PHBs are configured on the interface?

21. When configuring a 2950 switch with the **auto qos voip cisco-phone** command, what PHBs are configured on the interface?

22. When configuring a 2950 switch with the **auto qos voip cisco-phone** command, what version of CDP is required in order for AutoQoS to work?

23. When planning to use AutoQoS on a 2950 switch, what types of ports are generally configured with the **trust** option, and what type are generally configured with the **cisco-phone** option?

24. When using AutoQoS on a 6500 running Cat-OS, describe the difference in using the **ciscosoftphone** setting and the **trust dscp** setting.

25. When using AutoQoS on a 6500 running Cat-OS, describe when you might choose to use the **ciscosoftphone** option versus the **trust dscp** option.

26. When using AutoQoS on a 6500 running Cat-OS, describe when you might choose to use the **ciscoipphone** setting versus the **trust cos** setting.

27. When using AutoQoS on a 6500 running Cat-OS, the **set port qos autoqos 3/1 voip ciscoipphone** command has been configured. Describe what else must be true before AutoQoS will trust incoming CoS values for frames on port 3/1.

28. Comparing the CLI of older QoS options in a Cisco router, MQC, and AutoQoS, which takes the least time to implement?

29. Comparing the CLI of older QoS options in a Cisco router, MQC, and AutoQoS, which is considered to be the most modular?

30. Comparing the CLI of older QoS options in a Cisco router, MQC, and AutoQoS, which is considered to be the most difficult to use?

QOS Exam Topics

This chapter covers the following exam topics specific to the QoS exam:

- Explain how link layer and network layer markings are used to define service classes and the different applications represented by each of these service classes

- Given a network and a description of QoS issues, use MQC CLI commands to classify packets

- Given a network and a description of QoS issues, use class-based marking to assign packets to a specific service class

- Describe the function of Network Based Application Recognition

- Describe the purpose of pre-classification to support QoS in various VPN (IPSEC, GRE, L2TP) configurations

- Describe QoS trust boundaries and their significance in LAN based classification and marking

CHAPTER 4

Classification and Marking

QoS classification tools categorize packets by examining the contents of the frame, cell, and packet headers, whereas marking tools allow the QoS tool to change the packet headers for easier classification. Many QoS tools rely on a classification function to determine to which traffic the tool applies. To place voice and data traffic in separate queues, for example, you must use some form of classification to differentiate the two types of traffic and place the identified traffic in the proper queue. Marking provides a way for QoS tools to change bits in the packet header to indicate the level of service this packet should receive from other QoS tools. For instance, you can use marking tools to change the marking in voice packets to ensure that a classification tool can differentiate a voice packet from a data packet. Without the marking feature, the frame, packet, or cell remains unchanged.

Marking involves placing a value into one of the small number of well-defined frame, packet, or cell header fields specifically designed for QoS marking. By marking a packet, other QoS functions can perform classification based on the marked field inside a header. Marking simplifies the network's QoS design, it simplifies configuration of other QoS tools, and it reduces the overhead required by each of the other QoS tools to classify the packets.

Although classification and marking tools do not directly affect the bandwidth, delay, jitter, or loss experienced by traffic in the network, classification and marking tools are the building blocks for all other QoS tools. With these tools, all traffic on the network is identified for the next QoS tool to act upon.

The concepts that apply to all classification and marking are covered in the first section of this chapter, including the terminology, fields used, and the meaning behind each of the available marked fields. Following that, this chapter covers several classification and marking tools, with example configurations, as well as **show**, and **debug** commands.

"Do I Know This Already?" Quiz Questions

The purpose of the "Do I Know This Already?" quiz is to help you decide whether you really need to read the entire chapter. If you already intend to read the entire chapter, you do not necessarily need to answer these questions now.

The 10-question quiz, derived from the major sections in "Foundation Topics" portion of the chapter, helps you determine how to spend your limited study time.

Table 4-1 outlines the major topics discussed in this chapter and the "Do I Know This Already?" quiz questions that correspond to those topics.

Table 4-1 *"Do I Know This Already?" Foundation Topics Section-to-Question Mapping*

Foundation Topics Section Covering These Questions	Questions	Score
Classification and Marking Concepts	1–4	
Classification and Marking Tools	5–8	
Classification Issues when Using VPNs	9–10	
Total Score		

CAUTION   The goal of self-assessment is to gauge your mastery of the topics in this chapter. If you do not know the answer to a question or are only partially sure of the answer, mark this question wrong for purposes of the self-assessment. Giving yourself credit for an answer you correctly guess skews your self-assessment results and might provide you with a false sense of security.

You can find the answers to the "Do I Know This Already?" quiz in Appendix A, "Answers to the 'Do I Know This Already?' Quizzes and Q&A Sections." The suggested choices for your next step are as follows:

- **8 or less overall score**—Read the entire chapter. This includes the "Foundation Topics," the "Foundation Summary," and the "Q&A" sections.

- **9 or 10 overall score**—If you want more review on these topics, skip to the "Foundation Summary" section and then go to the "Q&A" section. Otherwise, move to the next chapter.

Classification and Marking Concepts Questions

1. Which of the following tools can be used to classify packets generated on behalf of an application that uses static well-known TCP port numbers?

   a. CB Marking

   b. ECN

   c. NBAR

   d. Pre-classify

2. Which of the following tools can be used to classify packets generated on behalf of an application that dynamically allocates the TCP ports numbers used by the application?

   a. CB Marking

   b. ECN

   c. NBAR

   d. Pre-classify

3. Which of the following header fields are part of the IEEE 802.1Q header?

   a. DE

   b. User Priority

   c. QoS

   d. DSCP

   e. ToS

4. Imagine a PC, connected to an IP phone via an Ethernet cable, with the IP phone connected to a 2950 switch. The switch is cabled to an access router, which in turn has Frame Relay connectivity to the central site. Assuming trunking issued between the IP phone and the switch, where is the recommended trust boundary for data coming from the PC towards the central site?

   a. PC

   b. Phone

   c. Switch

   d. Access router

   e. Frame Relay cloud

Classification and Marking Tools Questions

5. Imagine a router configuration with several **class-map** commands, with a policy map referring to the service classes defined in the **class-map** commands. The **policy map** has been enabled for incoming packets on interface Fa0/1. What command would you look for in order to tell if Class Based Marking was in use, as opposed to some other MQC command?

   a. **match**

   b. **match-all**

   c. **priority**

   d. **mark**

   e. **set**

6. Examine the following example of commands typed in configuration mode in order to create a class map. Assuming that the **class fred** command was used inside a policy map, and the policy map was enabled on an interface, which of the following would be true in regards to packets classified by the class map?

```
Router(config)#class-map fred
Router(config)#match ip dscp ef
Router(config)#match ip dscp af31
```

   a. Matches packets with both DSCP EF or AF31

   b. Matches packets with either DSCP EF or AF31

   c. Matches all packets that are neither EF or AF31

   d. Matches no packets

   e. Matches packets with precedence values of 3 and 5

7. Examine the following configuration snippet, and assume that all commands related to the **class-map** and all interface commands are shown. Which of the following answer best explains why the **show** command shows that class barney is not matching any packets?

```
class-map dino
 match protocol rtp audio
!
policy-map barney
 class dino
  set ip dscp ef
!
interface fastethernet0/0
 ip address 1.1.1.1 255.255.255.0
 service-policy input barney
```

   a. There is no RTP audio traffic currently in the network

   b. You cannot enable CB Marking as an input function

   c. The **show** command only works when the **mls enable counters** interface subcommand is used

   d. The **ip cef** global command is required .

   e. The **show policy-map interface fa0/0** command lists configuration information, but not packet counters

8. Assume that a router is configured correctly so that voice payload packets are marked with DSCP value EF. Which of the following commands could have been used inside the policy-map to cause CB Marking to set that value?

- a. **set ip dscp ef**
- b. **set ip dscp 46**
- c. **set dscp ef**
- d. **set dscp 46**
- e. **All of the above**
- f. **None of the above**

Classification Issues when Using VPNs Questions

9. Router A is the endpoint of an IPSEC VPN tunnel. Packets entering router A before being encrypted into the tunnel have been marked with meaningful DSCP values. What causes router A to copy the ToS byte from the original packet into the new VPN IP header?

- a. It works automatically, without any commands required
- b. The **ip cef** global command is needed
- c. The **mls qos** global command is needed
- d. The **qos pre-classify** global command is needed
- e. The **qos pre-classify** command is needed on the IPSEC crypto map

10. Router A is the endpoint of an IPSEC VPN tunnel. Packets entering router A on interface fa 0/0 will be encrypted and then forwarded to a central site out interface S0/0. You want to enable CB Marking on egress packets on the serial0/0 interface, but you want to look at the fields in the IP, TCP, and UDP headers of the original packet, before encryption. What must be done to allow your policy map to work?

- a. It works automatically, without any commands required
- b. The **ip cef** global command is needed
- c. The **mls qos** global command is needed
- d. The **qos pre-classify** global command is needed
- e. The **qos pre-classify** command is needed on the IPSEC crypto map

Foundation Topics

The contents of the "Foundation Topics" section of this chapter, and most of the rest of the chapters in this book, follow the same overall flow. Each chapter describes a type of category of QoS tool. Each "Foundation Topics" section begins with coverage of the concepts behind these tools. Then, each tool is examined, with coverage of how each tool works like the other tools, and how it works differently than the other tools. So, most of the core concepts are explained in the first part of the chapter; some of the concepts may be explained in the section about a specific tool, however, particularly if the concepts apply only to that tool.

The second part of the chapter covers class-based marking (CB Marking), Network Based Application Recognition (NBAR), and VPN tunnel pre-classification. For each tool, the pertinent configuration, **show**, and **debug** commands are also covered.

Classification and Marking Concepts

Most QoS tools classify traffic, which allows for each class of traffic to receive a different level of treatment from other traffic classes. These different types or classes of traffic are typically called *service classes* in QoS terminology. Classification allows the devices to decide which packets are part of each service class, which then allows the devices to perform other QoS functions differently based on the service class.

Classification and marking tools not only classify packets into service classes, but they also mark the packets in the same service class with the same value in a field in the header. By marking the packets, other QoS tools that examine the packet later can examine the marked bits to more easily classify packets.

Classification

Almost every QoS tool uses classification to some degree. To put one packet into a different queue than another packet, the IOS must somehow differentiate between the two packets. To perform header compression on Real Time Protocol (RTP) packets, but not on other packets, the IOS must determine which packets have RTP headers. To shape data traffic going into a Frame Relay network, so that the voice traffic gets enough bandwidth, the IOS must differentiate between Voice over IP (VoIP) and data packets. If an IOS QoS feature needs to treat two packets differently, it must use classification.

Because most QoS tools need to differentiate between packets, most QoS tools have classification features. In fact, many of you will already know something about several of the QoS tools described in this book, and you will realize that you already know how to perform classification using some of those tools. For instance, many QoS tools enable you to classify using access-control lists (ACLs). If ACL 101 *permits* a packet, a queuing tool might put the packet into one queue; if ACL 102 permits a packet, it is placed in a second queue; and so on. In one way of thinking, queuing could instead be called *classification and queuing*, because the queuing feature must somehow decide which packets end up in each queue. Similarly, traffic shaping could be called *classification and traffic shaping*, policing could be called *classification and policing*, and so on. Because most QoS tools classify traffic, however, the names of most QoS tools never evolved to mention the classification function of the tool.

Most classification and marking tools, like the other types of QoS tools, generally operate on packets that are entering or exiting an interface. The logic works something like an ACL, but the *action* is marking, as opposed to allowing or denying (dropping) a packet. More generally, classification and marking logic for ingress packets can be described as follows:

■ For packets entering an interface, if they match criteria 1, mark a field with a value.

■ If the packet was not matched, compare it to criteria 2, and then mark a potentially different field with a potentially different value.

■ Keep looking for a match of the packet, until it is matched

■ If the packet is not matched, no specific action is taken with the packet, and it is forwarded just like it would have been if no QoS had been configured.

> **NOTE** This book uses the following terms describe the data structures used when sending data:
>
> ■ **Frame**—Bits that include the data link layer header and trailer (for example, Ethernet frame and Frame Relay frame)
>
> ■ **Cell**—Specifically, an Asynchronous Transfer Mode (ATM) cell
>
> ■ **Packet**—Bits that include the network layer header, but does not include the data link header (for instance, an IP packet)
>
> ■ **Segment**—Bits that include the TCP or UDP header, but not the data link or network layer header

Class-Based Marking

This chapter focuses on Class-Based Marking (CB-Marking). CB Marking can classify packets into service classes by directly examining frame, cell, packet, and segment headers. CB Marking can also refer to access control lists (ACLs) to match packets, with packets permitted by an ACL being considered to match the logic used by CB Marking. For reference, Table 4-2 lists many of the most popular things that can be matched with an IP ACL; Table 4-3 lists the fields directly matchable by CB Marking in router IOS (as of Cisco IOS Software Release 12.2(15)T5):

Table 4-2 *Popular IP Extended ACL Matchable Fields*

Field	Comments
Source IP address	A range of source IP addresses can be matched by using a wildcard mask.
Destination IP address	A range of source IP addresses can be matched by using a wildcard mask.
IP Precedence*	Format of command uses names for precedence The decimal value for each name is as follows: <table><tr><td>**name**</td><td>IP Precedence Value</td></tr><tr><td>**routine**</td><td>0</td></tr><tr><td>**priority**</td><td>1</td></tr><tr><td>**immediate**</td><td>2</td></tr><tr><td>**flash**</td><td>3</td></tr><tr><td>**flash-override**</td><td>4</td></tr><tr><td>**critic/critical**</td><td>5</td></tr><tr><td>**internet**</td><td>6</td></tr><tr><td>**network**</td><td>7</td></tr></table>
IP DSCP*	Format of the command allows use of differentiated services code point (DSCP) names, as well as decimal values.
IP ToS	Can check to see whether a single Type of Service (ToS) field bit is toggled on; keywords are **normal** (binary **0000**), **max-reliability** (binary **1000**), **max-throughput** (binary **0100**), **min-delay** (binary **0010**), and **min-monetary-cost** (binary **0001**).
TCP ports	Can check source and destination ports; can also check a range of port numbers, whether a port number is larger or smaller than a single value.
TCP Established	Although not typically useful for QoS classification, ACLs can match all TCP segments after the initial segment used for connection establishment.
UDP	Checks the source and destination ports; can also check a range of port numbers, whether a port number is larger or smaller than a single value.
ICMP	Checks a larger variety of ICMP messages and code types (for example, echo request and echo reply).
IGMP	Checks for Internet Group Management Protocol (IGMP) message types.

* Although IP Precedence and DSCP can be matched with an ACL, with CB Marking, the fields can be matched directly without use of an ACL.

Table 4-3 *Fields Directly Matchable by CB Marking*

Field	Comments
Source MAC address	CB Marking uses the **match** command and can match multiple values in one command.
IP Precedence	CB Marking uses the **match** command and can match a multiple values in one command.
MPLS Experimental	CB Marking uses the **match** command and can match multiple values in one command.
CoS	Checks incoming ISL/802.1P CoS bits. Can match multiple values in one command. Only valid on Ethernet trunks.
Destination MAC address	Checks for destination MAC address. Can match multiple values in one command.
Input Interface	Checks for input interface. Can match multiple values in one command.
IP DSCP	Checks for IP DSCP field. Can match multiple values in one command.
RTP's UDP port-number range	RTP uses even-numbered UDP ports from 16,384 to 32,767. This option allows matching a subset of these values, even-numbered ports only, because RTP only uses even-numbered ports.
QoS Group	The QoS Group field is used to tag packets internal to a single router.
NBAR protocol types	Refer to the "Network Based Application Recognition (NBAR)" section in this chapter for more details.
NBAR Citrix applications	NBAR can recognize different types of Citrix applications; CB Marking can use NBAR to classify based on these application types.
Host name and URL string	NBAR can also match URL strings, including the host name, using regular expressions. CB Marking can use NBAR to match these strings for classification.

Classification with NBAR

CB Marking can be configured to look at many of the fields in Tables 4-2 and 4-3 to directly classify packets. However, CB Marking can also use NBAR to classify packets. NBAR provides a router with the capability to classify packets, particularly hard-to-identify packets. Independently, NBAR can be configured to keep counters of traffic types and traffic volume for each type.

NBAR classifies packets that are normally difficult to classify. For instance, some applications use dynamic port numbers, so a statically configured **match** command, looking for a particular UDP or TCP port number, simply could not classify the traffic. NBAR can look past the UDP and TCP header, and refer to the host name, URL, or MIME type in HTTP requests. (This deeper examination of the packet contents is sometimes called *deep packet inspection*.) NBAR can also look past the TCP and UDP headers to recognize application-specific information. For instance, NBAR allows recognition of different Citrix application types, and allows searching for a portion of a URL string.

You can easily recognize when CB Marking is using NBAR for classification. When the **match protocol** command is used, CB Marking is looking to match a protocol discovered by NBAR.

Whether or not NBAR is used with CB Marking, it can be used to gather and report statistics about packets entering and exiting an interface. To see an exhaustive list of protocols, use the **show ip nbar protocol-discovery** command on a router that has NBAR enabled on one or more interfaces. Because CB Marking can take advantage of NBAR's powerful packet matching capabilities, you should be aware of some of the more popular and more useful types of packets that NBAR can match. Table 4-4 lists those values.

Table 4-4   *Popular Fields Matchable by CB Marking by Using NBAR*

Field	Comments
RTP Audio versus video	RTP uses even-numbered UDP ports from 16,384 to 32,767. The odd-numbered port numbers are used by RTCP for call control traffic. NBAR allows matching the even-numbered ports only, allowing classification of voice payload into a different service class than voice signaling.
NBAR Citrix applications	NBAR can recognize different types of published Citrix applications
Host name, URL string, MIME type	NBAR can also match URL strings, including the host name and the MIME type, using regular expressions for matching logic.
Peer-to-peer applications	Can find file sharing applications like KaZaa, Morpheus, Grokster, and Gnutella.

NOTE   Some documents refer to NBAR's capability to look past the Layer 4 header as deep packet inspection and subport inspection.

Cisco IOS Software Release 12.2(15)T and later include the Cisco NBAR Protocol Discovery (CNPD) MIB. You can configure NBAR and monitor statistics, including providing the capability for the router to send a trap when user-defined thresholds are crossed. Also, you can configure the NBAR MIB to send traps to the management station when new protocols are discovered on the network, which can be useful for both QoS and for security purposes.

Marking

Marking involves setting some bits inside a data link or network layer header, with the goal of letting other devices' QoS tools classify based on the marked values. You can mark a wide variety of fields, and each has a particular purpose. Some fields are more widely used, and some are less widely used. Some marking options make sense for all devices on the LAN, whereas others only when using specific hardware platforms. Marking at the WAN is possible, too.

The following sections list the header fields that you can use for marking, along with explanations of when it is most useful to use that particular field. Recommendations follow these sections as to when to use classification and marking.

IP Header QoS Fields: Precedence and DSCP

The two most popular marking fields for QoS are the IP Precedence and IP DSCP fields that were introduced in Chapter 2, "QoS Tools and Architectures." QoS tools frequently use these two fields in part because the IP packet header exists from endpoint to endpoint in a network, as shown in Figure 4-1.

Figure 4-1 *Headers Used During Typical Packet Flow*

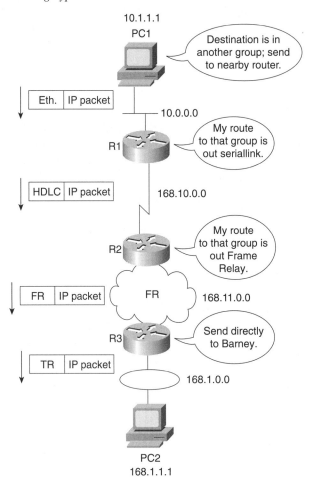

As seen in Figure 4-1, the IP packet en route to host PC2 stays intact throughout the network, whereas the data-link headers only exist while a frame is crossing between a host and a router, or between routers.

Figure 4-2 outlines the two marking fields and their positions inside an IP header.

You can mark the Precedence and DSCP fields with any valid binary value of either 3 or 6 bits, respectively. Chapter 2 contains detailed discussion of the recommended values used in these two fields. Briefly, Precedence field values should grow in importance, and in QoS behavior, as the number gets higher. DSCP differs in that several per-hop behavior (PHB) RFCs define suggested DSCP values for which the larger number does not always get a better QoS treatment.

Figure 4-2 *IP Precedence and IP DSCP Fields*

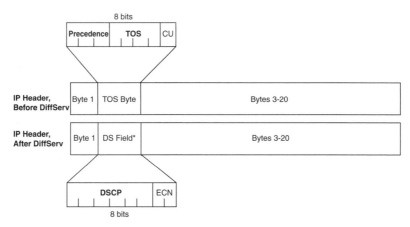

Table 4-5 lists the IP precedence and DSCP values, and their names, for review. Note that not all DSCP values are listed; only the DSCP values suggested by the DiffServ RFCs are listed in the table. Router QoS tools that are capable of setting DSCP can set any of the actual 64 values. (As you will read in Chapter 9, the 2950 cannot set all 64 DSCP values.)

Table 4-5 *IP Precedence and DSCP—Popular Values and Names*

Field and Value (Decimal)	Binary Value	Name	Defined by This RFC
Precedence 0	**000**	**routine**	791
Precedence 1	**001**	**priority**	791
Precedence 2	**010**	**immediate**	791
Precedence 3	**011**	**flash**	791
Precedence 4	**100**	**flash override**	791
Precedence 5	**101**	**critic**	791
Precedence 6	**110**	**internetwork control**	791
Precedence 7	**111**	**network control**	791
DSCP 0	**000**000	**best effort** or **default**	2475
DSCP 8	**001**000	CS1	2475
DSCP 16	**010**000	CS2	2475
DSCP 24	**011**000	CS3	2475
DSCP 32	**100**000	CS4	2475

continues

Table 4-5 *IP Precedence and DSCP—Popular Values and Names (Continued)*

Field and Value (Decimal)	Binary Value	Name	Defined by This RFC
DSCP 40	**101**000	CS5	2475
DSCP 48	**110**000	CS6	2475
DSCP 56	111000	CS7	2475
DSCP 10	**001**010	AF11	2597
DSCP 12	**001**100	AF12	2597
DSCP 14	**001**110	AF13	2597
DSCP 18	**010**010	AF21	2597
DSCP 20	**010**100	AF22	2597
DSCP 22	**010**110	AF23	2597
DSCP 26	**011**010	AF31	2597
DSCP 28	**011**100	AF32	2597
DSCP 30	**011**110	AF33	2597
DSCP 34	**100**010	AF41	2597
DSCP 36	**100**100	AF42	2597
DSCP 38	**100**110	AF43	2597
DSCP 46	**101**110	EF	2598

The two IP header QoS marking fields do not provide all the QoS marking fields needed today. One day, all other Layer 3 protocols besides IP may no longer be used. One day, all LAN switches will be capable of looking at IP headers, including IP DSCP and Precedence, and perform QoS based on those fields. Likewise, one day, all WAN services, including Frame Relay and ATM switches, will be able to perform QoS based on these same fields. However, today's reality is that even as more and more devices become capable of marking and reacting to IP precedence and DSCP, it will be a long time before all networking devices are both capable and configured to use these fields for QoS purposes. So, other QoS marking fields are needed.

LAN Class of Service (CoS)

Many LAN switches today can mark and react to a Layer 2 3-bit field called the Class of Service (CoS) located inside an Ethernet header. The CoS field only exists inside Ethernet frames when 802.1Q or Inter-Switch Link (ISL) trunking is used. (The IEEE 802.1P standard actually defines the usage of the CoS bits inside the 802.1Q header.) You can use the field to set 8 different binary values, which can be used by the classification features of other QoS tools, just like IP precedence and DSCP. Figure 4-3 shows the general location of the CoS field inside ISL and 802.1P headers.

Figure 4-3   *LAN CoS Fields*

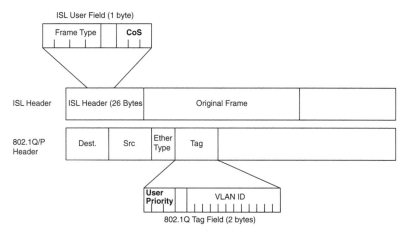

The term *CoS* really refers to two different fields — a field inside either the 802.1Q trunking header, or a field inside the ISL header. The IEEE 802.1Q standard uses the 3 most-significant bits of the 2-byte Tag Control field, called the user-priority bits. The Cisco proprietary ISL specification uses the 3 least-significant bits from the 1-byte User field, which is found inside the ISL header's user field byte. In general conversation, and in the QoS courses from Cisco, the term CoS applies to either of these two fields.

When can CoS be marked, and when can it be useful for classification to a QoS tool? First of all, trunking with 802.1Q or ISL must be enabled before the CoS field even exists! Second, as soon as the packet experiences Layer 3 forwarding, either with a router or some Layer 3 switch, the old LAN header gets discarded — which means you lose the CoS field. After a CoS field has been created and populated with the desired markings, routers and switches have several QoS tools that can react to these markings. Consider, for instance, a typical trunking environment, as shown in Figure 4-4, where all LAN switches are only performing Layer 2 switching.

Figure 4-4 *CoS — Trunking Locations in a Typical Network, Layer 2 Switches Only*

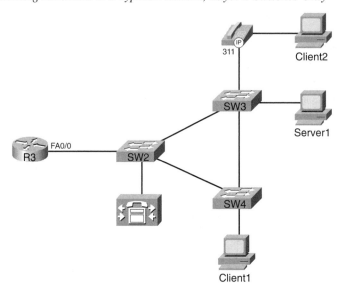

To mark the CoS bits, trunking must be used — and in Figure 4-4, trunking could be used on every Ethernet segment. Switches typically use trunking on the Ethernet segments to other switches, routers, and to IP Phones. Typically, switches do not need to use trunking on segments connected to PCs or servers. Because some networking cards have the capability to support 802.1Q or ISL trunking, however, servers and PCs can set the CoS bits.

> **NOTE** Trunking requires a Fast Ethernet interface, or Gigabit, or 10 Gigabit — it is not supported over 10-Mbps Ethernet. This book does not distinguish among the different types of Ethernet upon each mention.

Both routers and switches use QoS tools that can react to the marked CoS bits. Cisco routers can indeed mark CoS bits for frames exiting an Ethernet interface that supports trunking. For instance, R3 could mark CoS 5 on a frame it forwards out its FA 0/0 interface. Other Cisco router QoS tools can react to the marked CoS bits on incoming frames as well. For instance, R3 could mark packets entering its FA0/0 interface with a particular DSCP value based on the incoming CoS value. Later in this chapter, you will see a sample configuration for class-based marking that performs both of these functions.

Cisco switches vary widely regarding their capabilities to set CoS bits and react to previously marked CoS bits. Switches can support marking of CoS, and more often today support marking of

IP precedence and DSCP as well. LAN switches that do support QoS features generally perform output queuing, and sometimes input queuing, choosing queues based on CoS values. Congestion avoidance using Weighted Random Early Detection (WRED) is another typical switch QoS feature. In addition, some switches support policing tools, also based on CoS. Chapter 9, "LAN QoS," covers LAN QoS in additional depth.

Other Marking Fields

You can use single-bit fields in Frame Relay and ATM networks to mark a frame or cell for Layer 2 QoS. Unlike IP precedence, IP DSCP, and 802.1P/ISL CoS, however, these two fields are not intended for general, flexible use. Each of these single-bit fields, when set, imply that the frame or cell is a better candidate to be dropped, as compared with frames or cells that do not have the bit set. In other words, you can mark the bit, but the only expected action by another QoS tool is for the tool to drop the frame or cell.

Frame Relay defines the discard eligibility (DE) bit, and ATM defines the cell loss priority (CLP) bit. The general idea is that when a device, typically a WAN switch, experiences congestion, it needs to discard some frames or cells. If a frame or cell has the DE or CLP bit set, respectively, the switch may choose to discard those frames or cells, and not discard other frames or cells. If the DE or CLP bit is set, there is no requirement that the Frame Relay and ATM switches react to it—just like there is no guarantee that an IP packet with DSCP EF will get special treatment by another router. It's up to the owner of the Frame Relay or ATM switch to decide whether it will consider the DE and CLP bits, and how to react differently.

You can use two other QoS marking fields in specialized cases. The MPLS Experimental bits comprise a 3-bit field that you can use to map IP precedence into an MPLS label. Also, instead of simply mapping IP precedence to the MPLS Experimental field, you can perform CB Marking at the edge of the MPLS network, classifying on any of the fields mentioned in Tables 4-2, 4-3, and 4-4, and marking the appropriate MPLS experimental bits. This allows MPLS routers to perform QoS features indirectly based on the original IP Precedence field inside the IP packets encapsulated by MPLS, without the need to spend resources to open the IP packet header and examine the IP Precedence field.

Finally, the QoS Group field, an internal marking that exists only within the router, may be set as a packet passes through the fabric of a Cisco gigabit switch router (GSR) or edge services router (ESR). QoS processing can be performed more quickly inside the switching fabric by using the QoS group. Therefore, you may want to configure GSRs and ESRs to mark the QoS group on ingress so that QoS processing occurs more rapidly.

Summary of Marking Fields

Not all these marked fields receive the same amount of attention on the QoS exams. Refer to the Introduction of this book, and the website suggested there, for the latest information about where to focus your attention. Table 4-6 summarizes the marking fields.

Table 4-6 *Names of Marking Fields*

Field	Location	Length	Comments
IP Precedence	IP header	3 bits	Contained in the first 3 bits of the ToS byte.
IP DSCP	IP header	6 bits	Contained in the first 6 bits of the DS field, which replaces the ToS byte.
DS	IP header	1 byte	Replaces ToS byte per RFC 2475.
ToS	IP header	1 byte	Replaced by DS field per RFC 2475.
ToS	IP header	4 bits	A field inside the ToS byte; superseded by RFC 2475.
CoS	ISL and 802.1Q/P	3 bits	Cisco convention uses "CoS" to describe either trunking headers' QoS field.
Priority bits	802.1Q/P	3 bits	The name used by IEEE 802.1P for the CoS bits.
Discard Eligible (DE)	Frame Relay header	1 bit	Frame Relay switches may discard DE- marked frames, avoiding discarding frames without DE marked, under congestion.
Cell Loss Priority (CLP)	ATM cell header	1 bit	ATM equivalent of the DE bit
MPLS Experimental values(s)	MPLS header	3 bits	Used to pass QoS marking information across an MPLS network.
QoS Group	Headers internal to IOS	N/A	Uses values between 1–99 inclusive. Used for marking only internal to a single router, and only on specific models of routers.

The names of the various marking fields can be confusing. Quality of service (QoS) does not refer to any specific marking field, but it is a term that refers to a broad set of tools that effect bandwidth, delay, jitter, and loss. In other words, this whole book is about QoS. Class of service (CoS) refers to both of the two 3-bit fields in Ethernet trunking headers — one in the ISL header, and one in the 802.1Q trunking header. However, CoS also refers to a 2-bit field inside Systems Network Architecture (SNA) Layer 3 headers, which is also used for QoS functions. Type of service (ToS) is my personal favorite — ToS is the 1-byte field in the IP header, which includes a 3-bit Precedence field, and 4 ToS bits. And of course, DiffServ re-defines the ToS Byte as the DS-byte, with the DSCP field in the first 6 bits. Make sure you remember the true meanings of QoS, CoS, ToS, Precedence, and DSCP.

Classification and Marking Design Choices

Classification and marking tools provide many options, but sometimes sorting out the best way to use the tools can be difficult. Classification and marking tools can classify based on a large number of frame and packet header fields. They can also mark a number of fields, the most notable being the IP Precedence and DSCP fields. You can use the classification and marking tools on all routers in the network, on many LAN switches, and even on IP Phones and host computers. This brief section discusses some of the classification and marking design choices.

The first step in making good classification and marking design choices is to choose where to mark. The general rule for choosing where to mark is as follows:

> Mark as close to the ingress edge of the network as is possible.

Figure 4-5 diagrams a typical enterprise IP network, which will be used to look more closely at the options for where to mark packets.

Figure 4-5 *Typical Enterprise Network*

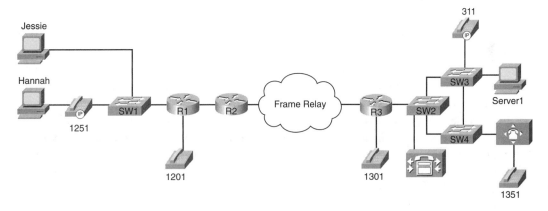

Consider packets that flow left to right in Figure 4-5. The marking efforts for data sent by the PC and phone on the left, up to R1, can be summarized as follows:

■   Hannah and Jessie, both client PCs, can mark IP precedence and IP DSCP, but it is unlikely that 802.1Q trunking would be used because most end-user Ethernet NICs do not support trunking.

- The IP Phone internally marks its own voice bearer traffic DSCP EF and CoS 5 by default, its own voice signaling traffic DSCP 31 and CoS 3.

- The phone needs to set the CoS value for frames sent to it by the PC, before sending the frame over the trunk to the switch. The switch can be configured to tell the switch to set the CoS to 0, which is typical.

- SW1, depending on the type of switch, might be able to re-mark CoS, precedence, or DSCP, or make general (multifield) classification and marking decisions—in other words, it might be able to look at some of the fields listed earlier in Tables 4-2 and 4-3.

- Finally, R1 can use general multifield classification and marking before sending the packet over the WAN.

So marking can be done in many places near the ingress edge of the network — but whom do you trust? Classification and marking should not be performed before the frame/packet reaches a trusted device. This location in the network is called the *trust boundary*. For instance, Jessie formerly marked her packets with DSCP default, but because the user of the PC can change that value, Jessie changed to use DSCP EF to get better service. In most cases, the end-user PCs are beyond the trust boundary. IP Phones can reset CoS, Hannah's traffic, and rely on the IP phone's markings with CoS 5, precedence 5, and DSCP EF — with the added benefit that the phone user cannot reset those values. The IP Phone trust settings are controlled by the connected Cisco Catalyst switch, enabling the system administrator to trust markings received from the IP Phone while rewriting the CoS value received from the attached PC.

The final consideration when deciding where to mark involves the function of the various devices, and personal preferences. For instance, IP Phones provide three classes based on CoS — one for voice bearer traffic, one for voice signaling traffic, and one for all packets from the PC. However, a network may need multiple classes for data traffic, so further classification may be required by a switch or router. Some switches provide robust Layer 3 QoS classification and marking functions — in these cases, classification and marking may be performed on the switch; otherwise classification and marking must be performed on the router. (note: the classification and marking features on Cisco LAN switches are covered in chapter 9.) Figure 4-6 shows three typical paths for frames between the end-user device and the first router. The first instance shows a typical installation near the end users — a switch that performs only Layer 2 QoS, and PCs connected to it. *Only Layer 2 QoS* just means that the switch can react to, or possibly set, CoS, but it cannot react to or mark IP precedence or DSCP. In this case, classification and marking is typically performed as packets enter R1's Ethernet interface. In addition, because SW1 can support CoS, but not precedence or DSCP, R1 may want to map incoming CoS values to the Precedence or DSCP fields.

Figure 4-6 *Three Classification and Marking Placement Strategies*

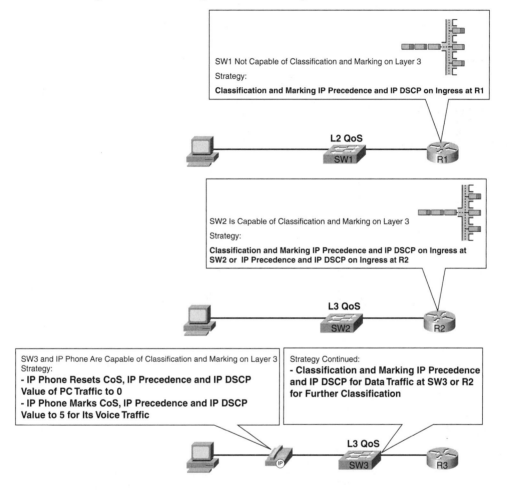

The second part of Figure 4-6 shows a network with a Layer 3 QoS-capable switch. Depending on the type of switch, this switch may not be able to perform Layer 3 switching, but it does have the capability to react to or mark IP precedence or DSCP. In this case, you should classify and mark on the switch. Classification and marking on the Layer 3 switch allows classification and marking closer to the trust boundary of the network, and offers the added benefits of queuing, congestion avoidance, and policing based on the marked values. If only a few sites in the network have Layer 3 QoS-capable switches, you may prefer to perform classification and marking on the router, so all sites' configurations are similar. However, classifying and marking in the router places additional overhead on the router's CPU.

Finally, the third example shows a PC cabled through an IP Phone to a Layer 3 QoS-capable switch. The IP Phone can easily take care of classification and marking into two categories— voice and nonvoice. The switch and router can take advantage of those marked values. If more classes are needed for this network's QoS policy, SW3, or R3, can perform classification and marking. Of course, if the QoS policy for this network only requires the three classes—one for voice bearer traffic, one for voice signaling traffic, one for nonvoice—and all PCs are connected through the switch in the IP Phone, no classification and marking is needed on SW3 or R3!

Figure 4-7 summarizes some of the design options for where to classify and mark, showing the remote site from Figure 4-5.

Figure 4-7 *Classification and Marking Options Applied to a Typical Enterprise Network*

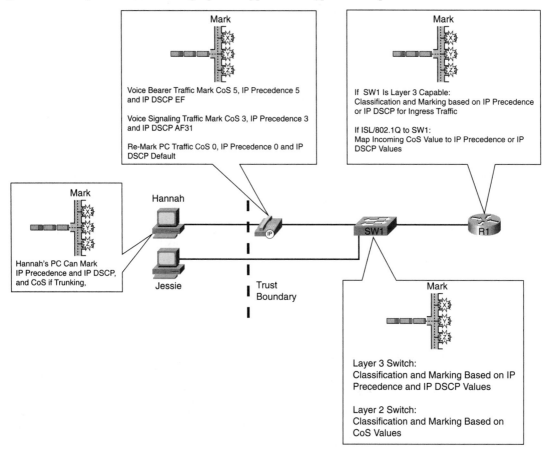

The choices of where to perform classification and marking can be summarized as follows:

■ Classify and mark as close to the ingress edge as possible.

- Consider the trust boundary in the network, making sure to mark or re-mark traffic after it reaches a trusted device in the network

- Because the two IP QoS marking fields — Precedence and DSCP — are carried end to end, mark one of these fields to maximize the benefits of reducing classification overhead by the other QoS tools enabled in the network.

Typically, when the packet makes it to the first WAN router, the initial marking has occurred. However, there may be other instances where marking should take place. Consider Figure 4-8, which shows several additional options for where marking can occur.

Figure 4-8 *Classification and Marking Options — Typical Enterprise WAN*

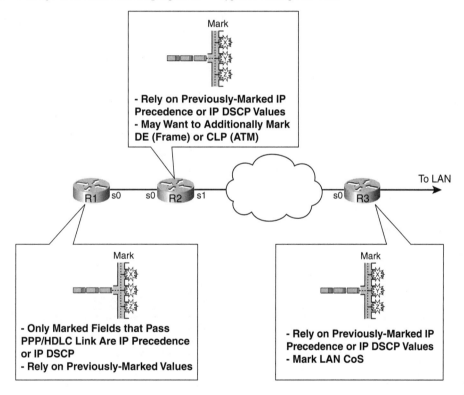

Most QoS tools can classify based on IP precedence and DSCP. However, the Frame Relay or ATM switches can also react to the DE and CLP bits, respectively. Therefore, you might want to set DE or CLP for the least-important traffic. If the LAN switches connected to R3 react to CoS settings, but not precedence or DSCP, which is typical of switches that only support Layer 2 QoS, you might want to mark the CoS bits on R3 before sending frames onto the Ethernet.

Finally, when you do mark CoS, IP precedence, and IP DSCP, what values should you use? Well, the "bigger is better" attitude is suggested for CoS and precedence. The DiffServ RFCs make recommendations for which markings to use for certain types of traffic, and most current Cisco products (as of publication date) use those recommendations. For instance, the DiffServ RFC's suggest marking voice signaling traffic as AF31, and Cisco IP Phones indeed do that. Table 4-7 lists these recommended values.

Table 4-7 *DiffServ RFC Recommended Values for Marking*

Type of Traffic	CoS	Precedence	DSCP
Voice payload	5	5	EF
Video payload	4	4	AF41
Voice/Video signaling	3	3	AF31
Best Effort	0	0	BE

Cisco has also noted some newer, more complete recommendations for Marking DSCP values in packets. These recommendations are spelled out in Cisco's QoS course, and are based on research from Cisco engineers. It remains to be seen if these settings will become defaults in Cisco products, and if so, how soon they will be included – however, for exam preparation, you should be aware of these values as well. Table 4-8 lists the values.

Table 4-8 *RFC Recommended Values for Marking*

Type of Traffic	CoS	Precedence	DSCP
Voice payload	5	5	EF
Video payload	4	4	AF41
Voice/Video signaling	3	3	CS3
Mission Critical Data	3	3	AF31
			AF32
			AF33
Transactional Data	2	2	AF21
			AF22
			AF23

Table 4-8 *RFC Recommended Values for Marking (Continued)*

Type of Traffic	CoS	Precedence	DSCP
Bulk Data	1	1	AF11 AF12 AF13
Best Effort	0	0	BE
Scavenger (Less than best effort)	0	0	2 4 6

Also note that Cisco recommends not to use more than 4 or 5 different service classes for data traffic. By using more classes, the difference in behavior between the various classes tends to blur. Also, do not give too many data service classes high priority service, for the same reason.

In summary, classification and marking tools classify packets based on a large number of different fields inside data link and network layer headers. Based on the classification, the tools then mark a field in a frame or packet header, with the goal that other QoS tools can more easily classify and perform specific QoS actions based on these marked fields. Among all the fields that can be marked, IP Precedence and DSCP, because they are part of the IP header, are the only fields that can be marked and carried from end to end in the network.

Classification and Marking Tools

The second major section of this chapter covers several Classification and Marking tools. First, Class-Based Marking will be covered in detail, followed by NBAR, which can be used by CB Marking to classify packets. Next, the text moves on to an explain some of the issues faced by CB Marking when tunnels are in use, and how IOS can be configured to still classify the packets correctly.

Class-Based Marking (CB Marking) Configuration

As with the other QoS tools whose names begin with the phrase Class Based, you use MQC commands to configure it. The logic used by CB Marking, now that you know the concepts, it is actually pretty straightforward:

1. Classify packets into service classes using the **match** command inside an MQC class map.

2. Mark the packets in each service class using the set command inside an MQC policy map.

3. Enable the CB Marking logic, as defined in a policy map, using the MQC **service-policy** command under an interface.

In Chapter 3, you read about the syntax of the MQC commands, and how policy maps use class maps to classify packets. Armed with that knowledge, you now only need to be reminded of all the fields with which you can match packets for classification using the MQC **match** command, and what fields you can mark with the MQC **set** command. Table 4-9 lists the options for the **match** command, which are applicable to all MQC QoS features. Table 4-10 lists the options on the **set** command, and Table 4-11 lists the **show** commands related to CB Marking. (Because the options for the **match** command are the same for all of the other MQC-based QoS tools inside a router, the rest of the chapters will refer back to Table 4-9 instead of repeating this same information in each chapter.)

Table 4-9 *Match Configuration Command Reference for CB Marking*

Command	Function
match [ip] precedence *precedence-value* [*precedence-value precedence-value precedence-value*]	Matches precedence in IPV4 packets when the **ip** parameter is included; matches IPV4 and IPV6 packets when **ip** parameter is missing.
match access-group {*access-group* | **name** *access- group-name*}	Matches an ACL by number or name
match any	Matches all packets
match class-map class-map-name	Matches based on another class –map
match cos *cos-value* [*cos-value cos-value cos-value*]	matches a CoS value
match destination-address mac *address*	matches a destination MAC address
match fr-dlci *dlci-number*	Matches a particular Frame Relay DLCI
match input-interface *interface-name*	matches an input interface
match ip dscp *ip-dscp-value* [*ip-dscp-value ip-dscp- value ip-dscp-value ip-dscp-value ip-dscp-value ip- dscp-value ip-dscp-value*]	Matches DSCP in IPV4 packets when the **ip** parameter is included; matches IPV4 and IPV6 packets when the **ip** parameter is missing.
match ip rtp *starting-port-number port-range*	Matches the RTP's UDP port-number range, even values only
match mpls experimental *number*	Matches an MPLS Experimental value
match mpls experimental topmost value	When multiple labels are in use, this command matches the MPLS EXP field in the top-most label.
match not match-criteria	Reverses the matching logic, in other words, things matched by the matching criteria do not match the class-map.

Table 4-9 *Match Configuration Command Reference for CB Marking*

match packet length {**max** *maximum-length-value* [**min** *minimum-length-value*] | **min** *minimum-length-value* [**max** *maximum-length-value*]}	Matches packets based on the minimum length, maximum length, or both.
match protocol citrix app *application-name-string*	Matches NBAR Citrix applications
match protocol http [**url** *url-string* | **host** *hostname- string* | **mime** *MIME-type*]	Matches a host name and URL string
match protocol *protocol-name*	Matches NBAR protocol types
match protocol rtp [**audio** | **video** | **payload-type** *payload-string*]	Matches RTP audio or video payload, based on the payload type. Also allows explicitly specified payload types.
match qos-group *qos-group-value*	Matches a QoS group
match source-address mac *address-destination*	Matches a source MAC address

Table 4-10 **set** *Configuration Command Reference for CB Marking*

Command	Function
set [ip] precedence *ip-precedence-value*	Marks the value for IP Precedence for IPV4 and IPV6 packets if the **ip** parameter is omitted; sets only IPV4 packets if **ip** parameter is included.
set [ip] dscp *ip-dscp-value*	Marks the value for IP DSCP for IPV4 and IPV6 packets if the **ip** parameter is omitted; sets only IPV4 packets if **ip** parameter is included.
set cos *cos-value*	Marks the value for CoS
set qos-group *group-id*	Marks the value for the QoS group
set atm-clp	Marks the value for the ATM CLP bit
set fr-de	Marks the value for the Frame Relay DE bit

Table 4-11 *EXEC Command Reference for CB Marking*

Command	Function
show policy-map *policy-map-name*	Lists configuration information about a policy map
show policy-map *interface-spec* [*input* | *output*] [**class** *class-name*]	Lists statistical information about the behavior of a policy map when enabled on an interface

You should read over the commands presented in the preceding tables to get familiar with the many options. However, you should not have to memorize all the options at this point. If you continue reading the chapters, and practice a little on real lab gear, you should be prepared for answering QoS exam questions.

QoS configuration should follow the process of planning the QoS policies for the network. After those policies have been defined, and the location of where to perform the marking functions has been determined, however, the CB Marking configuration that follows becomes an exercise in deciding how to match or classify the packets, and how to configure the commands correctly. In the first MQC configuration example, for example, the policy has been defined as follows:

■ All VoIP traffic should be marked with DSCP EF.

■ All other traffic should be marked with DSCP Default.

Figure 4-9 is used for many example configurations in this book. In the first example, marking is performed for packets entering R3's FA0/0 interface. In reality, it also makes sense to mark packets near R1 for packet flows from left to right in the figure. To keep the configurations less cluttered, however, only one direction, right to left, is shown. Example 4-1 lists the configuration for this first example.

Figure 4-9 *CB Marking Sample Configuration 1*

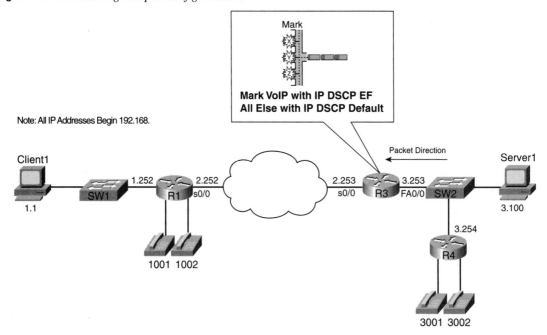

Example 4-1 *CB Marking: Sample 1 Configuration (Continued)*

```
R3#conf t
Enter configuration commands, one per line.  End with CNTL/Z.
R3(config)#ip cef
R3(config)#class-map voip-rtp
R3(config-cmap)#match ip rtp 16384 16383
R3(config-cmap)#policy-map voip-and-be
R3(config-pmap)# class voip-rtp
R3(config-pmap-c)# set ip dscp ef
R3(config-pmap-c)# class class-default
R3(config-pmap-c)#  set ip dscp default
R3(config-pmap-c)#interface fa 0/0
R3(config-if)# service-policy input voip-and-be
R3(config-if)#end
R3#
R3#show running-config
Building configuration...
!Portions removed to save space…
ip cef
!
class-map match-all voip-rtp
  match ip rtp 16384 16383
!
!
policy-map voip-and-be
  class voip-rtp
   set dscp ef
  class class-default
   set dscp default
!
interface Fastethernet0/0
 description connected to SW2, where Server1 is connected
 ip address 192.168.3.253 255.255.255.0
 service-policy input voip-and-be
```

First, focus on the command prompts in Example 4-1. Note that the **class-map** command moves the CLI into class map configuration mode, with the prompt **R3(config-cmap)**. The **policy-map** command moves the CLI into policy map configuration mode, and the **class** command that follows (not **class-map**, but just **class**) moves the CLI into an additional subconfiguration mode that has no specific name.

> **NOTE**   I tend to call configuration mode you are in after using the **policy-map** command, and then the **class** command, the *policy map class* mode when teaching QoS classes.

Next, examine the **match** commands. The solution could have referred to IP ACL 101 with the **match ip access-group 101** command, with ACL 101 matching UDP ports between 16,384 and 32,767, inclusive, to match all VoIP traffic. However, the **match ip rtp** command matches only the even-numbered ports in this same UDP port range. (VoIP payload only uses the even port numbers.) Therefore, the **match ip rtp** command is more efficient for matching VoIP, easier to configure, and only matches the VoIP payload.

Continuing down the configuration, examine the **policy-map set** commands. The first command sets a DSCP of EF for all traffic that matches **class-map voip-rtp**. The other **set** command, which follows the **class class-default** command, sets DSCP of Default for traffic that matches the **class-default class-map**. In other words, the policy map sets DSCP EF for packets that match one class, and DSCP Default, using the keyword **default**, for the other class. IOS includes a class that matches all remaining traffic, called **class-default**, in every policy map. Although the command **class class-default** was not specified in the configuration, note that the **class class-default** command is automatically added to the end of a policy map to match all unspecified traffic. **class-default** was used in the policy map to match all remaining traffic and then mark that traffic as BE.

> **NOTE** Earlier IOS releases required the keyword **ip** in the CB Marking **set** command when setting DSCP—for instance, in the command **set ip dscp ef**, the **ip** keyword was required. With IOS 12.2T, the **ip** keyword is optional. If it is used, IOS removes it from the command when recording the **set** command in both the running and startup configuration.

Finally, the **service-policy** command enables CB Marking for ingress packets with the **service-policy input voip-and-be** interface subcommand. When enabled, IOS applies the policy map classes in the order they appear in the **policy-map** command. In this example, for instance, the VoIP-RTP class is used to examine the packet first; if a match appears, the packet is marked with DSCP EF. After the packet has been matched and marked, it exits the policy map. If no match occurs, only then is the next class, class-default, used to examine the packet.

The next example is a CB Marking configuration that uses the same network as the one used in Example 4-1. R3 is performing the CB Marking function again, but this time R3 expects that SW2 has already set CoS bits to either 0 or 5. The engineers in the meeting to discuss QoS policies for this network decided that SW2 would mark CoS with either 0 or 5, and then R3 would map CoS 0 to DSCP Default, and CoS 5 to DSCP EF. For packets moving left to right, R3 should map DSCP Default back to CoS 0, and DSCP EF back to CoS 5. Figure 4-10 depicts the network and QoS policies, and Example 4-2 lists the configuration.

Figure 4-10 *CB Marking Sample Configuration 2*

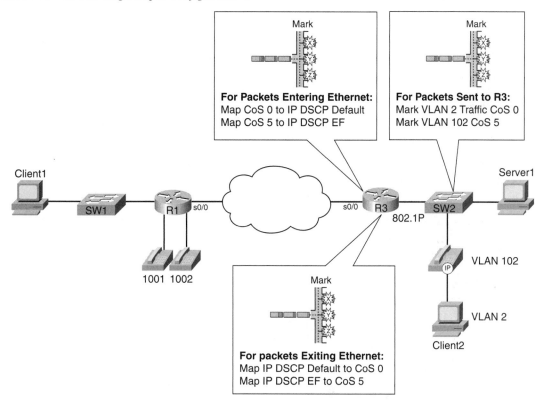

Example 4-2 *CB Marking: Sample 2 Configuration*

```
class-map cos0
 match cos 0
!
class-map cos5
 match cos 5
!
class-map BE
 match ip dscp default
!
class-map EF
 match ip dscp EF
!
policy-map map-cos-to-dscp
 class cos0
  set ip DSCP default
 class cos5
  set ip DSCP EF
```

continues

Example 4-2 *CB Marking: Sample 2 Configuration (Continued)*

```
class class-default
  set ip dscp default
!
policy-map map-dscp-to-cos
 class BE
  set cos 0
 class EF
  set cos 5
 class class-default
   set cos 0
!
interface FastEthernet0/0
!
interface FastEthernet0/0.1
 encapsulation dot1Q 102
 service-policy input map-cos-to-dscp
 service-policy output map-dscp-to-cos
!
interface FastEthernet0/0.2
 encapsulation dot1Q 2 native
```

As you learned earlier in this chapter, to mark and classify CoS values, a VLAN trunking header must exist on the packet. On R3 in this example, subinterface Fast Ethernet 0/0.1 and subinterface Fast Ethernet 0/0.2 have been created and assigned to the voice VLAN 102 and the data VLAN 2, respectively, using 802.1Q trunking. This configuration creates an 802.1Q header for traffic in the voice VLAN 102, without creating a VLAN header for the data VLAN 2 traffic because VLAN2 will be the private VLAN on this trunk.

The QoS policy required two policy maps in this example. Policy map map-cos-to-dscp matched CoS values for frames entering R3's FA 0/0.1 interface, and marked DSCP values, for packets flowing right to left in the figure. Therefore, the policy map was enabled on input of R3's FA 0/0.1 interface. Policy map map-dscp-to-cos matched DSCP values on packets exiting R3's FA 0/0.1 interface, and marked CoS, for packets flowing left to right in the figure. Therefore, the policy map was enabled on output of R3's FA 0/0.1 interface. Neither policy map could be applied on the WAN interface, because only interfaces configured for 802.1Q accept **service-policy** commands that reference policy maps that either classify or mark based on CoS.

Note that you cannot enable a policy map that refers to CoS on interface FA0/0.2 in this example. That subinterface is in the native VLAN, meaning that no 802.1Q header is used. In a real network, you would probably want to enable a policy map on the subinterface in order to mark traffic, but it must classify based on something beside CoS.

Network-Based Application Recognition (NBAR)

CB Marking, and other MQC-based tools, can use NBAR to help classify traffic. By using the **match protocol** class map subcommand, MQC can match protocols recognized by NBAR. This section describes how to configure CB Marking using NBAR for classification.

The connection between NBAR and CB Marking, or any other MQC tool, is through the **match protocol** class map subcommand. An MQC tool can include the **match protocol** command under a **class-map** command, and as a result, IOS uses NBAR to actually match the packets.

A sample configuration and statistical display may help you make sense of NBAR. Tables 4-12 and 4-13 list the NBAR configuration and exec commands, respectively. Following the tables, Figure 4-11 diagrams the familiar network, where R3 performs CB Marking based on NBAR classification of the URL string. Finally, Example 4-3 lists a sample NBAR and CB Marking configuration, where CB Marking matches a portion of an HTTP URL. The example includes a listing of NBAR statistics gathered on the interface.

Table 4-12   *Configuration Command Reference for NBA*

Command	Mode and Function
ip nbar protocol-discovery	Interface mode; enables NBAR for traffic entering and exiting the interface.
ip nbar port-map *protocol-name* [**tcp** I **udp**] *port-number*	Global; tells NBAR to search for a protocol using a different port number than the well-known port. Also defines ports to be used by custom packet description language modules (PDLMs).
ip nbar pdlm *pdlm-name*	Global; extends the list of protocols recognized by NBAR by adding additional PDLMs.
snmp-server enable traps cnpd	Global; enables the sending of NBAR traps.

NOTE   You can download additional PDLMs from Cisco.com:
www.cisco.com/cgi-bin/tablebuild.pl/pdlm

Table 4-13   *EXEC Command Reference for NBAR*

Command	Function
show ip nbar protocol-discovery [**interface** *interface-spec*] [**stats** /**byte-count** I **bit-rate** I **packet-count**}][{**protocol** *protocol-name* I **top-n** *number*}]	Lists information about statistics for the discovered protocols. Statistics can be listed by interface, by protocol, or for just the top *n* protocols by volume.
show ip nbar port-map [*protocol-name*]	Lists the current ports in use by the discovered protocols.

Figure 4-11 *CB Marking Sample Configuration 3*

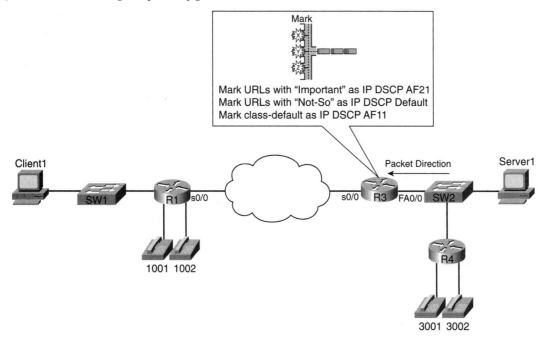

Example 4-3 uses the following criteria for marking packets:

■ Any HTTP traffic whose URL contains the string "important" anywhere in the URL is marked with AF21.

■ Any HTTP traffic whose URL contains the string "not-so" anywhere in the URL is marked with DSCP default.

■ All other traffic is marked with AF11.

Example 4-3 shows the configuration.

Example 4-3 *Sample 3: CB Marking Based on URLs, Using NBAR for Classification*

```
ip cef
!
class-map http-impo
 match protocol http url "*important*"
!
class-map http-not
 match protocol http url "*not-so*"
```

Example 4-3 *Sample 3: CB Marking Based on URLs, Using NBAR for Classification (Continued)*

```
!
policy-map http
 class http-impo
  set ip dscp AF21
!
 class http-not
  set ip dscp default
!
 class class-default
  set ip DSCP AF11
!
interface fastethernet 0/0
 ip nbar protocol-discovery
 service-policy input http
!
!

R3# show ip nbar protocol-discovery top-n 5

 FastEthernet0/0
                        Input                   Output
    Protocol            Packet Count            Packet Count
                        Byte Count              Byte Count
                        5 minute bit rate (bps) 5 minute bit rate (bps)
    -------------------- ------------------------ ------------------------
    eigrp               76                      0
                        5624                    0
                        0                       0
    bgp                 0                       0
                        0                       0
                        0                       0
    citrix              0                       0
                        0                       0
                        0                       0
    cuseeme             0                       0
                        0                       0
                        0                       0
    custom-01           0                       0
                        0                       0
                        0                       0
    unknown             5610                    0
                        5665471                 0
                        135000                  0
    Total               5851                    0
                        5845277                 0
                        135000                  0
```

continues

Example 4-3 *Sample 3: CB Marking Based on URLs, Using NBAR for Classification (Continued)*

```
R3#show ip nbar protocol-discovery interface fastethernet 0/0 stats packet-count top-n 5

FastEthernet0/0
                                Input                   Output
        Protocol                Packet Count            Packet Count
        -----------------       ----------------        ----------------
        http                    721                     428
        eigrp                   635                     0
        netbios                 199                     0
        icmp                    1                       1
        bgp                     0                       0
        unknown                 46058                   63
        Total                   47614                   492
```

Notice that the class map configuration does not specifically use the term NBAR. Two class maps, http-impo and http-not, use the **match** command, with the **protocol** keyword, which implies that the actual classification uses NBAR. NBAR has been enabled on FA0/0 with the **ip nbar protocol discovery** command, although it is not required for CB Marking to work. Also note that CEF forwarding must be enabled if using NBAR matching inside a policy map. To enable CEF, the **ip cef** global command is required.

> **NOTE** In earlier IOS releases, the **ip nbar protocol-discovery** command was required on an interface before using a **service-policy** command that used NBAR matching. With 12.2T train releases, the command is no longer required.

NBAR can match URLs exactly, or with some wildcards. You can use the asterisk (*) to match any characters of any length. In this case, as long as the phrases "important" or "not-so" appear in the URL, the packets are matched by one of the two class maps, respectively. Interestingly, when downloading an object with HTTP, the URL does not flow in every packet. *When classifying based on URL, NBAR matches all packets beginning with the matched URL until it sees another HTTP request.*

Also note that the order of the **class** commands inside the **policy-map** is important. Each packet is compared to each **class's** matching criteria in order, and once the first match is made, the packet is considered to be in that class. So, the order of the **class** commands can impact the logic. Also, if many **class** commands are used, and many packets are not matched until one of the last **class** commands, the matching process will require more CPU cycles.

When NBAR has been enabled with the **ip nbar protocol discovery** interface subcommand, the **show ip nbar protocol-discovery** command lists statistics for NBAR-classified packets. However, just using that command in live networks does not help much, because it lists three lines of output per type of protocol that can be discovered by NBAR — not just the protocols NBAR actually discovered. Therefore, the optional parameters on the command are more useful. For instance, both commands shown in the preceding example use the **top-n** parameter to limit the output based on the highest-volume protocols. The **show** command can also limit the statistics for a single interface, or it can limit the statistics to just packet count, or byte count, or bit rate.

Unlike most other IOS features, you can upgrade NBAR without changing to a later IOS version. Cisco uses a feature called packet descriptor language modules (PDLMs) to define new protocols that NBAR should match. When Cisco decides to add one or more new protocols to the list of protocols that NBAR should recognize, it creates and compiles a PDLM. You can then download the PDLM from Cisco, copy it into Flash memory, and add the **ip nbar pdlm** *pdlm- name* command to the configuration, where *pdlm-name* is the name of the PDLM file in Flash memory. NBAR can then classify based on the protocol information from the new PDLM.

CB Marking show Commands

CB Marking provides only one **show** command that provides statistical information: **show policy-map interface**. The statistics do provide some good insight to the packet volumes being marked by CB Marking. The next sample configuration includes a new configuration and several variations of the **show policy-map** command.

The same network is used for the next example as was used in the other CB Marking examples, but with different marking criteria. In this case, traffic is generated so that the **show** command output is more meaningful. The following traffic is generated:

■ Two G.711 VoIP calls between R4 and R1 using Foreign Exchange Station (FXS) cards on these two routers. Voice Activity Detection (VAD) is disabled.

■ One FTP connection from the client PC to the server, with an FTP get of a 40-MB file called big.zip.

■ One Microsoft NetMeeting video/audio conference between the client and server.

■ One web page download from the server to the client. The web page has a few small objects. The web page includes two panes, each with a different JPG file: one called important.jpg; the other called not-so.jpg. The JPGs are exact copies of each other, and each JPG is 687 KB. In later examples, the differing performance of the download of these examples is used to demonstrate the behavior of other QoS tools.

Figure 4-12 depicts the same familiar network, and lists the criteria in with the figure for easy reference.

The new criteria for Example 4-4 is as follows:

■ VoIP payload is marked with DSCP EF.

■ NetMeeting video traffic is marked with DSCP AF41.

■ Any HTTP traffic whose URL contains the string "important" anywhere in the URL is marked with AF21.

■ Any HTTP traffic whose URL contains the string "not-so" anywhere in the URL is marked with AF23.

■ All other traffic is marked with DSCP Default.

Figure 4-12 *Three Classification and Marking Placement Strategies*

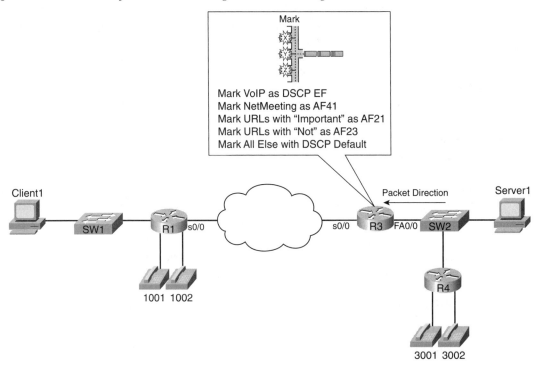

Example 4-4 shows the configuration, including the appropriate **show** commands.

Example 4-4   *CB Marking Sample 4, with* **show** *Command Output*

```
ip cef

!
class-map voip-rtp
 match protocol rtp audio
!
class-map http-impo
 match protocol http url "*important*"
!
class-map http-not
 match protocol http url "*not-so*"
!
class-map match-any NetMeet
 match protocol rtp payload-type 4
 match protocol rtp payload-type 34
!
policy-map laundry-list
!
 class voip-rtp
  set ip dscp EF
!
 class NetMeet
  set ip dscp AF41
!
class http-impo
  set ip dscp AF21
!
 class http-not
  set ip dscp AF23
!
 class class-default
  set ip DSCP default
!
 interface Fastethernet 0/0
 service-policy input laundry-list
end
R3#show policy-map
  Policy Map laundry-list
    Class voip-rtp
      set ip dscp 46
    Class NetMeet
      set ip dscp 34
    Class http-impo
      set ip dscp 18
    Class http-not
      set ip dscp 22
    Class class-default
```

continues

Example 4-4 *CB Marking Sample 4, with* **show** *Command Output (Continued)*

```
             set ip dscp 0

R3#show policy-map laundry-list
  Policy Map laundry-list
    Class voip-rtp
      set ip dscp 46
    Class NetMeet
      set ip dscp 34
    Class http-impo
      set ip dscp 18
    Class http-not
      set ip dscp 22
    Class class-default
      set ip dscp 0
R3#show policy-map interface fastethernet 0/0 input
 Fastethernet0/0

  Service-policy input: laundry-list

    Class-map: voip-rtp (match-all)
      35268 packets, 2609832 bytes
      5 minute offered rate 59000 bps, drop rate 0 bps
      Match: protocol rtp audio
      QoS Set
        ip dscp 46
         Packets marked 35268

    Class-map: NetMeet (match-any)
      817 packets, 328768 bytes
      5 minute offered rate 19000 bps, drop rate 0 bps
      Match: protocol rtp payload-type 4
             protocol rtp payload-type 34
      QoS Set
        ip dscp 34
         Packets marked 817

    Class-map: http-impo (match-all)
      2843 packets, 3462611 bytes
      5 minute offered rate 56000 bps, drop rate 0 bps
      Match: protocol http url "*important*"
      QoS Set
        ip dscp 18
         Packets marked 2855

    Class-map: http-not (match-all)
      2828 packets, 3445409 bytes
      5 minute offered rate 56000 bps, drop rate 0 bps
```

Example 4-4 *CB Marking Sample 4, with* **show** *Command Output (Continued)*

```
        Match: protocol http url "*not-so*"
        QoS Set
          ip dscp 22
           Packets marked 2842

    Class-map: class-default (match-all)
      33216 packets, 43649458 bytes
      5 minute offered rate 747000 bps, drop rate 0 bps
      Match: any
      QoS Set
        ip dscp 0
        Packets marked 33301
```

Review the configuration before taking a closer look at the **show** commands. The only part of the configuration that was not covered in the first three examples on CB Marking is the matching of the Microsoft NetMeeting traffic. NetMeeting uses RTP for the video flows, and by default uses G.723 for audio and H.323 for video. To match both the audio and video for NetMeeting, a class map that matches either of the two RTP payload subtypes for G.723 and H.323 is needed. So, the **NetMeet** class map uses match-any logic, and matches on RTP payload types 4 (G.723) and 34 (H.323).

> **NOTE**   For more background information on RTP payload types, refer to http://www.cisco.com/warp/public/cc/pd/iosw/prodlit/nbarw_wp.htm.

Also note that the NetMeet class map uses a combination of capital letters and lowercase letters, as does the **class** command that refers to it. Class map names are case sensitive — you may want to choose to use only uppercase or lowercase letters for names to avoid confusion.

The **show policy-map laundry-list** command just lists a summary of the configuration. You can gather the same information with a **show running-config** command, but it is summarized nicely with **show policy-map**. The **show policy-map** command lists the same configuration information, but it lists the information for all the configured policy maps in this router.

The **show policy-map** command using the **interface** option provides statistical information about the number of packets and bytes that have matched each class inside the policy maps. Because CB Marking is configured, it also notes the number of packets that have been marked. You can select all interfaces, just one interface, either input or output, and even select a single class inside a single policy map for display.

Finally, the **load-interval** interface subcommand can also be useful when looking at any QoS tool's statistics. The **load-interval** command defines the time interval over which IOS measures packet and bit rates on an interface. With a lower load interval, the statistics change more quickly; with a larger load interval, the statistics change more slowly. In a lab when you are just learning to use QoS tools, set the load interval to the minimum of 30 seconds, so you can see the results of new traffic, or changes to the configuration, quickly. (The default setting is 5 minutes.)

Miscellaneous Features of Class-Based Marking

The examples in this chapter highlight just some of the features of CB Marking, while the list of classification and marking options in Tables 4-9 and 4-10 provides a lot of details. This final section on CB Marking highlights some of the more important small features of CB Marking that so far have only been mentioned as part of the generic commands in Tables 4-9 and 4-10.

The **class-map** command actually has two optional keywords after the name of the class map, namely **match-any** and **match-all**. If you need to refer to multiple match criteria inside a class map, you can use multiple **match** subcommands. These two keywords can then be used to specify whether all matches must be true (**match-all**) or if just one needs to be true (**match-any**). **match-all** is the default.

The **match** subcommand under **class-map** can be used to match up to four IP Precedence values in one command. For instance, **match ip precedence 0 1 2** matches packets with any of the three values. Similarly, up to eight DSCP values can be matched with the **match ip dscp** command, and up to four CoS values can be matched in one **match cos** command.

Another small but interesting feature is the **match not** command. Inside a **class-map**, you can use **match not** to match all packets that *do not* match the remaining criteria in the command. For instance, to match packets that are not permitted by ACL 153, you could use the **match not access-group 153** command. You could of course just change the ACL to do the opposite of what it was matching originally, but in some cases, it might be more convenient to use **match not**. For instance, if you might want two classes—one for packets that match ACL 153, and one for those that do not.

All the CB Marking examples in this chapter show a single field being set by a policy map. However, you can actually mark multiple fields in the same policy map for the same packet. For instance, you might want to classify voice payload traffic, and mark it with DSCP EF. However, if the policy map will be enabled for outgoing traffic on a FastEthernet interface that trunks, you might also want to set the CoS field as well. To mark both, you would use two **set** commands under a single **class** command. For instance, inside **class voice**, you might see the commands **set ip dscp ef** and **set cos 5**.

If you have a spare router, it's a good idea to spend some time experimenting and getting familiar with the many options available with CB Marking, particularly with the **match** and **set** commands.

Classification Issues when Using VPNs

Virtual private networks (VPNs) provide a way for Enterprise networks to create a network in which packet contents are kept private, but the packets actually flow over the public Internet. To create a private VPN over a public Internet, VPN hardware or software encapsulates the private IP packets into another IP packet, typically encrypting the original IP packet in order to maintain privacy.

This short section points out a few of the challenges associated with QoS classification in the presence of VPNs.

Classification and Marking Before Entering the VPN Tunnel

In the earlier sections of this chapter, you read about the many things that Class-Based Marking can examine in order to classify a packet. However, once a packet has been encapsulated and probably encrypted as part of a VPN, those header fields are no longer available for examination. Figure 4-13 depicts a typical site-to-site VPN environment, using IPSEC tunnels:

Figure 4-13 *Typical Site-to-Site IPSEC VPN*

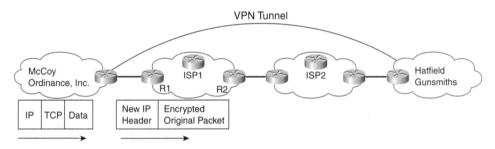

Figure 4-13 shows a router at each Enterprise site performing the encapsulation and encryption of the packets. The routers inside the ISP network see an IP header, but it's not the original IP header. Also, the original IP and TCP header in this example are part of the encrypted payload, making the packet unavailable to routers inside the ISP network. The application headers that NBAR can examine are also encrypted when the packet passes through the ISP. In short, the only thing that the ISP routers can examine are the VPN-created IP headers.

Thankfully, with a good classification and marking strategy, QoS can be extended into the ISP network, even with VPNs in use. When a Cisco router performs the VPN functions, for instance, IPSEC tunnel mode, the router copies the ToS byte from the original IP packet into the newly-created IP header. With proper classification and marking before the packet enters the VPN tunnel, the ISP will at least be able to look at the ToS byte, which includes the DSCP and ECN fields, in order to perform QoS functions. Figure 4-14 depicts the general idea.

Figure 4-14 *Cisco IOS VPN Copies Original ToS Byte*

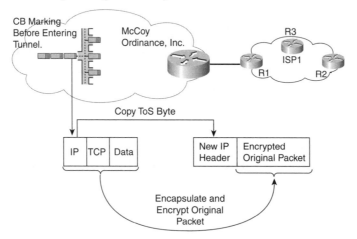

Without any overt action or configuration (beyond configuring VPN features as always) IOS copies the ToS byte to the new IP header. That's true whether using IPSec transport mode, tunnel mode, GRE tunnels, or any of the other Cisco IOS VPN features. So if an enterprise marks a packet with a DSCP value before sending it over a VPN connection, the ISP routers at least have the opportunity to examine the DSCP value to perform QoS functions.

NOTE IPSec uses either tunnel mode, where the original IP header is encrypted, and transport mode, where the original IP header is not encrypted. With tunnel mode, the original IP ToS byte is copied into the encapsulating IP header; with transport, the original ToS byte is not encrypted, and can be examined by QoS mechanisms. Regardless, the original ToS byte information is referencable by the QoS tools.

Classification and Marking on the Router Creating the VPN Tunnel

VPN tunnel encapsulation and encryption can be done by routers, firewalls, software on a PC, or specialized VPN hardware, like the Cisco 3000 series VPN concentrators. This section of the book looks at a specific implementation issue when performing VPN functions in a Cisco router.

Figure 4-14 depicted the original IP packet being encapsulated, encrypted, and copying the original ToS byte into the new IP header. A router performs these steps after the packet is received, but before the packet is forwarded to the outgoing interface. Once the new VPN packet has been created, the packet is then forwarded to the correct outgoing interface, based on the routing table, and transmitted. As a result, the following general statements can be made:

■ Packets entering a router interface, not yet in a VPN tunnel, can be processed with ingress QoS features on that interface just like always.

■ Packets exiting a router interface, after encapsulation and encryption by that router into a VPN tunnel, cannot be processed with egress QoS features on that interface just like always. The Egress QoS features can only examine the post-encapsulation IP header.

In many cases, these points do not matter a lot. You already know that the DSCP is copied into the new VPN IP header, and effective marking of DSCP before the packet is encapsulated might be all you need to do. However, in some cases, you might want to perform QoS features at egress on some interface, and you might simply want to be able to look at fields inside the original IP packet.

Cisco IOS includes a feature called *QoS Pre-classification*, just for this specific case. On routers that are VPN endpoints, you can configure the router such that it can refer to the original packet headers for QoS decisions, even seemingly after the original packet has been encapsulated and encrypted.

The QoS Pre-classification feature does allow the router that encapsulates and encrypts the original packet into the tunnel to look at the original headers for QoS functions. This feature does not, however, allow the ensuing routers to be able to look at the original headers—they are indeed encrypted. Internally, in the router performing the encapsulation and encryption, IOS keeps the original unencrypted packet in memory until the QoS actions have been taken.

Figure 4-15 summarizes the behavior of a router in terms of when it can and can't look at the original headers for QoS features, based on the presence or absence of QoS Pre-classification:

Keep in mind that this feature applies only to the router performing the encapsulation and not other routers. Also, the ToS byte is copied from the original IP header to the encapsulating VPN header automatically as a totally separate and unrelated feature.

Figure 4-15 *Locations Where the Original Classifications Fields are and are not Available*

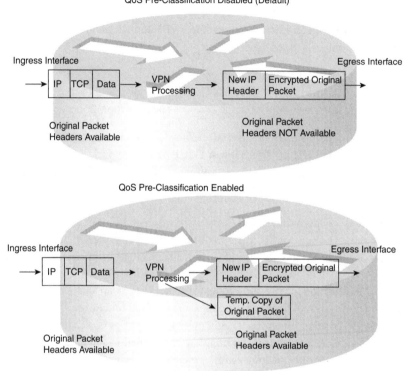

Configuring QoS Pre-classification

Configuring QoS Pre-classification is relatively simple. First, the command to enable it is **qos pre-classify.** The only hard part is knowing where to use the command. With IOS, depending on the type of VPN tunnel being created, you might use one of three general styles of configuration. Table 4-14 lists the modes in which you might type the commands, according to the type of VPN configured:

Table 4-14 *Rules for Where to Configure the **qos pre-classify** command*

Configuration Command Under Which the Command qos pre-classify Is Configured	Type of VPN
interface tunnel	GRE and IPIP
interface virtual-template	L2F and L2TP
crypto map	IPSEC

Although the configuration is simple, a few example commands can help. Figure 4-16 shows a sample network, with two remote sites connecting through an ISP. R4 and R1 have been configured such that IPSEC is used when someone at R4's branch Telnets to R1's Loopback IP address (10.1.1.1). Figure 4-16 depicts the network, and Example 4-5 that follows shows the configuration on R4, as well as some **show** commands.

Figure 4-16   *Site-to-Site VPN for Telnet Traffic: QoS Pre-classify*

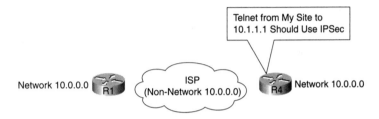

Example 4-5   *QoS Pre-classification Commands on R4*

```
!
crypto isakmp policy 2
 authentication pre-share
crypto isakmp key cisco address 192.168.2.1
!
!
crypto ipsec transform-set branch ah-md5-hmac esp-des esp-md5-hmac
!
crypto map mccoy 10 ipsec-isakmp
 set peer 192.168.2.1
 set transform-set branch
 match address 150
 qos pre-classify
!
!
!
 class-map match-all telnet
  match access-group 152
!
 policy-map test-preclass
  class telnet
!
interface Loopback0
 ip address 10.1.4.4 255.255.255.0
!
interface FastEthernet0/0
 ip address 192.168.3.4 255.255.255.0
 service-policy output test-preclass
 load-interval 30
```

continues

Example 4-5 *QoS Pre-classification Commands on R4 (Continued)*

```
  crypto map mccoy
 !
 access-list 150 permit tcp any host 10.1.1.1 eq telnet
 !
 access-list 152 permit tcp any eq telnet any
 access-list 152 permit tcp any any eq telnet

 R4#clear counters
 Clear "show interface" counters on all interfaces [confirm]
 R4#
 03:07:51: %CLEAR-5-COUNTERS: Clear counter on all interfaces by vty0 (192.168.2.1)
 !
 ! (Generated several screens worth of telnet traffic next…
 !
 R4#show policy-map interface fastEthernet 0/0
  FastEthernet0/0

   Service-policy output: test-preclass

     Class-map: telnet (match-all)
       263 packets, 34524 bytes
       30 second offered rate 1000 bps
       Match: access-group 152

     Class-map: class-default (match-any)
       3 packets, 228 bytes
       30 second offered rate 0 bps, drop rate 0 bps
       Match: any

 R4#show crypto map
 Crypto Map "mccoy" 10 ipsec-isakmp
         Peer = 192.168.2.1
         Extended IP access list 150
             access-list 150 permit tcp any host 10.1.1.1 port = 23
         Current peer: 192.168.2.1
         Security association lifetime: 4608000 kilobytes/3600 seconds
         PFS (Y/N): N
         Transform sets={
                 branch,
         }
         QOS pre-classification
         Interfaces using crypto map mccoy:
                 FastEthernet0/0

 R4#configure terminal
 Enter configuration commands, one per line.  End with CNTL/Z.
 R4(config)#crypto map mccoy 10 ipsec-isakmp
 R4(config-crypto-map)#no qos pre-classify
```

Example 4-5 *QoS Pre-classification Commands on R4 (Continued)*

```
R4(config-crypto-map)#^Z

R4#clear counters
Clear "show interface" counters on all interfaces [confirm]
R4#
03:10:59: %CLEAR-5-COUNTERS: Clear counter on all interfaces by vty0 (192.168.2.1)
!
! (Generated several screens worth of telnet traffic next…
!
R4#show policy-map interface fastEthernet 0/0
 FastEthernet0/0

  Service-policy output: test-preclass

    Class-map: telnet (match-all)
      0 packets, 0 bytes
      30 second offered rate 0 bps
      Match: access-group 152

    Class-map: class-default (match-any)
      28 packets, 28227 bytes
      30 second offered rate 2000 bps, drop rate 0 bps
      Match: any

R4#show crypto map
Crypto Map "mccoy" 10 ipsec-isakmp
        Peer = 192.168.2.1
        Extended IP access list 150
            access-list 150 permit tcp any host 10.1.1.1 port = 23
        Current peer: 192.168.2.1
        Security association lifetime: 4608000 kilobytes/3600 seconds
        PFS (Y/N): N
        Transform sets={
                branch,
        }
        Interfaces using crypto map mccoy:
                FastEthernet0/0
!
! Note that command output is missing the "QoS Pre-classification" Line
!
```

The example shows a test with **qos pre-classify** enabled, and then the same example with it disabled. The initial configuration uses IPSEC so that when someone near R4 Telnets to R1's Loopback IP address (10.1.1.1), IPSec is used to encrypt the packets. The **crypto map mccoy** global command includes the **qos pre-classify** subcommand. So, any QoS features that might be enabled on R4's

Fa0/0 interface (the outgoing interface for the traffic) should be able to look at the headers for these IPSEC encrypted packets.

To prove the function, **policy-map test-preclass** was created and enabled for output packets on R4's FA0/0 interface. This policy map has a single class called **telnet**, which matches all Telnet packets. All other types of packets will match the class-default class. (To test, I simply Telnetted to match the crypto map, and did several commands to generate Telnet traffic.) As the output from the **show policy-map interface** command indicates, the counters in **class telnet** show packets and bytes as matching that class. The small amount of traffic in class-default was simply overhead traffic.

Next, the example shows the **no qos pre-classify** subcommand, which removes the pre-classification function from the crypto map. The same test is run, but now notice the counters in **class class-default** have grown, but nothing has been matched in **class telnet**, demonstrating that the egress QoS policy map on R4's FA0/0 interface cannot look at the pre-VPN headers.

Also note the output of the **show crypto map** command, both with and without **qos pre-classify** enabled. When enabled, an extra line shows near the end of the output, stating that qos pre-classification is enabled. This line is simply missing if the feature has not been configured.

Foundation Summary

The "Foundation Summary" is a collection of tables and figures that provide a convenient review of many key concepts in this chapter. For those of you already comfortable with the topics in this chapter, this summary could help you recall a few details. For those of you who just read this chapter, this review should help solidify some key facts. For any of you doing your final prep before the exam, these tables and figures are a convenient way to review the day before the exam.

Table 4-15 shows the list of items that can be matched using the MQC **match** command, and Table 4-16 lists the fields that can be marked using CB Marking.

Table 4-15 *Match Configuration Command Reference for CB Marking*

Command	Function
match [ip] precedence *precedence-value* [*precedence-value precedence-value precedence-value*]	Matches precedence in IPV4 packets when the **ip** parameter is included; matches IPV4 and IPV6 packets when **ip** parameter is missing.
match access-group {*access-group* | **name** *access-group-name*}	Matches an ACL by number or name
match any	Matches all packets
match class-map class-map-nam*e*	Matches based on another class-map
match cos *cos-value* [*cos-value cos-value cos-value*]	Matches a CoS value
match destination-address mac *address*	Matches a destination MAC address
match fr-dlci *dlci-number*	Matches a particular Frame Relay DLCI
match input-interface *interface-name*	Matches an input interface
match ip dscp *ip-dscp-value* [*ip-dscp-value ip-dscp-value ip-dscp-value ip-dscp-value ip-dscp-value ip-dscp-value ip-dscp-value*]	Matches DSCP in IPV4 packets when the **ip** parameter is included; matches IPV4 and IPV6 packets when **ip** parameter is missing.
match ip rtp *starting-port-number port-range*	Matches the RTP's UDP port-number range, even values only
match mpls experimental *number*	Matches an MPLS Experimental value
match mpls experimental topmost value	When multiple labels are in use, this command matches the MPLS EXP field in the top-most label.

continues

Table 4-15 *Match Configuration Command Reference for CB Marking (Continued)*

Command	Function
match not match-criteria	Reverses the matching logic, in other words, things matched by the matching criteria do not match the class-map.
match packet length {**max** *maximum-length-value* [**min** *minimum-length-value*] | **min** *minimum-length-value* [**max** *maximum-length-value*]}	Matches packets based on the minimum length, maximum length, or both.
match protocol citrix app *application-name-string*	Matches NBAR Citrix applications
match protocol http [**url** *url-string* | **host** *hostname-string* | **mime** *MIME-type*]	Matches a host name and URL string
match protocol *protocol-name*	Matches NBAR protocol types
match protocol rtp [**audio** | **video** | **payload-type** *payload-string*]	Matches RTP audio or video payload, based on the payload type. Also allows explicitly specified payload types.
match qos-group *qos-group-value*	Matches a QoS group
match source-address mac *address-destination*	Matches a source MAC address

Table 4-16 set *Configuration Command Reference for CB Marking*

Command	Function
set [**ip**] **precedence** *ip-precedence-value*	Marks the value for IP Precedence for IPV4 and IPV6 packets if the **ip** parameter is omitted; sets only IPV4 packets if **ip** parameter is included.
set [**ip**] **dscp** *ip-dscp-value*	Marks the value for IP DSCP for IPV4 and IPV6 packets if the **ip** parameter is omitted; sets only IPV4 packets if **ip** parameter is included.
set cos *cos-value*	Marks the value for CoS
set qos-group *group-id*	Marks the value for the QoS group
set atm-clp	Marks the value for the ATM CLP bit
set fr-de	Marks the value for the Frame Relay DE bit

Figure 4-17 outlines the two IP marking fields and their positions inside an IP header.

Figure 4-17   *IP Precedence and IP DSCP Fields*

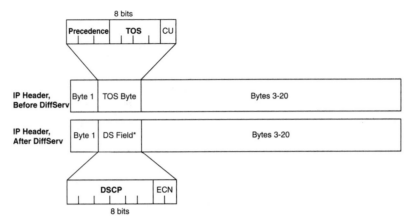

Figure 4-18 shows the general location of the CoS field inside ISL and 802.1P headers.

Figure 4-18   *LAN Class Of Service Fields*

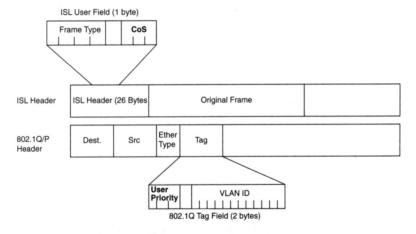

Table 4-17 summarizes the marking fields.

Table 4-17 *Names of Marking Fields*

Field	Location	Length	Comments
IP Precedence	IP header	3 bits	Contained in the first 3 bits of the ToS byte.
IP DSCP	IP header	6 bits	Contained in the first 6 bits of the DS field, which replaces the ToS byte.
DS	IP header	1 byte	Replaces ToS byte per RFC 2475.
ToS	IP header	1 byte	Replaced by DS field per RFC 2475.
ToS	IP header	4 bits	A field inside the ToS byte; superseded by RFC 2475.
CoS	ISL and 802.1Q/p	3 bits	Cisco convention uses "CoS" to describe either trunking headers' QoS field.
Priority bits	802.1Q/p	3 bits	The name used by IEEE 802.1P for the CoS bits.
Discard Eligible (DE)	Frame Relay header	1 bit	Frame Relay switches may discard DE- marked frames, avoiding discarding frames without DE marked, under congestion.
Cell Loss Priority (CLP)	ATM cell header	1 bit	ATM equivalent of the DE bit
MPLS Experimental values(s)	MPLS header	3 bits	Used to pass QoS marking information across an MPLS network.
QoS Group	Headers internal to IOS	N/A	Uses values between 1–99 inclusive. Used for marking only internal to a single router, and only on specific models of routers.

Table 4-18 lists the modes in which you might type the commands, according to the type of VPN configured:

Table 4-18 *Rules for Where to Configure the **qos pre-classify** command*

Configuration Command Under Which the qos pre-classify Command Is Configured	Type of VPN
interface tunnel	GRE and IPIP
interface virtual-template	L2F and L2TP
crypto map	IPSec

For Further Reading

This book attempts to cover the breadth and depth of QoS as covered on the QoS exam (642-642). However, you may want to read more about topics in this chapter, or other classification and marking topics.

For more on the topics in this chapter:

■ Cisco IOS 12.3 QOS Configuration Guide (http://www.cisco.com/univercd/cc/td/doc/product/software/ios123/123cgcr/qos_vcg.htm)

For more on other Classification and Marking topics:

■ For NBAR: http://www.cisco.com/warp/public/cc/pd/iosw/prodlit/nbarw_wp.htm

■ Appendix B, Additional QoS Reference Materials (found on this book's accompanying CD-ROM):

— Committed Access Rate (CAR)

— Policy-Based Routing (PBR)

— Dial-Peers

— QoS Policy Propagation Using BGP (QPPB)

For design related guidance:

■ Cisco's document "Cisco AVVID Network Infrastructure Enterprise Quality of Service Design" document at http://cisco.com/application/pdf/en/us/guest/netsol/ns17/c649/ccmigration_09186a00800d67ed.pdf

Q&A

As mentioned in the Introduction, you have two choices for review questions. The questions that follow next give you a more difficult challenge than the exam itself by using an open-ended question format. By reviewing now with this more difficult question format, you can exercise your memory better, and prove your conceptual and factual knowledge of this chapter. You can find the answers to these questions in Appendix A.

The second option for practice questions is to use the CD-ROM included with this book. It includes a testing engine and more than 200 multiple-choice questions. You should use this CD-ROM nearer to the end of your preparation, for practice with the actual exam format. You can even customize the CD-ROM exam to include, or not include, the topics that are only on the CCIP QoS.

1. Describe the difference between classification and marking.

2. Describe, in general, how a queuing feature could take advantage of the work performed by a classification and marking feature.

3. Characterize what must be true before the CoS field may be useful for marking packets.

4. Most other QoS tools, besides classification and marking tools, also have a classification feature. Describe the advantage of classification, in terms of overall QoS design and policies, and explain why classification and marking is useful, in spite of the fact that other tools also classify the traffic.

5. Which of the following classification and marking tools can classify based on the contents of an HTTP URL: class-based marking (CB Marking), QoS Pre-classification, network-based application recognition (NBAR), or cos-to-dscp maps?

6. Describe the differences between IP extended ACLs as compared with NBAR for matching TCP and UDP port numbers.

7. Which of the following QoS marking fields are carried inside an 802.1Q header: QoS, CoS, DE, ToS byte, User Priority, ToS bits, CLP, Precedence, QoS Group, DSCP, MPLS Experimental, or DS?

8. Which of the following QoS marking fields are carried inside an IP header: QoS, CoS, DE, ToS byte, User Priority, ToS bits, CLP, Precedence, QoS Group, DSCP, or MPLS Experimental?

9. Which of the following QoS marking fields are never marked inside a frame that exits a router: QoS, CoS, DE, ToS byte, User Priority, ToS bits, CLP, Precedence, QoS Group, DSCP, MPLS Experimental, or DS?

10. Describe the goal of marking near the edge of a network in light of the meaning of the term "trust boundary."

11. What configuration command lists the classification details when configuring CB Marking? What configuration mode must you use to configure the command? What commands must you issue to place the configuration mode user into that mode?

12. What configuration command lists the marking details when configuring CB Marking? What configuration mode must you use to configure the command? What commands must you issue to place the configuration mode user into that mode?

13. What configuration command enables CB Marking? What configuration mode must you use to configure the command? What commands must you issue to place the configuration mode user into that mode?

14. Describe how you can mark multiple DSCP values with a single class map. How many can you match with a single command?

15. What configuration command lets you match RTP audio without also matching RTP video traffic?

16. Describe the process by which NBAR can be updated to support new protocols, without upgrading IOS.

17. What CB Marking command implies that a policy map requires NBAR in order to match packets?

18. What command enables NBAR on an interface for incoming packets? For outgoing packets?

19. Describe the reason why you might see multiple **set** commands inside a single service class in a policy map, and give one example.

20. Imagine you are supposed to update a router configuration. The current configuration includes a class-map that refers to ACL 101, which has 23 ACL clauses (separate **access-list** commands). How could you easily create a new class map that matches the traffic denied by the ACL?

21. A router is configred to create a VPN tunnel. Explain the required steps you must take to cause a router to copy the ToS byte of the original packet into the ToS byte of the new IP header used to encapsulate the packet.

22. A router is configred to create a VPN tunnel, with unencrypted packets entering interface Fa0/0, and the encrypted packets going over a link to the internet (S0/0). Assuming as many defaults as possible were taken, could a policy map for packets entering the router's FA0/0 interface examine the packet headers as originally created by the end user device? Why?

23. A router is configred to create a VPN tunnel, with unencrypted packets entering interface Fa0/0, and the encrypted packets going over a link to the internet (S0/0). Assuming as many defaults as possible were taken, could a policy map for packets exiting the router's S0/0 interface examine the packet headers as originally created by the end user device? Why or why not?

24. A router is configred to create a VPN tunnel, with unencrypted packets entering interface Fa0/0, and the encrypted packets going over a link to the Internet (S0/0). Assuming the **qos pre-classify** command was configured correctly, could a policy map for packets entering the router's FA0/0 interface examine the packet headers as originally created by the end user device? Why or why not?

25. Name the three configuration areas in which you might use the **qos pre-classify** command in order to enable pre-classification.

QoS Exam Topics

This chapter covers the following exam
topics specific to the QoS exam:

- List and explain the different queuing
  algorithms

- Explain the components of hardware and
  software queuing systems on Cisco
  routers and how they are affected by
  tuning and congestion

- Describe the benefits and drawbacks of
  using WFQ to implement QoS

- Explain the purpose and features of
  Class-Based WFQ (CBWFQ)

- Explain the purpose and features of Low
  Latency Queuing (LLQ)

- Identify the Cisco IOS commands
  required to configure and monitor LLQ
  on a Cisco router

CHAPTER 5

Congestion Management

Most people understand the basic concepts of queuing, because most of us experience queuing every day. We wait in line to pay for groceries, we wait for a bank teller, we wait to get into a ride at an amusement park, and so on. So, most of the queuing concepts inside this chapter are intuitive.

Cisco uses the term "congestion management" to refer to queuing systems in their products. This chapter begins with coverage of some queuing concepts inside Cisco routers, including the distinction between hardware and software queues, and where software queues can be used. (Queuing inside LAN switches, particularly the Cisco 2950 series switches, is covered in Chapter 9, "LAN QoS.")

Following that, the second and third sections of the three major sections in this chapter cover specifics about several Queuing mechanisms available inside Cisco routers. The first of these two sections covers only concepts about several older Queuing tools. The final section covers both concepts and configuration for the three major queuing mechanisms covered by the current QoS exam, namely WFQ, CBWFQ, and LLQ.

"Do I Know This Already?" Quiz

The purpose of the "Do I Know This Already?" quiz is to help you decide if you really need to read the entire chapter. If you already intend to read the entire chapter, you do not necessarily need to answer these questions now.

The 12-question quiz, derived from the major sections in "Foundation Topics" portion of the chapter, helps you determine how to spend your limited study time.

Table 5-1 outlines the major topics discussed in this chapter and the "Do I Know This Already?" quiz questions that correspond to those topics.

Table 5-1 *"Do I Know This Already?" Foundation Topics Section-to-Question Mapping*

Foundation Topics Section Covering These Questions	Questions	Score
Cisco Router Queuing Concepts	1–3	
Scheduling Concepts: FIFO, PQ, CQ, and MDRR	4–6	
Concepts and Configuration: WFQ, CBWFQ, and LLQ	7–12	
Total Score		

CAUTION The goal of self-assessment is to gauge your mastery of the topics in this chapter. If you do not know the answer to a question or are only partially sure of the answer, mark this question wrong for purposes of the self-assessment. Giving yourself credit for an answer you correctly guess skews your self-assessment results and might provide you with a false sense of security.

You can find the answers to the "Do I Know This Already?" quiz in Appendix A, "Answers to the 'Do I Know This Already?' Quizzes and Q&A Sections." The suggested choices for your next step are as follows:

- **10 or less overall score**—Read the entire chapter. This includes the "Foundation Topics," the "Foundation Summary," and the "Q&A" sections.

- **11 or 12 overall score**—If you want more review on these topics, skip to the "Foundation Summary" section and then go to the "Q&A" section. Otherwise, move to the next chapter.

Cisco Router Queuing Concepts Questions

1. What is the main benefit of the hardware queue on a Cisco router interface?

    a. Prioritizes latency-sensitive packets so that they are always scheduled next

    b. Reserves a minimum amount of bandwidth for particular classes of traffic

    c. Provides a queue so that as soon as the interface is available to send another packet, the packet can be sent, without requiring an interrupt to the router CPU

    d. Allows configuration of a percentage of the remaining link bandwidth, after allocating bandwidth to the LLQ and the class-default queue

2. A set of queues associated with a physical interface, for the purpose of prioritizing packets exiting the interface, are called which of the following?

    a. Hardware queues

    b. Software queues

   c. Shaping queues

   d. TX-queues

3. Which of the following commands could change the length of a hardware queue?

   a. **hardware queue-length 10**

   b. **tx-queue length 10**

   c. **hardware 10**

   d. **tx-ring-limit 10**

Scheduling Concepts: FIFO, PQ, CQ, and MDRR Questions

4. What is the main benefit of having FIFO queuing enabled on a Cisco router interface?

   a. Prioritizes latency-sensitive packets so that they are always scheduled next

   b. Reserves a minimum amount of bandwidth for particular classes of traffic

   c. Provides a place to hold packets in RAM until space becomes available in the hardware queue for the interface.

   d. Provides a queue so that as soon as the interface is available to send another packet, the packet can be sent, without requiring an interrupt to the router CPU

   e. Allows configuration of a percentage of the remaining link bandwidth, after allocating bandwidth to the LLQ and the class-default queue

5. What are the main benefits of CQ being enabled on a Cisco router interface?

   a. Prioritizes latency-sensitive packets so that they are always scheduled next

   b. Reserves a minimum amount of bandwidth for particular classes of traffic

   c. Provides a place to hold packets in RAM until space becomes available in the hardware queue for the interface.

   d. Provides a queue so that as soon as the interface is available to send another packet, the packet can be sent, without requiring an interrupt to the router CPU

   e. Allows configuration of a percentage of the remaining link bandwidth, after allocating bandwidth to the LLQ and the class-default queue

6. What is the main benefit of enabling PQ on a Cisco router interface?

   a. Prioritizes latency-sensitive packets so that they are always scheduled next

   b. Reserves a minimum amount of bandwidth for particular classes of traffic

   c. Provides a place to hold packets in RAM until the interface becomes available for sending the packet

    d. Provides a queue so that as soon as the interface is available to send another packet, the packet can be sent, without requiring an interrupt to the router CPU

    e. Allows configuration of a percentage of the remaining link bandwidth, after allocating bandwidth to the LLQ and the class-default queue

Concepts and Configuration: WFQ, CBWFQ, and LLQ Questions

7. Which of the following are reasons why WFQ might discard a packet instead of putting it into the correct queue?

    a. The hold-queue limit for all combined WFQ queues has been exceeded.

    b. The queue length for the flow has passed the WRED minimum drop threshold.

    c. The WFQ queue length for the queue where the newly-arrived packet should be placed has exceeded the CDT

    d. ECN feedback has been signaled, requesting that the TCP sender slow down

8. Which of the following settings cannot be configured for WFQ on the **fair-queue** interface subcommand?

    a. CDT

    b. Number of queues

    c. Number of RSVP-reserved queues

    d. Hold Queue limit

    e. WRED thresholds

9. Examine the following configuration snippet. If a new class, called class3, was added to the policy-map, which of the following commands could be used to reserve 25 kbps of bandwidth for the class?

```
policy-map fred
 class class1
  priority 20
 class class2
  bandwidth 30
!
interface serial 0/0
 bandwidth 100
 service-policy output fred
```

    a. **priority 25**

    b. **bandwidth 25**

    c. **bandwidth percent 25**

    d. **bandwidth remaining-percent 25**

10. Examine the following configuration snippet. How much bandwidth does IOS assign to class2?

```
policy-map fred
 class class1
  priority percent 20
 class class2
  bandwidth remaining percent 20
interface serial 0/0
 bandwidth 100
 service-policy output fred
```

   a. 10 kbps

   b. 11 kbps

   c. 20 kbps

   d. 21 kbps

   e. Not enough information to tell

11. What is the largest number of classes inside a single policy map that can be configured as an LLQ?

   a. 1

   b. 2

   c. 3

   d. more than 3

12. To prevent non-LLQ queues from being starved, LLQ can police the low-latency queue. Looking at the configuration snippet below, what must be changed or added to cause this policy-map to police traffic in class1?

```
policy-map fred
 class class1
  priority 20
 class class2
  bandwidth remaining percent 20
interface serial 0/0
 bandwidth 100
 service-policy output fred
```

   a. Change the **priority 20** command to **priority 20 500**, setting the policing burst size

   b. Add the **police 20000** command under class1

   c. Nothing – the **priority** command implies that policing will also be performed

   d. Add the **LLQ-police** global configuration command

Foundation Topics

Queuing has an impact on all four QoS characteristics directly — bandwidth, delay, jitter, and packet loss. Many people, upon hearing the term "QoS," immediately think of queuing, but QoS includes many more concepts and features than just queuing. Queuing is certainly the most often deployed and most important QoS tool.

This chapter begins by explaining the core concepts about queuing. Following that, most queuing tools are covered, including additional concepts specific to that tool, configuration, monitoring, and troubleshooting.

Cisco Router Queuing Concepts

Most people already understand many of the concepts behind queuing. First, this section explains the basics and defines a few terms. Afterward, some of the IOS-specific details are covered.

IOS stores packets in memory while processing the packet. When a router has completed all the required work except actually sending the packet, if the outgoing interface is currently busy, the router just keeps the packet in memory waiting on the interface to become available. To manage the set of packets sitting around in memory waiting to exit an interface, IOS creates a queue. A queue just organizes the packets waiting to exit an interface; the queue itself is nothing more than a series of pointers to the memory buffers that hold the individual packets that are waiting to exit the interface.

The most basic queuing scheme uses a single queue, with first-in, first-out (FIFO) scheduling. What does that mean? Well, when the IOS decides to take the next packet from the queue, of those packets still in the queue, it takes the one that arrived earlier than all the other packets in the queue. Figure 5-1 shows a router, with an interface using a single FIFO queue.

Figure 5-1 *Single FIFO Queue*

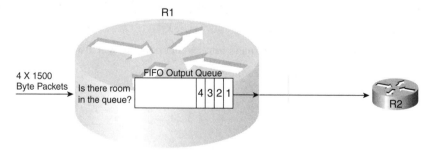

Although a single FIFO queue seems to provide no QoS features at all, it actually does affect drop, delay, and jitter. Because there is only one queue, the router need not classify traffic to place it into different queues. Because there is only one queue, the router need not worry about how to decide from which queue it should take the next packet — there is only one choice. And because this single queue uses FIFO logic, the router need not reorder the packets inside the queue.

However, the size of the output queue affects delay, jitter, and loss. Because the queue has a finite size, it may fill. If it fills, and another packet needs to be added to the queue, tail drop would cause the packet to be dropped. One solution to the drops would be to lengthen the queue, which decreases the likelihood of tail drop. With a longer queue, however, the average delay increases, because packets may be enqueued behind a larger number of other packets. In most cases when the average delay increases, the average jitter increases as well. The following list summarizes the key concepts regarding queue length:

- With a longer queue length, the chance of tail drop decreases as compared with a shorter queue, but the average delay increases, with the average jitter typically increasing as well.

- With a shorter queue length, the chance of tail drop increases as compared with a longer queue, but the average delay decreases, with the average jitter typically decreasing as well.

- If the congestion is sustained such that the offered load of bytes trying to exit an interface exceeds the interface speed for long periods, drops will be just as likely whether the queue is short or long.

To appreciate most queuing concepts, you need to consider a queuing system with at least two queues. Consider Figure 5-2, which illustrates two FIFO output queues.

Figure 5-2 *Dual FIFO Output Queues*

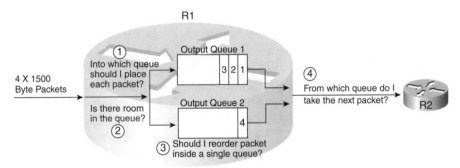

Figure 5-2 illustrates the questions that are answered by the queuing tool. Step 1, the classification step, works like classification and marking tools, except the resulting action is to place a packet in a queue, as opposed to marking a packet. So, at Step 1, the packet header is examined, and depending on the matched values, the packet is placed into the appropriate queue. Before placing the packet in the queue, the router must make sure that space is available, as shown in Step 2 in Figure 5-2. If no space is available, the packet is dropped. Inside each queue, the packets can be reordered (step 3): in this example, however, each queue uses FIFO logic inside each queue, so the packets would never be reordered inside the queue. Finally, the queuing system must choose to take the next packet for transmission from either Queue 1 or Queue 2 (Step 4). The *scheduler* makes the decision at Step 4.

Although the classification portion of each queuing tool is relatively obvious, consider two related points when thinking about classification by a queuing tool. First, with a QoS strategy that causes classification and marking to occur near the ingress edge of the network, the queuing tool may enqueue packets that have already been marked. So, the queuing tool can classify based on these marked fields, which was the whole point in marking them in the first place! Second, for each category of traffic for which you want to provide different queuing treatment, you need a different queue. For instance, you may want to classify traffic into six classes for queuing, so each class can get different treatment in a different queue. If the queuing tool only supports four different queues, you may need to consider a different queuing tool to support your QoS policy.

Inside each queue, the queuing methods use FIFO Queuing. The interesting logic for queuing occurs after the packets have been enqueued, when the router decides from which queue to take the next packet. *Queue scheduling* describes the process of the device, in this case a router, choosing which queue to service next. This process is also called a *service algorithm*, or a queue service algorithm. The scheduler may reserve amounts of bandwidth, or a percentage of link bandwidth, for a particular queue. The scheduler may always service one queue first, which means the packets in that queue will experience very low delay and jitter.

For the exams, you need to know what each queuing tool's scheduler accomplishes; for some tools, however, you also need to know the internals of how the scheduler actually works.

NOTE   Cisco leads the industry in making details about their products public (being the first large networking vendor to publish bug reports, for instance). However, Cisco must also protect their intellectual assets. So, for some of the newer queuing tools, Cisco has not yet published every detail about how the scheduling algorithm works. For some of the older queuing tools, the details are published. Frankly, the details of how the scheduling code works inside IOS might be interesting, but it is not really necessary for a deep understanding of what a queuing tool does. For the QoS exams, you need to know what each queuing tool's scheduler accomplishes; for some tools, however, you also need to know the internals of how the scheduler actually works. When necessary, this book gives you plenty of details about the internal scheduling algorithms to help prepare you for the exams.

A final comment about the core concepts of queuing: The size of each packet does not affect the length of the queue, or how many packets it can hold. A queue of length 10 holds ten 1500-byte packets as easily as it holds ten 64-byte packets. Queues actually do not hold the packets themselves, but instead just hold pointers to the packets, whose contents are held in buffers.

Table 5-2 summarizes the key concepts of queuing. This table is used to compare the various queuing tools in the "Queuing Tools" section of this chapter.

Table 5-2 *Key Concepts When Comparing Queuing Tools*

Feature	Definition	QoS Characteristic Affected
Classification	The capability to examine packets to determine into which queue the packet should be placed. Many options are available.	None
Drop policy	When the queue has been determined, the drop policy defines the rules by which the router chooses to drop the packet. Tail drop, modified tail drop, WRED (Weighted Random Early Detect), and ECN (Explicit Congestion Notification) are the main options.	Loss
Scheduling inside a single queue	In almost all cases, packets inside a single queue are scheduled using FIFO logic.	Bandwidth, delay, jitter, and loss
Scheduling between different queues	The logic that defines how queuing chooses the queue from which to take the next packet and place it in the TX Queue (Transmit Queue).	Bandwidth, delay, jitter, and loss
Maximum number of queues	The maximum number of different queues the queuing tools support, which in turn implies the maximum number of traffic classifications that can be treated differently by the queuing method.	None
Maximum queue length	The maximum number of packets in a single queue.	Loss, delay

Software Queues and Hardware Queues

The queues described so far in this chapter are created by the software in a router, namely Cisco IOS. However, when a queuing scheduler decides which packet to send next, the packet does not move directly out the interface. Instead, the router moves the packet from the interface software queue to another small FIFO queue on each interface. Cisco calls this separate, final queue either the *Transmit Queue* (TX Queue) or *Transmit Ring* (TX Ring), depending on the model of the router. Regardless of which name is used, for the purposes of this book and the QoS exam, you can call this small FIFO queue a Hardware Queue, TX Queue, or TX Ring. Throughout this book, you can consider all three names for the hardware queue to be equivalent.

The Hardware Queue's objective is to drive the link utilization to 100 percent when packets are waiting to exit an interface. The Hardware Queue holds outgoing packets so that the interface does not have to rely on the general-purpose processor in the router in order to start sending the next packet. The Hardware Queue can be accessed directly by the application-specific integrated circuits (ASICs) associated with an interface, so even if the general processor is busy, the interface can begin sending the next packet without waiting for the router CPU. Because the most constrained resource in a router is typically the bandwidth on the attached interfaces, particularly on WAN interfaces, the router hopes to always be able to send the next packet immediately when the interface finishes sending the last packet. The Hardware Queue provides a key component to reach that goal.

However, the existence of the Hardware Queue does impact queuing to some extent. Figure 5-3 depicts the Hardware Queue, along with a single FIFO software queue.

Figure 5-3 *Single FIFO Software Queue, with a Single Hardware Queue*

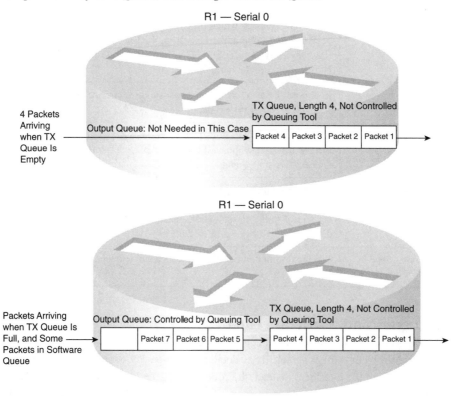

Two different examples are outlined in Figure 5-3. In the top part of the figure, the scenario begins with no packets in the software queue, and no packets in the Hardware Queue. Then, four packets arrive. With a Hardware Queue with room for four packets, all four packets are placed into the Hardware Queue.

In the second example, any new packets that arrive will be placed into the software queue. Assuming that the software queue and the Hardware Queue were empty before the seven packets shown in the figure arrived, the first four packets would have been placed in the Hardware queue, and the last three in the software queue. So, any new packets will be placed at the end of the software queue.

All the queuing tools in IOS create and manage interface Software queues, not interface Hardware Queues. Each interface uses one TX Queue (or TX Ring), and the Hardware Queue is a FIFO queue, unaffected by the queuing configuration on the interface.

In Figure 5-3, the packets are sent in the same order that they would have been sent if the Hardware Queue did not exist. In some cases, however, the Hardware Queue impacts the results of the software queuing scheduler. For instance, consider Figure 5-4, where queuing is configured with two software queues. In this scenario, six packets arrive, numbered in the order in which they arrive. The software queuing configuration specifies that the first two packets (1 and 2) should be placed into Queue 2, and the next four packets (numbered 3 through 6) should be placed into Queue 1.

Many people assume that the router behaves as shown in the top part of Figure 5-4, with the scheduler determining the order in which packets exit the interface. In reality, IOS behaves as shown in the bottom half of Figure 5-4. In the top half of the figure, if all six packets were to arrive instantaneously, all six packets would be placed into the appropriate software queue. If this particular queuing tool's scheduler always serviced packets from Queue 1, and only serviced Queue 2 if Queue 1 was empty, the packets will leave in a different order than they arrived. In fact, packets 3 through 6 would exit in order, and then packets 1 and 2 would be sent. Ultimately, the order would just depend on the logic of the scheduling part of the queuing tool.

In this particular example, however, the packets would actually exit the interface in the same order that the packets were received because of the existence of the Hardware Queue. As mentioned earlier, when the router identifies the output interface for a packet, it checks the Hardware Queue for that interface. If space is available, the packet is placed in the Hardware Queue, and no output queuing is performed for that packet. In the example, because the scenario assumes that no other packets were waiting to exit R1's S0/0 interface before these six packets arrive, the first two packets are placed in the Hardware Queue. When packet 3 arrives, S0/0's Hardware Queue is full, so packets 3 through 6 are placed into an interface software queue, based on the queuing configuration for R1's S0/0 interface. The queuing classification logic places packets 3 through 6 into Queue 1. The router drains the packets in order from the TX Queue, and moves packets 3, 4, 5, and 6, in order, from Queue 1 into the Hardware Queue. The actual order that the packets exit S0 is the same order as they arrived.

Figure 5-4 *Potential Impact of Hardware Queue on Software Queues 1*

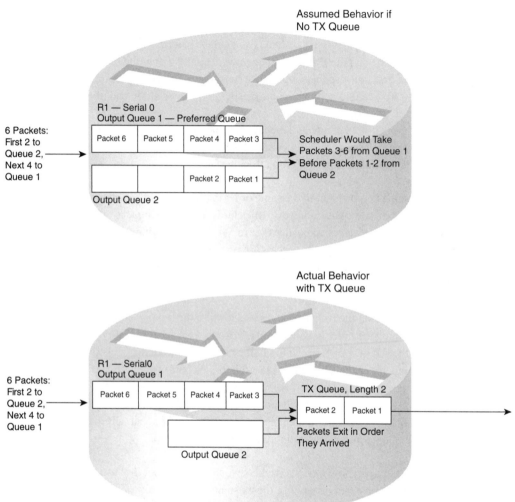

IOS automatically attempts to minimize the impact of the Hardware Queue to the IOS queuing tools. The IOS maintains the original goal of always having a packet in the Hardware Queue, available for the interface to immediately send when the interface completes sending the previous packet. When any form of software queuing tool is enabled on an interface, IOS on lower-end routers typically reduces the size of the Hardware Queue to a small value, often times to a length of 2. The smaller the value, the less impact the TX Queue has on the effects of the queuing method.

In some cases, you may want to change the setting for the size of the Hardware Queue. For instance, the QoS course makes a general recommendation of size 3 for slow speed serial interfaces, although

I personally believe that size 2 works well, and is the default setting on many router platforms once queuing has been configured. Also, ATM interfaces typically require a little thought for Hardware Queue lengths, as described at http://www.cisco.com/en/US/tech/tk39/tk824/technologies_tech_note09186a00800fbafc.shtml. (If you can't find the URL, go to www.cisco.com, and search on "Understanding and Tuning the tx-ring-limit Value.") Example 5-1 lists several commands that enable you to examine the size of the Hardware Queue, and change the size. (Keep in mind the other names for the Hardware Queue—TX Ring and TX Queue.)

Example 5-1 *TX Queue Length: Finding the Length, and Changing the Length*

```
R3#show controllers serial 0/0
Interface Serial0/0
Hardware is PowerQUICC MPC860
DCE V.35, clock rate 1300000
idb at 0x8108F318, driver data structure at 0x81096D8C
SCC Registers:
General [GSMR]=0x2:0x00000030, Protocol-specific [PSMR]=0x8
Events [SCCE]=0x0000, Mask [SCCM]=0x001F, Status [SCCS]=0x06
Transmit on Demand [TODR]=0x0, Data Sync [DSR]=0x7E7E
Interrupt Registers:
Config [CICR]=0x00367F80, Pending [CIPR]=0x00008000
Mask   [CIMR]=0x40204000, In-srv  [CISR]=0x00000000
Command register [CR]=0x600
Port A [PADIR]=0x1100, [PAPAR]=0xFFFF
       [PAODR]=0x0000, [PADAT]=0xEFFF
Port B [PBDIR]=0x09C0F, [PBPAR]=0x0800E
       [PBODR]=0x0000E, [PBDAT]=0x3E77D
Port C [PCDIR]=0x00C, [PCPAR]=0x000
       [PCSO]=0xC20,  [PCDAT]=0xFC0, [PCINT]=0x00F
Receive Ring
       rmd(68012830): status 9000 length 1F address 3D3FC84
       rmd(68012838): status 9000 length 42 address 3D41D04
       rmd(68012840): status 9000 length F address 3D43D84
       rmd(68012848): status 9000 length 42 address 3D43084
       rmd(68012850): status 9000 length 42 address 3D3E904
       rmd(68012858): status 9000 length 157 address 3D43704
Transmit Ring
       tmd(680128B0): status 5C00 length 40 address 3C01114
       tmd(680128B8): status 5C00 length D address 3C00FD4
       tmd(680128C0): status 5C00 length 40 address 3C00FD4
       tmd(680128C8): status 5C00 length D address 3C00E94
       tmd(680128D0): status 5C00 length 11A address 3D6E394
       tmd(680128D8): status 5C00 length 40 address 3C019D4
       tmd(680128E0): status 5C00 length 40 address 3C01ED4
       tmd(680128E8): status 5C00 length D address 3D58BD4
       tmd(680128F0): status 5C00 length 40 address 3D58954
       tmd(680128F8): status 5C00 length 40 address 3D59214
       tmd(68012900): status 5C00 length D address 3D59494
```

continues

Example 5-1 *TX Queue Length: Finding the Length, and Changing the Length (Continued)*

```
          tmd(68012908): status 5C00 length 40 address 3D59AD4
          tmd(68012910): status 5C00 length 40 address 3C00214
          tmd(68012918): status 5C00 length D address 3C01C54
          tmd(68012920): status 5C00 length 40 address 3C005D4
          tmd(68012928): status 7C00 length 40 address 3C00714

tx_limited=0(16)

SCC GENERAL PARAMETER RAM (at 0x68013C00)
Rx BD Base [RBASE]=0x2830, Fn Code [RFCR]=0x18
Tx BD Base [TBASE]=0x28B0, Fn Code [TFCR]=0x18
Max Rx Buff Len [MRBLR]=1548
Rx State [RSTATE]=0x18008440, BD Ptr [RBPTR]=0x2840
Tx State [TSTATE]=0x18000548, BD Ptr [TBPTR]=0x28C8

SCC HDLC PARAMETER RAM (at 0x68013C38)
CRC Preset [C_PRES]=0xFFFF, Mask [C_MASK]=0xF0B8
Errors: CRC [CRCEC]=0, Aborts [ABTSC]=0, Discards [DISFC]=0
Nonmatch Addr Cntr [NMARC]=0
Retry Count [RETRC]=0
Max Frame Length [MFLR]=1608
Rx Int Threshold [RFTHR]=0, Frame Cnt [RFCNT]=65454
User-defined Address 0000/0000/0000/0000
User-defined Address Mask 0x0000

buffer size 1524

PowerQUICC SCC specific errors:
0 input aborts on receiving flag sequence
0 throttles, 0 enables
0 overruns
0 transmitter underruns
0 transmitter CTS losts
0 aborted short frames
!!!!!!!!!!!!!!!!!!!!!!!!!!!!!!!!!!!!!!!!!!!!!!!!!!!!!!!!!!!!!!!!!!!!!!
R3#conf t
Enter configuration commands, one per line.  End with CNTL/Z.
R3(config)#int s 0/0
R3(config-if)#priority-group 1
R3(config-if)#^Z
!!!!!!!!!!!!!!!!!!!!!!!!!!!!!!!!!!!!!!!!!!!!!!!!!!!!!!!!!!!!!!!!!!!!!!
R3#show controllers serial 0/0
01:03:09: %SYS-5-CONFIG_I: Configured from console by console
Interface Serial0/0
!!!!! Lines omitted to save space
tx_limited=1(2)
!!!!! Lines omitted to save space
```

Example 5-1 *TX Queue Length: Finding the Length, and Changing the Length (Continued)*

```
!!!!!!!!!!!!!!!!!!!!!!!!!!!!!!!!!!!!!!!!!!!!!!!!!!!!!!!!!!!!!!!!!!!!!!!!!
R3#conf t
Enter configuration commands, one per line.  End with CNTL/Z.
R3(config)#int s 0/0
R3(config-if)#no priority-group 1
R3(config-if)#tx-ring-limit 1
R3(config-if)#^Z
!!!!!!!!!!!!!!!!!!!!!!!!!!!!!!!!!!!!!!!!!!!!!!!!!!!!!!!!!!!!!!!!!!!!!!!!!
R3#show controllers serial 0/0
Interface Serial0/0
! Lines omitted to save space

tx_limited=0(1)

! Lines omitted to save space
```

The **show controllers serial 0/0** command lists the size of the TX Queue or TX Ring. In the shaded output in Example 5-1, the phrase "tx_limited=0(16)" means that the TX Ring (Hardware Queue) holds 16 packets. The zero means that the queue size is not currently limited due to a queuing tool being enabled on the interface. For the first instance of **show controllers**, no queuing method is enabled on the interface, so a zero signifies that the size of the TX Ring has not been limited automatically.

After enabling Priority Queuing with the **priority-group** interface subcommand, the next **show controllers** command lists "tx_limited=1(2)." The new length of the TX Ring is 2, and 1 means that the length is automatically limited as a result of queuing being configured. Next, Priority Queuing is disabled with the **no priority-group** interface subcommand, but the length of the TX Ring is explicitly defined with the **tx-ring-limit 1** interface subcommand. On the final **show controllers** command, the "tx_limited=0(1)" output implies that the size is not limited, because no queuing is enabled, but that the length of the TX Ring is 1.

The following list summarizes the key points about Hardware Queues in relation to their effect on software queuing:

■ The Hardware Queue always performs FIFO scheduling, and cannot be changed.

■ The Hardware Queue uses a single queue, per interface.

■ IOS shortens the interface Hardware Queue automatically when an software queuing method is configured.

■ The Hardware Queue length can be configured to a different value.

Queuing on Interfaces Versus Subinterfaces and Virtual Circuits (VCs)

IOS queuing tools create and manage Software Queues associated with an interface, and then the packets drain into the Hardware Queue associated with the interface. IOS also supports queuing on Frame Relay subinterfaces and individual Frame Relay VCs when traffic shaping is also enabled, as well as for individual ATM VCs. Shaping queues, created by the traffic-shaping feature, drain into the interface output queues, which then drain into the Hardware Queue. Like the interface Software Queues, the shaping queues and ATM per-VC queues can be managed with IOS queuing tools. (In this book, the specific coverage shows queuing tools applied to the queues created by Shaping tools for Frame Relay.)

The interaction between shaping queues associated with a subinterface or VC, and software queues associated with a physical interface, is not obvious at first glance. So, before moving into the details of the various queuing tools, consider what happens on subinterfaces, VCs, and physical interfaces so that you can make good choices about how to enable queuing in a router.

Figure 5-5 provides a reasonable backdrop from which to explain the interaction between queues. R1 has many Frame Relay permanent virtual circuits (PVCs) exiting its S0/0 physical interface. The figure shows queues associated with two of the PVCs, a single software queue for the physical interface, and the Hardware Queue for the interface.

Figure 5-5 *Subinterface Shaping Queues, Software Queues, and Hardware Queue*

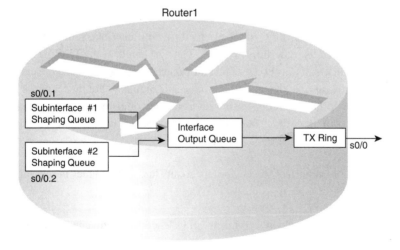

In this particular example, each subinterface uses a single FIFO shaping queue; a single software queue is associated with the physical interface. At first glance, it seems simple enough: a packet arrives, and the forwarding decision dictates that the packet should exit subinterface S0/0.1. It is placed into the subinterface 0/0.1 shaping queue, and then into the physical interface software queue, and then into the Hardware Queue. Then, it exits the interface.

In some cases, the packet moves from the shaping queues directly to the Hardware Queue. You may recall that packets are not even placed in the software queue if the Hardware Ring is not full! If no congestion occurs on the interface, the Hardware Ring does not fill. If no congestion occurs in the Hardware Ring, the interface software queue does not fill, and the queuing tool enabled on the interface has no effect on the packets exiting the interface.

In some cases, IOS does not place the packets into a shaping queue as they arrive, but instead the packets are placed into the Software queue or TX Queue. When the shaping features knows that a newly arrived packet does not exceed the shaping rate, there is no need to delay the packet. In that case, a queuing tool used for managing the shaping queue would also have no effect on that particular packet.

Traffic shaping can cause subinterface shaping queues to fill, even when there is no congestion on the physical interface. Traffic shaping, enabled on a subinterface or VC, slows down the flow of traffic leaving the subinterface or VC. In effect, traffic shaping on the subinterface creates congestion between the shaping queues and the physical interface software queues. On a physical interface, packets can only leave the interface at the physical clock rate used by the interface; similarly, packets can only leave a shaping queue at the traffic-shaping rate.

For example, the VC associated with subinterface S0/0.1 uses a 64 kbps committed information rate (CIR), and S0/0 uses a T/1 circuit. Without traffic shaping, more than 64 kbps of traffic could be sent for that PVC, and the only constraining factor would be the access rate (T/1). The Frame Relay network might discard some of the traffic, because the router may send more (up to 1.5 Mbps) on the VC, exceeding the traffic contract (64-kbps CIR). So, traffic shaping could be enabled on the subinterface or VC, restricting the overall rate for this PVC to 64 kbps, to avoid frame loss inside the Frame Relay network. If the offered load of traffic on the subinterface exceeds 64 kbps for some period, traffic shaping delays sending the excess traffic by placing the packets into the shaping queue associated with the subinterface, and draining the traffic from the shaping queue at the shaped rate.

Figure 5-6 shows an updated version of Figure 5-5; this one's PVC is currently exceeding the shaping rate, and the other PVC is not exceeding the shaping rate. In Figure 5-6, packets arrive and are routed out of each of the two subinterfaces. Traffic for subinterface 0/0.1 exceeds the shaping rate, and packets for subinterface 0/0.2 do not. Therefore, IOS places some packets into the shaping queue for subinterface 0/0.1, because traffic shaping delays packets by queuing the packets. On subinterface 0/0.2, IOS does not queue the packets, because the shaping rate has not been exceeded.

Figure 5-6 *Shaping Active on One VC, and Not Active on the Other*

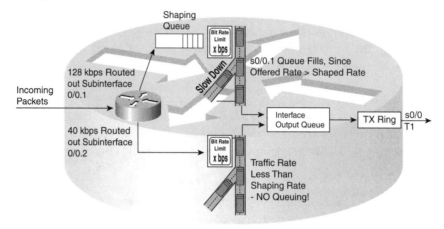

You can configure queuing tools to create and manage the software queues on a physical interface, as well as the shaping queues created by traffic shaping. The concepts in this chapter apply to using software queuing on both the main interface, and on any shaping queues. However, this chapter only covers the configuration of queuing to manipulate the interface software queues. Chapter 6, "Traffic Policing and Shaping," which covers traffic shaping, explains how to configure queuing for use on shaping queues. When reading the next chapter, keep these queuing concepts in mind and watch for the details of how to enable your favorite queuing tools for shaping queues.

Summary of Queuing Concepts

For the remainder of this chapter, queuing tools are compared based on the six general points listed in this section. Figure 5-7 outlines these points in the same sequence that each point is listed in the upcoming sections on each queuing tool.

Figure 5-7 *Six Comparison Points for IOS Queuing Tools*

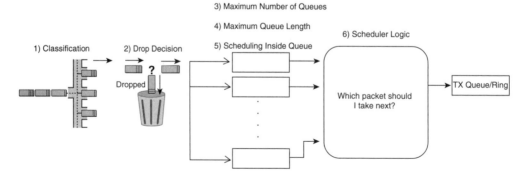

Scheduling gets the most attention when network engineers choose which queuing tool to use for a particular application. However, the other components of queuing are important as well. For instance, if the classification part of a queuing tool cannot classify the traffic as defined in the QoS policy for the network, either the policy must be changed or another tool must be used. One such example would be that PQ and CQ cannot take direct advantage of network-based application recognition (NBAR), but CBWFQ and LLQ can. In addition, some queuing tools allow a drop policy for each queue, which becomes particularly important when voice and video compete with data traffic in a converged network.

Scheduling Concepts: FIFO, PQ, CQ, and MDRR

For the purposes of QOS exam preparation, you need to know how Cisco IOS Queuing tools perform scheduling. Scheduling refers to the logic a queuing tool uses to pick the queue from which it will take the next packet. For some Queuing tools, you need to understand only the basic concepts, focusing on the scheduling logic. Those tools and concepts are covered in this section.

Later, in the last and most detailed section of this chapter, you will read about three of the most popular Queuing tools—WFQ, CBWFQ, and LLQ. For these tools, you need to know both the concepts and how to configure the tools.

FIFO Queuing

The first reason that a router needs software queues is to hold a packet while waiting for the interface to become available for sending the packet. Whereas the other queuing tools in this chapter also perform other functions, like reordering packets through scheduling, FIFO Queuing just provides a means to hold packets while they are waiting to exit an interface.

FIFO Queuing does not need the two most interesting features of the other queuing tools, namely classification and scheduling. FIFO Queuing uses a single software queue for the interface. Because there is only one queue, there is no need for classification to decide the queue into which the packet should be placed. Also there is no need for scheduling logic to pick which queue from which to take the next packet. The only really interesting part of FIFO Queuing is the queue length, which is configurable, and how the queue length affects delay and loss.

FIFO Queuing uses tail drop to decide when to drop or enqueue packets. If you configure a longer FIFO queue, more packets can be in the queue, which means that the queue will be less likely to fill. If the queue is less likely to fill, fewer packets will be dropped. However, with a longer queue, packets may experience more delay and jitter. With a shorter queue, less delay occurs, but the single FIFO queue fills more quickly, which in turn causes more tail drops of new packets. These facts are true for any queuing method, including FIFO.

Figure 5-8 outlines simple FIFO Queuing. R1 uses FIFO Queuing on the interface connected to R2. The only decision required when configuring FIFO Queuing is whether to change the length of the queue.

Figure 5-8 *Simple FIFO Queuing*

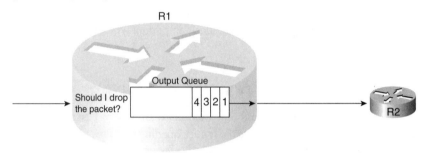

Remember to consider two steps when configuring FIFO Queuing. First, configuring FIFO Queuing actually requires you to turn off all other types of queuing, as opposed to just configuring FIFO Queuing. Cisco IOS uses WFQ as the default queuing method on serial interfaces running at E1 speeds and slower. However, IOS does not supply a command to enable FIFO Queuing; to enable FIFO Queuing, you must first disable WFQ by using the **no fair-queue** interface subcommand. If other queuing tools have been explicitly configured, you should also disable these. Just by removing all other queuing configuration from an interface, you have enabled FIFO!

The second FIFO configuration step that you might consider is to override the default queue length. To do so, use the **hold-queue x out** interface subcommand to reset the length of the queue.

Example 5-2 shows a sample FIFO Queuing configuration.

Example 5-2 *FIFO Queuing Configuration*

```
R3#conf t
Enter configuration commands, one per line.  End with CNTL/Z.
R3(config)#int s 0/0
R3(config-if)#no fair-queue
R3(config-if)#^Z
R3#sh int s 0/0
Serial0/0 is up, line protocol is up
 Hardware is PowerQUICC Serial
 Description: connected to FRS port S0. Single PVC to R1.
 MTU 1500 bytes, BW 1544 Kbit, DLY 20000 usec,
 reliability 255/255, txload 1/255, rxload 1/255
 Encapsulation FRAME-RELAY, loopback not set
 Keepalive set (10 sec)
 LMI enq sent 80, LMI stat recvd 73, LMI upd recvd 0, DTE LMI up
```

Example 5-2 *FIFO Queuing Configuration (Continued)*

```
LMI enq recvd 0, LMI stat sent 0, LMI upd sent 0
LMI DLCI 1023 LMI type is CISCO frame relay DTE
Broadcast queue 0/64, broadcasts sent/dropped 171/2, interface broadcasts 155
Last input 00:00:02, output 00:00:03, output hang never
Last clearing of "show interface" counters 00:13:48
Input queue: 0/75/0/0 (size/max/drops/flushes); Total output drops: 0
Queueing strategy: fifo
Output queue :0/40 (size/max)
30 second input rate 0 bits/sec, 0 packets/sec
30 second output rate 0 bits/sec, 0 packets/sec
235 packets input, 14654 bytes, 0 no buffer
Received 0 broadcasts, 0 runts, 0 giants, 0 throttles
2 input errors, 0 CRC, 2 frame, 0 overrun, 0 ignored, 0 abort
264 packets output, 15881 bytes, 0 underruns
0 output errors, 0 collisions, 6 interface resets
0 output buffer failures, 0 output buffers swapped out
10 carrier transitions
DCD=up  DSR=up  DTR=up  RTS=up  CTS=up

R3#conf t
Enter configuration commands, one per line.  End with CNTL/Z.
R3(config)#int s 0/0
R3(config-if)#hold-queue 50 out
R3(config-if)#^Z
!
R3#sh int s 0/0
Serial0/0 is up, line protocol is up
 Hardware is PowerQUICC Serial
! Lines omitted for brevity
 Queueing strategy: fifo
 Output queue :0/50 (size/max)
! Line omitted for brevity
```

Example 5-2 shows FIFO Queuing being configured by removing the default WFQ configuration with the **no fair-queue** command. The **show interface** command lists the fact that FIFO Queuing is used, and the output queue has 40 entries maximum. After configuring the output queue to hold 50 packets with the **hold-queue 50 out** command, the **show interface** output still lists FIFO Queuing, but now with a maximum queue size of 50.

FIFO Queuing is pretty basic, but it does provide a useful function: It provides the basic queuing function of holding packets until the interface is no longer busy.

Priority Queuing

Priority Queuing's most distinctive feature is its scheduler. PQ schedules traffic such that the higher-priority queues always get serviced, with the side effect of starving the lower-priority queues. With a maximum of four queues, called High, Medium, Normal, and Low, the complete logic of the scheduler can be easily represented, as is shown in Figure 5-9.

Figure 5-9 *PQ Scheduling Logic*

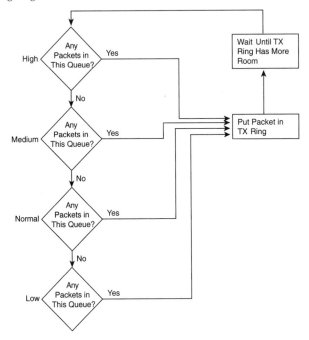

As seen in Figure 5-9, if the High queue always has a packet waiting, the scheduler will always take the packets in the High queue. If the High queue does not have a packet waiting, but the Medium queue does, one packet is taken from the Medium queue—and then the process always starts over at the High queue. The Low queue only gets serviced if the High, Medium, and Normal queues do not have any packets waiting.

The PQ scheduler has some obvious benefits and drawbacks. Packets in the High queue can claim 100 percent of the link bandwidth, with minimal delay, and minimal jitter. The lower queues suffer, however. In fact, when congested, packets in the lower queues take significantly longer to be serviced than under lighter loads. When the link is congested, user applications may stop working if their packets are placed into lower-priority queues.

The fact that PQ starves lower priority queues makes it a relatively unpopular choice for queuing today. Also, LLQ tends to be a better choice, because LLQ's scheduler has the capability to service high priority packets first while preventing the higher priority queues from starving the lower priority queues. If you would like to read more about the concepts behind PQ, as well as how to configure it, refer to Appendix B, "Additional QoS Reference Materials," (found on the book's accompanying CD-ROM).

Custom Queuing

Historically, Custom Queuing (CQ) followed PQ as the next IOS queuing tool added to IOS. CQ addresses the biggest drawback of PQ by providing a queuing tool that does service all queues, even during times of congestion. It has 16 queues available, implying 16 classification categories, which is plenty for most applications. The negative part of CQ, as compared to PQ, is that CQ's scheduler does not have an option to always service one queue first — like PQ's High queue — so CQ does not provide great service for delay- and jitter-sensitive traffic.

As with most queuing tools, the most interesting part of the tool is the scheduler. The CQ scheduler reserves an approximate percentage of overall link bandwidth to each queue. CQ approximates the bandwidth percentages, as opposed to meeting an exact percentage, due to the simple operation of the CQ scheduler. Figure 5-10 depicts the CQ scheduler logic.

Figure 5-10   *CQ Scheduling Logic for Current Queue*

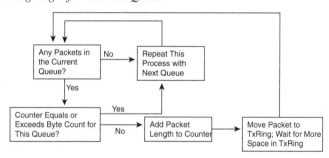

The CQ scheduler performs round-robin service on each queue, beginning with Queue 1. CQ takes packets from the queue, until the total byte count specified for the queue has been met or exceeded. After the queue has been serviced for that many bytes, or the queue does not have any more packets, CQ moves on to the next queue, and repeats the process.

CQ does not configure the exact link bandwidth percentage, but rather it configures the number of bytes taken from each queue during each round-robin pass through the queues. Suppose, for example, that an engineer configures CQ to use five queues. The engineer assigns a byte count of 10,000 bytes for each queue. With this configuration, the engineer has reserved 20 percent of the link bandwidth for each queue. (If each queue sends 10,000 bytes, a total of 50,000 bytes are sent per cycle, so each queue sends 10,000/50,000 of the bytes out of the interface, or 20 percent.) If instead the engineer has assigned byte counts of 5,000 bytes for the first 2 queues, 10,000 for the next 2 queues, and 20,000 for the fifth queue, the total bytes sent in each pass through the queues would again total 50,000 bytes. Therefore, Queues 1 and 2 would get 5,000/50,000, or 10 percent of the link bandwidth. Queues 3 and 4 would get 10000/50000, or 20 percent of the bandwidth, and Queue 5 would get 20000/50000, or 40 percent. The following formula calculates the implied bandwidth percentage for Queue x:

(Byte Count for Queue x)/(Sum of Byte Counts for All Queues)

The CQ scheduler essentially guarantees the minimum bandwidth for each queue, while allowing queues to have more bandwidth under the right conditions. Imagine that 5 queues have been configured with the byte counts of 5,000, 5,000, 10,000, 10,000, and 20,000 for queues 1 through 5, respectively. If all 5 queues have plenty of packets to send, the percentage bandwidth given to each queue is 10 percent, 10 percent, 20 percent, 20 percent, and 40 percent, as described earlier. However, suppose that Queue 4 has no traffic over some short period of time. For that period, when the CQ scheduler tries to service Queue 4, it notices that no packets are waiting. The CQ scheduler moves immediately to the next queue. Over this short period of time, only Queues 1 through 3 and Queue 5 have packets waiting. In this case, the queues would receive 12.5 percent, 12.5 percent, 25 percent, 0 percent, and 50 percent of link bandwidth, respectively. (The math to get these percentages is number-of-bytes-per-cycle/40,000 because around 40,000 bytes should be taken from the four active queues per cycle.) Note also that queues that have not been configured are automatically skipped.

Unlike PQ, CQ does not name the queues, but it numbers the queues 1 through 16. No single queue has a better treatment by the scheduler than another, other than the number of bytes serviced for each queue. So, in the example in the last several paragraphs, Queue 5, with 20000 bytes serviced on each turn, might be considered to be the "best" queue with this configuration. Do not be fooled by that assumption! If the traffic classified into Queue 5 comprises 80 percent of the offered traffic, the traffic in Queue 5 may get the worst treatment among all 5 queues. And of course, the traffic patterns will change over short periods of time, and over long periods. Therefore, whereas understanding the scheduler logic is pretty easy, choosing the actual numbers requires some traffic analysis, and good guessing to some degree.

If you would like to read more about CQ, refer to Appendix B.

Modified Deficit Round-Robin

Modified Deficit Round-Robin (MDRR) is specifically designed for the Gigabit Switch Router (GSR) models of Internet routers. In fact, MDRR is supported only on the GSR 12000 series routers, and the other queuing tools (WFQ, CBWFQ, PQ, CQ, and so on) are not supported on the GSRs. Don't worry—you won't have to know the details of MDRR configuration, but you should at least know how the MDRR scheduler works.

The MDRR scheduler is similar to the CQ scheduler in that it reserves a percentage of link bandwidth for a particular queue. As you probably recall, the CQ scheduler uses a round-robin approach to services queues. By taking one or more packets from each configured queue, CQ gives the packets in each queue a chance to be sent out the interface.

The MDRR scheduler uses a round-robin approach, but the details differ slightly from CQ in order to overcome a negative effect of CQ's scheduler. The CQ scheduler has a problem with trying to provide an exact percentage bandwidth.

For example, suppose a router uses CQ on an interface, with three queues, with the byte counts configured to 1500, 1500, and 1500. Now suppose that all the packets in the queues are 1500 bytes. (This is not going to happen in real life, but it is useful for making the point.) CQ takes a 1500-byte packet, notices that it has met the byte count, and moves to the next queue. In effect, CQ takes one 1500-byte packet from each queue, and each queue gets one third of the link bandwidth. Now suppose that Queue 3 has been configured to send 1501 bytes per queue service, and all the packets in all queues are still 1500 bytes long. CQ takes 1 packet from Queue 1, 1 from Queue 2, and then 2 packets from Queue 3! CQ does not fragment the second 1500-byte packet taken from Queue 3. In effect, Queue 3 sends two 1500-byte packets for every one packet sent from Queues 1 and 2, effectively giving 25 percent of the bandwidth each to Queues 1 and 2, and 50 percent of the link bandwidth to Queue 3.

MDRR supports two types of scheduling, one of which uses the same general algorithm as CQ. MDRR removes packets from a queue, until the quantum value (QV) for that queue has been removed. The QV quantifies a number of bytes, and is used much like the byte count is used by the CQ scheduler. MDRR repeats the process for every queue, in order from 0 through 7, and then repeats this round-robin process. The end result is that each queue gets some percentage bandwidth of the link.

MDRR deals with the CQ scheduler's problem by treating any "extra" bytes sent during a cycle as a "deficit." If too many bytes were taken from a queue, next time around through the queues, the number of "extra" bytes sent by MDRR is subtracted from the QV. In effect, if more than the QV is sent from a queue in one pass, that many less bytes are taken in the next pass. As a result, the MDRR scheduler provides an exact bandwidth reservation.

Figure 5-11 shows an example of how MDRR works. In this case, MDRR is using only two queues, with QVs of 1500 and 3000, respectively, and with all packets at 1000 bytes in length.

Figure 5-11 *MDRR: Making Up Deficits*

Note: All Packets are 1000 bytes long!

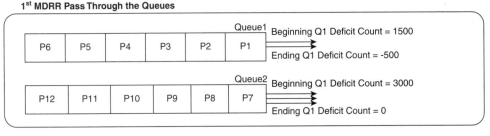

1st MDRR Pass Through the Queues

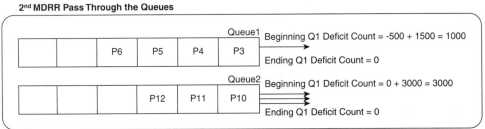

2nd MDRR Pass Through the Queues

First, some extra information on how to interpret Figure 5-11 might help. The figure shows the action during the first round-robin pass in the top half of the figure, and the action during the second pass in the lower half of the figure. The example begins with six packets (labeled P1 through P6) in Queue 1, and six packets (labeled P7 through P12) in Queue 2. Each arrowed line, attached to the right sides of the queues, and pointing to the right, represents the choice by MDRR to send a single packet.

When a queue first fills, the queue's deficit counter (DC) is set to the QV for that queue, which is 1500 for Queue 1, and 3000 for Queue 2. In Figure 5-11, MDRR begins by taking one packet from Queue 1, decrementing the DC to 500, and deciding that the DC has not been decremented to 0 (or less). MDRR takes a second packet from Queue 1, decrementing the DC to –500. MDRR then moves on to Queue 2, taking three packets, after which the DC for Queue 2 has decremented to 0.

That concludes the first round-robin pass through the queues. MDRR has taken 2000 bytes from Queue 1, and 3000 from Queue 2, giving the queues 40 percent and 60 percent of link bandwidth, respectively.

In the second round-robin pass, shown in the lower half of Figure 5-11, the process begins by MDRR adding the QV for each queue to the DC for each queue. Queue 1's DC becomes 1500 + –500, or 1000, to begin the second pass. During this pass, MDRR takes P3 from Queue 1, decrements DC to 0, and then moves on to Queue 2. After taking three more packets from Queue 3, decrementing Queue 2's DC to 0, MDRR completes the second pass. Over these two round-robin passes, MDRR has taken 3000 bytes from Queue 1, and 6000 from Queue 2—which is the same ratio as the ratio between the QVs.

With the deficit feature of MDRR, over time each queue receives a guaranteed bandwidth based on the following formula:

$$\frac{\text{QV for Queue X}}{\text{Sum of all QVs}}$$

> **NOTE**   For additional examples of the operation of the MDRR deficit feature, refer to http://www.cisco.com/warp/public/63/toc_18841.html. Alternatively, you can go to www.cisco.com and search for "Understanding and Configuring MDRR and WRED on the Cisco 12000 Series Internet Router."

Concepts and Configuration: WFQ, CBWFQ, and LLQ

The previous section explained four different types of queuing, focusing on the scheduler for each tool. Of those schedulers, one of the best features is the low latency treatment of packets in PQ's high priority queue. Packets in PQ's high queue always get serviced first, and spend very little time sitting in the queue. The other very useful scheduling feature was the capability to essentially reserve bandwidth for a particular queue with CQ or MDRR.

In this section, you will read about both the concepts and configuration for the three most commonly used Queuing tools in Cisco routers. CBWFQ uses a scheduler similar to CQ and MDRR, reserving link bandwidth for each queue. LLQ combines the bandwidth reservation feature of CBWFQ with a PQ-like high priority queue, called a Low Latency Queue, which allows delay-sensitive traffic to spend little time in the queue. But first, this section begins with WFQ, which uses a completely different scheduler.

Weighted Fair Queuing (WFQ)

Weighted Fair Queuing differs from PQ and CQ in several significant ways. The first and most obvious difference is that WFQ does not allow classification options to be configured! WFQ classifies packets based on flows. A *flow* consists of all packets that have the same source and destination IP address, and the same source and destination port numbers. So, no explicit matching is configured. The other large difference between WFQ versus PQ and CQ is the scheduler, which simply favors low-volume, higher-precedence flows over large-volume, lower-precedence flows. Also because WFQ is flow based, and each flow uses a different queue, the number of queues becomes rather large—up to a maximum of 4096 queues per interface. And although WFQ uses tail drop, it really uses a slightly modified tail-drop scheme—yet another difference.

Ironically, WFQ requires the least configuration of all the queuing tools in this chapter, yet it requires the most explanation to achieve a deep understanding. The extra work to read through the conceptual details will certainly help on the exam, plus it will give you a better appreciation for WFQ, which may be the most pervasively deployed QoS tool in Cisco routers.

WFQ Classification

Flow-Based WFQ, or just WFQ, classifies traffic into flows. Flows are identified by at least five items in an IP packet:

- Source IP address

- Destination IP address

- Transport layer protocol (TCP or UDP) as defined by the IP Protocol header field

- TCP or UDP source port

- TCP or UDP destination port

- IP Precedence

Depending on what document you read, WFQ also classifies based on the ToS byte, or more specifically, the IP Precedence field inside the ToS byte. Most documentation just lists the first five fields in the preceding list.

Whether WFQ uses the ToS byte or not when classifying packets, practically speaking, does not matter much. Good design suggests that packets in a single flow ought to have their Precedence or DSCP field set to the same value — so the same packets would get classified into the same flow, regardless of whether WFQ cares about the ToS byte or not for classification. (Regardless of whether you think of WFQ as classifying on ToS, or precedence, it is definitely true that the precedence of a packet impacts how the WFQ scheduler works.)

The term "flow" can have a couple of different meanings. For instance, imagine a PC that is downloading a web page. The user sees the page appear, reads the page for 10 seconds, and clicks a button. A second web page appears, the user reads the page for 10 seconds, and clicks another button. All the pages and objects came from a single web server, and all the pages and objects were loaded using a single TCP connection between the PC and the server. How many different combinations of source/destination, address/port, and transport layer protocol, are used? How many different flows?

From a commonsense perspective, only one flow exists in this example, because only one TCP connection is used. From WFQ's perspective, no flows may have occurred, or three flows existed, and possibly even more. To most people, a single TCP flow exists as long as the TCP connection stays up, because the packets in that connection always have the same source address, source port, destination address, and destination port information. However, WFQ considers a flow to exist only as long as packets from that flow need to be enqueued. For instance, while the user is reading the web pages for 10 seconds, the routers finish sending all packets sent by the web server, so the queue for that flow is empty. Because the intermediate routers had no packets queued in the queue for that flow, WFQ removes the flow. Similarly, even while transferring different objects that comprise a web page, if WFQ empties a flow's queue, it removes the queue, because it is no longer needed.

Why does it matter that flows come and go quickly from WFQ's perspective? With class-based schemes, you always know how many queues you have, and you can see some basic statistics for each queue. With WFQ, the number of flows, and therefore the number of queues, changes very quickly. Although you can see statistics about active flows, you can bet on the information changing before you can type the **show queue** command again. The statistics show you information about the short-lived flow — for instance, when downloading the third web page in the previous example, the **show queue** command tells you about WFQ's view of the flow, which may have begun when the third web page was being transferred, as opposed to when the TCP connection was formed.

WFQ Scheduler: The Net Effect

Cisco publishes information about how the WFQ scheduler works. Even with an understanding of how the scheduler works, however, the true goals behind the scheduler are not obvious. This section reflects on what WFQ provides, and the following sections describe how WFQ accomplishes the task.

The WFQ scheduler has two main goals. The first is to provide fairness among the currently existing flows. To provide fairness, WFQ gives each flow an equal amount of bandwidth. If 10 flows exist for an interface, and the bandwidth is 128 kbps, each flow effectively gets 12.8 kbps. If 100 flows exist, each flow gets 1.28 kbps. In some ways, this goal is similar to a time-division multiplexing (TDM) system, but the number of time slots is not preset, but instead based on the number of flows currently exiting an interface. Also keep in mind that the concept of equal shares of bandwidth for each flow is a goal — for example, the actual scheduler logic used to accomplish this goal is much different from the bandwidth reservation using byte counts with CQ.

With each flow receiving its fair share of the link bandwidth, the lower-volume flows prosper, and the higher-volume flows suffer. Think of that 128-kbps link again, for instance, with 10 flows. If Flow 1 needs 5 kbps, and WFQ allows 12.8 kbps per flow, the queue associated with Flow 1 may never have more than a few packets in it, because the packets will drain quickly. If Flow 2 needs 30 kbps, then packets will back up in Flow 2's queue, because WFQ only gives this queue 12.8 kbps as well. These packets experience more delay and jitter, and possibly loss if the queue fills. Of course, if Flow 1 only needs 5 kbps, the actual WFQ scheduler allows other flows to use the extra bandwidth.

The second goal of the WFQ scheduler is to provide more bandwidth to flows with higher IP precedence values. The preference of higher-precedence flows is implied in the name — "Weighted" implies that the fair share is weighted, and it is weighted based on precedence. With 10 flows on a 128-kbps link, for example, if 5 of the flows use precedence 0, and 5 use precedence 1, WFQ might want to give the precedence 1 flows twice as much bandwidth as the precedence 0 flows. Therefore, 5 precedence 0 flows would receive roughly 8.5 kbps each, and 5 precedence 1 flows would receive roughly 17 kbps each. In fact, WFQ provides a fair share roughly based on the ratio of each flow's precedence, plus one. In other words, precedence 7 flows get 8 times more bandwidth than does precedence 0 flows, because $(7 + 1) / (0 + 1) = 8$. If you compare precedence 3 to precedence 0, the ratio is roughly $(3 + 1) / (0 + 1) = 4$.

So, what does WFQ accomplish? Ignoring precedence for a moment, the short answer is lower-volume flows get relatively better service, and higher-volume flows get worse service. Higher-precedence flows get better service than lower-precedence flows. If lower-volume flows are given higher-precedence values, the bandwidth/delay/jitter/loss characteristics improve even more.

In a network where most of the delay-sensitive traffic is lower-volume traffic, WFQ is a great solution. It takes one command to enable it, and it is already enabled by default! Its default behavior favors lower-volume flows, which may be the more important flows. In fact, WFQ came out when many networks' most important interactive flows were Telnet and Systems Network Architecture (SNA) encapsulated in IP. These types of flows used much less volume than other flows, so WFQ provided a great default, without having to worry about how to perform prioritization on encapsulated SNA traffic.

WFQ Scheduler: The Process

WFQ gives each flow a weighted percentage of link bandwidth. However, WFQ does not predefine queues like class-based queuing tools do, because WFQ dynamically creates queues to hold the packets in each flow. And although WFQ ends up causing each flow to get some percentage of link bandwidth, the percentage changes, and changes rapidly, because flows come and go frequently. Because each flow may have different precedence values, the percentage of link bandwidth for each flow will change, and it will change very quickly, as each flow is added or removed. In short, WFQ simply could not be implemented by assigning a percentage of bandwidth, or a byte count, to each queue.

The WFQ scheduler is actually very simple. When the Hardware Queue frees a slot, WFQ can move one packet to the Hardware Queue, just like any other queuing tool. The WFQ scheduler takes the packet with the lowest *sequence number* (SN) among all the queues, and moves it to the Hardware Queue. The SN is assigned when the packet is placed into a queue, which is where the interesting part of WFQ scheduling takes place.

> **CAUTION** The Cisco QoS course uses the term "Finish Time" (FT) instead of Sequence Number, but its usage is identical to the coverage shown here. You should be aware of both terms for the exam.

For perspective on the sequence of events, marking the SN, and serving the queues, examine Figure 5-12.

Figure 5-12 *WFQ: Assigning Sequence Numbers and Servicing Queues*

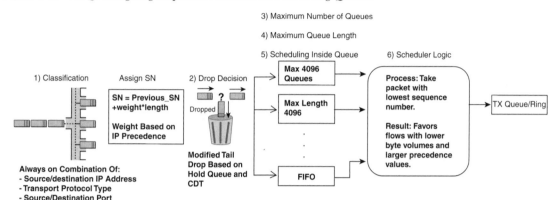

WFQ calculates the SN before adding a packet to its associated queue. In fact, WFQ calculates the SN before making the drop decision, because the SN is part of the modified tail-drop logic. The WFQ scheduler considers both packet length and precedence when calculating the SN. The formula for calculating the SN for a packet is as follows:

Previous_SN + (weight * new_packet_length)

Where "weight" is calculated as follows:

Weight = 32,384 / (IP_Precedence + 1)

The formula considers the length of the new packet, the weight of the flow, and the previous SN. By considering the packet length, the SN calculation results in a higher number for larger packets, and a lower number for smaller packets. The formula considers the SN of the most recently enqueued packet in the queue for the new sequence number. By including the SN of the previous packet enqueued into that queue, the formula assigns a larger number for packets in queues that already have a larger number of packets enqueued.

The third component of the formula, the weight, is the most interesting part. The WFQ scheduler sends the packet with the lowest SN next, and WFQ wants to give more bandwidth to the higher-precedence flows. So, the weight values are inversely proportional to the precedence values. Table 5-5 lists the weight values used by WFQ as of 12.0(5)T/12.1.

Table 5-3 *WFQ Weight Values, as of 12.0(5)T/12.1*

Precedence	After 12.0(5)T/12.1
0	32384
1	16192
2	10794
3	8096
4	6476
5	5397
6	4626
7	4048

As seen in the table, the larger the precedence value, the lower the weight, in turn making the SN lower. An example certainly helps for a fuller understanding. Consider the example in Figure 5-13, which illustrates one existing flow and one new flow.

Figure 5-13 *WFQ Sequence Number Assignment Example*

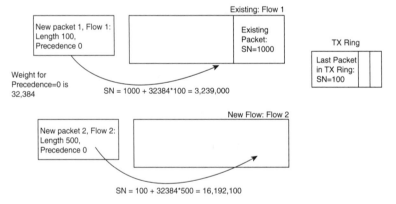

When adding new packet 1 to the queue for Flow 1, WFQ just runs the formula against the length of the new packet (100) and the weight, adding the SN of the last packet in the queue to which the new packet will be added. For new flows, the same formula is used; because there are no other packets in the queue, however, the SN of the most recently sent packet, in this case 100, is used in the formula. In either case, WFQ assigns larger SN values for larger packets and for those with lower IP precedence.

A more detailed example can show some of the effects of the WFQ SN assignment algorithm and how it achieves its basic goals. Figure 5-14 shows a set of four flow queues, each with four packets of varying lengths. For the sake of discussion, assume that the SN of the previously sent packet is zero in this case. Each flow's first packet arrives at the same instant in time, and all packets for all flows arrive before any more packets can be taken from the WFQ queues.

Figure 5-14 *WFQ Sequence Number Assignment Example 2*

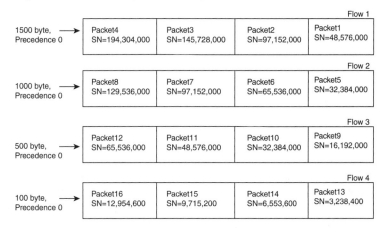

In this example, each flow had four packets arrive, all with a precedence of zero. The packets in Flow 1 were all 1500 bytes in length; in Flow 2, the packets were 1000 bytes in length; in Flow 3, they were 500 bytes; and finally, in Flow 4, they were 100 bytes. With equal precedence values, the Flow 4 packets should get better service, because the packets are much smaller. In fact, all four of Flow 4's packets would be serviced before any of the packets in the other flows. Flow 3's packets are sent before most of the packets in Flow 1 and Flow 2. Thus, the goal of giving the lower-volume flows better service is accomplished, assuming the precedence values are equal.

NOTE   For the record, the order the packets would exit the interface, assuming no other events occur, is 13 first, then 14, followed by 15, 16, 9, 5, 1, 11, 6, 12, 2, 7, 8, 10, 3, 4.

To see the effect of different precedence values, look at Figure 5-15, which lists the same basic scenario but with varying precedence values.

Figure 5-15 *WFQ Sequence Number Assignment with Varying Precedence Values*

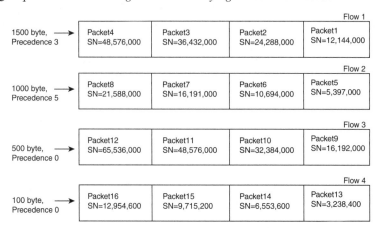

The SNs for Flow 1 and Flow 2 improve dramatically with the higher precedence values of 3 and 5, respectively. Flow 4 still gets relatively good service, even at precedence 0. Two packets from Flow 2, and one from Flow 1, will be serviced before Flow 4's fourth packet (SN 12,954,600), which is an example of how the higher precedence value gives the packets in this flow slightly better service. So, the lower-volume, but lower-precedence flows will have some degradation in service relative to the higher-volume, but higher-precedence flows.

> **NOTE** For the record, the order the packets would exit the interface, assuming no other events occur, is 13, 5, 14, 15, 6, 1, 16, 7, 9, 2, 8, 10, 3, 4, 11, 12.

Finally, a router using WFQ can experience a phenomenon called *too fair*. With many flows, WFQ will give some bandwidth to every flow. In the previous example, what happens if 200 new flows begin? Each of those new flows will get a relatively low SN, because the SN of the most recently sent packet is used in the formula. The packets that are already in the existing queues will have to wait on all the new packets. In an effort to give each flow some of the link bandwidth, WFQ may actually not give some or most of the flows enough bandwidth for them to survive.

WFQ Drop Policy, Number of Queues, and Queue Lengths

WFQ uses a slightly modified tail-drop policy for choosing when to drop packets. The decision is based on several factors, one being the SN of the packet.

WFQ places an absolute limit on the number of packets enqueued among all queues; this value is called the *hold-queue limit*. If a new packet arrives, and the hold-queue limit has been reached, the packet is discarded. That part of the decision is based not on a single queue, but on the whole WFQ queuing system for the interface.

The next decision is based on an individual queue. If a packet needs to be placed into a queue, and that queue's *congestive discard threshold* (CDT) has been reached, the packet may be thrown away. CDT is a little like a maximum queue length for each flow's queue, but WFQ puts a little twist on how the concept is used (hence the use of another term, instead of just calling it the maximum queue length). To appreciate how the CDT is used, examine Figure 5-16.

Figure 5-16   *WFQ Modified Tail Drop and Congestive Discard Threshold*

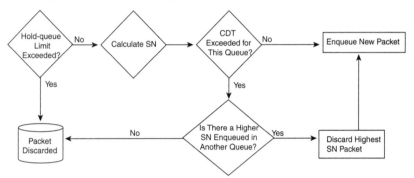

The hold-queue size limits the total number of packets in all of the flow or conversation queues. However, CDT limits the number of packets in each individual queue. If CDT packets are already in the queue into which a packet should be placed, WFQ considers discarding the new packet. Normally, the new packet is discarded. If a packet with a larger SN has already been enqueued in a different queue, however, WFQ instead discards the packet with the larger SN! It's like going to Disneyland, getting in line, and then being told that a bunch of VIPs showed up, so you cannot ride the ride, and you will have to come back later. (Hopefully Disney would not take you out of the line and send you to the bit bucket, though!) In short, WFQ can discard a packet in another flow when the queue for a different flow has exceeded CDT but still has lower sequence numbers. You can configure the CDT to a value between 1 and 4096, inclusive.

Finally, WFQ can be configured for a maximum of 4096 queues, but interestingly, the actual value can only be a power of 2 between 16 and 4096, inclusive. The IOS restricts the values because WFQ performs a hash algorithm to classify traffic, and the hash algorithm only works when the number of queues is one of these valid values.

Special WFQ Queues

Although you do not really need to know much detail for the QOS exam, there are a couple of types of WFQ queues about which you should at least be aware. First, WFQ keeps eight hidden queues for overhead traffic generated by the router. WFQ uses a very low weight for these queues in order to give preference to the overhead traffic.

The other type of queue isn't really hidden, but most people simply don't notice them. You can configure RSVP on the same interface as WFQ. As you might recall from Chapter 2, "QoS Tools and Architectures," RSVP reserves bandwidth on an interface. To reserve the bandwidth, RSVP asks WFQ to create a queue for each RSVP-reserved flow, and to give it a very low weight. As you will read in the next section, you can configure WFQ for the number of concurrent RSVP queues that can be used on an interface.

WFQ Configuration

Although WFQ requires a little deeper examination to understand all the underlying concepts, configuration is simple. IOS uses WFQ by default on all serial interfaces with bandwidths set at T/1 and E/1 speeds and below. None of WFQ's parameters can be set for an individual queue, so at most, the WFQ configuration will be one or two lines long. An example configuration for WFQ follows Tables 5-6 and 5-7. Tables 5-6 and 5-7 list the configuration and exec commands related to WFQ respectively.

Table 5-4 *Configuration Command Reference for WFQ*

Command	Mode and Function
fair-queue [*congestive-discard-threshold* [*dynamic-queues* [*reservable-queues*]]]	Interface configuration mode; enables WFQ, sets the CDT, sets maximum number of queues, and sets the number reserved for RSVP use
hold-queue *length* **out**	Interface configuration mode; changes the length of the hold queue

Table 5-5 *EXEC Command Reference for WFQ*

Command	Function
show queue *interface-name interface-number* [**vc** [*vpi/*] *vci*]]	Lists information about the packets that are waiting in a queue on the interface
show queueing [**custom** | **fair** | **priority** | **random-detect** [**interface** *atm-subinterface* [vc [[*vpi/*] *vci*]]]]	Lists configuration and statistical information about the queuing tool on an interface

In the next example, R3 uses WFQ on its S0/0 interface. R3 marks the packets as they enter E0/0, using CB marking. Two voice calls, plus one FTP download, and a large web page download generate the traffic. The web page is the same one used throughout the book, with competing frames on the left and right side of the page. Note that each of the two frames in the web page uses two separate TCP connections. The marking logic performed by CB marking is as follows:

■ VoIP payload — DSCP EF

■ HTTP traffic for web pages with "important" in the URL—DSCP AF21

- HTTP traffic for web pages with "not" in the URL—DSCP AF23

- All other—DSCP BE

Repetitive examples do not help much with WFQ, because there is little to configure. Example 5-3 shows the basic configuration, followed by some **show** commands. After that, it shows a few of the optional parameters being set. The example uses the familiar network diagram, as repeated in Figure 5-17.

Figure 5-17 *Sample WFQ Network—WFQ on R3's S0/0 Interface*

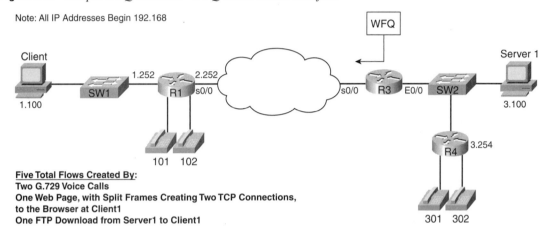

Note: All IP Addresses Begin 192.168

Five Total Flows Created By:
Two G.729 Voice Calls
One Web Page, with Split Frames Creating Two TCP Connections,
to the Browser at Client1
One FTP Download from Server1 to Client1

Example 5-3 *WFQ Configuration and **show** Commands*

```
R3#conf t
Enter configuration commands, one per line.  End with CNTL/Z.
R3(config)#int s 0/0
R3(config-if)#fair-queue
R3(config-if)#^Z
R3#sh int s 0/0
Serial0/0 is up, line protocol is up
  Hardware is PowerQUICC Serial
  Description: connected to FRS port S0. Single PVC to R1.
  MTU 1500 bytes, BW 1544 Kbit, DLY 20000 usec,
     reliability 255/255, txload 9/255, rxload 8/255
  Encapsulation FRAME-RELAY, loopback not set
  Keepalive set (10 sec)
  LMI enq sent  171, LMI stat recvd 163, LMI upd recvd 0, DTE LMI up
  LMI enq recvd 0, LMI stat sent  0, LMI upd sent  0
  LMI DLCI 1023  LMI type is CISCO  frame relay DTE
  Broadcast queue 0/64, broadcasts sent/dropped 378/2, interface broadcasts 347
  Last input 00:00:01, output 00:00:00, output hang never
  Last clearing of "show interface" counters 00:28:46
  Input queue: 0/75/0/0 (size/max/drops/flushes); Total output drops: 8249
```

continues

Example 5-3 *WFQ Configuration and **show** Commands (Continued)*

```
      Queueing strategy: weighted fair
      Output queue: 126/1000/64/8249 (size/max total/threshold/drops)
         Conversations  6/7/256 (active/max active/max total)
         Reserved Conversations 0/0 (allocated/max allocated)
         Available Bandwidth 1158 kilobits/sec
      5 minute input rate 52000 bits/sec, 97 packets/sec
      5 minute output rate 58000 bits/sec, 78 packets/sec
         36509 packets input, 2347716 bytes, 0 no buffer
         Received 0 broadcasts, 0 runts, 0 giants, 0 throttles
         1 input errors, 0 CRC, 1 frame, 0 overrun, 0 ignored, 0 abort
         28212 packets output, 2623792 bytes, 0 underruns
         0 output errors, 0 collisions, 5 interface resets
         0 output buffer failures, 0 output buffers swapped out
         10 carrier transitions
         DCD=up  DSR=up  DTR=up  RTS=up  CTS=up
R3#show queueing fair
Current fair queue configuration:

   Interface        Discard    Dynamic  Reserved  Link    Priority
                    threshold  queues   queues    queues  queues
   Serial0/0        64         256      0         8       1
   Serial0/1        64         256      0         8       1


R3#show queueing fair int s 0/0
Current fair queue configuration:

   Interface        Discard    Dynamic  Reserved  Link    Priority
                    threshold  queues   queues    queues  queues
   Serial0/0        64         256      0         8       1


R3# show queue s 0/0
   Input queue: 0/75/0/0 (size/max/drops/flushes); Total output drops: 11027
   Queueing strategy: weighted fair
   Output queue: 79/1000/64/11027 (size/max total/threshold/drops)
      Conversations  4/8/256 (active/max active/max total)
      Reserved Conversations 0/0 (allocated/max allocated)
      Available Bandwidth 1158 kilobits/sec


! Next stanza lists info about one of the VoIP calls
   (depth/weight/total drops/no-buffer drops/interleaves) 37/5397/1359/0/0
   Conversation 15, linktype: ip, length: 64
   source: 192.168.3.254, destination: 192.168.2.251, id: 0x013B, ttl: 253,
TOS: 184 prot: 17, source port 16772, destination port 19232
! Next stanza lists info about one of the VoIP calls
   (depth/weight/total drops/no-buffer drops/interleaves) 37/5397/1359/0/0
   Conversation 125, linktype: ip, length: 64
   source: 192.168.3.254, destination: 192.168.2.251, id: 0x0134, ttl: 253,
```

Example 5-3   *WFQ Configuration and **show** Commands (Continued)*

```
    TOS: 184 prot: 17, source port 16638, destination port 19476


! Next stanza lists info about one of the HTTP TCP connections
  (depth/weight/total drops/no-buffer drops/interleaves) 1/10794/36/0/0
  Conversation 33, linktype: ip, length: 1404
  source: 192.168.3.100, destination: 192.168.1.100, id: 0xFF50, ttl: 127,
    TOS: 72 prot: 6, source port 80, destination port 1067


! Next stanza lists info about one of the HTTP TCP connections
  (depth/weight/total drops/no-buffer drops/interleaves) 2/10794/34/0/0
  Conversation 34, linktype: ip, length: 1404
  source: 192.168.3.100, destination: 192.168.1.100, id: 0xFF53, ttl: 127,
    TOS: 88 prot: 6, source port 80, destination port 1068


! Notice the TOS values versus the weight in the last two stanzas!

R3#configure terminal
Enter configuration commands, one per line.  End with CNTL/Z.
R3(config)#int s 0/0
R3(config-if)#fair-queue 100 64 10
R3(config-if)#hold-queue 500 out
R3(config-if)#^Z
!
R3#show interface serial 0/0
Serial0/0 is up, line protocol is up
  Hardware is PowerQUICC Serial
  Description: connected to FRS port S0. Single PVC to R1.
  MTU 1500 bytes, BW 1544 Kbit, DLY 20000 usec,
     reliability 255/255, txload 9/255, rxload 8/255
  Encapsulation FRAME-RELAY, loopback not set
  Keepalive set (10 sec)
  LMI enq sent  198, LMI stat recvd 190, LMI upd recvd 0, DTE LMI up
  LMI enq recvd 0, LMI stat sent  0, LMI upd sent  0
  LMI DLCI 1023  LMI type is CISCO  frame relay DTE
  Broadcast queue 0/64, broadcasts sent/dropped 442/2, interface broadcasts 406
  Last input 00:00:01, output 00:00:00, output hang never
  Last clearing of "show interface" counters 00:33:14
  Input queue: 0/75/0/0 (size/max/drops/flushes); Total output drops: 12474
  Queueing strategy: weighted fair
  Output queue: 95/500/100/12474 (size/max total/threshold/drops)
     Conversations  5/6/64 (active/max active/max total)
     Reserved Conversations 0/0 (allocated/max allocated)
     Available Bandwidth 1158 kilobits/sec

! lines omitted for brevity

R3#show queueing fair
```

continues

Example 5-3 *WFQ Configuration and **show** Commands (Continued)*

```
Current fair queue configuration:

  Interface          Discard    Dynamic  Reserved  Link    Priority
                     threshold  queues   queues    queues  queues
  Serial0/0          100        64       10        8       1
  Serial0/1          64         256      0         8       1
R3#sh queue s 0/0
  Input queue: 0/75/0/0 (size/max/drops/flushes); Total output drops: 13567
  Queueing strategy: weighted fair
  Output queue: 125/500/100/13567 (size/max total/threshold/drops)
     Conversations  5/7/64 (active/max active/max total)
     Reserved Conversations 0/0 (allocated/max allocated)
     Available Bandwidth 1158 kilobits/sec

  (depth/weight/total drops/no-buffer drops/interleaves) 61/5397/654/0/0
  Conversation 61, linktype: ip, length: 64
  source: 192.168.3.254, destination: 192.168.2.251, id: 0x0134, ttl: 253,
  TOS: 184 prot: 17, source port 16638, destination port 19476

  (depth/weight/total drops/no-buffer drops/interleaves) 61/5397/653/0/0
  Conversation 15, linktype: ip, length: 64
  source: 192.168.3.254, destination: 192.168.2.251, id: 0x013B, ttl: 253,
  TOS: 184 prot: 17, source port 16772, destination port 19232

  (depth/weight/total drops/no-buffer drops/interleaves) 1/10794/15/0/0
  Conversation 34, linktype: ip, length: 1404
  source: 192.168.3.100, destination: 192.168.1.100, id: 0x00A5, ttl: 127,
  TOS: 88 prot: 6, source port 80, destination port 1068

  (depth/weight/total drops/no-buffer drops/interleaves) 1/10794/15/0/0
  Conversation 33, linktype: ip, length: 1404
  source: 192.168.3.100, destination: 192.168.1.100, id: 0x00A7, ttl: 127,
  TOS: 72 prot: 6, source port 80, destination port 1067

  (depth/weight/total drops/no-buffer drops/interleaves) 1/32384/12/0/0
  Conversation 29, linktype: ip, length: 1404
  source: 192.168.3.100, destination: 192.168.1.100, id: 0x00A1, ttl: 127,
  TOS: 0 prot: 6, source port 1353, destination port 1065
```

To enable WFQ, the **fair-queue** interface subcommand is used. After enabling WFQ, the **show interface** command output shows the fact that WFQ is enabled. (See the highlighted portion of the first **show interface** command in Example 5-3.) Note that the hold queue default size of 1000 is shown in the **show interface** output as well. The **show interface** command and the **show queueing fair** commands both list the CDT (default 64), along with the maximum number of queues (256).

The most interesting **show** command for WFQ is the **show queue** command. Note that a summary section is listed first, followed by a stanza of output for each active flow. Each stanza lists statistics about the current queue size, number of drops, and so on. Each stanza also lists the details used for classification. For instance, each stanza of the first **show queue** command includes a comment added by me. Knowing that two voice calls, one TCP connection for FTP, and two TCP connections for HTTP were being used, I could look at the source and destination addresses and ports numbers and decide which WFQ flows correlated to each of these user flows.

You can understand the usage of the ToS byte by WFQ with a little closer examination of the output of the **show queue** command. You may recall that the two HTTP transfers were marked with different DSCP values; note that the two HTTP flows in the command output have ToS byte values of 72 and 80. Which of these values corresponds to DSCP AF21 (important HTTP URLs per CB marking) and AF23 ("not" important URLs per CB marking)? Table 5-8 lists the pertinent details needed to correlate DSCP, ToS, and precedence values used in the example.

Table 5-6 *DSCP, ToS Byte, and WFQ Weight Values Used in Example 5-3*

DSCP Name	Type of Traffic Marked in This Example	Binary DSCP, with Precedence Portion in Bold	Binary ToS, with 0s Padded for Last 2 Bits	ToS Byte Decimal Value	Precedence Value (Decimal)
EF	VoIP	**101**110	**101**11000	184	5
AF21	HTTP URLs with "important"	**010**010	**010**01000	72	2
AF23	HTTP URLs with "not"	**010**110	**010**11000	88	2
BE	All else	**000**000	**000**00000	0	0

WFQ always weights the packets based on the first 3 bits of the ToS byte — in other words, based on the Precedence field. However, the **show queue** command output lists the entire contents of the ToS byte, which in this case included 6 bits marked by CB marking, and two trailing binary 0s. Therefore, the ToS byte values in the command lists the same values shown in the table. Even though CB marking marked a different DSCP for each type of HTTP traffic, as far as WFQ is concerned, each receives the same amount of weight. This is because WFQ does not look past the Precedence field when determining the weight.

Finally, the second half of Example 5-3 just shows some configuration changes and the resulting changes in the **show** command output. The configuration changes the CDT, the maximum number of queues, and the length of the hold queue. The highlighted portions of the **show interface**, **show queueing**, and **show queue** commands reflect the details of the configuration changes.

WFQ Summary

WFQ works well for networks where the most delay-sensitive traffic requires less bandwidth than the average flow. Also flows with higher precedence work well, with low-volume, high-precedence flows receiving exceptional treatment. Best of all, WFQ requires no classification configuration. As a result, WFQ provides a great default queuing choice, particularly when traffic characteristics are unpredictable and difficult to qualify.

WFQ works poorly for voice and interactive video traffic, because both need low delay and low jitter. WFQ does not provide a priority queue in order to minimize delay and jitter. Also delay can increase when too many concurrent flows occur, due to WFQ being "too fair," allowing some bandwidth to each flow, which may cause the voice or video flows to not get enough bandwidth.

Table 5-9 summarizes some of the key features of WFQ.

Table 5-7 *WFQ Functions and Features*

WFQ Feature	Explanation
Classification	Classifies without configuration, based on source/destination IP address/ port, protocol type (TCPIUDP), and ToS.
Drop policy	Modified tail drop.
Number of queues	4096.
Maximum queue length	Congestive discard threshold per queue (max 4096), with an overall limit based on the hold queue for all queues (max 4096).
Scheduling inside a single queue	FIFO.
Scheduling among all queues	Serves lowest sequence number (SN). The SN is assigned when the packet is placed into the queue, as a function of length and precedence.

Class-Based WFQ (CBWFQ)

Of the other Queuing tools covered in this chapter, CBWFQ is most like CQ, in that it can be used to reserve minimum bandwidth for each queue. It does differ from CQ in that you can configure the actual percentage of traffic, rather than a byte count. CBWFQ is like WFQ in that CBWFQ can actually use WFQ inside one particular queue, but it differs from WFQ in that it does not keep up with flows for all the traffic.

To begin the coverage of CBWFQ, examine Figure 5-18, which outlines the typical queuing features in sequence.

Figure 5-18 *CBWFQ—Summary of Main Features*

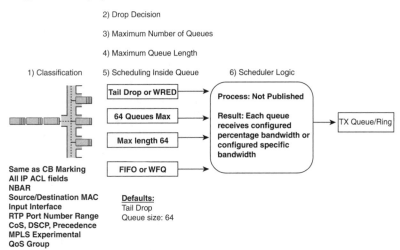

Starting left to right in the figure, CBWFQ classifies packets using the exact same set of fields that CB marking uses to classify packets. In fact, CBWFQ uses the exact same configuration commands, all of which are part of the Modular QoS CLI (MQC) commands described in Chapter 3, "MQC, QPM, and AutoQoS." CBWFQ's use of MQC makes learning the configuration for CBWFQ easy, assuming you remember how to configure CB marking from the preceding chapter. And unlike WFQ, which use flow-based classifiers, CBWFQ does not classify based on the flow, but on anything you can match with the MQC commands.

> **NOTE** CBWFQ uses the terms "class" and "queue" to refer to the single queue that is associated with a class that can be defined with CBWFQ. The terms "class" and "queue" are often used interchangeably when describing CBWFQ.

CBWFQ supports two types of drop policy, namely tail drop and WRED. Chapter 7, "Congestion Avoidance Through Drop Policies," covers WRED in detail, but the general idea is to discard packets before the queue actually fills, with the intent of making some TCP connections react to the lost packet and slow down sending packets. By having a few TCP connections slow down, the queue may not fill, reducing congestion.

You can enable WRED on any of the 64 queues available with CBWFQ. However, WRED is a good option for some queues, and not for others. If a queue holds on to VoIP payload, for example, you do not really want to drop any packets, because if you drop voice packets, the voice quality degrades. In queues holding less-drop-sensitive traffic, such as data, WRED is a good option, but WRED works poorly in queues holding voice and video traffic.

CBWFQ supports 64 queues, with a maximum and default queue length varying depending on the model of router and the amount of memory installed. All 64 queues can be configured, but one class queue, called *class-default*, is automatically configured. If the explicitly configured classification does not match a packet, IOS places the packet into the class-default class. You are allowed to change the configuration details regarding this default class, but this one class always exists.

So far, the other queuing tools in this chapter supported only FIFO logic inside a single queue. In fact, some of you may have been wondering why "step 5" was included in illustrations such as the one shown in Figure 5-19. Currently, CBWFQ can use either FIFO or WFQ inside the class-default queue. With Flow-Based WFQ in the class-default queue, when CBWFQ decides to take one or more packets from the queue, it takes the packet with the best sequence number (SN) — just like WFQ normally does.

> **NOTE**   Cisco 7500 series routers support either FIFO or WFQ inside each and every CBWFQ queue, whereas other platforms only support both FIFO and WFQ inside CBWFQ's class-default queue.

CBWFQ provides a great advantage by allowing WFQ to be used in the class-default queue. You may recall that WFQ is actually a very good default choice for queuing, because it treats low-volume flows well, and many low-volume flows are also interactive flows. WFQ also treats packets with high precedence well. So, with CBWFQ, for the traffic you know about, you classify it, and reserve the right amount of bandwidth for the class. For the traffic you cannot characterize, you let it default into the class-default queue, where you can dynamically apply some fairness to the default traffic by using WFQ. The capability to reserve bandwidth for some packets, and fairly assign the rest of the bandwidth with WFQ, makes CBWFQ a very powerful queuing tool.

Finally, Cisco does tell us the general idea behind how the CBWFQ scheduler works. The scheduler gives a percentage of the bandwidth to each class, based on the configured values. For instance, four classes, including class-default, may be configured with bandwidth percentages that total 100 percent. The scheduler ensures that each queue receives that percentage of bandwidth. If some queues do not need their bandwidth for a short period, the bandwidth is spread across the other classes. Cisco does not really offer more details about how the scheduler works—so you do not need to worry more about how CBWFQ works for the exams!

Table 5-10 summarizes some of the key features of CBWFQ.

Table 5-8   *CBWFQ Functions and Features*

CBWFQ Feature	Description
Classification	Classifies based on anything that MQC commands can match, just like CB marking. Includes all extended IP ACL fields, NBAR, incoming interface, CoS, precedence, DSCP, source/destination MAC, MPLS Experimental, QoS group, and RTP port numbers
Drop policy	Tail drop or WRED, configurable per queue.
Number of queues	64
Maximum queue length	Varies per router model and memory.
Scheduling inside a single queue	FIFO on 63 queues; FIFO or WFQ on class-default queue*.
Scheduling among all queues	Algorithm is not published. The result of the scheduler provides a percentage guaranteed bandwidth to each queue.

* Except on 7500 series, where you can use FIFO or WFQ in all the CBWFQ queues.

CBWFQ Configuration

CBWFQ configuration uses many of the same MQC commands as covered in Chapter 3 and Chapter 4. As a result, CBWFQ configuration should be relatively easy to understand. The commands used for CBWFQ configuration are listed Tables 5-9 and 5-10.

Table 5-9   *Command Reference for CBWFQ*

Command	Mode and Function
class-map *class-map-name*	Global config; names a class map, where classification options are configured
match ...	Class map subcommand; defines specific classification parameters
match access-group {*access-group* | **name** *access-group- name*}	Access control list (ACL)
match source-address mac *address*	Source MAC address
match ip precedence *ip-precedence-value* [*ip-precedence- value ip-precedence-value ip-precedence-value*]	IP precedence
match mpls experimental *number*	MPLS Experimental

continues

Table 5-9 *Command Reference for CBWFQ (Continued)*

Command	Mode and Function
match cos *cos-value* [*cos-value cos-value cos-value*]	CoS
match destination-address mac *address*	Destination MAC address
match input-interface *interface-name*	Input interface
match ip dscp *ip-dscp-value* [*ip-dscp-value ip-dscp-value ip-dscp-value ip-dscp-value ip-dscp-value ip-dscp-value ip-dscp-value*]	IP DSCP
match ip rtp *starting-port-number port-range*	RTP's UDP port number range
match qos-group *qos-group-value*	QoS group
match protocol *protocol-name*	NBAR protocol types
match protocol citrix [**app** *application-name-string*].	NBAR Citrix applications
match protocol http [**url** *url-string*	**host** *hostname-string*	**mime** *MIME-type*]	Host name and URL string
match any	Matches any and all packets
policy-map *policy-map-name*	Global config; names a policy, which is a set of actions to perform
class *name*	Policy map subcommand; identifies the packets to perform QoS actions on by referring to the classification logic in a class map
bandwidth {*bandwidth-kbps*	**percent** *percent*}	Class subcommand; sets literal or percentage bandwidth for the class. Must use either use actual bandwidth or percent on all classes in a single policy map
bandwidth {**remaining percent** *percent*}	Class subcommand; sets percentage of remaining bandwidth for the class. Remaining bandwidth is bandwidth minus other explicit bandwidth reservations
queue-limit *queue-limit*	Class subcommand; sets the maximum number of packets in the queue for that class

Table 5-9 *Command Reference for CBWFQ (Continued)*

Command	Mode and Function
fair-queue [**queue-limit** *queue-value*]	Class subcommand; enables WFQ in the class (class-default only)
random-detect dscp *dscpvalue min-threshold max- threshold* [*mark-probability-denominator*]	Class subcommand; enables DSCP- based WRED in the class
random-detect precedence *precedence min-threshold max- threshold mark-prob-denominator*	Class subcommand; enables precedence-based WRED in the class
max-reserved-bandwidth *percent*	Interface subcommand; defines the percentage of link bandwidth that can be reserved for CBWFQ queues besides class-default

Table 5-10 *EXEC Command Reference for CBWFQ*

Command	Function
show policy-map *policy-map-name*	Lists configuration information about all MQC-based QoS tools
show policy-map *interface-spec* [**input** | **output**] [**class** *class-name*]	Lists statistical information about the behavior of all MQC-based QoS tools

The remainder of this section includes several familiar lab scenarios, with example configurations and **show** commands. In the first CBWFQ example, R3 uses CBWFQ on its S0/0 interface. The engineer configuring R3 decided that voice traffic could benefit from being placed into a different queue than all other traffic, so a simple QoS policy has been devised, which includes the following:

- All VoIP payload traffic is placed in a queue.

- All other traffic is placed in another queue.

- Give the VoIP traffic 50 percent of the bandwidth.

- WFQ and WRED should be used on the non-VoIP traffic.

Figure 5-19 reminds you of the now-familiar example network, which shows the router in which the configuration is applied. Example 5-4 shows the configuration and **show** commands.

Figure 5-19 *Network Used with CBWFQ Configuration Examples*

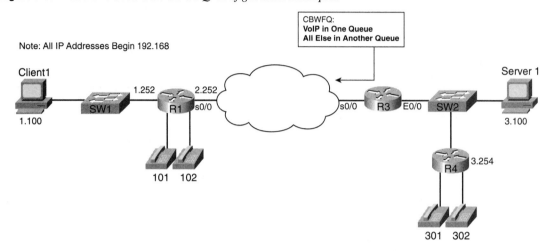

Example 5-4 *CBWFQ, VoIP in High Queue, Everything Else in Normal Queue*

```
R3#show running-config
Building configuration...

! Portions omitted for brevity
!
ip cef
!
class-map match-all voip-rtp
  match ip rtp 16384 16383
!
policy-map queue-voip
  class voip-rtp
   bandwidth percent 50
  class class-default
   fair-queue
! Portions omitted for brevity
!
interface Serial0/0
 description connected to FRS port S0. Single PVC to R1.
 no ip address
 encapsulation frame-relay
 load-interval 30
 bandwidth 128
 service-policy output queue-voip
 clockrate 128000
!
interface Serial0/0.1 point-to-point
 description point-point subint global DLCI 103, connected via PVC to DLCI 101 (
```

Example 5-4   *CBWFQ, VoIP in High Queue, Everything Else in Normal Queue (Continued)*

```
R1)
 ip address 192.168.2.253 255.255.255.0
 frame-relay interface-dlci 101
! Portions omitted for brevity


R3#show policy-map int s 0/0

 Serial0/0

  Service-policy output: queue-voip

   Class-map: voip-rtp (match-all)
      136435 packets, 8731840 bytes
      30 second   offered rate 51000 bps, drop rate 0 bps
      Match: ip rtp 16384 16383
      Weighted Fair Queueing
        Output Queue: Conversation 265
        Bandwidth 50 (%) Max Threshold 64 (packets)
        (pkts matched/bytes matched) 48550/3107200
        (depth/total drops/no-buffer drops) 14/0/0


   Class-map: class-default (match-any)
      1958 packets, 1122560 bytes
      30 second offered rate 59000 bps, drop rate 0 bps
      Match: any
      Weighted Fair Queueing
        Flow Based Fair Queueing
        Maximum Number of Hashed Queues 256
        (total queued/total drops/no-buffer drops) 15/0/0

R3#show policy-map int s 0/0 output class class-default Serial0/0
  Service-policy output: queue-voip

   Class-map: class-default (match-any)
      2217 packets, 1417985 bytes
      30 second offered rate 71000 bps, drop rate 0 bps
      Match: any
      Weighted Fair Queueing
        Flow Based Fair Queueing
        Maximum Number of Hashed Queues 256
        (total queued/total drops/no-buffer drops) 10/0/0

R3#show policy-map
  Policy Map queue-voip
    Class voip-rtp
      Weighted Fair Queueing
            Bandwidth 50 (%) Max Threshold 64 (packets)
    Class class-default
```

continues

Example 5-4 *CBWFQ, VoIP in High Queue, Everything Else in Normal Queue (Continued)*

```
        Weighted Fair Queueing
             Flow based Fair Queueing Max Threshold 64 (packets)


R3#show interface s 0/0
Serial0/0 is up, line protocol is up
  Hardware is PowerQUICC Serial
  Description: connected to FRS port S0. Single PVC to R1.
  MTU 1500 bytes, BW 1544 Kbit, DLY 20000 usec,
     reliability 255/255, txload 9/255, rxload 8/255
  Encapsulation FRAME-RELAY, loopback not set
  Keepalive set (10 sec)
  LMI enq sent  132, LMI stat recvd 132, LMI upd recvd 0, DTE LMI up
  LMI enq recvd 0, LMI stat sent  0, LMI upd sent  0
  LMI DLCI 1023  LMI type is CISCO  frame relay DTE
  FR SVC disabled, LAPF state down
  Broadcast queue 0/64, broadcasts sent/dropped 307/0, interface broadcasts 285
  Last input 00:00:02, output 00:00:00, output hang never
  Last clearing of "show interface" counters 00:22:02
  Input queue: 0/75/0/0 (size/max/drops/flushes); Total output drops: 0
  Queueing strategy: weighted fair
  Output queue: 16/1000/64/0 (size/max total/threshold/drops)
     Conversations  4/8/256 (active/max active/max total)
     Reserved Conversations 1/1 (allocated/max allocated)
     Available Bandwidth 1158 kilobits/sec
  30 second input rate 52000 bits/sec, 102 packets/sec
  30 second output rate 59000 bits/sec, 101 packets/sec
     126301 packets input, 8141304 bytes, 0 no buffer
     Received 0 broadcasts, 0 runts, 0 giants, 0 throttles
     0 input errors, 0 CRC, 0 frame, 0 overrun, 0 ignored, 0 abort
     126197 packets output, 8550371 bytes, 0 underruns
     0 output errors, 0 collisions, 2 interface resets
     0 output buffer failures, 0 output buffers swapped out
     0 carrier transitions
     DCD=up  DSR=up  DTR=up  RTS=up  CTS=up
R3#configure terminal
Enter configuration commands, one per line.  End with CNTL/Z.
R3(config)#policy-map queue-voip
R3(config-pmap)#class class-default
R3(config-pmap-c)#no fair-queue
R3(config-pmap-c)#^Z

R3#show policy-map
  Policy Map queue-voip
    Class voip-rtp
      Weighted Fair Queueing
            Bandwidth 50 (%) Max Threshold 64 (packets)
    Class class-default
```

The configuration for CBWFQ requires many commands, but the logic is straightforward. **class-map voip-rtp** matches all VoIP payload by matching with the **match ip rtp 16384 16383** command. The **policy-map queue-voip** policy assigns VoIP traffic 50 percent of the bandwidth based on the **bandwidth percent 50** command. But 50 percent of what? Well, the actual bandwidth is derived from the percentage of the bandwidth configured on the **bandwidth** interface subcommand. In this case, the bandwidth is set to 128, so the **voip-rtp** class gets 64 kbps, which is enough for the two G.729a VoIP calls. Just like with CB marking, the **service-policy output** command enables the policy on the interface, in this case S0/0.

The **show policy-map interface serial 0/0** command lists the most interesting statistical information about CBWFQ. (This paragraph, and the rest of the text that describes Example 5-4, explains the commands in the example in the same sequence as they are shown in the example.) It lists a stanza of information for each class, listing the configured matching parameters and bandwidth percentages. The offered rate of traffic that has been classified into each queue is listed, along with drop statistics. These values are useful when monitoring the configuration to decide whether the configuration values should be changed. Also note that in class-default, the output implies that Flow-Based WFQ is in use inside the queue.

The **show policy-map** command also has other options that reduce the amount of output, which can be large. For instance, the **show policy-map int s 0/0 output class class-default** shown in the example lists only information about class class-default.

The **show policy-map** command just lists a summary of the configured policy maps. Interestingly, the class-default stanza of the command output lists Weighted Fair Queuing, and then says it is "flow based." In this case, the command output is reminding you that inside the class-default queue, Flow-Based WFQ is applied to each flow. For comparison, at the end of the example, the configuration has been changed to disable WFQ in the class-default queue. The **show policy-map** command no longer lists Flow-Based WFQ for class-default.

Although some of the CBWFQ command output references WFQ in sections describing queues other than class-default, CBWFQ does not use Flow-Based WFQ inside any of these queues. CBWFQ on most Cisco router models can only use Flow-Based WFQ inside one queue—the class-default queue. (On the 7500, WFQ can be used inside each CBWFQ queue.)

Good QoS design calls for the marking of packets close to the source of the packet. Example 5-5 accomplishes the same queuing goals as the preceding example, but CBWFQ relies on the fact that the packets have been marked before reaching R3's S0/0 interface. In a real network, the packets could be marked on one of the LAN switches, or in an IP Phone, or by the computers in the network.

This example shows the packets being marked upon entering R3's E0/0 interface, just like Example 4-1 in Chapter 4. Example 5-5 shows the revised configuration based on the following criteria:

■ All VoIP payload traffic has been marked with DSCP EF; place this traffic in a queue.

■ All other traffic has been marked with DSCP BE; place this traffic in a different queue.

■ Give the VoIP traffic 58 kbps of the bandwidth on the link.

■ Use WRED and WFQ on the non-VoIP traffic.

Example 5-5 *CBWFQ, DSCP EF in One Queue, Everything Else in Another Queue*

```
R3#show running-config
class-map match-all voip-rtp
  match ip rtp 16384 16383
!
class-map match-all dscp-ef
  match ip dscp ef
!
!
policy-map voip-and-be
  class voip-rtp
   set ip dscp 46
  class class-default
   set ip dscp 0
!
policy-map queue-on-dscp
  class dscp-ef
   bandwidth 58
   queue-limit 30
  class class-default
   random-detect dscp-based
   fair-queue
!
interface Ethernet0/0
 description connected to SW2, where Server1 is connected
 ip address 192.168.3.253 255.255.255.0
 service-policy input voip-and-be
!
interface serial0/0
 clock rate 128000
 bandwidth 128
 service-policy output queue-on-dscp
R3#
R3#show policy-map interface serial 0/0
 Serial0/0

  Service-policy output: queue-on-dscp
```

Example 5-5 *CBWFQ, DSCP EF in One Queue, Everything Else in Another Queue (Continued)*

```
          Class-map: dscp-ef (match-all)
            8654 packets, 553856 bytes
            30 second offered rate 51000 bps, drop rate 0 bps
            Match: ip dscp ef
            Weighted Fair Queueing
              Output Queue: Conversation 41
              Bandwidth 58 (kbps) Max Threshold 30 (packets)
              (pkts matched/bytes matched) 8442/540288
              (depth/total drops/no-buffer drops) 8/0/0

          Class-map: class-default (match-any)
            673 packets, 779357 bytes
            30 second offered rate 71000 bps, drop rate 0 bps
            Match: any
            Weighted Fair Queueing
              Flow Based Fair Queueing
              Maximum Number of Hashed Queues 32
              (total queued/total drops/no-buffer drops) 14/0/0
              exponential weight: 9

          dscp      Transmitted      Random drop      Tail drop       Minimum Maximum  Mark
                    pkts/bytes       pkts/bytes       pkts/bytes      thresh  thresh   prob
          af11      0/0              0/0              0/0             32      40   1/10
          af12      0/0              0/0              0/0             28      40   1/10
          af13      0/0              0/0              0/0             24      40   1/10
          af21      0/0              0/0              0/0             32      40   1/10
          af22      0/0              0/0              0/0             28      40   1/10
          af23      0/0              0/0              0/0             24      40   1/10
          af31      0/0              0/0              0/0             32      40   1/10
          af32      0/0              0/0              0/0             28      40   1/10
          af33      0/0              0/0              0/0             24      40   1/10
          af41      0/0              0/0              0/0             32      40   1/10
          af42      0/0              0/0              0/0             28      40   1/10
          af43      0/0              0/0              0/0             24      40   1/10
          cs1       0/0              0/0              0/0             22      40   1/10
          cs2       0/0              0/0              0/0             24      40   1/10
          cs3       0/0              0/0              0/0             26      40   1/10
          cs4       0/0              0/0              0/0             28      40   1/10
          cs5       0/0              0/0              0/0             30      40   1/10
          cs6       23/2219          0/0              0/0             32      40   1/10
          cs7       0/0              0/0              0/0             34      40   1/10
          ef        0/0              0/0              0/0             36      40   1/10
          rsvp      0/0              0/0              0/0             36      40   1/10
          default   9/117            0/0              0/0             20      40   1/10

R3#show policy-map
```

continues

Example 5-5 *CBWFQ, DSCP EF in One Queue, Everything Else in Another Queue (Continued)*

```
Policy Map voip-and-be
  Class voip-rtp
    set ip dscp ef
  Class class-default
    set ip dscp default

Policy Map queue-on-dscp
  Class dscp-ef
    Weighted Fair Queueing
          Bandwidth 58 (kbps) Max Threshold 30 (packets)
  Class class-default
    Weighted Fair Queueing
          Flow based Fair Queueing
          exponential weight 9

          dscp      min-threshold    max-threshold    mark-probability
          --------------------------------------------------------------

          af11       -              -                1/10
          af12       -              -                1/10
          af13       -              -                1/10
          af21       -              -                1/10
          af22       -              -                1/10
          af23       -              -                1/10
          af31       -              -                1/10
          af32       -              -                1/10
          af33       -              -                1/10
          af41       -              -                1/10
          af42       -              -                1/10
          af43       -              -                1/10
          cs1        -              -                1/10
          cs2        -              -                1/10
          cs3        -              -                1/10
          cs4        -              -                1/10
          cs5        -              -                1/10
          cs6        -              -                1/10
          cs7        -              -                1/10
          ef         -              -                1/10
          rsvp       -              -                1/10
          default    -              -                1/10
```

The configuration is again detailed, but straightforward. **policy-map voip-and-be** marks packets as they enter E0/0, matching and marking VoIP packets with DSCP EF, and matching and marking all other packets, marking them with DSCP BE. The **class-map match-all dscp-ef** command creates a class that matches all DSCP EF traffic. **policy-map queue-on-dscp** refers to **class dscp-ef** in order to match all VoIP traffic, giving the voice traffic 58 kbps with the **bandwidth 58** command. That same class includes the **queue-limit 30** command, which changes the maximum queue size to 30. CBWFQ uses tail drop in each class by default, so under the **class class-default** command, the **random-detect dscp-based** command is used to enable WRED in the default class. In addition, of course, the **service-policy** command enables the service policy on the interface.

The **show** commands do not provide much new information, other than the statistics about WRED operation. The details about this part of the output are covered in Chapter 6.

You may have found it strange to see a configuration with classification and marking happening as the packet entered E0/0 in R3, and then another round of classification for packets exiting R3's S0/0 interface. One of the great advantages of classification and marking is that after the packets are marked, the configuration of the tools providing each per-hop behavior (PHB) is simple. Another advantage is that after the packet has been marked, other devices can perform the simpler matching of just looking for DSCP or IP precedence.

If the QoS policy calls for applying PHBs only for packets exiting WAN interfaces, and the policy does not call for PHBs between packets entering and exiting LAN interfaces, the classification and marking, and the queuing, may be performed with a single configuration. Example 5-6 shows a similar configuration to the preceding example, but with both the marking and queuing performed for packets exiting R3's S0/0 interface.

Example 5-6 *CBWFQ and CB Marking Combined*

```
R3#show running-config
class-map match-all voip-rtp
  match ip rtp 16384 16383
!
policy-map mark-and-queue
  class voip-rtp
    set ip dscp ef
    bandwidth 58
  class class-default
    set ip dscp 0
    random-detect dscp
    fair-queue
!
interface Ethernet0/0
 description connected to SW2, where Server1 is connected
! No service policy on E0/0!
!
interface serial0/0
 clock rate 128000
 bandwidth 128
 service-policy output mark-and-queue
```

Two classes are used in this example: voip-rtp, which matches all VoIP payload UDP ports; and class-default, which matches all other packets. Inside **policy-map mark-and-queue**, each class includes a **set** command to set the DSCP value. The voip-rtp class includes a **bandwidth** command to reserve bandwidth; class-default automatically gets 25 percent of the bandwidth. The **service-policy output mark-and-queue** command enables the policy for packets exiting R3's S0/0 interface. In this example, you get the benefits of classification and marking, a shorter configuration, and only one classification step inside this router, reducing overhead.

CBWFQ provides several variations of how to configure the bandwidth reserved for each queue. For instance, the **bandwidth 64** class subcommand reserves 64 kbps of bandwidth, regardless of the bandwidth setting on the interface. The **bandwidth percent 25** class subcommand would also reserve 64 kbps for a class if the interface bandwidth had been set to 256 kbps, using the **bandwidth 256** interface subcommand.

Both styles of the **bandwidth** commands do the same thing in this case, but which is better? Well, if your intent is to truly give a particular queue 25 percent of the bandwidth, regardless of the actual bandwidth, use the **percent** option. That way, if you actually increase the speed of the link in the future, all you have to do is change the setting for the **bandwidth** interface subcommand to reflect the increased bandwidth into CBWFQ. However, if you specifically engineer a queue to use a set amount of bandwidth, and that bandwidth requirement should not be increased even if the link speed increases, then use the **bandwidth** class subcommand without the **percent** option.

Example 5-7 shows these two variations on the bandwidth class subcommand, along with a few caveats.

Example 5-7 *Use of the Bandwidth Command, with and without the Percent Option*

```
R3#conf t
Enter configuration commands, one per line.  End with CNTL/Z.
R3(config)#class-map class1
R3(config-cmap)#match ip dscp af31
R3(config-cmap)#class-map class2
R3(config-cmap)#match ip dscp af32
R3(config-cmap)#class-map class3
R3(config-cmap)#match ip dscp af33
R3(config-cmap)#class-map class4
R3(config-cmap)#match ip dscp af21
R3(config-cmap)#policy-map explicit-bw
R3(config-pmap)#class class1
R3(config-pmap-c)#bandwidth 64
R3(config-pmap-c)#class class2
R3(config-pmap-c)#bandwidth percent 25
All classes with bandwidth should have consistent units
R3(config-pmap-c)#bandwidth 32
 !
```

Example 5-7   *Use of the Bandwidth Command, with and without the Percent Option (Continued)*

```
!
R3(config-pmap-c)#policy-map percent-bw
R3(config-pmap)#class class3
R3(config-pmap-c)#bandwidth percent 25
R3(config-pmap-c)#class class4
R3(config-pmap-c)#bandwidth 64
All classes with bandwidth should have consistent units
R3(config-pmap-c)#bandwidth percent 25
R3(config-pmap-c)#int s 0/1
R3(config-if)#bandwidth 64
R3(config-if)#service-policy output explicit-bw
 I/f Serial0/1 class class1 requested bandwidth 64 (kbps), available only 48 (kbps)
R3(config-if)#service-policy output percent-bw
R3(config-if)#^Z
R3#show running-config
00:05:05: %SYS-5-CONFIG_I: Configured from console by console
Building configuration...

! Portions omitted for brevity
!
class-map match-all class4
  match ip dscp af21
 class-map match-all class3
  match ip dscp af33
class-map match-all class2
  match ip dscp af32
 class-map match-all class1
  match ip dscp af31
!
 policy-map explicit-bw
  class class1
   bandwidth 64
  class class2
   bandwidth 32
!
 policy-map percent-bw
  class class3
   bandwidth percent 25
  class class4
   bandwidth percent 25
!
R3#show policy-map interface s 0/1
 Serial0/1

  Service-policy output: percent-bw

    Class-map: class3 (match-all)
```

continues

Example 5-7 *Use of the Bandwidth Command, with and without the Percent Option (Continued)*

```
      0 packets, 0 bytes
      5 minute offered rate 0 bps, drop rate 0 bps
      Match: ip dscp af33
      Queueing
        Output Queue: Conversation 25
        Bandwidth 25 (%)
        Bandwidth 16 (kbps) Max Threshold 64 (packets)
        (pkts matched/bytes matched) 0/0
        (depth/total drops/no-buffer drops) 0/0/0

    Class-map: class4 (match-all)
      0 packets, 0 bytes
      5 minute offered rate 0 bps, drop rate 0 bps
      Match: ip dscp af21
      Queueing
        Output Queue: Conversation 26
        Bandwidth 25 (%)
        Bandwidth 16 (kbps) Max Threshold 64 (packets)
        (pkts matched/bytes matched) 0/0
        (depth/total drops/no-buffer drops) 0/0/0

    Class-map: class-default (match-any)
      0 packets, 0 bytes
      5 minute offered rate 0 bps, drop rate 0 bps
      Match: any
```

This example shows a couple of important points about the options on the **bandwidth** class subcommand. First, inside a single policy map, you cannot use **bandwidth** commands with an explicitly stated bandwidth as well as a percent bandwidth. The error message, shown in the example, doesn't state it quite so exactly, but in both the **explicit-bw** and **percent-bw** policy maps, you can see that once one style of **bandwidth** command was used, the other style was rejected.

The other problem relates to the **bandwidth** interface subcommand setting, which tells IOS how much bandwidth is considered to be available to the interface. In the example, under **interface serial 0/1**, the **bandwidth 64** command specified 64 kbps of bandwidth. When the **service-policy output explicit-bw** command was attempted, IOS rejected it. That's because CBWFQ defaults to a **max-reserved-bandwidth** setting of 75 percent on each interface, meaning that by default a policy map cannot reserve more than 75 percent of the bandwidth defined on an interface. In this case, 48 kbps is 75 percent of the interface's configured 64-kbps bandwidth, and the **explicit-bw** policy map has attempted to reserve 64 kbps inside **class class1**, so the **service-policy** command was rejected.

However, the **service-policy output percent-bw** command was not rejected. Because it only uses percentages, the two classes took their configured percentages (25 percent each) from the interface's configured (64 kbps) bandwidth, giving each queue 16 kbps. If you look to the end of the example, you will see a **show policy-map** command that lists the percentages as well as the calculated 16 kbps for each queue.

CBWFQ Summary

CBWFQ combines some of the best features of the various queuing tools into a single tool. Like CQ, CBWFQ can reserve a guaranteed amount of bandwidth per queue, but without the negative side effects of the CQ scheduler. CBWFQ can use WFQ as the default behavior for unclassified traffic inside class class-default. Packet loss behavior can take advantage of WRED for each queue, which reduces the possibilities of global synchronization. In addition, of all the queuing tools, CBWFQ has the largest variety of directly matchable fields for classifying packets.

CBWFQ does have some drawbacks, however. Most drawbacks are minor, but one negative is the lack of a PQ-like feature. Delay- and jitter-sensitive traffic still suffers, even when enough bandwidth has been reserved by CBWFQ, because the CBWFQ scheduler can serve other queues when a VoIP or video packet is waiting in a queue. The next feature covered in the book, namely Low Latency Queuing (LLQ), overcomes this problem.

Low Latency Queuing (LLQ)

Low Latency Queuing sounds like the best queuing tool possible, just based on the name. What packet wouldn't want to experience low latency? As it turns out, for delay (latency) sensitive traffic, LLQ is indeed the queuing tool of choice.

LLQ is simple to understand and simple to configure, assuming you already understand CBWFQ. LLQ is not really a separate queuing tool, but rather a simple option of CBWFQ applied to one or more classes. CBWFQ treats these classes as strict-priority queues. In other words, CBWFQ always services packets in these classes if a packet is waiting, just as PQ does for the High queue.

> **NOTE** This section uses examples with only a single LLQ class in most cases. However, you can have more than one low-latency priority queue at the same time. It is very important that you read the section titled "LLQ with More Than One Priority Queue," just after the section about configuring LLQ. This section not only explains why you might want more than one low-latency queue, but it also covers some important information for the exam.

LLQ introduces some new lingo that you may find a little tricky. From one perspective, something like PQ has been added to CBWFQ, so you can expect to read or hear phrases that refer to the low-latency queue as "the PQ." Someone might say, "What did you put in the PQ?" What he really wants to know is what type of packets you classified and placed into the queue in which you enabled the LLQ feature of CBWFQ. In addition, the queue in which LLQ is enabled is sometimes just called "the LLQ." Therefore, if you use CBWFQ, and use the **priority** command to enable LLQ in one of the classes, you are really using LLQ, and a class with the **priority** command is "the LLQ" or "the PQ."

Terminology aside, the simple addition of LLQ logic to CBWFQ is depicted in Figure 5-20.

Figure 5-20 *Servicing Queues with LLQ and CBWFQ*

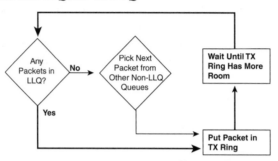

Note that like PQ, the LLQ scheduler always checks the low-latency queue first, and takes a packet from that queue. If there are no packets in the low-latency queue, the normal, scheduler logic applies to the other non-low-latency queue queues, giving them their guaranteed bandwidth.

For delay-sensitive traffic, the addition of a low-latency queue overcomes the one big negative of CBWFQ. In fact, with all the other queuing tools covered in this chapter so far, only PQ gave voice traffic the best quality. Of course, PQ had the negative side effect of almost destroying the performance of the lower-priority applications when the link was congested. With LLQ, you get the best of both worlds — low latency for the traffic in one queue, and guaranteed bandwidth for the traffic in other queues. Notice the thicker lines in Figure 5-20. If you follow these lines, you can see a path through the logic for LLQ in which only the low-latency queue gets any service. How can LLQ guarantee the other queues their respective bandwidths, with logic that never lets those queues get serviced? Well, the real answer is that Figure 5-20 is only part of the story. To prevent LLQ from having the same problem as PQ, where packets in the highest-priority queue could dominate and take all the available bandwidth, LLQ's scheduler actually operates as shown in Figure 5-21.

LLQ actually *polices* the PQ based on the configured bandwidth. By doing so, the packets in the queue that are forwarded still have very low latency, but LLQ also prevents the low-latency traffic from consuming more than its configured amount of bandwidth. By discarding excess traffic, LLQ can still provide bandwidth guarantees to the non-priority queues. The policing function works like policing as described in Chapter 6, but it is automatic in the low-latency queue — no additional policing configuration is required.

Figure 5-21 *Services Queues with LLQ and CBWFQ—The Real Story*

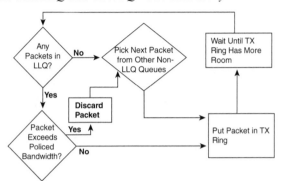

The policing function of LLQ takes care of protecting the other queues from the low-latency queue, but it does discard packets to accomplish that goal. Take a moment to reflect on the types of traffic that need to be classified into the low-latency queue. VoIP traffic, and in most cases, video traffic, need the low-latency, low-jitter performance of the low-latency queue. However, these are the same types of traffic that are most sensitive to dropped packets. So, although putting voice and interactive video into the low-latency queue may be good for queuing, discarding packets that exceed the configured rate for the queue would be harmful to those types of traffic. (Remember, interactive video needs low latency, but one-way video does not.)

The solution to the LLQ policing feature's bad effect on VoIP and interactive video traffic lies outside the control of LLQ. The solution requires the engineer to use whatever means necessary to prevent more than the reserved bandwidth for a low-latency queue from getting introduced into the network. If the low-latency queue has 30 kbps reserved, for example, a single G.729 call will never cause the policer to discard a packet. If a second call occurs, the policer will discard packets, and both voice calls will sound bad. The solution requires some engineering, and some use of call admission control (CAC) tools, to prevent the low-latency queue from being oversubscribed.

LLQ Configuration

LLQ configuration requires one more command in addition to the commands used for CBWFQ configuration. Instead of using the **bandwidth** command on a class, use the **priority** command. The syntax of the **priority** command is as foloows:

    priority {*bandwidth-kbps* | **percent** *percentage*} [*burst*]

This class subcommand enables LLQ in this class, reserves bandwidth, and enables the policing function. You can also configure the burst for the policer with this command, and it defaults to 20 percent of the configured policing rate.

The **priority** command sets the guaranteed minimum bandwidth, which is also the maximum bandwidth! As mentioned earlier, LLQ polices the traffic in a class that uses the **priority** command and discards excess traffic. The **burst** parameter works just like bursts do for policing tools described in Chapter 6; refer to Chapter 6 for more details on the concepts behind policing.

In the following example, the final lab scenario used in the CBWFQ section is repeated, except that LLQ is also enabled. The class with VoIP traffic has reserved 58 kbps again, but this time using the **priority** command. With two VoIP calls, the voice sounds fine. The same familiar traffic flows are used — two VoIP calls, a NetMeeting video conference, HTTP with two different frames (important.jpg and not-so.jpg), and an FTP download. The configuration shows CB marking on ingress of R3's E0/0, and CBWFQ on egress at R3's S0/0. The criteria for each type of traffic is as follows:

- R3's S0/0 is clocked at 128 kbps.

- VoIP payload is marked with DSCP EF, and placed in its own queue, using tail drop. This class gets 58 kbps.

- NetMeeting voice and video from Server1 to Client1 is marked with DSCP AF41, and placed in its own queue, using tail drop. This class gets 22 kbps.

- Any HTTP traffic whose URL contains the string "important" anywhere in the URL is marked with AF21, and placed in its own queue. This class gets 20 kbps.

- Any HTTP traffic whose URL contains the string "not-so" anywhere in the URL is marked with AF23, and placed in its own queue. This class gets 8 kbps.

- All other traffic is marked with DSCP BE, and placed in its own queue, using WRED and WFQ. This class gets the remaining 20 kbps.

Example 5-8 shows the configuration.

Example 5-8 *LLQ for VoIP, CBWFQ for NetMeeting, HTTP "important," HTTP "not-so" Important, and Everything Else*

```
R3#show running-config
Building configuration...
!
!Portions omitted for brevity
!
ip cef
!
class-map match-all dscp-ef
  match ip dscp ef
class-map match-all dscp-af41
  match ip dscp af41
```

Example 5-8 *LLQ for VoIP, CBWFQ for NetMeeting, HTTP "important," HTTP "not-so" Important, and Everything Else (Continued)*

```
class-map match-all dscp-af21
  match ip dscp af21
class-map match-all http-impo
  match protocol http url "*important*"
class-map match-all dscp-af23
  match ip dscp af23
class-map match-all http-not
  match protocol http url "*not-so*"
class-map match-all voip-rtp
  match ip rtp 16384 16383
class-map match-all NetMeet
  match access-group 101
!
!
policy-map laundry-list
  class voip-rtp
   set ip dscp ef
  class NetMeet
   set ip dscp af41
  class http-impo
   set ip dscp af21
  class http-not
   set ip dscp af23
  class class-default
   set ip dscp default
policy-map queue-on-dscp
  class dscp-ef
   priority 58
  class dscp-af41
   bandwidth 22
  class dscp-af21
   bandwidth 20
   random-detect dscp-based
  class dscp-af23
   bandwidth 8
   random-detect dscp-based
  class class-default
   fair-queue
   random-detect dscp-based
!
interface Ethernet0/0
 description connected to SW2, where Server1 is connected
 ip address 192.168.3.253 255.255.255.0
 ip nbar protocol-discovery
 half-duplex
 service-policy input laundry-list
```

continues

Example 5-8 *LLQ for VoIP, CBWFQ for NetMeeting, HTTP "important," HTTP "not-so" Important, and Everything Else (Continued)*

```
!
interface Serial0/0
 description connected to FRS port S0. Single PVC to R1.
 bandwidth 128
 no ip address
 encapsulation frame-relay
 load-interval 30
 max-reserved-bandwidth 85
 service-policy output queue-on-dscp
 clockrate 128000
!
interface Serial0/0.1 point-to-point
 description point-point subint global DLCI 103, connected via PVC to DLCI 101 (R1)
 ip address 192.168.2.253 255.255.255.0
 frame-relay interface-dlci 101
!
access-list 101 permit udp host 192.168.3.100 range 16384 32767 192.168.1.0
  0.0.0.255 range 16384 32767
! portions omitted for brevity
R3#show policy-map queue-on-dscp
    Policy Map queue-on-dscp
    Class dscp-ef
      Weighted Fair Queueing
            Strict Priority
            Bandwidth 58 (kbps) Burst 1450 (Bytes)
    Class dscp-af41
      Weighted Fair Queueing
            Bandwidth 22 (kbps) Max Threshold 64 (packets)
    Class dscp-af21
      Weighted Fair Queueing
            Bandwidth 20 (kbps) Max Threshold 64 (packets)
    Class dscp-af23
      Weighted Fair Queueing
            Bandwidth 8 (kbps) Max Threshold 64 (packets)
    Class class-default
      Weighted Fair Queueing
            Flow based Fair Queueing
            exponential weight 9
            dscp    min-threshold   max-threshold   mark-probability
            ------------------------------------------------------------

            af11       -               -              1/10
            af12       -               -              1/10
            af13       -               -              1/10
            af21       -               -              1/10
```

Example 5-8 *LLQ for VoIP, CBWFQ for NetMeeting, HTTP "important," HTTP "not-so" Important, and Everything Else (Continued)*

```
              af22     -              -              1/10
              af23     -              -              1/10
              af31     -              -              1/10
              af32     -              -              1/10
              af33     -              -              1/10
              af41     -              -              1/10
              af42     -              -              1/10
              af43     -              -              1/10
              cs1      -              -              1/10
              cs2      -              -              1/10
              cs3      -              -              1/10
              cs4      -              -              1/10
              cs5      -              -              1/10
              cs6      -              -              1/10
              cs7      -              -              1/10
              ef       -              -              1/10
              rsvp     -              -              1/10
              default  -              -              1/10


R3#show policy-map interface s 0/0 output class dscp-ef
 Serial0/0

  Service-policy output: queue-on-dscp

    Class-map: dscp-ef (match-all)
      227428 packets, 14555392 bytes
      30 second offered rate 52000 bps, drop rate 0 bps
      Match: ip dscp ef
      Weighted Fair Queueing
        Strict Priority
        Output Queue: Conversation 40
        Bandwidth 58 (kbps) Burst 1450 (Bytes)
        (pkts matched/bytes matched) 12194/780416
        (total drops/bytes drops) 0/0

R3#configure terminal
Enter configuration commands, one per line.  End with CNTL/Z.
R3(config)#policy-map queue-on-dscp
R3(config-pmap)#class dscp-ef
R3(config-pmap-c)#priority 48
R3(config-pmap-c)#^Z
R3#show policy-map interface s 0/0 output class dscp-ef
 Serial0/0

  Service-policy output: queue-on-dscp
```

continues

Example 5-8 *LLQ for VoIP, CBWFQ for NetMeeting, HTTP "important," HTTP "not-so" Important, and Everything Else (Continued)*

```
    Class-map: dscp-ef (match-all)
      279830 packets, 17909120 bytes
      30 second offered rate 51000 bps, drop rate 2000 bps
      Match: ip dscp ef
      Weighted Fair Queueing
        Strict Priority
        Output Queue: Conversation 40
        Bandwidth 48 (kbps) Burst 1200 (Bytes)
        (pkts matched/bytes matched) 64402/4121728
        (total drops/bytes drops) 97/6208
R3#
```

The only change to this configuration, when compared with the CBWFQ configuration in Example 5-8 is that in the dscp-ef class, inside **policy-map queue-on-dscp**, the **priority** command rather than the **bandwidth** command was used to reserve bandwidth. As seen in the output from the **show policy-map** command, IOS now performs strict-priority queuing on the traffic in class dscp-ef. Also note that the **show policy-map** output shows a burst value was defined (1450 bytes), which is used by the policing function of LLQ. The default burst size is equal to 200 milliseconds of traffic; 58000 bits/second * .2 seconds equals 11600 bits, or 1450 bytes.

Note also the drops experienced by the voice traffic as shown with the **show policy-map interface s 0/0 output class dscp-ef** command. The low-latency queue in this example has experienced zero drops, while providing the lowest possible latency for the voice traffic — which is exactly what you want for voice.

At the end of the example, the **priority** command was changed to reserve only 48 kbps. The two G.729 calls need about 52 kbps, and we know that LLQ polices. Notice that some packets have been dropped according to the final **show policy** command; this particular command was issued less than 10 seconds after changing the **priority** command to use only 48 kbps! In the time it took me to write this paragraph, the number of dropped packets had increased to 2000. Thus, the counters reinforce the fact that LLQ does indeed police the traffic. Therefore, you would need to use CAC mechanisms to prevent oversubscription of the low-latency queue.

LLQ with More Than One Priority Queue

Some Cisco documentation claims that you can only have one low-latency queue inside a single policy map. In other words, only one class can use the **priority** command, making it a low-latency queue. Other Cisco documentation claims that you can have more than one low-latency queue in a single policy map.

As it turns out, you can have multiple low-latency queues in a single policy map. Why would you need more than one low-latency queue in a policy map, and how would it work? Well, it's actually pretty simple, now that you know how to configure LLQ.

First, imagine a policy map that has one low-latency queue configured with the **priority 400** command. This queue needs 320 kbps for a single video conference call, plus three G.729 voice calls totaling about 80 kbps. If only the three voice calls and the single video-conference call occur, the LLQ configuration works fine, the policer does not drop any packets, and the voice and video packets are processed as FIFO within that LLQ class. As always, packets in the low- latency queue get serviced ahead of packets in the other non-LLQ classes.

Compare that configuration to a policy map with two low-latency queues defined — one for voice with a **priority 80** command, and another for video conferencing with **priority 320** configured. What's really different about this than the first configuration? The policing, but not the queuing.

With multiple low-latency queues, each class is policed at the configured rate. For instance, with all voice calls going into the class with **priority 80**, three G.729 calls are supported, but not more than that. With video-conferencing traffic going into the class with **priority 320**, only that single video call is supported.

The fact that the different types of traffic are policed separately in the second example provides the motivation to use multiple low-latency queues. Suppose that a fourth voice call were made, and the CAC tools in place did not prevent the call, meaning that more than 80 kbps of voice traffic was being sent. With a single low-latency queue, both video and some voice packets would be discarded due to policing, because the cumulative rate for all traffic would exceed 400 kbps. The policer would have no way to decide to discard just the extra voice, but not video, because the policer acts on all traffic in the class. However, with the two low-latency queues configuration, only the voice calls would lose packets due to policing, and the video conference would not have any packets dropped by the policer.

In effect, with multiple low-latency queues, you get more granularity in what you police. In fact, the most typical reason to use multiple low-latency queues is to support voice in one queue, and video in another.

Queuing does not differ when comparing using a single low-latency queue with multiple low-latency queues in a single policy map. IOS always takes packets from the low-latency queues first, as compared with the non-low-latency queues (those with a **bandwidth** command), just like before. However, IOS does not reorder packets between the various low-latency queues inside the policy map. In other words, IOS treats all traffic in all the low-latency queues with FIFO logic.

In short, using multiple low-latency queues in one policy map does enable you to police traffic more granularly, but it does not reorder packets among the various low-latency queues.

LLQ and the bandwidth *remaining percent* Command

When planning an LLQ configuration, you might frequently think of the LLQ traffic as needing an explicit amount of bandwidth. For instance, you plan for two G.729 calls, so you reserve 56 kbps for the call with the **priority 56** class subcommand. In that case, you need a specific amount of bandwidth, not a percentage of the interface bandwidth.

Alternatively, if the interface had a **bandwidth 256** command configured under it, you could have chosen to configure the **priority percent 22** command, which would also reserve 56 kbps. However, if you ever increased the speed of the link, and updated the interface to use **bandwidth 384**, then the LLQ would end up with more bandwidth — 22 percent of 384 kbps, or 84 bbps — but you might have still just wanted to support two voice calls. As a result, LLQ **priority** commands oftentimes show the explicitly configured bandwidth. So, more often than not, LLQ configurations define an explicit amount of link bandwidth, rather than a percentage.

Conversely, when reserving bandwidth for data, engineers often simply want to distribute the bandwidth by percentage. Earlier in this chapter, you read that you could use either the **bandwidth** class subcommand to reserve an explicit amount of bandwidth (for instance, **bandwidth 56**), or a percentage of the bandwidth defined for the interface (for instance, **bandwidth percent 25**). You can use either style of command. Either way works, but for data applications, a percentage of the bandwidth tends to work well.

Cisco provides yet another option for allocated bandwidth inside a policy map — an option that is particularly useful in many LLQ configurations. The command is **bandwidth remaining percent**, and it is particularly useful when an engineer wants a policy map that meets the following general concepts:

1. One or more LLQ classes need to be included in the policy map.

2. Some bandwidth is allocated for the class-default queue (that's not a choice by the engineer — IOS always does this.)

3. For all the rest of the bandwidth, it would be best to subdivide the bandwidth based on a percentage of the bandwidth that was not already allocated — in other words, subdivide the remaining bandwidth after meeting the first two bandwidth requirements.

In short, if the goal is to create an LLQ configuration, with some non-LLQ queues, and you want to subdivide the bandwidth amongst the non-LLQs based on percentages, the **bandwidth remaining**

percent command does the job. Example 5-9 shows an example configuration, along with some discussion of the numbers following the example.

Example 5-9 *Examples Using the **bandwidth** remaining percent Command*

```
R3#show running-config
Building configuration...
! Portions omitted for brevity
 policy-map remaining-2
  class class1
   priority 55
  class class2
   bandwidth remaining percent 25
  class class3
   bandwidth remaining percent 35
  class class4
   bandwidth remaining percent 40
!
! Output omitted for brevity
!
interface Serial0/1
 bandwidth 256
 service-policy output remaining-2

R3#show policy-map interface s0/1
 Serial0/1

  Service-policy output: remaining-2

    Class-map: class1 (match-all)
      0 packets, 0 bytes
      5 minute offered rate 0 bps, drop rate 0 bps
      Match: ip dscp af41
      Queueing
        Strict Priority
        Output Queue: Conversation 72
        Bandwidth 55 (kbps) Burst 1375 (Bytes)
        (pkts matched/bytes matched) 0/0
        (total drops/bytes drops) 0/0

    Class-map: class2 (match-all)
      0 packets, 0 bytes
      5 minute offered rate 0 bps, drop rate 0 bps
      Match: ip dscp af42
      Queueing
        Output Queue: Conversation 73
        Bandwidth remaining 25 (%) Max Threshold 64 (packets)
        (pkts matched/bytes matched) 0/0
```

continues

Example 5-9 *Examples Using the* **bandwidth** *remaining percent Command*

```
         (depth/total drops/no-buffer drops) 0/0/0

  Class-map: class3 (match-all)
    0 packets, 0 bytes
    5 minute offered rate 0 bps, drop rate 0 bps
    Match: ip dscp af43
    Queueing
      Output Queue: Conversation 74
      Bandwidth remaining 35 (%) Max Threshold 64 (packets)
      (pkts matched/bytes matched) 0/0
      (depth/total drops/no-buffer drops) 0/0/0

  Class-map: class4 (match-all)
    0 packets, 0 bytes
    5 minute offered rate 0 bps, drop rate 0 bps
    Match: ip dscp af31
    Queueing
      Output Queue: Conversation 75
      Bandwidth remaining 40 (%) Max Threshold 64 (packets)
      (pkts matched/bytes matched) 0/0
      (depth/total drops/no-buffer drops) 0/0/0

  Class-map: class-default (match-any)
    0 packets, 0 bytes
    5 minute offered rate 0 bps, drop rate 0 bps
    Match: any
```

In this example, the policy map provides the following bandwidth to the queues:

- 55 kbps to the LLQ (explicitly defined)

- 64 kbps for the class-default queue (25 percent of interface bandwidth)

- 34 kbps (25 percent of 137 kbps) to class 2

- 48 kbps (35 percent of 137 kbps) to class 3

- 55 kbps (40 percent of 137 kbps) to class 4

Two items are subtracted from the configured interface bandwidth in order to find the remaining bandwidth. As a quick review, the **max-reserved-bandwidth** command can be used to define how much interface bandwidth can be assigned to CBWFQ and LLQ classes, with the remainder being reserved for the class-default queue. In this case, 75 percent of 256 kbps is available to the all the non-class-default queues (192 kbps), with the rest (64 kbps) for the class-default queue. While you could change the **max-reserved-bandwidth** command setting under the interface, it is not generally recommended.

In this case, the remaining bandwidth for the non-LLQ queues ends up at 137 kbps. The logic flows like this:

1. Find the interface bandwidth as set with the bandwidth interface subcommand—in this case 256 kbps.

2. Subtract the bandwidth reserved for the class-default queue—in this case 64 kbps.

3. Subtract all bandwidth defined in LLQs—in this case 55 kbps.

4. The remaining amount of bandwidth is the bandwidth that is subdivided using the bandwidth remaining percent class subcommand, in this case, 137kbps.

> **NOTE** The example showed how to use the **bandwidth** *remaining percent* class subcommand in conjunction with an LLQ configuration. However, you can also use it without LLQ, with a standard CBWFQ configuration. In that case, only the class-default bandwidth is subtracted from the interface bandwidth, with the remaining bandwidth being allocated using the **bandwidth** *remaining percent* command.

Comparisons of WFQ, CBWFQ, and LLQ

WFQ, CBWFQ, and LLQ each have an important role to play with QoS implementations in Cisco routers. WFQ works well as a default queuing mechanism when there are no low-latency requirements due to its very simple configuration and fair treatment of typically more important low volume flows. When an engineer takes the time to figure out what types of traffic need particular levels of service, CBWFQ provides bandwidth reservation with each class. When those types of traffic include classes with low latency and low jitter requirements, LLQ allows bandwidth reservation, priority service, with protection for the lower priority queues. Table 5-11 lists a few of the more important points about these queuing tools, with comments about their support of each point.

Table 5-11 *Comparisons of WFQ, CBWFQ, and LLQ*

Concept	WFQ	CBWFQ	LLQ
Requires complex classification configuration	No	Yes	Yes
Uses MQC	No	Yes	Yes
Prefers low volume, high precedence flows	Yes	Not flow based	Not flow based
Experiences problems with large numbers of flows	Yes	No*	No
Can reserve bandwidth per queue	No	Yes	Yes
Provide low delay, low jitter queuing	No	No	yes

*With WFQ enabled inside the a CBWFQ class-default queue, that class can experience problems with large numbers of flows.

Foundation Summary

The "Foundation Summary" is a collection of tables and figures that provide a convenient review of many key concepts in this chapter. For those of you already comfortable with the topics in this chapter, this summary could help you recall a few details. For those of you who just read this chapter, this review should help solidify some key facts. For any of you doing your final preparation before the exam, these tables and figures are a convenient way to review the day before the exam.

The following list summarizes the key points about TX Rings and TX Queues in relation to their effect on queuing:

- The TX Queue/TX Ring always performs FIFO scheduling, and cannot be changed.

- The TX Queue/TX Ring uses a single queue, per interface.

- IOS shortens the interface TX Queue/TX Ring automatically when an output queuing method is configured

- You can configure the TX Ring/TX Queue length to a different value.

Figure 5-22 shows how Hardware Queues affect queuing. With queuing configured with two queues, seven packets arrive, numbered in the order in which they arrive. The output queuing configuration specifies that the first two packets (1 and 2) should be placed into Queue 2, and the next four packets (numbered 3 through 6) should be placed into Queue 1.

Figure 5-22 *Two Output Queues, with Scheduler Always Servicing Queue 1 Rather Than Queue 2 When Packets Are in Queue 1*

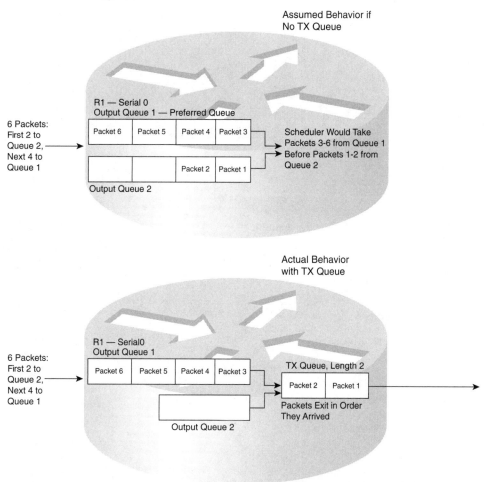

To delay the traffic, traffic shaping places the packets into the queue associated with the subinterface or DLCI and drains the traffic from the shaping queue at the shaped rate. Figure 5-23 shows the structure of the queues on a subinterface, interface, and the TX Queue, when shaping is enabled.

Figure 5-23 *Shaping Queues, Interface Queues, and TX Ring*

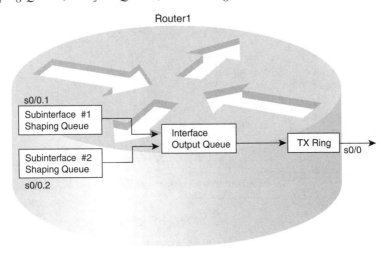

Flow-Based WFQ, or simply WFQ, classifies traffic into flows. Flows are identified by at least five items in an IP packet.

- Source IP address

- Destination IP address

- Transport layer protocol (TCP or UDP) as defined by the IP Protocol header field

- TCP or UDP source port

- TCP or UDP destination port

- IP Precedence

WFQ calculates the sequence number (SN) (also called Finish Time (FT)) before adding a packet to its associated queue. The formula for calculating the SN for a packet is as follows:

Previous_SN + weight * new_packet_length

Table 5-12 lists the weight values used by WFQ as of 12.0(5)T/12.1.

Table 5-12 *Weight Values Used by WFQ*

Precedence	After 12.0(5)T/12.1
0	32384
1	16192

Table 5-12 *Weight Values Used by WFQ (Continued)*

Precedence	After 12.0(5)T/12.1
2	10794
3	8096
4	6476
5	5397
6	4626
7	4048

WFQ discards some packet when a queue's *congestive discard threshold* (CDT) has been reached. To appreciate how the CDT is used, examine Figure 5-24.

Figure 5-24 *WFQ Modified Tail Drop and Congestive Discard Threshold*

Table 5-13 summarizes some of the key features of WFQ.

Table 5-13 *WFQ Functions and Features*

WFQ Feature	Explanation
Classification	Classifies without configuration, based on source/destination IP address/ port, protocol type (TCP|UDP), and ToS.
Drop policy	Modified tail drop.

continues

Table 5-13 *WFQ Functions and Features (Continued)*

WFQ Feature	Explanation
Number of queues	4096.
Maximum queue length	Congestive discard threshold per queue (max 4096), with an overall limit based on the hold queue for all queues (max 4096).
Scheduling inside a single queue	FIFO.
Scheduling among all queues	Serves lowest sequence number (SN). The SN is assigned when the packet is placed into the queue, as a function of length and precedence.

Table 5-14 summarizes some of the key features of CBWFQ.

Table 5-14 *CBWFQ Functions and Features*

CBWFQ Feature	Description
Classification	Classifies based on anything that MQC commands can match, just like CB marking. Includes all extended IP ACL fields, NBAR, incoming interface, CoS, precedence, DSCP, source/destination MAC, MPLS Experimental, QoS group, and RTP port numbers
Drop policy	Tail drop or WRED, configurable per queue.
Number of queues	64.
Maximum queue length	Varies per router model and memory.
Scheduling inside a single queue	FIFO on 63 queues; FIFO or WFQ on class-default queue*.
Scheduling among all queues	Algorithm is not published. The result of the scheduler provides a percentage guaranteed bandwidth to each queue.

* Except on 7500 series, where you can use FIFO or WFQ in all the CBWFQ queues.

To prevent LLQ from having the same problem as PQ, where packets in the highest-priority queue could dominate, LLQ's scheduler actually works as shown in Figure 5-25.

Figure 5-25 *Servicing Queues with LLQ and CBWFQ—The Real Story*

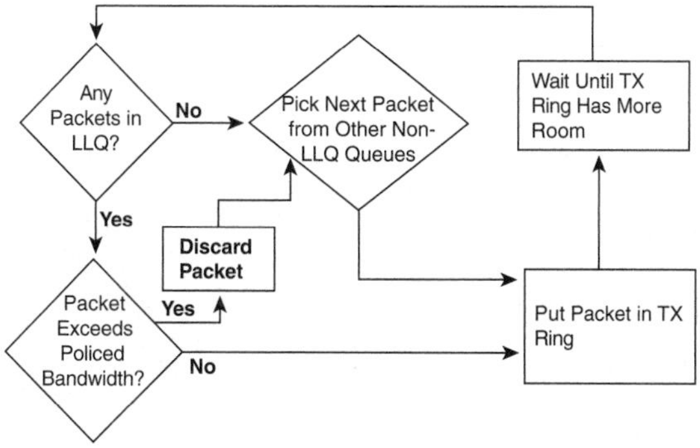

Table 5-15 lists a few of the more important points about these queuing tools, with comments about their support of each point.

Table 5-15 *Comparisons of WFQ, CBWFQ, and LLQ*

Concept	WFQ	CBWFQ	LLQ
Requires complex classification configuration	No	Yes	Yes
Uses MQC	No	Yes	Yes
Prefers low volume, high precedence flows	Yes	Not flow based	Not flow based
Experiences problems with large numbers of flows	Yes	No*	No
Can reserve bandwidth per queue	No	Yes	Yes
Provide low delay, low jitter queuing	No	No	yes

*With WFQ enabled inside the a CBWFQ class-default queue, that class can experience problems with large numbers of flows.

For Further Reading

This book attempts to cover the breadth and depth of QoS as covered on the QoS exam (642-642). However, you may want to read more about topics in this chapter, or other classification and marking topics.

For more on the topics in this chapter:

■ Cisco IOS 12.3 QOS Configuration Guide (http://www.cisco.com/univercd/cc/td/doc/product/software/ios123/123cgcr/qos_vcg.htm)

For more on other Classification and Marking topics:

■ Appendix B, "Additional QoS Reference Materials" (found on the book's accompanying CD-ROM):

— Priority Queuing (PQ)

— Custom Queuing (CQ)

— Modified Deficit Round Robin (MDRR)

For design related guidance:

■ Cisco's document "Cisco AVVID Network Infrastructure Enterprise Quality of Service Design" document at http://cisco.com/application/pdf/en/us/guest/netsol/ns17/c649/ccmigration_09186a00800d67ed.pdf

Q&A

As mentioned in the Introduction, you have two choices for review questions. The questions that follow next give you a more difficult challenge than the exam itself by using an open-ended question format. By reviewing now with this more difficult question format, you can exercise your memory better, and prove your conceptual and factual knowledge of this chapter. You can find the answers to these questions in Appendix A.

The second option for practice questions is to use the CD included with this book. It includes a testing engine and more than 200 multiple-choice questions. You should use this CD nearer to the end of your preparation, for practice with the actual exam format.

1. Describe the benefits of having a single FIFO output queue.

2. Explain the effects of changing a single FIFO queue's length to twice its original value. Include comments about how the change affects bandwidth, delay, jitter, and loss.

3. Explain the purpose of a TX Ring and TX Queue in a Cisco router.

4. Explain how a long TX Ring might affect the behavior of a queuing tool.

5. Describe the command output that identifies the length of the TX Ring or TX Queue, and whether the length was automatically lowered by IOS.

6. Explain under what circumstances the TX Ring, interface output queues, and subinterface output queues both fill and drain, and to where they drain.

7. Assume a queuing tool has been enabled on interface S0/0. Describe the circumstances under which the queuing tool would actually be used.

8. Explain the circumstances under which it would be useful to enable a queuing tool on a subinterface.

Scheduling Concepts: FIFO, PQ, CQ, and MDRR

9. Describe the process and end result of the scheduling feature of Priority Queuing.

10. Describe the process and end result of the scheduling feature of Custom Queuing.

11. Describe how the Modified Deficit Round-Robin scheduler works, and specifically why the word "deficit" refers to part of the scheduler logic.

Concepts and Configuration: WFQ, CBWFQ, and LLQ

12. WFQ classifies packets based on their flow. Other than a typical flow from an end user device, identify the other two types of flows recognized by WFQ.

13. Characterize the effect the WFQ scheduler has on different types of flows.

14. Describe the WFQ scheduler process. Include at least the concept behind any formulas, if not the specific formula.

15. You previously disabled WFQ on interface S0/0. List the minimum number of commands required to enable WFQ on S0/0.

16. What commands list statistical information about the performance of WFQ?

17. Define what comprises a flow in relation to WFQ.

18. You just bought and installed a new 3600 series router. Before adding any configuration to the router, you go ahead and plug in the new T1 Frame Relay access link to interface S0/0. List the minimum number of commands required to enable WFQ on S0/0.

19. Describe the CBWFQ scheduler process, both inside a single queue and among all queues.

20. Describe how LLQ allows for low latency while still giving good service to other queues.

21. Compare and contrast the CBWFQ command that configures the guaranteed bandwidth for a class with the command that enables LLQ for a class.

22. Describe the CBWFQ classification options. List at least five fields that can be matched without using an ACL.

23. Name the two CBWFQ global configuration commands that define classification options, and then the per-hop behaviors, respectively. Also list the command that enables CBWFQ on an interface.

24. Examine the following configuration (Example 5-10). Which of the five policy maps would certainly enable LLQ for voice payload traffic, based only of the information in the configuration?

Example 5-10 *Exhibit for CBWFQ Configuration Questions*

```
!
class-map match-all class1
  match ip rtp 16384 16383
class-map match-all class2
  match access-group 101
class-map match-all class3
  match ip rtp 16384 32767
class-map match-all class4
  match ip dscp ef
```

Example 5-10 *Exhibit for CBWFQ Configuration Questions (Continued)*

```
class-map match-all class5
  match access-group 102
!
policy-map pmap1
 class class1
  priority 60
policy-map pmap2
 class class2
  priority 60
policy-map pmap3
 class class3
  priority 60
policy-map pmap4
 class class4
  priority 60
policy-map pmap5
 class class5
  priority 60
!
interface Serial0/0
 service-policy output ?????
!
access-list 101 permit udp any gt 16383 any gt 16383
access-list 102 permit udp any range 16383 32767 any range 16383 32767
!
```

25. Using the same exhibit as in the preceding example, describe what must also be true for **pmap4** to queue voice payload traffic successfully, and only voice payload traffic, in a low-latency queue.

26. Which of the following queuing tools can always service a particular queue first, even when other queues have packets waiting? First-In, First-Out Queuing (FIFO); Priority Queuing (PQ); Custom Queuing (CQ); Weighted Fair Queuing (WFQ); Class-Based WFQ (CBWFQ); Low Latency Queuing (LLQ).

27. Which of the following queuing tools allows for a percentage bandwidth to be assigned to each queue? First-In, First-Out Queuing (FIFO); Priority Queuing (PQ); Custom Queuing (CQ); Weighted Fair Queuing (WFQ); Class-Based WFQ (CBWFQ); Low Latency Queuing (LLQ).

28. Which queuing tools could be configured to provide the lowest possible latency for voice traffic? Of these, which does Cisco recommend as the best option for voice queuing today?

29. Which of the following queuing tools can use flow-based classification? First-In, First-Out Queuing (FIFO); Priority Queuing (PQ); Custom Queuing (CQ); Weighted Fair Queuing (WFQ); Class-Based WFQ (CBWFQ); Low Latency Queuing (LLQ).

30. Which of the following queuing tools uses the Modular QoS CLI? First-In, First-Out Queuing (FIFO); Priority Queuing (PQ); Custom Queuing (CQ); Weighted Fair Queuing (WFQ); Class-Based WFQ (CBWFQ); Low Latency Queuing (LLQ).

31. Which of the following queuing tools allows for a value to be configured, which then results in a specific number of bytes being taken from each queue during a round-robin pass through the queues? First-In, First-Out Queuing (FIFO); Priority Queuing (PQ); Custom Queuing (CQ); Weighted Fair Queuing (WFQ); Class-Based WFQ (CBWFQ); Low Latency Queuing (LLQ).

32. What model of Cisco router supports WFQ inside CBWFQ classes other than class-default?

33. Give an explanation for the following comment: "WFQ can become too fair when it has a large number of active flows"?

34. Imagine the following commands in Example 5-11 were typed in configuration mode, in order. Also assume that class maps **class1**, **class2**, and **class3** have already been correctly defined. How much bandwidth will class **class3** be assigned on interface S0/0?

Example 5-11 *Exhibit for CBWFQ Configuration Questions*

```
!
policy-map pmap1
 class class1
   priority 60
class class2
   bandwidth percent 30
class class3
   bandwidth percent 45
!
policy-map pmap2
 class class1
   priority percent 20
class class2
   bandwidth remaining percent 30
class class3
   bandwidth remaining percent 70
!
policy-map pmap3
class class1
   priority percent 20
class class2
   bandwidth 30
class class3
   bandwidth percent 30
!
interface Serial0/0
 service-policy output pmap1
!
```

Example 5-11 *Exhibit for CBWFQ Configuration Questions (Continued)*

```
interface Serial0/1
bandwidth 512
 service-policy output pmap2
 !
interface Serial0/2
bandwidth 256
 service-policy output pmap3
 !
```

35. In the same example, what could be done so that the **service-policy output pmap1** command would be accepted under interface serial0/0—without changing the policy map? Assuming that was done, what actual bandwidth could be assigned to class3?

36. In the same example, how much bandwidth would class1 be assigned on interface serial 0/1?

37. In the same example, how much bandwidth would **class2** and **class3** be assigned on interface serial 0/1?

38. In the same example, how much bandwidth would **class2** and **class3** be assigned on interface serial 0/2?

QoS Exam Objectives

This chapter covers the following exam topics specific to the QoS exam:

- Describe the purpose of traffic conditioning using traffic policing and traffic shaping and differentiate between the features of each

- Explain how network devices measure traffic rates using single rate or dual rate, single or dual token bucket mathematical models

- Identify the Cisco IOS commands required to configure and monitor single rate and dual rate CB-Policing

- Identify the Cisco IOS commands required to configure and monitor percentage based CB-Policing

- Explain how the two rate limits, average rate and peak rate, can be used to rate limit traffic

- Identify the Cisco IOS commands required to configure and monitor CB-Shaping

- Identify the Cisco IOS commands required to configure and monitor Frame Relay adaptive CB-Shaping on Frame Relay interfaces

CHAPTER 6

Traffic Policing and Shaping

Traffic policing allows devices in one network to enforce a traffic contract. *Traffic contracts* define how much data one network can send into another, typically expressed as a committed information rate (CIR) and a committed burst (Bc). *Policing* measures the flow of data, and discards packets that exceed the traffic contract.

Similarly, traffic shaping allows packets to conform to a traffic contract. In cases where packets that exceed the traffic contract might be discarded, the sending device may choose just to slow down its sending rate, so that the packets are not discarded. The process of sending the traffic more slowly than it could be sent, to conform to a traffic contract, is called shaping.

In short, policing typically drops out-of-contract traffic, whereas shaping typically delays it.

Shaping and policing share several concepts and mechanisms. Both need to measure the rate at which data is sent or received, and take action when the rate exceeds the contract. Often when policing is used for packets entering a network, shaping is also used on devices sending into that network. Although shaping and policing are not always used in the same networks, there are more similarities than differences, so both are covered in this single chapter.

"Do I Know This Already?" Quiz

The purpose of the "Do I Know This Already?" quiz is to help you decide whether you really need to read the entire chapter. If you already intend to read the entire chapter, you do not necessarily need to answer these questions now.

The 12-question quiz, derived from the major sections in "Foundation Topics" section of this chapter, helps you determine how to spend your limited study time.

Table 6-1 outlines the major topics discussed in this chapter and the "Do I Know This Already?" quiz questions that correspond to those topics.

Table 6-1 *"Do I Know This Already?" Foundation Topics Section-to-Question Mapping*

Foundations Topics Section	Questions Covered in This Section	Score
Shaping and Policing Concepts	1–5	
Configuring Class-Based Shaping	6–8	
Configuring Class-Based Policing	9–12	
Total Score		

CAUTION   The goal of self-assessment is to gauge your mastery of the topics in this chapter. If you do not know the answer to a question or are only partially sure of the answer, mark this question wrong for purposes of the self-assessment. Giving yourself credit for an answer you correctly guess skews your self-assessment results and might provide you with a false sense of security.

You can find the answers to the "Do I Know This Already?" quiz in Appendix A, "Answers to the 'Do I Know This Already?' Quizzes and Q&A Sections." The suggested choices for your next step are as follows:

■ **10 or less overall score**—Read the entire chapter. This includes the "Foundation Topics," the "Foundation Summary," and the "Q&A" sections.

■ **11 or 12 overall score**—If you want more review on these topics, skip to the "Foundation Summary" section and then go to the "Q&A" section. Otherwise, move to the next chapter.

Shaping and Policing Concepts Questions

1. How big is the token bucket used by CB Shaping when no excess bursting is configured?

    a. Bc bytes

    b. Bc + Be bytes

    c. Bc bits

    d. Bc + Be bits

2. Which of the following are true about Policers in general, but not true about Shapers?

    a. Monitors traffic rates using concept of token bucket

    b. Can discard traffic that exceeds a defined traffic rate

    c. Can delay packets by queuing in order to avoid exceeding a traffic rate

    d. Can re-mark a packet

3. If shaping was configured with a rate of 128Kbps, and a Bc of 3200, what value would be calculated for Tc?

    a. 125 ms

    b. 125 sec

    c. 25 ms

    d. 25 sec

    e. Shaping doesn't use a Tc

    f. Not enough information to tell

4. With dual-rate policing, upon what value does the policer base the size of the token bucket associated with the second, higher policing rate?

    a. Bc

    b. Be

    c. CIR

    d. PIR

    e. Not based on any other value—it must be statically configured.

5. With single-rate policing, with three possible actions configured, how does the policer replenish tokens into the excess token bucket?

    a. By filling Bc * Tc tokens into the first bucket each time interval, with spilled tokens refilling the excess token bucket.

    b. By refilling the first bucket, based on a pro-rated amount of Bc, with spilled tokens refilling the excess token bucket.

    c. By Be * Tc each time interval

    d. By putting a pro-rated amount of Be into the excess token bucket directly.

    e. By Be tokens each second

Configuring Class-Based Shaping

6. Which of the following commands, when typed in the correct configuration mode, enables shaping at 128 kbps, with no excess burst?

    a. **shape average 128000 8000 0**

    b. **shape average 128 8000 0**

    c. **shape average 128000**

    d. **shape peak 128000 8000 0**

    e. **shape peak 128 8000 0 0**

    f. **shape peak 128000**

7. Examine the following configuration, noting the locations of the comments lines labeled "point 1", point 2", and so on. Assume that a correctly-configured policy map that implements CBWFQ, called queue-it, is also configured but not shown. In order to enable CBWFQ for the packets queued by CB Shaping, what command is required, and at what point in the configuration would the command be required?

```
policy-map shape-question
! point 1
 class class-default
! point 2
  shape average 256000 5120
! point 3
interface serial 0/0
! point 4
  service-policy output shape-question
! point 5
interface s0/0.1 point-to-point
! point 6
  ip address 1.1.1.1
! point 7
  frame-relay interface-dlci 101
! point 8
```

a. **service-policy queue-it**, at point 1

b. **service-policy queue-it**, at point 3

c. **service-policy queue-it**, at point 5

d. **service-policy queue-it**, at point 6

e. **shape queue service-policy queue-it**, at point 1

f. **shape queue service-policy queue-it**, at point 3

g. **shape queue service-policy queue-it**, at point 5

h. **shape queue service-policy queue-it**, at point 6

8. Using the same configuration snippet as in the previous question, what command would list the calculated Tc value, and what would that value be?

a. **show policy-map**, Tc = 125 ms

b. **show policy-map**, Tc = 20 ms

c. **show policy-map**, Tc = 10 ms

d. **show policy-map interface s0/0**, Tc = 125 ms

e. **show policy-map interface s0/0**, Tc = 20 ms

f. **show policy-map interface s0/0**, Tc = 10 ms

Configuring Class-Based Policing

9. Which of the following commands, when typed in the correct configuration mode, enables CB policing at 128 kbps, with no excess burst?

   a. **police 128000 conform-action transmit exceed-action transmit violate-action discard**

   b. **police 128 conform-action transmit exceed-action transmit violate-action discard**

   c. **police 128000 conform-action transmit exceed-action discard**

   d. **police 128 conform-action transmit exceed-action discard**

   e. **police 128k conform-action transmit exceed-action discard**

10. Examine the following configuration. Which of the following commands would be required to change this configuration so that the policing function would be a dual-rate policer, with CIR of 256 kbps and double that for the peak rate?

```
policy-map police-question
 class class-default
  police 256000 conform-action transmit exceed-action set-dscp-transmit af11
violate-action discard
interface serial 0/0
  service-policy input police-question
interface s0/0.1 point-to-point
  ip address 1.1.1.1
  frame-relay interface-dlci 101
```

   a. Replace the existing **police** command with **police cir 256000 Bc 4000 Be 4000 conform-action transmit exceed-action transmit violate-action drop**

   b. Replace the existing **police** command with **police cir 256000 pir 512000 conform-action transmit exceed-action set-dscp-transmit af11 violate-action drop**

   c. Replace the existing **police** command with **police 256000 512000 conform-action transmit exceed-action transmit violate-action drop**

   d. Replace the existing **police** command with **police cir 256000 pir 2x conform-action transmit exceed-action transmit violate-action drop**

11. In the previous question, none of the answers specified the settings for Bc and Be. What would CB policing calculate for Bc and Be when policing at rates of 256 kbps and 512 kbps with a dual-rate policing configuration?

   a. 4000 and 4000, respectively

   b. 4000 and 8000, respectively

   c. 8000 and 16000, respectively

   d. 32000 and 64000, respectively

12. Examine the following configuration, which shows all commands pertinent to this question. Which of the following **police** commands would be required to enable single-rate policing at approximately 128 kbps, with the Bc set to cause Tc = 10ms? (Note that a comment line shows where the **police** command would be added to the configuration.)

```
policy-map police-question2
 class class-default
 ! police command goes here
interface serial 0/0
   service-policy input police-question2
interface s0/0.1 point-to-point
   ip address 1.1.1.1
   frame-relay interface-dlci 101
```

   a. **police cir 128000 Bc 1280 conform-action transmit exceed-action transmit violate-action discard**

   b. **police cir percent 8 conform-action transmit exceed-action transmit violate-action discard**

   c. **police cir 128000 Tc 10 conform-action transmit exceed-action transmit violate-action discard**

   d. **police cir percent 8 Bc 10 ms conform-action transmit exceed-action transmit violate-action discard**

Foundation Topics

Traffic shaping solves some of the most important issues relating to quality of service (QoS) in networks today. Even when policing is not also used, traffic shaping solves a category of delay and loss problems called *egress blocking*, which can occur in all multiaccess WANs, such as Frame Relay and ATM networks. Traffic shaping is covered extensively in CCNP and CCIE exams and labs, so the coverage in this chapter will help you with other exams as well.

Policing solves specific problems relating to network capacity and traffic engineering. Suppose, for example, that an Internet service provider (ISP) engineers their network to effectively forward packets at rate x. Suppose further that the Sales department sells enough access so that the customers all together pay for x capacity. However, the customers can collectively send $10x$ into the ISP's network, so everyone suffers. Policing just gives a network engineer the ability to "enforce the law" by discarding excess traffic, much like a real policeman just enforces the law of the local community. Policing can also prevent a single customer from taking too much bandwidth, even if the provider has enough capacity to handle the extra traffic.

This chapter first explains the core concepts of traffic shaping and policing, including descriptions of how each uses the concept of token buckets. Following that, the chapter devotes separate sections to the configuration for the MQC-based tools for each function—Class-Based Shaping and Class-Based Policing.

Traffic Policing and Traffic Shaping Concepts

Traffic shaping and traffic policing both measure the rate at which data is sent or received. *Policing* discards excess packets, so that the overall policed rate is not exceeded. *Shaping* enqueues the excess packets, which are then drained from the queue at the shaping rate. In either case, both policing and shaping prevent the traffic from exceeding the bit rate defined to the policer or shaper.

This section covers concepts related to both shaping and policing. It starts with some of the motivations for using shaping and policing. One classic reason to choose to shape occurs when the device at the other end of the link is policing. Suppose, for instance, that R1 sits in an enterprise, and R2 is inside an ISP. R1 sends packets to R2, and R2 polices traffic, discarding any traffic beyond x bits per second (bps). The ISP might have chosen to police at R2 to protect the network from accepting too much traffic. R1 could be configured to shape the traffic it sends to R2 to the same rate as the policer at R2, instead of having the excess packets discarded by R2. Other less-obvious reasons for both shaping and policing exist. The upcoming section discusses these.

This section also discusses the mechanisms shaping and policing use to perform their functions. For instance, both policers and shapers must measure bit rates. To measure a rate, a number of bits or bytes over a time period must be observed and calculated. To keep the process simple, shaping and policing use similar mechanisms to account for the numbers of bits and bytes sent over time. First, however, we start with the motivations for using shaping and policing.

When and Where to Use Shaping and Policing

Most implementations of shaping and policing occur at the edges between two different networks. For instance, consider Figure 6-1, which illustrates the two typical cases for shaping and policing. The figure shows PB Tents Enterprise network, with a Frame Relay service, and Internet connectivity using ISP1.

Figure 6-1 *Connection to an ISP, and to a Frame Relay Network*

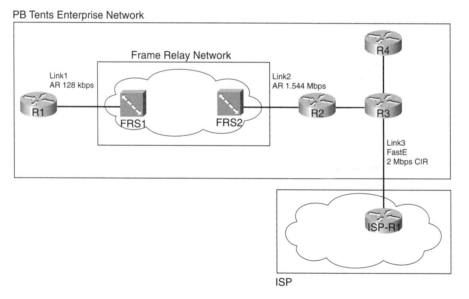

In this case, PB Tents has three separate boundaries between different networks. Link1, between R1 and the Frame Relay network switch labeled FRS1, is the first boundary. The second boundary is between the switch FRS2 and R2. Finally, a boundary exists between R3 and ISP-R1, over Link3.

For each boundary, the legal documents that detail the agreement between PB Tents and the Frame Relay service provider, and the documents that detail the agreement with ISP1, include something called a *traffic contract*. The need for the contract makes the most sense in the context of Frame Relay, but it also applies to the Internet connection. For instance, R2 uses a T/1 access link into the Frame Relay network. However, the virtual circuit (VC) between R2 and R1 may only include a committed information rate (CIR) of 64 kbps. Similarly, R1 has a 128-kbps access link, and the CIR of the VC to R2 still has a CIR of 64 kbps. When R1 sends a packet, the packet is transmitted at 128 kbps — that's the only speed that physically works! Likewise, R2 must send at 1.5 Mbps. However, the traffic contract may just state that the VC from R1 to R2 allows only 64 kbps in each direction.

Similarly, PB Tents and ISP1 may agree to install a link that is faster than PB Tents actually needs right now, expecting that PB Tent's Internet traffic loads will grow. When PB Tents needs more capacity to the Internet, each party can just agree to a new traffic contract, and PB Tents will pay ISP1 more money. For instance, metro Ethernet/Fast Ethernet/Gigabit Ethernet services have become more common; most sites do not really need 100 Mbps of bandwidth to the Internet. If PB Tents connected to ISP1 using a Fast Ethernet connection, but the traffic contract stated that PB Tents gets only 2 Mbps of service, however, the same mismatch between physical capability and legal ability, as seen with Frame Relay, occurs on the Internet connection.

In short, policing and shaping can play a role in cases where a router can send more traffic than the traffic contract allows. Shaping just slows the rate of sending packets so that the traffic contract is not exceeded. Policing discards some packets so that the traffic contract is not exceeded.

Policing: When and Where?

Whenever the physical clock rate exceeds the traffic contract, policing may be needed. Suppose, for instance, that ISP1 has 1000 customers, just like PB Tents, each with a 100-Mbps connection, and a contract for support of 2 Mbps. What happens over time? Well, without something to prevent it, each customer will send and receive more and more traffic. For a while, all the customers are happy, because their packets make it through the overbuilt ISP1 core. Even if ISP1 has enough capacity to support 10 Mbps of traffic from every customer, eventually, ISP1's network will become overrun, because their customers keep sending more and more traffic, so eventually all traffic will suffer. Queues become congested frequently, causing dropped packets. Multimedia traffic suffers through the poor performance as a result of high delay and jitter. TCP sessions continually decrease their window sizes because of the lost packets, causing synchronization effects inside ISP1. ISP1 can add capacity, but that probably means that ISP1 should start charging more to their customers, who may not be willing to upgrade to a higher-traffic contract.

In actual ISP networks, the network engineers design the core of the network expecting some degree of oversubscription. The term "oversubscription" means that the customer has sent and received more traffic than was contracted, or subscribed. As in the example of ISP1 in the preceding paragraph, ISPs and Frame Relay providers build their network expecting some oversubscription. However, they may not build the core expecting every customer to send traffic at full access rate, all the time.

Policing protects a network from being overrun by traffic. If ISP1 just policed traffic from each customer, discarding packets that exceed the traffic contract, it would protect itself from being overrun. However, the decision to add policing to a network can be politically difficult. Suppose that ISP1 has these 1000 customers, each of whom contracted for 2 Mbps of traffic. Each customer sends and receives more, averaging 10 Mbps, so that ISP1's network is becoming too congested. ISP1 chooses to implement policing, using the contracted rate, discarding packets that exceed 2 Mbps of traffic. Of course, most of their customers will be very unhappy! Such a move may be a career-ending, if not business-ending, choice.

Policers can also just mark down the traffic, instead of discarding it. To do so, the policer marks the packet with a different IP precedence or DSCP value when the traffic rate is exceeded, but it still lets the packet through. Later QoS functions, including policers and packet-drop tools such as Weighted Random Early Detection (WRED), can more aggressively discard marked-down packets as compared with those that have not been marked down. Essentially, the policer can increase the chance that a packet will get discarded somewhere else in the network if that packet causes the traffic rate to be exceeded. Generally speaking, when policers mark down packets, if the network is not currently congested, the packet can get through the network; if congested, the packet is much more likely to be discarded.

ISPs make the business choice of whether to police, and how aggressively to police. The options reduce to the following three basic options:

■ **Do not police**—To support the traffic, build the network to support the traffic as if all customers will send and receive data at the clock rate of the access link. From a sales perspective, close deals by claiming that no policing will be done, but encourage customers who exceed their contracts to pay for more bandwidth.

■ **Police at the contracted rate**—To support these traffic levels, the network only needs to be built to support the collective contracted rates, although the core would be overbuilt to support new customers. From a sales perspective, encourage customers that are beginning to exceed their contracts to upgrade, and give incentives.

■ **Police somewhere in between the contracted rate and the access-link clock rate**—For instance, ISP1 might police PB Tents at 5 Mbps, when the contract reads 2 Mbps. The network can be built to support the collective policed rates. The sales team can encourage customers to buy a larger contracted rate when they consistently exceed the contracted rate, but keep customer satisfaction higher by pointing out their generosity by only policing at rates much higher than the contracted rates.

Policing can be useful in multiaccess WANs (Frame Relay and ATM networks) for the same reason that it was useful for the ISP connection described earlier. Whenever data can be sent faster than the contracted rate, the danger exists that a network will be overrun when many sites exceed their contract at the same time. An example will help you understand a few of the issues. Figure 6-2, the network diagram for PB Tents network, has been expanded to show 12 branches, with a single central site.

Figure 6-2 *PB Tents Network, 12 Frame Relay Branches, 1 Central Site*

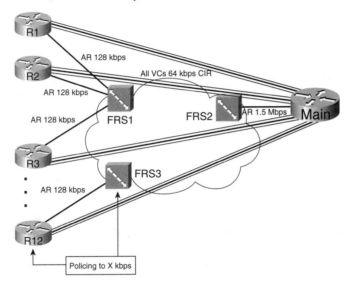

Each branch can send traffic at 128 kbps, but each branch only has a contracted 64-kbps CIR on their respective VCs to the main site. If all 12 sites conform to their CIRs, the Frame Relay network should be able to handle the load. If all 12 sites offer 128 kbps of traffic for long periods, however, the provider may still go ahead and try to forward all the traffic, because most Frame Relay providers overbuild their core networks. They also like to imply in their sales pitch that the customer gets to send excess packets for free.

Of course, at some point, if every customer of this provider sent traffic at full line rates for a period of time, the network would probably congest. The same options exist for the Frame Relay network as for an ISP — not to police but build more capacity; police to CIR, and deal with the sales and customer satisfaction issues; or police at something over CIR, and deal with the sales and customer satisfaction issues in slightly different ways.

To police the network in Figure 6-2, the Frame Relay switches can be configured to perform the policing, or the routers can be used. Traditionally, policing is performed as packets enter a network, which would suggest policing as packets enter the Frame Relay switches from the customer. If the service provider actually controls the edge routers in the enterprise network, however, the policing feature can be performed as packets exit the routers, going toward the Frame Relay cloud. If the customer controls the routers at the edge of the cloud, policing in these routers may be risky for the service provider, just because of the possibility that some customers might turn off policing to get more capacity for free.

The Cisco QoS exam covers policing in IOS routers using CB Policing. The exam does not cover policing in Frame Relay switches, or in LAN switches, although the basic concepts are the same.

Traffic Shaping—When and Where?

Networks use traffic shaping for two main reasons:

- To shape the traffic at the same rate as policing (if the service provider polices traffic)

- To avoid the effects of egress blocking

For instance, consider Branches 1 and 24 in Figure 6-3. Branch 1 does not shape, whereas Branch 24 does shape to 96 kbps. In both cases, the Frame Relay switches they are configured to police packets at a 96-kbps rate. (The CIR in each case is 64 kbps. Therefore, the service provider is not policing aggressively. The PB Tents engineer wants to get as much bandwidth as possible out of the service, so he shapes at 96 kbps rather than the 64-kbps CIR.)

Figure 6-3 *PB Tents Network, Policing and Shaping, Versus Just Policing*

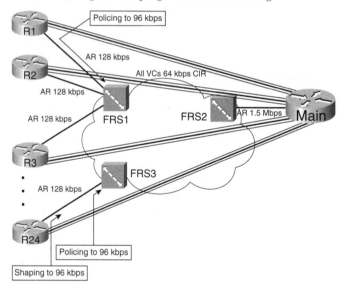

For Branch 1, the absence of shaping ensures that R1 will not artificially delay any packets. However, the policing performed at FRS1 will discard some packets when R1 sends more than 96-kbps worth of traffic. Therefore, some packets will be dropped, although the packets that are not dropped will not experience extra shaping delay. This strategy makes sense when the traffic from Branch 1 is not drop sensitive, but may be delay and jitter sensitive.

For Branch 24, the presence of shaping ensures that R24 will artificially delay some packets. However, the policing performed at FRS3 will not discard packets, because R24 will not send more than 96-kbps worth of traffic. Therefore, no packets will be dropped, although some packets will experience more delay and jitter. This strategy makes sense when the traffic from Branch 24 is drop sensitive, but not delay and jitter sensitive.

The other reason to use shaping is to avoid the effects of egress blocking. *Egress blocking* occurs when packets try to exit a multiaccess WAN, such as Frame Relay and ATM, and cannot exit the network because of congestion. Automobile traffic patterns cause the same kinds of behavior as egress blocking. In the morning, for instance, everyone in the state may try to commute to the same small, downtown area of a big city. Even though an eight-lane highway leads into the city, it may seem that everyone living in the surrounding little towns tries to get off at the few exits of the highway between 7 and 8 a.m. each morning. The highway and exits in the downtown area become congested. Similarly, in the afternoon, if everyone tries to reach the suburbs through one exit off the highway at 5:30 p.m., the eight-lane highway feeding into the two-lane exit road becomes congested. Likewise, although plenty of capacity may exist in a network, egress blocking can occur for packets trying to exit the network.

Figure 6-4 illustrates what happens with egress blocking, using a Frame Relay network as an example.

Figure 6-4 *PB Tents Network, Egress Blocking*

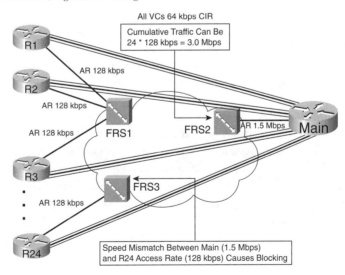

Suppose that all 24 branches shape at 64 kbps. The cumulative traffic sent by the branches to the main site is 1.5 Mbps, if each branch simultaneously sends 64 kbps. Because the Main router has a T/1 installed, FRS2 should not experience congestion when forwarding packets out of the access link to the Main router. However, what if shaping were not used at the branches? If all 24 branches were to send traffic at 128 kbps (access rate) for a period of time, the cumulative offered load would be about 3 Mbps. Packets would begin to queue trying to exit FRS2's interface connected to the Main router. The packets would experience more delay, more jitter, and eventually more packet drops as the FRS2 output queue filled. Notice that the service provider did not do any policing — egress blocking still occurred, because the branches could collectively overload the egress link between the cloud and the main site.

Interestingly, even if policing were used, and shaping at the branches, egress blocking could still occur. In Figure 6-3, shaping and policing were configured at 96 kbps, because the service provider did not want to be too aggressive in enforcing the traffic contract. With all 24 branches sending 96 kbps at the same time, about 2.25 Mbps of traffic needs to exit FRS2 to get to the Main router. Again, egress blocking can occur, even with policing and shaping enabled!

Similarly, egress blocking can occur right to left in the figure as well. Imagine that the Main router receives 11 consecutive 1500-byte packets from a LAN interface, destined to Branch 24. It takes the Main router roughly 100 milliseconds to send the packets into the Frame Relay network, because its access link is a T/1. When the frames arrive in FRS1, they need to be sent out the access link to R24. However, this access link runs at 128 kbps. To send these 11 packets, it takes slightly more than 1 second just to serialize the packets over the link! Most of the packets then wait in the output queue on FRS3, waiting their turn to be sent. This simple case is another example of egress blocking, sometimes just referred to as a *speed mismatch*.

One solution to the egress blocking problem is to shape the traffic. In the example network, shaping all VCs at the branches to 64 kbps would ensure that the cumulative offered load did not exceed the access rate at the main site. Similarly, if the Main router shaped the VC to R1 to 64 kbps, or even 128 kbps, the egress blocking problem on FRS1 would be solved.

In both cases, however, delay and jitter occurs as a result of the shaping function. Instead of having more queuing delay in the Frame Relay switches, shaping delays occur in the router, because packets wait in router shaping queues. With the queuing occurring in the routers, however, the features of IOS queuing tools can be used to better manipulate the traffic, and give better delay characteristics to delay-sensitive traffic. For instance, with the shaping queues forming in a router, the router can use Low Latency Queuing (LLQ) to dequeue Voice over IP (VoIP) packets first. A Frame Relay switch cannot perform complicated queuing, because the Frame Relay switch does not examine fields outside the Frame Relay or IP header when making forwarding and queuing decisions.

Table 6-2 summarizes some of the key points about the rationale behind when you should use policing and shaping.

Table 6-2 *Policing and Shaping: When to Use Them, and Where*

Topic	Rationale
Why police?	If a neighboring network can send more traffic than the traffic contract specifies, policing can be used to enforce the contract, protecting the network from being overrun with too much traffic.
Where to police?	Typically, policing is performed as packets enter the first device in a network. Egress policing is also supported, although it is less typical.
Why shape?	The first of two reasons for shaping is when the neighboring network is policing. Instead of waiting for the neighboring policer to discard traffic, a shaper can instead delay traffic so that it will not be dropped. The second reason has to do with the effects of egress blocking. By shaping, egress blocking can be avoided, or minimized, essentially moving the queues from inside the service provider cloud, and back into the enterprise routers. By doing so, the router queuing tools can selectively give better QoS performance to particular types of traffic.
Where to shape?	Shaping is always an egress function. Typically, shaping is performed on packets exiting a router, going into another network. This may be the edge between a router and a multiaccess WAN, or possibly just a link to an ISP.

How Shaping Works

Shaping only makes sense when the physical clock rate of a transmission medium exceeds a traffic contract. The most typical case for shaping involves a router connected to a Frame Relay or ATM network. More often today, however, connections to ISPs use a point-to-point serial link or an Ethernet link between an enterprise and the ISP, with a traffic contract defining lower traffic volumes than the physical link.

Routers can only send bits out an interface at the physical clock rate. To have the average bit rate, over time, be lower than the clock rate, the router just has to send some packets for some specified time period, and then not send any packets for another time period. To average sending at a packet rate of half the physical link speed, the router should send packets half of the time, and not send the other half of the time. To make the average rate equal to 1/4 of the physical link speed, the router should send 1/4 of the time, and not send packets 3/4 of the time. Over time, it looks like a staccato series of sending, and silence.

You can understand traffic-shaping logic by reviewing just a few simple examples. Of course, you need to know a few more details for the exam! However, the basics follow these simple examples: If R1 has a 128-kbps access rate, and a 64-kbps CIR, and the engineer wants to shape the traffic to match CIR (64 kbps), R1 just has to send traffic on the link half of the time. If, over time, R1 sends traffic half of the time, at 128 kbps (because that's the only rate it can actually send traffic), the average over that time is 64 kbps. The concept is that simple!

A few more simple examples here emphasize the point. Referring to Figure 6-4, assume R1 wants to shape at 96 kbps, because the Frame Relay switch is policing at 96 kbps. With a 128-kbps access rate, to shape to 96 kbps, R1 should send 3/4 of the time, because 96/128 = 3/4.

Again from Figure 6-4, if the Main router wants to shape the VC connecting it to R24 at 128 kbps, to avoid the egress-blocking problem, the Main router needs to send packets 128/1536 (actual available bit rate for T/1 is 1.536 Mbps), or 1/12 of the time. If the Main router wants to shape that same VC to 64 kbps, to match the CIR, the Main router should send packets over that VC at 64/1536, or 1/24, of the time.

Traffic shaping implements this basic logic by defining a measurement interval, and a number of bits that can be sent in that interval, so that the overall shaped rate is not exceeded. Examples help, but first, Table 6-3 lists some definitions.

Table 6-3 *Shaping Terminology*

Term	Definition
Tc	Time interval, measured in milliseconds, over which the committed burst (Bc) can be sent. With many shaping tools, Tc = Bc/CIR.
Bc	Committed burst size, measured in bits. This is the amount of traffic that can be sent over the interval Tc. Typically also defined in the traffic contract.
CIR	Committed information rate, in bits per second, defines the rate defined in the traffic contract.
Shaped Rate	The rate, in bits per second, to which a particular configuration wants to shape the traffic. In some cases, the shaped rate is set to the same value as CIR; in others, the shaped rate is set to a larger value, with the hope of sending more traffic through the network.
Be	Excess burst size, in bits. This is the number of bits beyond Bc that can be sent after a period of inactivity.

The actual processes used by traffic shaping, and the terms in Table 6-3, will make much more sense to you with a few examples. The first example, as outlined in Figure 6-5, shows the familiar case where R1 shapes to 64 kbps, with a 128-kbps access link.

Figure 6-5 *Mechanics of Traffic Shaping—128-kbps AR, 64-kbps Shaped Rate*

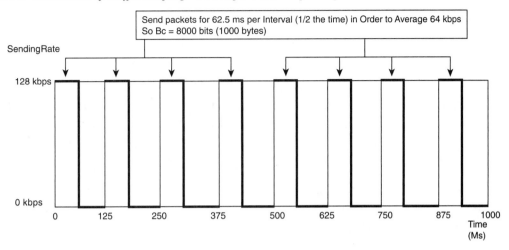

The router should send literally half of the time to average sending 64 kbps on a 128-kbps link. Traffic shaping accomplishes this by sending up to half of the time in each Tc.

As shown in the figure, R1 sends at line rate for 62.5 ms, and then is silent for 62.5 ms, completing the first interval. (The Tc defaults to 125 ms for many shaping tools; CB Shaping happens to default to another Tc in this case, but the concept is still valid.) As long as packets are queued and available, R1 repeats the process during each interval. At the end of 1 second, for instance, R1 would have been sending for 62.5 ms in 8 intervals, or 500 ms—which is .5 seconds. By sending for half of the second at 128 kbps, R1 will have sent traffic at an average rate of 64 kbps.

IOS traffic shaping does not actually start a timer for 62.5 ms, and then stop sending when the timer stops. IOS actually calculates, based on the configuration, how many bits could be sent in each interval so that the shaped rate would be met. This value is called the *committed burst* (Bc) for each interval. It is considered a burst, because the bits actually flow at the physical line rate. The burst is committed, because if you send this much every interval, you are still conforming to the traffic contract. In this example, the Bc value is set to 8000 bits, and the actual process allows the shaper to send packets in each interval until 8000 bits have been sent. At that point, the shaper waits until the Tc has ended, and another interval starts, with another Bc worth of bits sent in the next interval. With an interval of 125 ms, and 8000 bits per interval, a 64-kbps shaped rate is achieved.

The Bc value is calculated using the following formulas:

$$Bc = Tc * CIR$$

or

$$Bc = Tc * Shaped\ rate$$

In the first formula, which is scattered throughout the Cisco documentation, the formula assumes that you want to shape at the CIR. In some cases, however, you want to shape to some other rate, so the second formula gives the more exact formula. For instance, if a Shaping tool had a default of 125 ms for Tc, and with a shaped rate of 64 kbps, the Bc would be

Bc = .125 seconds * 64000 bits/second = 8000 bits

When configuring shaping, you typically configure the shaping rate and optionally the Bc. If you configure both values, IOS changes the Tc so that the formula is met; you never actually configure the value of Tc. If you just configure the shaping rate, depending on the Shaping tools, IOS assumes a particular value for Tc or Bc, and then calculates the other value.

The section covering CB Shaping later in this chapter covers how CB Shaping calculates Tc and Bc assuming that only the shaping rate has been configured. However, if you configure both the shaping rate and the Bc, IOS calculates Tc as follows:

Tc = Bc/CIR

or

Tc = Bc/Shaped rate

Again, the formula referring to CIR assumes that you shape to the CIR value, whereas the second formula refers to the shaping rate, because you can configure shaping to shape at a rate different from CIR.

Additional examples should bring the concepts together. Previously you read the example of the PB Tents company shaping at 96 kbps over a link using a 128-kbps clock rate, because the Frame Relay provider policed at 96 kbps. If the shaping function is configured with a shaping rate of 96 kbps, assuming a Tc of 125 ms, the formulas specify the following:

Bc = .125 sec * 96,000 bits/sec = 12,000 bits

Figure 6-6 shows what happens in this example. For each interval, shaping can release 12,000 bits, which takes 91.25 ms. 91.25/125 = 3/4, implying that the router will average sending bits at 3/4 of the clock rate, or 96 kbps.

Traffic shaping uses the idea of a number of bits per interval for implementation because it's much more efficient than calculating rates all the time. The shaper just grabs the next packet, decrements the Bc values by the number of bits in the packet, and keeps doing that until the Bc value is consumed. At that point, shaping waits until the Tc has expired, when shaping gets to send another Bc worth of bits.

Figure 6-6 *Mechanics of Traffic Shaping — 128-kbps Access Rate, 96-kbps Shaped Rate*

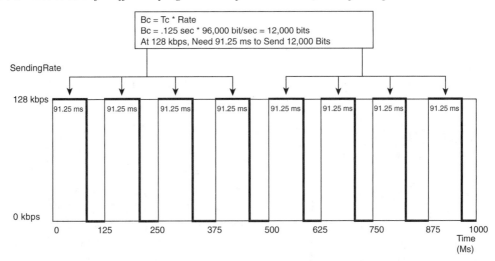

The length of Tc may have some impact on the delay and jitter characteristics of the packets being shaped. Consider another example, with the Main router sending packets to R24, shaping at 128 kbps, but with a T/1 access link. Figure 6-7 shows the shaping details.

Figure 6-7 *Mechanics of Traffic Shaping—Main Router with 1.536 Access Rate, 128-kbps Shaped Rate*

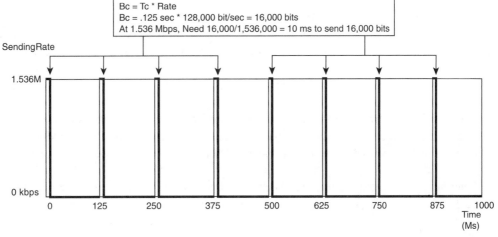

Simply put, at T/1 speeds, it does not take long to send the Bc worth of bits per interval. However, The Tc value of 125ms may be a poor choice for delay-sensitive traffic. Suppose that a VoIP packet arrives at Main, and it needs to be sent to R24. Main uses LLQ, and classifies VoIP into the low-latency queue, so the new VoIP packet will be sent next. That's true—unfortunately, the packet sent just prior to the new VoIP packet's arrival consumed all of Bc for this Tc. How long does the VoIP packet have to wait before the current Tc will end and a new one will begin? Well, it only took 10 ms to send the Bc worth of bits, so another 115 ms must pass before the current Tc ends, and the VoIP packet can be sent! With one-way delay budgets of 150 to 200 ms, a single shaping delay of 115 ms just will not work. Therefore, Cisco recommends that when you have delay-sensitive traffic, configure Bc such that Tc is 10 ms or less. In this same example, if the Bc were configured to 1280 bits, Tc = 1280/128,000 = .010 seconds, or 10 ms.

NOTE   Many of you might be concerned about the relatively small Bc of 1280 bits, or only 160 bytes! Most packets exceed that length. Well, as it turns out, you will also typically use fragmentation in the exact same cases. To accommodate the same delay-sensitive traffic, the fragments will be of similar size—in fact, as you will read in Chapter 8, "Link Efficiency Tools," the fragmentation size will likely be 160 bytes in this particular example. Therefore, with delay-sensitive traffic, you will drive Tc down to about 10 ms by lowering Bc, and the Bc value will essentially allow a single fragment per Tc. By doing so, you reduce the shaping delay waiting on the next Tc to occur, and you reduce the serialization delay by fragmenting packets to smaller sizes.

The next several sections continue the discussion of how traffic shaping works, covering excess burst, queuing, adaption, and some concepts about enabling shaping.

Traffic Shaping with No Excess Burst

Traffic shaping includes the capability to send more than Bc in some intervals. The idea is simple: Data traffic is bursty, so after a period of inactivity, it would be nice if you could send more than Bc in the first interval after traffic occurs again. This extra number of bits is called the *burst excess*, or Be. Traffic-shaping tools allow Be as an option.

The underlying operation of traffic shaping to allow for Be requires a little more insight into how traffic shaping works, and it also requires us to understand the concept of token buckets. Token buckets can be used to describe how shaping and policing are implemented.

Ignoring Be for a moment, imagine a bucket filled with tokens, like subway tokens. In the token-bucket scenario, each token lets you buy the right to send 1 bit. One token bucket is used for formal operation of traffic shaping as discussed earlier; this bucket has a size of Bc.

Two main actions revolve around the token bucket and the tokens:

■   The re-filling of the bucket with new tokens

■   The consumption of tokens by the Shaper to gain the right to forward packets

For filling the token bucket, the bucket is filled to its maximum capacity, but no more, at the beginning of each Tc (assuming that Be = 0 for the time being). Another way you can think of it as if the Shaper dumps Bc worth of tokens into the bucket at the beginning of every interval; however, if there's not enough room in the bucket, because not all the tokens were used during the previous time interval, some tokens spill out. Those spilled tokens can't be used. The net result, either way you look at it, is that the interval starts with a full token bucket of size Bc. Figure 6-8 shows the basic idea:

Figure 6-8 *Mechanics of Filling the Shaping Token Bucket*

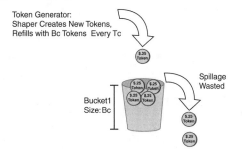

Every time a packet is sent, traffic shaping spends tokens from the token bucket to buy the right to send the packet. If the packet is 1000 bits long, 1000 tokens are removed from the bucket. When traffic shaping tries to send a packet, and the bucket does not have enough tokens in it to buy the right to send the packet, traffic shaping must wait until the next interval, when the token bucket is refilled.

An analogy of token bucket is a child and the allowance the child receives every Saturday morning. For the sake of argument, assume the weekly allowance is $10. The child may spend the money every week; if the child doesn't spend it, he may save up to buy something more expensive. Imagine that the child's parents are looking at the child's piggybank every Saturday morning, however, and if they find some leftover money, they just add a little more money so that the child always starts Saturday morning with $10! After a few weeks of this practice, the child would likely try to spend all the money each week, knowing that he would never be able to save any more than $10. Similarly, the Bc of bits, or the tokens in the bucket if you prefer, are only usable in that individual Tc interval, and the next Tc (interval) always starts with Bc tokens in the bucket, but never any more.

Traffic Shaping with Excess Burst

Traffic shaping implements Be by making the bucket bigger. In fact, to support an excess burst, the bucket now contains Bc plus Be worth of tokens. The filling of tokens into the bucket at the beginning of each interval, and the draining of tokens to gain the right to send packets, remains the same. For instance, at the beginning of each interval, the Shaper still tries to fill the bucket with Bc tokens. If some spill out, because there's no more room for more tokens in the bucket, those tokens are wasted.

The key advantage gained by having Be—in other words, having a token bucket of size Bc plus Be—is that the token bucket is larger. As a result, after some time during which the actual bit rate is lower than the shaping rate, the token bucket fills with tokens. If in the next interval more than Bc bits needed to be sent, the Shaper could send them—up to the number of tokens in the bucket, namely Bc + Be. Basically, the Shaper allows the amount of data passed by the shaper to burst.

Figure 6-9 shows a graph of how shaping works when using Be. The shaper represented by the graph shapes to a CIR of 64 kbps, over a 128-kbps link. The Bc has been set to 8000 bits, with an additional 8000 bits for Be.

Figure 6-9 *Bc and Be, After a Period of Inactivity*

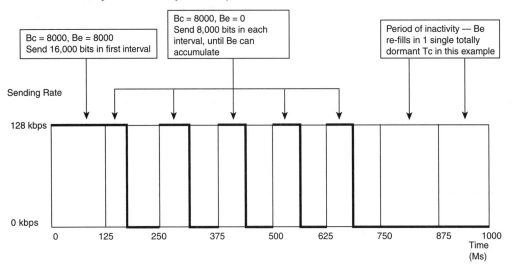

The example in Figure 6-9 assumes that enough inactive or slow periods have occurred, just prior to this example, so that the token bucket is full. In other words, the token bucket holds Bc + Be tokens, which is 16,000 tokens in this example. A large amount of traffic shows up, so traffic shaping sends as fast as it can until it runs out of tokens.

In the first interval, traffic shaping can send a total of 16,000 bits. On a 128-kbps link, assuming a 125-ms Tc, all 125 ms are required to send 16,000 bits! Effectively, in this particular case, after a period of inactivity, R1 sends continuously for the entire first interval.

To begin the second interval, Shaping adds Bc (8000) tokens to the bucket. Those tokens do not fill the bucket, but it does allow the shaper to pass 8000 bits, which requires half the time interval. So, in this example, the shaper will send for 187.5 ms (the entirety of the first 125 ms interval, plus half of the second interval) until traffic shaping artificially slows down the traffic. Thus, the goal of allowing a burst of data traffic to get started quickly is accomplished with Be.

Traffic-Shaping Adaption

The rate at which the shaping function shapes traffic can vary over time. The adaption or adaptation process causes the shaper to recognize congestion and reduce the shaping rate temporarily, to help reduce congestion. Similarly, adaption notices when the congestion abates and returns the shaping rate to the original rate.

Two features define how adaption works. First, the shaper must somehow notice when congestion occurs, and when it does not occur. Second, the shaper must adjust its rate downward and upward as the congestion occurs and abates.

Figure 6-10 represents three different ways in which the main router can notice congestion. Three separate lines represent three separate frames sent to the main router, signifying congestion. Two of the frames are data frames with the Frame Relay backward explicit congestion notification (BECN) bit set. This bit can be set inside any Frame Relay frame header, signifying whether congestion has occurred in the direction opposite to the direction of the frame with the bit set. The third (bottom) message is a Foresight message. Stratacom, and later Cisco after they acquired Stratacom, defined Foresight as a signaling protocol in Frame Relay and ATM networks, used to signal information about the network, such as congestion information. If the Frame Relay network consists of Cisco/Stratacom WAN switches, the switch can send Foresight messages, and Cisco routers can react to those messages. Following the figure, each of the three variations for the Main router to recognize that congestion is occurring is explained in detail.

Figure 6-10 *FECN, BECN, and Foresight Feedback*

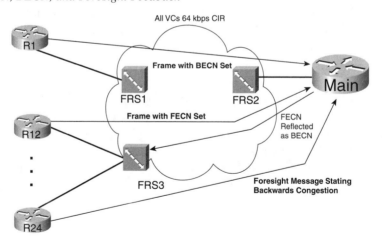

First consider the BECN frame. Backward means that the congestion exists in the opposite, or backward, direction, as compared with the direction of the frame. Therefore, if FRS1 notices congestion trying to send frames to R1 (right to left in the figure), on the next frame sent by R1 (left to right in the figure), FRS1 can mark the BECN bit. In fact, any device can set the forward explicit congestion notification (FECN) and BECN bits — however, in some networks, the Frame Relay switches do set the bits, and in some, they do not.

If the BECN bit is set, the Main router, if using adaptive shaping, reduces its shaping rate on the VC to R1. Because the congestion occurs right to left, as signaled by a BECN flowing left to right, router Main knows it can slow down and help reduce the congestion. If Main receives another frame with BECN set, Main slows down more. Eventually, Main slows down the shaping rate until it reaches a minimum rate, sometimes called the *minimum information rate* (MIR), and other times called the *mincir*.

Similarly, if Main receives a Frame from R12 with FECN set, the congestion is occurring left to right. It does not help for Main to slow down, but it does help for R12 to slow down. Therefore, the Main router can "reflect" the FECN, by marking the BECN bit in the next frame it sends on the VC to R12. R12, receiving a BECN, can reduce the shaping rate.

Finally, Foresight messages are separate, nondata signaling frames. Therefore, when the congestion occurs, Foresight does not need to wait on a data frame to signal congestion. In addition, Foresight sends messages toward the device that needs to slow down. For instance, a switch notices congestion right to left on the VC between Main and R24. The switch generates and sends a Foresight message to Main, using that same VC, so Main knows it needs to slow down its shaping rate on that VC temporarily. When configuring adaptive shaping, you configure the minimum and maximum shaping rate. With no congestion, CB Shaping uses the maximum rate. When the Shaper receives a BECN or Foresight message, it slows down by 25 percent of the maximum rate. In order to slow down, CB Shaping actually simply decreases Bc and Be by 25%, keeping the Tc value the same. In other words, CB Shaping allows fewer bits to pass in each time interval. If the Shaper continues to receive BECNs, the Shaper continues to slow down by 25 percent of the maximum rate per Tc , until the minimum rate is reached.

The rate grows again after 16 consecutive intervals occur without a BECN or Foresight congestion message. The shaping rate grows by 1/16 of the maximum rate during each Tc, until the maximum rate is reached again. To do that, the formerly-reduced Bc and Be values are increased by 1/16 oftheir configured values each Tc. Because of that, the formula for calculating how much CB Shaping increases the rate per time interval as actually showing the increase in BC and Be values. The formula for the amount of increase per interval is:

$$\frac{(Bc + Be)}{16}$$

Where to Shape: Interfaces, Subinterfaces, and VCs

Shaping can be applied to the physical interface, a subinterface, or in some cases, to an individual VC. Depending on the choice, the configuration causes traffic shaping to occur separately for each VC, or it shapes several VCs together. In most cases, engineers want to shape each VC individually.

When shaping is applied to an interface for which VCs do not exist, shaping is applied to the main interface, because there are no subinterfaces or VCs on those interfaces. On Frame Relay and ATM interfaces, however, some sites have multiple VCs terminating in them, which means that subinterfaces will most likely be used. In some cases, more than one VC is associated with a single multipoint subinterface; in other cases, point-to-point subinterfaces are used, with a single VC associated with the subinterface. The question becomes this: To shape per VC, where do you enable traffic shaping?

First, consider a typical branch office, such as R24 in Figure 6-11. R24 has a single VC to the Main site at PB Tents. Because R24 only has the single VC, the configuration on R24 may not even use subinterfaces at all. If the configuration does not use subinterfaces on R24's serial link, traffic shaping can be configured on the physical interface. If the configuration includes a subinterface, you can enable traffic shaping on the physical interface, or on the subinterface. Because there is only one VC, it does not really matter whether shaping is enabled on the physical interface, or the subinterface — the behavior is the same.

Figure 6-11 *PB Tents Network: Shaping on Subinterfaces and VCs*

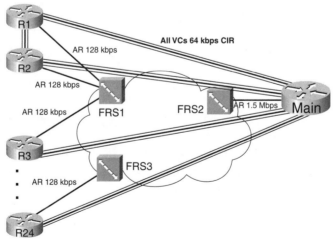

Now consider the Main router. It has a VC to each remote site. (Also notice that a VC has been added between R1 and R2, just to make things interesting.) So, on the main router, point-to-point subinterfaces are used for the VCs to branches 3 through 24, and a multipoint subinterface is used for the two VCs to R1 and R2. To shape each VC to branches 3 through 24 separately, shaping can be configured on the subinterface. However, shaping applied to a multipoint subinterface shapes all the traffic on all VCs associated with the subinterface. To perform shaping on each VC, you need to enable shaping on each individual data-link connection identifier (DLCI).

As it turns out, CB Shaping can be applied per subinterface, but not per-VC on multipoint subinterfaces. In the example in Figure 6-11, CB Shaping could shape all traffic from router Main to both R1 and R2, but it could not shape traffic to R1 separately from the traffic going to R2.

In summary, most QoS policies call for shaping on each VC. The configuration commands used to enable shaping differ slightly based on the number of VCs, and how they are configured. Table 6-4 summarizes the options.

Table 6-4 *Options of How to Enable Shaping for per-VC Shaping*

Location	Requirements for Shaping per VC
No VCs, for example, point-to-point links	Shape on the main interface. Shaping occurs for all traffic on interface.
Physical interface, 1 VC, no subinterfaces	Shaping shapes the individual VC associated with this interface. Shaping can be enabled on the physical interface.
Physical interface, 1 VC, 1 subinterface	Shaping shapes the individual VC associated with this interface. Shaping can be enabled on the physical interface, the subinterface, or the VC (DLCI).
Multiple VCs on 1 interface, point-to-point subinterfaces only	Shaping can be enabled on the subinterface, or per DLCI. Both methods work identically.
Multiple VCs on 1 interface, some multipoint subinterfaces with > 1 VC per subinterface	Must enable shaping on each DLCI to shape per VC.

Queuing and Traffic Shaping

Shaping tools support a variety of queuing tools that can be applied to the packets waiting in the shaping queue(s). At the same time, IOS supports queuing tools for the interface software queue(s) associated with the physical interface. Deciding when to use queuing tools on shaping queues, when to use them on the interface software queues, and how the configurations differ in each case, can be a little confusing. This section attempts to clear up some of that confusion.

> **NOTE**   The current QoS exam does not cover any details about the other Shaping tools besides CB Shaping. However, the idea of how to use Queuing tools for Shaping, and to also use Queuing tools for the interface software queues, confuses many people. The rest of the details in this short section on "Queuing and Traffic Shaping" discuss those details. This material is probably outside what you'll see on the exam, but is important enough to include coverage.

To begin, Table 6-5 lists the traffic-shaping tools, and the queuing tools supported by each for the shaping queues.

Table 6-5 *Options for Queuing in Traffic-Shaping Tools*

Shaping Tool	Queuing Tools Supported for the Shaping Queue(s)
GTS	WFQ
CB shaping	FIFO, WFQ, CBWFQ, LLQ
DTS	FIFO, WFQ, CBWFQ, LLQ
FRTS	FIFO, WFQ, CBWFQ, LLQ, PQ, CQ

When a Shaper uses a queuing tool, instead of creating a single FIFO shaping queue, it creates multiple shaping queues based on the Queuing tool. For instance, if FRTS were configured to use Priority Queuing (PQ) for the shaping queues, it would create four queues for shaping, named High, Medium, Normal, and Low. Figure 6-12 shows the basic idea, with shaping enabled on the physical interface, FIFO Queuing on the physical interface, and PQ configured for shaping the only VC.

Figure 6-12 *FRTS, with FIFO Queuing for the Physical Interface, Plus PQ for the Shaping Queue*

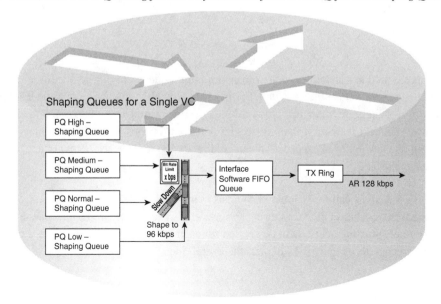

The shaping queues exist separately from the interface software queues, as seen in Figure 6-12. With PQ applied to the Shaper, four shaping queues exist for this VC. When the Shaper decides to allow another packet to be sent, it takes the next packet from the PQ shaping queues, according to PQ scheduler logic. Those packets are placed into software queues associated with the physical interface and then forwarded out the interface—in this case shown as a single FIFO queue.

In some cases, the shaping queues are bypassed, and in other cases, the interface software queues are bypassed. To understand why, consider Figure 6-13, which demonstrates part of the logic behind the decision for determining when each queue should be used.

Figure 6-13   *Decision Logic for Queuing with Shaping Enabled*

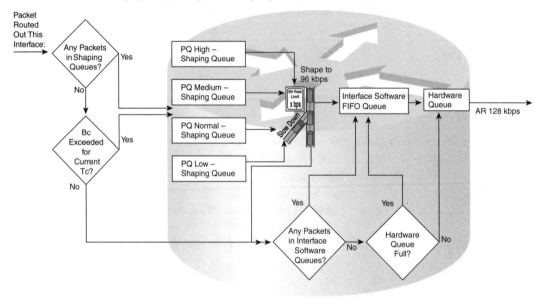

Packets are held in a shaping queue or interface output queue only if there is some reason why the packet must wait to take the next step. For instance, you already know that if the Hardware Queue is not full, packets are immediately placed into the Hardware Queue, bypassing the interface Software Queue. Likewise, if shaping decides that a packet does not need to be delayed, because the shaping rate has not been exceeded, it can go directly to the interface output queue, or even to the Hardware Queue.

Many QoS designs call for shaping per VC, as mentioned in the preceding section. Suppose that a router has two 64-kbps CIR VCs sharing an access link, each configured on a separate point-to-point subinterface. Shaping queues will be created for each VC. A single set of interface output queues will be created, too. Figure 6-14 depicts the overall idea.

Figure 6-14   *Fancy Queuing for the Physical Interface and for Two Sets of Shaping Queues*

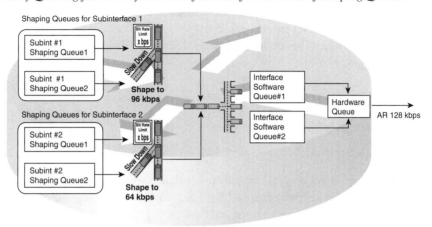

The shaping tool creates a set of queues for each subinterface or VC, based on the queuing tool configured for use by the shaper. IOS creates only one set of interface software queues for the physical interface, based on the queuing configuration on the physical interface, as covered in Chapter 5, "Congestion Management." In Figure 6-14, two sets of shaping queues have been created, one per VC. Both VCs feed the single set of interface output queues.

Finally, in this particular example, congestion can occur at the physical interface. The total of the two shaping rates listed in Figure 6-14 is 160 kbps, which exceeds the access rate (128 kbps). Because interface output queues can fill, it helps to apply a queuing tool to the interface output queues in this case.

How Policing Works

Policers, like Shapers, need to determine whether a packet is within the traffic contract. To do so, it performs a metering process to effectively measure the cumulative byte-rate of the arriving packets. Based on that metering process, the policer acts on the packet as follows:

■   Allowed to pass

■   Dropped

■   Re-marked with a different IP precedence or IP DSCP value.

Policers can be a little more complicated than Shapers. Like CB Shaping, CB Policing uses token buckets for the mechanics of how to monitor traffic and decide which packets are outside the traffic contract. If you want CB Policing to decide if a packet either conforms to or exceeds the contract, it will use a single token bucket, like CB Shaping. You can think of this style of policing as having two classes, as determined by the metering process. The two categories are *conforming* and *exceeding*.

However, CB Policing can be configured to use three categories about whether a packet is conforming to the contract:

■ **Conforming**—Packet is inside the contract

■ **Exceeding**—Packet is using up a excess burst capability

■ **Violating**—Packet is totally outside the contract

When configuring CB Policing, you can choose to define with the conforming and exceeding actions, or you can choose to configure all three actions. If you use only two categories, the policer is sometimes called a "two-color" policer, and it uses a single token bucket. If you configure all three categories, CB Policing uses dual token buckets, and is called a "three-color" policer. (The ideas behind the three-color policing function are described further in RFC 2697, "A Single-rate Three Color Marker".)

CB Policing also allows the concept of a dual-rate policer, which means that the policer actually monitors two different rates, called the Committed Information Rate (CIR) and the Peak Information Rate (PIR). To do that, CB Policing must use another twist on the logic of how the two token buckets are used. This more advanced style of policing allows a router to enforce traffic contracts for two sustained rates, which gives service providers a lot more flexibility in terms of what they offer to their customers. This concept of policing and monitoring two rates is defined in RFC 2698, "A Dual-rate Three-Color Marker".

The sections that follow cover, in order, single rate, single bucket (two-color) CB Policing; single rate policing, but with two token buckets (three-color); and finally the RFC 2698 concept of a two-rate, three-color policer, meaning two token buckets, and two separate policing rates.

CB Policing: Single-Rate, Two-Color (1 Bucket)

When using token buckets for policing, two important things happen. First, tokens are replenished into the bucket. Later, when the policer wants to decide if a packet conforms to the contract or not, the policer will look into the bucket, and try to get enough tokens to allow the packet through. If there's enough, the policer will "spend" the tokens, removing them from the bucket, in order to have the right to allow the packet past the policer.

With Policing, think of each token as the right to send a single byte; with Shaping, each token represented a bit. First, consider how CB Policing fills the single token bucket. Unlike CB Shaping, CB policing replenishes tokens in the bucket in response to a packet arriving at the policing function, as opposed to using a regular time interval (Tc). Every time a packet is policed, CB policing puts some tokens back into the Bucket. The number of tokens placed into the Bucket is calculated as follows:

$$\frac{(Current\_packet\_arrival\_time - Previous\_packet\_arrival\_time) * Police\_rate}{8}$$

Note that the arrival times' units are in seconds, and the police rate is in bits per second, with the result being a number of tokens. Each token represents the right to send 1 byte, so the formula includes the division by 8 in order to convert the units to bytes instead of bits.

The idea behind the formula is simple — essentially, a small number of tokens are replenished before each packet is policed, with an end result of having tokens replenished at the policing rate. Suppose, for instance, that the police rate is 128,000 bps (which happens to equal 16,000 bytes per second.) If 1 second has elapsed since the previous packet arrived, CB Policing would replenish the bucket with 16,000 tokens. If 0.1 seconds had passed since the previous packet had arrived, CB Policing would replenish the bucket with 0.1 seconds worth of tokens, or 1600 tokens. If .01 seconds had passed, CB Policing would replenish 160 tokens at that time. Essentially, the Bucket is replenished with a prorated number of tokens based on how long ago it was last replenished.

The second part of using a bucket relates to the policer's choice as to whether a packet conforms to the contract or not. CB Policing compares the number of bytes in the packet to the number of tokens the token bucket. CB policing's decision is simple, as noted here:

■   If the number of bytes in the packet is less than or equal to (<=) the number of tokens in the bucket, the packet conforms. CB policing removes tokens from the bucket equal to the number of bytes in the packet, and performs the action for packets that conform to the contract.

■   If the number of bytes in the packet is greater than (>) the number of tokens in the bucket, the packet exceeds the contract. CB policing does not remove tokens from the bucket, and performs the action for packets that exceed the contract.

Therefore, the logic used by a single-rate, two-color policer is simple. The bucket gets replenished with tokens based on packet arrival time. If the packet conforms, CB Policing either forwards, discards, or re-marks the packet, and some tokens are then removed from the bucket. If the packet exceeds, CB Policing either forwards, discards, or re-marks the packet, but no tokens are removed from the bucket. (Note that discarding packets that conform is a valid configuration option, but it is not particularly useful.)

CB Policing: Dual Token Bucket (Single-Rate)

When you want the policer to support both a committed burst (Bc) and an excess burst (Be), the policer uses two token buckets. By using two token Buckets, CB Policing can categorize packets into three groups:

- Conform

- Exceed

- Violate

The intent of these three categories is to allow the policer to decide if packets totally conform, whether they are using the excess burst capability (exceed), or whether the packet puts the data beyond even the excess burst (violate).

> **NOTE**   There is no official name for the two token buckets, so I will refer to them simply as the Bc bucket and the Be bucket in this section.

Just like with a single token bucket, to understand how CB Policing works with two buckets is to understand how the buckets are filled and drained. CB Policing continues to replenish the Bc bucket when a packet arrives. However, any spilled tokens when filling the Bc bucket are not simply wasted. If the Bc bucket is full, the extra, or spilled tokens, replenish the Be bucket. If the Be bucket fills, the excess tokens spill out and are wasted. Figure 6-15 shows the basic process:

Figure 6-15   *Refilling Dual Token Buckets with CB Policing*

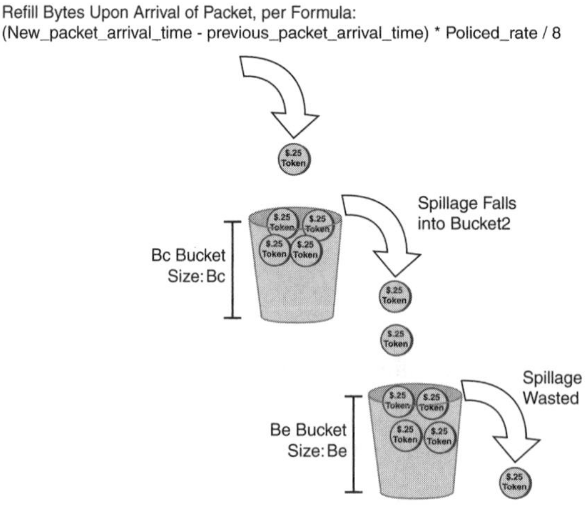

With Bc and Be configured, CB policing uses dual token buckets, and the algorithm is simple:

1. If the number of bytes in the packet is less than or equal to (<=) the number of tokens in the Bc Bucket, the packet *conforms*. CB policing removes tokens from the Bc Bucket equal to the number of bytes in the packet, and performs the action for packets that conform to the contract.

2. If the packet does not conform, and the number of bytes in the packet is less than or equal to (<=) the number of tokens in the Be Bucket, the packet *exceeds*. CB policing removes tokens from the Be Bucket equal to the number of bytes in the packet, and performs the action for packets that exceed the contract.

3. If the packet neither conforms nor exceeds, it *violates* the traffic contract. CB policing does not remove tokens from either bucket, and performs the action for packets that violate the contract.

Essentially, packets that fit within Bc conform, those that require the extra bytes allowed by Be exceed, and those that go beyond even Be are considered to violate the traffic contract.

CB Policing: Dual Token Bucket (Dual Rate)

Dual Token Bucket CB Policing with a single rate provides a very useful function. After a period of low activity, a larger burst of data can be considered to either conform to or exceed the traffic contract, without violating the traffic contract. Because data tends to be bursty, the idea of a policer with bursting capability makes a lot of sense.

Dual Token Bucket with Dual-rate policing also provides a bursting feature, but with dual-rate, the CB Policer allows you to essentially set two different sustained rates. Packets that fall under the lower rate—the Committed Information Rate (CIR)—conform to the traffic contract. A second sustained rate—the Peak Information Rate (PIR)—defines a traffic rate above CIR. Packets that happen to exceed the CIR, but fall below PIR, are considered to exceed the contract, but not to violate it. Finally, packets beyond even the PIR are considered to violate the contract.

As usual, the mechanics of how it all works behind the scenes relates to how the policer replenishes tokens into the buckets, and how the policer then takes tokens from the buckets during the process of deciding if a packet conforms, exceeds, or violates the traffic contract. First, consider Figure 6-16, which shows the refill process works for the two buckets. In this case, the buckets are referred to as the CIR bucket and the PIR bucket, respectively.

Figure 6-16 *Refilling CIR and PIR Dual Token Buckets with CB Policing*

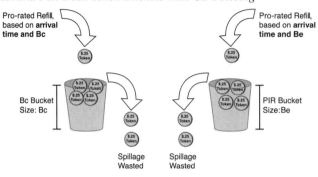

A couple of differences exist between the token refilling process of the single rate, three-color policing of the previous section. First, note that both buckets are filled upon the arrival of a packet that needs to be policed. However, the PIR bucket is refilled with tokens directly, instead of having to rely on spillage from the refilling of the CIR bucket. Essentially, this means that the PIR bucket does not have to rely on a period of low or no activity in order to get more tokens. Also note that when refilling, any tokens that spill from either bucket are wasted.

The refilling of the two buckets based on two different rates is very important. For example, imagine you set a CIR of 128 kbps (16 kilobytes/second), and a PIR of 256 kbps (32 kilobytes/second). If .1 seconds passed before the next packet arrived, then the CIR bucket would be replenished with 1.6 kilobytes of tokens (1/10 of 1 seconds worth of tokens, in bytes), while the PIR bucket would be replenished with 3.2 kilobytes of tokens. So, there are more tokens to use in the PIR bucket, as compared to the CIR bucket.

As usual, the second part of the process involves how the policer thinks about the tokens in the buckets in order to decide if the packet conforms, exceeds, or violates the traffic contract. The logic is similar to the single rate, two bucket policing described earlier, but with a twist for what happens for conforming packets:

1. If the number of bytes in the packet is less than or equal to (<=) the number of tokens in the CIR bucket, the packet *conforms*. CB Policing removes tokens from the CIR equal to the number of bytes in the packet, and performs the action for packets that conform to the contract. *CB Policing also removes the same number of tokens from the PIR bucket.*

2. If the packet does not conform, and the number of bytes in the packet is less than or equal to (<=) the number of tokens in the PIR bucket, the packet *exceeds*. CB Policing removes tokens from the PIR bucket equal to the number of bytes in the packet, and performs the action for packets that exceed the contract.

3. If the packet neither conforms nor exceeds, it *violates* the traffic contract. CB Policing does not remove tokens from either bucket, and performs the action for packets that violate the contract.

Even before you read this list, you probably guessed the base logic. If there are enough tokens in the CIR bucket, the packet conforms; if not, and there's enough in the PIR bucket, it exceeds; if not, the packet violates the contract. The new part revolves around the fact that even if the packet conforms, the policer takes tokens from the PIR bucket.

An example can help. Imagine that CB Policing has been configured for the following:

- CIR 128 kbps (16 kilobytes/second)

- Bc of 8000 bytes

- PIR of 256 kbps (32K kilobytes/second)

- Be of 16,000 bytes

Effectively, PIR and Be are double the values of CIR and Bc. Now imagine that both buckets are full of tokens, and a bunch of packets arrive at the same instant. Because they arrive at the same instant, the replenishment of tokens into the buckets is either 0, or negligible — so for the sake of discussion, assume no new tokens are added to either bucket during this example.

The first 8000 bytes worth of packets pass through the policer, with the packets considered to conform. The CIR bucket is decremented to 0. At the same time, the PIR bucket is also decremented, from 16,000 to 8,000 tokens.

For the next 8000 bytes of packets, the policer decides that the packets exceed the contract, and the policer removes tokens from the PIR bucket. Finally, after the rest of the packets are considered to violate the traffic contract, at least until some time passes, allowing more tokens to be added to the two buckets.

Summary of CB Policing Mechanics

CB Policing includes a lot of small details about how it chooses which packets conform to, exceed, or violate a traffic contract. To help with exam prep, Table 6-6 lists the key points about how CB Policing uses token buckets.

Table 6-6 *Summary of CB Policing Mechanics*

Feature	Behavior of Single-Rate, Two-Color	Behavior of Single-Rate, Three-Color	Behavior of Dual-Rate, Three-Color
Size of "first" bucket	Bc (bytes)	Bc (bytes)	Bc (bytes)
Size of "second" bucket	N/A	Be (bytes)	Be (bytes)

Table 6-6 *Summary of CB Policing Mechanics (Continued)*

Feature	Behavior of Single-Rate, Two-Color	Behavior of Single-Rate, Three-Color	Behavior of Dual-Rate, Three-Color
Refill of first bucket	Prorated portion of Bc based on packet arrival time	Prorated portion of Bc based on packet arrival time	Prorated portion of Bc based on packet arrival time
Refill of second bucket	N/A	Filled by spilled Tokens from refill of first bucket	Prorated portion of Be based on packet arrival time
Logic for "conform" action	1st bucket => packet size; decrement 1st bucket by packet size	1st bucket => packet size; decrement 1st bucket by packet size	1st bucket => packet size; decrement both buckets by packet size
Logic to choose "exceed" action	All packets that do not conform	Doesn't conform, but 2nd bucket => packet size; decrement 2nd bucket by packet size	Doesn't conform, but 2nd bucket => packet size; decrement 2nd bucket by packet size
Logic to choose "violate" action	N/A	All other packets	All other packets

Policing, but Not Discarding

Shapers queue excess packets, and policers discard excess packets. However, policers allow a sort of compromise, where the packets are not discarded, but they are marked so that if congestion occurs later, this particular packet is more likely to be discarded. Consider Figure 6-17, for instance, and the policing function on R1.

Figure 6-17 *Marking Down Packets with Policing*

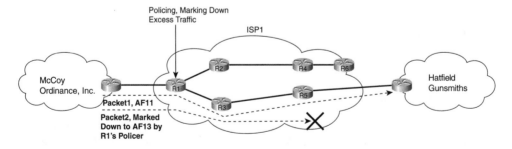

In the figure, two packets travel over a route marked with dotted lines. Each is marked with DSCP AF11 as they enter R1. R1's policer decides that Packet1 conforms, but that Packet2 exceeds the policing rate. R1's policer re-marks Packet2 as AF13. DiffServ suggests that AF13 should be in the same queuing class as AF11, but with a higher drop preference than AF11. If no congestion occurs, both packets get through the network. If some congestion occurs, however, Packet2 has a higher chance of being discarded, because it has a DSCP that implies a higher preference to be dropped than does Packet1.

Policing by marking down the packet provides a compromise option. The ISP can protect the network from being overrun by aggressively discarding marked-down packets at the onset of congestion. Customer satisfaction can be improved by letting the customers take advantage of the capacity when it is available.

The same concept, on a limited basis, can be applied in Frame Relay and ATM networks. Frame Relay headers include the discard eligibility (DE) bit, and ATM headers include the cell loss priority (CLP) bit. Each of these single bits can be used to imply that the frame or cell is a better frame or cell to discard when congestion occurs.

Finally, when choosing to re-mark a packet, you might actually want to mark multiple fields. For instance, you might want to mark down a packet from AF11 to AF13, inside the DSCP field of the IP header. You might also want to mark ATM CLP, or 802.1p CoS as well. When a policer is configured to mark multiple fields for packets that fall into a single policing category, the policer is said to be a *multi-action* policer.

Class-Based Shaping Configuration

Cisco IOS Software includes four different Shaping tools. Of those, CB Shaping and Frame Relay Traffic Shaping (FRTS) are the most popular. Interestingly, the four shaping tools all basically work the same way internally. In fact, the four shaping tools share much of the underlying shaping code in IOS. Although some features differ, and the configurations certainly differ, most of the core functions behave the same. So, rather than cover all four Traffic Shaping tools, the current QoS exam focuses on CB Shaping, which uses the Modular QoS command-line interface (MQC).

> **NOTE**   If you are interested in more information about FRTS, you can refer to Appendix B on the CD-ROM that comes with this book, which includes the old FRTS coverage from the first edition of this book.

CB Shaping has many features. First, the underlying processes, including the use of a single token bucket, work like the Shaping processes described earlier in this chapter. CB Shaping can be enabled on a large variety of interfaces. It can also adapt the rate based on BECN signals, and reflect BECNs on a VC after receiving an FECN. Additionally, CB Shaping can also perform shaping on a subset of the traffic on an interface. Finally, the configuration for CB Shaping is simple, because like all other QoS features starting with the words "class based," CB shaping uses the Modular QoS command-line interface (MQC) for configuration.

In addition to its core features, CB Shaping can also take advantage of IOS queuing tools. Shapers queue traffic in order to slow the overall traffic rate. CB Shaping defaults to use a single FIFO queue when delaying packets, but it also supports several queuing methods for the shaping queues, including WFQ, CBWFQ, and LLQ. With these additional queuing tools, multiservice traffic can be better supported. For instance, LLQ can be applied to the shaping queues, providing a low-latency service for voice and video traffic.

As mentioned earlier, like all QoS tools whose names begin with "Class Based", CB Shaping using MQC for configuration. Tables 6-7 and 6-8 list the configuration and **show** commands pertinent to CB shaping. The MQC **match** commands are omitted, but they can be found in Table 3-2 in Chapter 3.)

Table 6-7 *Command Reference for Class-Based Shaping*

Command	Mode and Function
shape [**average** | **peak**] *mean-rate* [[*burst- size*] [*excess-burst-size*]]	Policy map class configuration mode; enables shaping for the class, setting the shaping rate, and optionally Bc and Be. The average option causes shaping as normal; the peak option causes Bc + Be to be sent per Tc.
shape [**average** | **peak**] **percent** *percent* [[*burst- size*] [*excess-burst-size*]]	Policy map class configuration mode; enables shaping for the class, setting the rate as a percentage of link bandwidth
Shape adaptive *min-rate*	Policy map class configuration mode; enables the minimum rate for adaptive shaping. The maximum rate is configured with the **shape average** or **shape peak** command.
Shape fecn-adapt	Policy map class configuration mode; enables reflection of BECN signals upon receipt of an FECN.
service-policy {**input** | **output**} *policy-map-name*	Interface or subinterface configuration mode; enables CB shaping on the interface.
class-map *class-map-name*	Global configuration; names a class map, where classification options are configured.
shape max-buffers *number-of-buffers*	Sets the maximum queue length for the default FIFO shaping queue

Table 6-8 *EXEC Command Reference for Class-Based Shaping*

Command	Function
show policy-map *policy-map-name*	Lists configuration information about all MQC-based QoS tools
show policy-map *interface-spec* [**input** | **output**] [**class** *class-name*]	Lists statistical information about the behavior of all MQC-based QoS tools

As usual, the best way to understand the generic commands is to see them used in an example. The first example configuration shows R3, with a 128-kbps access rate, and a 64-kbps Frame Relay VC connecting to R1. The criteria for the configuration is as follows:

- Shape all traffic at a 64Kbps rate.

- Use the default setting for Tc.

- Enable the configuration on the subinterface.

- Use WFQ on the physical interface.

- Use the default queuing method for the shaping queues.

In each example, the client downloads one web page, which has two frames inside the page. The web page uses two separate TCP connections to download two separate large JPG files. The client also downloads a file using FTP get. In addition, a VoIP call is placed between extension 302 and 102. Example 6-1 shows the configuration and some sample **show** commands, and Figure 6-18 shows the network diagram.

Figure 6-18 *Sample Network Used for CB Shaping Configuration Examples*

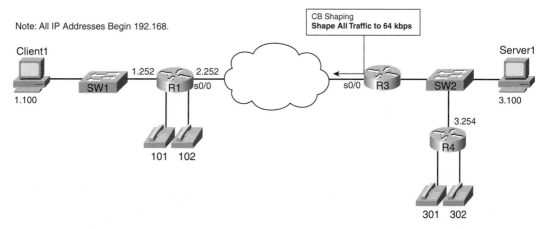

Example 6-1 *CB Shaping on R3, 64-kbps Shape Rate*

```
policy-map shape-all
 class class-default
  shape average 64000
!
interface serial0/0
 bandwidth 64
 load-interval 30
 fair-queue
```

continues

Example 6-1   *CB Shaping on R3, 64-kbps Shape Rate (Continued)*

```
interface serial0/0.1
 service-policy output shape-all

R3#show queue serial 0/0
  Input queue: 0/75/1/0 (size/max/drops/flushes); Total output drops: 5965
  Queueing strategy: weighted fair
  Output queue: 0/1000/64/90 (size/max total/threshold/drops)
     Conversations  0/7/256 (active/max active/max total)
     Reserved Conversations 0/0 (allocated/max allocated)
     Available Bandwidth 1158 kilobits/sec

R3#show policy-map
  Policy Map shape-all
    Class class-default
      Traffic Shaping
         Average Rate Traffic Shaping
                CIR 64000 (bps) Max. Buffers Limit 1000 (Packets)

R3#show policy-map interface s0/0.1

 Serial0/0.1

  Service-policy output: shape-all

    Class-map: class-default (match-any)
      7718 packets, 837830 bytes
      30 second offered rate 69000 bps, drop rate 5000 bps
      Match: any
      Traffic Shaping
          Target/Average   Byte    Sustain   Excess    Interval  Increment
            Rate           Limit   bits/int  bits/int  (ms)      (bytes)
            64000/64000    2000    8000      8000      125       1000


        Adapt  Queue    Packets   Bytes    Packets   Bytes     Shaping
        Active Depth                       Delayed   Delayed   Active
         -       56      6393      692696   6335      684964    yes
```

The CB shaping configuration uses the default class (class-default), and a policy map (shape-all),
which is enabled on serial 0/0.1 using the **service-policy output shape-all** command. The command
class-map class-default matches all packets. The command **policy-map shape-all** only refers to
the class-default class—essentially, classification is configured, but it matches all traffic. Inside
class class-default, the **shape average 64000** command shapes the traffic to 64 kbps.

Just like with other MQC-based tools, the **show policy-map** and **show policy-map interface
serial0/0.1** commands provide all the interesting information about this example. Note that **show**

policy-map just lists the same information in the configuration, whereas **show policy-map interface** lists statistics, tells you whether shaping is currently active, and lists the computed values, such as Bc and Be in this case.

CB Shaping calculates a value for Bc and Be if the **shape** command does not include a value. From those values, CB Shaping calculates the Tc. At lower shaping rates (less than 320 kbps), CB Shaping assumes a Bc of 8000 bits, and calculates Tc based on the formula Tc = Bc/CIR, with some rounding as necessary. At 320 kbps, the calculated Tc would be 25 ms, or .025 seconds. Note that in this first example, Tc = 125 ms, because 8000/64,000 = 1/8 of a second.

For speeds higher than 320 kbps, CB Shaping instead uses a default Tc of .025 seconds, and calculates Bc based on the same formula, which with a little easy algebra translates to Bc = Tc * CIR. For instance, at 640 kbps, Bc = .025 * 640 kbps = 16,000 bits.

> **NOTE**   The QoS course currently suggests letting IOS pick Bc and Be values. If you are sending latency-sensitive multiservice traffic, you should set Bc to drive the calculation of Tc down to 10 ms. This recommendation has been made by Cisco in other documents.

A close examination of the output of the **show policy-map interface s0/0.1** command in Example 6-1 provides a refresher of how Shaping works with its token bucket. First, Be defaults to be equal to Bc. Bc defaults to 8000 bits because the shaping rate (64 kbps) is less than 320 kbps. These two values are shown in the command output as **Sustain bits/int** and **Excess bits/int**. Also note the heading **Byte Limit**—it represents the size of the token bucket. Bc + Be equals 16,000 bits, or 2000 bytes in this case. Finally, the last column in that same part of the command output lists **Increment (bytes)**, which indicates how many bytes worth of tokens are replenished each Tc. The number of bits replenished into the token bucket each time period, and 8000 bits is of course equal to 1000 bytes. Essentially, the command output lists the details of how the Shaper's token bucket logic will work.

In this example, packets are enqueued on the subinterface due to shaping, but few packets are enqueued on the physical interface software queues. With a 128-kbps clock rate, and a shaping rate for all traffic on the interface of 64 kbps, no congestion should occur on the physical interface.

By default, CB shaping uses simple FIFO Queuing for the shaping queue. A common misconception about CB shaping is that because the MQC commands are used, CBWFQ is automatically used — but that is not true! In this example, FIFO Queuing is used for the shaping queue.

Setting Bc to Tune Tc

You can explicitly set the Bc and Be values in addition to the shaping rate. As a result, you will have supplied two of the three variables in the Tc = Bc/CIR formula, and CB Shaping can simply calculate the Tc value implied by your configuration. The next example shows how to set Bc to affect Tc.

For the second configuration, imagine that the Frame Relay provider actually polices the VC from R3 to R1 at 96 kbps. You engineer the network to support a single G.729 VoIP call, which takes about 28 kbps. You decide that you want to be very careful about packet drops, latency, and jitter for this voice traffic, so you decide to shape all traffic except voice. To avoid drops inside the cloud, you shape the rest of the traffic to a rate of 64 kbps (so that the combined single VoIP call, and the Shaped rate of 64 kbps, do not exceed the policing rate in the Frame Relay network). The next example shows the configuration, and the criteria for the configuration is as follows:

■ Shape non-VoIP traffic at 64 kbps.

■ Choose values so Tc is 50 ms.

■ Enable the configuration on the subinterface.

In this case, a single VoIP call and one web page connection with two frames inside the page are used, plus an FTP get. Example 6-2 shows the configuration and some sample **show** commands.

Example 6-2 *CB Shaping on R3, 64-kbps for Non-Voice Traffic, Tc = 50 ms*

```
ip cef
!
class-map match-all voip-rtp
  match ip rtp 16384 16383
!
policy-map shape-non-voip
  class voip-rtp
  class class-default
    shape average 64000 3200
!
interface serial0/0
 bandwidth 64
 load-interval 30
 fair-queue
interface serial0/0.1
 service-policy output shape-non-voip

R3#show policy-map
  Policy Map shape-non-voip
    Class voip-rtp
    Class class-default
      Traffic Shaping
        Average Rate Traffic Shaping
              CIR 64000 (bps) Max. Buffers Limit 1000 (Packets)
          Bc 3200

R3#show policy-map interface serial 0/0.1

Serial0/0.1
```

Example 6-2 *CB Shaping on R3, 64-kbps for Non-Voice Traffic, Tc = 50 ms (Continued)*

```
Service-policy output:shape-non-voip

  Class-map: voip-rtp (match-all)
    50379 packets, 3224256 bytes
    30 second offered rate 25000 bps
    Match: ip rtp 16384 16383

  Class-map: class-default (match-any)
    5402 packets, 6634217 bytes
    30 second offered rate 66000 bps, drop rate 0 bps
    Match: any
    Traffic Shaping
         Target/Average   Byte   Sustain    Excess     Interval  Increment
             Rate         Limit  bits/int   bits/int   (ms)      (bytes)
         64000/64000      800    3200       3200       50        400


      Adapt  Queue    Packets   Bytes    Packets   Bytes    Shaping
      Active Depth                       Delayed   Delayed  Active
        -      8        31      40168      30      38764    yes

R3#show queue serial 0/0
  Input queue: 0/75/0/0 (size/max/drops/flushes); Total output drops: 6083
  Queueing strategy: weighted fair
  Output queue: 0/1000/64/0 (size/max total/threshold/drops)
    Conversations  0/7/256 (active/max active/max total)
    Reserved Conversations 0/0 (allocated/max allocated)
    Available Bandwidth 1158 kilobits/sec
```

The configuration in the example is relatively simple, but detailed. It begins with some familiar MQC commands configuring LLQ. The **class-map match-all voip-rtp** command creates a new class map, with parameters to match all VoIP payload traffic. The **policy-map shape-non-voip** command refers to **class voip-rtp**, with no parameters. With no parameters, no actions are taken for packets in the class, which includes no shaping action. **class class-default** refers to the class that matches all traffic, with the **shape average 64000 3200** command shaping to 64 kbps, with a Bc of 3200 bits. (CB shaping then calculates Tc as 3200/64000, or 50 ms.) Note that because **class voip-rtp** occurs first in the policy map, all VOIP traffic matches that class, and is not shaped.

The **show policy-map** command just restates the information in the configuration. Note the absence of commands under **class voip-rtp**—remember, no commands were added under the command **class voip-rtp** — effectively creating a "do nothing" class. The **class class-default** command matches all other traffic, shaping to 64 kbps. In the **show policy-map interface s0/0.1** command, you see that shaping is enabled only for **class class-default**, but not for **class voip-rtp**.

Note that Be, which was not configured, is defaulted to be equal to Bc as in the previous example.

While this example does show how CB Shaping can be configured to shape a subset of the traffic—which allows you to avoid shaping voice traffic—it also shows how to set Bc, and how it impacts the calculated Tc value. If you need to apply shaping in a network that includes VoIP traffic, the example in the next section shows a better choice for how to configure CB Shaping.

Tuning Shaping for Voice Using LLQ and a Small Tc

In the preceding example, the motivation to shape was based on the Frame Relay provider's policing of the VC at 96 kbps. If the VoIP call was not active, the data still only gets 64 kbps worth of bandwidth! Although that's great for the single voice call, it may not be a good choice for the data. The real requirement is for high-quality voice, with good treatment of the data as a secondary goal, knowing that the service provider is policing at 96 kbps.

A better solution is to use CB shaping's capability to include CBWFQ or LLQ as the queuing tools for the shaping queues. In the first two examples, the shaping queue was a single FIFO queue, because no queuing was configured. In the next example, CB shaping will shape all traffic, including voice, at 96 kbps, but with LLQ used on the shaping queues to ensure good voice quality. Because it will shape voice traffic, this configuration forces Tc down to 10 ms, which is the recommended value for Tc when delay-sensitive voice and video traffic is shaped. The revised requirements are as follows:

■ Ensure high-quality VoIP for one G.729 call, through low loss, low delay, and low jitter.

■ Achieve VoIP loss goal by not exceeding the policing rate of the service provider.

■ Achieve VoIP delay and jitter goal by using LLQ.

■ Choose values so Tc is 10 ms.

■ Shape all traffic, including voice, because LLQ will always take the voice traffic next anyway.

Example 6-3 shows the configuration.

Example 6-3 *CB Shaping on R3, 96-kbps Shape Rate, with LLQ for Shaping Queues*

```
ip cef
!

class-map match-all voip-rtp
 match ip rtp 16384 16383
 !
 !
 ! The following Policy map is used for queuing (LLQ)
 !
```

Example 6-3 *CB Shaping on R3, 96-kbps Shape Rate, with LLQ for Shaping Queues (Continued)*

```
policy-map queue-voip
  class voip-rtp
   priority 32
  class class-default
   fair-queue
!
!!!!!!!!!!!!!!!!!!!!!!!!!!!!!!!!!!!!!!!!!!!!!!!!!!!!!!!!!!!!!!!!!!!
! The following Policy map is used for Shaping;
! It refers to policy-map queue-voip
!
policy-map shape-all
  class class-default
   shape average 96000 960
   service-policy queue-voip
!
interface serial0/0
 bandwidth 64
 load-interval 30
 fair-queue
interface serial0/0.1
  service-policy output shape-all

R3#show policy-map
  Policy Map shape-all
    Class class-default
      Traffic Shaping
         Average Rate Traffic Shaping
               CIR 96000 (bps) Max. Buffers Limit 1000 (Packets)
            Bc 960
        service-policy queue-voip

  Policy Map queue-voip
    Class voip-rtp
      Weighted Fair Queueing
          Strict Priority
          Bandwidth 32 (kbps) Burst 800 (Bytes)
    Class class-default
      Weighted Fair Queueing
          Flow based Fair Queueing Max Threshold 64 (packets)

R3#show policy-map interface serial 0/0.1

 Serial0/0.1

  Service-policy output: shape-all

   Class-map: class-default (match-any)
```

continues

Example 6-3 *CB Shaping on R3, 96-kbps Shape Rate, with LLQ for Shaping Queues (Continued)*

```
    5189 packets, 927835 bytes
    30 second offered rate 91000 bps, drop rate 0 bps
  Match: any
  Traffic Shaping
        Target/Average    Byte    Sustain   Excess    Interval  Increment
        Rate              Limit   bits/int  bits/int  (ms)      (bytes)
        96000/96000       1200    960       960       10        120

    Adapt  Queue     Packets   Bytes    Packets   Bytes     Shaping
    Active Depth                        Delayed   Delayed   Active
    -      17        5172      910975   4002      831630    yes


      Service-policy : queue-voip
        Class-map: voip-rtp (match-all)
          4623 packets, 295872 bytes
          30 second offered rate 25000 bps, drop rate 0 bps
          Match: ip rtp 16384 16383
          Weighted Fair Queueing
            Strict Priority
              Output Queue: Conversation 24
              Bandwidth 32 (kbps) Burst 800 (Bytes)
              (pkts matched/bytes matched) 3528/225792
              (total drops/bytes drops) 0/0

        Class-map: class-default (match-any)
          566 packets, 631963 bytes
          30 second offered rate 65000 bps, drop rate 0 bps
          Match: any
          Weighted Fair Queueing
            Flow Based Fair Queueing
            Maximum Number of Hashed Queues 16
          (total queued/total drops/no-buffer drops) 17/0/0
```

Example 6-3 contains a lot of interesting command output. It begins with the configuration, which is followed by several **show** commands. The configuration contains two policy maps; one configures shaping, and the other configures LLQ. Inside the shaping policy map (**shape-all**), the **service-policy queue-voip** command is used, which tells IOS to enable the **queue-voip policy-map** to the Shaping queues.

Because the interaction between the two policy maps can be confusing, Figure 6-19 shows the general idea behind what is happening in the configuration.

Figure 6-19   *Interaction Between Shaping Policy Map shape-all and Queuing Policy Map queue-voip*

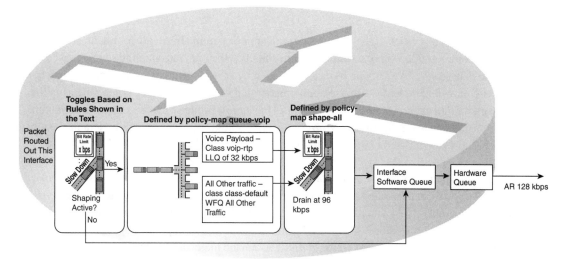

Scanning the figure from left to right, packets are first routed out the subinterface. Then the IOS checks to see whether shaping is active. Shaping becomes active when a single packet exceeds the traffic contract; shaping only becomes inactive when all the shaping queues are drained, and the ensuing packets are not exceeding the traffic contract. Therefore, the shaper must be involved at this step to decide whether to try to queue the packet into the shaping queue.

If the packet exceeds the contract, the shaper needs to queue the packet. In this case, instead of a single FIFO queue, you have a queuing system for the shaping queues as defined by **policy-map queue-voip**. This policy map defines two queues, with one being a 32-kbps low-latency queue into which all voice payload is placed. This queue was created with the **class voip-rtp** command inside **policy-map queue-voip**. Because queue-voip defines queuing, and no other details have been configured, all the rest of the packets go into a second queue, associated with the class-default class. (WFQ is applied to the packets inside the class-default queue, by default, but it can be disabled.)

The next step in the process really shows how integrated the queuing and shaping functions are in with this configuration. After packets have been enqueued in one of the shaping queues, CB shaping must decide *when* to take a packet from a queue. However, the shaper does not decide *which* packet to take — the queuing logic as defined in **policy-map queue-voip** determines which packet to dequeue next. Therefore, the **shape average 96000 960** command tells CB shaping the rate and Bc values to use when deciding when it can next dequeue packets from the shaping queues. When CB shaping releases the next packet from the shaping queues, the packet is placed into the interface software queue, and it finally exits the serial interface.

The interaction between CB shaping, and the queuing tool used for the shaping queues (LLQ in this case) can be a bit confusing. In particular, the shaper must make the decision about whether to put a packet into the shaping queue, and then the shaper decides when the next packet can be taken from a shaping queue. Between those points, the queuing scheduler decides which packet to service next from the shaping queues.

Now taking a closer look at the configuration. The **policy-map shape-all** command creates the shaping configuration, with the **shape average 96000 960** command enabling shaping and defining a Bc so that Tc = 960/96,000, or 10 ms. Although a Bc of 960 bits may seem smaller than a typical packet, you would typically also use a fragmentation tool on this interface when VoIP is in the network. Fragmentation would happen to cause the largest frame size to be shorter than 960 bits. In addition, the **service-policy queue-voip** command enables LLQ inside the class-default class inside policy map shape-all — thereby enabling LLQ for the shaping queues.

A closer look at **policy-map queue-voip** reveals two classes. The **class voip-rtp** command matches all VoIP payload, and is assigned 32 kbps with the **priority 32** command, making it the low-latency queue. Remember, LLQ actually polices the traffic in the low-latency queue at this rate, so this queue can send only 32 kbps. Because all traffic is shaped at 96 kbps, 64 kbps remains, which is guaranteed for queuing; the **class class-default** command matches all other traffic, guaranteeing the remaining 64 kbps to the class.

Finally, the **service-policy output shape-all** subcommand on interface s 0/0.1 enables the policy on the subinterface, which enables CB shaping. Therefore, the CB shaping logic, and related LLQ logic, is applied to all packets exiting subinterface serial 0/0.1.

The **show policy-map** commands reflect the details in the configuration. The command lists **policy-map shape-all** as performing traffic shaping, and **policy-map queue-voip** as performing LLQ. The **show policy-map interface s0/0.1** command lists the shaping parameters and statistics, just like it did in the earlier examples. However, halfway through the command output, a new section has appeared, with details about **policy-map shape-all**'s use of the LLQ **policy-map queue-voip**. The same information seen in CBWFQ and LLQ **show policy-map interface** commands in Chapter 5 appears in this area, including packet rates and byte rates.

This example allows the G.729 call to work well, because LLQ will always service the voip-rtp class when a packet is waiting. If no VoIP calls are up, however, the rest of the traffic can be sent at 96 kbps, the maximum sending rate for shaping. In other words, the rest of the traffic is guaranteed 64 kbps, with a maximum limit of the shaping rate. With LLQ, the VoIP always receives good treatment when the call is up, unless the VoIP traffic exceeds the LLQ policed rate of 32 kbps.

You should be aware of a couple of terms relating to this configuration on the test. When one policy map refers to another, the configuration are sometimes referred to as "hierarchical" policy maps. Other times, they are called "nested" policy maps. Or you can just think of it as how CBWFQ and LLQ can be configured for the shaping queues.

Shaping to a Peak Rate

In all the examples of CB Shaping so far, the command that enabled shaping always began with the words **shape average**. However, there is another option instead of "average", as seen in the generic form of the following command:

```
shape [average ¦ peak] mean-rate [[burst- size] [excess-burst-size]]
```

When you use the **peak** option, CB Shaping changes how it decides if a packet conforms to or exceeds the traffic contract. As a reminder, using the Shaping logic covered so far in this chapter, Bc bits are sent each Tc. If there's been a period of low or no activity, and the Shaper has been configured with a Be value, then for a short time, more than Bc can be sent—specifically, Be more. With **shape peak**, the shaper allows Bc and Be bits to be sent in each interval, even if there has not been a period of little or no activity. In effect, **shape peak** means that the shaper actually shapes assuming you can send the configured burst during every time period.

Frankly, most people find how it works a little odd, so an example comparing **shape average** with **shape peak**, using the same settings, can help. First, consider shaping configured with the following command:

```
shape average 64000
```

As covered earlier in this section, CB Shaping assumes a Bc of 8000, a Be of the same value, and then calculates Tc of .125 seconds. (Those numbers can be seen in Example 6-3.) The token bucket will be size Bc + Be, or 16,000 bits. After a period of inactivity, 16,000 bits can be sent. Under consistently high offered load, 8,000 bits can be sent each Tc, because the token bucket is filled at Bc bits (8000 bits) per interval.

Compare the following command to the **shape average** command:

```
shape peak 64000
```

Just as with **shape average**, CB Shaping assumes a Bc of 8000, a Be of the same value, and then calculates Tc of .125 seconds. And just as with **shape average,** the token bucket will be size Bc + Be, or 16,000 bits. However, instead of replenishing the token bucket with Bc bits each Tc, **shape peak** tells CB Shaping to replenish Bc + Be tokens per Tc. Translated, that means that the shaper gets the right to send the committed burst, and the excess burst, every time period.

Interestingly, the **shape peak 64000** command actually shapes packets at a rate higher than 64 kbps. To calculate the actual rate, you would use the following formula:

Shaping_rate = configured_rate (1 + Be/Bc)

For instance, in this example, the actual shaping rate would be 128 kbps:

64 (1 + 8000/8000) = 128

Example 6-4 lists an example configuration using shape peak, along with a few comments confirming the math behind the use of this command.

Example 6-4 *CB Shaping on R3, 96-kbps Shape Rate, with LLQ for Shaping Queues*

```
! Portions omitted for brevity
policy-map test1
  class class-default
    shape peak 64000
!
interface Serial0/0
 service-policy output test1
!
R3#show policy-map interface s 0/0

 Serial0/0

  Service-policy output: test1

    Class-map: class-default (match-any)
      20 packets, 1245 bytes
      5 minute offered rate 0 bps, drop rate 0 bps
      Match: any
      Traffic Shaping
```

Target/Average Rate	Byte Limit	Sustain bits/int	Excess bits/int	Interval (ms)	Increment (bytes)
128000/64000	2000	8000	8000	125	2000

Adapt Active	Queue Depth	Packets	Bytes	Packets Delayed	Bytes Delayed	Shaping Active
-	0	0	0	0	0	no

To interpret the example, first remember that Bc defaults to 8000 bits at speeds lower than 320 kbps, and that Be = Bc by default. The **show policy-map interface s0/0** command lists the target rate as 128,000 bits/second, as confirmed with the math that precedes the example. Also, the column labeled **Increment (bytes)** refers to the number of bytes worth of tokens added back to the token bucket in each interval. To support the peak rate, instead of just adding Bc worth of tokens (1000 bytes), Bc + Be (2000 bytes) worth of tokens are added.

Miscellaneous CB Shaping Configuration: Adaptive Shaping

This chapter covered the concepts behind adaptive shaping a little earlier. To configure adaptive shaping with CB Shaping, you need to use the **shape** command twice inside a single **policy-map**. Example 6-5 shows an example:

Example 6-5 *Adaptive CB Shaping Configuration*

```
!
policy-map shape-all
  class class-default
    shape average 96000 9600
    shape adaptive 32000
interface serial0/0
 bandwidth 64
 load-interval 30
 fair-queue
interface serial0/0.1
 service-policy output shape-all
```

As you can see in the example, the **shape average** command is configured, along with the **shape adaptive** command, inside the same policy map class (class-default). The **shape average** command enables shaping; with that command alone, CB Shaping shapes at 96 kbps all the time. With **shape adaptive 32000** configured in the same class, CB Shaping will reduce the shaping rate in reaction to received BECNs, all the way down to 32 kbps. The rate is reduced by 25 percent of the previous actual shaping rate for each BECN received. But the shaping rate will never fall below 32 kbps—so you can think of that rate as the minimum rate, and the 96-kbps rate as the maximum rate.

As a reminder, after 16 consecutive intervals with no received BECNs, this router would start increasing the Shaping rate by 1/16 of the original 96-kbps shaping rate each Tc. To do so, CB Shaping actually starts replenishing the token bucket with a little more each Tc, specifically by (Bc + Be)/16 each Tc. As a result, the rate will likely increase a little more slowly than it decreased in the presence of BECNs.

Miscellaneous CB Shaping Configuration: Shaping by Percent

The **shape** command also allows you to configure the shaping rate based on a percentage of link bandwidth, if you prefer. That's true whether or not you are configuring CB shaping with the **shape average** or **shape peak** commands. For instance, if you had a Frame Relay interface whose access rate (the physical clock rate) was 128 kbps, but you wanted to configure shaping for 64 kbps, you could use the **shape average percent 50** command.

Be aware that the calculation of the actual shaping rate, when enabled on a physical interface, is based on the interface's configured bandwidth. For instance, in this same example, the default setting of the interface's **bandwidth** command is 1544, meaning T/1 speed. The shaping rate would then be calculated as 50 percent of that, or 772 kbps.

Note also that with the **percent** option, Bc and Be are configured with units of milliseconds. Interestingly, configuring Bc with the **percent** option actually sets Tc, with CB Shaping calculating

Bc based on the Bc = Tc * CIR formula. Example 6-6 shows an example configuration, along with the calculated Bc and Be values.

Example 6-6 *Shaping Based on Percent*

```
R3#show running-config
Building configuration...
!
! Portions omitted for brevity
!
policy-map percent-test
  class class-default
    shape average percent 50 125 ms
interface Serial0/1
 bandwidth 128
 service-policy output percent-test

R3#show policy-map interface s 0/1
 Serial0/1

  Service-policy output: percent-test

    Class-map: class-default (match-any)
      0 packets, 0 bytes
      5 minute offered rate 0 bps, drop rate 0 bps
      Match: any
      Traffic Shaping
            Target/Average   Byte    Sustain    Excess     Interval  Increment
               Rate          Limit   bits/int   bits/int   (ms)      (bytes)
            50 (%)                    125 (ms)      0 (ms)
              64000/64000    2000    8000       8000       125       1000


        Adapt   Queue   Packets   Bytes   Packets   Bytes    Shaping
        Active  Depth                     Delayed   Delayed  Active
          -       0       0         0       0         0        no
```

In the configuration, the **shape average percent 50 125 ms** command enables shaping for a rate of 50 percent of the interface's bandwidth. In this case, on S0/1, the bandwidth has been set to 128 kbps, so when the **service-policy output percent-test** command is used, CB Shaping calculates the rate as 50 percent of 128 kbps. Please note that the command requires the **ms** keyword after the number of ms configured for the Bc value (as shown), and for the Be value (not shown in this example.)

The output of the **show policy-map interface** command lists several interesting bits of information as well. For instance, note that the calculated rate of 64000 bits/second is shown. Also, the configured Bc time period of 125 ms shows up as the time interval. CB Shaping then calculated Bc = 64,000 * .125, or 8000 bits.

Comparing CB Shaping and FRTS

The QoS exam does not cover the other three IOS shaping tools, other than a possible need to simply know about the existence of GTS, DTS, and FRTS. Interestingly, the QoS exam does cover Frame Relay Fragmentation, which happens to require FRTS configuration, so you may want to glance over the FRTS coverage in Appendix B which is found on the CD-ROM.

It is good to review the features of CB Shaping now that you have read about the concepts and the configuration. At the same time, because many installations still use FRTS, it seems appropriate to compare the two QoS tools here, in spite of the fact that the exam objectives certainly don't mention FRTS.

Table 6-9 summarizes the key points for comparison between the CB Shaping and FRTS, with a few words of explanation following.

Table 6-9 *Comparison of CB Shaping and FRTS Features*

Feature	CB Shaping	FRTS
Supports ATM, FR, HDLC, PPP, LAN interfaces	Yes	No
Can be enabled on interfaces and subinterfaces	Yes	Yes
Can be enabled per Frame Relay DLCI to support per-VC shaping on multipoint interfaces	No	Yes
Supports adaptive shaping	Yes	Yes
Supports concurrent FRF.12 Frame Relay fragmentation	No	Yes
Supports MLP over Frame and ATM Fragmentation	Yes	Yes
Queuing methods in shaping queue	FIFO, WFQ, CBWFQ, LLQ	FIFO, WFQ, CBWFQ, LLQ, PQ, CQ
Concurrent queuing methods on Physical interface	All	FIFO, FRF*
Can be configured using MQC commands	Yes	No
Can classify traffic to shape a subset of the traffic on an interface/VC	Yes	No
Default Tc	Variable	125 ms

* The Cisco QoS course claims WFQ is supported on the physical interface. In addition, FRF is not technically a queuing tool, although its feature of using two queues does achieve the same effect.

A few words explaining the content of the table can help. First, FRTS only supports Frame Relay—otherwise it'd be a really poor choice of name—but CB Shaping supports any type of data link protocol. If you configure Frame Relay to use multipoint subinterfaces, FRTS does allow you to shape for each VC, whereas CB Shaping does not.

Another point that used to be very important, but isn't today, relates to CB Shaping's non-support of Frame Relay fragmentation. Fragmentation, covered in Chapter 8 of this book, is very important for supporting latency-sensitive traffic. However, there is a fragmentation option available, called Multi-link PPP over Frame Relay Fragmentation, which allows CB Shaping to be used on Frame Relay interfaces concurrently with fragmentation.

Class Based Policing Configuration

CB policing performs policing using three separate actions for packets that conform, exceed, or violate the traffic contract. (The exact meanings of each of these three categories were covered in the "How Policing Works" section earlier in this chapter.) Generally speaking, CB policing considers packets that happen to arrive when enough Bc tokens are available as "conforming" packets. Packets that arrive when Bc is consumed, but Be is not, are considered "exceeding"; and packets that arrive after Bc and Be have been consumed are considered "violating" packets.

For each category (conform, exceed, violate), CB policing can use a variety of actions. Table 6-11, a little later in the chapter, lists the action keywords used in the **police** command. In general, the choices are to drop the packet, transmit the packet, or to first re-mark some QoS field, and then transmit the packet. CB policing uses MQC commands for configuration. Because it is class based, CB policing can police subsets of the traffic on the interface or subinterface on which it is enabled. CB policing uses the same familiar MQC classification commands that all the other MQC-based tools use; again, you only need to learn one more MQC command to know how to configure another MQC QoS feature.

The **police** command configures CB policing inside a policy map. On the **police** command, you define the policing rate in bps, the **Bc** in bytes, and the **Be** in bytes. Note that CB Shaping's settings for Bc and Be were in bits, not bytes!

Two examples of configuration for CB policing (Examples 6-7 and 6-8) follow Tables 6-10 through 6-12. Table 6-10 lists the CB policing configuration commands. Table 6-11 lists the actions that you can configure on the **police** command. (The MQC **match** commands, which can be used with any of the MQC-based features, are not listed, but can be seen in Table 3-2 in Chapter 3.) Table 6-12 lists the CB policing **show** commands.

Table 6-10 *Command Reference for Class-Based Policing*

Command	Mode and Function
police *bps burst-normal burst-max* **conform-action** *action* **exceed-action** *action* [**violate-action** *action*]	**policy-map** class subcommand; enables policing for the class, setting the police rate, Bc, and Bc + Be values, and actions taken. Actions are **drop**, **set-clp-transmit**, **set-dscp-transmit**, **set-prec-transmit**, **set-qos-transmit**, **transmit**.
police cir percent *percent* [**bc** *conform-burst-in-msec*] [**pir percent** *percent*] [**be** *peak-burst-in-msec*] [**conform-action** action [**exceed-action** action [**violate-action** action]]]	**policy-map** class subcommand; enables policing for the class, based on percentage of link bandwidth, for a dual-rate policer
police {**cir** cir} [**bc** conform-burst] {**pir** pir} [**be** peak-burst] [**conform-action** action [**exceed-action** action [**violate-action** action]]]	**policy-map** class subcommand; enables dual-rate policing
service-policy {**input** | **output**} *policy-map-name*	Interface or subinterface configuration mode; enables CB policing on the interface.
class-map *class-map-name*	Global config; names a class map, where classification options are configured.
policy-map *policy-map-name*	Global config; names a policy, which is a set of actions to perform.
class *name*	**policy-map** subcommand; identifies which packets on which to perform some action by referring to the classification logic in a class map.

Table 6-11 *Options for Actions Taken with the **police** Command*

Command	Mode and Function
drop	Drops the packet
set-dscp-transmit	Sets the DSCP and transmits the packet
set-prec-transmit	Sets the IP precedence (0 to 7) and sends the packet

continues

Table 6-11 *Options for Actions Taken with the **police** Command*

Command	Mode and Function
set-qos-transmit	Sets the QoS group ID (1 to 99) and sends the packet
set-clp-transmit	Sets the ATM CLP bit (ATM interfaces only) and sends the packet
transmit	Sends the packet

Table 6-12 *EXEC Command Reference for Class-Based Policing*

Command	Function
show policy-map *policy-map-name*	Lists configuration information about all MQC-based QoS tools
show policy-map *interface-spec* [*input* | *output*] [**class** *class-name*]	Lists statistical information about the behavior of all MQC-based QoS tools

The actions to take on each packet, whether it conforms, exceeds, or violates the contract, boil down to either dropping the packet, transmitting the packet, or re-marking and transmitting the packet. The **drop** and **transmit** options are pretty obvious. However, CB policing includes keywords such as **set-prec-transmit** and **set-dscp-transmit**, which allow the policer to transmit the packet, but first mark the IP Precedence or DSCP field with a lower value. You may recall from the "How Policing Works" section that marking down a packet can be useful because the marked-down packet can have a higher likelihood for discard later, but if no congestion occurs, the packet can be delivered. You can also configure CB Policing to use multiple actions, for instance, mark DSCP and LAN CoS for packets that exceed the contract.

You can use CB policing to police all traffic, or a subset of the traffic, entering or exiting an interface. In the first example, router ISP-edge polices all ingress traffic from an enterprise network. The criteria for the first CB policing example is as follows:

- Create a single-rate, three-color policing configuration.

- All traffic policed at 96 kbps at ingress to the ISP-edge router.

- Bc of 1 second's worth of traffic is allowed.

- Be of 0.5 second's worth of traffic is allowed.

- Traffic that violates the contract is discarded.

- Traffic that exceeds the contract is marked down to DSCP Be.

- Traffic that conforms to the contract is forwarded with no re-marking.

Figure 6-20 shows the network in which the configuration is applied, and Example 6-7 shows the configuration.

Figure 6-20 *Example Network for Policing Examples*

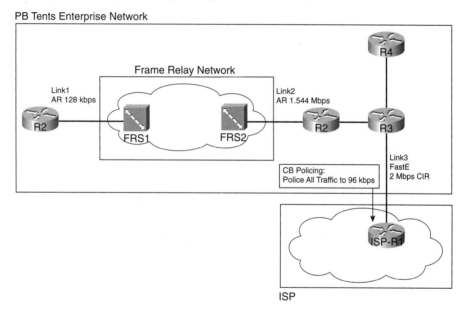

Example 6-7 *Single-rate Three-color CB Policing at 96 kbps at ISP-edge Router*

```
ISP-edge#show running-config
Building configuration...
!
!Lines omitted for brevity
!
ip cef
!
policy-map police-all
  class class-default
! note: the police command wraps around to a second line.
     police cir 96000 bc 12000 be 6000 conform-action transmit exceed-action
set-dscp- transmit 0 violate-action drop
```

continues

Example 6-7 *Single-rate Three-color CB Policing at 96 kbps at ISP-edge Router (Continued)*

```
!
interface Serial1/0
 description connected to FRS port S1. Single PVC to R3.
 no ip address
 encapsulation frame-relay
 load-interval 30
 service-policy input police-all
 no fair-queue
 clockrate 1300000
!
interface Serial1/0.1 point-to-point
 description point-point subint global DLCI 101, connected via PVC to Ent-edge
 ip address 192.168.2.251 255.255.255.0
 frame-relay interface-dlci 103
!
! Lines omitted for brevity
!

ISP-edge#show policy-map
  Policy Map police-all
    Class class-default
! note: the next output lines describes the police command, which
! wraps around to a second line.
      police cir 96000 conform-burst 12000 excess-burst 6000 conform-action
transmit exceed-action set-dscp-transmit 0 violate-action drop

ISP-edge#show  policy-map  interface s 1/0

 Serial1/0

  Service-policy input: police-all

    Class-map: class-default (match-any)
      8375 packets, 1446373 bytes
      30 second offered rate 113000 bps, drop rate 15000 bps
      Match: any
      police:
        cir 96000 bps, conform-burst 12000, excess-burst 6000
        conformed 8077 packets, 1224913 bytes; action: transmit
        exceeded 29 packets, 17948 bytes; action: set-dscp-transmit 0
        violated 269 packets, 203512 bytes; action: drop
 conformed 95000 bps, exceed 0 bps violate 20000 bps
```

The example takes advantage of the fact that in any policy map, all traffic that does not match a class gets placed into the class-default class. Because one design goal was to police all traffic, no explicit class maps were needed—all traffic matches the class-default class inside every policy map by default. Therefore, inside new policy map police-all, the **police cir 96000 bc 12000 be 18000 conform-action transmit exceed-action set-dscp-transmit 0 violate-action drop** command enables policing for the class-default class.

The parameters of the **police** command set the policing rate to 96,000 bps, with 12,000 *bytes* of burst capability. The shaping tools configure Bc and Be as a number of bits; IOS policers configure these values as a number of bytes. The requirements for this example stated 1 second's worth of Bc, and 12,000 bytes can be sent in 1 second with a CIR of 96,000 bps. The **excess-burst** configuration parameter is 6000 bytes, or half of Bc. The stated goals asked for a Be of 0.5 seconds of traffic, and it does indeed take 0.5 seconds to send 6000 bytes at 96 kbps.

Keep in mind that all IOS shapers use bits as the unit when setting Bc and Be; both policers use bytes as the unit.

The **police** command defines a single rate, but the fact that it is a three-color policing configuration, and not a two-color configuration, is not obvious at first glance. To configure a three-color policer, you need to either configure a Be value larger than 0, or configure a violate action, or both. In this case, both are configured, telling IOS to use two token buckets, thereby enabling three categories for the packets.

In Example 6-7, the **police** command transmits packets that *conform*, marks down packets that *exceed* to a DSCP value of zero, and drops packets that *violate* the values. The **show policy- map** command repeats the same details as shown in the configuration command, as highlighted in the example. The **show policy-map interface s1/0** command lists statistics about the number of packets that conformed, exceeded, and violated the contract.

Policing a Subset of the Traffic

One of the advantages of CB policing is the ability to perform policing per class. The next example, Example 6-8, shows CB policing with web traffic classified and policed differently than the rest of the traffic. The criteria for the next CB policing example is as follows:

- Police web traffic at 80 kbps at ingress to the ISP-edge router. Transmit conforming and exceeding traffic, but discard violating traffic.

- Police all other traffic at 16 kbps at ingress to the ISP-edge router. Mark down exceeding and violating traffic to DSCP 0.

- Bc of 1 second's worth of traffic is allowed.

- Be of 0.5 second's worth of traffic is allowed.

Example 6-8 shows the configuration.

Example 6-8 *CB Policing 80 kbps for Web Traffic, 16 kbps for the Rest with Markdown to Be, at ISP-edge Router*

```
ISP-edge#show running-config
Building configuration...
!
!Lines omitted for brevity
!
ip cef
!
class-map match-all match-web
  match protocol http
!
policy-map police-web
  class match-web
      police cir 80000 bc 10000 be 5000 conform-action transmit exceed-action transmit
violate-action drop
  class class-default
      police cir 16000 bc 2000 be 1000 conform-action transmit exceed-action
transmit violate-action set-dscp-transmit 0
!
interface Serial1/0
 description connected to FRS port S1. Single PVC to R3.
 no ip address
 ip nbar protocol-discovery
 encapsulation frame-relay
 load-interval 30
 service-policy input police-web
 no fair-queue
 clockrate 1300000
!
interface Serial1/0.1 point-to-point
 description point-point subint global DLCI 101, connected via PVC to DLCI 103 (R3)
 ip address 192.168.2.251 255.255.255.0
 frame-relay interface-dlci 103
!
!
!Lines omitted for brevity
!
ISP-edge#show policy-map
  Policy Map police-web
    Class match-web
! note: the police command wraps around to a second line.
      police cir 80000 conform-burst 10000 excess-burst 5000 conform-action
transmit exceed-action transmit violate-action drop
    Class class-default
! note: the police command wraps around to a second line.
```

Example 6-8   *CB Policing 80 kbps for Web Traffic, 16 kbps for the Rest with Markdown to Be, at ISP-edge Router (Continued)*

```
        police cir 16000 conform-burst 2000 excess-burst 1000 conform-action
transmit exceed-action transmit violate-action set-dscp-transmit 0

ISP-edge#show policy-map interface s 1/0

 Serial1/0

  Service-policy input: police-web

    Class-map: match-web (match-all)
      736 packets, 900505 bytes
      30 second offered rate 90000 bps, drop rate 14000 bps
      Match: protocol http
      police:
        cir 80000 bps, conform-burst 10000, excess-burst 5000
        conformed 625 packets, 748645 bytes; action: transmit
        exceeded 13 packets, 14268 bytes; action: transmit
        violated 98 packets, 137592 bytes; action: drop
        conformed 75000 bps, exceed 0 bps violate 17000 bps


    Class-map: class-default (match-any)
      3751 packets, 241636 bytes
      30 second offered rate 26000 bps, drop rate 0 bps
      Match: any
      police:
        cir 16000 bps, conform-burst 2000, excess-burst 1000
        conformed 2330 packets, 149928 bytes; action: transmit
        exceeded 46 packets, 2944 bytes; action: transmit
        violated 1376 packets, 88808 bytes; action: set-dscp-transmit 0
        conformed 16000 bps, exceed 0 bps violate 9000 bps
```

If you are becoming comfortable with MQC configurations now, this configuration should be relatively easy to decipher. The **class-map match-all match-web** command creates a new class, which matches all web traffic using NBAR. The **policy-map police-web** command creates a new policy map, which uses **class match-web** to classify web traffic, and **class class-default** to classify all other traffic.

Inside each class of the policy-map, a **police** command is used, setting the parameters as outlined in the stated goals. For instance, the **police cir 80000 bc 10000 be 5000 conform- action transmit exceed-action transmit violate-action drop** command sets the rate at 80 kbps, with a 1-second Bc value of 10,000 bytes, and a configured Be of 5,000 bytes.

The **show policy-map interface s1/0** command lists statistics as always, in this case showing the two classes in the policy map police-web. As you would expect, separate policing statistics are shown per class, because CB policing is enabled per class.

Configuring Dual-Rate Policing

The first two examples in this section on CB Policing configuration showed single rate policing with two token buckets. By using two token buckets, CB Policing could create three categories for the packets—conforming, exceeding, and violating. Using terminology from RFC 2496, CB Policing was configured as a single-rate three-color policer in each case, with the word "color" implying the three categories (conform, exceed, violate).

> **NOTE**   To create a single rate two-color CB Policing configuration, you simply do not include the **violate-action** keyword and the Be value in the **police** command.

This section shows an example of configuring a dual-rate three-color policer. As you might recall from the earlier section titled "CB Policing: Dual Rates, Three-Color (2 Buckets)", a dual-rate policer uses two rates, one called CIR, and one called PIR. The goal of a dual-rate policer is to let the engineer define the two rates, with packets below the CIR considered to conform, packets above CIR but below PIR considered to exceed, and all other packets considered to violate the contract.

To allow configuration of two different rates, the **police** command is still used. However, the syntax differs slightly from the earlier use of the command. The generic syntax is as follows:

```
police {cir cir} [bc conform-burst] {pir pir} [be peak-burst]
    [conform-action action [exceed-action action [violate-action action]]]
```

Note that with the syntax of this command, you are required to configure a CIR and a PIR setting. (The curly brackets mean that the parameter is required.) The command includes a place to set the Bc value and the Be values as well, plus the same set of options for conform, exceed, and violate actions.

For example, if you wanted to perform dual-rate policing, with a CIR of 96 kbps and a PIR of 128 kbps, you would simply use a command like **police cir 96000 pir 128000.**

CB Policing Miscellany

There are a few more miscellaneous points you should be aware of with CB Policing. This short section outlines the remaining points.

Multi-action Policing

If a packet violates the contract, instead of discarding it, you might mark down DSCP to 0. That way, if the rest of the network is not congested, the packet makes it through, but if the network is congested, another router will be more likely to discard the packet.

On occasion, an engineer might want to mark more than one field in a packet header. For instance, Frame Relay switches might choose to discard frames with DE marked in the Frame Relay header, rather than those with DE unmarked, if congestion does occur. An engineer might want to mark both DSCP and FR DE when a packet violates the contract.

Cisco supports marking multiple fields for a single category with policing. To do so, first the police command is used to set the rate(s), but the actions are not configured in the police command. Instead, by omitting the actions, the police command places the user into another submode, in which the actions can be added on individual lines. To configure multiple actions, multiple conform-action, exceed-action, or violate-action subcommands are used. Example 6-9 shows an sample, with marking of DSCP 0 and FR DE for packets that violate the traffic contract:

Example 6-9 *Multi-action Policing*

```
R3#conf t
Enter configuration commands, one per line.  End with CNTL/Z.
R3(config)#policy-map testpol1
R3(config-pmap)#class class-default
R3(config-pmap-c)#police 128000 256000
R3(config-pmap-c-police)#conform-action transmit
R3(config-pmap-c-police)#exceed-action transmit
R3(config-pmap-c-police)#violate-action set-dscp-transmit 0
R3(config-pmap-c-police)#violate-action set-frde-transmit
```

Note that the preceding is not a *single **police*** command, but instead, it uses a sub-command mode after the police command. In particular, note that there are two instances of the **violate-action** subcommand, with different actions listed.

Policing by Percentage

Like for the **shape** command, IOS supports a version of the police command that allows you to configure the policing rate as a percentage of link bandwidth. You can also configure the Bc and Be values as a number of milliseconds, from which IOS calculates the actual Bc and Be values based on how many bits can be sent in that many milliseconds. Example 6-10 shows an example of a dual-rate policing configuration using the percentage option.

Example 6-10 *Configuring Percentage-Based Policing*

```
R3#show running-config
! Portions omitted for Brevity
 policy-map test-pol6
  class class-default
    police cir percent 25 bc 500 ms pir percent 50 be 500 ms
 !
 !
interface serial0/0
 bandwidth 256
 service-policy output test-pol6
 !
R3#show policy-map interface s0/0
 Serial0/0

  Service-policy output: test-pol6

    Class-map: class-default (match-any)
      4 packets, 156 bytes
      5 minute offered rate 0 bps, drop rate 0 bps
      Match: any
      police:
          cir 25 % bc 500 ms
          cir 64000 bps, bc 4000 bytes
          pir 50 % be 500 ms
          pir 128000 bps, be 8000 bytes
        conformed 0 packets, 0 bytes; actions:
          transmit
        exceeded 0 packets, 0 bytes; actions:
          drop
        violated 0 packets, 0 bytes; actions:
          drop
        conformed 0 bps, exceed 0 bps, violate 0 bps
  R3#
```

The syntax of the **police** command includes the percent keyword, telling IOS to interpret the CIR and PIR values as link percentages. Once enabled on **interface serial0/0**, which has a **bandwidth 256** command, IOS can interpret the percentages into actual bit rates. For instance, the output of the **show policy-map interface s0/0** command lists CIR as 25 percent on one line, and then as 64000 bps on the next. The math is simply the percentage times the interface bandwidth, or 25 percent of 256 kbps. The PIR is calculated the same way, in this case as 50 percent of the PIR, or 50 percent of 256 kbps.

Note that the Bc and Be values are configured as a number, followed by the keyword **ms** (meaning milliseconds). To calculate the actual Bc and Be, the math is again simple. IOS figures out how many bits would be sent in that many milliseconds at the stated rate. For instance, Bc was set to 500 ms; at a CIR of 64 kbps, you can send 32,000 bits in 500 ms (.5 seconds times 64,000 bits/second). So Bc is calculated as 32,000 bits, but for policing, Bc and Be units are bytes—so the **show policy-map interface** command lists a Bc of 4,000 bytes. Similarly, the Be is calculated as PIR * number_of_milliseconds, or 128,000 bits/second multiplied by .5 seconds, or 64,000 bits. Converted to bytes, that's 8000 bytes, which is indeed reflected in the **show policy-map interface** command output in the example.

CB Policing Defaults for Bc and Be

If you do not configure a Bc value, then CB Policing configures a default value based on the following formula:

$$Bc = CIR/32$$

Although the math is easy, this formula may seem to be a little random at first. What logic behind it is essentially to figure out how many bytes could be sent at the CIR speed in 1/4 of a second. And remember, the CIR is in bits/second, and the Bc setting is in bytes. So, a different look at the formula may make more sense:

$$Bc = \frac{(CIR * .25 \text{ seconds})}{8 \text{ bits/byte}}$$

Also note that CB Policing will not allow the calculated default to be less than 1500—if the math works out to a number less than 1500, CB Policing uses 1500 instead.

For Be, the default depends on whether you configure a single bucket (two color) policer, or a two bucket (three color) policer. To configure to use a single bucket/two colors, just leave off the Be and violate-action options. In this case, Be defaults to 0. However, if you configure a violate action, or set Be to something besides 0, IOS thinks you want to use a two bucket/three color policing function. In that case, IOS defaults Be = Bc.

When dual-rate policing is used, and Bc and Be are not configured, IOS calculates the value for Bc using the same formula as shown previously. For Be, IOS using a slightly-different formula, with the same intent, but based on PIR:

$$Be = \frac{(PIR * .25 \text{ seconds})}{8 \text{ bits/byte}} = PIR/32$$

Table 6-13 summarizes the small details about the defaults for Bc and Be. The table lists all three cases, plus a reminder of how to know which style of configuration is being used.

Table 6-13 *Summary of Default Calculations for Bc and Be with CB Policer*

Type of Policing Configuration	Telltale signs in the police command	Defaults
Single Rate, Single Bucket/ Two color	No violate-action or Be configured, no PIR configured	Bc = CIR/32 Be = 0
Single Rate, Dual Bucket/ Three color	violate-action and/or Be is configured, no PIR configured	Bc = CIR/32 Be = Bc
Dual Rate, Dual Bucket/Three color	PIR is configured	Bc = CIR/32 Be = PIR/32

Policing by Percent

Like the **shape** command, the **police** command now includes an option for configuring the rate using a percentage of link bandwidth. The concept works the same way as it does the **shape** command. For instance, if an interface had a **bandwidth** setting of 128 kbps, to police at 64 kbps, the **police cir percent 50** command could be used. The generic form of the **police** command, using the percent option, is as follows:

```
police cir percent percent [bc conform-burst-in-msec] [pir percent percent]
  [be peak-burst-in-msec] [conform-action action [exceed-action action
  [violate-action action]]]
```

When using the **police** command with the **percent** option, you only have to configure the CIR percentage. To configure a single-rate policer, simply don't include the **pir** option; to configure a dual-rate policer, include the **pir** option. Regardless of whether the command defines single-rate or dual-rate policing, if Bc and Be are not configured, IOS calculates the value to use for each using the same rules as described in the previous section of this chapter.

CB Policing Configuration Summary

CB Policing inside Cisco IOS has many features, most of which are covered in this chapter. The syntax of the commands, the ways the **police** command can be used, and the meaning of the output of the related **show** commands are all important. Also, the core features of how Cisco implements CB Policing in Cisco IOS are also important, and are summarized in the list that follows.

- Supports Single-rate, two-color policing, which uses a single token bucket, and two action categories (conform and exceed)

- Single-rate, three-color policing, which uses two token buckets, and three action categories (conform, exceed, and violate)

- Dual-rate, three-color policing, using two buckets, supporting both CIR and PIR rates

- "Two Color" and "Three color" terminology refers to the actions categories that can be determined by the policer – namely conform, exceed, and violate

- Supports policing of a subset of traffic by using MQC classes, with the **police** command enabled in the traffic classes that include the packets that need to be policed

- Support for multiactions policing by repeating the conform-action, exceed-action, and/or violate-action keywords.

- For single-rate policing, if Bc and Be are not configured, IOS calculates the values as Be = 0 and Bc as the larger of either 1500 or CIR/32.

- For dual-rate policing, if Bc and Be are not configured, IOS calculates the values as follows: Bc as the larger of either 1500 or CIR/32, and Be as the larger of either 1500 or PIR/32.

- The **police** command allows configuration of the rates as percentages of link bandwidth, with Bc and Be being set as a number of milliseconds.

Foundation Summary

The "Foundation Summary" is a collection of tables and figures that provide a convenient review of many key concepts in this chapter. For those of you already comfortable with the topics in this chapter, this summary could help you recall a few details. For those of you who just read this chapter, this review should help solidify some key facts. For any of you doing your final prep before the exam, these tables and figures are a convenient way to review the day before the exam.

ISPs make the business choice of whether to police, and how aggressively to police. The options reduce to the following three basic options:

- Do not police. To support the traffic, build the network to support the traffic as if all customers will send and receive data at the clock rate of the access link. From a sales perspective, close deals by claiming that no policing will be done, but encourage customers who exceed their contracts to pay for more bandwidth.

- Police at the contracted rate. To support these traffic levels, the network only needs to be built to support the collective contracted rates, although the core would be overbuilt to support new customers. From a sales perspective, encourage customers that are beginning to exceed their contracts to upgrade, and give incentives.

- Police somewhere in between the contracted rate and the access-link clock rate. For instance, ISP1 might police PB Tents at 5 Mbps, when the contract reads 2 Mbps. The network can be built to support the collective policed rates. The sales team can encourage customers to buy a larger contracted rate when they consistently exceed the contracted rate, but keep customer satisfaction higher by pointing out their generosity by only policing at rates much higher than the contracted rates.

Figure 6-21 points out two cases of egress blocking, using a Frame Relay network as an example.

Figure 6-21   *PB Tents Network, Egress Blocking*

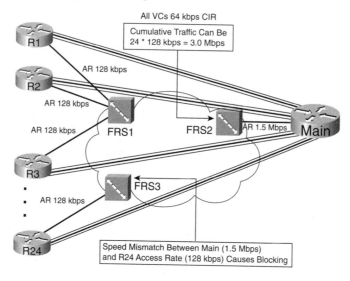

Table 6-14 summarizes some of the key points about when and where you should consider using policing and shaping.

Table 6-14   *Policing and Shaping: When to Use Them, and Where*

Topic	Rationale
Why police?	If a neighboring network can send more traffic than the traffic contract specifies, policing can be used to enforce the contract, protecting the network from being overrun with too much traffic.
Where to police?	Typically, policing is performed as packets enter the first device in a network. Egress policing is also supported, although it is less typical.
Why shape?	The first of two reasons for shaping is when the neighboring network is policing. Instead of waiting for the neighboring policer to discard traffic, a shaper can instead delay traffic so that it will not be dropped. \n\n The second reason has to do with the effects of egress blocking. By shaping, egress blocking can be avoided, or minimized, essentially moving the queues from inside the service provider cloud, and back into the enterprise routers. By doing so, the router queuing tools can selectively give better QoS performance to particular types of traffic.
Where to shape?	Shaping is always an egress function. Typically, shaping is performed on packets exiting a router, going into another network. This may be the edge between a router and a multiaccess WAN, or possibly just a link to an ISP.

Traffic shaping implements this basic logic by defining a measurement interval, and a number of bits that can be sent in that interval, so that the overall shaped rate is not exceeded. Table 6-15 lists some related definitions.

Table 6-15 *Shaping Terminology*

Term	Definition
Tc	Time interval, measured in milliseconds, over which the committed burst (Bc) can be sent. With many shaping tools, Tc = Bc/CIR.
Bc	Committed burst size, measured in bits. This is the amount of traffic that can be sent over the interval Tc. Typically also defined in the traffic contract.
CIR	Committed information rate, in bits per second, defines the rate defined in the traffic contract.
Shaped Rate	The rate, in bits per second, to which a particular configuration wants to shape the traffic. In some cases, the shaped rate is set to the same value as CIR; in others, the shaped rate is set to a larger value, with the hope of sending more traffic through the network.
Be	Excess burst size, in bits. This is the number of bits beyond Bc that can be sent after a period of inactivity.

Traffic Shaping uses a token bucket to control the mechanics of deciding which packets conform to the shaping rate, and which exceed the rate. Two main actions revolve around the token bucket and the tokens:

■ The re-filling of the bucket with new tokens

■ The consumption of tokens by the Shaper to gain the right to forward packets.

For filling the token bucket, the bucket is filled to the brim, but no more, at the beginning of each Tc (assuming that Be = 0 for the time being). Another way you can think of it as if the Shaper dumps Bc worth of tokens into the Bucket at the beginning of every interval—but if there's not enough room in the bucket, because not all the tokens were used during the previous time interval, some tokens spill out—and those spilled tokens can't be used. The net result, either way you look at it, is that the interval starts with a full token bucket of size Bc. Figure 6-22 shows the basic idea:

Figure 6-22 *Mechanics of Filling the Shaping Token Bucket*

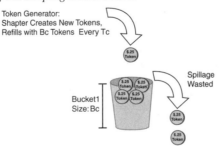

With Be configured, the size of the single token bucket used by shaping is Bc + Be, but the tokens are still only refilled with Bc every time interval. This effectively lets the shaper save extra tokens after a period of inactivity in order to burst longer. Figure 6-23 lists the overall process used by shaping, with both a Bc and Be value configured.

Figure 6-23 *Bc and Be, After a Period of Inactivity (Both Buckets Full)*

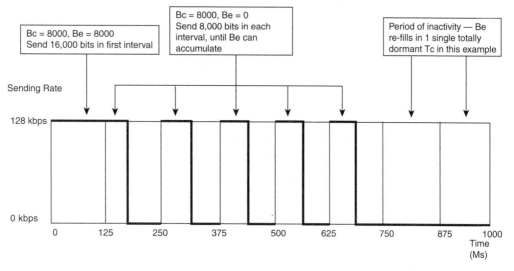

The formulas IOS uses to calculate Tc when you configure both the shaping rate and the Bc are as follows:

$$Tc = Bc/CIR$$

Or

$$Tc = Bc/\text{Shaped rate}$$

CB Shaping calculates a value for Bc and Be if the **shape** command does not include a value. From that, it calculates the Tc. At lower shaping rate (less than 320Kbs), CB Shaping assumes a Bc of 8000 bits, and calculates Tc based on the formula Tc = Bc/CIR, with some rounding as necessary. Note that at 320 kbps, the calculated Tc would be 25 ms, or .025 seconds.

For speeds higher than 320 kbps, CB Shaping instead uses a default Tc of .025 seconds (250 ms), and calculates Bc based on the same formula, which with a little easy algebra translates to Bc = Tc * CIR. For instance, at 640 kbps, Bc = .025 * 640 kbps = 16,000 bits.

CB Shaping defaults Be to be equal to Bc.

CB Shaping can adapt its shaping rate based on the receipt of BECNs or Foresight messages. When the shaper receives a BECN or Foresight message, it slows down by 25 percent of the maximum rate, repeating the process for each received BECN or Foresight message, until the minimum rate is reached. The rate grows again after 16 consecutive intervals occur without a BECN or Foresight congestion message. The shaping rate grows by 1/16 of the maximum rate during each Tc, until the maximum rate is reached again. This process results in an increase in the shaping rate based on the following formula: (Bc + Be)/16.

When a shaper uses a queuing tool, instead of having a single shaping queue, multiple shaping queues exist. If FRTS were configured to use PQ, for example, up to four queues could be created for shaping. Figure 6-24 shows the basic idea, with shaping enabled on the physical interface, FIFO Queuing on the physical interface, and PQ configured for the shaping queue.

Figure 6-24 *FIFO Queuing for the Physical Interface, Plus PQ for the Shaping Queue*

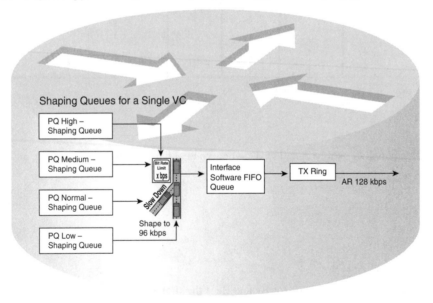

Many QoS designs call for shaping per VC. For the same router, with two 64-kbps CIR VCs (each configured on a separate point-to-point subinterface) shaping queues are created for each subinterface, with the familiar output queues as well. Figure 6-25 depicts the overall idea.

Figure 6-25 *Fancy Queuing for the Physical Interface as well as for Two Sets of Shaping Queues*

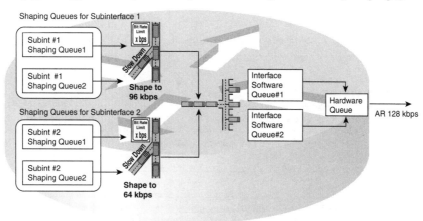

The CB Shaping **shape** command has an option for peak-rate shaping. For instance, the **shape peak 64000** command actually shapes packets at a rate higher than 64 kbps. To calculate the actual rate, you would use the following formula:

Shaping_rate = configured_rate (1 + Be/Bc)

For instance, the actual shaping rate would be 128 kbps, assuming the default value 8000 for both Bc and Be:

64 (1 + 8000/8000) = 128

Table 6-16 summarizes the key points for comparison between the CB Shaping and FRTS, with a few words of explanation following.

Table 6-16 *Comparison of CB Shaping and FRTS Features*

Feature	CB Shaping	FRTS
Supports ATM, FR, HDLC, PPP, LAN interfaces	Yes	No
Can be enabled on interfaces and subinterfaces	Yes	Yes
Can be enabled per Frame Relay DLCI to support per-VC shaping on multipoint interfaces	No	Yes
Supports adaptive shaping	Yes	Yes
Supports concurrent FRF.12 Frame Relay fragmentation	No	Yes
Supports MLP over Frame and ATM Fragmentation	Yes	Yes
Queuing methods in shaping queue	FIFO, WFQ, CBWFQ, LLQ	FIFO, WFQ, CBWFQ, LLQ, PQ, CQ
Concurrent queuing methods on Physical interface	All	FIFO, FRF*
Can be configured using MQC commands	Yes	No
Can classify traffic to shape a subset of the traffic on an interface/VC	Yes	No
Default Tc	Variable	125 ms

* The Cisco QoS course claims WFQ is supported on the physical interface. In addition, FRF is not technically a queuing tool, although its feature of using two queues does achieve the same effect.

CB Policing includes a lot of small details about how it chooses which packets conform to, exceed, or violate a traffic contract. To help with exam prep, Table 6-17 lists the key points about how CB Policing uses token buckets.

Table 6-17 *Summary of CB Policing Mechanics*

Feature	Behavior of Single-Rate, Two-Color	Behavior of Single-Rate, Three-Color	Behavior of Dual-Rate, Three-Color
Size of "first" bucket	Bc (bytes)	Bc (bytes)	Bc (bytes)
Size of "second" bucket	N/A	Be (bytes)	Be (bytes)
Refill of first bucket	Prorated portion of Bc based on packet arrival time	Prorated portion of Bc based on packet arrival time	Prorated portion of Bc based on packet arrival time
Refill of second bucket	N/A	Filled by spilled Tokens from refill of first bucket	Prorated portion of Be based on packet arrival time
Logic for "conform" action	1st bucket => packet size; decrement 1st bucket by packet size	1st bucket => packet size; decrement 1st bucket by packet size	1st bucket => packet size; decrement 1st and 2nd bucket by packet size
Logic to choose "exceed" action	All packets that do not conform	Doesn't conform, but 2nd bucket => packet size; decrement 2nd bucket by packet size	Doesn't conform, but 2nd bucket => packet size; decrement 2nd bucket by packet size
Logic to choose "violate" action	N/A	All other packets	All other packets

Figure 6-26 shows how a single-rate, three-color policer replenishes the tokens in the dual token buckets.

Figure 6-26 *Refilling Dual Token Buckets with CB Policing*

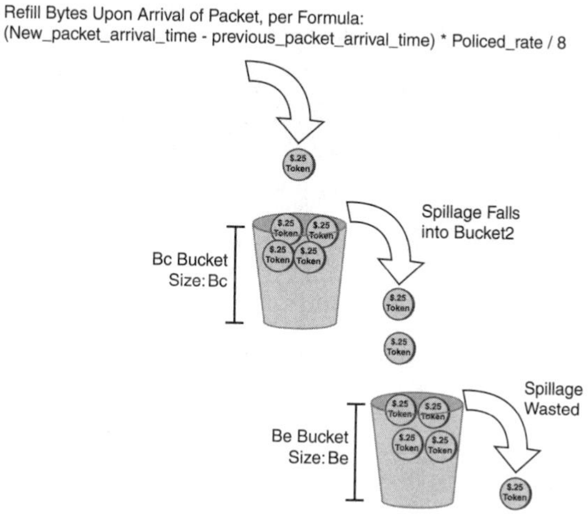

Refill Bytes Upon Arrival of Packet, per Formula:
(New_packet_arrival_time - previous_packet_arrival_time) * Policed_rate / 8

Bc Bucket Size: Bc

Spillage Falls into Bucket2

Be Bucket Size: Be

Spillage Wasted

Figure 6-27 depicts the mechanics of how a dual-rate, three-color policer works in regards to refilling tokens into the dual token buckets:

Figure 6-27 *Refilling CIR and PIR Dual Token Buckets with CB Policing*

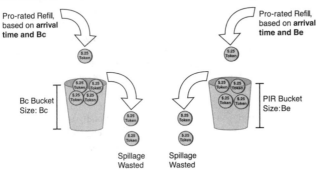

Table 6-18 summarizes the small details about the defaults for Bc and Be. The table lists all three cases, plus a reminder of how to know which style of configuration is being used.

Table 6-18 *Summary of Default Calculations for Bc and Be with CB Policer*

Type of Policing Configuration	Telltale signs in the police command	Defaults
Single Rate, Single Bucket/ Two color	No violate-action or Be configured, no PIR configured	Bc = CIR/32 Be = 0
Single Rate, Dual Bucket/ Three color	violate-action and/or Be is configured, no PIR configured	Bc = CIR/32 Be = Bc
Dual Rate, Dual Bucket/Three color	PIR is configured	Bc = CIR/32 Be = PIR/32

Table 6-19 lists the various actions associated with CB policing.

Table 6-19 *Policing Actions Used by CAR and CB Policing*

Command	Mode and Function
drop	Drops the packet
set-dscp-transmit	Sets the DSCP and transmits the packet
set-prec-transmit	Sets the IP precedence (0 to 7) and sends the packet
set-qos-transmit	Sets the QoS group ID (1 to 99) and sends the packet
set-clp-transmit	Sets the ATM CLP bit (ATM interfaces only) and sends the packet
transmit	Sends the packet

The list that follows summarizes the core features of how Cisco implements CB Policing.

- Supports Single-rate, two-color policing, which uses a single token bucket, and two action categories (conform and exceed)

- Single-rate, three-color policing, which uses two token buckets, and three action categories (conform, exceed, and violate)

- Dual-rate, three-color policing, using two buckets, supporting both CIR and PIR rates

- "Two Color" and "Three color" terminology refers to the actions categories that can be determined by the policer – namely conform, exceed, and violate

- Supports policing of a subset of traffic by using MQC classes, with the police command enabled in the traffic classes that include the packets that need to be policed

- Support for multiactions policing by repeating the conform-action, exceed-action, and/or violate-action keywords.

- For single-rate policing, if Bc and Be are not configured, IOS calculates the values as Be = 0 and Bc as the larger of either 1500 or CIR/32.

- For dual-rate policing, if Bc and Be are not configured, IOS calculates the values as follows: Bc as the larger of either 1500 or CIR/32, and Be as the larger of either 1500 or PIR/32.

- The **police** command allows configuration of the rates as percentages of link bandwidth, with Bc and Be being set as a number of milliseconds.

Q&A

As mentioned in the Introduction, you have two choices for review questions. The questions that follow next give you a more difficult challenge than the exam itself by using an open-ended question format. By reviewing now with this more difficult question format, you can exercise your memory better, and prove your conceptual and factual knowledge of this chapter. You can find the answers to these questions in Appendix A.

The second option for practice questions is to use the CD included with this book. It includes a testing engine and more than 200 multiple-choice questions. You should use this CD nearer to the end of your preparation, for practice with the actual exam format. You can even customize the CD exam to include, or not include, the topics that are only on the CCIP QoS.

Traffic Policing and Traffic Shaping Concepts

1. Explain the points during the process of a single router receiving and forwarding traffic at which shaping and policing can be enabled on a router.

2. Compare and contrast the actions that shaping and policing take when a packet exceeds a traffic contract.

3. Compare and contrast the effects that shaping and policing have on bandwidth, delay, jitter, and loss.

4. Describe the typical locations to enable shaping and policing in an internetwork.

5. Describe the reasons behind egress blocking in a Frame Relay network with a T1 access link at the main site, 128-kbps access links at each of 20 remote sites, with 64-kbps CIR VCs from the main site to each remote site.

6. If a router has CB Shaping configured, with a shaping rate of 256 kbps, and a Bc of 16,000 bits, what Tc value does the shaping tool use?

7. If a router has CB Shaping configured, with a shaping rate of 512 kbps, and a Be of 16,000 bits, what Tc value does the shaping tool use?

8. Define the terms Tc, Bc, Be, and CIR.

9. Describe the concept of traffic-shaping adaption.

10. Describe the difference between interface output queues and shaping queues, and explain where the queues could exist on a router with 1 physical interface and 20 subinterfaces.

11. How many token buckets are used by the CB Shaping internal processes with Be = 0? How big is the bucket(s)?

12. How many token buckets are used by the CB Shaping internal processes with Be = 8000? How big is the bucket(s)?

13. How many token buckets are used by the CB Policing internal processes with Be = 0? How big is the bucket(s)?

14. How many token buckets are used by CB Policing internal processes, configured for single-rate policing, with Be = 8000? How big is the bucket(s)?

15. How many token buckets are used by CB Policing internal processes, configured for dual-rate policing, with Be = 8000? How big is the bucket(s)?

16. Imagine a CB Shaping configuration with a rate of 128000, Bc = 8000, and Be = 16000. What is the Tc value, and how many tokens are refilled into the first bucket during each Tc?

17. Imagine a CB Shaping configuration with a rate of 128000, Bc = 8000, and Be = 16000. At the beginning of the next time interval, the token bucket is full. If the physical clock rate of the interface on which shaping is enabled is 256 kbps, describe how much traffic that will be sent in this next Tc, and why.

18. If a policer is called a "two color" policer, what does that mean?

19. If a policer is called a "three color" policer, what does that mean?

20. With CB Policing, how are tokens refilled into the bucket associated with the CIR policing rate?

21. With a dual-rate policer, how are tokens refilled into the token bucket associated with PIR?

22. With a single-rate policer, with Be > 0, how are tokens refilled into the excess token bucket?

23. With a single-rate policer, with Be = 0, what must be true for the policer to decide that a packet exceeds the traffic contract?

24. With a single-rate policer, with Be > 0, what must be true for the policer to decide that a packet exceeds the traffic contract?

25. With a single-rate policer, with Be > 0 what must be true for the policer to decide that a packet violates the traffic contract?

26. With a single-rate policer, regardless of Be setting, what must be true for the policer to decide that a packet conforms to the traffic contract?

27. For policing configurations that use two buckets, a packet is classified as conforming, exceeding, or violating the traffic contract. When processing a new packet, in which of these three cases does the policer then also remove or spend the tokens?

28. Comparing the logic used for a single-rate and dual-rate policer, when both use two token buckets, their logic differs slightly in terms of how the tokens are removed from the buckets when policing a packet. Explain that difference.

29. Comparing the logic used for a single-rate and dual-rate policer, when both use two token buckets, their logic differs slightly in terms of how the tokens are added to the buckets before policing a newly-arrived packet. Explain that difference.

Class Based Shaping Configuration

30. Along with the **class-map**, **policy-map**, and **service-policy** commands, CB shaping requires one specific command that actually sets values used for the shaping function. List the command, with the correct syntax, that sets a shaped rate of 128 kbps, a Bc of 8000, and a Be of 8000, when using CB shaping. Do not assume any defaults; explicitly set the values in the command.

31. Explain the context inside the configuration mode under which the service-policy command can be used to enable LLQ on a CB shaping queue. ("Context" means what part of configuration mode—for instance, global-configuration mode, interface configuration mode, and so on.)

32. CB shaping has been configured under subinterface s0/0.1. What **show** command lists statistics for CB shaping behavior just for that subinterface?

33. Which of the traffic-shaping tools can be enabled on each VC on a Frame Relay multipoint subinterface?

34. At what rate would CB Shaping actually shape traffic when using the command **shape peak 64000 8000 16000**?

35. Assume that two class maps have already been defined, called C1 and C2. You decide to add a policy map, and enable it on **interface serial 0/1**, so that the policy map has both classes C1 and C2 in it. For class C1, you do not use any shaping, but for class C2, you will shape with a rate of 128 kbps. Create the rest of the syntactically-correct configuration commands to meet this requirement.

36. Assume the same general requirements as the previous question. Create the configuration, defining the shaping rate as a percentage, assuming the interface already has a **bandwidth 256** command under it.

37. Assume the same general requirements as the previous question, except now you want to tune the Tc down to 10ms, and not have any excess burst capability. Create the configuration.

38. Assume the same general requirements as the previous question, except now you want to keep the default Bc, but make Be equal to twice Bc. Create the configuration.

39. Assume the same general requirements as the previous question, except now you want to adapt the shaping rate to 50 percent of the originally configured rate upon the receipt of Frame Relay BECNs. Create the configuration.

Class Based Policing Configuration

40. Assume that two class maps have already been defined, called C1 and C2. You decide to add a **policy-map**, and enable it on **interface serial 0/1**, so that the policy-map has both classes C1 and C2 in it. For class C1, will configure policing at a rate of 128 kbps, and for class C2, you will police at a rate of 256 kbps. You want to transmit packets that conform to the contract, and re-mark to DSCP AF13 for those that exceed the contract. Create the rest of the syntactically-correct configuration commands to meet this requirement.

41. Assume the same general requirements as the previous question, but in this case, you want to create a two-bucket/three-color policer, and drop packets that violate the traffic contract. Create the configuration commands.

42. Assume that two class maps have already been defined, called C1 and C2. You decide to add a policy map, and enable it on **interface serial 0/1**, so that the policy map has both classes C1 and C2 in it. For class C1, will configure policing at a rate of 128 kbps, and for class C2, you will police at a rate of 256 kbps. You can configure any actions you like for the three categories. However, you need to change the Bc setting such that the first token bucket's size is equal to 1 second's worth of data. Create the configuration commands.

43. Assume the same general requirements as the previous question, but now you decide to create a dual-rate policer for class C2, with the PIR set at double the CIR of 256 kbps. Create the configuration commands. Assuming you didn't configure Be, what would CB Policing calculate for the Be setting?

44. Assume the same general requirements as the previous question, but now configure the **police** commands assuming that **interface serial 0/1** has a **bandwidth 512** command configured, and you have to use the percent option in both **police** commands.

45. CB Policing has been configured under subinterface s0/0.1. What **show** command would list statistics for CB Policing behavior just for that subinterface?

46. List the command, with the correct syntax, that sets a Policed rate of 512 kbps, a Bc of 1 second's worth of traffic, and a Be of an additional .5 seconds worth of traffic, when using CB Policer. Do not assume any defaults; explicitly set the values in the command. You can choose any other settings needed for the command.

47. Explain the concept behind re-marking policed packets versus discarding the packets.

QoS Exam Objectives

This chapter covers the following exam topics specific to the QoS exam:

- Describe the drawbacks tail drop as a congestion control mechanism

- Describe the elements of a RED traffic profile

- Describe Weighted Random Early Detection and how it can be used to prevent congestion

- Identify the Cisco IOS commands required to configure and monitor DSCP-based CB-WRED

- Explain how ECN interacts with WRED in Cisco IOS

CHAPTER 7

Congestion Avoidance Through Drop Policies

Quality of service (QoS) congestion-avoidance tools help prevent congestion before it occurs. These tools monitor queue depth, and before the queue fills, they drop some packets. The computers sending the packets might reduce the frequency of sending packets in reaction to the packet loss, particularly if the application sending the data uses TCP. In the moments after the congestion-avoidance tool discards packets, congestion is reduced, because less traffic is sent into the network.

Cisco congestion-avoidance tools rely on the behavior of TCP to reduce congestion. TCP flows slow down after packet loss. By discarding some TCP packets before congestion gets bad, congestion-avoidance tools may actually reduce the overall number of packets dropped, and reduce congestion, thereby indirectly reducing delay and jitter.

The first section of this chapter begins with a review of TCP and a description of how TCP slows down after packet loss. Following that, several of the problems that can be solved using congestion-avoidance tools are described, namely tail drop, global synchronization, and TCP starvation. The concepts section of this chapter ends with coverage of Random Early Detection (RED), which defines several algorithms, which are the basis of IOS congestion-avoidance tools.

Weighted RED (WRED) and Explicit Congestion Notification (ECN) are two congestion-avoidance tools available in IOS. These are covered in sequence, with the differences between the two highlighted at the end of the chapter.

"Do I Know This Already?" Quiz

The purpose of the "Do I Know This Already?" quiz is to help you decide whether you really need to read the entire chapter. If you already intend to read the entire chapter, you do not necessarily need to answer these questions now.

The 9-question quiz, derived from the major sections in "Foundation Topics" section of this chapter, helps you determine how to spend your limited study time.

Table 7-1 outlines the major topics discussed in this chapter and the "Do I Know This Already?" quiz questions that correspond to those topics.

Use Table 7-1 to record your score.

Table 7-1 *"Do I Know This Already?" Foundation Topics Section-to-Question Mapping*

Foundation Topics Section Covering These Questions	Questions	Score
Congestion-Avoidance Concepts and RED	1 to 3	
WRED	4 to 7	
ECN	8 to 9	
Total Score		

> **CAUTION** The goal of self-assessment is to gauge your mastery of the topics in this chapter. If you do not know the answer to a question or are only partially sure of the answer, mark this question wrong for purposes of the self-assessment. Giving yourself credit for an answer you correctly guess skews your self-assessment results and might provide you with a false sense of security.

You can find the answers to the "Do I Know This Already?" quiz in Appendix A, "Answers to the 'Do I Know This Already?' Quizzes and Q&A Sections." The suggested choices for your next step are as follows:

- **7 or less overall score**—Read the entire chapter. This includes the "Foundation Topics," the "Foundation Summary,", and "Q&A" sections.

- **8 or 9 overall score**—If you want more review on these topics, skip to the "Foundation Summary" section and then go to the "Q&A" section. Otherwise, move to the next chapter.

Congestion-Avoidance Concepts and RED Questions

1. TCP Slow Start controls the rate a TCP sender sends data by controlling:

   a. Growth of the Advertised Window

   b. Growth of the Congestion Window

   c. Calculation of the Average Queue Depth

   d. The wait-for-acknowledgement timer

2. For which of the following WRED categories will WRED discard all packets?

   a. Tail Drop

   b. Full Drop

   c. Random Drop

   d. Partial Drop

   e. No Drop

3. For which of the following WRED categories will WRED discard a subset of the packets?

   a. Tail Drop

   b. Full Drop

   c. Random Drop

   d. Partial Drop

   e. No Drop

WRED Questions

4. On which of the following types of queues can you enable WRED on routers that are not part of the 7500-series router line?

   a. On the physical interface

   b. On a CBWFQ class that has been configured with the **bandwidth** command

   c. On an LLQ class that has been configured with the **priority** command

   d. On a single FIFO queue created by CB Shaping

The next three questions refer to the following configuration snippet:

```
ip cef
!
! The following classes are used in the LLQ configuration applied to S0/0
!
class-map match-all class1
  match protocol http url "*important*"
class-map match-all class2
  match protocol http url "*not-so*"
class-map match-all class3
  match protocol http
!
policy-map wred-q
  class class1
   bandwidth percent 25
   random-detect dscp-based
   random-detect dscp af22 25 35 50
  class class2
   bandwidth percent 20
```

```
    random-detect
    random-detect precedence 2 25 35 50
   class class3
     bandwidth percent 15
     random-detect dscp-based
     random-detect dscp af22 50 25 35
   class class-default
     random-detect dscp-based
     random-detect dscp af22 2 25 50
  !
  interface s0/0
   ip address 1.1.1.1 255.255.255.0
   random-detect dscp-based
   random-detect dscp af22 50 25 35
   !
  interface s0/1
   ip address 2.2.2.2 255.255.255.0
   service-policy output wred-q
```

5. For which of the following will WRED discard 2% of packets of some precedence or DSCP value, when the average queue depth approaches the maximum threshold?

   a. On physical interface S0/0

   b. On serial 0/1, class class1

   c. On serial 0/1, class class2

   d. On serial 0/1, class class3

   e. On serial 0/1, class class-default

   f. None of the above

6. Imagine a packet marked as AF22. Out which interface or class must the packet be forwarded in order to have a 35% chance of being discarded, assuming that WRED's average queue depth calculation was approaching the maximum threshold?

   a. On physical interface S0/0

   b. On serial 0/1, class class1

   c. On serial 0/1, class class2

   d. On serial 0/1, class class3

   e. On serial 0/1, class class-default

   f. None of the above

7. Assuming the commands in the configuration snippet were typed into configuration mode in a router, one of the **random-detect** commands would be rejected. Under which configuration mode can that erroneous command be found?

   a. On physical interface S0/0

   b. On serial 0/1, class class1

   c. On serial 0/1, class class2

   d. On serial 0/1, class class3

   e. On serial 0/1, class class-default

   f. None of the above

ECN Questions

8. Imagine that WRED with ECN has been configured for a CBWFQ class. Under which of the following cases could WRED randomly choose to discard a packet, but instead, mark the ECN bits inside the packet header and allowing the packet to pass?

   a. Average queue depth between the min and max thresholds, plus the incoming packet ECN field set to 00

   b. Average queue depth between the min and max thresholds, plus the incoming packet ECN field set to 01 or 10

   c. Average queue depth above max threshold, plus the incoming packet ECN field set to 01 or 10

   d. Average queue depth between the min and max thresholds, plus the incoming packet TCP ECE flag must be set to "1", and ECN field must be set to 01

9. Referring to the configuration snippet before question 5, what command would be required to enable ECN for class2 in **policy-map wred-q**?

   a. **ecn enable**

   b. **no ecn disable**

   c. **random-detect ecn**

   d. None required – WRED automatically does it if the TCP sender sets the ECN bits correctly

Foundation Topics

The term "congestion avoidance" describes a small set of IOS tools that help queues avoid congestion. Queues fill when the cumulative offered load from the various senders of packets exceeds the line rate of the interface (or the shaping rate if shaping is enabled). When more traffic needs to exit the interface than the interface can support, queues form. Queuing tools help us manage the queues; congestion-avoidance tools help us reduce the level of congestion in the queues by selectively dropping packets.

Once again, a QoS tool gives you the opportunity to make tradeoffs between QoS characteristics — in this case, packet loss versus delay and jitter. However, the tradeoff is not so simple in this case. It turns out that by selectively discarding some packets before the queues get completely full, cumulative packet loss can be reduced, and queuing delay and queuing jitter can also be reduced! When you prune a plant, you kill some of the branches, but the plant gets healthier and more beautiful through the process. Similarly, congestion-avoidance tools discard some packets, but in doing so achieve the overall effect of a healthier network.

This chapter begins by explaining the core concepts that create the need for congestion-avoidance tools. Following this discussion, the underlying algorithms, which are based RED, are covered. Finally, the chapter includes coverage of configuration and monitoring for two IOS congestion-avoidance tools, WRED and ECN.

Congestion-Avoidance Concepts and Random Early Detection (RED)

Congestion-avoidance tools rely on the behavior of TCP to reduce congestion. A large percentage of Internet traffic consists of TCP traffic, and TCP senders reduce the rate at which they send packets after packet loss. By purposefully discarding a percentage of packets, congestion-avoidance tools cause some TCP connections to slow down, which reduces congestion.

This section begins with a discussion of User Datagram Protocol (UDP) and TCP behavior when packets are lost. By understanding TCP behavior in particular, you can appreciate what happens as a result of tail drop, which is covered next in this section. Finally, to close this section, RED is covered. The two IOS congestion-avoidance tools both use the underlying concepts of RED.

TCP and UDP Reactions to Packet Loss

UDP and TCP behave very differently when packets are lost. UDP, by itself, does not react to packet loss, because UDP does not include any mechanism with which to know whether a packet was lost. TCP senders, however, slow down the rate at which they send after recognizing that a packet was lost. Unlike UDP, TCP includes a field in the TCP header to number each TCP segment (sequence number), and another field used by the receiver to confirm receipt of the packets (acknowledgment number). When a TCP receiver signals that a packet was not received, or if an acknowledgment is not received at all, the TCP sender assumes the packet was lost, and resends the packet. More importantly, the sender also slows down sending data into the network.

TCP uses two separate window sizes that determine the maximum window size of data that can be sent before the sender must stop and wait for an acknowledgment. The first of the two different windowing features of TCP uses the Window field in the TCP header, which is also called the *receiver window* or the *advertised window*. The receiver grants the sender the right to send x bytes of data before requiring an acknowledgment, by setting the value x into the Window field of the TCP header. The receiver grants larger and larger windows as time goes on, reaching the point at which the TCP sender never stops sending, with acknowledgments arriving just before a complete window of traffic has been sent.

The second window used by TCP is called the *congestion window*, or CWND, as defined by RFC 2581. Unlike the advertised window, the congestion window is not communicated between the receiver and sender using fields in the TCP header. Instead, the TCP sender calculates CWND. CWND varies in size much more quickly than does the advertised window, because it was designed to react to congestion in networks.

The TCP sender always uses the lower of the two windows to determine how much data it can send before receiving an acknowledgment. The receiver window is designed to let the receiver prevent the sender from sending data faster than the receiver can process the data. The CWND is designed to let the sender react to network congestion by slowing down its sending rate. It is the variation in the CWND, in reaction to lost packets, which RED relies upon.

To appreciate how RED works, you need to understand the processes by which a TCP sender lowers and increases the CWND. CWND is lowered in response to lost segments. CWND is raised based on the logic defined as the TCP slow start and TCP congestion-avoidance algorithms. In fact, most people use the term "slow start" to describe both features together, in part because they work closely together. The process works like this:

- A TCP sender fails to receive an acknowledgment in time, signifying a possible lost packet.

- The TCP sender sets CWND to the size of a single segment.

- Another variable, called slow start threshold (SSTHRESH) is set to 50 percent of the CWND value before the lost segment.

- After CWND has been lowered, slow start governs how fast the CWND grows up until the CWND has been increased to the value of SSTHRESH.

- After the slow start phase is complete, congestion avoidance governs how fast CWND grows after CWND > SSTHRESH.

Therefore, when a TCP sender fails to receive an acknowledgment, it reduces the CWND to a very low value (one segment size of window). This process is sometimes called *slamming the window* or *slamming the window shut*. The sender progressively increases CWND based first on slow start, and then on congestion avoidance. As you go through this text, remember that the TCP windows use a unit of bytes in reality. To make the discussion a little easier, I have listed the windows as a number of segments, which makes the actual numbers more obvious.

Slow start increases CWND by the maximum segment size for every packet for which it receives an acknowledgment. Because TCP receivers may, and typically do, acknowledge segments well before the full window has been sent by the sender, CWND grows at an exponential rate during slow start—a seemingly contradictory concept. Slow start gets its name from the fact that CWND has been set to a very low value at the beginning of the process, meaning it starts slowly, but slow start does cause CWND to grow quickly.

Figure 7-1 outlines the process of how the TCP sender grows CWND upon the receipt of each acknowledgement.

Figure 7-1 *Growing CWND for each Received Acknowledgement*

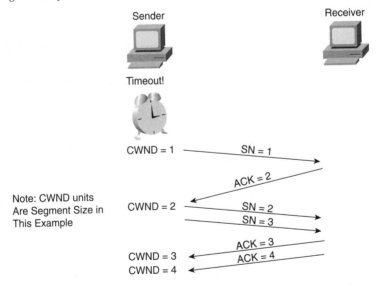

By increasing CWND when each acknowledgment is received, CWND actually increases at an exponential rate. So, Slow Start might be better called *slow start but fast recovery*.

Congestion avoidance is the second mechanism that dictates how quickly CWND increases after being lowered. As CWND grows, it begins to approach the original CWND value. If the original packet loss was a result of queue congestion, letting this TCP connection increase back to the original CWND may then induce the same congestion that caused the CWND to be lowered in the first place. *Congestion avoidance* just reduces the rate of increase for CWND as it approaches the previous CWND value. Once slow start has increased CWND to the value of SSTHRESH, which was set to 50 percent of the original CWND, congestion-avoidance logic replaces the slow start logic for increasing CWND. Congestion avoidance uses a formula that allows CWND to grow more slowly, essentially at a linear rate.

Figure 7-2 shows a graph of CWND with just slow start, and with slow start and congestion avoidance, after the sender times out waiting for an acknowledgment.

Figure 7-2   *Graphs of CWND with Slow Start and Congestion Avoidance*

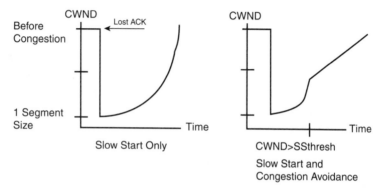

Many people do not realize that the slow start process consists of a combination of the slow start algorithm and the congestion-avoidance algorithm. With slow start, CWND is lowered, but it grows quickly. With congestion avoidance, the CWND value grows more slowly as it approaches the previous CWND value. In summary, UDP and TCP react to packet loss in the following ways:

- UDP senders do not reduce or increase sending rates as a result of lost packets.

- TCP senders do reduce their sending rates as a result of lost packets.

- TCP senders decide to use either the receiver window or the CWND, based on whichever is smaller at the time.

- TCP slow start and congestion avoidance dictate how fast the CWND rises after the window was lowered due to packet loss.

NOTE   Depending on the circumstances, TCP sometimes halves CWND in reaction to lost packets, and in some cases it lowers CWND to one segment size, as was described in this first section. The more severe reaction of reducing the window to one segment size was shown in this section for a more complete description of slow start and congestion avoidance. The course upon which the QoS exam combines all these concepts under the term *Slow Start*.

Tail Drop, Global Synchronization, and TCP Starvation

Tail drop occurs when a packet needs to be added to a queue, but the queue is full, so the router must discard the packet. Yes, tail drop is indeed that simple. However, tail drop results in some interesting behavior in real networks, particularly when most traffic is TCP based, but with some UDP traffic. Of course, the Internet today delivers mostly TCP traffic, because web and email traffic use TCP.

The preceding section described the behavior of a single TCP connection after a single packet loss. Now imagine an Internet router, with 100,000 or more TCP connections running their traffic out of a high-speed interface. The amount of traffic in the combined TCP connections finally exceeds the output line rate, causing the output queue on the interface to fill, which in turn causes tail drop.

What happens to those 100,000 TCP connections after many of them have at least one packet dropped? The TCP connections reduce their CWND; the congestion in the queue abates; the various CWND values increase with slow start, and then with congestion avoidance. Eventually, however, as the CWND values of the collective TCP connections approach the previous CWND value, the congestion occurs again, and the process is repeated. When a large number of TCP connections experience near simultaneous packet loss, the lowering and growth of CWND at about the same time causes the TCP connections to *synchronize*. The result is called *global synchronization*. The graph in Figure 7-3 shows this behavior.

Figure 7-3 *Graph of Global Synchronization*

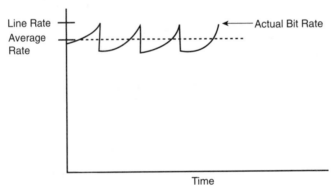

The graph shows the results of global synchronization. The router never fully utilizes the bandwidth on the link because the offered rate keeps dropping as a result of synchronization. Note that the overall rate does not drop to almost nothing because not all TCP connections happen to have packets drop when tail drop occurs, and some traffic uses UDP, which does not slow down in reaction to lost packets.

Weighted RED (WRED), when applied to the interface that was tail dropping packets, significantly reduces global synchronization. WRED allows the average output rates to approach line rate, with even more significant throughput improvements, because avoiding congestion and tail drops decreases the overall number of lost packets. Figure 7-4 shows an example graph of the same interface, after WRED was applied.

Figure 7-4 *Graph of Traffic Rates After the Application of WRED*

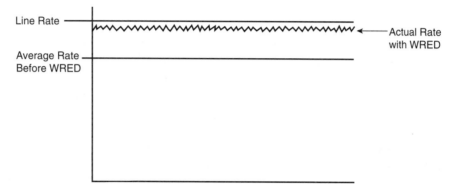

Another problem can occur if UDP traffic competes with TCP for bandwidth and queue space. Although UDP traffic consumes a much lower percentage of Internet bandwidth than TCP does, UDP can get a disproportionate amount of bandwidth as a result of TCP's reaction to packet loss. Imagine that on the same Internet router, 20 percent of the offered packets were UDP, and 80 percent TCP. Tail drop causes some TCP and UDP packets to be dropped; however, because the TCP senders slow down, and the UDP senders do not, additional UDP streams from the UDP senders can consume more and more bandwidth during congestion.

Taking the same concept a little deeper, imagine that several people crank up some UDP-based audio or video streaming applications, and that traffic also happens to need to exit this same congested interface. The interface output queue on this Internet router could fill with UDP packets. If a few high-bandwidth UDP applications fill the queue, a larger percentage of TCP packets might get tail dropped—resulting in further reduction of TCP windows, and less TCP traffic relative to the amount of UDP traffic.

The term "TCP starvation" describes the phenomena of the output queue being filled with larger volumes of UDP, causing TCP connections to have packets tail dropped. Tail drop does not distinguish between packets in any way, including whether they are TCP or UDP, or whether the flow uses a lot of bandwidth or just a little bandwidth. TCP connections can be starved for bandwidth because the UDP flows behave poorly in terms of congestion control. Flow-Based WRED (FRED), which is also based on RED, specifically addresses the issues related to TCP starvation. FRED has limited applicability, and is not currently mentioned in the QoS exam topics. However, if you would like to read more about it, you can refer to Appendix B, "Additional QoS Reference Materials," which contains coverage of FRED from the previous edition of this book.

Random Early Detection (RED)

Random Early Detection (RED) reduces the congestion in queues by dropping packets so that some of the TCP connections temporarily send fewer packets into the network. Instead of waiting until a queue fills, causing a large number of tail drops, RED purposefully drops a percentage of packets before a queue fills. This action attempts to make the computers sending the traffic reduce the offered load that is sent into the network.

The name "Random Early Detection" itself describes the overall operation of the algorithm. RED randomly picks the packets that are dropped after the decision to drop some packets has been made. RED detects queue congestion early, before the queue actually fills, thereby avoiding tail drops and synchronization. In short, RED discards some randomly picked packets early, before congestion gets really bad and the queue fills.

> **NOTE** IOS supports three RED-based tools: Weighted RED (WRED), Explicit Congestion Notification (ECN), and Flow-Based WRED (FRED). RED itself is not supported in IOS.

RED logic contains two main parts. RED must first detect when congestion occurs; in other words, RED must choose under what conditions it should discard packets. When RED decides to discard packets, it must decide how many to discard.

First, RED measures the *average queue depth* of the queue in question. RED calculates the average depth, and then decides whether congestion is occurring based on the average depth. RED uses the average depth, and not the actual queue depth, because the actual queue depth will most likely change much more quickly than the average depth. Because RED wants to avoid the effects of synchronization, it needs to act in a balanced fashion, not a jerky, sporadic fashion. Figure 7-5 shows a graph of the actual queue depth for a particular queue, compared with the average queue depth.

Figure 7-5 *Graph of Actual Queue Depth Versus Average Queue Depth*

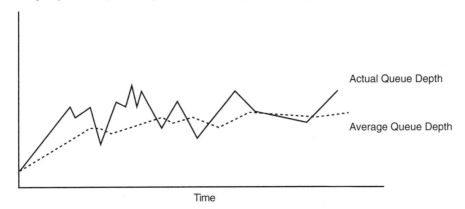

As seen in the graph, the calculated average queue depth changes more slowly than does the actual queue depth. RED uses the following algorithm when calculating the average queue depth:

$$\text{New average} = (\text{Old\_average} * (1 - 2^{-n})) + (\text{Current\_Q\_depth} * 2^{-n})$$

For you test takers out there, do not worry about memorizing the formula, but focus on the idea. WRED uses this algorithm, with a default for n of 9. This makes the equation read as follows:

$$\text{New average} = (\text{Old\_average} * .998) + (\text{Current\_Q\_depth} * .002)$$

In other words, the current queue depth only accounts for .2 percent of the new average each time it is calculated. Therefore, the average changes slowly, which helps RED prevent overreaction to changes in the queue depth. When configuring WRED, you can change the value of n in this formula by setting the *exponential weighting constant* parameter. By making the exponential weighting constant smaller, you make the average change more quickly; by making it larger, the average changes more slowly.

RED decides whether to discard packets by comparing the average queue depth to two thresholds, called the *minimum threshold* and *maximum threshold*. Table 7-2 describes the overall logic of when RED discards packets, as illustrated in Figure 7-6.

Table 7-2 *Three Categories of When RED Will Discard Packets and How Many*

Average Queue Depth Versus Thresholds	Action	Name
Average < minimum threshold	No packets dropped.	No Drop
Minimum threshold < average depth < maximum threshold	A percentage of packets dropped. Drop percentage increases from 0 to a maximum percent as the average depth moves from the minimum threshold to the maximum.	Random Drop
Average depth > maximum threshold	All new packets discarded similar to tail dropping.	Full Drop

When the average queue depth is very low or very high, the actions are somewhat obvious. As seen in Table 7-2 and Figure 7-6, RED does not discard packets when the average queue depth falls below the minimum threshold. When the average depth rises above the maximum threshold, RED discards all packets. While this action might seem like a Tail Drop action, technically it is not, because the actual queue might not be full yet. So, to distinguish between true Tail Drop, and the case when the RED average queue depth exceeds the maximum threshold, RED calls this action category *Full Drop*.

In between the two thresholds, however, RED discards a percentage of packets, with the percentage growing linearly as the average queue depth grows. The core concept behind RED becomes more obvious if you notice that the maximum percentage of packets discarded is still much less than discarding all packets. Once again, RED wants to discard some packets, but not all packets. As congestion increases, RED discards a higher percentage of packets. Eventually, the congestion can increase to the point that RED discards all packets.

Figure 7-6 *RED Discarding Logic Using Average Depth, Minimum Threshold, and Maximum Threshold*

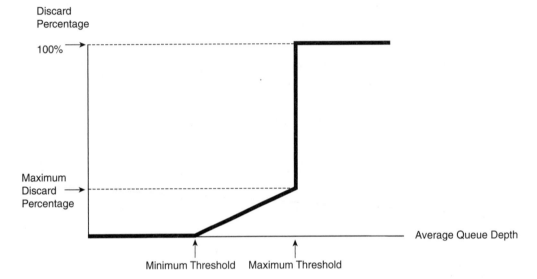

You can set the maximum percentage of packets discarded by WRED by setting the mark probability denominator (MPD) setting in IOS. IOS calculates the maximum percentage using the formula 1/MPD. For instance, an MPD of 10 yields a calculated value of 1/10, meaning the maximum discard rate is 10 percent.

RED discards a larger percentage of packets as the average queue depth approaches the maximum threshold, as shown in the graph of Figure 7-6. RED also randomly picks the packets that will be discarded.

Table 7-3 summarizes some of the key terms related to RED.

Table 7-3 *RED Terminology*

Term	Meaning
Actual queue depth	The actual number of packets in a queue at a particular point in time.
Average queue depth	Calculated measurement based on the actual queue depth and the previous average. Designed to adjust slowly to the rapid changes of the actual queue depth.

Table 7-3 *RED Terminology (Continued)*

Term	Meaning
Minimum threshold	Compares this setting to the average queue depth to decide whether packets should be discarded. No packets are discarded if the average queue depth falls below this minimum threshold.
Maximum threshold	Compares this setting to the average queue depth to decide whether packets should be discarded. All packets are discarded if the average queue depth falls above this maximum threshold.
Mark probability denominator	Used to calculate the maximum percentage of packets discarded when the average queue depth falls between the minimum and maximum thresholds.
Exponential weighting constant	Used to calculate the rate at which the average queue depth changes as compared with the current queue depth. The larger the number, the slower the change in the average queue depth.
No Drop	State in which RED's average queue depth falls below the minimum threshold. No packets are discarded.
Random Drop	State in which RED's average queue depth falls between the minimum and maximum thresholds. A percentage of randomly-selected packets are discarded.
Full Drop	State in which RED's average queue depth exceeds the maximum threshold. All packets are dropped

The next two sections in this chapter cover WRED and ECN, including their respective configurations.

Weighted RED (WRED)

WRED behaves almost identically to RED, as described in the preceding section of this chapter. It calculates the average queue depth, and decides whether to discard packets, and what percentage of packets to discard, based on all the same variables as RED.

The difference between RED and WRED lies in the fact that WRED creates a *WRED profile* for each precedence or DSCP value. A WRED profile is a set of minimum and maximum thresholds plus a packet discard percentage. The minimum and maximum thresholds are defined as a number of entries in the queue. Instead of directly configuring the discard percentage, you configure the Mark Probability Denominator (MPD), with the percentage being 1/MPD. By using a different WRED profile for each IP Precedence or DSCP value, WRED can treat packets differently.

The other major concept that needs to be covered, before diving into WRED configuration, relates to where WRED can be enabled, and how it interoperates with queuing tools. Interestingly, although WRED can be enabled on a physicalinterface, it cannot be concurrently enabled along with any other queuing tool! When using Modular QoS command-line interface (MQC) to configure queuing, however, WRED can be used for individual class queues.

The following sections cover the following:

■ How WRED weights packets

■ When WRED can be enabled

■ When WRED can be enabled to work with other queuing tools

■ WRED configuration

How WRED Weights Packets

WRED bases its decisions about when to discard packets, and what percentage to discard, on the following four factors:

■ The average queue depth

■ The minimum threshold

■ The maximum threshold

■ The MPD

First, just like RED, WRED calculates the average queue depth. WRED then compares the average queue depth to the minimum and maximum thresholds to decide whether it should discard packets. If the average queue depth is between the two thresholds, WRED discards a percentage of the packets, with the percentage based on the MPD; if the average queue depth exceeds the maximum threshold, WRED discards all new packets.

To weight based on precedence or DSCP markings, WRED sets the minimum threshold, maximum threshold, and the MPD to different values per precedence or DSCP value. The average queue depth calculation, however, is not based on the precedence or DSCP value, but is instead calculated for all packets in the queue, regardless of the precedence or DSCP value.

An example of how WRED weights packets can help you make more sense out of how WRED behaves differently than RED. First, consider Figure 7-7, which happens to show the default settings for precedence 0; these settings together define the WRED profile for Precedence 0 traffic.

Figure 7-7 *Default WRED Profile for Precedence 0*

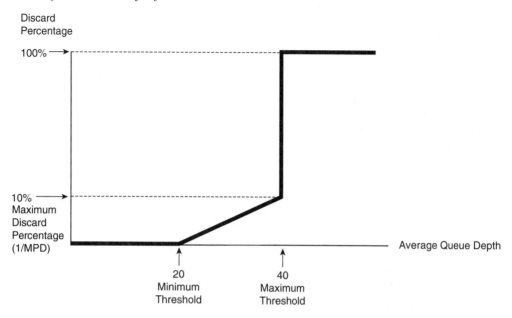

WRED calculates the average queue depth just like RED, ignoring precedence, but it decides when to discard packets based on the precedence or DSCP value. Suppose, for instance, that the average queue depth just passed 20. For new precedence 0 packets that need to be placed into the queue, WRED begins discarding some packets. If the average queue depth continues to increase toward 40, WRED continues to discard precedence 0 packets, but more aggressively, up to a rate of 10 percent, when the average queue depth reaches 40. After the average queue depth passes 40, WRED discards all new precedence 0 packets. In fact, if all packets were precedence 0, RED and WRED would behave identically.

The real differences between RED and WRED can be seen with more than one IP precedence value. Figure 7-8 shows the WRED profile for both precedence 0 and precedence 3. (The settings in the figure do not match WRED's precedence 3 defaults, which are listed later in this section.)

Suppose that the queue associated with the interface has a bunch of packets in it, marked with different precedence values, and the average queue depth just passed 20. For new precedence 0 packets that need to be placed into the queue, WRED begins discarding some precedence 0 packets, because the minimum threshold for precedence 0 is 20. WRED does not discard any precedence 3 packets, however, because the precedence 3 minimum threshold is 30. After the average queue depth reaches 30, WRED starts discarding precedence 3 packets as well. As the average queue depth reaches 40, precedence 0 packets are discarded at a rate approaching 10 percent, but precedence 3 packets are only discarded 5 percent of the time, because the MPD is set to 20, and 1/20 is 5 percent.

Figure 7-8 *Example WRED Profiles for Precedences 0 and 3*

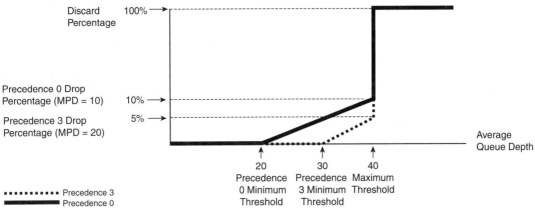

With these two WRED profiles, WRED discards precedence 0 packets earlier, and at a higher rate, as compared to precedence 3 packets. In short, the weighting feature of WRED just determines when WRED begins discarding a percentage of the packets (per-precedence minimum threshold), the maximum percentage discarded (based on per-precedence MPD), and the point at which WRED discards all packets of that precedence (based on the per-precedence maximum threshold).

IOS uses logical choices for the default settings for all WRED parameters. However, you can choose to override the parameters with configuration commands. Tables 7-4 and 7-5 list the IOS default values for minimum threshold, maximum threshold, and MPD with precedence-based WRED (Table 7-4) and DSCP-based WRED (Table 7-5).

Table 7-4 *Cisco IOS Software-Default WRED Profiles for Precedence-Based WRED*

Precedence	Minimum Threshold	Maximum Threshold	Mark Probability Denominator	Calculated Maximum Percent Discarded
0	20	40	10	10%
1	22	40	10	10%
2	24	40	10	10%
3	26	40	10	10%
4	28	40	10	10%

Table 7-4 *Cisco IOS Software-Default WRED Profiles for Precedence-Based WRED (Continued)*

Precedence	Minimum Threshold	Maximum Threshold	Mark Probability Denominator	Calculated Maximum Percent Discarded
5	31	40	10	10%
6	33	40	10	10%
7	35	40	10	10%
RSVP*	37	40	10	10%

*RSVP = Resource Reservation Protocol

Table 7-5 *Cisco IOS Software Default WRED Profiles for DSCP-Based WRED**

DSCP**	Minimum Threshold	Maximum Threshold	Mark Probability Denominator	Calculated Maximum Percent Discarded
AF11, AF21, AF31, AF41	33	40	10	10%
AF12, AF22, AF32, AF42	28	40	10	10%
AF13, AF23, AF33, AF43	24	40	10	10%
EF	37	40	10	10%

*Stated Values for IOS 12.2 Mainline Software

**Class selector DSCP values use the same WRED profile settings as their corresponding precedence values.

Cisco IOS Software follows the suggested meaning of all DSCP values, including the fact that these four AF DSCP values should be given equal treatment. The last digit of the name of the AF DSCP value identifies the drop preference, with 3 being most likely to be dropped, and 1 being least likely to be dropped. Note, for instance, that the settings for assured forwarding (AF) DSCPs AF11, AF21, AF31, and AF41 are all identical. For the same reason, AF12, AF22, AF32, and AF42 have the same defaults, as do AF13, AF23, AF33, and AF43.

WRED and Queuing

WRED relies on the average queue depth concept, which calculates a rolling average of the queue depth of some queue. But which queue? Well, first consider a serial interface on a router, on which Weighted Fair Queuing (WFQ) is enabled by default. In this case, however, WFQ has been disabled, leaving a single first-in, first-out (FIFO) output queue on the interface. Figure 7-9 shows the basic idea.

Figure 7-9 *FIFO Output Queue and WRED Interaction*

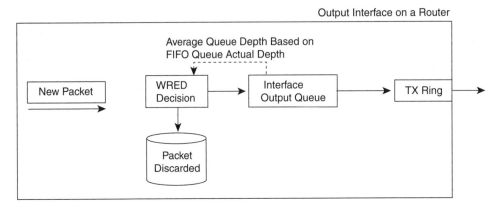

As was covered in depth in Chapter 5, "Congestion Management," each interface has a TX Queue or TX Ring. If the TX Ring/TX Queue fills, IOS places new packets into the software queue(s) awaiting transmission. In this example, a single FIFO output queue is used, as shown. With WRED also enabled, WRED calculates the average queue depth of the single FIFO output queue. As new packets arrive, before being placed into the FIFO output queue, WRED logic decides whether the packet should be discarded, as described in detail earlier in this chapter.

With WRED enabled directly on a physical interface, IOS supports FIFO Queuing, and FIFO Queuing only! That fact certainly makes the explanation easier, because there is less to cover! So, WRED works just like Figure 7-9 when it is enabled directly on a physical interface, because WRED can only work with a single FIFO queue in that case.

You might recall that of all the queuing tools listed in Chapter 5, CBWFQ and Low Latency Queuing (LLQ, which is merely a variation of CBFWQ) are the only queuing tools that claim to be capable of using WRED. To use WRED with CBWFQ or LLQ, you need to configure CBWFQ or LLQ as you normally would, and then enable WRED inside the individual classes as needed. However, you cannot enable WRED inside a class configured as the low-latency queue (in other words, you cannot use WRED in a class that uses the **priority** command.) Figure 7-10 illustrates an expanded diagram of CBWFQ, with the details that include WRED's part of the process.

As you recall, CBWFQ classifies traffic into various classes. Each class has a single FIFO queue inside the class, so WRED bases its average queue depth calculation on the actual depth of each per-class FIFO queue, respectively. In other words, a different instance of WRED operates on each of the FIFO queues in each class. WRED might be discarding packets aggressively in one congested class, without discarding any packets in a class that is not congested.

Figure 7-10 *WRED with CBWFQ*

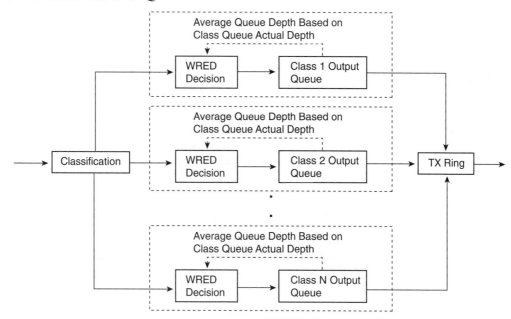

WRED can be enabled for some CBWFQ classes, and not for others. For instance, with LLQ, voice traffic is typically placed into the priority queue. Because voice is drop sensitive, and UDP based, it would be better not to just apply WRED to the voice class. Instead, you can apply WRED to the data classes that serve predominantly TCP flows. This way, WRED can be used to limit the queue congestion for the interface without performing drops on the voice traffic.

Now that you understand the basic operation of WRED, along with the meaning of the parameters that can be tuned, you can configure WRED.

WRED Configuration

WRED requires very little configuration if you want to take the IOS defaults for the various tunable settings, such as per-precedence and per-DSCP thresholds. If you want to change the defaults, the configuration details can become quite large.

This section begins with a table of configuration commands (Table 7-6) and **show** commands (Table 7-7), followed by three separate examples.

Table 7-6 *Command Reference for WRED*

Command	Mode and Function
random-detect [*dscp-based* | *prec-based*]	Interface or class configuration mode; enables WRED, specifying whether to react to precedence or DSCP.
random-detect [**attach** *group-name*]	Interface configuration mode; enables per-VC* WRED on ATM interfaces by referring to a **random-detect- group**.
random-detect-group *group-name* [*dscp- based* | *prec-based*]	Global configuration mode; creates a grouping of WRED parameters, which can be enabled on individual ATM VCs using the **random-detect attach** command.
random-detect precedence *precedence min- threshold max- threshold mark-prob- denominator*	Interface, class, or random-detect-group configuration modes; overrides default settings for the specified precedence, for minimum and maximum WRED thresholds, and for percentage of packets discarded.
random-detect dscp *dscpvalue min- threshold max-threshold* [*mark- probability- denominator*]	Interface, class, or random-detect-group configuration modes; overrides default settings for the specified DSCP, for minimum and maximum WRED thresholds, and for the percentage of packets discarded.
random-detect exponential- weighting- constant *exponent*	Interface, class, or random-detect-group configuration modes; overrides default settings for exponential weighting constant. Lower numbers make WRED react quickly to changes in queue depth; higher numbers make WRED react less quickly.

* VC = virtual circuit

Table 7-7 *EXEC Command Reference for WRED*

Command	Function
show *queue interface-name interface- number* [**vc** [*vpi*/] *vci*]]	Lists information about the packets that are waiting in a queue on the interface
show queueing random-detect [**interface** *atm-subinterface* [**vc** [[*vpi*/] *vci*]]]	Lists configuration and statistical information about the queuing tool on an interface.
show interfaces	Mentions whether WRED has been enabled on the interface
show interface random-detect	Lists information about WRED when distributed WRED is running on a VIP* interface
show policy-map [**interface** *interface-name interface-number*]	Lists WRED information when it is enabled inside an MQC policy map

*VIP = Versatile Interface Processor

In the first example, R3 enables WRED on its S0/0 interface. WRED treats packets differently based on the IP precedence value, which has been marked with CB marking as the packets enter R3's E0/0 interface. The marking logic performed by CB marking is as follows:

- VoIP payload: DSCP EF

- HTTP traffic for web pages with "important" in the URL: DSCP AF21

- HTTP traffic for web pages with "not-so" in the URL: DSCP AF23

- All other: DSCP default

To generate traffic in this network, two voice calls will be made between the analog phones attached to R1 and R4. Multiple web browsers will load the standard page (this is the same page we have used in other chapters in this book) with two TCP connections created by each browser—one to get a file with the word "important" in it, and the other getting a file with "not-so" in it. An FTP download of a large file will also be initiated from the Server to Client1.

Example 7-1 shows the basic configuration and **show** commands output. Only the required commands and parameters have been used, with defaults for all other settings. The example uses the familiar network diagram, as repeated in Figure 7-11.

Figure 7-11 *Sample Network for All WRED Examples—Configuration on R3*

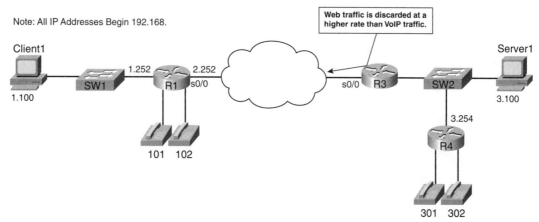

Example 7-11 *WRED Default Configuration, R3, S0/0*

```
R3#show running-config
!
hostname R3
!
no ip domain-lookup
```

continues

Example 7-11 *WRED Default Configuration, R3, S0/0 (Continued)*

```
ip host r4 192.168.3.254
ip host r2 192.168.23.252
ip host r1 192.168.1.251
!
ip cef
!
class-map match-all voip-rtp
  match ip rtp 16384 16383
class-map match-all http-impo
  match protocol http url "*important*"
class-map match-all http-not
  match protocol http url "*not-so*"
class-map match-all class-default
  match any
!
!
policy-map laundry-list
  class voip-rtp
   set ip dscp ef
  class http-impo
   set ip dscp af21
  class http-not
   set ip dscp af23
  class class-default
   set ip dscp default
!
call rsvp-sync
!
interface Ethernet0/0
 description connected to SW2, where Server1 is connected
 ip address 192.168.3.253 255.255.255.0
half-duplex
 service-policy input laundry-list
!
interface Serial0/0
 description connected to FRS port S0. Single PVC to R1.
 no ip address
 encapsulation frame-relay
 load-interval 30
 random-detect
 clockrate 128000
!
interface Serial0/0.1 point-to-point
 description point-point subint global DLCI 103, connected via PVC to DLCI 101 (
R1)
 ip address 192.168.2.253 255.255.255.0
 frame-relay interface-dlci 101
```

Example 7-11 *WRED Default Configuration, R3, S0/0 (Continued)*

```
!
! Lines omitted for brevity.
!
R3#show queueing interface serial 0/0
Interface Serial0/0 queueing strategy: random early detection (WRED)
    Exp-weight-constant: 9 (1/512)
    Mean queue depth: 37

class   Random drop      Tail drop       Minimum Maximum  Mark
        pkts/bytes       pkts/bytes      thresh  thresh   prob
0       1776/315688      1012/179987       20      40     1/10
1       0/0              0/0               22      40     1/10
2       5/4725           16/17152          24      40     1/10
3       0/0              0/0               26      40     1/10
4       0/0              0/0               28      40     1/10
5       0/0              0/0               31      40     1/10
6       0/0              0/0               33      40     1/10
7       0/0              0/0               35      40     1/10
rsvp    0/0              0/0               37      40     1/10

R3#show queue s 0/0
Output queue for Serial0/0 is 57/0

Packet 1, linktype: ip, length: 64, flags: 0x88
  source: 192.168.3.254, destination: 192.168.2.251, id: 0x053E, ttl: 253,
  TOS: 184 prot: 17, source port 18378, destination port 17260
    data: 0x47CA 0x436C 0x0028 0x0000 0x8012 0x3F73 0x4C7E
          0x8D44 0x18D1 0x03FE 0xFC77 0xA2A7 0x35A2 0x54E7

Packet 2, linktype: ip, length: 64, flags: 0x88
  source: 192.168.3.254, destination: 192.168.2.251, id: 0x0545, ttl: 253,
  TOS: 184 prot: 17, source port 16640, destination port 17178
    data: 0x4100 0x431A 0x0028 0x0000 0x8012 0x6330 0x21B4
          0x82AF 0x05C9 0x03FE 0x1448 0x8706 0xAFD9 0xD364
!
! Output omitted for brevity.
!

R3#show interfaces s 0/0
Serial0/0 is up, line protocol is up
  Hardware is PowerQUICC Serial
  Description: connected to FRS port S0. Single PVC to R1.
  MTU 1500 bytes, BW 1544 Kbit, DLY 20000 usec,
    reliability 255/255, txload 20/255, rxload 4/255
  Encapsulation FRAME-RELAY, loopback not set
  Keepalive set (10 sec)
  LMI enq sent  591, LMI stat recvd 591, LMI upd recvd 0, DTE LMI up
```

continues

Example 7-11 *WRED Default Configuration, R3, S0/0 (Continued)*

```
   LMI enq recvd 0, LMI stat sent  0, LMI upd sent  0
   LMI DLCI 1023  LMI type is CISCO  frame relay DTE
   FR SVC disabled, LAPF state down
   Broadcast queue 0/64, broadcasts sent/dropped 2726/0, interface broadcasts 252
2
   Last input 00:00:02, output 00:00:00, output hang never
   Last clearing of "show interface" counters 01:38:28
   Input queue: 0/75/0/0 (size/max/drops/flushes); Total output drops: 4391
   Queueing strategy: random early detection(RED)
   30 second input rate 29000 bits/sec, 58 packets/sec
   30 second output rate 122000 bits/sec, 91 packets/sec
      23863 packets input, 1535433 bytes, 0 no buffer
      Received 0 broadcasts, 0 runts, 0 giants, 0 throttles
      2 input errors, 0 CRC, 2 frame, 0 overrun, 0 ignored, 0 abort
      36688 packets output, 5638653 bytes, 0 underruns
      0 output errors, 0 collisions, 4 interface resets
      0 output buffer failures, 0 output buffers swapped out
      0 carrier transitions
      DCD=up  DSR=up  DTR=up  RTS=up  CTS=up
```

The WRED part of the configuration is quite short. The configuration shows the **random-detect** interface subcommand under serial 0/0. As you will see later, the command actually disables WFQ if configured. The rest of the highlighted configuration commands show the CB marking configuration, which implements the functions listed before the example. (For more information about CB marking, see Chapter 4, "Classification and Marking.")

After the configuration, the **show queueing interface serial 0/0** command output lists the WRED settings, and the statistics for each precedence value. The defaults for the exponential weighting constant, and the per-precedence defaults of minimum threshold, maximum threshold, and MPD are all listed. In addition, the command lists statistics for bytes/packets dropped by WRED, per precedence value. For those of you who did not memorize the DSCP values, you may not be able to correlate the DSCP values set by CB marking, and the precedence values interpreted by WRED. WRED just looks at the first 3 bits of the IP ToS byte when performing precedence-based WRED. So, DSCP best effort (BE) equates to precedence 0, DSCP AF21 and AF23 both equate to precedence 2, and DSCP expedited forwarding (EF) equates to precedence 5.

The **show queueing** command also lists a column of statistics for tail drop as well as random drops. In this example, WRED has dropped several packets, and the queue has filled, causing tail drops, as shown with the nonzero counters for random drops and tail drops in the **show queueing** command output.

The **show queue serial 0/0** command lists the same type of information seen in earlier chapters. However, this command lists one particularly interesting item relating to WRED in the first line of the command output. The actual queue depth for the single FIFO queue used with WRED is listed at 57 entries in this particular example. The earlier **show queueing** command lists an *average queue depth* of 37 just instants before. These two numbers just give us a small reminder that WRED decides to drop based on average queue depth, as opposed to actual queue depth.

Finally, the **show interfaces** command at the end of the example reminds us that WRED does not work with any other queuing method directly on the interface. The command uses the statement "Queueing strategy: random early detection (RED)" to remind us of that fact. WRED uses a single FIFO queue, and measures its average queue depth based on the queue depth of the FIFO queue.

The second WRED configuration example uses WRED on R3's S0/0 interface again, but this time with DSCP WRED, and a few changes to the defaults. In fact, Example 7-2 just shows the changed configuration, with most of the configuration staying the same. For instance, the same CB marking configuration is used to mark the traffic, so the details are not repeated in the example. The example uses the familiar network diagram that was also used in the preceding example.

Example 7-12 *DSCP-Based WRED on R3 S0/0*

```
R3#configure terminal
Enter configuration commands, one per line.  End with CNTL/Z.
R3(config)#interface serial 0/0
R3(config-if)#random-detect dscp-based
R3(config-if)#random-detect dscp af21 50 60
R3(config-if)#random-detect dscp af23 20 30
R3(config-if)#random-detect ?
  dscp                           parameters for each dscp value
  dscp-based                     Enable dscp based WRED on an interface
  exponential-weighting-constant weight for mean queue depth calculation
  flow                           enable flow based WRED
  prec-based                     Enable prec based WRED on an interface
  precedence                     parameters for each precedence value
  <cr>
R3(config-if)#random-detect exponential-weighting-constant 5
R3(config-if)#^Z

R3#show queue serial 0/0
Output queue for Serial0/0 is 37/0

Packet 1, linktype: ip, length: 64, flags: 0x88
  source: 192.168.3.254, destination: 192.168.2.251, id: 0x0545, ttl: 253,
  TOS: 184 prot: 17, source port 16640, destination port 17178
    data: 0x4100 0x431A 0x0028 0x0000 0x8012 0xAB15 0x21E1
          0x71CF 0x05C9 0x03FE 0x7AA3 0x770B 0x2408 0x8264

Packet 2, linktype: ip, length: 64, flags: 0x88
  source: 192.168.3.254, destination: 192.168.2.251, id: 0x053E, ttl: 253,
```

continues

Example 7-12 *DSCP-Based WRED on R3 S0/0*

```
   TOS: 184 prot: 17, source port 18378, destination port 17260
      data: 0x47CA 0x436C 0x0028 0x0000 0x8012 0x8759 0x4CAB
            0x7D04 0x18D1 0x03FE 0xDC15 0x3E4A 0x4E92 0x5447


R3#show queueing interface s 0/0
Interface Serial0/0 queueing strategy: random early detection (WRED)
      Exp-weight-constant: 5 (1/32)
      Mean queue depth: 38
```

dscp	Random drop pkts/bytes	Tail drop pkts/bytes	Minimum thresh	Maximum thresh	Mark prob
af11	0/0	0/0	33	40	1/10
af12	0/0	0/0	28	40	1/10
af13	0/0	0/0	24	40	1/10
af21	8/9904	18/21288	50	60	1/10
af22	0/0	0/0	28	40	1/10
af23	13/18252	33/34083	20	30	1/10
af31	0/0	0/0	33	40	1/10
af32	0/0	0/0	28	40	1/10
af33	0/0	0/0	24	40	1/10
af41	0/0	0/0	33	40	1/10
af42	0/0	0/0	28	40	1/10
af43	0/0	0/0	24	40	1/10
cs1	0/0	0/0	22	40	1/10
cs2	0/0	0/0	24	40	1/10
cs3	0/0	0/0	26	40	1/10
cs4	0/0	0/0	28	40	1/10
cs5	0/0	0/0	31	40	1/10
cs6	0/0	0/0	33	40	1/10
cs7	0/0	0/0	35	40	1/10
ef	0/0	0/0	37	40	1/10
rsvp	0/0	0/0	37	40	1/10
default	16/16254	20/23216	20	40	1/10

The configuration begins with a change from precedence-based WRED to DSCP-based WRED using the **random-detect dscp-based** interface subcommand. The **random-detect dscp af21 50 60** changes the default minimum and maximum thresholds for AF21 to 50 and 60, respectively, with the **random-detect dscp af23 20 30** changing these same values for AF23. In addition, although Cisco does not recommend changing the exponential weighting constant, the configuration does offer an example of the syntax with the **random-detect exponential- weighting-constant 5** command. By setting it to a smaller number than the default (9), WRED will more quickly change the average queue depth calculation, more quickly reacting to changes in the queue depth.

The command output from the various **show** commands do not differ much compared to when DSCP-based WRED is enabled. The format now includes DSCP values rather than precedence values, as you may notice with the counters that point out drops for both AF21 and AF23, which were previously both treated as precedence 2.

WRED suffers from the lack of concurrent queuing tool support on an interface. However, WRED can be enabled inside a CBWFQ class, operating on the queue for the class, effectively enabling WRED concurrently with CBWFQ. The final WRED example shows a configuration for WRED using LLQ.

The last WRED configuration example repeats base configuration similar to one of the CBWFQ examples from Chapter 5. Voice, HTTP, and FTP traffic compete for the same bandwidth, with WRED applied per-class for the two HTTP classes and one FTP class. Note that because voice traffic is drop sensitive, WRED is not enabled for the low-latency queue. Because WRED can be enabled per class in conjunction with CBWFQ, WRED calculates average queue depth based on the per-class queue.

The criteria for each type of traffic is as follows:

- R3's S0/0 is clocked at 128 kbps.

- VoIP payload is marked with DSCP EF using CB marking on ingress to R3 E0/0. On egress of R3's S0/0 interface, DSCP EF traffic is placed in its own queue, *without WRED*. This class gets 58 kbps.

- Any HTTP traffic whose URL contains the string "important" anywhere in the URL is marked with AF21 using CB marking on ingress to R3 E0/0. On egress of R3's S0/0 interface, DSCP AF21 traffic is placed in its own queue, *with WRED*. This class gets 20 kbps.

- Any HTTP traffic whose URL contains the string "not-so" anywhere in the URL is marked with AF23 using CB marking on ingress to R3 E0/0. On egress of R3's S0/0 interface, DSCP AF23 traffic is placed in its own queue, *with WRED*. This class gets 8 kbps.

- All other traffic is marked with DSCP BE using CB marking on ingress to R3 E0/0. On egress of R3's S0/0 interface, DSCP BE traffic is placed in its own queue, *with WRED*. This class gets 20 kbps.

Example 7-3 lists the configuration and **show** commands used when WRED is enabled in LLQ classes dscp-af21, dscp-af23, and class-default.

Example 7-13 *WRED Used in LLQ Classes dscp-af21, dscp-af23, and class-default*

```
R3#show running-config
Building configuration...
!
!Portions omitted for brevity
!
```

continues

Example 7-13 *WRED Used in LLQ Classes dscp-af21, dscp-af23, and class-default*

```
ip cef
!
! The following classes are used in the LLQ configuration applied to S0/0
!
class-map match-all dscp-ef
  match ip dscp ef
class-map match-all dscp-af21
  match ip dscp af21
class-map match-all dscp-af23
  match ip dscp af23
!
! The following classes are used on ingress for CB marking
!
class-map match-all http-impo
  match protocol http url "*important*"
class-map match-all http-not
  match protocol http url "*not-so*"
class-map match-all class-default
  match any
class-map match-all voip-rtp
  match ip rtp 16384 16383
!
! Policy-map laundry-list creates CB marking configuration, used on
! ingress on E0/0
!
policy-map laundry-list
  class voip-rtp
   set ip dscp ef
  class http-impo
   set ip dscp af21
  class http-not
   set ip dscp af23
  class class-default
   set ip dscp default
!


! Policy-map queue-on-dscp creates LLQ configuration, with WRED
! inside three classes
!
policy-map queue-on-dscp
  class dscp-ef
    priority 58
  class dscp-af21
   bandwidth 20
   random-detect dscp-based
  class dscp-af23
```

Example 7-13   *WRED Used in LLQ Classes dscp-af21, dscp-af23, and class-default*

```
      bandwidth 8
       random-detect dscp-based
     class class-default
       fair-queue
       random-detect dscp-based
     !
     interface Ethernet0/0
      description connected to SW2, where Server1 is connected
      ip address 192.168.3.253 255.255.255.0
      ip nbar protocol-discovery
      half-duplex
      service-policy input laundry-list
     !
     interface Serial0/0
      description connected to FRS port S0. Single PVC to R1.
      bandwidth 128
      no ip address
      encapsulation frame-relay
      load-interval 30
      max-reserved-bandwidth 85
      service-policy output queue-on-dscp
      clockrate 128000
     !
     interface Serial0/0.1 point-to-point
      description point-point subint global DLCI 103, connected via PVC to DLCI 101 (R1)
      ip address 192.168.2.253 255.255.255.0
      frame-relay interface-dlci 101
     !
     R3#show policy-map interface serial 0/0

      Serial0/0

       Service-policy output: queue-on-dscp

         Class-map: dscp-ef (match-all)
           46437 packets, 2971968 bytes
           30 second offered rate 0 bps, drop rate 0 bps
           Match: ip dscp ef
           Weighted Fair Queueing
             Strict Priority
             Output Queue: Conversation 264
             Bandwidth 58 (kbps) Burst 1450 (Bytes)
             (pkts matched/bytes matched) 42805/2739520
             (total drops/bytes drops) 0/0

         Class-map: dscp-af21 (match-all)
           2878 packets, 3478830 bytes
```

continues

Example 7-13 *WRED Used in LLQ Classes dscp-af21, dscp-af23, and class-default*

```
      30 second offered rate 76000 bps, drop rate 0 bps
      Match: ip dscp af21
      Weighted Fair Queueing
        Output Queue: Conversation 266
        Bandwidth 20 (kbps)
        (pkts matched/bytes matched) 2889/3494718
        (depth/total drops/no-buffer drops) 11/26/0
        exponential weight: 9
        mean queue depth: 5
```

dscp	Transmitted pkts/bytes	Random drop pkts/bytes	Tail drop pkts/bytes	Minimum thresh	Maximum thresh	Mark prob
af11	0/0	0/0	0/0	32	40	1/10
af12	0/0	0/0	0/0	28	40	1/10
af13	0/0	0/0	0/0	24	40	1/10
af21	2889/3494718	8/9904	18/21288	32	40	1/10
af22	0/0	0/0	0/0	28	40	1/10
af23	0/0	0/0	0/0	24	40	1/10
af31	0/0	0/0	0/0	32	40	1/10
af32	0/0	0/0	0/0	28	40	1/10
af33	0/0	0/0	0/0	24	40	1/10
af41	0/0	0/0	0/0	32	40	1/10
af42	0/0	0/0	0/0	28	40	1/10
af43	0/0	0/0	0/0	24	40	1/10
cs1	0/0	0/0	0/0	22	40	1/10
cs2	0/0	0/0	0/0	24	40	1/10
cs3	0/0	0/0	0/0	26	40	1/10
cs4	0/0	0/0	0/0	28	40	1/10
cs5	0/0	0/0	0/0	30	40	1/10
cs6	0/0	0/0	0/0	32	40	1/10
cs7	0/0	0/0	0/0	34	40	1/10
ef	0/0	0/0	0/0	36	40	1/10
rsvp	0/0	0/0	0/0	36	40	1/10
default	0/0	0/0	0/0	20	40	1/10

```
    Class-map: dscp-af23 (match-all)
      1034 packets, 1250984 bytes
      30 second offered rate 32000 bps, drop rate 0 bps
      Match: ip dscp af23
      Weighted Fair Queueing
        Output Queue: Conversation 267
        Bandwidth 8 (kbps)
        (pkts matched/bytes matched) 1047/1266140
        (depth/total drops/no-buffer drops) 11/46/0
        exponential weight: 9
```

Example 7-13 *WRED Used in LLQ Classes dscp-af21, dscp-af23, and class-default*

```
           mean queue depth: 5

dscp    Transmitted       Random drop      Tail drop       Minimum Maximum  Mark
        pkts/bytes        pkts/bytes       pkts/bytes      thresh  thresh   prob
af11    0/0               0/0              0/0             32      40       1/10
af12    0/0               0/0              0/0             28      40       1/10
af13    0/0               0/0              0/0             24      40       1/10
af21    0/0               0/0              0/0             32      40       1/10
af22    0/0               0/0              0/0             28      40       1/10
af23    1047/1266140      13/18252         33/34083        24      40       1/10
af31    0/0               0/0              0/0             32      40       1/10
af32    0/0               0/0              0/0             28      40       1/10
af33    0/0               0/0              0/0             24      40       1/10
af41    0/0               0/0              0/0             32      40       1/10
af42    0/0               0/0              0/0             28      40       1/10
af43    0/0               0/0              0/0             24      40       1/10
cs1     0/0               0/0              0/0             22      40       1/10
cs2     0/0               0/0              0/0             24      40       1/10
cs3     0/0               0/0              0/0             26      40       1/10
cs4     0/0               0/0              0/0             28      40       1/10
cs5     0/0               0/0              0/0             30      40       1/10
cs6     0/0               0/0              0/0             32      40       1/10
cs7     0/0               0/0              0/0             34      40       1/10
ef      0/0               0/0              0/0             36      40       1/10
rsvp    0/0               0/0              0/0             36      40       1/10
default 0/0               0/0              0/0             20      40       1/10


    Class-map: class-default (match-any)
      847 packets, 348716 bytes
      30 second offered rate 2000 bps, drop rate 0 bps
      Match: any
      Weighted Fair Queueing
        Flow Based Fair Queueing
        Maximum Number of Hashed Queues 256
        (total queued/total drops/no-buffer drops) 0/0/0
        exponential weight: 9

dscp    Transmitted       Random drop      Tail drop       Minimum Maximum  Mark
        pkts/bytes        pkts/bytes       pkts/bytes      thresh  thresh   prob
af11    0/0               0/0              0/0             32      40       1/10
af12    0/0               0/0              0/0             28      40       1/10
af13    0/0               0/0              0/0             24      40       1/10
af21    0/0               0/0              0/0             32      40       1/10
af22    0/0               0/0              0/0             28      40       1/10
af23    0/0               0/0              0/0             24      40       1/10
```

continues

Example 7-13 *WRED Used in LLQ Classes dscp-af21, dscp-af23, and class-default*

```
af31        0/0             0/0             0/0             32    40   1/10
af32        0/0             0/0             0/0             28    40   1/10
af33        0/0             0/0             0/0             24    40   1/10
af41        0/0             0/0             0/0             32    40   1/10
af42        0/0             0/0             0/0             28    40   1/10
af43        0/0             0/0             0/0             24    40   1/10
cs1         0/0             0/0             0/0             22    40   1/10
cs2         0/0             0/0             0/0             24    40   1/10
cs3         0/0             0/0             0/0             26    40   1/10
cs4         0/0             0/0             0/0             28    40   1/10
cs5         0/0             0/0             0/0             30    40   1/10
cs6         0/0             0/0             0/0             32    40   1/10
cs7         0/0             0/0             0/0             34    40   1/10
ef          0/0             0/0             0/0             36    40   1/10
rsvp        0/0             0/0             0/0             36    40   1/10
default     59/767          0/0             0/0             20    40   1/10
```

The example lists a large configuration, but only a small amount pertains to WRED. Two sets of class maps have been configured — one set is used by the CB marking policy called laundry-list, and the other set is used by the LLQ policy map called queue-on-dscp. In **policy-map queue-on-dscp**, inside classes dscp-af21, dscp-af23, and class-default, the **random-detect dscp-based** command enables WRED. These three **random-detect** commands are highlighted in the **show running-config** output in the example.

Also note that WRED is not enabled on interface serial 0/0 in this configuration, because WRED applies to the output queues used by each class. Because WRED is not enabled on the main interface, to see statistics for WRED, you must use the **show policy-map interface** command. This command in the example lists WRED statistics inside each class in which WRED has been enabled. For the classes in which WRED is not enabled, such as the dscp-ef class, no additional WRED statistical information is listed. The default values for exponential weighting constant, and the per-DSCP defaults for minimum threshold, maximum threshold, and MPD are all listed in the command output.

WRED Summary

WRED provides a valuable tool for managing congestion in queues. Cisco IOS uses defaults that conform to the DiffServ Assured Forwarding conventions, which reduce the likelihood that you will need to configure thresholds for WRED. WRED can be particularly effective when used with MQC-based queuing tools, but when enabled directly on an interface, WRED has the unfortunate side effect of disallowing other queuing tools to be used. Table 7-8 lists some of WRED's key points.

Table 7-8 *WRED Feature Summary*

Feature	WRED
Discards packets to avoid congestion	Yes
Can be enabled on physical interface concurrently with a queuing tool	No
Can be combined with CBWFQ or LLQ policy map	Yes
Bases drop decision, at least in part, on different thresholds per precedence or DSCP value	Yes

Explicit Congestion Notification

ECN is very much interrelated with WRED. This section begins with a description of how ECN works with WRED, followed by a short section on ECN configuration.

ECN Concepts

WRED's main goal is to get some TCP senders to temporarily slow down the rate at which they send data into the network. By doing so, the temporary congestion may abate, avoiding problems such as tail drop and global synchronization. However, to cause TCP senders to slow down, WRED resorts to an inherently harmful action—the discarding of packets. It's a classic case of doing some harm now, in order to prevent more harm later.

Explicit Congestion Notification (ECN) provides the same benefit as WRED, without discarding packets. In fact, ECN is really just a feature of WRED in which TCP senders are signaled to slow down by setting bits in the packet headers. By signaling TCP senders to slow down, congestion may abate, all the while avoiding the use of packet drop.

When ECN is enabled, a router's WRED logic works almost exactly as before. For instance, WRED profiles are defined for each precedence or DSCP value. Average queue depths are calculated. WRED compares the average queue depth with the thresholds, and decides whether to drop nothing, to randomly drop a percentage of the packets, or to perform full drop.

The difference lies in what WRED does once it randomly chooses a packet to be discarded, which happens when the average queue depth is between the minimum and maximum threshold. With ECN enabled, WRED still randomly picks the packet, but instead of discarding it, WRED marks a couple of bits in the packet header, and forwards the packet. Marking these bits begins a process, defined in RFC 3168, which causes the sender of the TCP segment to reduce the congestion window (CWND) by 50 percent.

ECN causes the sender of the randomly-chosen packet to slow down. To do so, the sender of the packet must be told that congestion occurred, and ECN wants it to slow down. To trigger the process, the router, which notices the congestion, needs some bits to set in order to signal that the packet experienced congestion. Figure 7-12 shows the bits that are set by the router.

Figure 7-12 *ECN Bits in DSCP Byte*

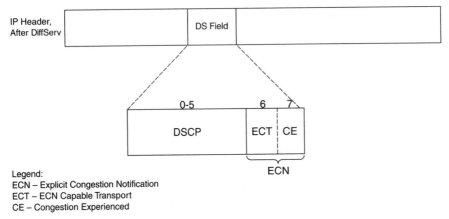

You might recall from back in Chapter 2, "QoS Tools and Architectures," that the two low-order bits in the DSCP byte were formerly unused, but they were later defined for use by ECN. With RFC 3168, which defines ECN, the two extra bits have been defined as the ECT and CE bits—together known as the ECN field.

To see how these bits are used, Figure 7-13 shows a full example. When looking at the figure, and the explanation that follows, keep in mind these two important points:

■ Routers, not the TCP endpoints, notice congestion, and then want to get the TCP senders to slow down.

■ TCP senders must somehow learn that a router is congested, so it can choose to slow down.

While Figure 7-13 holds several details, the general idea is that the router sets some bits in the packet instead of discarding it. In order to get the original sender of the packet to slow down, bits need to be set in the next packet sent back to the original sender. In other words, the router can set bits in the packet flowing left-to-right in the figure, but some other bits must be set in the packet flowing in the opposite direction (right-to-left) in order for PC Client2 to know to slow down.

Figure 7-13 *Example of ECN Signaling to Reduce CWND*

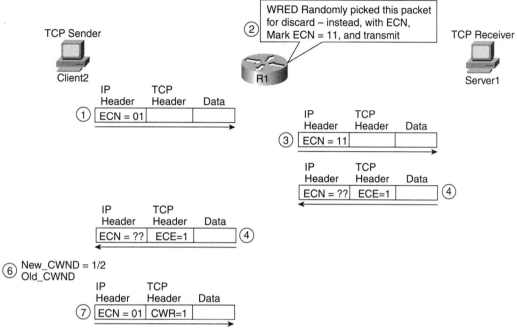

The following steps explain the contents of Figure 7-13, with the text following the circled numbers in the figure:

1. A TCP sender has negotiated a TCP connection, and both endpoints agree that they can support ECN. To indicate that support, the TCP sender sets the ECN bits to either 01 or 10. (If a TCP sender does not support ECN, the bits should be set to 00.)

2. The router uses WRED to recognize congestion, and the router randomly chooses this packet for discard. However, with ECN configured, the router checks the packet's ECN bits, and finds them set to "01". So, the router sets the bits to "11", and forwards the packet instead of discarding it.

3. The packet continues on its trip to the TCP receiver.

4. The TCP receiver receives the packet, and notices ECN = 11. As a result, the receiver sets a TCP flag in the next TCP segment it sends back to the TCP sender. The flag is called the Explicit Congestion Experienced (ECE) flag. (The ECN bit settings are not important in the packet at step 4, but they can be used to signal congestion in the right-to-left direction in this example.)

5. The packet passes through the router just like any other packet—there is no need for the router to watch for this return packet, or to set any other bits at this point.

6. The TCP sender receives the TCP segment with TCP ECE flag set, telling it to slow down. So, the TCP sender reduces its congestion window (CWND) by half.

7. The TCP sender wants the TCP receiver to know that it "got the message" and slowed down. To do so, the TCP sender, in it's next TCP segment, sets another new TCP flag called the *Congestion Window Reduced* (CWR) flag.

As you can see, the sender does indeed slow down by reducing its CWND, and the router didn't have to discard any packets. Overall, it's a better solution than WRED without ECN. However, this process depends on whether the TCP implementations on the endpoint hosts supports ECN or not. For instance, if Client2 and Server1 had negotiated about ECN when initializing the TCP connection, and one of them didn't support ECN, they would decide not to use ECN. Packets sent for this TCP connection would set ECN = 00. Under these circumstances, even with ECN configured on the router, the router's WRED logic could still discard the packet. That's because the router's ECN logic first checks to see whether ECN is supported for the underlying TCP connection; if not supported, the router uses the same old WRED logic, and discards the packet.

In summary, the WRED ECN logic works just like WRED without ECN, until a packet has been randomly chosen for discard (when average queue depth is between the min and max thresholds). At that point:

If ECN = 00, discard the packet

Otherwise, set ECN = 11, and forward the packet.

ECN Configuration

As you can understand from the details, ECN relies on routers that can mark the ECN bits, as well as IP hosts that support ECN with their TCP implementations. Implementation on Cisco routers is relatively easy, with one additional command required for configuration as compared with WRED configuration. Example 7-4 lists a simple WRED configuration, with ECN enabled, along with a few **show** commands.

Example 7-14 *WRED Used in LLQ Classes dscp-af21, dscp-af23, and class-default*

```
R3#show running-config
Building configuration...
!
!Portions omitted for brevity
!
ip cef
!
class-map match-all class1
  match protocol http
!
 policy-map ecn-test
```

Example 7-14 *WRED Used in LLQ Classes dscp-af21, dscp-af23, and class-default (Continued)*

```
  class class1
    bandwidth percent 50
    random-detect dscp-based
    random-detect ecn
!
!
interface Serial0/0
 no ip address
 service-policy output ecn-test
 encapsulation frame-relay
 clockrate 128000
!
interface Serial0/0.1 point-to-point
 bandwidth 128
 ip address 192.168.2.3 255.255.255.0
 frame-relay interface-dlci 143
!
! The rest has been omitted for brevity
!
R3#show policy-map interface s0/0

 Serial0/0

  Service-policy output: ecn-test

    Class-map: class1 (match-all)
      0 packets, 0 bytes
      5 minute offered rate 0 bps, drop rate 0 bps
      Match: protocol http
      Queueing
        Output Queue: Conversation 265
        Bandwidth 50 (%)
        Bandwidth 772 (kbps)
        (pkts matched/bytes matched) 0/0
        (depth/total drops/no-buffer drops) 0/0/0
         exponential weight: 9
         explicit congestion notification
         mean queue depth: 0

    dscp    Transmitted     Random drop     Tail drop     Minimum Maximum  Mark
            pkts/bytes      pkts/bytes      pkts/bytes    thresh  thresh   prob
    af11      0/0             0/0             0/0           32      40     1/10
    af12      0/0             0/0             0/0           28      40     1/10
    af13      0/0             0/0             0/0           24      40     1/10
    af21      0/0             0/0             0/0           32      40     1/10
    af22      0/0             0/0             0/0           28      40     1/10
    af23      0/0             0/0             0/0           24      40     1/10
```

continues

Example 7-14 *WRED Used in LLQ Classes dscp-af21, dscp-af23, and class-default (Continued)*

```
     af31      0/0            0/0            0/0          32   40  1/10
     af32      0/0            0/0            0/0          28   40  1/10
     af33      0/0            0/0            0/0          24   40  1/10
     af41      0/0            0/0            0/0          32   40  1/10
     af42      0/0            0/0            0/0          28   40  1/10
     af43      0/0            0/0            0/0          24   40  1/10
      cs1      0/0            0/0            0/0          22   40  1/10
      cs2      0/0            0/0            0/0          24   40  1/10
      cs3      0/0            0/0            0/0          26   40  1/10
      cs4      0/0            0/0            0/0          28   40  1/10
      cs5      0/0            0/0            0/0          30   40  1/10
      cs6      0/0            0/0            0/0          32   40  1/10
      cs7      0/0            0/0            0/0          34   40  1/10
       ef      0/0            0/0            0/0          36   40  1/10
     rsvp      0/0            0/0            0/0          36   40  1/10
  default      0/0            0/0            0/0          20   40  1/10

! note this new statistical section that follows:
     dscp      ECN Mark
               pkts/bytes
     af11       0/0
     af12       0/0
     af13       0/0
     af21       0/0
     af22       0/0
     af23       0/0
     af31       0/0
     af32       0/0
     af33       0/0
     af41       0/0
     af42       0/0
     af43       0/0
      cs1       0/0
      cs2       0/0
      cs3       0/0
      cs4       0/0
      cs5       0/0
      cs6       0/0
      cs7       0/0
       ef       0/0
     rsvp       0/0
  default       0/0

  Class-map: class-default (match-any)
     0 packets, 0 bytes
     5 minute offered rate 0 bps, drop rate 0 bps
     Match: any
```

The configuration is indeed quite simple. Notice the inclusion of the **random-detect ecn** command inside **policy-map ecn-test**. The rest of the configuration looks like normal CBWFQ configuration, with WRED enabled. Remember, ECN is really just a feature of WRED, with the same details of WRED thresholds and discard percentages, per DSCP. ECN simply means that if WRED randomly chooses to discard a packet, if that packet supports ECN (ECN field is 01 or 10), then the router marks ECN=11, and doesn't discard it.

Note that the ECN logic also means that randomly-chosen packets that have ECN set as 00 will be discarded like WRED normally would. So, the WRED section of the **show policy-map interface s0/0** command has the same types of statistics for discarded packets. A separate new section of output is included later to count the number of packets marked with ECN = 11. The new section is denoted with a heading in gray background near the end of the example.

Foundation Summary

The "Foundation Summary" is a collection of tables and figures that provide a convenient review of many key concepts in this chapter. For those of you already comfortable with the topics in this chapter, this summary could help you recall a few details. For those of you who just read this chapter, this review should help solidify some key facts. For any of you doing your final prep before the exam, these tables and figures are a convenient way to review the day before the exam.

Figure 7-14 shows a graph of CWND after packet loss just using slow start, and another with slow start plus congestion avoidance.

Figure 7-14 *Graphs of CWND with Slow Start and Congestion Avoidance*

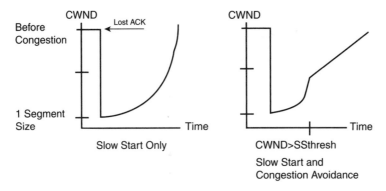

The key information about TCP and UDP operation when packets are dropped is summarized in the following list:

- UDP senders do not reduce or increase sending rates as a result of lost packets.

- TCP senders do reduce their sending rates as a result of lost packets.

- TCP senders decide to use either the receiver window or the CWND, based on whichever is lower at the time.

- TCP slow start and congestion avoidance dictate how fast the CWND rises after the window was lowered due to packet loss.

Table 7-9 describes the overall logic of when RED discards packets, with the same ideas outlined in Figure 7-15.

Table 7-9 *Three Categories of When RED Will Discard Packets, and How Many*

Average Queue Depth Versus Thresholds	Action	Name
Average < minimum threshold	No packets dropped.	No Drop
Minimum threshold < average depth < maximum threshold	A percentage of packets dropped. Drop percentage increases from 0 to a maximum percent as the average depth moves from the minimum threshold to the maximum.	Random Drop
Average depth > maximum threshold	All new packets discarded similar to tail dropping.	Full Drop

Figure 7-15 *RED Discarding Logic Using Average Depth, Minimum Threshold, and Maximum Threshold*

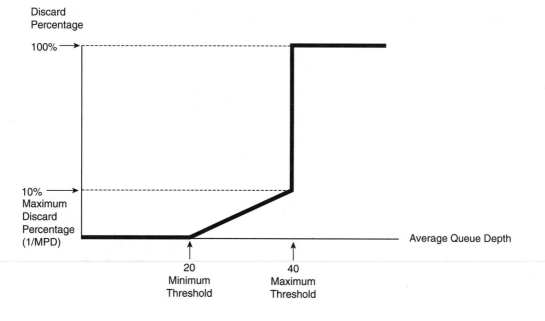

Table 7-10 summarizes some of the key terms related to RED.

Table 7-10   *RED Terminology*

Term	Meaning
Actual queue depth	The actual number of packets in a queue at a particular point in time.
Average queue depth	Calculated measurement based on the actual queue depth and the previous average. Designed to adjust slowly to the rapid changes of the actual queue depth.
Minimum threshold	Compares this setting to the average queue depth to decide whether packets should be discarded. No packets are discarded if the average queue depth falls below this minimum threshold.
Maximum threshold	Compares this setting to the average queue depth to decide whether packets should be discarded. All packets are discarded if the average queue depth falls above this maximum threshold.
Mark probability denominator	Used to calculate the maximum percentage of packets discarded when the average queue depth falls between the minimum and maximum thresholds.
Exponential weighting constant	Used to calculate the rate at which the average queue depth changes as compared with the current queue depth. The larger the number, the slower the change in the average queue depth.
No Drop	State in which RED's average queue depth falls below the minimum threshold. No packets are discarded.
Random Drop	State in which RED's average queue depth falls between the minimum and maximum thresholds. A percentage of randomly-selected packets are discarded.
Full Drop	State in which RED's average queue depth exceeds the maximum threshold. All packets are dropped

Figure 7-16 shows the default WRED settings for precedence 0, with some nondefault settings for precedence 3 traffic.

Figure 7-16   *Example WRED Profile for Precedences 0 and 5*

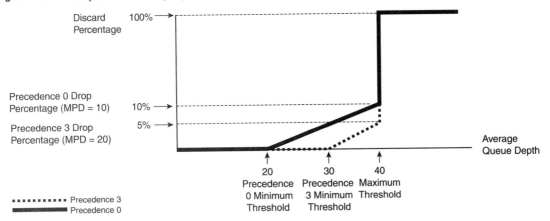

WRED measures the average queue depth of the FIFO queue on an interface, as shown in Figure 7-17.

Figure 7-17 *FIFO Output Queue and WRED Interaction*

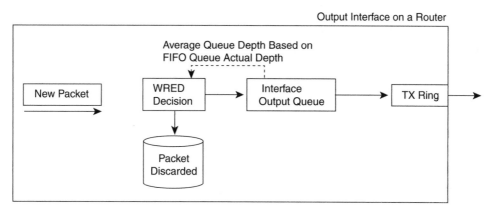

ECN allows WRED to signal a TCP sender to slow down, instead of discarding a packet sent by that TCP sender. Figure 7-18 shows the entire process.

Figure 7-18 *ECN Signaling to Slow Down TCP Sender*

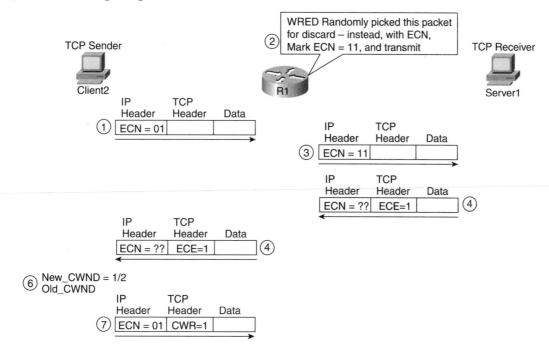

Q&A

As mentioned in the Introduction, you have two choices for review questions. The questions that follow next give you a more difficult challenge than the exam itself by using an open-ended question format. By reviewing now with this more difficult question format, you can exercise your memory better, and prove your conceptual and factual knowledge of this chapter. You can find the answers to these questions in Appendix A.

The second option for practice questions is to use the CD-ROM included with this book. It includes a testing engine and more than 200 multiple-choice questions. You should use this CD-ROM nearer to the end of your preparation, for practice with the actual exam format.

Congestion-Avoidance Concepts and Random Early Detection (RED)

1. Describe the function of the congestion window in TCP, and how it is changed as a result of packet loss.

2. Identify the two TCP windowing mechanisms, and describe when each is used.

3. Describe the process of TCP slow start, and when it occurs.

4. Describe the meaning of the term "global synchronization," and discuss what causes it.

5. Define the meaning of the term "tail drop."

6. Define the meaning of the term "TCP starvation."

7. Does RED compare the actual queue depth or the average queue depth to queue thresholds when deciding whether it should discard a packet? Why this one, and not the other?

8. Describe how RED uses actual queue depth to calculate average queue depth. Do not list the formula, but just describe the general idea.

9. Assume the RED minimum threshold is 20, the maximum threshold is 40, and the mark probability denominator is 10. What must be true for RED to discard all new packets?

10. Assume the RED minimum threshold is 20, the maximum threshold is 40, and the mark probability denominator is 10. What must be true for RED to discard 5 percent of all new packets?

11. Define how RED uses the mark probability denominator. Give one example.

12. Define the term "exponential weighting constant." If the value is lowered compared to the default setting of 9, how does RED behave differently?

13. Define the term "WRED Profile."

14. Explain how you can tune how fast or slow that WRED changes the calculated average queue depth over time.

Weighted RED (WRED)

15. Spell out the words represented by the initials RED, WRED, and FRED.

16. List the three WRED terms that name the separate states in which WRED discards no packets, a percentage of packets, and all packets.

17. List the queuing tools that can be concurrently supported on an interface when WRED has been enabled directly on a serial interface, assuming no retrictions on the particular model of router.

18. Identify the most important difference between RED operation and WRED operation.

19. Describe how WRED "weights" packets.

20. List the queuing tools that can enable WRED for use with some or all of their queues, effectively enabling WRED concurrently with the queuing tool, assuming no retrictions on the particular model of router.

21. What command enables you to look at WRED drop statistics when WRED is configured inside an MQC class?

22. Taking as many defaults as possible, list the configuration commands needed to configure precedence-based WRED on interface S1/1.

23. Taking as many defaults as possible, list the configuration commands needed to configure DSCP-based WRED on interface S1/1.

24. Taking as many defaults as possible, list the configuration commands needed to configure DSCP-based WRED inside class class1, inside policy map my-policy. (You can assume that the CBWFQ configuration has already been completed, and you just entered global configuration mode. Assume that you need just to enable WRED in class class1.)

25. List the command needed to set the minimum threshold to 25, the maximum threshold to 50, and the mark probability denominator to 4, for precedence 2.

26. What show command lists detailed statistics about random drops on interface S1/1?

Explicit Congestion Notification

27. For a single WRED profile, WRED can be either dropping no packets, randomly choosing packets to discard, or dropping all packets. For which of these three states does ECN impact WRED's discard actions? How does it change what WRED does to the packets?

28. Identify the bits in the IP header used with ECN, by name and location.

29. Imagine a router on which WRED and ECN are enabled, and WRED decides to randomly discard a packet. What must be true in order for WRED to discard the packet, instead of using ECN logic to mark and forward the packet? Explain the role of any other devices besides the router.

30. Imagine a router on which WRED and ECN are enabled, and WRED decides to randomly discard a packet. What must be true in order for WRED to use ECN logic to mark and forward the packet, instead of discarding the packet? Explain the role of any other devices besides the router.

31. Imagine a policy map with WRED already configured for **class class-web**. What additional command is required to also enable ECN for the packets in that class?

QoS Exam Topics

This chapter covers the following exam topics specific to the QoS exams:

- Explain the various link efficiency mechanisms and their function

- Identify the Cisco IOS commands required to configure and monitor CB header compression

- Given a list of link speeds and a specific delay requirement, determine the proper fragment size to use at each link speed and identify the typical delay requirement for VoIP packets

- Identify the Cisco IOS commands required to configure and monitor Multilink PPP with Interleaving

- Identify the Cisco IOS commands required to configure and monitor FRF.12

CHAPTER 8

Link Efficiency Tools

Most WAN links are leased from a service provider, with one of the variables affecting the pricing being the bandwidth on the link. For instance, the distance and the bandwidth, or clock rate, on the link affect leased line pricing. Frame Relay service providers base their prices in part based on the access rate of the access links into the Frame Relay network, and the committed information rate (CIR) of the various virtual circuits (VCs).

If the offered load on the network consistently exceeds the bandwidth or clock rate of the link the traffic must flow across, unpredictable behavior can result. For example, queues consistently fill, causing more delay, jitter, and drops. If the offered load far exceeds the clock rate for a period of time, most data applications slow down significantly, with voice and video streams possibly even becoming unusable. Depending on how you configure quality of service (QoS) in the network, some traffic types may perform as expected, but with a likely result of allowing some other traffic types to degrade even more quickly, because most QoS tools by design end up favoring one type of traffic over another.

This chapter covers two classes of QoS tools that directly impact the usage of the bandwidth in a network—compression tools and link fragmentation and interleaving (LFI) tools. Compression tools compress the number of bytes in a packet so that fewer bytes need to be sent over a link.

LFI tools directly impact serialization delays—and serialization delay is impacted by actual link bandwidth. The slower the link, the longer it takes to serialize a packet. If a small packet must wait on a large packet to be serialized onto a link, the small packet may experience too much delay, particularly on slow-speed links. LFI tools reduce the delay experienced by a short packet by breaking larger packets into smaller pieces, and by transmitting the original small packets in between the fragments of the original larger packets. Smaller packets get better service, and in many cases, smaller packets are part of a delay-sensitive application, such as Voice over IP (VoIP).

"Do I Know This Already?" Quiz

The purpose of the "Do I Know This Already?" quiz is to help you decide whether you really need to read the entire chapter. If you already intend to read the entire chapter, you do not necessarily need to answer these questions now.

The 10-question quiz, derived from the major sections in "Foundation Topics" section of the chapter, helps you determine how to spend your limited study time.

Table 8-1 outlines the major topics discussed in this chapter and the "Do I Know This Already?" quiz questions that correspond to those topics.

Table 8-1 *"Do I Know This Already?" Foundation Topics Section-to-Question Mapping*

Foundation Topics Section Covering These Questions	Questions	Score
Compression	1–5	
Link Fragmentation and Interleave	6–10	
Total Score		

CAUTION The goal of self-assessment is to gauge your mastery of the topics in this chapter. If you do not know the answer to a question or are only partially sure of the answer, mark this question wrong for purposes of the self-assessment. Giving yourself credit for an answer you correctly guess skews your self-assessment results and might provide you with a false sense of security.

You can find the answers to the "Do I Know This Already?" quiz in Appendix A, "Answers to the 'Do I Know This Already?' Quizzes and Q&A Sections." The suggested choices for your next step are as follows:

- **8 or less overall score**—Read the entire chapter. This includes the "Foundation Topics," the "Foundation Summary," and the "Q&A" sections.

- **9 or 10 overall score**—If you want more review on these topics, skip to the "Foundation Summary" section and then go to the "Q&A" section. Otherwise, move to the next chapter.

Compression Questions

1. With CB RTP header compression, which of the following are compressed?

    a. RTP header

    b. TCP header

   c. IP header

   d. UDP header

   e. Data

2. With CB TCP header compression, which of the following are compressed?

   a. RTP header

   b. TCP header

   c. IP header

   d. UDP header

   e. Data

3. With Layer 2 payload compression, which of the following could be compressed?

   a. RTP header

   b. TCP header

   c. IP header

   d. UDP header

   e. Data

4. Which of the following Modular QoS Command-Line Interface (MQC) **class** subcommands enables CB RTP header compression?

   a. **compression ip header rtp**

   b. **compression header ip rtp**

   c. **compression ip rtp**

   d. **compression header**

   e. **compression header ip**

5. In the **show policy-map interface** command output, with TCP or RTP header compression enabled, what does "efficiency improvement factor" mean?

   a. The number of bytes that would have been sent without compression, per second

   b. The ratio of bytes actually sent, over the number of bytes that would have been sent without compression

   c. The ratio of bytes that would have been sent without compression, over the number of bytes actually sent

   d. The compression ratio

Link Fragmentation and Interleave Questions

6. What fragment size, in bytes, should be used on a 256-Kbps link in order to ensure each fragment has less than or equal to 10 ms of serialization delay?

    a. 80

    b. 160

    c. 214

    d. 240

    e. 320

    f. 480

7. What serialization delay, in milliseconds, would be experienced by a 160 byte fragment on a 64-kbps link?

    a. 5

    b. 10

    c. 15

    d. 20

    e. 25

    f. 30

    g. 35

    h. 40

8. A router has MLP LFI configured on **interface s0/0.** The **bandwidth 128** command is already configured on the multilink interface. Which of the following commands is used under a multilink interface in order to set the fragment size to 160 bytes?

    a. **ppp multilink fragment-delay 10**

    b. **ppp multilink fragment-size 160**

    c. **ppp multilink interleave**

    d. **ppp fragment-delay 10**

    e. **ppp fragment-size 160**

9. A router has FRF.12 configured for all VC's on **interface s0/0**. The **bandwidth 128** command is already configured on the interface. Which of the following commands is used under the **map-class frame-relay** command in order to set the fragment size to 160 bytes?

    a. **frame-relay fragment 10**

    b. **frame-relay fragment 160**

    c. **frame-relay traffic-shaping**

    d. **fragment 10**

    e. **fragment 160**

10. Which of the following commands list statistics about the number of fragments created with FRF.12?

    a. **show queueing interface**

    b. **show fragments**

    c. **show interfaces**

    d. **show frame-relay fragment**

Foundation Topics

Payload and Header Compression

Compression involves mathematical algorithms that encode the original packet into a smaller string of bytes. After sending the smaller encoded string to the other end of a link, the compression algorithm on the other end of the link reverses the process, reverting the packet back to its original state.

Over the years, many mathematicians and computer scientists have developed new compression algorithms that behave better or worse under particular conditions. For instance, each algorithm takes some amount of computation, some memory, and they result in saving some number of bytes of data. In fact, you can compare compression algorithms by calculating the ratio of original number of bytes, divided by the compressed number of bytes—a value called the *compression ratio*. Depending on what is being compressed, the different compression algorithms have varying success with their compression ratios, and each uses different amounts of CPU and memory.

In Cisco routers, compression tools can be divided into two main categories: payload compression and header compression. *Payload compression* compresses headers and the user data, whereas header compression only compresses headers. As you might guess, payload compression can provide a larger compression ratio for larger packets with lots of user data in them, as compared to header compression tools. Conversely, *header compression* tools work well when the packets tend to be small, because headers comprise a large percentage of the packet. Figure 8-1 shows the fields compressed by payload compression, and by both types of header compression. (Note that the abbreviation DL stands for data link, representing the data-link header and trailer.)

Figure 8-1 *Payload and Header Compression*

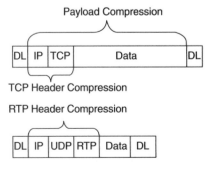

Both types of compression tools require CPU cycles and memory. Payload compression algorithms tend to take a little more computation and memory, just based on the fact that they have more bytes to process, as seen in Figure 8-1. With any of the compression tools, however, the computation time required to perform the compression algorithm certainly adds delay to the packet. The bandwidth gained by compression must be more important to you than the delay added by compression processing, otherwise you should choose not to use compression at all!

Figure 8-2 outlines an example showing the delays affected by compression. The compression and decompression algorithms take time, of course. However, serialization delay decreases, because the packets are now smaller. Queuing delay also decreases. In addition, on Frame Relay and ATM networks, the network delay decreases, because the network delay is affected by the amount of bits sent into the network.

Figure 8-2 *Delay Versus Bandwidth with Compression*

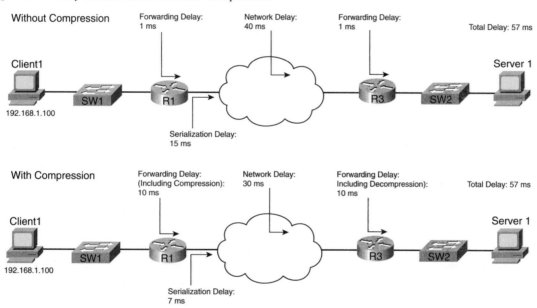

This example uses contrived numbers to make the relevant points. The example assumes a 2:1 compression ratio, with a 1500-byte packet, and 768-kbps access links on both ends. The various delay components in the top half of the figure, without compression, add up to 57 ms. In the lower figure, with compression, the delay is still 57 ms. Because a 2:1 compression ratio was achieved, twice as much traffic can be sent without adding delay—it seems like an obvious choice to use compression! However, compression uses CPU and memory, and it is difficult to predict how compression will work on a particular router in a particular network. Compression requires that you try it, monitor CPU utilization, look at the compression ratios, and experiment before just deciding to add it to all routers over an entire network. In addition, although this example shows no increase in delay, in most cases, just turning on software compression will probably increase delay slightly, but still with the benefit of increasing the amount of traffic you can send over the link.

Compression hardware minimizes the delay added by compression algorithms. Cisco offers several types of hardware compression cards that reduce the delay taken to compress the packets. Cisco offers compression service adapters on 7200, 7300, 7400, 7500 routers, compression advanced integration modules (AIMs) on 3660 and 2600 routers, and compression network modules for 3620s and 3640s. On 7500s with Versatile Interface Processors (VIPs), the compression work can be distributed to the VIP cards, even if no compression adapters are installed. Thankfully, when the compression cards are installed and compression is configured, IOS assumes that you want the compression to occur on the card by default, requiring you to specifically configure software compression if you do not want to use the compression hardware for some reason.

Header Compression

Header compression algorithms take advantage of the fact that the headers are predictable. If you capture the frames sent across a link with a network analyzer, for instance, and look at IP packets from the same flow, you see that the IP headers do not change a lot, nor do the TCP headers, or UDP and RTP headers if RTP is used. Therefore, header compression can significantly reduce the size of the headers with a relatively small amount of computation. In fact, TCP header compression compresses the IP and TCP header (originally 40 bytes combined) down to between 3 and 5 bytes. Similarly, RTP header compression compresses the IP, UDP, and RTP headers (originally 40 bytes combined) to 2 to 4 bytes. (The variation in byte size for RTP headers results from the presence of a UDP checksum. Without the checksum, the RTP header is 2 bytes; with the checksum, the RTP header is 4 bytes.)

TCP header compression results in large compression ratios if the TCP packets are relatively small. For instance, with a 64-byte packet, with 40 of those being the IP and TCP headers, the compressed packet is between 27 and 29 bytes! That gives a compression ratio of 64/27, or about 2.37, which is pretty good for a compression algorithm that uses relatively little CPU. However, a 1500-byte packet with TCP header compression saves 35 to 37 bytes of the original 1500-byte packet, providing a compression ratio of 1500/1463, or about 1.03, a relatively insignificant savings in this case.

RTP header compression typically provides a good compression result for voice traffic, because VoIP tends always to use small packets. For instance, G.729 codecs in Cisco routers uses 20 bytes of data, preceded by 40 bytes of IP, UDP, and RTP headers. After compression, the headers are down to 4 bytes, and the packet size falls from 60 bytes to 24 bytes! Table 8-2 lists some of the overall VoIP bandwidth requirements, and the results of RTP header compression.

Table 8-2 *Bandwidth Requirements for Various Types of Voice Calls With and Without cRTP*

Codec	Payload Bandwidth (in kbps)	IP/UDP/RTP Header size (in bytes)	Layer 2 header Type	Size of Layer 2 header plus trailer (in bytes)*	Total Bandwidth (in kbps)
G.711	64	40	Ethernet	18	87.2
G.711	64	40	FR	9	83.6
G.711	64	2 (cRTP)	FR	9	68.4
G.729	8	40	Ethernet	18	31.2
G.729	8	40	FR	9	27.6
G.729	8	2 (cRTP)	FR	9	12.4

* Some tables circulating in Cisco documents and older Cisco courses only include the header size in the calculations; this table includes the Data Link header and Trailer.

Class-Based TCP and RTP Header Compression Configuration

Cisco has supported TCP and RTP header compression natively in Cisco IOS Software for the last several major revisions. With Release 12.2(13)T, Cisco added IOS support for these two compression tools as Modular QoS Command-Line Interface (MQC)-based features. As a result, the configuration is painfully simple.

As with other MQC-based tools, you need to configure class maps and policy maps. And like the other MQC tools, there is one particular configuration command (**compression header ip [tcp | rtp]**) that enables the function, with this command added inside a class inside a policy map. The only slightly unusual task, as compared with other MQC-based tools, is that compression must be enabled on both sides of a point-to-point link or Frame Relay VC. Simply put, configuring compression tells a router to compress packets it will send, and to decompress packets it receives; if only one router on the end of a link or VC compresses and decompresses, the other router will become confused, and the packets will be discarded.

Table 8-3 lists the single configuration command for CB compression, along with a reference to the best **show** command to use with CB Compression.

Table 8-3 *Command Reference for Class Based Header Compression*

Command	Mode and Function
compression header ip [tcp | rtp]	Class configuration mode; enables RTP, TCP, or both kinds of compression for packets in that class
show policy-map interface *interface-name* **[input | output]**	Lists statistics for all MQC features enabled inside the policy map for packets entering or exiting the interface

You can see the power and simplicity of CB Compression with one single example network (see Figure 8-3) and configuration.

Figure 8-3 *Payload and Header Compression*

Note: All IP Addresses Begin 192.168.

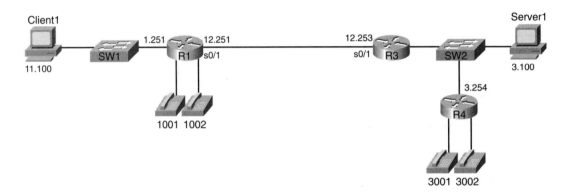

The network in Figure 8-3 has voice traffic, lots of email and web traffic, some Telnet traffic, and several other small TCP/IP applications. Because RTP can significantly reduce the amount of overhead, RTP header compression will be used. Also, TCP header compression is mostly beneficial with smaller TCP segments, so compressing Telnet traffic, and not compressing other traffic, makes good sense. So the choices made in this particular network are as follows:

- Use CB RTP Header Compression for voice traffic

- Use CB TCP Header Compression for Telnet traffic

- Do not compress other traffic

To test, a single G.729 VoIP call was made between phones off R4 and R1, along with a single Telnet connection from R4 to R1. Example 8-1 shows the configuration on R3.

Example 8-1 *CB Header Compression on R3*

```
R3#show running-config
Building configuration...
!
! Portions omitted for brevity
!
hostname R3
!
ip cef
!
 class-map match-all telnet-only
  match protocol telnet
 class-map match-all voice-only
  match protocol rtp audio
!
!
 policy-map test-compress
  class voice-only
   priority 30
   compression header ip rtp
  class telnet-only
   compression header ip tcp
   bandwidth 20
!
!
interface Serial0/1
 ip address 192.168.4.3 255.255.255.0
 service-policy output test-compress
 load-interval 30
 clockrate 64000
!
R3#show policy-map interface s0/1
 Serial0/1

  Service-policy output: test-compress

    Class-map: voice-only (match-all)
      2880 packets, 184320 bytes
      30 second offered rate 25000 bps, drop rate 0 bps
      Match: protocol rtp audio
      Queueing
        Strict Priority
        Output Queue: Conversation 264
        Bandwidth 30 (kbps) Burst 750 (Bytes)
```

continues

Example 8-1 *CB Header Compression on R3 (Continued)*

```
        (pkts matched/bytes matched) 2/54
        (total drops/bytes drops) 0/0
    compress:
        header ip rtp
        UDP/RTP compression:
        Sent: 2880 total, 2880 compressed,
              106560 bytes saved, 66240 bytes sent
              2.60 efficiency improvement factor
              100% hit ratio, five minute miss rate 0 misses/sec, 0 max
              rate 9000 bps

  Class-map: telnet-only (match-all)
    261 packets, 28399 bytes
    30 second offered rate 0 bps, drop rate 0 bps
    Match: protocol telnet
    compress:
        header ip tcp
        TCP compression:
        Sent: 259 total, 242 compressed,
              7877 bytes saved, 19390 bytes sent
              1.40 efficiency improvement factor
              99% hit ratio, five minute miss rate 0 misses/sec, 0 max
              rate 0 bps

    Queueing
      Output Queue: Conversation 265
      Bandwidth 20 (kbps) Max Threshold 64 (packets)
      (pkts matched/bytes matched) 39/9832
      (depth/total drops/no-buffer drops) 0/0/0

  Class-map: class-default (match-any)
    850 packets, 55734 bytes
    30 second offered rate 0 bps, drop rate 0 bps
    Match: any
```

First, examine the configuration for **policy-map test-compress**. Two classes are referencd, one for voice (class **voice-only**) and one for Telnet (class **telnet-only**). For voice, the **compress header ip rtp** command tells IOS to compress RTP flows that end up in this class. Similarly, the **compress header ip tcp** command tells IOS to use TCP header compression on flows that end up in class **telnet-only**.

> **NOTE** If you omit the RTP and TCP keywords on the **compress** command, IOS performs both RTP and TCP header compression in that class.

Although not shown, a similar configuration is required on R1. Both routers on each end of the serial link need to enable RTP and TCP header compression for the exact same TCP and RTP flows. In reality, you will most likely use identical class maps on each router. The problem is that if one router tries to compress TCP packets, and the other does not expect to need to decompress the packets, then the TCP connection will fail. So, you essentially need the exact same policy map and classes on each side of the link when doing compression.

The output from the **show policy-map interface serial 0/1** command lists statistics about the number of packets compressed, the bytes that would have been sent, and the number of bytes actually sent. By reverse engineering the counters, you can see the compression ratio and savings with CB RTP compression. For instance, the output claims a "2.6 Efficiency Improvement Factor" (for class **voice-only**), which is a fancy term for compression ratio. The counters state that the router sent and compressed 2880 total packets, with 106,560 bytes saved, and 66,240 bytes actually sent. Another way to interpret those numbers is to say that (106,560 + 66,240) bytes would have been sent without compression, and only 66,240 were sent with compression. So, the compression ratio would be (106,560 + 66,240) / 66,240, which is indeed a compression ratio of 2.6.

Another bit of interesting math with the counters can be seen by examining the number of bytes saved (106,560) versus the number of packets compressed (2880). The number of bytes saved per packet is 37, because 106,560/2880 is exactly 37. So, CB RTP compression is indeed compressing the 40-byte IP/UDP/RTP header into 3 bytes on average, saving 37 bytes per packet on average.

Link Fragmentation and Interleaving

Both types of QoS tools covered in this chapter address bandwidth constraints to some degree. Compression tools directly attack bandwidth constraints by lowering the bandwidth required to forward packets. Link fragmentation and interleaving (LFI) tools directly lower delay by defeating a side effect of a small transmit clock speed, namely serialization delay.

A quick review of serialization delay should help you make more sense out of LFI tools. Serialization is the time required to send a frame over a physical link. If a link has a physical clock rate of x bps, it takes $1/x$ seconds to send a single bit. If a frame has y bits in it, it takes y/x seconds to serialize the frame. The faster the link, the lower the serialization delay. On a 56-kbps link, for example, it takes 1/56,000 of a second to send 1 bit. A 1500-byte frame (12,000 bits) takes 12,000/56,000 seconds to serialize, or roughly 214 ms.

When a router starts to send a frame out of an interface, it sends the complete frame. If a small, delay-sensitive frame needs to exit an interface, and the router has just begun to send a large frame, the small frame must wait until the whole large frame has been sent before the router will send the small, delay-sensitive frame. As seen in the preceding example, a 1500-byte frame takes 214 ms to serialize at 56 kbps, which is far too long for the small frame to wait if it is part of a VoIP stream.

LFI tools attack the serialization delay problem by ensuring that large packets do not delay smaller packets. It accomplishes this by dividing larger packets (fragmentation) and interleaving later-arriving smaller packets in between the fragments from the larger packet. The smaller, delay-sensitive interleaved packets, typically VoIP, are defined in your QoS policy. Figure 8-4 outlines the basic process.

Figure 8-4 *Basic Concept Behind LFI Tools*

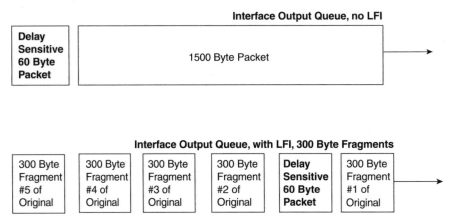

As shown in the upper queue in the figure, without LFI, the small 60-byte packet must wait for the full 1500-byte packet to be forwarded. In the lower queue, with LFI enabled, IOS can choose to let the smaller packet exit the interface ahead of some of the fragments of the larger packet.

Before examining LFI in more detail, you need to take a closer look at the terms "packet" and "frame." In most cases in this book, these terms have been used interchangeably. However, it is important to realize what really gets placed into the queues, and what really gets fragmented, when discussing LFI tools.

First, we need a shared definition of what each of the two terms mean. *Packet* refers to the entity that flows through the network, including the Layer 3 header, all headers from layers above Layer 3, and the end-user data. Packets do not include the data-link (Layer 2) headers and trailers. *Frames* include the packet, as well as the data-link (Layer 2) header and trailer.

Queuing tools actually place frames into the queues. For instance, Weighted Fair Queuing (WFQ) on a PPP serial interface places PPP frames into the queues. Concerning queuing tools, the distinction does not really have much bearing on the choices you make. In addition, because most people tend to use the term "packet" more often, this book just uses packet when it does not matter whether you care about the packet or the frame.

LFI tools require you to think about what happens to the packet, *and* what happens to the frame. Consider Figure 8-5, which shows some of the details of an unfragmented frame, and a fragmented frame, using Frame Relay.

Figure 8-5 *LFI Application to Packets and Frames, 1500-Byte Packet*

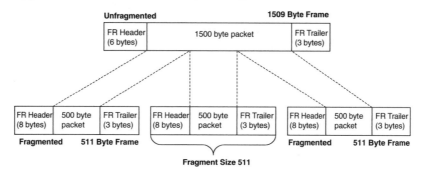

In the upper part of the figure, a 1500-byte packet has an extra 9 bytes of Frame Relay header and trailer added to it, to form a 1509-byte frame. In the lower part of the figure, the 1500-byte packet has been fragmented into three 500-byte fragments, and then placed into Frame Relay frames. It turns out that with FRF.12 LFI, an additional 2 bytes of header are needed to manage the fragments, so each of the three frames totals 511 bytes in length.

Technically, the fragment size used in the figure is 511 bytes, not 500. Most people would tend to think something like "the router fragmented the 1500-byte packet into three 500-byte fragments." In reality, the router performs logic like in the following list:

■ The router fragments the *packet* into smaller pieces.

■ The router adds the appropriate data-link headers and trailers, including any headers specifically needed for fragmentation support.

■ The length of the resulting *frames* (including data-link headers/trailers) does not exceed the fragmentation size configured.

■ The router adds these frames to the appropriate queue.

So, the router fragments packets into smaller pieces, but the size of the pieces is determined by the fragment size, which is based on the frame size. Therefore, does LFI really fragment packets, or frames? Frankly, either term works. When you are choosing the size of the fragments, however, always remember that the fragment size determines the size of the frames, *not* the packets. Therefore, you *should* consider the length of the data-link headers and trailers when choosing the size of the fragments.

Multilink PPP LFI

The core concept behind LFI, and its benefits, is very straightforward. The details, however, can be a little confusing, mainly because IOS LFI tools interact directly with IOS queuing tools. In addition, the two LFI tools covered on the Cisco QoS exam happen to behave differently as to how they interact with queuing tools. So to understand where LFI functions take place, you need to examine each tool specifically. This section covers multilink PPP LFI (MLP LFI), with Frame Relay fragmentation (FRF) covered in the next section of this chapter. Figure 8-6 depicts how MLP LFI works with a queuing tool on an interface.

Figure 8-6 *MLP LFI Interaction with Queuing*

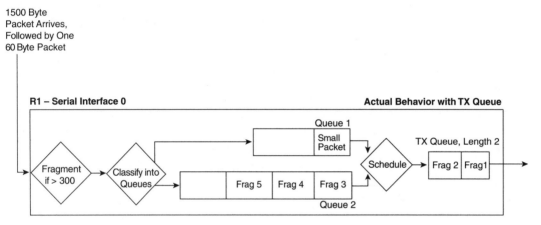

The figure outlines a lot of the detailed concepts behind LFI. In this example, a 1500-byte packet first arrives at R1, followed by a 60-byte packet. The fragmentation logic has been configured to fragment the frames down to a little more than 300 bytes, to make room for 300 bytes from the packet, and a little more for the data-link headers and trailers. After fragmentation, the queuing tool on the interface classifies the frames into their respective queues, which in this example happens to be two different queues. (The queuing tool's classification step works exactly as described in Chapter 5, "Congestion Management.")

Now look to the far right side of the figure. The TX Queue is shown, with a queue length of 2. In this example, an assumption has been made that the small packet arrived after IOS had placed the first two fragments of the large packet into the two available slots in the TX Queue, with the last three fragments being placed into Queue 2. The TX Queue is always *absolutely* a single FIFO queue, as described in Chapter 5. In other words, the small packet does not interrupt the router while it is in the middle of sending fragment 1, nor does the small packet have a chance to be sent before fragment 2, because fragment 2 is already in the TX Queue. The best behavior the small packet can hope for is to be the next packet placed onto the end of the TX Queue. Therefore, for now, the small packet has been placed into Queue 1.

Now look just to the left of the TX Queue, between the two interface output queues and the TX Queue. The term "schedule" reminds us that the queuing scheduler chooses the next packet to be moved from the output queues to the TX Queue (as described in Chapter 5). The queuing tool's scheduler may decide to take the next packet from Queue 1 or Queue 2 — a decision totally based on the logic of the queuing tool.

Interleaving occurs when the queuing scheduler decides to service the queue that holds the small packet next, rather than the queue holding the next fragment of the large packet. If Low Latency Queuing (LLQ) has been configured, and Queue 1 is the low-latency queue, the scheduler takes the small packet next, meaning that the small packet would be interleaved between fragments of the larger packet. If the queuing tool was Custom Queuing (CQ), and the queuing scheduler were able to send more bytes from Queue 2 in this cycle, fragment 3 would be sent next.

Maximum Serialization Delay and Optimum Fragment Sizes

How large should the fragments be to reduce serialization delay to an acceptable level? Well, the real answer lies in an analysis of the delay budgets for your network. From that analysis, you determine the maximum serialization delay you can have on each link.

The delay budget includes many delay components, such as queuing delay, propagation delay, shaping delay, network delay, and serialization delay. Based on that delay budget, you determine how much serialization delay you can afford on a particular link. Figure 8-7 depicts example delay values for various delay components.

Figure 8-7   *Review of Delay Components, Including Serialization Delay*

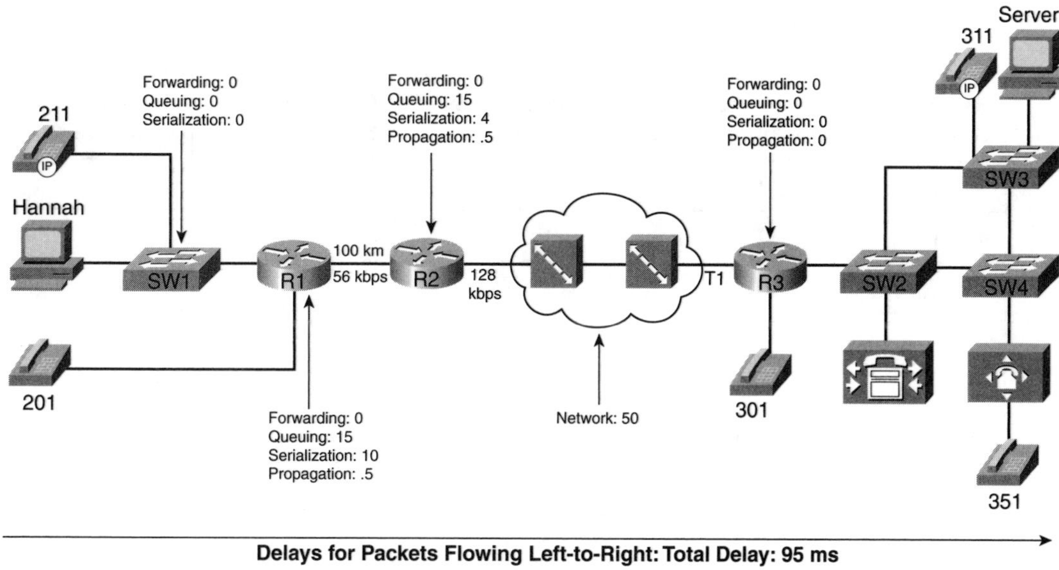

Delays for Packets Flowing Left-to-Right: Total Delay: 95 ms

Now imagine that you need to configure R1 in the figure to use MLP LFI. You already know that you want a maximum serialization delay of 10 ms, and conveniently, MLP LFI enables you to configure a max-delay parameter. MLP LFI then calculates the fragment size, based on the following formula:

Max-delay * bandwidth

In this formula, bandwidth is the value configured on the **bandwidth** interface subcommand, and max-delay is the serialization delay configured on the **ppp multilink fragment-delay** command. For instance, R1 in Figure 8-7 shows a budget for 10 ms of serialization delay. On a 56-kbps link, a 10-ms max-delay would make the fragment size 56,000 * .01, or 560 bits, which is 70 bytes.

Cisco generally suggests a maximum serialization delay per link of 10-15 ms in multiservice networks. Because serialization delay becomes less than 10 ms for 1500-byte packets at link speeds greater than 768 kbps, Cisco recommends that LFI be considered on links with a 768-kbps clock rate and below.

> **NOTE**   Earlier Cisco courses, and some other Cisco documents, make the recommendation to set fragment sizes such that the fragements require 10 ms or less. The 10-15 ms recommendation is stated in the current Cisco QoS course.

The math used to find the fragment size, based on the serialization delay and bandwidth, is pretty easy. For perspective, Table 8-4 summarizes the calculated fragment sizes based on the bandwidth and maximum delay.

Table 8-4   *Fragment Sizes Based on Bandwidth and Serialization Delay*

Bandwidth/Link Speed (Kbps)	Fragment size (bytes) with 10-ms Delay	Fragment size (bytes) with 20-ms Delay	Fragment size (bytes) with 30-ms Delay	Fragment size (bytes) with 40-ms Delay
56 kbps	70	140	210	280
64 kbps	80	160	240	320
128 kbps	160	320	480	560
256 kbps	320	640	960	1280
512 kbps	640	1280	1920*	2560*
768 kbps	1000	2000*	3000*	4000*
1536 kbps	2000*	4000*	6000*	8000*

*Values over 1500 exceed the typical maximum transmit unit (MTU) size of an interface. Fragmentation of sizes larger than MTU does not result in any fragmentation.

Frame Relay LFI Using FRF.12

Cisco IOS Software supports two flavors of Frame Relay LFI. The more popular option, FRF.12, is based on Frame Relay Forum Implementation Agreement 12, with the other option, FRF.11-C, being based on Frame Relay Forum Implementation Agreement 11, Annex C. FRF.12 applies to data VCs, and FRF.11-C applies to voice VCs. Because most Frame Relay VCs are data VCs, and because most service providers do not offer FRF.11 (VoFR) VCs, the exam focuses on FRF.12.

> **NOTE**   Another LFI feature, called *multilink PPP over Frame Relay and ATM*, also provides an option for LFI. This option is suited for environments that use Frame Relay/ATM internetworking and desire to run delay-sensitive applications such as VoIP on slow-speed WAN links.

FRF.12 varies greatly from MLP LFI in terms of how it works with queuing tools. To use FRF.12, IOS requires that Frame Relay Traffic Shaping (FRTS) also be used. The current QoS course does not focus on FRTS configuration as an end to itself. However, having read about and understood how CB Shaping works, you can learn about FRF.12 with only a little knowledge of FRTS.

> **NOTE**   Appendix B, "Additional QoS Reference Materials" (found on the book's accompanying CD-ROM) contains FRTS concepts and configuration details, based on the first edition of this book.

Like CB Shaping, FRTS delays packets so that the Shaping rate is not exceeded. You configure the shaping rate, and a Bc value, and optionally a Be value if you want an excess burst capability. Like CB Shaping, FRTS delays the packets by putting them into a single FIFO queue, called a Shaping queue (assuming that no queuing tool has been configured). However, like CB Shaping, FRTS can be configured to use a Queuing tool. For example, Figure 8-8 shows FRTS configured to use LLQ to create four class queues for Shaping.

FRTS can apply queuing tools to shaping queues associated with each VC, as shown in the figure. Figure 8-8 shows a single LLQ, with three other CBWFQ class queues. As FRTS decides to allow additional packets to leave those queues each time interval, the packets are placed into a FIFO interface queue, because FRTS typically uses a single FIFO queue on the physical interface. IOS then moves the packets from the interface FIFO software queue into the TX Queue, and then out the interface.

When you add FRF.12 to FRTS, however, two interface FIFO output queues are created rather than the single FIFO queue. Figure 8-9 shows the two FIFO interface output queues, called *Dual FIFO* queues, with FTRS and FRF.12.

Figure 8-8 *Interface Single FIFO Queues with FRTS and FRF.12*

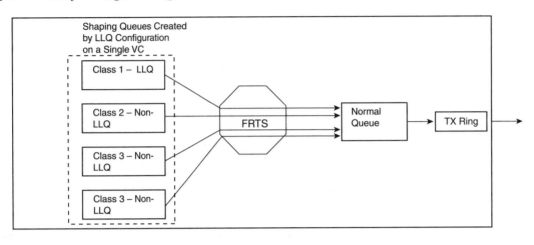

Figure 8-9 *Interface Dual FIFO Queues with FRTS and FRF.12*

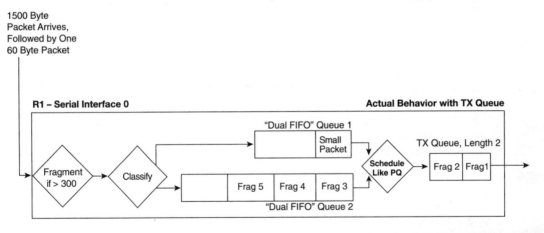

Figure 8-9 focuses on the interface software queues, ignoring the shaping queues. Just like in the figure that depicted MLP LFI, a 1500-byte packet arrives, followed by a 60-byte packet. The large packet is fragmented into five 300-byte packets, with the first two being placed into the TX Queue, and the last three ending up in one of the interface output queues. The small packet arrives next, and it is not fragmented, because it is less than 300 bytes in length. It is placed into the other Dual FIFO queue.

This two-queue Dual FIFO structure acts like the queuing tools described in Chapter 5 in many ways. It has classification logic that places packets into one queue or the other (more on that in a few paragraphs). It has a number of queues (always two), and it has particular behavior inside each queue (FIFO). It also performs scheduling between the two queues using an algorithm such as Priority Queuing's (PQ) scheduling algorithm. Therefore, to understand what happens, you need to take a closer look at the classification logic and the scheduling algorithm applied to the Dual FIFO queues.

First, when a packet passes through the fragmentation step in Figure 8-9, if there are no packets in either Dual FIFO queue, and there is room in the TX Queue/TX Ring, the fragments get placed into the TX Ring/TX Queue until it is full. That's why in Figure 8-9 the first two fragments of the large packet got placed into the 2-entry TX Queue. Then, when the TX Queue is full, packets are placed into one of the two Dual FIFO queues.

IOS schedules packets from the Dual FIFO interface queues into the interface TX Queue in a PQ-like fashion. The logic treats one of the two Dual FIFO queues like the PQ High queue, and the other like the PQ Normal queue. The scheduler always takes packets from the High queue first if one is available; otherwise, the scheduler takes a packet from the Normal queue. Just like PQ, the scheduler always checks the High queue for a packet before checking the Normal queue. Although IOS does not give a lot of information about the two Dual FIFO queues in **show** commands, one command (**show queueing interface**) does list counters for the High and Normal queues. (This book refers to these two queues as the High and Normal Dual FIFO queues, even though most other IOS documents and courses do not even name the two queues.)

Putting the classification logic together with the queue service logic makes one neat package. LFI wants to interleave the small packets between fragments of the larger packets. By classifying the unfragmented packets into the Dual-FIFO High queue, and the fragments into the Dual-FIFO Normal queue, the PQ-like queue service algorithm interleaves unfragmented packets in front of fragmented packets.

FRF.12 classifies packets into one of the Dual FIFO interface output queues based on the queuing configuration for the shaping queues on each VC. FRTS allows a large variety of queuing tools to be configured for the shaping queues. Two of these queuing tools, if enabled on the shaping Queue of a VC, cause packets to be placed in the High Dual FIFO queue on the physical interface. Figure 8-10 outlines the main concept.

Figure 8-10 *Classification Between FRTS LLQ Shaping Queues and Interface Dual FIFO Queues with FRF.12*

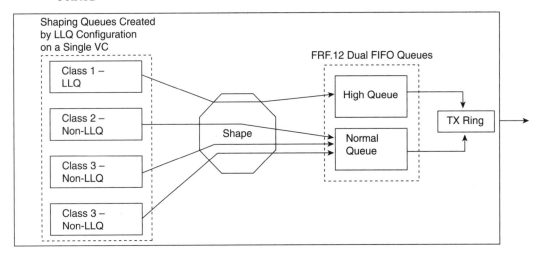

The figure depicts LLQ for the shaping queue on a single VC feeding into the interface Dual FIFO queues. The shaping logic remains unchanged, as does the LLQ logic for the shaping queues — in other words, with or without FRF.12 configured, the behavior of shaping acts the same. The only difference created by adding FRF.12 to FRTS comes when FRTS must decide which of the two interface Dual FIFO software queues to place the packet into after the shaper allows it to pass. (Without FRF.12, a single FIFO interface software queue exists, in which case classification logic is not needed.)

As shown in the figure, the only way a packet makes it to the High Dual FIFO queue is to have first been in the low-latency queue. In other words, FRF.12 determines which packets are interleaved based on which packets were placed into the low-latency queue in the shaping queue.

The classification logic and the scheduling logic make perfect sense if you consider the packets that need the minimal latency. When you purposefully configure LLQ for shaping queues, the class of packets you place into the low-latency queue must be the ones for which you want to minimize latency. FRF.12 should interleave those same packets to further reduce latency; therefore, FRF.12 just places those same packets into the Dual FIFO High queue.

NOTE Because the Dual FIFO queues created by FRF.12 essentially creates a high-priority queue appropriate for VoIP traffic, when you are using FRTS, Cisco also recommends configuring LFI on links that run at speeds greater than 768 kbps. However, you should configure the fragment size to something larger than the MTU — for instance, 1500 bytes. By doing so, no packets are actually fragmented, but VoIP packets can be placed in the high-priority queue in the Dual FIFO queuing system on the physical interface.

FRTS interaction and usage of queuing tools can be difficult to understand, let along trying to keep track of all the options. Interestingly, FRTS supports one set of queuing tools without FRF.12 enabled, and a subset with FRF.12 enabled, and with yet another subset of those (LLQ and IP RTP Priority) that actually interleave the packets. Table 8-5 summarizes the queuing tools and identifies when you can use them with FRTS and FRF.12.

Table 8-5 *Queuing Tool Support with FRTS and FRF.12 (Cisco IOS Software Release 12.2 Mainline)*

Desired Features	Queuing Tools Supported on Each VC (Shaping Queues)
FRTS only	FIFO, PQ, Custom Queuing (CQ), Weighted Fair Queuing (WFQ), Class-Based Weighted Fair Queuing (CBWFQ), LLQ, IP RTP Priority
FRTS with FRF.12 enabled	WFQ, CBWFQ, LLQ, IP RTP Priority
FRTS, FRF.12, with actual interleaving of packets	LLQ, IP RTP Priority

Choosing Fragment Sizes for Frame Relay

FRF.12 uses the same basic math as does MLP LFI to determine the fragment size—max-delay * bandwidth. But what do you use for bandwidth in the formula? CIR? Do you use the shaping or policing rate? Or the access rate, which is the clock rate used on the access link? Figure 8-11 shows a typical Frame Relay network that provides a backdrop from which to discuss which values to use.

Figure 8-11 *Example Frame Relay Network Used to Explain How to Choose Fragment Sizes*

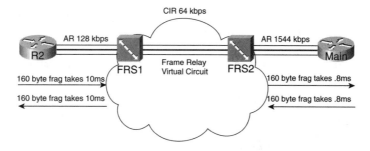

In most cases, you should choose to fragment based on the *slower access rate on either end of a VC*, which in this case is the 128-kbps access rate on R1. The reason you should use the lower of the two access rates becomes apparent only when you think of serialization delay inside the cloud, and in both directions. First, consider left-to-right flow in the network. To reduce serialization delay to 10 ms on a 128-kbps link, the fragment size should be set to 160 bytes (128,000 * .01 = 1280 bits). When R2 sends a packet, the serialization delay takes 10 ms. Moving from left to right, a full-sized fragment (160 bytes) sent from FRS1 to the Main router takes only 0.0008 seconds to serialize when passing over the T/1! Reversing the direction, a 160-byte fragment leaving router Main, going into the cloud, only takes 0.8 ms serialization delay, so you might be tempted to make the fragment size much larger for packets sent by router Main. When the packets get to FRS2, however, and need to cross the access link to R1, a small fragment size of 160 bytes gives you an advantage of low serialization delay. If you were to make the fragment size on the Main router a much larger size, the frame would experience a much larger serialization delay on the link from FRS1 to R1.

One common misconception is that fragmentation size should be based on the CIR of the VC, rather than on the access rate. Fragmentation attacks the problem of serialization delay, and serialization delay is based on how long it takes to encode the bits onto the physical interface, which in turn is determined by the physical clock rate on the interface. So, you should always *base FRF.12 fragmentation sizes on the clock rate (access rate) of the slower of the two access links*, *not* on CIR.

FRF.12 configuration does not let you set the maximum delay, as does MLP LFI. Instead, you configure the fragment size directly. When planning, you normally pick a maximum serialization delay for each link first. So before you can configure FRF.12, you need to calculate the fragmentation size. When you know the lower of the two access rates, and the maximum serialization delay desired, you can calculate the corresponding fragment size with the following formula:

Max-delay * bandwidth

For instance, to achieve 10-ms delay per fragment on a 128-kbps link, the fragment size would be:

.01 seconds * 128,000 bps, or 1280 bits (160 bytes)

Table 8-4, shown earlier in this section, lists some of the more common combinations of maximum delay and bandwidth, with the resulting fragment sizes.

MLP LFI and FRF both accomplish the same general task of reducing serialization delay for some packets. As seen in this chapter, the methods used by each differ in how each tool takes advantage of queuing tools. Table 8-6 summarizes the core functions of MLP LFI versus FRF.12, particularly how they each interact with the available queuing tools.

Table 8-6 *Comparisons Between MLP LFI and FRF.12*

Step in the Process	MLP LFI	FRF.12
Configures maximum delay, or actual fragment size	Maximum delay	Fragment size
Classification into the interface output queues	Based on the queuing tool enabled on the interface	All packets coming from LLQ or RTP Priority shaping queues placed in higher-priority queue

Table 8-6 *Comparisons Between MLP LFI and FRF.12 (Continued)*

Step in the Process	MLP LFI	FRF.12
Number of interface software queues	Based on the queuing tool enabled on the interface	2 queues, called *Dual FIFO*
How queue service algorithm causes interleaving to occur	Based on queuing tool's inherent queue service algorithm; PQ, LLQ, and RTP Priority most aggressively interleave packets	PQ-like algorithm, always servicing Dual-FIFO High queue over Normal queue

Multilink PPP Interleaving Configuration

Before you configure MLP LFI, think about why you would use MLP at all. If you have a point-to-point link, and need to perform LFI, you must migrate from your current Layer 2 protocol to MLP, to use MLP LFI. However, MLP itself has many benefits, and even a few brief thoughts about what MLP does will help you through some of the configuration tasks.

MLP enables you to have multiple parallel point-to-point links between a pair of devices, such as routers. The main motivation for MLP was to allow dial applications to continue adding additional switched WAN connections between the endpoints when more bandwidth was needed. For instance, maybe one dialed line was brought up, but when the utilization exceeded 60 percent, another line dialed, and then another, and so on.

MLP includes the inherent capability to load balance the traffic across the currently active lines, without causing reordering problems. To understand those concepts, consider Figure 8-12, with three parallel point-to-point links controlled by MLP.

Figure 8-12 *MLP Bundled with 3 Active Links — What Could Happen*

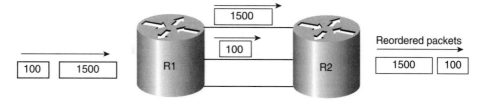

With three active links, MLP could reorder packets. If a 1500-byte packet arrives, for instance, immediately followed by a 100-byte packet, MLP might send the first packet over one link, and the next packet over the second link. Because the second packet is much smaller, its serialization delay will be much smaller. Assuming that both links speeds are equal, the 100-byte packet will arrive before the larger packet. Consequently, the 100-byte packet is forwarded first, before the 1500-byte packet. If both packets are part of the same flow, the endpoint computer may have to do more work to reorder the packets, which TCP could do if it is being used. However, some UDP-based applications could require that the out-of-order packets be re-sent, depending on the application. Over time, the three links will experience different utilization averages, depending on the random occurrence of traffic in the network.

MLP does not behave as shown in Figure 8-12. Instead, MLP, by its very nature, fragments packets. Figure 8-13 shows what really happens.

Figure 8-13 *MLP Bundle with 3 Active Links — What Does Happen*

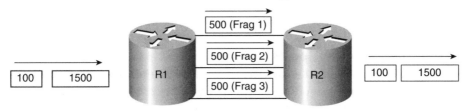

MLP always fragments PPP frames to load balance traffic equitably and to avoid out-of-order packets. Notice that the 1500-byte packet was fragmented into three 500-byte fragments, one for each link. By default, MLP fragments each packet into equal-sized fragments, one for each link. Suppose, for instance, that two links were active; the fragments would have been 750 bytes long. If four were active, each fragment would have been 375 bytes long. And yes, even the 100-byte packet would be fragmented, with one fragment being sent over each link.

The other point you should consider about basic MLP, before looking at MLP LFI configuration, is that the multiple links appear as one link from a Layer 3 perspective. In the figures, R1 and R2 each have one IP address that applies to all three links. To configure these details, most of the interface subcommands normally entered on the physical interface are configured somewhere else, and then applied to each physical interface that will comprise part of the same MLP bundle.

With those two basic MLP concepts in mind, you can now make more sense of the MLP LFI configuration. Tables 8-7 and 8-8 list the pertinent configuration and **show** commands, respectively, and are followed by some example configurations.

Table 8-7 *Configuration Command Reference for MLP Interleaving*

Command	Mode and Function
ppp multilink [bap]	Interface configuration mode; enables multilink PPP on the interface, dialer group, or virtual template
ppp multilink interleave	Interface configuration mode; enables interleaving of unfragmented frames with fragments of larger frames

Table 8-7 *Configuration Command Reference for MLP Interleaving (Continued)*

Command	Mode and Function
ppp multilink fragment delay *time*	Interface configuration mode; Enables MLP fragmentation, and defines fragment size, with formula bandwidth/time
ppp multilink fragment disable	Interface configuration mode; Disables MLP fragmentation
ppp multilink group *group-number*	Interface configuration mode; links a physical interface to a dialer group or virtual template

Table 8-8 *EXEC Command Reference for MLP Interleaving*

Command	Function
show ppp multilink	Lists information about the active links currently in the same MLP bundle
show interfaces	Lists statistics and status about each interface, including multilink virtual interfaces
show queueing [**interface** *atm-subinterface* [**vc** [[*vpi/*] *vci*]]]	Lists configuration and statistical information about the queuing tool on an interface

The first MLP LFI example shows a baseline configuration for MLP, without LFI. After this, the additional configuration commands for fragmentation, and then interleave, are added. Finally, the example ends with the addition of the **ip rtp priority** command, which enables one of the forms of queuing with a low-latency feature. (**ip rtp priority** simply puts all voice traffic in a PQ, and all other traffic is processed by the queuing tool enabled on the interface—in this case, WFQ. LLQ could have been used instead, with the same general result.) The explanation after the example explains how some traffic was interleaved (or not) at each step along the way.

The criteria for the configuration is as follows:

■ Clock rate is 128 kbps on the point-to-point link.

■ Fragment to 10-ms fragments.

■ Use RTP Priority.

In the example, Client 1 downloads two to three web pages, each of which has two frames inside the page. Each web page uses two separate TCP connections to download two separate large JPG files. Client 1 also downloads a file using FTP get. In addition, a VoIP call is placed between extensions 3002 and 1002. Figure 8-14 shows the network used for the example, and Example 8-2 shows the configuration and some sample **show** commands.

Figure 8-14 *Sample Network for MLP LFI Examples*

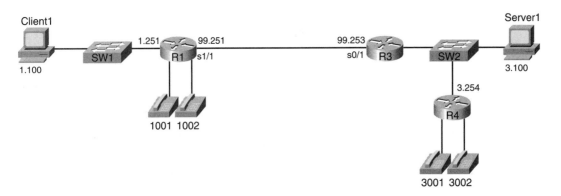

Note: All IP Addresses Begin 192.168.

Example 8-2 *MLP LFI Configuration*

```
!
! STEP 1 STEP 1 STEP 1 STEP 1 STEP 1 STEP 1 STEP 1 STEP 1 STEP 1 STEP 1 STEP 1 STEP 1
!
R3#show running-config
!
! Many lines  omitted for brevity
!
username R1 password 0 me
!
interface Multilink9
 bandwidth 128
 ip address 192.168.99.253 255.255.255.0
 no ip route-cache cef
 load-interval 30
 fair-queue
 no cdp enable
 ppp multilink
 multilink-group 9
!
!
interface Serial0/1
 bandwidth 128
 no ip address
 encapsulation ppp
 no ip mroute-cache
 load-interval 30
 clockrate 128000
 ppp multilink
```

Example 8-2   *MLP LFI Configuration (Continued)*

```
multilink-group 9
!
!
! STEP 2 STEP 2 STEP 2 STEP 2 STEP 2 STEP 2 STEP 2 STEP 2 STEP 2 STEP 2
!
! Adding Fragmentation for 10ms fragments. Added same command on R1 as well,
! No shown here for brevity.
!
R3#conf t
Enter configuration commands, one per line.  End with CNTL/Z.
R3(config)#interface multilink 9
R3(config-if)#ppp multilink fragment-delay 10
R3(config-if)#^Z

R3#show interfaces multilink 9
Multilink9 is up, line protocol is up
  Hardware is multilink group interface
  Internet address is 192.168.99.253/24
  MTU 1500 bytes, BW 128 Kbit, DLY 100000 usec,
     reliability 255/255, txload 233/255, rxload 43/255
  Encapsulation PPP, loopback not set
  Keepalive set (10 sec)
  DTR is pulsed for 2 seconds on reset
  LCP Open, multilink Open
  Open: IPCP
  Last input 00:00:02, output never, output hang never
  Last clearing of "show interface" counters 00:20:41
  Input queue: 0/75/0/0 (size/max/drops/flushes); Total output drops: 1056
  Queueing strategy: weighted fair
  Output queue: 64/1000/64/1055 (size/max total/threshold/drops)
     Conversations  5/11/32 (active/max active/max total)
     Reserved Conversations 0/0 (allocated/max allocated)
     Available Bandwidth 96 kilobits/sec
  30 second input rate 22000 bits/sec, 44 packets/sec
  30 second output rate 117000 bits/sec, 48 packets/sec
     4459 packets input, 273353 bytes, 0 no buffer
     Received 0 broadcasts, 0 runts, 0 giants, 0 throttles
     0 input errors, 0 CRC, 0 frame, 0 overrun, 0 ignored, 0 abort
     62241 packets output, 5141980 bytes, 0 underruns
     0 output errors, 0 collisions, 0 interface resets
     0 output buffer failures, 0 output buffers swapped out
     0 carrier transitions
!
! STEP 3 STEP 3 STEP 3 STEP 3 STEP 3 STEP 3 STEP 3 STEP 3 STEP 3 STEP 3
!
! Added Interleaving feature. Did same on R1, not shown here.
!
```

continues

Example 8-2 *MLP LFI Configuration (Continued)*

```
R3#conf t
Enter configuration commands, one per line.  End with CNTL/Z.
R3(config)#interface multilink 9
R3(config-if)#ppp multilink interleave
R3(config-if)#^Z
R3#show interfaces multilink 9
Multilink9 is up, line protocol is up
  Hardware is multilink group interface
  Internet address is 192.168.99.253/24
  MTU 1500 bytes, BW 128 Kbit, DLY 100000 usec,
     reliability 255/255, txload 227/255, rxload 29/255
  Encapsulation PPP, loopback not set
  Keepalive set (10 sec)
  DTR is pulsed for 2 seconds on reset
  LCP Open, multilink Open
  Open: IPCP
  Last input 00:00:00, output never, output hang never
  Last clearing of "show interface" counters 00:22:00
  Input queue: 0/75/0/0 (size/max/drops/flushes); Total output drops: 1406
  Queueing strategy: weighted fair
  Output queue: 27/1000/64/1405/164 (size/max total/threshold/drops/interleaves)
     Conversations  5/11/32 (active/max active/max total)
     Reserved Conversations 0/0 (allocated/max allocated)
     Available Bandwidth 96 kilobits/sec
  30 second input rate 15000 bits/sec, 30 packets/sec
  30 second output rate 114000 bits/sec, 54 packets/sec
     6386 packets input, 386857 bytes, 0 no buffer
     Received 0 broadcasts, 0 runts, 0 giants, 0 throttles
     0 input errors, 0 CRC, 0 frame, 0 overrun, 0 ignored, 0 abort
     66702 packets output, 6267446 bytes, 0 underruns
     0 output errors, 0 collisions, 0 interface resets
     0 output buffer failures, 0 output buffers swapped out
     0 carrier transitions
R3#

R3#show queue multilink 9
  Input queue: 0/75/0/0 (size/max/drops/flushes); Total output drops: 1906
  Queueing strategy: weighted fair
  Output queue: 64/1000/64/1905/16500 (size/max total/threshold/drops/interleaves)
     Conversations  5/11/32 (active/max active/max total)
     Reserved Conversations 0/0 (allocated/max allocated)
     Available Bandwidth 96 kilobits/sec

  (depth/weight/total drops/no-buffer drops/interleaves) 1/32384/4/0/982
  Conversation 4, linktype: ip, length: 74
  source: 192.168.3.100, destination: 192.168.1.100, id: 0xF513, ttl: 127,
  TOS: 0 prot: 6, source port 80, destination port 1517
```

Example 8-2   *MLP LFI Configuration (Continued)*

```
    (depth/weight/total drops/no-buffer drops/interleaves) 52/32384/1700/0/0
    Conversation 17, linktype: ip, length: 62
    source: 192.168.3.254, destination: 192.168.99.251, id: 0x08E5, ttl: 253,
    TOS: 0 prot: 17, source port 18490, destination port 17228
!
! Lines omitted for brevity
!
!
! STEP 4 STEP 4 STEP 4 STEP 4 STEP 4 STEP 4 STEP 4 STEP 4 STEP 4 STEP 4
!
! Adding RTP Priority Queuing configuration next. Did same on R1.
!
R3#conf t
Enter configuration commands, one per line.  End with CNTL/Z.
R3(config)#interface multilink 9
R3(config-if)#ip rtp priority 16384 16383 65
R3(config-if)#^Z
R3#

R3#show interfaces multilink 9
Multilink9 is up, line protocol is up
  Hardware is multilink group interface
  Internet address is 192.168.99.253/24
  MTU 1500 bytes, BW 128 Kbit, DLY 100000 usec,
     reliability 255/255, txload 231/255, rxload 41/255
  Encapsulation PPP, loopback not set
  Keepalive set (10 sec)
  DTR is pulsed for 2 seconds on reset
  LCP Open, multilink Open
  Open: IPCP
  Last input 00:00:03, output never, output hang never
  Last clearing of "show interface" counters 00:23:36
  Input queue: 0/75/0/0 (size/max/drops/flushes); Total output drops: 1784
  Queueing strategy: weighted fair
  Output queue: 17/1000/64/1783/4441 (size/max total/threshold/drops/interleaves)
     Conversations  5/11/32 (active/max active/max total)
     Reserved Conversations 0/0 (allocated/max allocated)
     Available Bandwidth 31 kilobits/sec
  30 second input rate 21000 bits/sec, 43 packets/sec
  30 second output rate 116000 bits/sec, 59 packets/sec
     10217 packets input, 618117 bytes, 0 no buffer
     Received 0 broadcasts, 0 runts, 0 giants, 0 throttles
     0 input errors, 0 CRC, 0 frame, 0 overrun, 0 ignored, 0 abort
     72195 packets output, 7661717 bytes, 0 underruns
     0 output errors, 0 collisions, 0 interface resets
     0 output buffer failures, 0 output buffers swapped out
```

continues

Example 8-2 *MLP LFI Configuration (Continued)*

```
        0 carrier transitions

R3#show queue multilink 9
  Input queue: 0/75/0/0 (size/max/drops/flushes); Total output drops: 1784
  Queueing strategy: weighted fair
  Output queue: 18/1000/64/1783/6643 (size/max total/threshold/drops/interleaves)
    Conversations  6/11/32 (active/max active/max total)
    Reserved Conversations 0/0 (allocated/max allocated)
    Available Bandwidth 31 kilobits/sec

  (depth/weight/total drops/no-buffer drops/interleaves) 1/0/0/0/0
  Conversation 40, linktype: ip, length: 62
  source: 192.168.3.254, destination: 192.168.99.251, id: 0x08E5, ttl: 253,
  TOS: 0 prot: 17, source port 18490, destination port 17228


  (depth/weight/total drops/no-buffer drops/interleaves) 1/32384/11/0/1282
  Conversation 0, linktype: ip, length: 74
  source: 192.168.3.100, destination: 192.168.1.100, id: 0xED88, ttl: 127,
  TOS: 0 prot: 6, source port 80, destination port 1513
!
! Lines omitted for brevity
!
!
! STEP 5 STEP 5 STEP 5 STEP 5 STEP 5 STEP 5 STEP 5 STEP 5 STEP 5 STEP 5
!
R3#show running-config
!
! Lines omitted for brevity



!
username R1 password 0 me
!
interface Multilink9
 bandwidth 128
 ip address 192.168.99.253 255.255.255.0
 no ip route-cache cef
 load-interval 30
 fair-queue
 no cdp enable
 ppp multilink
 ppp multilink fragment-delay 10
 ppp multilink interleave
 multilink-group 9
 ip rtp priority 16384 16383 65
!
interface Serial0/1
```

Example 8-2 *MLP LFI Configuration (Continued)*

```
bandwidth 128
no ip address
encapsulation ppp
no ip mroute-cache
load-interval 30
clockrate 128000
ppp multilink
multilink-group 9
!
! Lines omitted for brevity
!
```

Cisco IOS Software enables you to use a couple of styles of configuration to configure MLP. This example shows the use of a virtual interface called a *multilink interface*. MLP needs to make more than one physical point-to-point link behave like a single link. To make that happen, IOS uses multilink interfaces to group together commands that normally would be applied to a physical interface. Each physical interface that is part of the same multilink group takes on the shared characteristics of the multilink interface. For instance, three parallel serial links in the same multilink group share a single IP address on one end of the link.

Example 8-2 is rather long. To help you find your way, the example includes comments lines with Step 1, Step 2, and so on. The following list explains these comments:

Step 1   In the example, multilink group 9 defines the interesting parameters in this example. Under the **interface multilink 9** command, the IP address configuration (192.168.99.253), along with the **bandwidth** command, is listed. The **multilink ppp** command implies that this multilink group indeed uses multilink PPP. The **multilink group 9** command tells IOS that this interface (multilink 9) is part of multilink group 9; this same command links each physical interface to the multilink group configuration. Now the interface configuration details that will be shared by all links in the same MLP bundle have been configured.

To add R3's serial 0/1 interface to the MLP bundle, the **multilink group 9** interface subcommand is added under serial 0/1. After the equivalent configuration has been added to R1, a single leased point-to-point serial link was up between R3 and R1, and each router was able to ping the other across the link.

Step 2   The example next shows the addition of the **ppp multilink fragment-delay 10** command. Interestingly, this command does not enable fragmentation, but rather defines the maximum fragment size. Because the bandwidth was already set to 128, IOS calculates the fragment size as bandwidth * max-delay (in seconds), or 128,000 * .01, which results in a 1280 bit (160 byte) fragment size.

Before the **ppp multilink fragment-delay 10** command was added, in this example, MLP did not fragment. If the **ppp multilink fragment-delay** command had not been added, and four links were active in the MLP bundle, MLP would fragment frames into four equal-sized fragments. If three links were active, each frame would be fragmented into three equal-sized fragments, and so on. With one active link, MLP does not actually fragment the frames until the **ppp multilink fragment-delay** command is added.

After adding the **ppp multilink fragment-delay 10** command in the example, the voice-call quality did not improve. So far, the configuration asked for fragmentation, but not for interleaving. Without interleaving, the unfragmented packets still must wait on all the fragments of larger packets to be serialized. In the context of QoS, it seems rather silly not to automatically interleave the shorter, unfragmented frames. Remember, however, that MLP fragments frames to load balance across multiple links without running into the problems relating to out-of-order packets.

Step 3   To gain the QoS advantage of reducing serialization delay by interleaving packets, the **ppp multilink interleave** command is added to the configuration next. The **show interfaces** command that follows lists a (highlighted) line that now shows a counter for interleaved packets, with the counter indeed showing that some packets have been interleaved.

Now the example has added all the requirements for MLP LFI, and all seems well — but it is not! The voice quality is still barely tolerable, with long delay and many breaks in the speech. The voice quality still suffers because of the queuing tool, WFQ. Notice that the next command in the example, **show queue multilink 9**, lists a voice flow with some statistics highlighted for the voice flow. The command lists drops for the highlighted voice flow, which is making a large impact of voice quality. Although the voice packets that get serviced do get interleaved, causing the interleave counter in the **show interfaces** command to increment, the quality still suffers because of the queuing delay and drops.

Step 4   The best ways to prevent the drops is to enable Low Latency Queuing (LLQ) for the voice traffic. In this case, the configuration shows an older Queuing tool, IP RTP priority, which is enabled with the **ip rtp priority 65** command. (However, LLQ is still recommended today for voice traffic.) After adding the **ip rtp priority** command, the **show interfaces** command still shows interleaves, which is good, but the **show queue** command does not show any drops for the voice flow. In fact, the voice-call quality improved significantly to the point that all New Jersey housewives would give the call a Mean Opinion Score of 5!

Step 5   The final configuration on R3 is listed at the end of the example for completeness.

Frame Relay Fragmentation Configuration

The configuration of FRF.12 requires very little effort in itself. However, FRF.12 requires FRTS, and for the FRF.12 interleaving function to actually work, you need to enable IP RTP Priority or LLQ for the shaping queues on one or more VCs. Therefore, although the FRF.12 configuration details are brief, the related tools make the configuration a little longer.

The **show** commands related to FRF.12 give a fairly detailed view into what is actually happening with fragmentation and are covered as part of a couple of examples. Tables 8-9 and 8-10 list the configuration and **show** commands, respectively, and are followed by two FRF.12 examples.

Table 8-9 *Command Reference for Frame Relay Fragmentation*

Command	Mode and Function
frame-relay traffic-shaping	Interface subcommand; enables FRTS on the interface
class *name*	Interface DLCI subcommand; enables a specific FRTS map class for the DLCI
frame-relay class *name*	Interface or subinterface command; enables a specific FRTS map class for the interface or subinterface
map-class frame-relay *map-class-name*	Global configuration mode; Names a map class, and places user in map-class configuration mode.
frame-relay fragment *fragment_size*	Map-class configuration mode; enables FRF.12 for VCs using this class

Table 8-10 *EXEC Command Reference for Frame Relay Fragmentation*

Command	Function
show frame-relay fragment [**interface** *interface*] [*dlci*]	Shows fragmentation statistics
show frame-relay pvc [*interface-type interface-number*] [*dlci*]	Shows statistics about overall performance of a VC
show queueing [**interface** *atm-subinterface* [**vc** [[*vpi/*] *vci*]]]	Lists configuration and statistical information about the queuing tool on an interface

The criteria for the configuration is as follows:

- Clock rate is 128 kbps on the access links on each end of the VC between R3 and R1.

- Fragment to 10-ms fragments.

- Shape all traffic at a 64-kbps rate.

- Configure Tc for 10ms.

- Do not use a Be.

- Enable the configuration on the subinterface.

- Use WFQ for the Shaping Queues.

In the example, Client 1 downloads two to three web pages, each of which has two frames inside the page. Each web page uses two separate TCP connections to download two separate large JPG files. Client 1 also downloads a file using FTP get. In addition, a VoIP call is placed between extensions 3002 and 1002. Figure 8-15 shows the network used for the example, and Example 8-3 shows the configuration and some sample **show** commands.

Figure 8-15   *Sample Network for FRF.12 Configuration*

Note: All IP Addresses Begin 192.168.

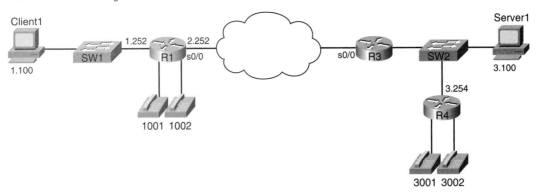

Example 8-3   *FRF.12 Configuration Sample (Continued)*

```
R3#show running-config
!
! Many lines  omitted for brevity
!
interface Serial0/0
```

Example 8-3 *FRF.12 Configuration Sample (Continued)*

```
 description connected to FRS port S0. Single PVC to R1.
 no ip address
 encapsulation frame-relay
 load-interval 30
 clockrate 128000
!
! REFERENCE POINT 4
!
 bandwidth 128
!
! REFERENCE POINT 1
!
 frame-relay traffic-shaping
!
interface Serial0/0.1 point-to-point
 description point-point subint global DLCI 103, connected via PVC to DLCI 101 (
 ip address 192.168.2.253 255.255.255.0
!
! REFERENCE POINT 2
!
 frame-relay class shape-all-64
 frame-relay interface-dlci 101 IETF
!
interface Serial0/0.2 point-to-point
 description point-to-point subint connected to DLCI 102 (R2)
 ip address 192.168.23.253 255.255.255.0
 frame-relay interface-dlci 102
!
!
! Many lines omitted for brevity
!
!
! REFERENCE POINT 3
!
map-class frame-relay shape-all-64
 frame-relay traffic-rate 64000 640
 no frame-relay adaptive-shaping
 frame-relay fair-queue
 frame-relay fragment 160
!
!
! REFERENCE POINT 5
!

R3#show frame-relay fragment interface s 0/0.1 101

fragment size 160                       fragment type end-to-end
```

continues

Example 8-3 *FRF.12 Configuration Sample (Continued)*

```
in fragmented pkts 52               out fragmented pkts 9367
in fragmented bytes 5268            out fragmented bytes 1511866
 in un-fragmented pkts 5552          out un-fragmented pkts 6320
 in un-fragmented bytes 341743       out un-fragmented bytes 405268
 in assembled pkts 5577              out pre-fragmented pkts 7387
 in assembled bytes 346749           out pre-fragmented bytes 1862784
 in dropped reassembling pkts 0      out dropped fragmenting pkts 0
 in timeouts 0
 in out-of-sequence fragments 0
 in fragments with unexpected B bit set 0
 in fragments with skipped sequence number 0
 out interleaved packets 0
!
! REFERENCE POINT 6
!
R3#show frame-relay fragment
interface        dlci  frag-type    frag-size  in-frag   out-frag  dropped-fr
ag
Serial0/0.1      101   end-to-end   160        54        9700      0


!
! REFERENCE POINT 7
!
R3#show frame-relay pvc

PVC Statistics for interface Serial0/0 (Frame Relay DTE)


            Active    Inactive    Deleted    Static
 Local        2          0           0          0
 Switched     0          0           0          0
 Unused       0          0           0          0


DLCI = 101, DLCI USAGE = LOCAL, PVC STATUS = ACTIVE, INTERFACE = Serial0/0.1

 input pkts 6094       output pkts 7926       in bytes 379217
 out bytes 1998660     dropped pkts 0         in FECN pkts 0
 in BECN pkts 0        out FECN pkts 0        out BECN pkts 0
 in DE pkts 0          out DE pkts 0
 out bcast pkts 31     out bcast bytes 2416
 pvc create time 00:25:19, last time pvc status changed 00:15:50
!
! REFERENCE POINT 8
!
R3#show interface s 0/0
Serial0/0 is up, line protocol is up
  Hardware is PowerQUICC Serial
  Description: connected to FRS port S0. Single PVC to R1.
```

Example 8-3 *FRF.12 Configuration Sample (Continued)*

```
    MTU 1500 bytes, BW 1544 Kbit, DLY 20000 usec,
       reliability 255/255, txload 20/255, rxload 4/255
    Encapsulation FRAME-RELAY, loopback not set
    Keepalive set (10 sec)
    LMI enq sent  14, LMI stat recvd 14, LMI upd recvd 0, DTE LMI up
    LMI enq recvd 0, LMI stat sent  0, LMI upd sent  0
    LMI DLCI 1023  LMI type is CISCO  frame relay DTE
    Broadcast queue 0/64, broadcasts sent/dropped 65/0, interface broadcasts 61
    Last input 00:00:03, output 00:00:00, output hang never
    Last clearing of "show interface" counters 00:02:20
    Queueing strategy: dual fifo
    Output queue: high size/max/dropped 0/256/0
    Output queue 77/128, 176 drops; input queue 0/75, 0 drops
    30 second input rate 26000 bits/sec, 51 packets/sec
    30 second output rate 122000 bits/sec, 126 packets/sec
       6599 packets input, 409250 bytes, 0 no buffer
       Received 0 broadcasts, 0 runts, 0 giants, 0 throttles
       0 input errors, 0 CRC, 0 frame, 0 overrun, 0 ignored, 0 abort
       17824 packets output, 2169926 bytes, 0 underruns
       0 output errors, 0 collisions, 0 interface resets
       0 output buffer failures, 0 output buffers swapped out
       0 carrier transitions
       DCD=up  DSR=up  DTR=up  RTS=up  CTS=up


!
! REFERENCE POINT 9
!
R3#show queueing interface s 0/0
Interface Serial0/1 queueing strategy: priority

Output queue utilization (queue/count)
       high/0 medium/0 normal/16513 low/0
!
! Many lines  omitted for brevity
!
```

Because this example is so long, and because FRTS is not covered in the main part of this book in this edition, the explanation that follows can be rather long. To help you correlate the upcoming explanations with the text in the example, the example contains reference numbers, which I'll refer to inside the explanations.

First, a brief look at FRTS configuration is in order. (If you want more background, take a few minutes and look over the FRTS section in Appendix B.) At REFERENCE POINT 1, the **frame-relay traffic-shaping** command sits under physical interface s0/0. This command enables FRTS on every VC on the interface.

However, the details of the FRTS configuration—the shaping rate, the Bc, and so on—are defined at REFERENCE POINT 3. Notice the **map-class frame-relay shape-all-64** command, which is followed by several subcommands. FRTS uses the **map-class** command to provide a configuration area where FRTS parameters can be configured. Those configuration parameters can be applied to one or more Frame Relay VCs using the **frame-relay class shape-all-64** interface subcommand, shown at REFERENCE POINT 2.

In short, the **frame-relay traffic-shaping** command enables FRTS on the interface, the **frame-relay class** command points to a set of configuration parameters, and the **map-class frame-relay** command is the configuration area where the FRTS parameters are configured.

Take a look at the map class created at REFERENCE POINT 3 in the configuration. FRF is configured with the **frame-relay fragment** command inside a **map-class** command. In this case, the fragment size was set to 160 bytes, which at a bandwidth of 128 kbps implies 10 ms of serialization delay for the longest frame. (The bandwidth was set under the interface—look for REFERENCE POINT 4, which is above REFERENCE POINT 1, to find it.) So the configuration calls for a fragment size that makes each fragment require 10 ms of serialization delay.

Now on to the **show** commands. The next command in the example (REFERENCE POINT 5), **show frame-relay fragment int s 0/0.1 101,** lists most of the detailed statistics about FRF behavior. The **show** command output lists counters for input and output packets and bytes as you might expect. In the example, 405,268 bytes have been sent in unfragmented frames, and 1,511,866 bytes in the fragmented frames, for a total of 1,917,134 bytes. It also lists a measurement of the number of output bytes that would have been sent had fragmentation not been used, as shown in the counters labeled "pre-fragmented." The number of prefragmented bytes, listed as 1,862,784 in the command output, implies that R3 sent about 55,000 more bytes than it otherwise would have had to send had fragmentation not been used. This result is due to the added Frame Relay header and trailer overhead added to each fragment.

The shorter version of the same command, **show frame-relay fragment** (REFERENCE POINT 6), lists the basic configuration settings and just the counter of input and output fragmented packets.

The **show frame-relay pvc** command (REFERENCE POINT 7) lists statistics for each VC, but the counters represent values before fragmentation occurs. To see how the counters in this command and the **show frame-relay fragment** command compare, examine the highlighted value for packets sent, and the value of prefragmented output packets in the **show frame-relay fragment** command. The **show frame-relay pvc** command lists 7926 packets sent. The **show frame-relay fragment** command lists 7387 prefragmented packets sent, which is only a few less than what was seen in the **show frame-relay pvc** command that was typed just a few seconds later. Therefore, the **show frame-relay pvc** command counters are based on the packets before fragmentation.

Next, at REFERENCE POINT 8, the **show interfaces serial 0/0** command lists a tidbit of insight into FRF operation. The highlighted portion of the command output lists the queuing method as Dual FIFO. As explained earlier, FRF causes two physical interface software queues to be used, as shown previously in Figure 8-9. The High queue gets PQ-like treatment, which is how FRF interleaves frames between the fragments in the other FRF output queue.

The final command in the example actually drives home two essential points (REFERENCE POINT 9). The **show queueing interface serial 0/0** command lists information about queuing on interface serial 0/0, just as was seen many times in Chapter 5. In this case, it describes the queuing on the physical interface, which we call Dual FIFO. Notice, however, that the command lists the queuing method as "priority," and it lists counters for four queues, named High, Medium, Normal, and Low. So although the queuing method is called Dual FIFO, it behaves like PQ, with only two queues in use.

You might have noticed that the only queue with nonzero counters in the **show queueing** command is the Normal queue. With FRF.12, the only way to get a packet into the High Dual-FIFO queue is to use IP RTP Priority or LLQ on an FRTS shaping queue. In Example 8-3, WFQ is used on the shaping queues (WFQ is enabled for FRTS with the **map-class** subcommand **frame-relay fair-queue**, near REFERENCE POINT 3 in the example.) Because WFQ does not have a PQ-like feature, none of the packets were interleaved into the Dual-FIFO High queue. In short, while the one important FRF.12 configuration command was used (**frame-relay fragment**), without a queuing tool to schedule packets into the Dual-FIFO high queue, it's a waste of time, and actually causes unnecessary overhead.

To cause interleaving by enabling LLQ in this example, the map class would need to have a command like **service-policy output do-llq**, instead of **frame-relay fair-queue**. A **policy-map do-llq** would be needed, with configuration for LLQ inside it. By enabling LLQ in that map class, IOS would interleave packets exiting the LLQ into the Dual-FIFO high queue.

The next example uses LLQ to interleave the packets. Networks that need FRF.12 most often are those supporting voice traffic. These same networks need to use LLQ in the shaping queues to help reduce delay and jitter, and use FRF to reduce serialization delay. Shaping should also be tuned with a low Tc value, to reduce the delay waiting for the next shaping interval. The next example uses a class map called shape-all-96-shortTC, which includes FRF.12, LLQ, with shaping using a 10-ms Tc.

This next example also oversubscribes the access link from R3 to the FR cloud. When supporting voice, Cisco recommends to not oversubscribe an access link. However, many data-oriented Frame Relay designs purposefully oversubscribe the access links. Therefore, when the time comes to add VoIP traffic, increasing the CIRs on all the VCs may not be financially possible. This example uses two VCs, with each shaped at 96 kbps, with a 128-kbps access rate. Figure 8-16 outlines the network.

Figure 8-16 *Frame Relay Network with the R3 Access Link Oversubscribed*

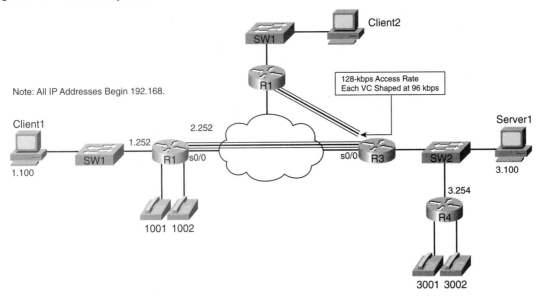

The criteria for the example is as follows:

■ Clock rate is 128 kbps on all access links.

■ Fragment to 10-ms fragments.

■ Shape all VCs at a 96-kbps rate.

■ Set Tc to 10 ms.

■ Do not use a Be.

■ Configure LLQ, with VoIP in the low-latency queue, and all other traffic in another queue.

In the example, Client 1 and Client 2 each download one web page, which has two frames inside the page. Each page download uses two separate TCP connections to download two separate large JPG files. Both PCs also download a file using FTP get. In addition, a VoIP call is placed between extensions 3002 and 1002. Figure 8-16 depicts the network used in the example. Example 8-4 shows the configuration and some sample **show** commands.

Example 8-4 *Oversubscribed Access Link, with FRF.12, LLQ, and Tc = 10 ms*

```
R3#show running-config
!
! Portions omitted for brevity
!
```

Example 8-4 *Oversubscribed Access Link, with FRF.12, LLQ, and Tc = 10 ms (Continued)*

```
class-map match-all voip-rtp
  match ip rtp 16384 16383
!
!
policy-map voip-and-allelse
  class voip-rtp
    priority 30
  class class-default
   fair-queue
!
interface Serial0/0
 description connected to FRS port S0. Single PVC to R1.
 no ip address
 encapsulation frame-relay
 load-interval 30
 clockrate 128000
 bandwidth 128
 frame-relay traffic-shaping
!
interface Serial0/0.1 point-to-point
 description point-point subint global DLCI 103, connected via PVC to DLCI 101 (
 ip address 192.168.2.253 255.255.255.0
 frame-relay class shape-all-96-shortTC
 frame-relay interface-dlci 101 IETF
!
interface Serial0/0.2 point-to-point
 description point-to-point subint connected to DLCI 102 (R2)
 ip address 192.168.23.253 255.255.255.0
 frame-relay class shape-all-96-shortTC
 frame-relay interface-dlci 102
!
map-class frame-relay shape-all-96-shortTC
 no frame-relay adaptive-shaping
 frame-relay cir 96000
 frame-relay bc 960
 service-policy output voip-and-allelse
 frame-relay fragment 160
!

R3#show traffic-shape serial 0/0.1

Interface   Se0/0.1
        Access Target   Byte   Sustain   Excess    Interval  Increment Adapt
VC      List   Rate     Limit  bits/int  bits/int  (ms)      (bytes)   Active
101            96000    120    960       0         10        120       -

R3#show traffic-shape serial 0/0.2
```

continues

Example 8-4 *Oversubscribed Access Link, with FRF.12, LLQ, and Tc = 10 ms (Continued)*

```
Interface    Se0/0.2
         Access Target   Byte   Sustain  Excess   Interval Increment Adapt
VC       List   Rate     Limit  bits/int bits/int (ms)     (bytes)   Active
102             96000    120    960      0        10       120       -

R3#show frame-relay fragment interface serial 0/0.1 101

fragment size 160                   fragment type end-to-end
in fragmented pkts 14               out fragmented pkts 843
in fragmented bytes 1386            out fragmented bytes 135638
in un-fragmented pkts 596           out un-fragmented pkts 1607
in un-fragmented bytes 35967        out un-fragmented bytes 103064
in assembled pkts 603               out pre-fragmented pkts 1706
in assembled bytes 37283            out pre-fragmented bytes 234764
in dropped reassembling pkts 0      out dropped fragmenting pkts 0
in timeouts 0
in out-of-sequence fragments 0
in fragments with unexpected B bit set 0
in fragments with skipped sequence number 0
out interleaved packets 662

R3#show frame-relay fragment interface serial 0/0.2 102
fragment size 160                   fragment type end-to-end
in fragmented pkts 0                out fragmented pkts 1541
in fragmented bytes 0               out fragmented bytes 235482
in un-fragmented pkts 285           out un-fragmented pkts 27
in un-fragmented bytes 12764        out un-fragmented bytes 1555
in assembled pkts 285              out pre-fragmented pkts 296
in assembled bytes 12764           out pre-fragmented bytes 227911
in dropped reassembling pkts 0      out dropped fragmenting pkts 0
in timeouts 0
in out-of-sequence fragments 0
in fragments with unexpected B bit set 0
in fragments with skipped sequence number 0
out interleaved packets 0

R3#show policy-map interface serial 0/0.2
 Serial0/0.2: DLCI 102 -

  Service-policy output: voip-and-allelse

    Class-map: voip-rtp (match-all)
      0 packets, 0 bytes
      30 second offered rate 0 bps, drop rate 0 bps
      Match: ip rtp 16384 16383
      Weighted Fair Queueing
```

Example 8-4   *Oversubscribed Access Link, with FRF.12, LLQ, and Tc = 10 ms (Continued)*

```
              Strict Priority
              Output Queue: Conversation 24
              Bandwidth 30 (kbps) Burst 750 (Bytes)
              (pkts matched/bytes matched) 0/0
              (total drops/bytes drops) 0/0

        Class-map: class-default (match-any)
           1440 packets, 1275806 bytes
           30 second offered rate 55000 bps, drop rate 0 bps
           Match: any

R3#show queueing interface serial 0/0
Interface Serial0/0 queueing strategy: priority

Output queue utilization (queue/count)
        high/9514 medium/0 normal/34038 low/0
```

The FRF.12 configuration portion of the example is comprised again of a single command, **frame-relay fragment 160**, configured inside **map-class frame-relay shape-all-96-shortTC**. The rest of the configuration meets the other requirements stated before the example. The map class includes a setting of CIR to 96,000 bps, and a Bc of 960 bits, yielding a Tc value of 960/96,000, or 10 ms. The **policy-map voip-and-allelse** command defines LLQ for VoIP, with all other traffic being placed in the class-default queue. The **service-policy output voip-and-allelse** command under **class-map frame-relay shape-all-96-shortTC** enables LLQ for all VCs that use the class. FRTS is of course enabled on the physical interface, with the **frame-relay class shape-all-96-shortTC** subinterface command causing each of the two VCs to use the FRTS parameters in the map class, rather than the FRTS defaults.

Immediately following the configuration in the example, two **show frame-relay traffic-shaping** commands verify the settings made in the configuration. Both show a calculated Tc value of 10 ms, and a Bc of 960.

Next comes a pair of **show frame-relay fragment interface** commands, one for subinterface s 0/0.1, and one for serial interface 0/0.2. On serial 0/0.1, the last line of output points out that interleaves did occur. For interleaves to occur, at least a small amount of congestion must occur on the physical interface. With two VCs shaped at 96 kbps, and a 128-kbps access link, and plenty of generated traffic, some congestion did occur. Notice however that serial 0/0.2 does not show any interleaved packets. All the traffic generated going from R3 to R2 was FTP and HTTP traffic, neither of which gets classified into the low-latency queue. In the **show policy-map interface serial 0/0.2** command that ends the example, for instance, notice that the counters show no packets have been in the low-latency queue. This example shows a perfect case where you have a VC (R3 to R2) that does not really need FRF for itself; FRF should be enabled, however, so that the small packets from other VCs can be interleaved.

The **show queueing interface serial 0/0** command shows incrementing counters for both the High queue and the Normal queue. Because one voice call is using the VC from R3 to R1, the voice packets get placed into the R3-to-R1 VC's low-latency queue, and then placed into the Dual FIFO High queue. (Interestingly, I did a few repetitive **show queueing** commands, once every 5 seconds, and saw the High queue counter increment about 250 packets per 5-second interval. With 20 ms of payload, each G.729 call sends 50 packets per second, so the counters reflected the fact that the voice packets from the low-latency queue were being placed into the Dual FIFO High queue.)

MLP LFI and FRF.12 Configuration: The Short Version

This last large section of this chapter, covering the configuration of MLP LFI and FRF.12, is relatively long, with some long configuration examples, and many configuration commands. However, if you boil away all the related discussion and examples, there are only a few configuration and **show** commands used specifically for MLP LFI and FRF.12. The rest of the commands relate to configuring the related features, namely MLP and FRTS.

To help you focus on the commands used specifically for LFI, Table 8-11 summarizes the commands and related information.

Table 8-11 *MLP LFI and FRF.12 Configuration: The Essentials*

Function	MLP LFI Behavior	FRF.12 Behavior
Config command	**ppp multilink fragment-delay** *delay* **ppp multilink interleave**	**frame-relay fragment** *size*
Config mode	The config mode reached by using the **interface multilink y** command	The config mode reached by using the **map-class frame-relay** command
Other required features	MLP	FRTS
How to configure Queuing to cause Interleaving	Enable a queuing tool with PQ, like LLQ, under the multilink interface	Enable a queuing tool with PQ, like LLQ, under the **map-class frame-relay** command
Important **show** commands	**show interface multilink**	**show frame-relay fragment** **show queueing interface** *x/y*
Info in those **show** commands	Statistics on numbers of fragments and interleaves	Statistics on numbers of fragments, plus stats on Dual-FIFO queue interleaving, respectively

Foundation Summary

The "Foundation Summary" is a collection of tables and figures that provide a convenient review of many key concepts in this chapter. For those of you already comfortable with the topics in this chapter, this summary could help you recall a few details. For those of you who just read this chapter, this review should help solidify some key facts. For any of you doing your final prep before the exam, these tables and figures are a convenient way to review the day before the exam.

Figure 8-17 shows the fields compressed by payload compression, and by both types of header compression. (The abbreviation "DL" stands for data link, representing the data-link header and trailer.)

Figure 8-17   *Payload and Header Compression*

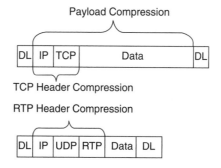

LFI tools attack the serialization delay problem by breaking the large packets into smaller pieces (fragmentation), and then sending the smaller frames ahead of most of the new fragments of the original large frame (interleaving). Figure 8-18 outlines the basic process.

Figure 8-18 *Basic Concept Behind LFI Tools*

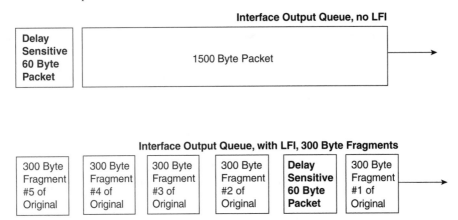

Figure 8-19 depicts how MLP LFI works with a queuing tool on an interface.

Figure 8-19 *MLP LFI Interaction with Queuing*

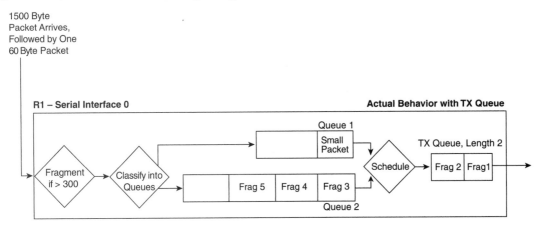

For perspective, Table 8-12 summarizes the calculated fragment sizes based on the bandwidth and maximum delay.

Table 8-12 *Fragment Sizes Based on Bandwidth and Serialization Delay*

Bandwidth/Link Speed	10-ms Delay	20-ms Delay	30-ms Delay	40-ms Delay
56 kbps	70	140	210	280
64 kbps	80	160	240	320
128 kbps	160	320	480	560
256 kbps	320	640	960	1280
512 kbps	640	1280	1920*	2560*
768 kbps	1000	2000*	3000*	4000*
1536 kbps	2000*	4000*	6000*	8000*

*Values over 1500 exceed the typical maximum transmit unit (MTU) size of an interface. Fragmentation of sizes larger than MTU does not result in any fragmentation.

Two of these queuing tools, if enabled on the shaping queue of a VC, cause packets to be placed in the High Dual FIFO queue on the physical interface. Figure 8-20 outlines the main concept.

Figure 8-20 *Classification Between FRTS LLQ Shaping Queues and Interface Dual FIFO Queues with FRF.12*

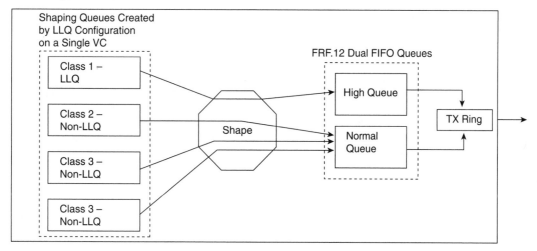

MLP, by its very nature, fragments packets. Figure 8-21 shows what really happens.

Figure 8-21 *MLP Bundle with 3 Active Links—What Does Happen*

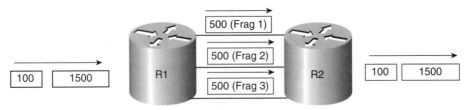

To help you focus on the commands used specifically for LFI, Table 8-13 summarizes the commands and related information.

Table 8-13 *MLP LFI and FRF.12 Configuration: The Essentials*

Function	MLP LFI Behavior	FRF.12 Behavior
Config command	**ppp multilink fragment-delay** *delay* **ppp multilink interleave**	**frame-relay fragment** *size*
Config mode	The config mode reached by using the **interface multilink y** command	The config mode reached by using the **map-class frame-relay** command
Other required features	MLP	FRTS
How to configure Queuing to cause Interleaving	Enable a queuing tool with PQ, like LLQ, under the multilink interface	Enable a queuing tool with PQ, like LLQ, under the **map-class frame-relay** command
Important **show** commands	**show interface multilink**	**show frame-relay fragment** **show queueing interface** *x/y*
Info in those **show** commands	Statistics on numbers of fragments and interleaves	Statistics on numbers of fragments, plus stats on Dual-FIFO queue interleaving, respectively

Q&A

As mentioned in the Introduction, you have two choices for review questions. The questions that follow next give you a more difficult challenge than the exam itself by using an open-ended question format. By reviewing now with this more difficult question format, you can exercise your memory better, and prove your conceptual and factual knowledge of this chapter. You can find the answers to these questions in Appendix A.

The second option for practice questions is to use the CD-ROM included with this book. It includes a testing engine and more than 200 multiple-choice questions. You should use this CD-ROM nearer to the end of your preparation, for practice with the actual exam format.

Compression Tools

1. Describe what is compressed, and what is not compressed, when using payload compression. Be as specific as possible regarding headers and data.

2. Describe what is compressed, and what is not compressed, when using TCP header compression. Be as specific as possible regarding headers and data.

3. Describe what is compressed, and what is not compressed, when using RTP header compression. Be as specific as possible regarding headers and data.

4. Suppose a packet is sent across a network with no compression. Later, a packet of the exact same size and contents crosses the network, but payload compression is used on the one serial link in the network. Describe the difference in bandwidth and delay in the network between these two packets.

5. How much bandwidth should a G.729 call require over Frame Relay, and how much should be required with cRTP?

6. When TCP header compression is used, what is the range of sizes of the part of the frame that can be compressed, and what is the range of sizes for this field of the frame after compression?

7. When RTP header compression is used, what is the range of sizes of the part of the frame that can be compressed, and what is the range of sizes for this field of the frame after compression?

The next several questions refer to the following configuration snippet.

```
!
hostname R1
!
ip cef
!
 class-map match-all class1
```

```
      match protocol telnet
 class-map match-all class2
  match protocol rtp audio
 !
 !
 policy-map test-compress
  class class2
   compression header ip
  class class1
   compression header ip tcp
   bandwidth 20
 !
 !
interface Serial0/1
 ip address 10.1.1.1 255.255.255.0
 service-policy output test-compress
 load-interval 30
 clockrate 64000
 !
```

```
 !
hostname R2
 !
ip cef
 !
 policy-map catch-all
  class class-default
   compression header ip
 !
 !
interface Serial0/1
 ip address 10.1.1.1 255.255.255.0
 service-policy output catch-all
 load-interval 30
```

8. The configuration snippet shows the configuration on two routers, R1 and R2, on the serial interfaces attached to a common serial link. Will VoIP RTP sessions be compressed, or even work at all? Explain why or why not in relation to what has been configured on the two routers.

9. The configuration snippet shows the configuration on two routers, R1 and R2, on the serial interfaces attached to a common serial link. Will telnet connections be compressed, or even work at all? Explain why or why not in relation to what has been configured on the two routers.

10. The configuration snippet shows the configuration on two routers, R1 and R2, on the serial interfaces attached to a common serial link. Will web TCP connections be compressed, or even work at all? Explain why or why not in relation to what has been configured on the two routers.

11. Without creating all the exact configuration commands, generally describe the types of changes to the configuration on R2 that would be required in order to ensure that none of the flows would fail due to one router wanting to compress, and the other one not wanting to compress.

LFI Tools

12. List the words represented by the abbreviation LFI.

13. Describe the main motivation for LFI tools in relation to the support of data, voice, and video traffic.

14. To achieve a 20-ms serialization delay on a 128-kbps link, how long can the fragments be?

15. To achieve a 10-ms serialization delay on a 64-kbps link, how long can the fragments be?

16. To achieve a 10-ms serialization delay on a 56-kbps link, how long can the fragments be?

17. To achieve a 30-ms serialization delay on a 128-kbps link, how long can the fragments be?

18. Suppose that a 1500-byte packet exits a 56-kbps serial interface, and LFI is not used. How long is the serialization delay?

19. Which queuing tools can you enable directly on a serial interface when using multilink Point-to-Point Protocol with link fragmentation and interleaving (MLP LFI), in order to interleave packets?

20. Which queuing tools can you enable with FRTS in order to actually interleave the traffic?

21. Explain the scheduling logic used by MLP LFI to determine which packets can be interleaved in front of fragments of other packets.

22. Suppose a 1500-byte packet arrives and needs to be sent over an MLP bundle that has two active links. LFI has not been configured. Which link does the packet flow across to achieve MLP load balancing?

23. What command can you use to determine the fragment size used for MLP LFI? What is the only parameter of the command?

24. What command enables the interleaving feature of MLP LFI?

25. What commands list counters for the number of interleaved packets using MLP LFI?

26. What other QoS feature for Frame Relay must you enable when you also configure FRF.12?

27. What command enables FRF and sets the fragment size?

28. What command lists counters for the numbers of packets and bytes that were fragmented and unfragmented by FRF.12?

29. What command lists counters for the numbers of packets and bytes that would have been sent if FRF.12 fragmentation had not been performed?

30. What command lists counters for the number of packets that end up in the High and Normal Dual-FIFO siftware queues, when using FRF.12?

QoS Exam Topics

This chapter covers the following exam topics specific to the QOS exam:

- Describe QoS trust boundaries and their significance in LAN-based classification and marking

- Describe and explain the different queuing capabilities available on the Cisco Catalyst 2950 Switch

CHAPTER 9

LAN QoS

"Why would I go through the hassle of configuring and managing QoS on my LAN, which is already overprovisioned? If I have to, I will just add more bandwidth!"

This is a common statement. Conventional wisdom dictates, "If you have enough bandwidth, you do not need QoS, which is used only for WAN links that do not have enough bandwidth. LANs have plenty of bandwidth, so you are safe."

Although this sounds reasonable, it is not entirely accurate. Bandwidth is only one of the factors that needs to be taken into consideration for a network that supports real-time applications.

This chapter discusses the QoS features that the Cisco Catalyst 2950 LAN switch offers and examines some recommended configurations designed to prioritized real-time applications across your LAN.

"Do I Know This Already?" Quiz

The purpose of the "Do I Know This Already?" quiz is to help you decide whether you need to read the entire chapter. If you already intend to read the entire chapter, you do not necessarily need to answer these questions now.

The 18-question quiz, derived from the major sections in the "Foundation Topics" portion of the chapter, helps you determine how to spend your limited study time.

Table 9-1 outlines the major topics discussed in this chapter and the "Do I Know This Already?" quiz questions that correspond to those topics.

Table 9-1 *"Do I Know This Already?" Foundation Topics Section-to-Question Mapping*

Foundation Topics Section Covering These Questions	Questions	Score
Classification and Marking	1–5	
Congestion Management	6–11	
Policing	12–14	
AutoQoS	15–18	
Total Score		

CAUTION The goal of self-assessment is to gauge your mastery of the topics in this chapter. If you do not know the answer to a question or are only partially sure of the answer, mark this question wrong for purposes of the self-assessment. Giving yourself credit for an answer you correctly guess skews your self-assessment results and might provide you with a false sense of security.

You can find the answers to the "Do I Know This Already?" quiz in Appendix A, "Answers to the 'Do I Know This Already?' Quizzes and Q&A Sections." The suggested choices for your next step are as follows:

- **8 or less overall score**—Read the entire chapter. This includes the "Foundation Topics," the "Foundation Summary," and the "Q&A" sections.

- **9 or 10 overall score**—If you want more review on these topics, skip to the "Foundation Summary" section and then go to the "Q&A" section. Otherwise, move to the next chapter.

Classification and Marking

1. What methods does a Catalyst 2950 currently use to classify traffic?

    a. CoS

    b. CoS and DSCP

    c. CoS, DSCP, and access lists

    d. CoS, DSCP, access lists, and NBAR

2. What QoS map needs to be modified on the Catalyst 2950 to allow the switch to match the Layer 2 and Layer 3 currently marked by Cisco IP Phones?

    a. DSCP to CoS

    b. CoS to DSCP

    c. CoS-to-IP Precedence map

   d. IP Precedence-to-CoS map

   e. DSCP-to-IP Precedence map

   f. IP Precedence-to-DSCP map

3. By default, what values does the Catalyst 2950 trust?

   a. CoS

   b. DSCP

   c. CoS and DSCP

   d. None of the above

4. Which of the following is *not* a trust option on the Catalyst 2950?

   a. Trust CoS

   b. Trust IP Precedence

   c. Trust DSCP

   d. Trust Cisco Phone

5. What does the command **mls qos trust cos pass-through dscp** do?

   a. Enables trust of CoS values only if a DSCP value is present

   b. Enables trust of CoS values and does not modify the DSCP value

   c. Enables trust of CoS only if the DSCP value matches the CoS-to-DSCP map

   d. Enables trust of DSCP only if a CoS value is present

Congestion Management

6. How many egress queues are present on each Ethernet interface of the Catalyst 2950?

   a. 1

   b. 2

   c. 4

   d. 8

7. Which three scheduling methods are supported on the Catalyst 2950?

   a. Strict priority scheduling

   b. Custom scheduling

   c. Strict priority and WRR scheduling

   d. MDRR scheduling

   e. WRR scheduling

   f. FIFO scheduling

8. Which scheduling method is configured by default on a Catalyst 2950?

   a. Strict priority scheduling

   b. Custom scheduling

   c. Strict priority and WRR scheduling

   d. MDRR scheduling

   e. WRR scheduling

   f. FIFO scheduling

9. Which scheduling method is recommended for networks that transport IP telephony traffic?

   a. Strict priority scheduling

   b. Custom scheduling

   c. Strict priority and WRR scheduling

   d. MDRR scheduling

   e. WRR scheduling

   f. FIFO scheduling

10. Which command is used to assign a CoS value of 5 to queue 4?

   a. **wrr-queue cos-map 5 4**

   b. **wrr-queue cos-assign 4 5**

   c. **wrr-queue cos-map 4 5**

   d. **wrr-queue cos-assign 5 4**

11. Which of the following commands is used to enable strict priority with WRR scheduling on the Catalyst 2950?

   a. **wrr-queue bandwidth 20 1 80 P**

   b. **wrr-queue bandwidth 0 20 1 80**

   c. **wrr-queue bandwidth 20 1 80 0**

   d. **wrr-queue bandwidth P 20 1 80**

Policing

12. What is a policer?

    a. A policer measures the data rate of arriving packets, identifies conforming and nonconforming traffic flows, and takes action on the traffic flows based upon the traffic contract.

    b. A policer measures the available bandwidth of an interface, identifies the traffic peaks, and takes action on peak traffic based upon the traffic contract.

    c. A policer measures the data rate of arriving packets, identifies known and unknown traffic flows, and takes action on the unknown traffic flows based upon the traffic contract.

    d. A policer measures the available bandwidth of an interface, identifies the known and unknown traffic flows, and takes action on the unknown traffic flows based upon the traffic contract.

13. What is out-of-profile or nonconforming traffic?

    a. Traffic routed out of the wrong interface

    b. Received traffic that exceeds the rate specified by the policer

    c. Received traffic that does not exceed the rate specified by the policer

    d. Received traffic that has not been defined by the policer

14. What can a policer do with nonconforming traffic on a Catalyst 2950?

    a. Drop it

    b. Remark the DSCP value

    c. Remark the CoS value

    d. A and B

    e. B and C

AutoQoS

15. Which of the following commands enables AutoQoS on the Catalyst 2950?

    a. **auto qos trust**

    b. **auto qos voip trust**

    c. **auto qos trust voip**

    d. **auto qos cisco-phone**

    e. **auto qos trust cisco-phone**

16. What does the command **auto qos voip trust** do?

    a. Enables trust of CoS on applied interface

    b. Enables trust of DSCP on applied interface

    c. Changes CoS-to-DSCP map

    d. Changes DSCP-to-CoS map

    e. Enables strict priority scheduling

    f. Enables strict priority queuing

    g. A, C, and F

    h. B, D, and E

    i. A, B, C, D, and F

17. What does the command **auto qos voip cisco-phone** do?

    a. Enables trust of CoS for a Cisco IP Phone

    b. Enables trust of DSCP for a Cisco IP Phone

    c. Changes CoS-to-DSCP map

    d. Changes DSCP-to-CoS map

    e. Enables strict priority scheduling

    f. Enables strict priority queuing

    g. A, C, and F

    h. B, D, and E

    i. A, B, C, D, and F

18. What command can you use to verify AutoQoS on a Catalyst 2950?

    a. **show qos auto**

    b. **show auto qos**

    c. **show auto cos**

    d. **show cos auto**

Foundation Topics

This chapter describes the concepts of LAN QoS for the Cisco Catalyst 2950 and discusses the following options available to you:

- Classification and marking

- Defining trust boundaries

- Congestion management

- Policing

- AutoQoS

The Need for QoS on the LAN

LAN quality of service (QoS) is often misunderstood and overlooked. Thanks to conventional wisdom, most network administrators think that they do not require LAN QoS. If your plans include the addition of real-time applications, such as IP telephony or video conferencing, you should include a strategy for LAN QoS while you are in the planning stages of your project. This up-front planning can result in the perceived success or failure of your project in the eyes of the end users.

Buffer Overflow (Overrun)

Suppose that is it 8:30 on a Monday morning. All your fellow employees report to work, simultaneously power on their computers, and begin their day. Their traffic flows through the access layer switches and converges on the uplink port to the distribution layer switch. If the uplink port is smaller than the input port, or the uplink port is oversubscribed, the buffer on the uplink port begins to fill, as shown in Figure 9-1.

Figure 9-1 *Buffer Overflow*

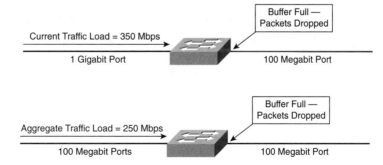

For an instant, the buffer of the uplink port can become full, potentially causing packets to drop. In a typical TCP/IP data-networking environment, this is not a concern because the packet is retransmitted. In an environment comprised of real-time applications, such as IP telephony and video conferencing, instantaneous buffer overruns (overflows) can affect the quality of the voice or video streams.

In a Cisco IP Telephony environment, a G.729 digital signal processor (DSP) can rebuild up to 30 ms of lost voice. If the Cisco standard 20 ms per packet has been deployed, a single packet can be dropped without degrading voice quality. If two consecutive voice packets are lost, resulting in 40 ms of lost voice conversation, the DSP cannot compensate, and a clip is heard in the conversation. If the Real-Time Transport Protocol (RTP) stream carries a fax or modem conversation, a single packet results in a modem retrain, whereas two consecutive packets result in a dropped connection.

You *cannot* remedy these problems by adding bandwidth. Although additional bandwidth capacity might reduce the periods during which congestion occurs, it does not prevent congestion entirely. Many data applications, such as FTP, are very bursty and greedy, consuming as much bandwidth as possible. If the total aggregate bandwidth consumes more than the uplink port's scheduler can transmit at any given moment in time, congestion can still occur. By classifying the real-time applications on your LAN and scheduling the desired level of service for each real-time application, you can avoid congestion. QoS tools are required to manage the switch's buffers to minimize loss, delay, and jitter. You must properly enable and configure the QoS parameters in order to set the desired priority by matching a traffic flow with the desired egress queue.

Bandwidth is *not* a substitute for LAN QoS! LAN QoS is a buffer management issue.

The Cisco Catalyst 2950

This chapter focuses on the capabilities and configuration needed to provide QoS on a Cisco Catalyst 2950 series switch. The previous edition of this book covered a broader range of LAN information. It is provided on the CD-ROM that is included with this book, for those of you interested in reading about the differences in switches. For those pursing the Implementing Cisco QOS exam, the Cisco Catalyst 2950 is the basis for the LAN QoS questions.

The Catalyst 2950 can be ordered with either a Standard or Enhanced Cisco IOS Software image. From a QoS perspective, the Enhanced IOS version is preferred over the Standard IOS version to deploy the LAN QoS needed to support real-time applications. Table 9-2 lists the key differences in QoS capabilities between the Enhanced and Standard OS versions available for the Catalyst 2950.

Table 9-2 *Enhanced Versus Standard IOS Images*

QoS Feature	Enhanced Image Support	Standard Image Support
Classification capability?	Layers 2 to 4	Layer 2 only
Marking capability?	Layer 2 and 3	Layer 2 only
Priority queue support?	Yes	Yes
Weighted Round Robin capability?	Yes	Yes
Policing capability?	Yes	No
AutoQoS capability?	Yes	No

Due to the additional QoS capabilities, the Enhanced IOS image should be used when deploying a network that will support real-time applications. The discussion of all QoS features in this chapter assumes that the Catalyst 2950 is running the enhanced IOS image.

> **NOTE** The Catalyst 2950 IOS version is hardware-dependent. This means that you cannot currently order a Catalyst 2950 with a standard IOS image and upgrade it to the Enhanced IOS image.

Classification and Marking

Classification describes how a particular traffic flow is identified. Classification is the method of differentiating one stream of traffic from another so that different levels of service can be applied to one traffic stream, while other traffic streams might receive only best-effort service. Classification is the first step in the process of providing QoS guarantees for real-time application traffic.

Marking describes the method used to change values in specific fields of a packet. By changing these values, marking provides a way to inform next-hop devices of a packet's classification or identification.

Classification on a Catalyst 2950 with the Enhanced IOS images can be achieved by examining the headers of an IP packet or Ethernet frame.

Layer 2 Header Classification and Marking

Classification and marking at Layer 2 takes place in the 3-bit User Priority field called class of service (CoS), which resides inside the header of an Ethernet frame. The CoS bits exist inside Ethernet frames only when 802.1Q trunking is used. The field can set eight different binary values, which can be used by the classification features of other QoS tools.

Figure 9-2 shows the general location of the CoS bits inside the 802.1Q headers.

Figure 9-2 *User Priority Fields*

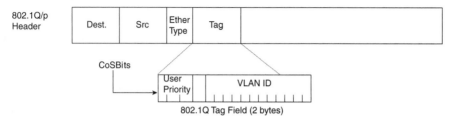

Layer 3 Header Classification and Marking

Classification and marking in the Layer 3 header takes place in the type of service (ToS) or Differentiated Services (DS) field. The Precedence and Differentiated Services Code Point (DSCP) fields can be marked with any valid binary value of either 3 or 6 bits, respectively. Figure 9-3 outlines the two fields and their positions inside an IP header.

Figure 9-3 *IP Precedence and IP DSCP Fields*

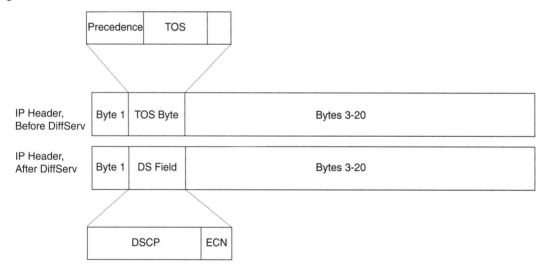

Layer 2-to-Layer 3 Mapping

The Catalyst 2950 has the capability to examine both Layer 2 CoS bits and Layer 3 DSCP bits, using either marking for classification of the received packet. Some devices connected to the switch might not have this capability. For example, a Layer 2 switch examines CoS bits, whereas a router generally is configured to examine the DSCP bits.

Consider a case in which a router, configured to examine the DSCP bits, is connected to a Layer 2 switch, configured to examine CoS bits. In this case, a packet transmitted from the router to the switch may be marked with the desired DSCP value; however, the switch cannot examine the DSCP bits and, therefore, uses the default CoS value configured for the ingress port of the switch, usually 0. This means that the switch cannot maintain the intended level of service for the received packet.

To maintain the intended level of service, the Cisco Catalyst 2950 has the capability to translate the tag from one layer to the other. If the switch receives an Ethernet frame with the CoS bit set to 5, the switch has the capability to mark the DSCP field of the received packet for downstream Layer 3 nodes to use for classification. Conversely, if the switch receives a packet with the DSCP value set to EF (Decimal 46), the switch has the capability to mark the CoS bits of the received frame for connected Layer 2 trunks to use for classification. The mechanisms used for this translation are CoS-DSCP maps and DSCP-CoS maps, respectively.

To show the current state of the CoS-to-DSCP map on the Catalyst 2950, use the **show mls qos map cos-dscp** command. Example 9-1 shows the CoS-to-DSCP map state of a Catalyst 2950 that has not been configured for QoS.

Example 9-1   *Default CoS-to-DSCP Map*

```
2950-ENH# show mls qos map cos-dscp
Cos-dscp map:
  cos:   0  1  2  3  4  5  6  7
  --------------------------------
       dscp:   0  8  16 24 32 40 48 56
```

In the default state, a CoS value of 3 is mapped to a DSCP decimal value of 24 (CS3), while a CoS value of 5 is mapped to a DSCP decimal value of 40 (CS5). Table 9-3 lists the DSCP classes associated with the DSCP decimal values.

Table 9-3   *DSCP Values*

DSCP Decimal Value	DSCP Class
0	default dscp (000000)
8	CS1(precedence 1) dscp (001000)
10	AF11 dscp (001010)
16	CS2 (precedence 2) dscp (010000)
18	AF21 dscp (010010)
24	CS3 (precedence 3) dscp (011000)

continues

Table 9-3   *DSCP Values (Continued)*

DSCP Decimal Value	DSCP Class
26	AF31 dscp (011010)
32	CS4(precedence 4) dscp (100000)
34	AF41 dscp (100010)
40	CS5(precedence 5) dscp (101000)
46	EF dscp (101110)
48	CS6(precedence 6) dscp (110000)
56	CS7(precedence 7) dscp (111000)

A Cisco IP Phone marks voice-signaling traffic with a CoS value of 3 and a DSCP class of AF31 (decimal 26). Voice-media traffic is marked with a CoS value of 5 and DSCP class of EF (decimal 46). To keep this marking consistent, CoS-to-DSCP mapping for CoS values of 3 and 5 needs to be modified. This can be accomplished by using the global **mls qos map cos-dscp** command, as demonstrated in Example 9-2.

Example 9-2   **show mls qos map cos-dscp** *After Modification*

```
2950-ENH(config)#mls qos map cos-dscp 0  8 16 26 32 46 48 56
2950-ENH#show mls qos map cos-dscp
   Cos-dscp map:
        cos:  0  1  2  3  4  5  6  7
   --------------------------------
       dscp:  0  8 16 26 32 46 48 56
```

The **show mls qos map cos-dscp** command verifies the change. Comparing the output in Example 9-2 with Example 9-1, you can see that the CoS value of 3 has been mapped to DSCP AF31 (decimal 26) instead of DSCP CS3 (decimal 24), and the CoS value of 5 has been mapped to DSCP EF (decimal 46) instead of DSCP CS5 (decimal 40). If you have used the **auto qos** option to configure the Catalyst 2950, the switch modifies the CoS-to-DSCP map automatically.

Whereas the CoS-to-DSCP mapping needs to be changed to keep the marking consistent, the DSCP-to-CoS values do not need to be changed. In the default state, the switch places a CoS value of 3 into the 802.1Q header for all packets that it receives with a DSCP value of CS3 (decimal 24) or AF31 (decimal 26) and place a CoS value of 5 in the 802.1Q header for all packets it receives with a DSCP value of CS5 (decimal 40) or EF (decimal 46). The **show mls qos map dscp-cos** command can be used to verify the DSCP-to-CoS mapping, as demonstrated in Example 9-3.

Example 9-3   show mls qos map dscp-cos

```
2950-ENH#show mls qos map dscp-cos
   Dscp-cos map:
        dscp:  0  8 10 16 18 24 26 32 34 40 46 48 56
        -------------------------------------------------
         cos:  0  1  1  2  2  3  3  4  4  5  5  6  7
```

Trust Boundaries

A *trust boundary* is the point in your network at which the received CoS or DSCP markings can be trusted. Placing this trust boundary as close as possible to the source of the traffic reduces the processing overhead of downstream devices by allowing all downstream devices to trust the marking they receive and schedule traffic in the proper queue.

By default, the Ethernet interfaces on a Catalyst 2950 are in the untrusted state. This means that any CoS value received on an interface will be overwritten with a CoS value of 0, by default. Because the CoS-to-DSCP map specifies that a CoS value of 0 maps to a DSCP value of 0, all DSCP markings are overwritten with a value of 0 as well. The **show mls qos interface** command verifies the trust state of a port. Example 9-4 shows the trust state of FastEthernet 0/1 in the default state.

Example 9-4   show mls qos interface

```
2950-ENH#show mls qos interface FastEthernet 0/1
FastEthernet0/1
trust state: not trusted
trust mode: not trusted
COS override: dis
default COS: 0
pass-through: none
trust device: none
```

To prioritize real-time traffic, you must be able to classify the real-time traffic, so you need some level of trust. Trust boundaries on a Catalyst 2950 can be based upon CoS, DSCP, or a Cisco IP Phone device. Table 9-4 lists the options for configuring the trust state.

Table 9-4 *Trust Boundaries*

Command	Function
mls qos trust [cos [pass-through]| device cisco-phone | dscp]	**mls qos trust cos [pass-through]** This command configures the interface to trust the CoS value for all Ethernet frames received. The **pass-through** option prevents the switch from overwriting the original DSCP value in the received packet with the values indicated in the CoS-to-DSPC map.
	mls qos trust device cisco-phone This command configures the interface to trust CoS values received only if a Cisco IP Phone is attached.
	mls qos trust dscp This command configures the interface to trust the DSCP value for all Ethernet packets received.
switchport priority extend [cos *value*| **trust]**	**switchport priority extend cos** *value* Used in conjunction with **mls qos trust device cisco-phone**, this command overwrites the original CoS value of all Ethernet frames received from a PC attached to an IP phone with the value specified. **switchport priority extend cos 0** is the default.
	switchport priority extend trust Used in conjunction with **mls qos trust device cisco-phone**, this command enables the switch to trust the CoS value of all Ethernet frames received from a PC attached to an IP phone.

CoS-Based Trust Boundaries

To enable the interface to trust the CoS value received for all Ethernet frames, use the **mls qos trust cos** command on the interface. Example 9-5 shows the trust state of Fast Ethernet 0/1 that has been configured to trust the received CoS value.

Example 9-5 *Trust CoS*

```
2950-ENH(config-if)#mls qos trust cos
2950-ENH#show mls qos interface FastEthernet 0/1
FastEthernet0/1
trust state: trust cos
```

Example 9-5 *Trust CoS (Continued)*

```
trust mode: trust cos
COS override: dis
default COS: 0
pass-through: none
trust device: none
```

In Example 9-5, the CoS value in the 802.1Q header is trusted and the DSCP value is marked based upon the CoS-DSCP map, discussed in the "Layer 2-to-Layer 3 Mapping" section later in this chapter. To enable trust of the received CoS values without modifying the received DSCP value, use the **mls qos trust cos pass-through dscp** command on the interface.

DSCP-Based Trust Boundaries

To trust the DSCP value received on an interface, use the **mls qos trust dscp** command. Example 9-6 shows the trust state of Fast Ethernet 0/1 that has been configured to trust the received DSCP value.

Example 9-6 *Trust DSCP*

```
2950-ENH(config-if)#mls qos trust dscp
2950-ENH#show mls qos interface FastEthernet 0/1
FastEthernet0/1
trust state: trust dscp
trust mode: trust dscp
COS override: dis
default COS: 0
pass-through: none
trust device: none
```

In Example 9-6, the switch will trust all DSCP values received on Fast Ethernet 0/1.

Cisco IP Phone–Based Trust Boundaries

So far, you have looked at trust based upon CoS and DSCP values received on an Ethernet interface. What happens when a Cisco IP Phone is connected to Fast Ethernet 0/3, but the IP phone has a PC connected to its local switch port? You need to be able to trust the IP Phone without trusting the attached PC. If you trust CoS or DSCP on Fast Ethernet 0/3, you are trusting all packets received on that interface. If the attached PC has the capability to mark its traffic, how will the switch know who to trust and who not to trust? This situation is not acceptable in an IP telephony environment. To trust the marking from a Cisco IP phone but not trust the marking from the attached PC, use the **mls**

qos trust device cisco-phone command on the Ethernet interface. Example 9-7 shows interface Fast Ethernet 0/3 configured to trust an attached Cisco IP Phone.

Example 9-7 *Trust Cisco IP Phones*

```
2950-ENH(config-if)#mls qos trust device cisco-phone
2950-ENH#show mls qos interface FastEthernet0/3
FastEthernet0/3
trust state: not trusted
trust mode: not trusted
COS override: dis
default COS: 0
pass-through: none
trust device: cisco-phone
```

Enabling trust based upon **device cisco-phone** tells the switch to detect an attached Cisco IP Phone using Cisco Discovery Protocol (CDP) version 2. If a Cisco IP Phone is not discovered on the interface, the trust state remains untrusted, and any markings received on this interface are overwritten with the default CoS value configured on the port. By default, this value is 0.

If a Cisco IP Phone is discovered on the interface, the switch will extend the trust boundary to the Cisco IP Phone. Voice-signaling packets marked with a CoS value of 3 and voice-medial traffic marked with a CoS value of 5 will be trusted by the switch. By default, the traffic from the attached PC will be overwritten with a CoS value of 0. This behavior can be modified to either substitute a different CoS value for the received traffic or trust the original values received from the PC attached to the IP phone. The interface command **switchport priority extend** [**cos** *value* | **trust**] modifies this behavior. Although it is possible to modify or trust the CoS values received from a PC attached to a Cisco IP Phone, recommended practice is to keep the default **switchport priority extend 0** on the interface.

Setting the Default CoS Value

At times, it is desirable to tag all incoming traffic with a specific CoS value. Suppose that you have an application server connected to interface Fast Ethernet 0/10 and that this interface does not have the ability to mark CoS or DSCP values. You have determined that this application server should receive better treatment than best effort but not quite as good as voice and video traffic. Assume that this class of service on your network is classified using a CoS value of 2. You need some mechanism to place this value on all untagged frames received on interface Fast Ethernet 0/10. You can use the **mls qos cos** command to accomplish this. Table 9-5 lists the options for configuring the default CoS value.

Table 9-5   *Default CoS Value*

Command	Function
mls qos cos [*value* | **override**]	**mls qos cos** *value* This command configures the interface to attach the specified CoS value to all untagged frames that are received.
	mls qos cos override This command configures the interface to overwrite the original CoS value received with the specified value.

Use the **mls qos cos 2** command to set the default CoS value of untagged Ethernet frames received on interface Fast Ethernet 0/10 to a value of 2. In Example 9-8, all untagged Ethernet frames received on interface Fast Ethernet 0/10 will be tagged with a CoS value of 2.

Example 9-8   *Default CoS Value*

```
2950-ENH(config-if)#mls qos cos 2
2950-ENH#show mls qos interface fastEthernet 0/10
02:38:06: %SYS-5-CONFIG_I: Configured from console by console
FastEthernet0/1
trust state: not trusted
trust mode: not trusted
COS override: ena
default COS: 2
pass-through: none
trust device: none
```

Suppose the application server connected to interface Fast Ethernet 0/10 does have the capability to mark CoS values; however, for whatever reason, the CoS value the switch receives is CoS 1. To maintain the same class of service, this value needs to be changed. Because the **mls qos cos 2** command marks untagged frames, it does not affect the frames received from the application server now that it is tagging frames with a CoS value of 1. Use the **mls qos cos override** command on interface Fast Ethernet 0/10 to overwrite the CoS value of 1 with the configured CoS value of 2. This command overrides any trust state of the interface, CoS or DSCP, and places the configured default CoS value of 2 in every frame.

Configuring Trust Boundaries in an IP Telephony Environment

Now that you know how to set a default CoS value or trust attached devices based upon CoS, DSCP, or device, you are ready to look at how these parameters would be configured in an IP telephony environment. Figure 9-4 illustrates a typical IP telephony network.

Figure 9-4 *Trust in an IP Telephony Network*

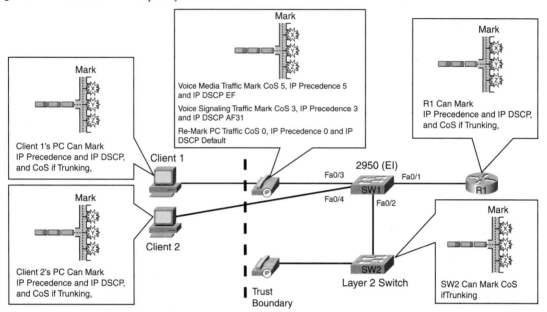

Notice the devices connected to the Catalyst 2950 (SW1). Interface Fast Ethernet 0/1 is connected to Router R1. If R1 supports 802.1Q, SW1 can be configured to trust the CoS value received on interface Fast Ethernet 0/1. However, routers typically classify and mark packets based upon Layer 3 markings and SW1 has the capability to perceive these same markings, so DSCP values can also be used to classify traffic. Because R1 is on the trusted side of the trust boundary, SW1 will be configured to trust all DSCP values received on interface Fast Ethernet 0/1.

Interface Fast Ethernet 0/2 is connected to switch SW2. Assume that an 802.1Q trunk exists between SW1 and SW2, which has the capability to classify and mark based only upon Layer 2 CoS values. Because SW2 is on the trusted side of the trust boundary, SW1 will be configured to trust the CoS values received on interface Fast Ethernet 0/2.

Interface Fast Ethernet 0/3 is connected to a Cisco IP Phone, which has a PC named Client 1 connected to its switch port. Client 1 has the capability to mark CoS and DSCP values. The Cisco IP Phone is on the trusted side of the trust boundary; however, the PC is on the untrusted side. SW1 will be configured to trust the device cisco-phone on interface Fast Ethernet 0/3. By default, all traffic from Client 1 will be reclassified with a CoS value of 0.

Interface Fast Ethernet 0/4 is connected to a PC named Client 2, which has the capability to mark CoS and DSCP values. Because Client 2 is on the untrusted side of the trust boundary, SW1 will leave interface Fast Ethernet in the default, or untrusted, state. This action causes any markings received on interface Fast Ethernet to be overwritten with a value of 0.

Example 9-9 shows the configuration necessary to implement the trust boundary.

Example 9-9 *Trust Configuration*

```
interface FastEthernet0/1
 switchport mode trunk
 mls qos trust dscp
!
interface FastEthernet0/2
 switchport mode trunk
 mls qos trust cos
!
interface FastEthernet0/3
 switchport voice vlan 100
 mls qos trust device cisco-phone
 spanning-tree portfast
!
interface FastEthernet0/4
!
```

Notice that interface Fast Ethernet 0/4 has no configuration, because the desired state for this interface is the default state of untrusted.

Using MQC for Classification and Marking

This section discusses how the Modular QoS CLI (MQC) can be used to classify and mark packets specifically on the Catalyst 2950. For more information about the classification and marking capabilities of MQC, refer to the "Cisco Modular QoS CLI" section of Chapter 3, "MQC, QPM, and AutoQoS."

MQC allows the Catalyst 2950 to identify inbound traffic and place a DSCP and CoS value on that traffic flow. Downstream nodes on the trusted side of the trust boundary can then use these marks to offer the desired level of service for that traffic. Figure 9-5 shows the addition of a video server into the IP telephony network

Figure 9-5 *MQC Classification and Marking*

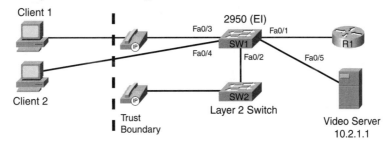

Assume that the video server does not have the capability to mark DSCP values; however, the desire is to offer priority to video traffic over best-effort traffic.

You have determined that this application should be classified with a DSPC value of AF41 (decimal 34). Although you could mark all inbound traffic with a CoS value of 4, upon consulting the CoS-to-DSCP map in Example 9-1, you see that a CoS of 4 is currently mapped to a DSCP value of CS4 (decimal 32). You need to classify this traffic with a DSCP value of AF41 (decimal 34), so you need to either change the CoS-to-DSCP map or use a method other than applying a default CoS. Assume that you chose the latter. The MQC can be used to classify the traffic from the video server and mark the DSCP value.

The first step in prioritizing the video traffic is to identify the traffic. Because the video server in this example is not capable of marking CoS or DSCP, you must use some other method of identification. The Catalyst 2950 has the capability to use Cisco traditional IP standard access lists, IP extended access lists, and MAC access lists to identify traffic. Using an IP standard access list that matches the source of the video server, traffic from the video server can be identified and placed into a class map. Assume that the IP address of the video server is 10.2.1.1. Example 9-10 shows the configuration necessary.

Example 9-10 *Identifying the Video Traffic Using an IP Access List*

```
class-map match-all video
   match access-group 1
!
access-list 1 permit 10.2.1.1
!
```

Once the video traffic has been identified, the Catalyst 2950 needs to place a mark on the traffic for the downstream node to act upon. The Catalyst 2950 offers the capability to set a DSCP value for this traffic. A policy map is used to set the traffic identified in class-map video to a DSCP value of AF41 (decimal 34). Finally, the policy map is applied to all incoming traffic on interface Fast Ethernet 0/5 using the **service-policy input** command. Example 9-11 shows the necessary configuration.

Example 9-11 *Marking the Video Traffic*

```
class-map match-all video
   match access-group 1
!
policy-map video
   class video
     set ip dscp 34
!
interface FastEthernet0/5
  service-policy input video
!
access-list 1 permit 10.2.1.1
!
```

The **service-policy input** command indicates the direction in which the policy map is applied. With this configuration, the switch places a DSCP value of AF31 in each packet received from the video server on interface Fast Ethernet 0/5. MQC on the Catalyst 2950 is used to modify traffic into the switch, so currently there is no option to apply a service policy in the outbound direction. A single **service-policy input** command can be used per Ethernet interface.

Suppose you need to identify the video traffic without specifying the IP address of the video server. You can use a MAC access list in this case. The marking process would remain the same as the IP access list example; however, the means of identifying the traffic would change. Assume that the MAC address of the video server is 0001.0000.0001. Example 9-12 shows the configuration needed to accomplish this.

Example 9-12 *Identifying the Video Traffic Using a MAC Access List*

```
class-map match-all videoMAC
  match access-group name videoMAC
!
policy-map videoMAC
  class videoMAC
    set ip dscp 34
!
mac access-list extended videoMAC
 permit host 0001.0000.0001 any
!
interface FastEthernet0/5
 service-policy input videoMAC
!
```

Because the switch has an internal DSCP-to-CoS map, the DSCP value of AF41 (decimal 34) in both examples will be automatically mapped to the CoS value of 4 by the Catalyst 2950 for use by connect 802.1Q trunks.

Verifying MQC Classification and Marking

The **show access-lists** command can be used to verify that the access lists are configured on the switch. Example 9-13 shows both the IP access list and MAC access list created in the previous section.

Example 9-13 **show access-lists**

```
2950-ENH#show access-lists
Standard IP access list 1
    permit 10.2.1.1
Extended MAC access list videoMAC
    permit host 0001.0000.0001 any
```

The **show class-map** [**class-map name**] command is used to verify that the class map has been configured with the desired match parameter. Example 9-14 shows the class maps for both the videoIP and videoMAC classes configured in the previous section.

Example 9-14   show class-map

```
2950-ENH#show class-map videoIP
 Class Map match-all videoIP (id 3)
   Match access-group  1
2950-ENH#show class-map videoMAC
 Class Map match-all videoMAC (id 5)
   Match access-group name videoMAC
```

The **show policy-map** [**policy-map name**] command is used to verify that the policy map has been configured with the desired class-map and set parameters. Example 9-15 shows the class maps for both the videoIP and videoMAC classes configured in the previous section.

Example 9-15   show policy-map

```
2950-ENH#show policy-map videoIP
 Policy Map videoIP
  class  videoIP
   set ip dscp 34
2950-ENH#show policy-map videoMAC
 Policy Map videoMAC
  class  videoMAC
   set ip dscp 34
```

Congestion Management

QoS is required only during the times of congestion on the network. If the switch has the capability to transmit packets as they are received and does not need to buffer packets, there is no need to use the configured QoS. The moment congestion occurs, the configured QoS parameters become necessary. The switch needs to prioritize the received traffic to allow some traffic to be immediately transmitted, such as real-time applications, while buffering other traffic that can be transmitted when congestion abates. This concept is called *congestion management*.

Each FastEthernet port on a Catalyst 2950 has a single ingress receive queue to service incoming traffic, and four egress transmit queues to schedule outgoing traffic. The ingress queue receives traffic as it is presented to the switch and classifies the traffic based upon the trust, marking, and MQC configuration. After the packet has been received and classified, the switch places the packet in the appropriate egress queue, based upon the CoS value of the Ethernet frame after classification has been completed. Figure 9-6 illustrates the treatment received by packets as they enter the switch.

The egress queues need to be configured to reflect the scheduling desired for each CoS value. Egress queues can be configured on a per-interface basis as strict priority scheduled, Weighted Round Robin (WRR) scheduled, or strict priority and WRR scheduled.

Figure 9-6 *Packet Flow*

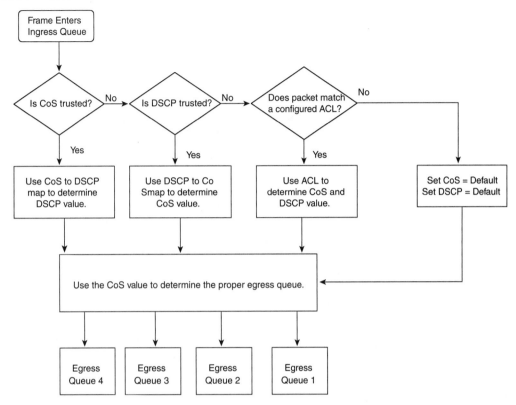

Strict Priority Scheduling

With the strict priority scheduling method, each of the four queues is weighted from 1 to 4, with 1 being the lowest priority and 4 being the highest priority. Traffic is transmitted from the highest priority queue (queue 4) until the queue is empty. After the highest priority queue has been emptied, the traffic in the next highest priority queue (queue 3) is transmitted. If a packet arrives in queue 4 while the switch is transmitting the traffic in queue 3, the switch stops transmitting the traffic waiting in queue 3 and begins to transmit the traffic in queue 4. If the switch does not receive additional traffic in queue 4, it continues to transmit the traffic in queue 3 until it is empty. At this point, if there is no traffic in either queue 4 or queue 3, the switch begins to transmit traffic from queue 2, and so on. Figure 9-7 illustrates the packet flow used by strict priority scheduling.

Figure 9-7 *Strict Priority Scheduling Flow*

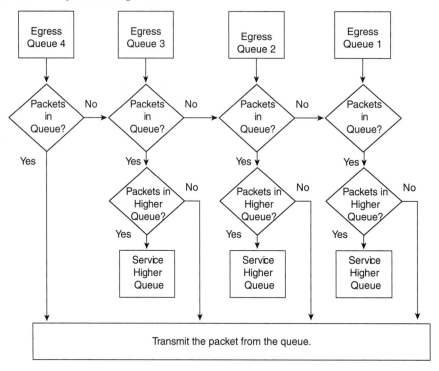

In strict priority scheduling, entrance into a queue is based upon the CoS marking of the packet after the switch has classified the traffic and performed the configured level of trust on the interface. The global **wrr-queue cos-map** [*queue id*] [*cos values*] command matches a specified priority queue with the desired CoS value.

Assume that you have IP telephony, video, and data applications on your network. Classification has already been configured and the desired CoS value is associated with the identified traffic. You now need to prioritize the applications at the egress queue in the following order, with the top application receiving the highest priority:

- IP telephony media streams: CoS 5

- Video and IP telephony signaling traffic: CoS 4 and CoS 3 respectively

- Premium data applications: CoS 2

- Best effort traffic: CoS 0 and CoS 1

Assigning traffic with a CoS value of 5 to queue 4 ensures that the IP telephony traffic is always serviced first. Assigning traffic with a CoS value of 4 or a CoS value of 3 to queue 3 ensures that video and IP telephony signaling are sent if there is currently no IP telephony media traffic in queue 4. And so on. Example 9-16 shows the configuration needed to prioritize traffic at the egress port in the specified order.

Example 9-16 *Strict Priority Scheduling*

```
2950-ENH(config)#wrr-queue cos-map 1 0 1
2950-ENH(config)#wrr-queue cos-map 2 2
2950-ENH(config)#wrr-queue cos-map 3 3 4 6 7
2950-ENH(config)#wrr-queue cos-map 4 5
```

CoS values 6 and 7 have been placed in queue 3. These values are reserved for other purposes such as routing updates and bridge protocol data units (BPDUs) and should never be placed in the lower priority queues.

Use the **show wrr-queue cos-map** command to verify that the correct CoS values is using the desired queue. Example 9-17 shows that the correct priority queues are populated with the desired CoS values as specified.

Example 9-17 *Verifying Strict Priority Scheduling*

```
2950-ENH#show wrr-queue cos-map
CoS Value      :  0  1  2  3  4  5  6  7

Priority Queue :  1  1  2  3  3  4  3  3
```

Strict priority scheduling offers the capability to guarantee that the highest priority traffic is always transmitted first, minimizing delay for that class of traffic. However, strict priority scheduling has the potential of starving the lower priority queues if the higher priority queues are consuming the full bandwidth of the interface for extended periods of time.

Strict priority scheduling is the default scheduling method used by the Catalyst 2950.

WRR Scheduling

Weighted Round Robin (WRR) scheduling eliminates the potential of starving the lower priority queues by assigning a weight to each queue. A *weight* is defined as the importance of a queue relative to the remaining queues. Simply stated, this means the number of packets that one queue will transmit is relative to the number of packets the remaining queues will transmit.

For example, assume that the strict priority scheduling from the previous section is in effect on your network. IP telephony traffic and video traffic are flowing without an issue. Premium data applications occasionally time out, but due to the heavy loads of higher priority traffic, the best-effort traffic continually stalls for brief periods of time. To remedy this situation, you can assign each of the four queues with a weight that specifies a minimum number of packets that must be consecutively transmitted. After this number of packets has been reached, the switch must then move on to the next queue and consecutively transmit the configured minimum number of packets configured for that queue. And so on. Figure 9-8 illustrates the packet flow used by WRR scheduling.

Figure 9-8 *Weighted Round Robin Scheduling Flow*

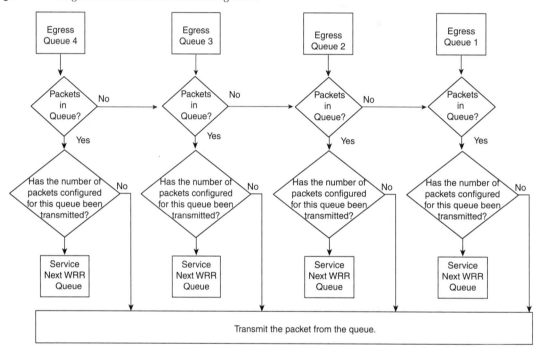

This guarantees that each queue will be able to

■ Transmit traffic for at least the number of packets specified by the weight value

■ Prevent starvation of the lower priority queues

Going back to the strict priority queue example, assume that you want to guarantee bandwidth to all queues to prevent starvation and you want to transmit a minimum of

■ 50 packets in queue 4

■ 25 packets in queue 3

■ 10 packets in queue 2

■ 5 packets in queue 1

This can be accomplished using the global **wrr-queue bandwidth** [*q1 weight*] [*q2 weight*] [*q3 weight*] [*q4 weight*] command, where *weight* is expressed in the number of packets relative to each queue. Example 9-18 shows the configuration necessary to implement WRR with the discussed values.

Example 9-18   *WRR Scheduling*

```
wrr-queue bandwidth 5 10 25 50
wrr-queue cos-map 1 0 1
wrr-queue cos-map 2 2
wrr-queue cos-map 3 3 4 6 7
wrr-queue cos-map 4 5
!
```

Use the **show wrr-queue bandwidth** command to verify that the desired number of packets will be transmitted from each queue. Example 9-19 shows that the number of packets scheduled for transmission from each queue follows the design specification.

Example 9-19   *Verifying WRR Scheduling*

```
2950-ENH#show wrr-queue bandwidth
WRR Queue  :   1   2   3   4

Bandwidth  :   5  10  25  50
```

WRR scheduling offers the capability to guarantee bandwidth to traffic in each queue. This configuration prevents queue starvation for the lower priority queues; however, it does not provide a delay guarantee for any traffic. Real-time applications such as voice traffic require a minimum amount of delay and may suffer if too many packets are transmitted in front of voice packets. In this example, the queues will transmit a total of 40 packets before the switch will transmit from queue 4 again

■ Queue 3 will transmit 25 packets.

■ Queue 2 will transmit 10 packets.

■ Queue 1 will transmit 5 packets.

This added delay might cause quality issues in a voice conversation if the voice packet arrives at the destination beyond the designed delay budget.

Strict Priority and WRR Scheduling

Strict priority and WRR scheduling combines the benefits of both strict priority scheduling and WRR scheduling by providing a scheduling method that allows for a single strict priority queue and a WRR scheduling method for the remaining three queues. Queue 4 is configured as the strict priority queue, offering the capability to guarantee a minimal amount of delay to traffic within this queue. The remaining three queues are configured with WRR scheduling, which guarantees a minimal amount of bandwidth to each queue when the single strict priority queue is not transmitting. By restricting access into the strict priority queue to real-time applications that require it, such as IP telephony media streams, starvation will not occur in the three remaining queues. Figure 9-9 illustrates the packet flow used by strict priority and WRR scheduling.

Figure 9-9   *Strict Priority Queuing Flow*

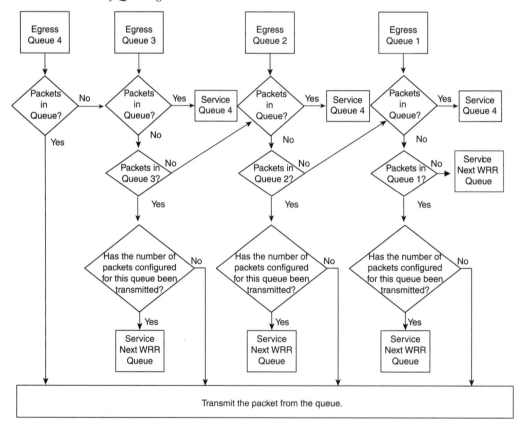

To enable strict priority and WRR scheduling on the Catalyst 2950, use the global **wrr-queue bandwidth** [*q1 weight*] [*q2 weight*] [*q3 weight*] [*q4 weight*] command, where the weight of queue 4

is configured as 0. Going back to the WRR scheduling example, suppose you needed to guarantee minimal delay for IP telephony media streams. Because this traffic has been classified with a CoS value of 5 and placed into queue 4, you simply need to change the weight assigned to queue 4 from 50 to 0. Example 9-20 shows the configuration necessary to implement strict priority and WRR scheduling.

Example 9-20 *Strict Priority Queuing*

```
wrr-queue bandwidth 5 10 25 0
wrr-queue cos-map 1 0 1
wrr-queue cos-map 2 2
wrr-queue cos-map 3 3 4 6 7
wrr-queue cos-map 4 5
!
```

The three remaining WRR queues use the assigned weights to determine the amount of remaining bandwidth that each WRR queue will receive after the strict priority queue has been serviced. In Example 9-20, queue 1 is configured for 5, queue 2 is configured for 10, and queue 3 is configured for 25. This means that queue 2 will receive twice as much of the remaining bandwidth as queue 1, while queue 3 will received five times as much of the remaining bandwidth as queue 1.

Use the **show wrr-queue bandwidth** command to verify that queue 4 has been configured as the priority queue and the desired number of packets will be transmitted from each of the remaining three queues. Example 9-21 shows that strict priority queuing has been enabled on queue 4 while the three remaining queues follow the WRR design specification.

Example 9-21 *Verifying Strict Priority Queuing*

```
2950-ENH#show wrr-queue bandwidth
WRR Queue   :   1   2   3   4

Bandwidth   :   5  10  25   0
```

Although three methods of scheduling are available to you, strict priority queuing is the preferred scheduling method for networks that support real-time applications, such as IP telephony. The addition of the strict priority queue guarantees minimal delay to real-time applications while the WRR scheduler provides bandwidth guarantees to the reaming three queues. Table 9-6 lists the commands used to configure the scheduling options discussed in this section.

Table 9-6 *Scheduling Commands*

Command	Function
wrr-queue cos-map *quid value*	This command assigns CoS values from 0 to 7 to one of the four egress queues. For example, **wrr-queue cos-map 4 5** places all frames with a CoS value of 5 in egress queue 4.
wrr-queue bandwidth *weight1 weight2 weight3 weight4*	This command allocates the amount of bandwidth the queues will use during WRR scheduling. For example, **wrr-queue bandwidth 20 1 80 0** schedules 20 packets from queue 1 for every 1 packet from queue 2 and every 80 packets from queue 3, while queue 4 uses strict priority scheduling.

Policing

At times, your network can become congested with unnecessary or unwanted traffic, such as an FTP server that is sending more data than desired. As the amount of this traffic grows, it can begin to starve out the more desirable traffic, causing business applications to timeout, hampering the productivity of your end users. A mechanism to limit the less desirable traffic needs to be implemented to prevent this situation. This mechanism is called *policing*.

A policer measures the data rate of arriving packets, identifies conforming and nonconforming traffic flows, and takes action on the traffic flows based upon the traffic contract.

Policing involves creating a policy, or traffic contract, that defines the acceptable amount of traffic for a particular class of service. After a policy has been established, a policer is configured to measure the data rate of arriving packets. The policer identifies conforming and nonconforming traffic flows and takes action on the traffic flows based on the traffic contract. Traffic within this defined limit is considered *in profile* or *conforming* traffic, while traffic that exceeds the defined limit is considered *out of profile* or *nonconforming* traffic. The policer has the capability to either drop or remark nonconforming traffic.

Consider the network in Figure 9-10.

An FTP server has been added to interface Fast Ethernet 0/6 of a Catalyst 2950. You have been instructed to limit the FTP traffic generated by the server to 5 Mbps; however, during periods of light utilization, you should allow the FTP server to use as much bandwidth as is available. You can use a policer to accomplish this task.

Figure 9-10 *Policing FTP Traffic*

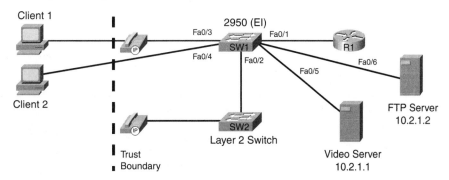

First you need to determine the priority level that will be offered to the FTP traffic in the conforming state and in the nonconforming state. Assume that the priority of applications configured on this network is in the following order, with the top application receiving the highest priority:

1. IP telephony media streams: DSCP EF

2. Video and IP telephony signaling traffic: DSCP AF41 and DSCP AF31, respectively

3. Premium data applications: DSCP AF21

4. Best-effort traffic: DSCP 0

From this priority list, you determine that the conforming FTP traffic will receive a DSCP value of AF21 while nonconforming traffic will receive a DSCP value of 0. This allows the network to treat the first 5 Mbps of FTP traffic as a premium data application, while treating FTP traffic that exceeds the 5-Mbps limit to best-effort service.

MQC needs to be configured to classify, mark, and police the FTP traffic. Because all FTP traffic originates from the FTP server, (the IP address for which is 10.2.1.2) you can use an access list to match the traffic. The access list will then be applied to the class map as demonstrated in Example 9-22.

Example 9-22 *Classifying FTP Traffic for Policing*

```
class-map match-all policeftp
  match access-group 2
!
access-list 2 permit 10.2.1.2
```

A policy map is created for the traffic that matches the class map **policeftp**. The class **policeftp** within the policy map **policeftp** will be configured to mark the IP DSCP value of all matched traffic to

DSCP AF21 (decimal 18). Next, you need to configure a policer for the class **policeftp**. Table 9-7 lists the options available to a policer on a Catalyst 2950.

Table 9-7 *Policer Options*

Command	Arguments	Function
police *rate-bps burst-byte* [**exceed-action** {**drop** | **dscp** *dscp-value*}]	*rate-bps*	The average receive rate at which the policer will accept conforming traffic

Acceptable values for 10/100 1000000 (1 Mbps) to 100000000 (100 Mbps) in multiples of 1000000 (1 Mbps)

Acceptable values for 1 Gigabit 8000000 (8 Mbps) to 1000000000 (1 Gbps) in multiples of 8000000 (8 Mbps) |
| | *burst-byte* | Allowable burst size that the policer will accept before marking traffic as nonconforming

Acceptable values for 10/100 4096 (4 kbps), 8192 (8 kbps), 16384 (16 kbps), 32768 (32 kbps), or 65536 (64 kbps)

Acceptable values for 1 Gigabit 4096 (4 kbps), 8192 (8 kbps), 16384 (16 kbps), 32768 (32 kbps), 65536 (64 kbps), 131072 (128 kbps), 262144 (256 kbps), or 524288 (512 kbps) |
| | **exceed-action drop** | Specifies that all nonconforming traffic will be dropped |
| | **exceed-action dscp** [*dscp value*] | Specifies that all nonconforming traffic will be remarked with the DSCP value specified and transmitted |

Because the design specifications call for 5000000 (5 Mbps) of conforming traffic with an **exceed** option of reclassifying all nonconforming traffic with a DSPC value of 0, the policer command you would need to use under the class **policeftp** would be **police 5000000 8192 exceed-action dscp 0**. The burst size was not specified in the design specification, so the minimum burst size (8 Kbps) is used because this is a required parameter. Finally, the **service-policy input policeftp** command will be configured on interface Fast Ethernet 0/6 to apply the policy map **policeftp** and activate classification, marking, and policing for this example. Example 9-23 shows the configuration for implementing classification, marking, and policing on interface FastEthernet 0/6.

Example 9-23 *Policing FTP Traffic*

```
class-map match-all policeftp
  match access-group 2
!
policy-map policeftp
  class policeftp
    set ip dscp 18
    police 5000000 8192 exceed-action dscp 0
!
!
interface FastEthernet0/6
 service-policy input policeftp
!
access-list 2 permit 10.2.1.2
!
```

Because a single policer can be applied to a class under the **policy-map** statement using MQC, you can define multiple policers per interface if multiple classes are defined under the policy map. 10/100 Fast Ethernet interfaces have the capability to support six different policers, configured under a single policy map. Gigabit Ethernet interfaces have the capability to support 60 different policers, configured under a single policy map. In both interface types, the **exceed-action** option allows for nonconforming traffic to be either dropped or reclassified with a different DSCP value. Notice that the **service-policy input** command was used to apply the policer to interface FastEthernet 0/6. Policing can be applied only to the ingress of the Catalyst 2950.

The **show policy-map** [*policy-map name*] command verifies that the policy map has been configured with the desired class map, policing, and marking. Example 9-24 shows the output for **show policy-map policeftp**.

Example 9-24 *Verifying Policing Policy-Map*

```
2950-ENH#show policy-map policeftp
 Policy Map policeftp
  class  policeftp
   set ip dscp 18
     police 5000000 8192 exceed-action dscp 0
```

For more information on policing concepts and configuration examples for Cisco routers, see Chapter 6, "Traffic Policing and Shaping."

AutoQoS

Understanding and configuring QoS across your network can be a complex and tricky undertaking. Several questions await you:

- Who should I trust?

- How do I trust them?

- Should I trust them at Layer 2?

- Layer 3?

- Higher?

After trust has been established, new questions arise:

- How do I identify the important applications on my network?

- How do I ensure that important applications are marked for easy identification by downstream nodes?

- How do I prioritize one application over another?

- Which egress queue should each application use?

- What percentage of bandwidth should each queue receive?

- Should I be using policing?

- Is the current classification acceptable for use by downstream nodes?

Encountering QoS for the first time can be a daunting experience. There are many factors to consider when planning a network to support real-time applications. Cisco has responded to this complexity dilemma by creating a method that simplifies the trust boundary, classification, and scheduling configuration by automatically applying Cisco QoS best practices for IP telephony traffic. This method is called *AutoQoS*.

AutoQoS on the Catalyst 2950 consists of the two commands listed and defined in Table 9-8.

Table 9-8 *AutoQoS Commands*

Command	Function
auto qos voip trust	This command enables the trust of CoS values on the interface it is applied to by adding the **mls qos trust cos** command on that interface. Additionally, this command automatically modifies the CoS-to-DSCP map and configures strict priority queuing for the Catalyst 2950.
auto qos voip cisco-phone	This command enables the trust of CoS values received from a Cisco IP Phone on the interface it is applied to by placing both the **mls qos trust device cisco-phone** command and the **mls qos trust cos** command on that interface. Additionally, this command automatically modifies the CoS-to-DSCP map and configures strict priority queuing for the Catalyst 2950.

Figure 9-11 illustrates where the commands might be placed.

Figure 9-11 *AutoQoS*

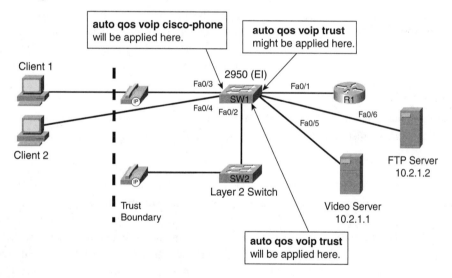

The **auto qos voip cisco-phone** command is configured on interface Fast Ethernet 0/3. This command enables the trust for the connected Cisco IP Phone by placing the commands **mls qos**

trust device cisco-phone and **mls qos trust cos** on interface Fast Ethernet 0/3. Example 9-25 shows this process.

Example 9-25 **auto qos voip cisco-phone** *Configuration*

```
2950-ENH(config-if)#interface FastEthernet 0/3
2950-ENH(config-if)#auto qos voip cisco-phone
2950-ENH#show running-config
Building configuration...
. . .
!
interface FastEthernet0/3
 switchport voice vlan 100
 mls qos trust device cisco-phone
 mls qos trust cos
 auto qos voip cisco-phone
 spanning-tree portfast
!
. . .
```

The switch uses CDP version 2 packets to determine if an IP phone is truly attached to this interface. If an IP phone is discovered by CDP, the trust boundary is extended to the IP phone and the switch then trusts the CoS values received from the IP phone for voice-media traffic (CoS 5) and voice-signaling traffic (CoS 3). By default, trust is not extended to the attached PC (Client 1), so packets received from Client 1 are reclassified with a CoS value of 0.

If an IP phone is not discovered on interface Fast Ethernet 0/3 using CDP version 2, the interface remains in the untrusted state. Any traffic received on this interface is reclassified with a CoS value of 0.

The **auto qos voip trust** command is used to trust the CoS values of connected devices. Unlike the **qos voip cisco-phone** command, the **auto qos voip trust** command does not verify a connected device before trusting received CoS values. If a connected device has the capability to mark a CoS value, it will be trusted, so the **auto qos voip trust** command is useful for extending the trust boundary to connect 802.1Q trunks. In Figure 9-11, the **auto qos voip trust** command is configured on interface Fast Ethernet 0/2 because a Layer 2 switch using an 802.1Q trunk is attached to that interface. This causes the switch to place the **mls qos trust cos** command on interface Fast Ethernet 0/2, indicating that all CoS values received on this interface will be trusted. Example 9-26 shows this process.

Example 9-26 *AutoQoS VoIP Trust*

```
2950-ENH(config)#interface FastEthernet 0/2
2950-ENH(config-if)#auto qos voip trust
2950-ENH#show running-config
```

Example 9-26 *AutoQoS VoIP Trust (Continued)*

```
Building configuration...
. . .
!
interface FastEthernet0/2
 switchport mode trunk
 mls qos trust cos
 auto qos voip trust
!
```

Interface Fast Ethernet 0/1 in Figure 9-11 states that "**auto qos voip trust** *might* be applied here."
The *might* depends on the configuration of the router attached to this interface. The **auto qos voip
trust** command places **mls qos trust** *cos* on the interface. If the attached router is capable and has
been configured to provide an 802.1Q trunk to the switch, adding the **auto qos voip trust** to
interface Fast Ethernet 0/1 will accomplish the desired effect. If the attached router is not capable or
has not been configured to provide an 802.1Q trunk to the switch, the switch will use the default
value for untagged frames, even though the attached router may be configured for classification
based upon DSCP. In this case, AutoQoS will not accomplish the desired result. The **mls qos trust
dscp** command needs to be placed on interface Fast Ethernet 0/1. Example 9-27 shows the
configuration needed.

Example 9-27 *Manual Trust of DSCP*

```
            2950-ENH(config)#interface FastEthernet 0/1
2950-ENH(config-if)#mls qos trust dscp
2950-ENH#show running-config
Building configuration...
. . .
!
interface FastEthernet0/1
 mls qos trust dscp
!
. . .
```

So far, this section has discussed the effect that AutoQoS has on trust boundaries. AutoQoS also
offers the benefit of automatically configuring classification and queue scheduling for an IP
telephony network. Placing either the **auto qos voip trust** command or the **auto qos voip cisco-
phone** command on an interface enables this automatic configuration. After AutoQoS is enabled,
the switch places all packets with a CoS value of 0, 1, 2, or 4 in egress queue 1. Egress queue 1 will
be allocated 20 packets for transmission or, expressed in other terms, 20 percent of the bandwidth
allocated to the WRR scheduler. All packets with a CoS value of 3, 6, or 7 will be placed in egress
queue number 3. Queue number 3 will be allocated 80 packets for transmission or, expressed in other
terms, 80 percent of the bandwidth allocated to the WRR scheduler. All packets with a CoS value of 5

will be placed in queue 4, which will be configured to act as the strict priority queue. Table 9-9 lists these values.

Table 9-9 *AutoQoS Classification and Scheduling*

Egress Queue	CoS Value	WRR Bandwidth Allocated
1	0, 1, 2, 4	20 percent WRR
2	Not used	Not used
3	3, 6, 7	80 percent WRR
4	5	Strict priority queue

You can verify these values by using the **show auto qos** command, as demonstrated in Example 9-28.

Example 9-28 **show auto qos**

```
2950-ENH#show auto qos
Initial configuration applied by AutoQoS:
wrr-queue bandwidth 20 1 80 0
no wrr-queue cos-map
wrr-queue cos-map 1 0 1 2 4
wrr-queue cos-map 3 3 6 7
wrr-queue cos-map 4 5
mls qos map cos-dscp 0 8 16 26 32 46 48 56
!
interface FastEthernet0/2
 mls qos trust cos
!
interface FastEthernet0/3
 mls qos trust device cisco-phone
 mls qos trust cos
```

Notice that the global command **wrr-queue bandwidth 20 1 80 0** has a **1** configured for egress queue 2; however, egress queue 2 is defined as not used. In this case, the value of 1 represents a single packet (1 percent) for every 80 (80 percent) from queue 3, and a single packet (1 percent) for every 20 (20 percent) from queue 1. This allows an easy translation from packets to percentages. Because there are no CoS values associated with egress queue 2, no traffic will ever reach that queue and, therefore, it will not be used to transmit traffic in this configuration.

Also notice that the global command **mls qos map cos-dscp 0 8 16 26 32 46 48 56** has been added to the configuration of the switch. Refer to the "Layer 2-to-Layer 3 Mapping" section of this chapter, which discussed that the default CoS-to-DSCP mapping did not match the values presented by Cisco IP Phones. Example 9-29 shows the default CoS-to-DSCP mapping for the Catalyst 2950.

Example 9-29 *Default* **mls qos map cos-dscp** *Configuration*

```
2950-ENH# show mls qos map cos-dscp
  Cos-dscp map:
        cos:   0  1  2  3  4  5  6  7
       -------------------------------
       dscp:   0  8 16 24 32 40 48 56
```

Because AutoQoS configures the QoS parameters based upon the needs of an IP telephony network, the CoS-to-DSCP mapping changes to match the values presented by Cisco IP Phones. A CoS value of 3 will be mapped to a DSCP value of 26, while a CoS value of 5 will by mapped to a DSCP value of 46 using the global command **mls qos map cos-dscp 0 8 16 26 32 46 48 56**. The **show mls qos map cos-dscp** command verifies the changes made by AutoQoS, as demonstrated in Example 9-30.

Example 9-30 *AutoQoS Changes to CoS Map*

```
2950-ENH#show mls qos map cos-dscp
  Cos-dscp map:
        cos:   0  1  2  3  4  5  6  7
       -------------------------------
       dscp:   0  8 16 26 32 46 48 56
```

Using AutoQoS can help simplify the configuration of QoS on your network by minimizing mistakes and omissions. AutoQoS is a great tool that is focused toward preparing your network for the addition of IP telephony. If you plan to use AutoQoS in your network, recommended practice is that you enable AutoQoS *before* you configure QoS parameters. QoS parameters can be modified to suit the needs of your network after AutoQoS has been enabled.

> **NOTE**   After reading this chapter, take a moment to review the section "AutoQoS VoIP Configuration for IOS Switches" in Chapter 3. For more information on AutoQoS and the benefits it offers other Cisco platforms, see the section "Cisco AutoQoS Feature" in Chapter 3.

Foundation Summary

The "Foundation Summary" is a collection of tables and figures that provides a convenient review of many key concepts in this chapter. For those of you already comfortable with the topics in this chapter, this summary can help you recall a few details. For those of you who just read this chapter, this review should help solidify some key facts. For any of you doing your final preparation before the exam, these tables and figures are a convenient way to review the day before the exam.

Table 9-10 lists the key differences in QoS capabilities between the Enhanced and Standard OS versions available for the Catalyst 2950.

Table 9-10 *Enhanced Versus Standard IOS Images*

QoS Feature	Enhanced Image Support	Standard Image Support
Classification capability?	Layers 2 to 4	Layer 2 only
Marking capability?	Layer 2 and 3	Layer 2 only
Priority queue support?	Yes	Yes
Weighted Round Robin capability?	Yes	Yes
Policing capability?	Yes	No
AutoQoS capability?	Yes	No

Figure 9-12 shows the general location of the CoS field inside the 802.1Q headers.

Figure 9-12 *User Priority Fields*

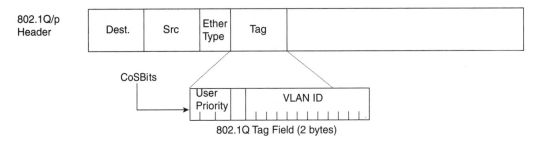

Figure 9-13 outlines the two fields and their positions inside an IP header.

Figure 9-13 *IP Precedence and IP DSCP Fields*

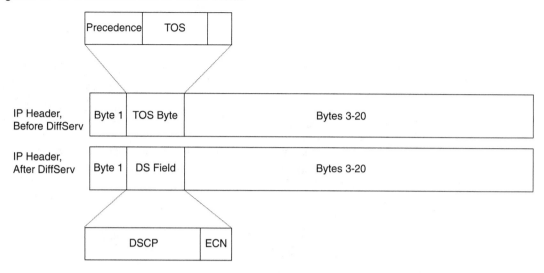

Table 9-11 lists the DSCP classes associated with the DSCP decimal values.

Table 9-11 *DSCP Values*

DSCP Decimal Value	DSCP Class
0	default dscp (000000)
8	CS1(precedence 1) dscp (001000)
10	AF11 dscp (001010)
16	CS2(precedence 2) dscp (010000)
18	AF21 dscp (010010)
24	CS3(precedence 3) dscp (011000)
26	AF31 dscp (011010)
32	CS4(precedence 4) dscp (100000)
34	AF41 dscp (100010)
40	CS5(precedence 5) dscp (101000)
46	EF dscp (101110)
48	CS6(precedence 6) dscp (110000)
56	CS7(precedence 7) dscp (111000)

Table 9-12 lists the options for configuring the trust state.

Table 9-12 *Trust Boundaries*

Command	Function
mls qos trust [**cos** {**pass-through**} | **device cisco-phone** | **dscp**]	**mls qos trust cos** {**pass-through**} This command configures the interface to trust the CoS value for all Ethernet frames received. The **pass-through** option prevents the switch from overwriting the original DSCP value in the received packet with the values indicated in the CoS to DSPC map.
	mls qos trust device cisco-phone This command configures the interface to trust CoS values received only if a Cisco IP phone is attached.
	mls qos trust dscp This command configures the interface to trust the CoS value for all Ethernet packets received.
switchport priority extend [**cos** *value*| **trust**]	**switchport priority extend cos** *value* Used in conjunction with **mls qos trust device cisco-phone**, this command overwrites the original CoS value of all Ethernet frames received from a PC attached to an IP phone with the value specified. **switchport priority extend cos 0** is the default.
	switchport priority extend trust Used in conjunction with **mls qos trust device cisco-phone**, this command enables the switch to trust the CoS value of all Ethernet frames received from a PC attached to an IP phone.

Table 9-13 lists the options for configuring the default CoS value.

Table 9-13 *Default CoS Value*

Command	Function
mls qos cos [*value*| **override**]	**mls qos cos** *value* This command configures the interface to attach the specified CoS value to all untagged frames that are received.
	mls qos cos override This command configures the interface to overwrite the original CoS value received with the specified value.

Figure 9-14 illustrates the treatment received by packets as they enter the switch.

Figure 9-14 *Packet Flow*

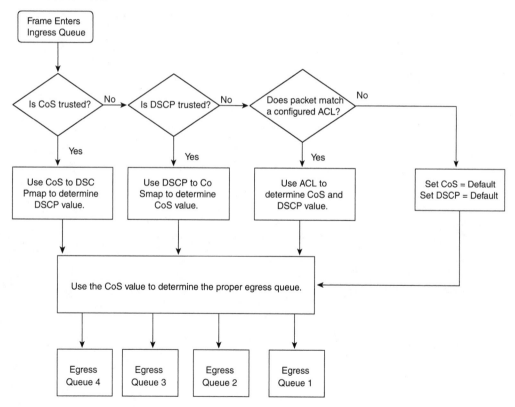

Figure 9-15 illustrates the packet flow used by strict priority scheduling.

Figure 9-15   *Strict Priority Scheduling Flow*

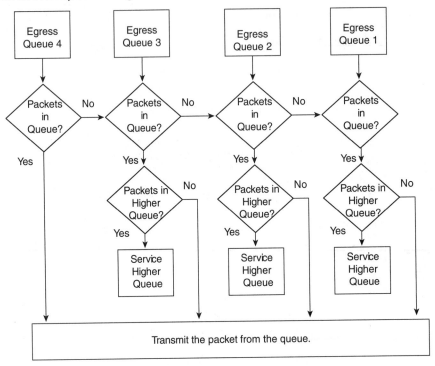

Figure 9-16 illustrates the packet flow used by WRR scheduling.

Figure 9-16   *Weighted Round Robin Scheduling Flow*

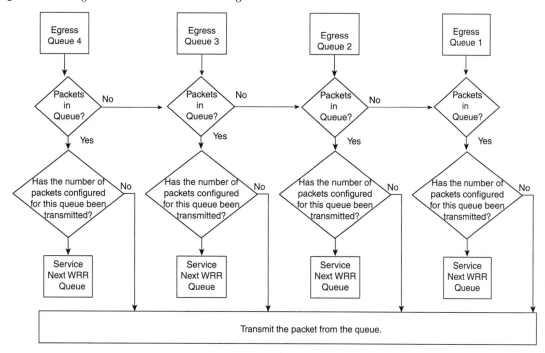

Figure 9-17 illustrates the packet flow used by strict priority queuing.

Figure 9-17 *Strict Priority Queuing Flow*

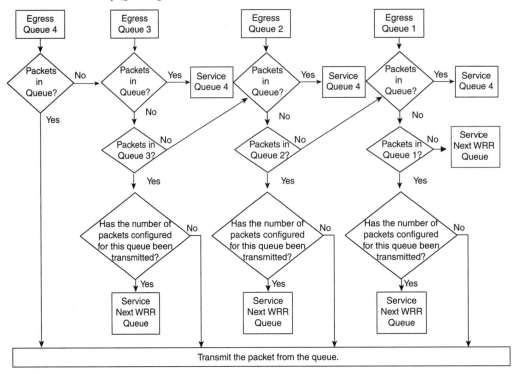

Table 9-14 lists the commands used to configure the available scheduling options.

Table 9-14 *Scheduling commands*

Command	Function
wrr-queue cos-map *quid value*	This command assigns CoS values from 0 to 7 to one of the four egress queues. For example, **wrr-queue cos-map 4 5** places all frames with a CoS value of 5 in egress queue 4.
wrr-queue bandwidth [1-255] [1-255] [1-255] [0-255]	This command allocates the amount of bandwidth the queues will use during WRR scheduling. For example, **wrr-queue bandwidth 20 1 80 0** allocates 20 packets to queue 1, 1 packet to queue 2, 80 packets to queue 3, and strict priority queuing to queue 4.

Table 9-15 lists the options available to a policer on a Catalyst 2950.

Table 9-15 *Policer Options*

Command	Arguments	Function
police *rate-bps burst-byte* [**exceed-action** {**drop** | **dscp** *dscp-value*}]	*rate-bps*	The average receive rate at which the policer will accept conforming traffic Acceptable values for 10/100 1000000 (1 Mbps) to 100000000 (100 Mbps) in multiples of 1000000 (1 Mbps) Acceptable values for 1 Gigabit 8000000 (8 Mbps) to 1000000000 (1 Gbps) in multiples of 8000000 (8 Mbps)
	burst-byte	Allowable burst size that the policer will accept before marking traffic as nonconforming Acceptable values for 10/100 4096 (4 kbps), 8192 (8 kbps), 16384 (16 kbps), 32768 (32 kbps), or 65536 (64 kbps) Acceptable values for 1 Gigabit 4096 (4 kbps), 8192 (8 kbps), 16384 (16 kbps), 32768 (32 kbps), 65536 (64 kbps), 131072 (128 kbps), 262144 (256 kbps), or 524288 (512 kbps)
	exceed-action drop	Specifies that all nonconforming traffic will be dropped
	exceed-action dscp [*dscp value*]	Specifies that all nonconforming traffic will be remarked with the DSCP value specified and transmitted

AutoQoS on the Catalyst 2950 consists of the two commands listed and defined in Table 9-16.

Table 9-16 *AutoQoS Commands*

Command	Function
auto qos voip trust	This command enables the trust of CoS values on the interface it is applied to by adding the **mls qos trust cos** command on that interface. Additionally, this command automatically modifies the CoS-to-DSCP map and configures strict priority queuing for the Catalyst 2950.
auto qos voip cisco-phone	This command enables the trust of CoS values received from a Cisco IP Phone on the interface it is applied to by placing both the **mls qos trust device cisco-phone** command and the **mls qos trust cos** command on that interface. Additionally, this command automatically modifies the CoS-to-DSCP map and configures strict priority queuing for the Catalyst 2950.

Figure 9-18 illustrates where the commands might be placed.

Figure 9-18 *AutoQoS*

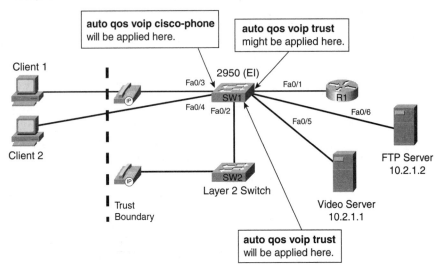

Table 9-17 lists the classification and scheduling options configured by AutoQoS.

Table 9-17 *AutoQoS Classification and Scheduling*

Egress Queue	CoS Value	WRR Bandwidth Allocated
1	0, 1, 2, 4	20 percent WRR
2	Not used	Not used
3	3, 6, 7	80 percent WRR
4	5	Strict Priority Queue

For Further Reading

This book attempts to cover the breadth and depth of QoS as covered on the QoS exam (642-641). However, you might want to read more about topics in this chapter, or other classification and marking topics.

For more on the topics in this chapter:

■   *Cisco 2950 QoS Configuration Guide* (http://www.cisco.com/univercd/cc/td/doc/product/lan/cat2950/12119ea1/2950scg/swqos.htm)

■   "Cisco AutoQoS White Paper" (http://cisco.com/en/US/tech/tk543/tk759/technologies_white_paper09186a00801348bc.shtml)

For design-related guidance:

■   "Cisco AVVID Network Infrastructure Enterprise Quality of Service Design" (http://cisco.com/application/pdf/en/us/guest/netsol/ns17/c649/ccmigration_09186a00800d67ed.pdf)

Q&A

As mentioned in the Introduction, you have two choices for review questions. The following questions give you a more difficult challenge than the exam itself by using an open-ended question format. By reviewing now with this more difficult question format, you can exercise your memory better, and prove your conceptual and factual knowledge of this chapter. You can find the answers to these questions in Appendix A.

The second option for practice questions is to use the CD-ROM included with this book, which includes a testing engine and more than 200 questions and drag-and-drop tasks. You should use this CD-ROM nearer to the end of your preparation, for practice with the actual exam format.

1. Why do you need QoS in the LAN?

2. What is buffer overflow and when does it occur?

3. What IOS types are available for the Catalyst 2950 and which one is preferred for QoS?

4. You have a Catalyst 2950 running the standard IOS image and need to migrate to a Catalyst 2950 running the enhanced IOS image. What are your options to migrate to a Catalyst 2950 running the enhanced IOS image?

5. What methods can a Catalyst 2950 currently use to classify traffic?

6. What map needs to be changed on the Catalyst 2950 to reflect the current markings of Cisco IP Phones?

7. What command is used to verify the CoS-to-DSCP map?

8. By default, a Catalyst 2950 maps voice-media traffic and voice-signaling traffic to which DSCP values?

9. To keep the DSCP values of the voice-media traffic and the voice-signaling traffic consistent between the IP phones and the Catalyst 2950, which DSCP values need to be configured on the Catalyst 2950?

10. By default, what values does the Catalyst 2950 trust?

11. Name two of the three markings or devices that the Catalyst 2950 can use to extend a trust boundary.

12. Where is the **trust** command configured on a Catalyst 2950?

13. What does the **switchport priority extend cos 0** command do?

14. What does the **mls qos trust cos pass-through dscp** command do?

15. What command enables the trust of a Cisco IP Phone on a Catalyst 2950?

16. How does the Catalyst 2950 determine whether a Cisco IP Phone is connected to a port configured to trust device cisco-phone?

17. What happens if an interface is configured to trust device cisco-phone and a PC is connected to the interface?

18. Which command set the default CoS value of an interface to 2 for all untagged frames received?

19. What does the command **mls qos cos override** do?

20. What command views the current trust state of interface Fast Ethernet 0/1?

21. A router that is not configured for 802.1Q is connected to interface 0/1 of the Catalyst 2950. The router interface forwards a voice-media packet to the switch. What CoS value will the switch receive?

22. A router that is not configured for 802.1Q is connected to interface 0/1 of the Catalyst 2950. The switch is configured to trust CoS on this interface. The router interface forwards a voice-media packet to the switch. What DSPC value will the switch use for this packet by default?

23. What can MQC be used for on the Catalyst 2950?

24. What is a class map used for?

25. What is a policy map used for?

26. How is a policy map applied to an interface?

27. In which direction can a service policy be applied on a Catalyst 2950?

28. How many ingress queues are present on each Ethernet interface of the Catalyst 2950?

29. How many egress queues are present on each Ethernet interface of the Catalyst 2950?

30. What scheduling methods are supported on the Catalyst 2950?

31. What mark does the Catalyst 2950 use to determine the proper queue for a packet?

32. Which scheduling method is configured by default on a Catalyst 2950?

33. Which scheduling method is recommended for networks that transport IP telephony traffic?

34. How does strict priority scheduling work?

35. What are the advantages and disadvantages of using strict priority scheduling?

36. How does Weighted Round Robin scheduling work?

37. What are the advantages and disadvantages of WRR scheduling?

38.   How does strict priority queuing work?

39.   What queue is configured for the strict priority queue when using strict priority queuing?

40.   What command assigns a CoS value of 5 to queue 4?

41.   What command assigns WRR scheduling with queue 1 servicing 5 packets, queue 2 servicing 10 packets, queue 3 servicing 25 packets, and queue 4 servicing 50 packets?

42.   What command enables the strict priority queue when using strict priority queuing?

43.   What command verifies that queue 4 has been configured for the priority queue?

44.   What is a policer?

45.   What is out of profile or nonconforming traffic?

46.   What can a policer do with nonconforming traffic on a Catalyst 2950?

47.   How many policers can be applied to a single 10/100 Ethernet interface on a Catalyst 2950? How about a Gigabit interface on a Catalyst 2950?

48.   What is the maximum burst size that a policer can use for a 10/100 interface on a Catalyst 2950?

49.   What is the maximum burst size that a policer can use for a Gigabit interface on a Catalyst 2950?

50.   What is the minimum traffic rate that a policer can use for conforming traffic for a 10/100 interface on a Catalyst 2950?

51.   What is the minimum traffic rate that a policer can use for conforming traffic for a Gigabit interface on a Catalyst 2950?

52.   What commands enables AutoQoS on the Catalyst 2950?

53.   Where are the **auto qos voip trust** and **auto qos voip cisco-phone** commands applied?

54.   What does the command **auto qos voip trust** do?

55.   What does the command **auto qos voip cisco-phone** do?

56.   When is configuring trust manually preferred over AutoQoS?

57.   When AutoQoS is enabled, what CoS values are mapped to queue 1? What percentage of the WRR scheduler does queue 1 receive?

58.   When AutoQoS is enabled, what CoS values are mapped to queue 2? What percentage of the WRR scheduler does queue 2 receive?

59.   When AutoQoS is enabled, what CoS values are mapped to queue 3? What percentage of the WRR scheduler does queue 3 receive?

60. When AutoQoS is enabled, what CoS values are mapped to queue 4? What percentage of the WRR scheduler does queue 4 receive?

61. What command can you use to verify AutoQoS?

QOS Exam Topics

This chapter covers the following exam topics specific to the QoS exam:

- Explain the QoS requirements of the different application types

- List typical enterprise traffic classes; then, identify the delay, jitter, packet-loss, and bandwidth requirements of each traffic class

- Explain the best practice QoS implementations and configurations within the campus LAN

- Explain the best practice QoS implementations and configurations on the WAN customer edge (CE) and provider edge (PE) routers

CHAPTER 10

Cisco QoS Best Practices

Today's applications require converged networks to provide predictable, measurable, and possibly guaranteed service to facilitate the productivity of your end users. As network applications grow in number and complexity, this simple truth becomes more and more apparent. The days of classifying all traffic into a single class that receives best-effort treatment is rapidly becoming a methodology of the past.

The previous nine chapters of this book describe in detail the various concepts and methods available to you for the configuration of classification, congestion management, and congestion avoidance on Cisco routers and switches. This chapter is designed to pull these concepts together, illustrating the Cisco best practices for a converged network.

"Do I Know This Already?" Quiz

The purpose of the "Do I Know This Already?" quiz is to help you decide whether you need to read the entire chapter. If you already intend to read the entire chapter, you do not necessarily need to answer these questions now.

The 15-question quiz, derived from the major sections in the "Foundation Topics" portion of the chapter, helps you determine how to spend your limited study time.

Table 10-1 outlines the major topics discussed in this chapter and the "Do I Know This Already?" quiz questions that correspond to those topics.

Table 10-1 *"Do I Know This Already?" Foundation Topics Section-to-Question Mapping*

Foundation Topics Section Covering These Questions	Questions	Score
Application Requirements	1–5	
Best Practices Methodology	6–10	
Best Practices Implementations	11–15	
Total Score		

CAUTION The goal of self-assessment is to gauge your mastery of the topics in this chapter. If you do not know the answer to a question or are only partially sure of the answer, mark this question wrong for purposes of the self-assessment. Giving yourself credit for an answer you correctly guess skews your self-assessment results and might provide you with a false sense of security.

You can find the answers to the "Do I Know This Already?" quiz in Appendix A, "Answers to the 'Do I Know This Already?' Quizzes and Q&A Sections." The suggested choices for your next step are as follows:

- **8 or less overall score**—Read the entire chapter. This includes the "Foundation Topics," the "Foundation Summary," and the "Q&A" sections.

- **9 or 10 overall score**—If you want more review on these topics, skip to the "Foundation Summary" section and then go to the "Q&A" section. Otherwise, move to the next chapter.

1. Which of the following traffic types provides a consistent packet exchange?

    a. Interactive video

    b. Voice media

    c. Voice signaling

    d. Mission-critical data

2. Which of the following factors influence the bandwidth requirements of a VoIP call?

    a. Layer 3 routing protocol

    b. Layer 2 media type

    c. Codec selection

    d. Speech samples per packet

3. The International Telecommunications Union (ITU) G.114 specification states that the one-way delay of a voice packet should not exceed how many milliseconds (ms)?

    a. 100

    b. 150

    c. 200

    d. 250

4.   How much bandwidth should be provisioned for a 384-kbps interactive video stream?

    a. 384 kbps—The average rate of the stream

    b. 460.8 kbps—The average rate of the stream + 20%

    c. 768 kbps—The average rate of the stream * 2

    d. 192 kbps—The size of H.264 compressed video

5.   How sensitive is mission-critical data to jitter? (Link: Data Traffic)

    a. Low

    b. Low to moderate

    c. Moderate to high

    d. High

6.   A converged network should be designed for less than what percentage of packet loss in the class that supports real-time applications?

    a. .5

    b. 1

    c. 1.5

    d. 5

7.   A converged network should be designed for less than how many milliseconds of jitter in the class that supports real-time applications?

    a. 10

    b. 20

    c. 30

    d. 40

8.   Where should traffic be classified?

    a. In the core

    b. As close to the source as possible

    c. As close to the destination as possible

    d. On the WAN router

9.   What is the recommended differentiated services code point (DSCP) value for scavenger traffic?

   a. 0

   b. CS0

   c. CS1

   d. AF13

10.   What is the recommended DSCP class for bulk data applications?

   a. AF1x

   b. AF2x

   c. AF3x

   d. EF

11.   What are the preferred methods of queuing on Cisco routers?

   a. PQ and CBWFQ

   b. PQ and CQ

   c. LLQ and CBWFQ

   d. LLQ and CQ

12.   When using LFI, what is the recommended serialization delay of a voice packet?

   a. 5–10 ms

   b. 10–15 ms

   c. 15–20 ms

   d. 20–25 ms

13.   Where does WRED perform the most effectively?

   a. When applied to the LLQ

   b. When applied to a CBWFQ that services UDP applications

   c. When applied to a CBWFQ that services TCP applications

   d. When applied to a CBWFQ that services both UDP and TCP applications

14. What QoS mechanism should never be used in the core of the campus LAN?

   a. Classification and marking

   b. Congestion management

   c. Congestion avoidance

15. If the service provider manages the CE router, what inbound policy is required on the PE router?

   a. Classification and marking

   b. Congestion management

   c. Policing

   d. All of the above

   e. None of the above

Foundation Topics

This chapter describes the Cisco QoS best practices for the implementation of QoS across a converged network by discussing the following topics:

■ The need for QoS best practices

■ End-to-end QoS

■ QoS service level agreements (SLAs)

■ Application requirements for QoS

■ QoS best practices methodology

■ QoS best practices case studies

The Need for QoS Best Practices

Imagine a world without standards or accepted conventions. Driving down the highway, you notice that the information on each sign is written in a different language. The information you need to know is there, but is represented in a manner you are not familiar with. How do you make sense of this information? Deciding to take the next exit to pull off the highway and get your bearings, you drive up the exit ramp only to discover the cars on this road are driving on the opposite side of the street. How can you predict which side to drive on if each road has its own conventions? Awkwardly, you merge into the traffic and begin to travel on what feels like the wrong side of the road. Looking up, you see a traffic light in front of you that changes colors from blue to orange. What do you do? This is not a normal convention that you are accustomed to. Does orange mean stop, go, or caution? Although this mixed-up world can function, simple tasks become complex and fraught with hazards. To function *efficiently* and *effectively*, standards need to be agreed upon and instituted throughout the highway infrastructure.

QoS configuration of your network parallels this example. With so many QoS configuration options available, it is sometimes difficult to decide which method is best for your network. Common questions include the following:

■ What is the best way to identify and classify my traffic?

■ At what point in my network should I classify my traffic?

■ At what point in my network do I trust the markings that I receive?

- What is the best way to ensure that my real-time applications always receive priority treatment without starving other mission-critical applications?

- How do I limit unwanted or unnecessary traffic throughout my network?

The goal of the Cisco QoS best practices methodology is to answer these questions and offer a standardized methodology that can be used throughout your network.

End-to-End QoS

End-to-end QoS is a term that describes the treatment a packet receives at every node as it travels across your network from the originating device to the terminating device. The Internet Engineering Task Force (IETF) has defined two models to accomplish this goal:

- **Integrated Services (IntServ)**—Requires that each node establish a guaranteed bandwidth, delay, and jitter before a single packet is sent

- **Differentiated Services (DiffServ)**—Requires that each node be configured to classify and schedule each packet as it is received on a per-hop basis

This chapter describes end-to-end QoS based upon the DiffServ model.

Consider the typical converged network depicted in Figure 10-1.

Figure 10-1 *Typical Converged Network*

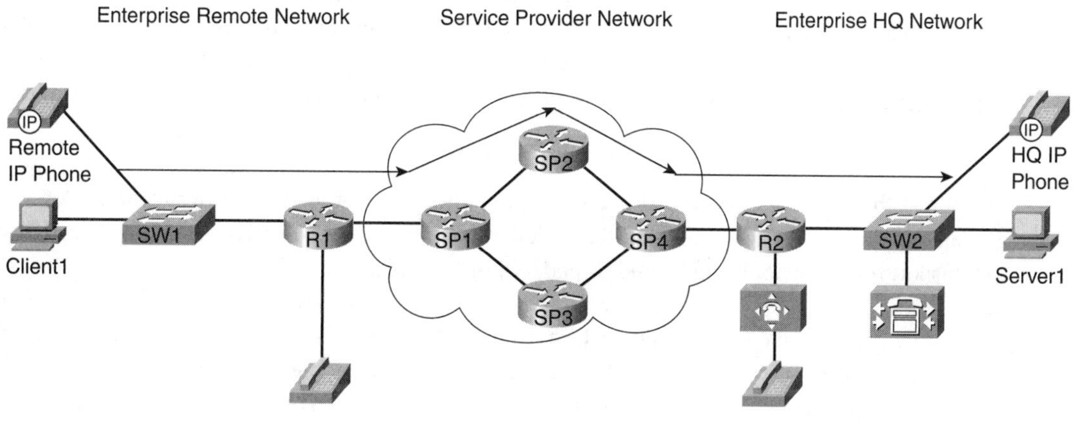

A packet leaves the Remote IP Phone at the enterprise remote site bound for its destination, HQ IP Phone at the enterprise HQ site. During the journey, the packet traverses switch SW1, Router R1, Router SP1, Router SP2, Router SP4, Router R2, and finally switch SW2. Each node along this path must have the capability to offer the same treatment, or class of service (CoS), to the packet. If any node along this path cannot offer the necessary CoS for this traffic, the end-to-end QoS of the network can be compromised, possibly resulting in an unintelligible conversation. End-to-end QoS is only as strong as the weakest node.

Achieving end-to-end QoS consists of identifying traffic flows and classifying them into groups that each node can recognize and act upon. This requires that an agreed-upon standard for classification and prioritization be in place for each node the packet traverses. This agreed-upon standard, or best practice, determines the action taken for each packet on its journey from originating source to final destination.

QoS Service Level Agreements

In the network in Figure 10-1, the network administrator has the ability to configure Routers R1 and R2 and Switches SW1 and SW2 to provide the CoS desired for each type of traffic on the network. However, the network administrator does not have direct control over the service provider's Routers SP1, SP2, SP3, and SP4. To maintain the desired classification and prioritization of the traffic over the service provider's network, there must be an agreement between the enterprise and the service provider to accomplish this. This agreement is called a service level agreement (SLA). An SLA is a contractual agreement that stipulates how each defined class of traffic will be treated and any penalties involved if this agreement is not met. The treatment may consist of bandwidth, delay, jitter, and high-availability guarantees, depending upon the level of service that is purchased.

In the past, service provider networks typically offered only bandwidth guarantees for data networks, without regard for other metrics such as delay and jitter. In a data network without real-time applications, this was an acceptable solution. If a TCP packet was delayed, experienced jitter, or was lost, the application would recover without affecting the productivity of the end users. In today's networks that transport real-time applications, delay, jitter, and packet loss are much more of a concern.

To address this concern, service providers are differentiating themselves by offering an SLA to guarantee delay, jitter, packet loss, and bandwidth rates to give their enterprise customers the ability to transport real-time applications end-to-end without degradation.

An SLA can be offered on a per interface basis, if the physical link is dedicated to a single customer, or on a per permanent virtual circuit (PVC) basis, if multiple customers share the physical link. A typical SLA offers the capability to classify and prioritize three to five classes of traffic. The class that services real-time applications typically receives a maximum-bandwidth guarantee, a delay guarantee, a jitter guarantee, and a packet-loss guarantee. The remaining classes typically transport data applications and offer a minimum-bandwidth (best-effort) guarantee. Depending on the needs of the data traffic, delay, jitter, and packet-loss guarantees can be purchased for these classes as well.

Consider the SLA offered by the service provider in Figure 10-2.

Figure 10-2   *Service Provider SLA*

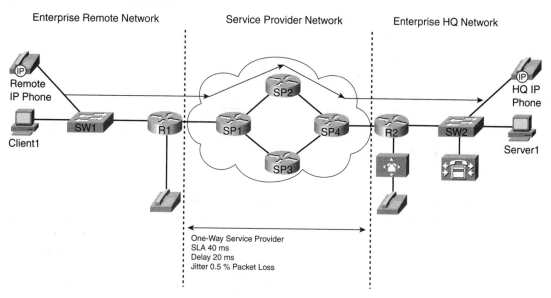

In this network, assume that the service provider offers an SLA of 40 ms of latency, 20 ms of jitter, and 0.5 percent packet loss for three classes of service:

- **Gold**—Gold traffic consists of real-time applications. Traffic within this class is guaranteed a maximum amount of bandwidth and guaranteed this level of service 90 percent of the time for traffic that does not exceed the maximum bandwidth. Traffic that exceeds the guaranteed maximum bandwidth will be reclassified as best-effort traffic.

- **Silver**—Silver traffic consists of premium data applications. Traffic within this class is guaranteed a minimum amount of bandwidth and guaranteed this level of service 75 percent of the time for traffic that does not exceed the minimum bandwidth. Traffic that exceeds the guaranteed minimum bandwidth will be reclassified as best-effort traffic.

- **Best-effort**—Best-effort traffic consists of all traffic that has been reclassified and any other unclassified application traffic. Traffic within this class is guaranteed a minimum amount of bandwidth and guaranteed this level of service 50 percent of the time. Traffic that exceeds the guaranteed minimum bandwidth will be sent if bandwidth is available. If no bandwidth is available, this traffic will be dropped.

Table 10-2 lists the SLA values used in this example.

Table 10-2 *SLA Example Values*

	Gold Class	**Silver Class**	**Best-Effort Class**
40 ms of Latency	90%	75%	50%
20 ms of Jitter	90%	75%	50%
0.5% Packet Loss	90%	75%	50%

With the SLA in place, the administrator of the enterprise network can plan for the implementation of end-to-end QoS and develop a QoS strategy for Routers R1 and R2 and Switches SW1 and SW2 to meet the needs of the enterprise applications.

Many service provides also offer the option of managing the customer's WAN edge router. In Figure 10-2, assume that the service provider manages Routers R1 and R2. In this case, Routers R1 and R2 would be configured and maintained by the service provider. The SLA offered by the service provider could then be extended to include the managed routers at the customer's premise. An additional class of traffic can then be defined to allow the prioritization of management traffic, such as Telnet and Simple Network Management Protocol (SNMP), to ensure that the service provider can access the routers during times of heavy congestion.

Application Requirements for QoS

The traffic flow generated by an application dictates the QoS needs for that application. Some applications generate a consistent traffic flow, consuming the same amount of bandwidth throughout the packet exchange, whereas other applications vary greatly throughout the packet exchange. Understanding how your applications behave on your network is important in order to plan for the proper QoS treatment of each application. This section discusses the traffic behavior of consistent and inconsistent real-time applications as well as data traffic.

Voice Traffic

Voice traffic is extremely consistent. After a voice conversation has been established, the bandwidth requirements remain the same for the life of the conversation.

To fully understand the QoS requirements for the Cisco implementation of voice traffic, you must first understand how voice traffic is transported across the network. A single voice packet consists of the voice payload, a Real-Time Transport Protocol (RTP) header, a User Datagram Protocol (UDP) header, an IP header, and a Layer 2 header, as shown in Figure 10-3.

Figure 10-3   *Voice Packet*

Layer 2	IP	UDP	RTP	Voice Payload
Variable Size Based on Layer 2 Protocol	20 Bytes	8 Bytes	12 Bytes	Variable Size Based on Codec Selection and the ms of Speech Included

IP headers (20 bytes), UDP headers (8 bytes), and RTP headers (12 bytes), without the use of compressed RTP, consistently use 40 bytes per packet.

The voice payload is dependant upon the codec selected and the amount of speech included, measured in milliseconds. In Cisco IP Telephony environments, the two most common codec specifications are as follows:

- **G.711**—Carries an uncompressed 64-kbps payload stream, known in the traditional telephony world as pulse code modulation (PCM). G.711 offers toll-quality voice conversations at the cost of bandwidth consumption. The G.711 codec is ideally suited for situations where bandwidth is abundant and quality is the primary driver, such as LAN environments.

- **G.729** —Carries a compressed 8-kbps payload stream, known in the traditional telephony world as Conjugate Structure Algebraic Code-Excited Linear Prediction (CS-ACELP). G.729 offers a reduction in bandwidth consumption at the cost of near toll-quality voice conversations. G.729 is ideally suited for situations where bandwidth is limited, such as WAN environments.

By default, the Cisco IP Telephony solutions place 20 ms of speech into a single G.711 or G.729 packet. This means that it takes 50 packets to generate a full second of the voice conversation, because

$$50 * 20 \text{ ms} = 1 \text{ second}$$

If the G.711 codec is selected using 50 packets per second (pps), the voice payload per packet will be 1280 bits, because

$$64,000 \text{ kbps} \div 50 \text{ pps} = 1280 \text{ bits}$$

Expressed in bytes, this becomes 160 bytes because

$$1280 \text{ bits} \div 8 = 160 \text{ bytes}$$

If the G.729 codec is selected using 50 pps, the voice payload per packet will be 160 bits because

$$8000 \text{ kbps} \div 50 \text{ pps} = 160 \text{ bits}$$

Expressed in bytes, this becomes 20 bytes because

160 bits ÷ 8 = 20 bytes

Discounting the Layer 2 headers and compressed RTP

A single G.711 packet @ 50 pps = the IP/UDP/RTP headers (40 bytes) + voice payload (160 bytes) = 200 bytes per packet

At 50 pps, this yields 10,000 bytes per voice stream or 80 kilobits per voice stream (10,000 * 8 = 80,000).

Discounting the Layer 2 headers and compressed RTP

A single G.729 packet @ 50 pps = IP/UDP/RTP headers (40 bytes) + voice payload (20 bytes) = 60 bytes per packet

At 50 pps, this yields 3000 bytes per voice stream or 24 kilobits per voice stream (3000 × 8 = 24,000).

Increasing the amount of speech included in a single packet from 20 ms to 30 ms decreases the number of packets required to transport that same second of voice. In this case, approximately 33 packets are needed (33 * 30 ms is approximately = to 1 second).

The voice payload of a G.711 packet @ 33 pps contains approximately 1939 bits (64,000 ÷ 33) or approximately 240 bytes (1939 ÷ 8). Adding the IP/UDS/RTP headers, this becomes 280 bytes (240 + 40) per packet. At 33 pps, this yields 9240 bytes per voice stream or approximately 74 kilobits.

The voice payload of a G.729 packet @ 33 pps contains approximately 242 bits (8000 ÷ 33) or approximately 30 bytes. Adding the IP/UDS/RTP headers, this becomes 70 bytes (30 + 40) per packet. At 33 pps, this yields 2310 bytes per voice stream or approximately 19 kilobits.

Table 10-3 lists these common G.711 and G.729 rates.

Table 10-3 *Codec Selection*

Codec	Speech Samples Per Packet	Voice Payload	Packets per Second	Total Bandwidth Per Call
G.711	20 ms	160 bytes	50 pps	80 kbps
G.711	30 ms	240 bytes	33 pps	74 kbps
G.729	20 ms	20 bytes	50 pps	24 kbps
G.729	30 ms	30 bytes	33 pps	19 kbps

RTP Header Compression, also known as Compressed RTP (cRTP), voice activation detection (VAD), and Layer 2 headers also play a role in determining the bandwidth requirements of a voice conversation.

Header compression can be used to reduce the UDP/RTP header size on a per link basis. Typically, cRTP is used on slow-speed links to minimize the bandwidth requirements per voice conversation and to maximize the number of voice conversations that can be transported by reducing the UDP/RTP header from 20 bytes to 2–4 bytes. Although cRTP can offer significant bandwidth savings, the impact on the router's CPU performance increases for every voice conversation transported. Understand this impact on your hardware before enabling cRTP. For the purpose of bandwidth engineering in this section, cRTP will not be discussed.

Although VAD can be used to reduce the payload by transmitting 2 bytes of payload during silent times instead of the full payload size, for the purposes of bandwidth engineering, VAD should not be taken into account.

Layer 2 headers also play a role in determining the bandwidth requirements of voice conversations. Assume that a G.729 codec is used @ 50 pps, requiring 24 kbps per conversation and this conversation is carried over a Frame Relay circuit. The Frame Relay headers (8 bytes) need to be added to the required overhead for each frame. As discussed, each G.729 packet @ 50 pps consists of 60 bytes per packet. Adding the Frame Relay header brings the required bandwidth per frame to 68 bytes, or 544 bits per frame. At 50 pps, this yields 3400 bytes per voice stream or approximately 28 kilobits per voice stream.

Table 10-4 lists the common Layer 2 requirements and the total bandwidth required.

Table 10-4 *Layer 2 Headers*

Codec	802.1Q Ethernet (32 Bytes @ Layer 2)	MLP (13 Bytes @ Layer 2)	Frame Relay (8 Bytes @ Layer 2)	ATM (Variable Bytes @ Layer 2 Due to Cell Padding)
G.711 @ 50 pps	93 kbps	86 kbps	84 kbps	106 kbps
G.711 @ 33 pps	83 kbps	78 kbps	77 kbps	84 kbps
G.729 @ 50 pps	37 kbps	30 kbps	28 kbps	43 kbps
G.729 @ 33 pps	27 kbps	22 kbps	21 kbps	28 kbps

So far, this section has discussed the bandwidth required by voice media streams. To establish the media stream, you must first establish the properties of the stream. Referred to as *call signaling,* the list that follows presents just some of the included properties:

■ Dialed number

■ Calling number

■ Codec desired

Call signaling requires 150 bps plus the Layer 2 headers needed to transport the call signaling traffic across the network.

Bandwidth is only one of the QoS requirements needed to successfully transport voice across your network. Voice packets that are lost or delayed can lead to clipping, or missing parts of speech, in the voice conversation. The industry-standard algorithm used in Cisco digital signal processors (DSPs) has the capability to predict 30 ms of speech based upon previously received voice packets. This means that a single packet can be lost without the parties on the conversation noticing the loss. However, if more than one packet is lost in succession, the DSP cannot compensate and a clip will be heard in the conversation. Your network should be designed to limit packet loss of voice packets to less than 1 percent.

The International Telecommunications Union (ITU) G.114 specification states that the one-way delay of a voice packet from the source (the speaker's mouth) to the destination (the listener's ear) should not exceed 150 ms. Delays exceeding 200 ms can result in voice degradation.

Jitter is defined as the variation in delay. For example, if the first ten packets in a voice conversation arrive 20 ms apart and the eleventh packet arrives 30 ms after the tenth packet, the jitter of the eleventh packet is 10 ms. By default, Cisco IP Phones have an adaptive internal jitter buffer that buffer received voice packets and play the voice stream to the listener consistently, removing the small amount of received jitter. However, this adaptive jitter buffer can compensate for only 20–50 ms of received jitter. A packet received that has jitter greater than 50 ms will be discarded. Your network should be designed to limit jitter to 30 ms or less.

Table 10-5 lists the delay, jitter, and packet-loss requirements for transporting voice traffic.

Table 10-5 *Voice Delay, Jitter, and Packet Loss*

Delay	< or = 150 ms
Jitter	< or = 30 ms
Packet Loss	< 1 percent

Although voice traffic is very consistent, it is intolerant of delay and network congestion. To minimize the effects of delay, jitter, and packet loss, voice traffic should always be placed in the priority queue, using Low Latency Queuing (LLQ) whenever possible. Table 10-6 compares the QoS requirements of voice traffic with other types of traffic.

Table 10-6   *Voice Traffic Requirements*

	Voice	**Video**	**Mission-Critical/ Transactional Data**	**Bulk Data/ Best-Effort Data**
Bandwidth Requirements	*Low to Moderate*	Moderate	Low to Moderate	Moderate to High
Drop Sensitivity	*High*	High	Moderate to High	Low
Delay Sensitivity	*High*	High	Low to Moderate	Low
Jitter Sensitivity	*High*	High	Low to Moderate	Low
Smooth or Bursty	*Smooth*	Bursty	Both	Both
Benign or Greedy	*Benign*	Greedy	Both	Both

Video Traffic

Video traffic is fairly consistent, but does have the capability to burst. After a video stream has been established, the bandwidth requirements will fluctuate slightly during the life of the connection. A video stream begins by sending the entire picture being transmitted. After the picture has been established, the video stream sends only changes to the picture. If there is little movement in the displayed picture, few frames are sent, reducing the needed bandwidth. As movement increases, more frames need to be sent to compensate for this movement, increasing the required bandwidth.

Assume that you are participating in a videoconference and the average of the video stream is 384 kbps. During times of minimal movement, the transmit rate can drop significantly lower than 384 kbps; however, as you move around the camera, the transit rate begins to increase above 384 kbps. To compensate for these fluctuations in bandwidth requirements, video traffic should be provisioned by adding 20 percent to the average requirements. For example, the 384-kbps stream should be provisioned for 460.8 kbps, because 20 percent of 384 kbps is 76.8 kbps.

Interactive video traffic shares the same requirements for delay, jitter, and packet loss as voice traffic. Video packets that are lost or suffer too much delay or jitter can result in a lost picture or jerky video.

Table 10-7 lists the delay, jitter, and packet-loss requirements for transporting video traffic.

Table 10-7   *Video Delay, Jitter, and Packet Loss*

Delay	< or = 150 ms
Jitter	< or = 30 ms
Packet Loss	< 1 percent
Bandwidth Fluctuation	20 percent

Although video traffic is fairly consistent it is intolerant of delay and network congestion. To minimize the effects of delay, jitter, and packet loss, video traffic should always be placed in the priority queue, using LLQ whenever possible. Table 10-8 compares the QoS requirements of video traffic with other types of traffic.

Table 10-8   *Video Traffic Requirements*

	Voice	Video	Mission-Critical/ Transactional Data	Bulk Data/ Best-Effort Data
Bandwidth requirements	Low to Moderate	*Moderate*	Low to Moderate	Moderate to High
Drop Sensitivity	High	*High*	Moderate to High	Low
Delay Sensitivity	High	*High*	Low to Moderate	Low
Jitter Sensitivity	High	*High*	Low to Moderate	Low
Smooth or Bursty	Smooth	*Bursty*	Both	Both
Benign or Greedy	Benign	*Greedy*	Both	Both

Data Traffic

The QoS requirements of data applications vary based upon the needs of the particular application. Best practice is to have a baseline of each application on your network to determine the QoS requirements for your applications.

Data applications should be separated into no more than four or five distinct classes, with each class consisting of data applications that share the same QoS requirements. Typically, these classes consist of the following:

■ **Mission-critical applications**—Mission-critical applications are defined as the core applications that your business relies upon to function effectively and efficiently. These applications are greedy and use as much bandwidth as they can. Because they are usually

TCP-based, these applications are not sensitive to delay, jitter, and loss. These applications, which should be limited to three or less, will receive at least 50 percent of the bandwidth remaining after LLQ has serviced the priority traffic.

- **Transactional applications**—Transactional applications are typically client/server applications that support your core business. Unlike mission-critical applications that can be greedy, transactional applications typically exchange small packets when adding, updating, deleting, or retrieving text data from a central point. However, these applications are usually sensitive to delay and packet loss. Transactional applications include Enterprise Resource Planning (ERP) applications such as SAP or Oracle. These applications, which should be limited to three or less, will receive at least 20 percent of the bandwidth remaining after LLQ has serviced the priority traffic.

- **Best Effort applications**—Most applications use the best-effort class. These applications typically include e-mail, HTTP, and FTP traffic. The best-effort class will receive at least 25 percent of the bandwidth remaining after LLQ has serviced the priority traffic.

- **Scavenger (less than best-effort) applications**—Using a scavenger class allows you to identify and limit bandwidth to less-desirable traffic. This type of traffic typically consists of applications such as the peer-to-peer file-sharing program Kazaa. These applications should receive no more than 5 percent of the bandwidth remaining after LLQ has serviced the priority traffic.

Because data applications are typically tolerant of delay, jitter, and packet loss, each class of data traffic will be provisioned using Class-Based Weighted Fair Queuing (CBWFQ). Using CBWFQ guarantees that a percentage of bandwidth will be available for each class.

By limiting the data classes to four or five classes, you have the ability to offer a more-defined level of service between the classes. Defining too many classes or defining too many applications within a class nullifies the benefits of QoS. For example, if all data traffic uses the mission-critical class, you lose the ability to differentiate the traffic and provide the desired level of service—in effect, nullifying QoS.

After you have a baseline of the applications in your network and determine the classes needed to provide the desired level of service, it is important to group applications with common requirements into the same class. For example, an FTP application and a transactional application should never be placed into the same class. The FTP stream is bursty and greedy, taking as much bandwidth as it can. This might delay the time-sensitive transactional application, causing the session to time out. Placing these applications into separate classes allows each to operate without impacting the other.

Data traffic is extremely variable depending upon the data application. Table 10-9 compares the QoS requirements of mission-critical/transactional traffic and best-effort traffic with other types of traffic.

Table 10-9 *Data Traffic Requirements*

	Voice	Video	Mission-Critical/ Transactional Data	Bulk Data/ Best-Effort Data
Bandwidth Requirements	Low to Moderate	Moderate	*Low to Moderate*	*Moderate to High*
Drop Sensitivity	High	High	*Moderate to High*	*Low*
Delay Sensitivity	High	High	*Low to Moderate*	*Low*
Jitter Sensitivity	High	High	*Low to Moderate*	*Low*
Smooth or Bursty	Smooth	Bursty	*Both*	*Both*
Benign or Greedy	Benign	Greedy	*Both*	*Both*

QoS Best Practices Methodology

So far, the chapters in this book discuss the various ways that QoS can be applied to a Cisco infrastructure and the QoS requirements for different types of traffic. This section discusses the Cisco best practices methodology for classification, congestion management, congestion avoidance, and policing using a Cisco infrastructure.

> **NOTE** AutoQos VoIP chooses and configures automatically what it thinks are the appropriate QoS configuration settings. In some regards, those choices can be thought of as a set of best practices for VoIP traffic. Refer to Chapter 3, "MQC, QPM, and AutoQos," and particularly Tables 3-5, 3-6, and 3-8, for a brief review of QoS options with AutoQos VoIP, both on routers and switches.

Classification and Marking Best Practices

Put simply, *classification* is nothing more than identifying a flow of traffic and grouping into common groups the traffic flows that share QoS requirements. *Marking* is a means to place a mark in each packet of the identified traffic flow for later nodes to identify.

Classification is performed at the trust boundary, which should be as close to the source as possible. In an enterprise environment, the trust boundary is typically implemented at the access layer switches or distribution layer switches. In a service provider's network, the trust boundary is typically implemented at the CE or PE router. Performing classification as close to the source as possible simplifies the QoS configuration required by later nodes, because the downstream node will need to perform only congestion management and congestion avoidance.

Most Cisco routers and many Cisco switches offer the capability to identify and classify traffic through the use of the Network Based Application Recognition (NBAR) protocol. This capability greatly reduces the complexity of classifying traffic by automatically identifying the most common types of traffic found on today's networks. Some trusted devices, such as Cisco IP Phones, have the capability to mark packets for classification. Alternatively, you can use an access list to classify a traffic flow based upon Layer 2 through 7 markings.

After you determine the method of classification, you can group the traffic into classes with other traffic that shares the same QoS requirements.

Assume that your network consists of IP telephony traffic, interactive video traffic, streaming video traffic, IP routing protocols, network management applications, and various data applications. Using a combination of NBAR, trust of IP phones, and access lists, each traffic flow can be placed into the appropriate group.

A single class will be created for voice media traffic. This class will consist of voice media traffic only. Each packet in the stream will be marked using a DSCP value of EF and a CoS value of 5.

A second class will be created for interactive video. This class will consist of interactive video traffic only. Each packet in the stream will be marked using a DSCP value of AF41 and a CoS value of 4.

A third class will be created for streaming video. This class will consist of streaming video traffic only. Each packet in the stream will be marked using a DSCP value of CS4 and a CoS value of 4.

A fourth class will be created for routing protocols. This class will consist of routing update traffic only. Each packet in the stream will be marked using a DSCP value of CS6 and a CoS value of 6.

A fifth class will be created for network management. This class will consist of network management traffic only. Each packet in the stream will be marked using a DSCP value of CS2 and a CoS value of 2.

No more than five distinct data classes should be used. These classes include the following:

- **Mission-critical**—Using DSCP AF3x and CoS of 3

- **Transactional**—Using DSCP AF2x and CoS 2

- **Bulk transfers**—Using DSCP AF1x and CoS 1

- **Best Effort**—Using DSCP 0 and CoS 0

- **Scavenger traffic**—Using DSCP CS1 and CoS 1

At this point, all traffic in the example network has been classified into the proper group. Each network has its own distinct application requirements and traffic patterns. Your network might or might not require each class of traffic used in the example network. If your network does not have each class of traffic that is discussed, it is a good practice to plan a seamless implementation strategy in case you add these classes in the future.

Table 10-10 lists the discussed classes and shows the Cisco best practices for classification and marking of DSCP and CoS values for each traffic type.

Table 10-10 *Classification and Marking Best Practices*

Application or Protocol	DSCP Marking	DSCP Decimal Value	CoS Value
Voice traffic	EF	46	5
Bulk transfer traffic Web traffic, FTP traffic, large data-transfer applications, and so on	AF11 AF12 AF13	10	1
Transactional applications Database access, interactive traffic, and so on	AF21 AF22 AF23	18	2
Mission-critical applications Core business traffic	AF31 AF32 AF33	25	3
Interactive video traffic	AF41 AF42 AF43	34	4
IP routing BGP, OSPF, and so on	Class 6 (CS6)	48	6
Streaming video	Class 4 (CS4)	32	4
Voice and video signaling traffic SIP, H.323, and so on	AF31/Class 3 (CS3)	26/24	3

Table 10-10   *Classification and Marking Best Practices (Continued)*

Application or Protocol	DSCP Marking	DSCP Decimal Value	CoS Value
Network management traffic SNMP	Class 2 (CS2)	16	2
Scavenger traffic	Class 1 (CS1)	8	1
Unspecified or unclassified traffic	Best Effort or class 0 (CS0)	0	0

TIP   Notice that voice and video signaling traffic is listed with a DSCP value of AF31/CS3. As of this writing, Cisco IP Phones mark this traffic as AF31 by default. Within Cisco, a migration is underway to change the marking from AF31 to CS3, leaving the AF3 class available for mission-critical applications. Until this migration is complete, mission-critical applications should use a DSCP value of 25.

Congestion Management Best Practices

Congestion management describes how a router or switch handles each configured class of traffic during times of congestion. If there is no congestion on the router or switch for that period in time, congestion management does not come into play. However, when buffers and queues begin to fill, the router or switch must have a means to decide the order in which traffic will be transmitted.

LLQ and CBWFQ are the preferred methods for scheduling traffic. LLQ provides a guaranteed, minimal amount of delay and jitter through the router, making LLQ ideal for transporting voice and interactive video traffic.

CBWFQ is used to guarantee that each configured traffic class has a minimal level of bandwidth, thereby preventing starvation for each configured class of traffic.

Table 10-11 lists the congestion management best practices. Remember that the percentage of bandwidth allocated depends upon the applications on your network. In many cases, all the listed classes are not needed, as this allows for the bandwidth assigned to the unnecessary class to be allocated to a necessary class. If excess bandwidth is available, it is divided among the traffic classes in proportion to their configured bandwidths.

Table 10-11 *Congestion Management Best Practices*

Application or Protocol	DSCP Marking	Queue Used	Percentage of Queue
Voice traffic	EF	LLQ	The combination of voice and video traffic in LLQ should not use more than 33 percent of the total available link bandwidth (e.g., 20 percent of total bandwidth).
Bulk transfer traffic Web traffic, FTP traffic, large data-transfer applications, and so on	AF11 AF12 AF13	CBWFQ	This class will receive a moderate amount of the remaining bandwidth after LLQ has been serviced (e.g., 15 percent of remaining bandwidth).
Transactional applications Database access, interactive traffic, and so on	AF21 AF22 AF23	CBWFQ	This class will receive a small amount of the remaining bandwidth after LLQ has been serviced (e.g., 5 percent of remaining bandwidth).
Mission-critical applications Core business traffic	AF31 AF32 AF33	CBWFQ	This class will receive more of the remaining bandwidth after LLQ has been serviced (e.g., 25 percent of remaining bandwidth).
Interactive video traffic	AF41 AF42 AF43	LLQ	The combination of voice and video traffic in LLQ should not use more than 33 percent of the total available link bandwidth.
IP routing BGP, OSPF, and so on	Class 6 (CS6)	CBWFQ	This class will receive a moderate amount of the remaining bandwidth after LLQ has been serviced (e.g., 10 percent of remaining bandwidth).
Streaming video	Class 4 (CS4)	CBWFQ	This class will receive a moderate amount of the remaining bandwidth after LLQ has been serviced (e.g., 10 percent of remaining bandwidth).
Voice and video signaling traffic SIP, H.323, and so on	AF31/ Class 3 (CS3)	CBWFQ	This class will receive a small amount of the remaining bandwidth after LLQ has been serviced (e.g., 5 percent of remaining bandwidth).

Table 10-11   *Congestion Management Best Practices (Continued)*

Application or Protocol	DSCP Marking	Queue Used	Percentage of Queue
Network management traffic SNMP	Class 2 (CS2)	CBWFQ	This class will receive a small amount of the remaining bandwidth after LLQ has been serviced (e.g., 5 percent of remaining bandwidth).
Scavenger traffic	Class 1 (CS1)	CBWFQ	If used, this class will receive less than best-effort treatment. Packets in this class will be transmitted only if there are no other packets to transmit.
Unspecified or unclassified traffic	Best Effort or class 0 (CS0)	CBWFQ	This class will receive no guarantees. Some percentage of bandwidth can be specified that will be used by this class if all other classes have been transmitted (e.g., 5 percent of remaining bandwidth).

In this example the aggregate allocated bandwidth is 100 percent. By default, only 75 percent of the link bandwidth is available to LLQ/CBWFQ. If all applications on your network are accounted for and properly classified, the allocated bandwidth can be configured to use 100 percent of the link by using the **max-reserved-bandwidth 100** interface command. Be aware that this command reserves all the available interface bandwidth, meaning that any unclassified traffic might face starvation if the best-effort class is not able to transmit the packet due to heavy volume.

As a design guideline, the LLQ should contain only the real-time applications on your network and should not use more than 33 percent of the total available link bandwidth. When a packet has reached the LLQ, it is scheduled, or transmitted, on a first-in, first-out (FIFO) basis from the queue. If too many packets exist in the LLQ, the benefits of QoS are negated, because each packet must wait in the LLQ for scheduling. This guideline prevents LLQ from becoming overprovisioned.

After traffic has been scheduled into the appropriate queue, you must examine the physical links that the traffic needs to traverse. In the case of a low-speed serial link, such as a 256-kbps Frame Relay link, that will transport real-time applications, traffic shaping, Link Fragmentation and Interleaving (LFI), and compressed RTP (cRTP) must be considered.

Traffic shaping is needed to prevent packets from being transmitted at a rate greater than the committed information rate (CIR) of the Frame Relay circuit. This results in packets being marked as discard eligible (DE) by the Frame Relay network and poses the potential of being dropped. Applications using TCP will retransmit the packet; however, real-time applications have no means of recovering a dropped packet. By traffic shaping the sending rate to the CIR of the interface, you can ensure that packets are not marked DE and therefore not potentially dropped.

Recall from Chapter 6, "Traffic Policing and Shaping," that Cisco routers begin to send traffic on a Frame Relay circuit eight times a second. This results in a Tc value of 125 ms. In the worst case, a voice packet can experience a high amount of delay while waiting on the next send cycle. This can cause the voice packet to arrive too late for use and be discarded by the terminating device. To remedy this situation, the Tc value should be configured for 10 ms by stating the send cycle 100 times per second. This ensures that in the worst case a voice packet will experience only a small delay that can be compensated for by the jitter buffer in the terminating device.

Now that you are sending every 10 ms, what happens if a large data packet begins to serialize as a voice packet arrives? Even though the sending interval has been decreased, the voice packet will need to wait until the large data packet completes serialization before it can be transmitted. This too can cause the voice packet to experience a large delay. The solution to this problem is Link Fragmentation and Interleaving (LFI). LFI takes the large data packet and breaks it into smaller fragments that can be serialized more quickly. Because the recommended serialization delay of a voice packet is between 10 and 15 ms, LFI needs to be configured to fragment all packets so that each fragment can be serialized in 10 ms.

Congestion Avoidance Best Practices

Congestion avoidance is used to randomly drop packets to prevent the assigned queue from becoming congested. This congestion results in the tail drop of all subsequent received packets. Recall from Chapter 7, "Congestion Avoidance Through Drop Policies," that WRED uses a minimum threshold, average queue depth, and maximum threshold to determine if a packet should be dropped from a queue, while the mark probability denominator is used to calculate the number of packets that will be discarded.

As a rule of thumb, WRED performs more effectively when applied to a CBWFQ that services TCP applications, because these applications have the capability to retransmit lost packets. Some classes of traffic, such as best-effort and bulk transfer traffic, are good candidates for WRED. Real-time applications, which reside in the low latency queue, should never be eligible for WRED.

The type of applications present in each class of traffic and the potential congestion of the queues determine how WRED should be configured. By using the default DSCP drop probability, WRED has a means of randomly dropping packets from traffic flows that have been classified by the administrator as applications that can sustain the loss. From the default drop probability, a baseline can be gathered over time. The minimum and maximum thresholds and mark probability denominator can then be modified as needed.

Table 10-12 lists the best practices for congestion avoidance.

Table 10-12 *Congestion Avoidance Best Practices*

Application or Protocol	DSCP Marking	WRED Policy
Voice traffic	EF	WRED not applied.
Bulk transfer traffic	AF11	DSCP-based
Web traffic, FTP traffic, large data-transfer applications, and so on	AF12 AF13	The default minimum and maximum thresholds will be used for this class of traffic if WRED is enabled.
Transactional applications	AF21	DSCP-based
Database access, interactive traffic, and so on	AF22 AF23	The default minimum and maximum thresholds will be used for this class of traffic if WRED is enabled.
Mission-critical applications	AF31	DSCP-based
Core business traffic	AF32 AF33	The default minimum and maximum thresholds will be used for this class of traffic if WRED is enabled.
Interactive video traffic	AF41	DSCP-based
	AF42 AF43	The default minimum and maximum thresholds will be used for AF42 and AF43 if WRED is enabled. Interactive video, marked AF41, should use LLQ, and, therefore, WRED should not be applied.
IP routing	Class 6 (CS6)	DSCP-based
BGP, OSPF, and so on		The default minimum and maximum thresholds will be used for this class of traffic.
Streaming video	Class 4 (CS4)	DSCP-based
		The default minimum and maximum thresholds will be used for this class of traffic if WRED is enabled.
Voice and video signaling traffic	AF31/Class 3 (CS3)	DSCP-based
SIP, H.323, and so on		A high minimum threshold should be set for this class of traffic if WRED is enabled.

continues

Table 10-12 *Congestion Avoidance Best Practices (Continued)*

Application or Protocol	DSCP Marking	WRED Policy
Network management traffic SNMP	Class 2 (CS2)	DSCP-based The default minimum and maximum thresholds will be used for this class of traffic if WRED is enabled.
Scavenger traffic	Class 1 (CS1)	DSCP-based A low minimum threshold should be set for this class of traffic if WRED is enabled.
Unspecified or unclassified traffic	Best Effort or class 0 (CS0)	DSCP-based The default minimum and maximum thresholds will be used for this class of traffic if WRED is enabled.

Policing Best Practices

Policing limits unwanted traffic in the network by defining an allowable limit and specifying what action should be taken on traffic that exceeds the specified limit.

Unlike classification, congestion management, and to some extent congestion avoidance, there are no steadfast rules for policing that cover most situations. With the possible exception of scavenger traffic, no class of traffic requires policing. Policing should be used to limit the amount of inbound bandwidth used by acceptable traffic. The decision to use policing in the enterprise is typically based upon the need to maximize current throughput without purchasing additional bandwidth. In a service provider network, policing is typically used to limit the sending rate of the enterprise customer and either drop or remark nonconforming traffic.

Policing varies greatly between networks. By gathering a baseline of your network and understanding the acceptable sending rates of each traffic class, you can map a strategy for policing. For policing strategies available with a Cisco infrastructure, see Chapter 6.

QoS Case Studies

The following four QoS case studies examine Cisco best practices for QoS implementations in a typical converged network given the following setups:

■ Enterprise campus QoS implementations

■ Enterprise (CE) to service provider (PE) WAN QoS implementations

- Service provider (PE) to enterprise (CE) WAN QoS implementations

- Service provider backbone QoS implementations

Enterprise Campus QoS Implementations

Before you configure QoS in a campus environment, it is important to have a hieratical and redundant campus design to support real-time applications. This design should consist of an access layer, a distribution layer, and a core, as shown in Figure 10-4.

Figure 10-4 *Campus Network Design*

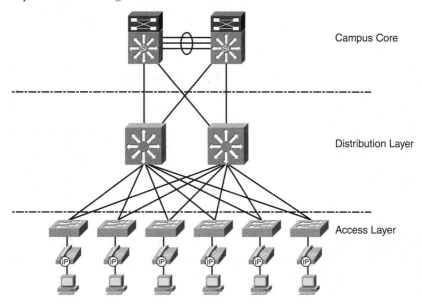

Typically, IP phones and client PCs are connected to access layer switches. The distribution layer switches provide connectivity and redundancy for access layer switches. This setup allows for the scalability and aggregation of access layer switches, which can provide IP phone and client connections for many floors or buildings. The core of the campus network typically consists of very high-speed links that connect the distribution layer switches. Due to these high-speed links, congestion is typically not an issue in the campus core. If the core of your network has the potential for congestion, scheduling should be configured to prioritize desired traffic.

Classification and marking should never be performed in the core of the network, because all traffic received by the core should arrive marked from a trusted source. This section addresses the QoS requirements for the access and distribution layers of the campus LAN. QoS for the core of the campus network will not be discussed.

Table 10-13 lists the QoS components that need to be configured in the access layer and distribution layer of the campus LAN.

Table 10-13 *QoS Components of the Access and Distribution Layers*

QoS Component	Component Function
Trust boundaries	Determines the devices to be trusted. Establishes the trust boundary as close to the source as possible. Access layer function.
Classification and marking	Identifies and marks traffic with desired DSCP/CoS values. Performs as close to the source as possible. Modifies CoS-to-DSCP map. Access layer function.
Congestion management	Schedules each class of traffic with the desired CoS. Access and distribution layer function.
Policing	Limits unwanted or excessive traffic. Access and distribution layer function.

The Cisco Catalyst 2950 and 3550 are common access layer switches seen in converged networks today. Chapter 9, "LAN QoS," discusses the QoS configuration options of the Catalyst 2950. In Figure 10-4, assume that the access layer switches are Catalyst 3550 switches and the distribution layer consists of Catalyst 4500 switches using a Supervisor III module.

By default, the switch transmits packets on a FIFO basis without regard for the received markings on each frame. To begin QoS configuration, you must enable QoS on the access layer switch. This is achieved with the global **mls qos** command. After you enable QoS, you need to determine which devices on your network you will trust. You should configure a trust boundary as close to the source as possible. This means the access layer should contain the initial trust boundary by extending trust to desired devices, such as IP phones, while not extending trust to undesired devices, such as the attached PCs. This is accomplished using the **mls qos trust device cisco-phone** command on the interface that connects a Cisco IP Phone. Additionally, you need to trust the DSCP or CoS markings received from the distribution layer. This is accomplished by placing either the **mls qos trust dscp** command or the **mls qos trust cos** command on the interface that connects to the distribution layer switch. In this example, both the access layer and the distribution layer switches have the capability to read the received DSCP marking, so trust will be based upon DSCP. Example 10-1 shows the configuration necessary to establish the trust boundary.

Example 10-1   *Catalyst 3550 Access Layer Switch Trust Boundaries*

```
interface FastEthernet0/1
 description Connection to Distribution Layer
 switchport trunk encapsulation dot1q
 switchport mode trunk
 no ip address
 mls qos trust dscp
!
interface FastEthernet0/2
description Connection to IP Phone
 switchport voice vlan 5
 no ip address
 mls qos trust device cisco-phone
!
```

After you establish the trust boundary, you can begin to classify desired traffic into the proper traffic groups. Assume that this network carries Cisco voice traffic as well as mission-critical data, transactional data, bulk data, and best-effort traffic. Table 10-14 lists the recommended DSCP and CoS marking for each of these traffic classes.

Table 10-14   *Campus LAN Classification*

Application or Protocol	DSCP Marking	DSCP Decimal Value	CoS Value
Voice traffic	EF	46	5
Bulk transfer traffic	AF11	10	1
Web traffic, FTP traffic, large data-transfer applications, and so on	AF12		
	AF13		
Transactional applications	AF21	18	2
Database access, interactive traffic, and so on	AF22		
	AF23		
Mission-critical applications	AF31	26	3
Core business traffic	AF32		
	AF33		

continues

Table 10-14 *Campus LAN Classification (Continued)*

Application or Protocol	DSCP Marking	DSCP Decimal Value	CoS Value
IP routing BGP, OSPF, and so on	Class 6 (CS6)	48	6
Voice and video signaling traffic SIP, H.323, and so on	AF31/Class 3 (CS3)	26/24	3
Network management traffic SNMP	Class 2 (CS2)	16	2
Unspecified or unclassified traffic	Best-effort or class 0 (CS0)	0	0

Cisco IP Phones have the capability to mark both voice signaling and voice media traffic; however, other applications, such as Cisco Softphone and certain Computer Telephony Integration (CTI) applications, may not. To ensure that each device or application in the network receives the proper treatment for all voice signaling and media traffic, it is important to classify this traffic using some other means:

- All Cisco voice media streams are carried across the network in UDP/RTP packets that use the port range of 16384 to 32767.

- All Cisco Skinny voice signaling packets are transported across the network using the TCP port range of 2000 to 2002.

- H.323 signaling packets use TCP port 1720 as well as the TCP range of 11000 to 11999.

- Media Gateway Control Protocol (MGCP) uses the UDP port 2427.

These protocols and port numbers can be used to classify this traffic. Similarly, the protocol and port number of traffic that comprises the mission-critical, transaction, bulk data, and network-management traffic can be used for classification. The best-effort class will match all other traffic. Example 10-2 shows the configuration necessary to classify and mark the desired traffic.

Example 10-2 *Catalyst 3550 Access Layer Switch Classification*

```
class-map match-all voice-media
 match access-group 100
class-map match-all voice-signaling
 match access-group 101
class-map match-all mission-critical
```

Example 10-2 *Catalyst 3550 Access Layer Switch Classification (Continued)*

```
 match access-group 102
class-map match-all transactional
 match access-group 103
class-map match-all bulkdata
 match access-group 104
class-map match-all netmanage
 match access-group 105
class-map match-all besteffort
 match any
!
policy-map mark-traffic
 class voice-media
  set ip dscp ef
class voice-signaling
  set ip dscp 24
class mission-critical
  set ip dscp af31
class transactional
  set ip dscp af21
class bulkdata
  set ip dscp af11
class netmanage
  set ip dscp cs2
class besteffort
  set ip dscp 0
!
access-list 100 permit udp any any range 16384 32767
access-list 101 permit tcp any any range 2000 2002
access-list 101 permit tcp any any eq 1720
access-list 101 permit tcp any any range 11000 11999
access-list 102 permit <Protocol / port for Mission Critical Traffic>
access-list 103 permit <Protocol / port for Transactional Traffic>
access-list 104 permit <Protocol / port for Bulk Data Traffic>
access-list 105 permit <Protocol / port for Network Management Traffic>
```

Finally, the **service-policy input** command is used to enable classification for each desired interface that connects to a Cisco IP Phone of a client PC, as shown in Example 10-3.

Example 10-3 *Catalyst 3550 Access Layer Service-Policy Input*

```
!
interface FastEthernet0/2
description Connection to IP Phone
 switchport voice vlan 5
 no ip address
 service-policy input mark-traffic
 mls qos trust device cisco-phone
```

When the access layer switch receives a packet with a DSCP value from a trusted interface or device, it automatically assigns a CoS value to the packet. Likewise, if the switch receives a packet with a CoS value, it automatically assigns a DSCP value to the packet. These assigned values can be modified using the **mls qos map dscp-cos** and **mls qos map cos-dscp** commands, respectively. Because DSCP uses 6 bits, as opposed to the 3 bits used by CoS, a wider range of DSCP values can be mapped to a single CoS value. For example, a received packet marked AF31, AF32, or AF33 will share the same CoS value of 3. Typically, this is desired behavior and so the DSCP-to-CoS map does not usually need to be modified. The CoS-to-DSCP map, however, has fewer options. By default, a received packet with a CoS value of 5 will be marked with a DSCP value of decimal 40, which is not the same as DSCP EF (decimal 46). Because a CoS value of 5 typically represents the marking for voice traffic, which should also be marked with a DSCP value of EF, you need to modify the CoS-to-DSCP map. The **mls qos map cos-dscp 0 8 16 24 32 46 48 56** command makes this modification.

> **TIP** Notice that the CoS value of 3 is mapped to DSCP CS3 (decimal 24) by default. This is different than the current DSCP value AF31 (decimal 26) marked by the Cisco IP Phone today and more in line with the Cisco migration strategy of changing the voice signaling DSCP marking from AF31 (decimal 26) to CS3 (decimal 24), as discussed in the earlier "Classification and Marking Best Practices" section of this chapter. To keep the voice signaling traffic consistent with the way Cisco IP Phones are marking traffic today, use the **mls qos map cos-dscp 0 8 16 24 32 46 48 56** command.

When trust, classification, and marking have been established, you need to determine the CoS each type of traffic will receive. To properly configure scheduling, it is important to understand the transmit-queuing capability of the access layer switches used in your network. Separating traffic into distinct hardware queues within the access layer switch is a requirement. The Catalyst 3550 in the sample network offers one strict priority transmit queue and three standard transmit queues (1p3q2t). Each standard queue has two drop thresholds and is serviced using a WRR scheduling method. This allows real-time applications, such as voice, to receive a guaranteed delay, jitter, and bandwidth, while the remaining three queues will receive a guaranteed bandwidth. Admission into each queue is dependant upon the CoS value received. Table 10-15 shows the default queue admission on a Catalyst 3550.

Table 10-15 *Catalyst 3550 Default Queue Admission*

CoS Value	Queue
0 and 1	1 – standard queue
2 and 3	2 – standard queue
4 and 5	3 – standard queue
6 and 7	4 – strict priority queue

Notice that Ethernet frames marked with a CoS value of 5 will be placed in standard queue 3. Because Cisco IP Phones mark voice media traffic with a CoS value of 5 by default, this means that all voice media traffic will not be placed into the strict priority queue. The **wrr-queue cos-map** command remaps received with a CoS value of 5 into the strict priority queue, queue number 4. Example 10-4 shows the necessary configuration.

Example 10-4 *Catalyst 3550 Access Layer WRR-Queue CoS-Map*

```
!
interface FastEthernet0/1
 description Connection to Distribution Layer
 switchport trunk encapsulation dot1q
 switchport mode trunk
 no ip address
 mls qos trust dscp
 wrr-queue cos-map 4 5
 priority-queue out
!
interface FastEthernet0/2
description Connection to IP Phone
 switchport voice vlan 5
 no ip address
 mls qos trust device cisco-phone
 wrr-queue cos-map 4 5
 priority-queue out
 spanning-tree portfast
!
```

Notice that the **priority-queue out** command is also placed under the interface. This command instructs the switch to treat queue number 4 as the strict priority queue. Without this command the Catalyst 3550 treats queue number 4 as a standard queue. After the strict priority queue has been defined and real-time traffic has been scheduled, you need to determine the scheduling treatment received for the remaining traffic. Assume that it has been determined that queue 1, consisting of frames marked with CoS values 0 and 1, transmits 25 frames per interval. Queue 2, consisting of frames marked with CoS values 2 and 3, transmits 50 frames per interval. Finally, queue 3, consisting of frames marked with a CoS value of 4, transmits 10 frames per interval. The **wrr-queue bandwidth** command can be placed upon the interface to specify the number of packets each queue is allowed to transmit before the next queue is serviced. Example 10-5 shows how the WRR bandwidth is configured for this example.

Example 10-5 *Catalyst 3550 Access WRR-Queue Bandwidth*

```
!
interface FastEthernet0/1
 description Connection to Distribution Layer
 switchport trunk encapsulation dot1q
```

continues

Example 10-5 *Catalyst 3550 Access WRR-Queue Bandwidth (Continued)*

```
switchport mode trunk
no ip address
mls qos trust dscp
wrr-queue bandwidth 25 50 10 15
wrr-queue cos-map 4 5
priority-queue out
!
```

Remember that this is just an example. Scheduling treatment will depend on the QoS requirements of the applications that exist on your network.

Notice that queue 4 has been configured to transmit 15 frames per interval. In a network that contains real-time applications, this will not suffice. Thankfully, the **priority-queue out** command overrides this configuration, changing queue 4 from a standard WRR queue to a strict priority queue. The WRR configuration of queue 4 comes into play only if the **priority-queue out** command is removed from the interface.

At this point, the access layer of the campus network has been configured to classify traffic into groups and provide for the QoS requirements of the desired applications. From the access layer, packets flow to the distribution layer switches. The distribution layer of the example network consists of Catalyst 4500 switches using Supervisor III modules. Because the distribution layer trusts markings received from the trust boundaries established in the access layer, you do not need to reclassify received traffic. This simplifies the QoS configuration of the distribution layer, by requiring only the configuration of scheduling the predefined traffic classes and the policing of any unwanted traffic.

By default, QoS is disabled on the Catalyst 4500. To enable QoS, use the global **qos** command. The **qos trust dscp** interface command is used on the interfaces that connect to the access layer in the example network. This allows the distribution layer switches to trust the received DSCP marking. Example 10-6 shows the distribution configuration needed to extend trust to the access layer.

Example 10-6 *Catalyst 4500 Trust*

```
interface GigabitEthernet1/1
description Connection to Access Layer
switchport trunk encapsulation dot1q
switchport mode trunk
qos trust dscp
```

The Supervisor III module offers one strict priority transmit queue and three standard transmit queues (1p3q2t). Each standard queue has two drop thresholds and is serviced using a WRR scheduling method. This allows real-time applications, such as voice, to receive a delay, jitter, and bandwidth guarantee, while the remaining three queues receive only a guaranteed bandwidth. Admission into each queue is dependant upon the DSCP or CoS value received. Table 10-16 shows the default queue admission on a Catalyst 4500 using a Supervisor III module.

Table 10-16 *Catalyst 4500 with Supervisor III Default Queue Admission*

DSCP/CoS Value	Queue
DSCP 0–15 CoS 0–1	1 – standard queue
DSCP 16–31 CoS 2–3	2 – standard queue
DSCP 32–47 CoS 4–5	3 – strict priority queue
DSCP 48–63 CoS 6–7	4 – standard queue

By default, each of the four queues will be allowed to transmit for 25 percent of the interface before moving to the next queue. As with the access layer switches, this will not provide the priority needed for real-time applications. To provide the necessary prioritization, you need to enable the strict priority queue. To enable the strict priority queue on the Catalyst 4500, use the **tx-queue 3** and **priority out** commands on each desired interface. Example 10-7 shows the necessary configuration.

Example 10-7 *Catalyst 4500 Strict Priority Queuing*

```
interface GigabitEthernet1/1
description Connection to Access Layer
switchport trunk encapsulation dot1q
switchport mode trunk
qos trust dscp
tx-queue 3
priority high
```

As with the access layer switches, the distribution layer switches have the capability to map a received CoS value to a DSCP value or a received DSCP value to a CoS value. If trust is based upon the received DSCP value of a packet, the appropriate CoS value will be placed upon the packet. If trust is based upon the CoS value received, the CoS-to-DSCP map may need to be modified. For example, a received CoS value of 5 will result in a DSCP value of decimal 40, which is not the same as DSCP EF or decimal 46. You can change the CoS-to-DSCP mapping with the global **qos map cos 5 to dscp 46** command.

Because the distribution layer provides aggregation service for all the access layer switches, this is an ideal place to limit traffic that might threaten congestion in the core. For example, assume that there is a large amount of unwanted FTP traffic, yet the core of your network is provisioned for a maximum of 5 Mbps of FTP traffic. The distribution layer can be used to limit the received FTP traffic to 5 Mbps and drop any additional FTP traffic received. Example 10-8 shows how this is accomplished.

Example 10-8 *Catalyst 4500 Policing*

```
class-map match-all policeftp
 match access-group 2
!
policy-map policeftp
 class policeftp
  police 5000000 8192 exceed-action drop
!
!
interface GigabitEthernet1/1
description Connection to Access Layer
service-policy input policeftp
switchport trunk encapsulation dot1q
switchport mode trunk
qos trust dscp
tx-queue 3
priority high
!
access-list 2 permit <IP Address of FTP server>
!
```

By identifying the desired traffic to police, defining the policed limit, and applying the limit to the interface, the distribution layer can prevent the transport of any unwanted traffic into the core of the campus network.

Enterprise (CE) to Service Provider (PE) WAN QoS Implementations

As traffic leaves the campus LAN and enters the enterprise WAN edge router, also known as the CE router, for transport across the service provider's network, the question of QoS configuration on the CE router arises. The exact QoS configuration depends upon who has configuration control of the CE router. In some cases, this router is under the administrative control of the enterprise, while in other cases, the service provider manages the CE router. The major difference between the two configurations becomes mostly a matter of trust. If the CE router is under the control of the enterprise, the DSCP markings received from the campus LAN can be trusted because the same administrative control extends to the campus LAN. However, if the service provider manages the CE router, a trust boundary will be established on the CE router because the service provider has no control over the campus LAN. In either case, some fundamental QoS configurations are consistent. Table 10-17 lists the QoS components required on the CE router.

Table 10-17 *QoS Components of the CE Router*

QoS Component	Component Function Managed Enterprise WAN Edge	Component Function Unmanaged Enterprise WAN Edge
SLA	Defines the supported classes of traffic and the level of service each class will receive. Enforced on the CE router.	Defines the supported classes of traffic and the level of service each class will receive. Enforced on the PE router.
Trust boundaries	Established on the CE router by the service provider. The service provider can then trust packets received from the CE, which removes the need for an inbound policy on the PE router.	Established on the CE router by the enterprise administrator. The service provider may not trust packets received from the CE and may remark traffic at the PE based upon the SLA.
Classification and marking	Traffic will be reclassified and marked on the CE based upon the classes offered in the SLA. The service provider can then trust markings received from the CE, which removes the need for an inbound policy on the PE router.	Traffic may be reclassified and marked on the CE based upon the classes offered in the SLA. The service provider may not trust packets received from the CE and may remark traffic at the PE based upon the SLA.
Congestion management	LLQ/CBWFQ queuing will be configured on the CE in accordance with the SLA. Traffic shaping, LFI, and cRTP may be configured depending upon the link type and speed.	LLQ/CBWFQ queuing will be configured on the CE in accordance with the SLA. Traffic shaping, LFI, and cRTP may be configured depending upon the link type and speed.
Congestion avoidance	WRED may be used to randomly drop best-effort traffic.	WRED may be used to randomly drop best-effort traffic.
Policing	Policing may be required on the CE router. The service provider can then trust the traffic rate received from the CE, which removes the need for an inbound policy on the PE router.	Policing will be required on the PE router. The service provider will reclassify or drop traffic that exceeds the limit specified in the SLA.

Notice that the SLA agreement is instrumental in each QoS component required. This is because the SLA provides the roadmap that will be used for all traffic that traverses the service provider's network. From this roadmap, QoS configuration for the CE router can be developed. Assume that Table 10-18 represents the SLA that has been reached between the enterprise and the service provider.

Table 10-18 *Sample SLA*

Class of Traffic	DSCP Value	Guarantee	Percentage of Link Speed or CIR
Gold	DSCP EF CS3	A maximum bandwidth Low latency No packet loss	25 percent of total link speed or CIR
Silver	DSCP AF31 DSCP AF32 DSCP AF32 CS6	A minimum bandwidth Minimal packet loss	50 percent of link speed or CIR after Gold traffic has been transmitted
Bronze	DSCP AF21 DSCP AF22 DSCP AF23	A minimum bandwidth Low to no packet loss	25 percent of link speed or CIR after Gold and Silver traffic have been transmitted
Default	DSCP 0	None—Best effort	25 percent of link speed or CIR after Gold, Silver, and Bronze traffic have been transmitted

In this example, the service provider will place traffic into each of these classes based upon the received DSCP value of each packet.

Assume that the link between the enterprise and the service provider is a Frame Relay circuit with a port speed and CIR of 256 kbps, as shown in Figure 10-5.

Figure 10-5 *Enterprise WAN Edge*

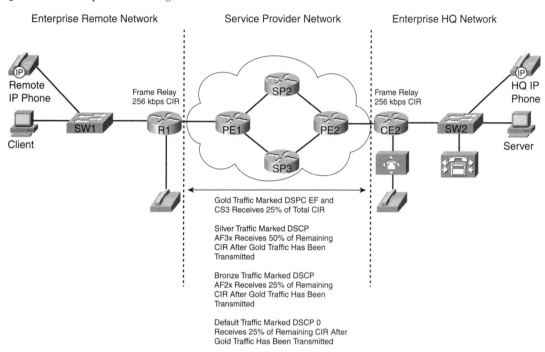

With the SLA and network topology in place, you can begin to build the required QoS configurations.

Classification of the enterprise traffic into the Gold, Silver, Bronze, and Default groups must be performed first. Because the campus LAN has more than four traffic classes defined, some classes must be combined to classify all traffic within the four classes the service provider offers in this example. Combining these classes requires that some traffic be reclassified and marked on the CE router. Table 10-19 lists the enterprise traffic classes, the original campus LAN DSCP marking, and the reclassified DSCP marking on the CE, if needed.

Table 10-19 *CE Reclassification*

Application or Protocol	Campus LAN Original DSCP Marking	CE/PE Reclassified DSCP Marking	SLA Traffic Class
Voice traffic	EF	EF	Gold
Bulk transfer traffic	AF11	AF22	Bronze
Web traffic, FTP traffic, large data-transfer applications, and so on	AF12 AF13		

continues

Table 10-19 *CE Reclassification (Continued)*

Application or Protocol	Campus LAN Original DSCP Marking	CE/PE Reclassified DSCP Marking	SLA Traffic Class
Transactional applications Database access, interactive traffic, and so on	AF21 AF22 AF23	AF32	Silver
Mission-critical applications Core business traffic	AF31 AF32 AF33	AF31	Silver
IP routing BGP, OSPF, and so on	Class 6 (CS6)	CS6	Silver
Voice and video signaling traffic SIP, H.323, and so on	AF31/Class 3 (CS3)	CS3	Gold
Network management traffic SNMP	Class 2 (CS2)	AF21	Bronze
Unspecified or unclassified traffic	Best-effort or class 0 (CS0)	0	Default

In this example, Gold traffic will consist of voice media and call setup traffic. Note that call setup traffic will use the marking of DSCP CS3 in this example to allow mission-critical traffic to use the AF31 marking. This assumes that call setup traffic has been marked as CS3 in the campus LAN. Silver traffic will consist of all mission-critical and transactional enterprise application traffic as well as IP routing traffic. Bronze traffic will consist of bulk transfer data and network management traffic. Default, or best-effort, traffic will consist of all other nonclassified traffic.

Notice that some application traffic, such as voice media traffic, does not need to be reclassified, because the DSCP marking of EF allows the voice media traffic admittance into the Gold traffic class. However, other application traffic will need to be remarked to gain admittance into the desired traffic class. For example, bulk transfer data traffic needs to be reclassified from AF1x to AF22 to gain admittance into the Bronze class.

If the CE is controlled by the enterprise, the classifications can be trusted from the campus LAN and passed on to the service provider, or they can be reclassified using MQC, NBAR, access lists, or any combination of these on the CE router before delivery to the service provider. If the service provider manages the CE router, traffic will most likely be reclassified using NBAR or access lists as specified in the SLA. This example assumes that the CE is managed by the enterprise. DSCP marking from the campus LAN is trusted and MQC is used to reclassify traffic into the Gold, Silver, Bronze, and Default traffic classes supported by the SLA. Example 10-9 shows this configuration.

Example 10-9 *CE Classification*

```
class-map match-any voice-media
  match ip dscp ef
class-map match-any voice-signaling
  match ip dscp cs3
 class-map match-any mission-critical
  match ip dscp af31
  match ip dscp af32
  match ip dscp af33
class-map match-any transactional
  match ip dscp af21
  match ip dscp af22
  match ip dscp af23
class-map match-any bulkdata
  match ip dscp af11
  match ip dscp af12
  match ip dscp af13
class-map match-any routing
  match ip dscp cs6
class-map match-any netmanage
  match ip dscp cs2
!
policy-map OutPolicy
  class voice-media
   set ip dscp ef
  class voice-signaling
   set ip dscp cs3
  class mission-critical
   set ip dscp af31
  class transactional
   set ip dscp af32
  class bulkdata
   set ip dscp af22
  class routing
   set ip dscp cs6
  class netmanage
   set ip dscp af21
  class class-default
   set ip dscp 0
!
```

Notice that some classes, such as the **bulkdata** class, have been remarked, while other classes, such as the **voice-media** class, remain unchanged. This allows the CE router to classify the traffic into groups supported in the SLA.

Queuing will use a combination of LLQ and CBWFQ in the **policy-map** command. LLQ will guarantee that all Gold traffic will receive 25 percent of the CIR. Because the Gold class consists of the **voice-media** class and the **voice-signaling** class, the allocated 25 percent of the link must be split between these two classes. In this example, the **voice-media** class will receive 21 percent of the link, while the **voice-signaling** class will receive 4 percent of the link.

CBWFQ will be used on the Silver and Bronze classes to guarantee that a minimum amount of bandwidth will be available for each enterprise traffic class.

The Silver class will consist of IP routing updates, mission-critical data, and transactional data traffic. All enterprise traffic classes in the Silver class will be allocated a minimum of 50 percent of the link after the Gold traffic class has been transmitted. In this example, IP routing updates will receive 5 percent, mission-critical traffic will receive 30 percent, and transaction data traffic will receive 15 percent.

The Bronze class will consist of bulk transfer data and network management traffic. All enterprise traffic classes in the Bronze class will be allocated a minimum of 25 percent of the link after the Gold traffic class has been transmitted. In this example, the bulk data class will receive 20 percent of the link, while network management traffic will receive 5 percent of the link.

The Default class will consist of all unclassified and best-effort traffic. This class will receive 25 percent of the link after the Gold class has been transmitted.

Example 10-10 shows the CE queuing configuration.

Example 10-10 *CE Queuing*

```
policy-map OutPolicy
  class voice-media
   priority percent 21
   set ip dscp ef
  class voice-signaling
   priority percent 4
   set ip dscp cs3
  class mission-critical
   bandwidth percent remaining 30
   set ip dscp af31
  class transactional
   bandwidth percent remaining 15
   set ip dscp af32
  class bulkdata
```

Example 10-10 *CE Queuing (Continued)*

```
    bandwidth percent remaining 20
     set ip dscp af22
    class routing
     bandwidth percent remaining 5
     set ip dscp cs6
    class netmanage
     bandwidth percent remaining 5
     set ip dscp af21
    class class-default
     bandwidth percent remaining 25
     set ip dscp 0
```

Notice that the **priority percent** and **bandwidth percent remaining** commands are used to specify the amount of bandwidth available to each class of traffic. These commands allow you to specify bandwidth per class without having to specify the exact amount of bandwidth. For example, 25 percent of the 256-kbps CIR is 64 kbps. The 64 kbps available to the priority queue could have been divided between the **voice-media** and **voice-signaling** classes and specified in terms of bandwidth to accomplish this same goal. Using the **percent** and **percent remaining** options simplifies QoS configuration because a single template can now be used across the enterprise.

Because this example network has a low-speed Frame Relay link, traffic shaping, LFI, and cRTP must be taken into consideration.

Traffic shaping will be configured to limit the total traffic sent to the CIR value of 256 kbps. This will prevent any frame from being marked as discard eligible and possibly being dropped by the service provider in time of congestion. While TCP traffic has a means of recovering lost packets, real-time applications do not.

Because delay is a major concern with real-time applications, it is important to minimize the serialization delay for the voice traffic in this network. The recommended serialization delay for voice packets is 10 to 15 ms. The recommended delay can be exceeded if a voice packet is waiting for a larger data packet to serialize before it can be transmitted. To minimize the serialization delay, all packets must be sized so that they will serialize within the 10–15 ms window. Modifying the default TC value and using LFI will accomplish this. For this example, TC will be modified to 10 ms by configuring the Bc to 2560, while Frame Relay fragmentation will be added to ensure that all packets are no larger than 320 bytes. Because the network in this example contains a slow Frame

Relay link, the RTP headers can be compressed to conserve bandwidth. Example 10-11 shows the configuration needed to address these concerns.

Example 10-11 *CE Traffic Shaping, LFI, and cRTP*

```
!
interface Serial0/0.1 point-to-point
 description to SP PE router
 ip address 10.254.14.2 255.255.255.252
 frame-relay interface-dlci 115
  class FR-Shape
!
map-class frame-relay FR-Shape
 frame-relay cir 256000
 frame-relay bc 2560
 frame-relay be 0
 frame-relay mincir 256000
 service-policy output OutPolicy
 frame-relay fragment 320
 frame-relay ip rtp header-compression
```

Finally, congestion avoidance should be configured on the bulk data and default, or Best Effort, traffic classes. This helps prevent tail drop in the default by randomly dropping packets from different flows in the bulk data and default classes. Example 10-12 shows this configuration.

Example 10-12 *CE Congestion Avoidance*

```
!
policy-map OutPolicy
  class voice-media
   priority percent 21
   set ip dscp ef
  class voice-signaling
   priority percent 4
   set ip dscp cs3
  class mission-critical
   bandwidth percent remaining 30
   set ip dscp af31
  class transactional
   bandwidth percent remaining 15
   set ip dscp af32
  class bulkdata
   bandwidth percent remaining 20
   set ip dscp af22
   random-detect dscp-based
  class routing
   bandwidth percent remaining 5
   set ip dscp cs6
```

Example 10-12 *CE Congestion Avoidance (Continued)*

```
 class netmanage
  bandwidth percent remaining 5
  set ip dscp af21
 class class-default
  set ip dscp 0
  random-detect dscp-based
!
```

Example 10-13 pulls the entire configuration together, showing the total QoS configuration of the CE router in the sample network.

Example 10-13 *CE QoS Configuration*

```
class-map match-any voice-media
  match ip dscp ef
class-map match-any voice-signaling
  match ip dscp cs3
 class-map match-any mission-critical
  match ip dscp af31
  match ip dscp af32
  match ip dscp af33
class-map match-any transactional
  match ip dscp af21
  match ip dscp af22
  match ip dscp af23
class-map match-any bulkdata
  match ip dscp af11
  match ip dscp af12
  match ip dscp af13
class-map match-any routing
  match ip dscp cs6
class-map match-any netmanage
  match ip dscp cs2
!
policy-map OutPolicy
  class voice-media
   priority percent 21
   set ip dscp ef
  class voice-signaling
   priority percent 4
   set ip dscp cs3
  class mission-critical
   bandwidth percent remaining 30
   set ip dscp af31
  class transactional
   bandwidth percent remaining 15
```

continues

Example 10-13 *CE QoS Configuration (Continued)*

```
     set ip dscp af32
    class bulkdata
     bandwidth percent remaining 20
     set ip dscp af22
     random-detect dscp-based
    class routing
     bandwidth percent remaining 5
     set ip dscp cs6
    class netmanage
     bandwidth percent remaining 5
     set ip dscp af21
    class class-default
     set ip dscp 0
     random-detect dscp-based
!
interface Serial0/0
 description to SP PE router
 encapsulation frame-relay
 frame-relay traffic-shaping
!
interface Serial0/0.1 point-to-point
 ip address 10.254.14.2 255.255.255.252
 frame-relay interface-dlci 115
  class FR-Shape
!
map-class frame-relay FR-Shape
 frame-relay cir 256000
 frame-relay bc 2560
 frame-relay be 0
 frame-relay mincir 128000
 service-policy output OutPolicy
 frame-relay fragment 320
 frame-relay ip rtp header-compression
```

Example 10-13 examined the QoS configuration of the CE router from the perspective of sending packets to the PE router. The assumption here is that traffic arriving from the PE router will be marked in accordance with the SLA. The use of NBAR or access lists will be required to remark the mission-critical data, transactional data, bulk transfer data, and network management traffic to the original campus LAN classification. The exact configuration required is dependant upon the applications that comprise each class.

Service Provider (PE) to Enterprise (CE) WAN QoS Implementations

The previous section discusses how traffic is treated as it leaves the CE router. This section looks at the treatment traffic receives on the service provider's WAN edge (PE) router. As with the previous section, the exact configuration depends upon the configuration control of the CE router.

Table 10-20 lists the QoS components required on the PE router.

Table 10-20 *QoS Components of the PE Router*

QoS Component	Component Function Managed Enterprise WAN Edge	Component Function Unmanaged Enterprise WAN Edge
SLA	Defines the supported classes of traffic and the level of service each class will receive. Enforced on the CE router.	Defines the supported classes of traffic and the level of service each class will receive. Enforced on the PE router.
Trust boundaries	Established on the CE router by the service provider. The service provider can then trust packets received from the CE router, which removes the need for an inbound policy on the PE router.	The service provider may not trust packets received from the CE router and may remark traffic on the PE router based upon the SLA.
Classification and marking	Traffic will be reclassified and remarked on the CE router based upon the classes offered in the SLA. The service provider can then trust markings received from the CE router, which removes the need for an inbound policy on the PE router.	Traffic may be reclassified and remarked on the PE router based upon the classes offered in the SLA.
Congestion management	LLQ/CBWFQ queuing will be configured in accordance with the SLA. Traffic shaping, LFI, and cRTP may be configured depending upon the link type and speed.	LLQ/CBWFQ queuing will be configured in accordance with the SLA. Traffic shaping, LFI, and cRTP may be configured depending upon the link type and speed.
Congestion avoidance	WRED may be used to randomly drop best-effort traffic.	WRED may be used to randomly drop best-effort traffic.
Policing	Policing may be required on the CE router. The service provider can then trust the traffic rate received from the CE, which removes the need for an inbound policy on the PE router.	Policing will be required on the PE router. The service provider will reclassify or drop traffic that exceeds the limit specified in the SLA.

As with the CE router QoS configuration, the PE router uses the SLA to determine the QoS configuration needed.

The service provider can trust the DSCP values received from the CE, or remark the values using NBAR or access lists based on the terms of the SLA. For this example, assume that the service provider trusts the DSCP value on each packet as long as the marking is consistent with the acceptable values specified in the SLA. Any other DSCP value received will be rewritten with a DSCP value of 0. Example 10-14 shows the configuration needed on the PE to accomplish this.

Example 10-14 *PE DSCP Classification and Marking*

```
class-map match-any gold
  match ip dscp ef
  match ip dscp cs3
 class-map match-any silver
  match ip dscp af31
  match ip dscp af32
  match ip dscp cs6
class-map match-any bronze
  match ip dscp af22
  match ip dscp af21
!
policy-map InPolicy
  class gold
  class silver
  class bronze
  class class-default
    set ip dscp 0
```

In this example network, the CE router is under the control of the enterprise. The service provider has no control over the amount of traffic being sent in each class. Therefore, the service provider must use policing to either drop or remark nonconforming traffic. The Gold class will be policed to 25 percent of the link. Nonconforming traffic received in this class will be dropped. The Silver class will be policed to a minimum of 50 percent of the link. Nonconforming traffic received in this class will be remarked to the Bronze class and sent. The Bronze class will be policed to a minimum of 25 percent of the link. Nonconforming traffic received in this class will be remarked to the Default class and sent. The Default class will not be policed. Example 10-15 shows the configuration needed on the PE to accomplish this.

Example 10-15 *PE Policing*

```
policy-map InPolicy
  class gold
    police percent 25
      conform-action transmit
      exceed-action drop
```

Example 10-15 *PE Policing (Continued)*

```
 class silver
  police percent 50
   conform-action transmit
   exceed-action set-dscp-transmit af22
 class bronze
  police percent 25
   conform-action transmit
   exceed-action set-dscp-transmit 0
 class class-default
  set ip dscp 0
```

So far, the discussion has focused on using DSCP values on the PE. This implies that the service provider's core network is using IP routing to pass along the DSCP value from router to router. If the service provider uses Multiprotocol Label Switching (MPLS), the MPLS experimental bit is the preferred marking. By mapping the DSCP value to the appropriate MPLS experimental value, the service provider can maintain the separate classes of service across the MPLS backbone. Example 10-16 shows how this might be configured.

Example 10-16 *PE MPLS Classification and Marking*

```
policy-map InPolicy
  class gold
   police percent 25
    conform-action set-mpls-exp-transmit 5
    exceed-action drop
  class silver
   police percent 50
    conform-action set-mpls-exp-transmit 4
    exceed-action set-mpls-exp-transmit 3
  class bronze
   police percent 25
    conform-action set-mpls-exp-transmit 3
    exceed-action set-mpls-exp-transmit 0
  class class-default
   set mpls experimental 0
```

Because traffic shaping, LFI, and cRTP have been configured on the CE router, the PE router must also be configured to reflect these values. Example 10-17 shows the configuration of traffic shaping, LFI, and cRTP on the PE router.

Example 10-17 *PE Policing*

```
interface Serial0/0
 description to Customer's CE router
 encapsulation frame-relay
```

continues

Example 10-17 *PE Policing (Continued)*

```
 frame-relay traffic-shaping
!
interface Serial0/0.1 point-to-point
 ip address 10.254.14.1 255.255.255.252
 frame-relay interface-dlci 125
  class FR-Shape
!
map-class frame-relay FR-Shape
 frame-relay cir 256000
 frame-relay bc 2560
 frame-relay be 0
 frame-relay mincir 128000
 service-policy input InPolicy
 frame-relay fragment 320
 frame-relay ip rtp header-compression
```

Finally, WRED will be configured on the Silver, Bronze, and Default classes to prevent tail drop from occurring. Example 10-18 shows the configuration needed to enable WRED.

Example 10-18 *PE Congestion Avoidance*

```
policy-map InPolicy
  class gold
   police percent 25
    conform-action transmit
    exceed-action drop
  class silver
   police percent 50
    conform-action transmit
    exceed-action set-dscp-transmit af22
   random-detect dscp-based
  class bronze
   police percent 25
    conform-action transmit
    exceed-action set-dscp-transmit 0
   random-detect dscp-based
  class class-default
   bandwidth percent remaining 25
   set ip dscp 0
   random-detect dscp-based
```

The preceding configurations examine how traffic received by the PE router is treated in accordance to the sample SLA. You must also consider traffic being sent from the PE to the CE. Because all traffic being sent from the PE should already be classified and marked with the appropriate DSCP value, this becomes a matter of queuing and congestion avoidance. You can create an output policy map, similar to the policy map used in the CE router, to define the queuing and WRED configurations. Example 10-19 shows the configuration for the output policy map on the PE router.

Example 10-19 *PE-to-CE Output Policy Map*

```
policy-map OutPolicy
  class gold
    priority percent 25
  class silver
    bandwidth percent remaining 50
    random-detect dscp-based
  class bronze
    bandwidth percent remaining 25
    random-detect dscp-based
  class class-default
    bandwidth percent remaining 25
    random-detect dscp-based
!
interface Serial0/0
 description to Customer's CE router
 encapsulation frame-relay
 frame-relay traffic-shaping
!
interface Serial0/0.1 point-to-point
 ip address 10.254.14.1 255.255.255.252
 frame-relay interface-dlci 125
  class FR-Shape
!
map-class frame-relay FR-Shape
 frame-relay cir 256000
 frame-relay bc 2560
 frame-relay be 0
 frame-relay mincir 256000
 service-policy input InPolicy
 service-policy output OutPolicy
 frame-relay fragment 320
 frame-relay ip rtp header-compression
```

Notice that WRED was also configured on the Silver, Bronze, and Default traffic classes. This mirrors the configuration on the service provider's input policy map.

Example 10-20 pulls the entire configuration together, showing the total QoS configuration of the PE router in the sample network.

Example 10-20 *CE QoS Configuration*

```
class-map match-any gold
  match ip dscp ef
  match ip dscp cs3
 class-map match-any silver
  match ip dscp af31
  match ip dscp af32
  match ip dscp cs6
class-map match-any bronze
  match ip dscp af22
  match ip dscp af21
!
policy-map InPolicy
  class gold
   police percent 25
    conform-action transmit
    exceed-action drop
  class silver
   police percent 50
    conform-action transmit
    exceed-action set-dscp-transmit af22
   random-detect dscp-based
  class bronze
   police percent 25
    conform-action transmit
    exceed-action set-dscp-transmit 0
   random-detect dscp-based
  class class-default
   bandwidth percent remaining 25
   set ip dscp 0
   random-detect dscp-based
!
policy-map OutPolicy
  class gold
   priority percent 25
  class silver
   bandwidth percent remaining 50
   random-detect dscp-based
  class bronze
   bandwidth percent remaining 25
   random-detect dscp-based
  class class-default
   bandwidth percent remaining 25
   random-detect dscp-based
```

Example 10-20 *CE QoS Configuration (Continued)*

```
!
interface Serial0/0
 description to Customer's CE router
 encapsulation frame-relay
 frame-relay traffic-shaping
!
interface Serial0/0.1 point-to-point
 ip address 10.254.14.1 255.255.255.252
 frame-relay interface-dlci 125
  class FR-Shape
!
map-class frame-relay FR-Shape
 frame-relay cir 256000
 frame-relay bc 2560
 frame-relay be 0
 frame-relay mincir 256000
 service-policy input InPolicy
 service-policy output OutPolicy
 frame-relay fragment 320
 frame-relay ip rtp header-compression
```

Note that the configuration in Example 10-20 assumes that the service provider is using DSCP instead of the MPLS experimental bit to mark traffic across the service provider backbone.

Service Provider Backbone QoS Implementations

The service provider's backbone typically consists of very high-speed links. Traditionally, service providers have planned for capacity on these links by provisioning double the amount of bandwidth for each link. For example, if a link averages 10 Gbps of data, it would be provisioned for a capacity of 20 Gbps of data. Although this will handle the traffic load on average, it offers no protection for real-time applications in times of heavy congestion. Assume that a denial-of-service attack is launched and all traffic is carried across this link. This link could quickly become saturated with traffic. Without a means of separating traffic into desired groups that can be prioritized, all applications on the 20-Gbps link would suffer. Implementing QoS in the service provider's backbone can prevent this issue from happening.

The service provider's network consists of Provider Edge (PE) and Provider Core (P) routers. The P routers make up the core of the backbone, while the PE routers connect the backbone to their customer's CE routers. Figure 10-6 illustrates a typical service provider backbone model.

Figure 10-6 *Service Provider Backbone*

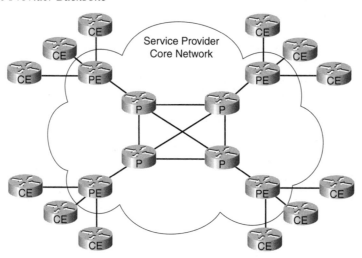

The service provider's backbone can use IP routing or MPLS to transport packets from network to network. In an MPLS network, the MPLS experimental bits are used to separate traffic classes, whereas DSCP is used to separate traffic classes in an IP network. This section discusses the configuration of the service provider's network using DSCP.

The service provider's backbone consists of high-speed links, which means there is no need for traffic shaping, LFI, or cRTP between the PE and P routers.

Trust boundaries are established on the PE routers. This frees the P routers from the task of classification, marking, and policing. All classification, marking, and policing in a service provider's backbone should be configured on the PE router. The previous section examined the inbound and outbound configuration of classification, marking, and policing needed on the PE router to support the four separate classes of traffic specified in the sample SLA. QoS configuration from the PE router to the P router and from the P router to the PE router becomes a matter of queuing and congestion avoidance for the four defined classes of traffic.

The queuing method used in the backbone will depend upon the type of router installed. Cisco Gigabit Series Routers (GSRs) use Modified Deficit Round Robin (MDRR) for queuing, whereas other routers, such as the Cisco 7500 Series routers, use LLQ for queuing. This example assumes that 7500 Series routers make up the service provider's backbone.

The same output policy map created in the previous section, "Service Provider (PE) to Enterprise (CE) WAN QoS Implementations," can be used to perform queuing and congestion avoidance from the PE router to the P router. This output policy provides the queuing specified in the sample SLA for each supported class of traffic and enables WRED on the Silver, Bronze, and Default classes of traffic. Example 10-21 shows this configuration.

Example 10-21 *PE-to-P Output Policy Map*

```
policy-map OutPolicy
  class gold
   priority percent 25
  class silver
   bandwidth percent remaining 50
   random-detect dscp-based
  class bronze
   bandwidth percent remaining 25
   random-detect dscp-based
  class class-default
   bandwidth percent remaining 25
   random-detect dscp-based
!
interface POS1/0
 description to P router
 service-policy output OutPolicy
```

Because the OutPolicy policy map was created in the "Service Provider (PE) to Enterprise (CE) WAN QoS Implementations" section of this chapter, the only change required to enable the policy map is the addition of the **service-policy output OutPolicy** command to the interface used to connect to the P router.

To perform the necessary queuing and congestion avoidance on the P router, the P router needs to identify the four classes of traffic using the existing DSCP values. After the traffic classes have been identified, they can be queued in accordance to the sample SLA. The configuration of the P router is similar to the PE outbound configuration, as shown in Example 10-22.

Example 10-22 *P-to-PE Output Policy Map*

```
class-map match-any gold
  match ip dscp ef
  match ip dscp cs3
 class-map match-any silver
  match ip dscp af31
  match ip dscp af32
  match ip dscp cs6
class-map match-any bronze
  match ip dscp af22
  match ip dscp af21
!
policy-map OutPolicy
  class gold
```

continues

Example 10-22 *P-to-PE Output Policy Map (Continued)*

```
   priority percent 25
  class silver
   bandwidth percent remaining 50
   random-detect dscp-based
  class bronze
   bandwidth percent remaining 25
   random-detect dscp-based
  class class-default
   bandwidth percent remaining 25
   random-detect dscp-based
 !
interface POS1/0
 description to PE router
 service-policy output OutPolicy
```

Because the P router trusts all markings received from neighbor routers, and because classification, marking, and policing will not be performed on the P router, there is no need for an inbound policy map.

Foundation Summary

The "Foundation Summary" is a collection of tables and figures that provide a convenient review of many key concepts in this chapter. For those of you already comfortable with the topics in this chapter, this summary can help you recall a few details. For those of you who just read this chapter, this review can help solidify some key facts. For any of you doing your final preparation before the exam, these tables and figures are a convenient way to review the day before the exam.

A single voice packet consists of the voice payload, an RTP header, a UDP header, an IP header, and a Layer 2 header, as shown in Figure 10-7.

Figure 10-7 *Voice Packet*

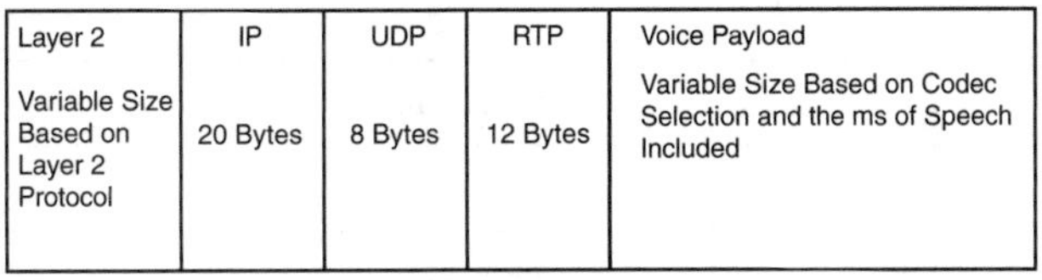

Layer 2	IP	UDP	RTP	Voice Payload
Variable Size Based on Layer 2 Protocol	20 Bytes	8 Bytes	12 Bytes	Variable Size Based on Codec Selection and the ms of Speech Included

Table 10-21 lists the common G.711 and G.729 rates without including Layer 2 overhead.

Table 10-21 *Codec Selection*

Codec	Speech Samples Per Packet	Voice Payload	Packets Per Second	Total Bandwidth Per Call
G.711	20 ms	160 bytes	50 pps	80 kbps
G.711	30 ms	240 bytes	33 pps	74 kbps
G.729	20 ms	20 bytes	50 pps	24 kbps
G.729	30 ms	30 bytes	33 pps	19 kbps

Table 10-22 lists the common G.711 and G.729 rates including Layer 2 overhead.

Table 10-22 *Layer 2 Headers*

Codec	802.1Q Ethernet (32 Bytes @ Layer 2)	MLP (13 Bytes @ Layer 2)	Frame Relay (8 Bytes @ Layer 2)	ATM (Variable Bytes @ Layer 2 Due to Cell Padding)
G.711 @ 50 pps	93 kbps	86 kbps	84 kbps	106 kbps

continues

Table 10-22 *Layer 2 Headers (Continued)*

Codec	802.1Q Ethernet (32 Bytes @ Layer 2)	MLP (13 Bytes @ Layer 2)	Frame Relay (8 Bytes @ Layer 2)	ATM (Variable Bytes @ Layer 2 Due to Cell Padding)
G.711 @ 33 pps	83 kbps	78 kbps	77 kbps	84 kbps
G729a @ 50 pps	37 kbps	30 kbps	28 kbps	43 kbps
G729a @ 33 pps	27 kbps	22 kbps	21 kbps	28 kbps

Table 10-23 lists the delay, jitter, and packet-loss requirements for transporting voice traffic.

Table 10-23 *Voice Delay, Jitter, and Packet Loss*

Delay	< or = 150 ms
Jitter	< or = 30 ms
Packet Loss	< 1 percent

Table 10-24 compares the QoS requirements of voice traffic with other types of traffic.

Table 10-24 *Voice Traffic Requirements*

	Voice	Video	Mission-Critical/ Transactional Data	Bulk Data/ Best-Effort Data
Bandwidth Requirements	*Low to Moderate*	Moderate	Low to Moderate	Moderate to High
Drop Sensitivity	*High*	High	Moderate to High	Low
Delay Sensitivity	*High*	High	Low to Moderate	Low
Jitter Sensitivity	*High*	High	Low to Moderate	Low
Smooth or Bursty	*Smooth*	Bursty	Both	Both
Benign or Greedy	*Benign*	Greedy	Both	Both

Table 10-25 lists the delay, jitter, and packet-loss requirements for transporting video traffic.

Table 10-25 *Video Delay, Jitter, and Packet Loss*

Delay	< or = 150 ms
Jitter	< or = 30 ms
Packet Loss	< 1 percent
Bandwidth Fluctuation	20 percent

Table 10-26 lists the Cisco best practices for classification and marking of DSCP and CoS values for each traffic type.

Table 10-26 *Classification and Marking Best Practices*

Application or Protocol	DSCP Marking	DSCP Decimal Value	CoS Value
Voice traffic	EF	46	5
Bulk transfer traffic	AF11	10	1
Web traffic, FTP traffic, large data-transfer applications, and so on	AF12		
	AF13		
Transactional applications	AF21	18	2
Database access, interactive traffic, and so on	AF22		
	AF23		
Mission-critical applications	AF31	26	3
Core business traffic	AF32		
	AF33		
Interactive video traffic	AF41	34	4
	AF42		
	AF43		
IP routing	Class 6 (CS6)	48	6
BGP, OSPF, and so on			
Streaming video	Class 4 (CS4)	32	4

continues

Table 10-26 *Classification and Marking Best Practices (Continued)*

Application or Protocol	DSCP Marking	DSCP Decimal Value	CoS Value
Voice and video signaling traffic SIP, H.323, and so on	AF31/Class 3 (CS3)	26/24	3
Network management traffic SNMP	Class 2 (CS2)	16	2
Scavenger traffic	Class 1 (CS1)	8	1
Unspecified or unclassified traffic	Best Effort or class 0 (CS0)	0	0

Table 10-27 lists the congestion management best practices. Remember that the percentage of bandwidth allocated depends upon the applications on your network. In many cases, all the listed classes will not be needed. This allows for the bandwidth assigned to the unnecessary class to be allocated to necessary classes.

Table 10-27 *Congestion Management Best Practices*

Application or Protocol	DSCP Marking	Queue Used	Percentage of Queue
Voice traffic	EF	LLQ	The combination of voice and video traffic in LLQ should not use more than 33 percent of the total available link bandwidth (e.g., 20 percent of total bandwidth).
Bulk transfer traffic Web traffic, FTP traffic, large data-transfer applications, and so on	AF11 AF12 AF13	CBWFQ	This class will receive a moderate amount of the remaining bandwidth after LLQ has been serviced (e.g., 15 percent of remaining bandwidth).
Transactional applications Database access, interactive traffic, and so on	AF21 AF22 AF23	CBWFQ	This class will receive a small amount of the remaining bandwidth after LLQ has been serviced (e.g., 5 percent of remaining bandwidth).
Mission-critical applications Core business traffic	AF31 AF32 AF33	CBWFQ	This class will receive more of the remaining bandwidth after LLQ has been serviced (e.g., 25 percent of remaining bandwidth).

Table 10-27 *Congestion Management Best Practices (Continued)*

Application or Protocol	DSCP Marking	Queue Used	Percentage of Queue
Interactive video traffic	AF41 AF42 AF43	LLQ	The combination of voice and video traffic in LLQ should not use more than 33 percent of the total available link bandwidth).
IP routing BGP, OSPF, and so on	Class 6 (CS6)	CBWFQ	This class will receive a moderate amount of the remaining bandwidth after LLQ has been serviced (e.g., 10 percent of remaining bandwidth).
Streaming video	Class 4 (CS4)	CBWFQ	This class will receive a moderate amount of the remaining bandwidth after LLQ has been serviced (e.g., 10 percent of remaining bandwidth).
Voice and video signaling traffic SIP, H.323, and so on	AF31/ Class 3 (CS3)	CBWFQ	This class will receive a small amount of the remaining bandwidth after LLQ has been serviced (e.g., 5 percent of remaining bandwidth).
Network management traffic SNMP	Class 2 (CS2)	CBWFQ	This class will receive a small amount of the remaining bandwidth after LLQ has been serviced (e.g., 5 percent of remaining bandwidth).
Scavenger traffic	Class 1 (CS1)	CBWFQ	If used, this class will receive less than best-effort treatment. Packets in this class will be transmitted only if there are no other packets to transmit.
Unspecified or unclassified traffic	Best Effort or class 0 (CS0)	CBWFQ	This class will receive no guarantees. Some percentage of bandwidth can be specified that will be used by this class if all other classes have been transmitted (e.g., 5 percent of remaining bandwidth).

Table 10-28 lists the best practices for congestion avoidance.

Table 10-28 *Congestion Avoidance Best Practices*

Application or Protocol	DSCP Marking	WRED Policy
Voice traffic	EF	WRED not applied.
Bulk transfer traffic	AF11	DSCP-based
Web traffic, FTP traffic, large data-transfer applications, and so on	AF12 AF13	The default minimum and maximum thresholds will be used for this class of traffic if WRED is enabled.
Transactional applications	AF21	DSCP-based
Database access, interactive traffic, and so on	AF22 AF23	The default minimum and maximum thresholds will be used for this class of traffic if WRED is enabled.
Mission-critical applications	AF31	DSCP-based
Core business traffic	AF32 AF33	The default minimum and maximum thresholds will be used for this class of traffic if WRED is enabled.
Interactive video traffic	AF41	DSCP-based
	AF42 AF43	The default minimum and maximum thresholds will be used for AF42 and AF43 if WRED is enabled. Interactive video, marked AF41, should use LLQ, and, therefore, WRED should not be applied.
IP routing BGP, OSPF, and so on	Class 6 (CS6)	DSCP-based The default minimum and maximum thresholds will be used for this class of traffic.
Streaming video	Class 4 (CS4)	DSCP-based The default minimum and maximum thresholds will be used for this class of traffic if WRED is enabled.
Voice and video signaling traffic SIP, H.323, and so on	AF31/Class 3 (CS3)	DSCP-based A high minimum threshold should be set for this class of traffic if WRED is enabled.

Table 10-28 *Congestion Avoidance Best Practices (Continued)*

Application or Protocol	DSCP Marking	WRED Policy
Network management traffic SNMP	Class 2 (CS2)	DSCP-based The default minimum and maximum thresholds will be used for this class of traffic if WRED is enabled.
Scavenger traffic	Class 1 (CS1)	DSCP-based A low minimum threshold should be set for this class of traffic if WRED is enabled.
Unspecified or unclassified traffic	Best Effort or class 0 (CS0)	DSCP-based The default minimum and maximum thresholds will be used for this class of traffic if WRED is enabled.

Table 10-29 lists the QoS components that need to be configured in the access layer and distribution layer of the campus LAN.

Table 10-29 *QoS Components of the Access and Distribution Layers*

QoS Component	Component Function
Trust boundaries	Determines the devices to be trusted. Establishes the trust boundary as close to the source as possible. Access layer function.
Classification and marking	Identifies and marks traffic with desired DSCP/CoS values. Performs as close to the source as possible. Modifies CoS-to-DSCP map. Access layer function.
Congestion management	Schedules each class of traffic with the desired CoS. Access and distribution layer function.
Policing	Limits unwanted or excessive traffic. Access and distribution layer function.

Table 10-30 lists the QoS components required on the CE router.

Table 10-30 *QoS Components of the CE Router*

QoS Component	Component Function Managed Enterprise WAN Edge	Component Function Unmanaged Enterprise WAN Edge
SLA	Defines the supported classes of traffic and the level of service each class will receive. Enforced on the CE router	Defines the supported classes of traffic and the level of service each class will receive. Enforced on the PE router.
Trust boundaries	Established on the CE router by the service provider. The service provider can then trust packets received from the CE, which removes the need for an inbound policy on the PE router.	Established on the CE router by the enterprise administrator. The service provider may not trust packets received from the CE and may remark traffic at the PE based upon the SLA.
Classification and marking	Traffic will be reclassified and marked on the CE based upon the classes offered in the SLA. The service provider can then trust markings received from the CE, which removes the need for an inbound policy on the PE router.	Traffic may be reclassified and marked on the CE based upon the classes offered in the SLA. The service provider may not trust packets received from the CE and may remark traffic at the PE based upon the SLA.
Congestion management	LLQ/CBWFQ queuing will be configured on the CE in accordance with the SLA. Traffic shaping, LFI, and cRTP may be configured depending upon the link type and speed.	LLQ/CBWFQ queuing will be configured on the CE in accordance with the SLA. Traffic shaping, LFI, and cRTP may be configured depending upon the link type and speed.
Congestion avoidance	WRED may be used to randomly drop best-effort traffic.	WRED may be used to randomly drop best-effort traffic.
Policing	Policing may be required on the CE router. The service provider can then trust the traffic rate received from the CE, which removes the need for an inbound policy on the PE router.	Policing will be required on the PE router. The service provider will reclassify or drop traffic that exceeds the limit specified in the SLA.

Table 10-31 lists the QoS components required on the PE router.

Table 10-31   *QoS Components of the PE Router*

QoS Component	Component Function Managed Enterprise WAN Edge	Component Function Unmanaged Enterprise WAN Edge
SLA	Defines the supported classes of traffic and the level of service each class will receive. Enforced on the CE router.	Defines the supported classes of traffic and the level of service each class will receive. Enforced on the PE router.
Trust boundaries	Established on the CE router by the service provider. The service provider can then trust packets received from the CE router, which removes the need for an inbound policy on the PE router.	The service provider may not trust packets received from the CE router and may remark traffic on the PE router based upon the SLA.
Classification and marking	Traffic will be reclassified and remarked on the CE router based upon the classes offered in the SLA. The service provider can then trust markings received from the CE router, which removes the need for an inbound policy on the PE router.	Traffic may be reclassified and remarked on the PE router based upon the classes offered in the SLA.
Congestion management	LLQ/CBWFQ queuing will be configured in accordance with the SLA. Traffic shaping, LFI, and cRTP may be configured depending upon the link type and speed.	LLQ/CBWFQ queuing will be configured in accordance with the SLA. Traffic shaping, LFI, and cRTP may be configured depending upon the link type and speed.
Congestion avoidance	WRED may be used to randomly drop best-effort traffic.	WRED may be used to randomly drop best-effort traffic.
Policing	Policing may be required on the CE router. The service provider can then trust the traffic rate received from the CE, which removes the need for an inbound policy on the PE router.	Policing will be required on the PE router. The service provider will reclassify or drop traffic that exceeds the limit specified in the SLA.

For Further Reading

This book attempts to cover the breadth and depth of QoS as covered on the QOS exam (643-642); however, you might want to read more about topics in this chapter.

For more on the topics in this chapter:

- QoS Classification best practices (http://www.cisco.com/en/US/support/index.html. Then follow this link path: **Technology Support > QoS (Quality of Service) > Classification & Marking > View All Documents**))

- "Implementing DiffServ for End-to-End Quality of Service Overview" (http://www.cisco.com/univercd/cc/td/doc/product/software/ios122/122cgcr/fqos_c/fqcprt7/qcfdfsrv.pdf)

For design-related guidance:

- "Cisco AVVID Network Infrastructure Enterprise Quality of Service Design" (http://cisco.com/application/pdf/en/us/guest/netsol/ns17/c649/ccmigration_09186a00800d67ed.pdf)

Q&A

1. What is end-to-end QoS?

2. What do service providers use to contractually guarantee specific delay, jitter, and packet loss to their customers?

3. When would an SLA be offered on a per PVC basis?

4. In a Cisco IP Telephony environment, which codec is best suited for the LAN?

5. In a Cisco IP Telephony environment, which codec is best suited for the WAN?

6. By default, how many milliseconds of speech are placed into every packet in a voice media stream?

7. How much bandwidth is required to transport a G.729 VoIP call @ 50 packets per second over a Frame Relay circuit? Assume that cRTP and VAD are not enabled.

8. Enabling cRTP can reduce the overhead of the IP/UDP/RTP header from 40 bytes to how many bytes?

9. Cisco DSPs have the capability to compensate for how many milliseconds of lost speech?

10. A Cisco IP Phone can compensate for how much jitter?

11. Data applications should be separated into no more than how many distinct classes?

12. In a converged network supporting voice, interactive video, streaming video, mission-critical data, transactional data, and best-effort traffic, which class or classes should use the low latency queue?

13. What tool is recommended to discover applications on your network?

14. What DSCP value do Cisco IP Phones currently mark voice media traffic with?

15. What CoS value do Cisco IP Phones currently mark voice media traffic with?

16. What DSCP value do Cisco IP Phones currently mark voice signaling traffic with?

17. What CoS value do Cisco IP Phones currently mark voice media signaling with?

18. What is the recommended CoS value for IP routing protocols?

19. What is the recommended DSCP value for IP routing protocols?

20. What is the recommended DSCP class for transactional applications?

21. Which type of queue should voice signaling traffic use in an enterprise network?

22. Which command is used to allocate 100 percent of the link to MQC?

23. What value should the Tc be configured for on a Frame Relay circuit that will transport voice media traffic?

24. What is needed in a campus LAN before QoS is implemented?

25. Where in the campus LAN is policing typically configured?

26. What is the recommended CoS value for IP routing protocols?

27. What QoS mechanism should never be implemented in the core of the campus LAN?

28. If Cisco IP Phones have the capability to mark voice media and voice signaling traffic, why is it necessary to use access lists to classify these types of traffic?

29. When is a CoS-to-DSCP map used?

30. When should the CoS-to-DSCP map be modified?

31. Which two queuing methods should be used in the service provider's backbone network?

Answers to the "Do I Know This Already?" Quizzes and Q & A Sections

Chapter 1

"Do I Know This Already" Quiz

QoS: Tuning Bandwidth, Delay, Jitter, and Loss Questions

1. Which of the following are not traffic characteristics that can be affected by QoS tools?

Answer: C

2. Which of the following characterize problems that could occur with voice traffic when QoS is not applied in a network?

Answer: A, B

VoIP does not retransmit packets, and VoIP does not use broadcasts.

3. What does a router base its opinion of how much bandwidth is available to a queuing tool on a serial interface?

Answer: E

A router always uses the bandwidth setting, which defaults to T1 speed.

4. Which of the following components of delay varies based on the varying sizes of packets sent through the network?

Answer: B

You could also make an argument that Queuing delay is indirectly increased with larger packets, because other packets must remain in the queue longer while the router serializes the longer packet.

5. Which of the following is the most likely reason for packet loss in a typical network?

    Answer: C

Traffic Characteristics of Voice, Video, and Data Questions

6. Ignoring Layer 2 overhead, how much bandwidth is required for a VoIP call using a G.729 coded?

    Answer: C

    The voice payload requires 8 kbps, and the overhead (IP, RTP, and UDP) requires 16 kbps.

7. Which of the following are components of delay for a VoIP call, but not for a data application?

    Answer: A, D

    The de-jitter buffer must be filled on the receiver before the receiver can play out the voice audio to the telephone user. Packetization delay refers to the time the codec must wait for the human to speak in order to collect 20ms of voice samples for processing.

8. Which of the following are true statements of both Voice and Video conferencing traffic?

    Answer: C, D

    Voice traffic is isochronous. Voice uses a single size packet for one voice call, and video traffic uses varying packet sizes.

Planning and Implementing QoS Policies

9. Which of the following are not one of the major planning steps when implementing QoS Policies?

    Answer: C

10. When planning QoS policies, which of the following are important actions to take when trying to identify traffic and its requirements?

    Answer: A, B

Q&A

1. List the four traffic characteristics that QoS tools can affect.

    Answer: Bandwidth, delay, jitter, and loss.

2.   Describe some of the characteristics of voice traffic when no QoS is applied in a network.

Answer: Voice is hard to understand; voice breaks up, sounds choppy; calls are disconnected; large delays make it difficult to know when the other caller has finished talking.

3.   Describe some of the characteristics of video traffic when no QoS is applied in a network.

Answer: Picture displays erratically; picture shows jerky movements; audio not in sync with video; movements slow down; video stream stops; picture black due to missing pixels; frozen video.

4.   Describe some of the characteristics of data traffic when no QoS is applied in a network.

Answer: Data arrives too late to be useful; erratic response times cause users to stop using application; customer care agents waiting on screen refresh, so customer waits.

5.   Interpret the meaning of the phrase, "QoS is both 'managed fairness,' and at the same time 'managed unfairness'."

Answer: QoS tools improve QoS characteristics for particular packets. However, improving one packet's behavior typically comes at the expense of another packet. The terms "managed fairness" and "managed unfairness" just refer to the fact that QoS policies may be fair to one packet but unfair to another.

6.   Define bandwidth. Compare and contrast bandwidth concepts over point-to-point links versus Frame Relay.

Answer: Bandwidth refers to the number of bits per second that can reasonably be expected to be successfully delivered across a network. With point-to-point networks, bandwidth is equal to the speed of the link—the clock rate. With Frame Relay, the actual bandwidth is difficult to define. Typically, the minimum bandwidth equals the CIR of a VC. However, engineers at the provider and at the customer typically expect more than CIR to get through the network. The maximum bandwidth would be bounded by the slower of the two access rates on the access links.

7.   Compare and contrast bandwidth and clock rate in relation to usage for QoS.

Answer: Bandwidth refers to the router's perceived bandwidth on the interface/ subinterface, and is referenced by QoS tools. Clock rate defines the physical encoding rate on router interfaces that provide clocking; QoS tools ignore the clock rate setting.

8. List the QoS tool types that affect bandwidth, and give a brief explanation of why each tool can affect bandwidth.

   Answer: Compression, CAC, and queuing affect bandwidth. Compression reduces the number of bits needed to transmit a frame, allowing more frames to be sent over the same amount of bandwidth. CAC reduces the overall load of voice and video traffic in the network by disallowing new calls. Queuing can reserve subsets of the bandwidth on a link for a particular queue, guaranteeing a minimum amount of bandwidth for that queue.

9. Define delay, compare/contrast one-way and round-trip delay, and characterize the types of packets for which one-way delay is important.

   Answer: Delay is the time taken from when a frame/packet is sent until it is received on the other side of the network. One-way delay just measures the delay for a packet from one endpoint in the network to its destination. Round-trip delay measures the time it takes to send a packet to one destination and for a response packet to be received. Voice and video are concerned with one-way delay.

10. List the categories of delay that could be experienced by all three types of traffic: data, voice, and video.

    Answer: Serialization, propagation, queuing, forwarding/processing, shaping, network. Note that codec, packetization, and de-jitter delays are unique to voice and video, so technically these delays should not have been part of your answer for this question.

11. Define, compare, and contrast serialization and propagation delay.

    Answer: Serialization delay defines the time it takes to encode a frame onto the physical link. For instance, on a point-to-point link of 56 kbps, a bit is encoded every 1/56,000 seconds; therefore, a frame that is 1000 bits long takes 1000/56000 seconds to encode on the link. So, serialization delay is a function of link speed and length of the frame. Propagation delay defines the time taken for a single bit to be delivered across some physical medium, and is based solely on the length of the physical link, and the speed of energy across that medium. If that same point-to-point link were 1000 km (approximately 620 miles) in length, the propagation delay would be $1,000,000m/2.1 * 10^8$ ms, or 4.8 milliseconds.

12. Define network delay.

    Answer: Network delay refers to the delay incurred by a packet inside a packet network, like ATM, Frame Relay, or MPLS networks. Because the customer does not know the details of these networks, and because many customers' packets share the carrier network, variable delays occur.

13. List the QoS tool types that affect delay and give a brief explanation of why each tool can affect delay.

Answer: Queuing, link fragmentation and interleaving, compression, and traffic shaping. Queuing methods use an algorithm to choose from which queue to take the next packet for transmission, which can decrease delay for some packets and increase delay for others. LFI tools break large frames into smaller frames, so that smaller delay-sensitive frames can be sent after the first short fragment, instead of having to wait for the entire large original frame to be sent. Compression helps delay because it reduces the overall load in the network, reducing congestion, reducing queue lengths, and reducing serialization delays. Finally, traffic shaping actually increases delay, but it can be applied for one type of traffic, allowing other traffic to be sent with less delay. Also, policing can have an indirect impact on delay by preventing other traffic from consuming too much of a link, thereby lessening the length of queues, and reducing queuing delay.

14. Define jitter. Give an example that shows a packet without jitter, followed by a packet with jitter.

Answer: Jitter measures the change in delay experienced by consecutive packets. If a PC sends four packets one after the other, practically at the same time, say 1 ms apart, so the departure times are T=0, T=1, T=2, and T=3, for instance, packets arrive at T=70, T=71, T=80, T=81, respectively. The second packet was sent 1 ms after the first, and arrived 1 ms after the first packet—so no jitter was experienced. However, the third packet arrived 9 ms after the second packet, after being sent 1 ms after the second packet— so 8 ms of jitter was experienced.

15. List the QoS tool types that affect jitter and give a brief explanation of why each tool can affect jitter.

Answer: Queuing, link fragmentation and interleaving, compression, and traffic shaping. These same QoS tools can be used for addressing delay issues. Queuing can always be used to service a jitter-sensitive queue first if packets are waiting, which greatly reduces delay and jitter. LFI decreases jitter by removing the chance that a jitter-sensitive packet will be waiting behind a very large packet. Compression helps by reducing overall delay, which has a net effect of reducing jitter. Traffic shaping may actually increase jitter, so it should be used with care—but if shaping is applied to jitter-insensitive traffic only, jitter-sensitive traffic will actually have lower delays and jitter.

16. Define packet loss and describe the primary reason for loss for which QoS tools can help.

Answer: Packet loss means that a packet, which has entered the network, does not get delivered to the endpoint—it is lost in transit. Routers and switches drop packets for many reasons. However, QoS tools can affect the behavior of loss when packets will be lost due to queues being too full. When a queue is full, and another packet needs to be added to the queue, tail drop occurs.

17. List the QoS tool types that affect loss and give a brief explanation of why each tool can affect loss.

Answer: Queuing and RED. Queuing tools allow definition of a longer or shorter maximum queue length; the longer the queue, the less likely that drops will occur. Also by placing traffic into different queues, more variable traffic may experience more loss, because those queues will be more likely to fill. RED tools preemptively discard packets before queues fill, hoping to get some TCP connections to slow down, which reduces the overall load in the network—which shortens queues, reducing the likelihood of packet loss.

18. Describe the contents of an IP packet carrying the payload for a G.729 VoIP call.

Answer: The IP packet contains an IP header, a UDP header, an RTP header, and the voice payload. With G.729, the payload uses 20 bytes, with an 8-byte UDP header, and a 12-byte RTP header. The IP header is 20 bytes long.

19. Describe the amount of bandwidth required for G.711 and G.729 VoIP calls, ignoring data-link header/trailer overhead.

Answer: G.711 consumes 64 kbps for payload, plus another 16 kbps for the IP, UDP, and RTP headers, for a total of 80 kbps. G.729 consumes 8 kbps for payload, plus another 16 kbps for IP, UDP, and RTP headers, for a total of 24 kbps.

20. List the delay components that voice calls experience, but which data-only flows do not experience.

Answer: Codec delay, packetization delay, and de-jitter initial playout delay.

21. Define the meaning of the term "packetization delay" in relation to a voice call.

Answer: Voice must be converted from sound waves to analog electrical signals, and finally to digital signals, and then placed into a packet. Before 20 ms of voice digital payload can be placed into a packet, the speaker must speak for 20 ms. Packetization delay refers to the (default) 20 ms of delay, waiting for the speaker to speak long enough to fill the packet with the correctly sized payload.

22. List the different one-way delay budgets as suggested by Cisco and the ITU.

Answer: The ITU in document G.114 suggests a budget of up to 150 ms for quality voice calls; Cisco suggests a delay budget of up to 200 ms one-way if you cannot meet the 150-ms goal.

23. Define the term "codec delay" and discuss the two components when using a G.729 codec.

   Answer: Voice calls incur codec delay when the codec converts the analog signal into digital voice payload. Every codec requires some time to process the incoming signal, which adds delay. With G.729, because it is predictive, it must also wait for some additional incoming voice to arrive, because it is algorithm-processing the voice sample to be encoded, plus a part of the next sample that will be encoded. The delay waiting for the additional voice is called "look-ahead" delay.

24. Describe the affects of a single lost packet versus two consecutive lost packets, for a G.729 voice call.

   Answer: Lost voice packets result in the receiver having a period of silence corresponding the length of voice payload inside the lost packet(s). With two consecutive G.729 packets lost, 40 ms of voice is lost; the G.729 codec cannot predict and generate replacement signals when more than 30 ms of consecutive voice is lost. A single lost G.729 packet would only cause a 20-ms break in the voice, which could be regenerated. So, a single lost packet is not perceived as loss in a G.729 call.

25. Describe a typical video payload flow in terms of packet sizes and packet rates.

   Answer: Video payloads use variable-length packets. The packet rates are also typically variable.

26. Discuss the delay requirements of video traffic.

   Answer: Interactive video (video conferencing, for instance) requires low delay because it is interactive. Delay budgets up to 200 ms are the norm. However, streaming video— one-way video—can tolerate long delays. When playing an e-learning video, for instance, the playout may start after 30 seconds of video has been received into a de-jitter buffer—but each packet may have experienced several seconds of delay.

27. List the basic differences between TCP and UDP traffic.

   Answer: TCP performs error recovery, whereas UDP does not. TCP also uses dynamic windowing to perform flow control, whereas UDP does not. Both use port numbers to multiplex among various applications running on a single computer.

28. Contrast the QoS characteristics needed by interactive data applications, as compared to the QoS needs of voice payload flows.

   Answer: Answering such a question requires one to understand that QoS requirements for data applications are more subjective than those for voice. Generally, interactive data wants consistent delay (low jitter), but relative to voice, more jitter is tolerable.

Bandwidth demands vary greatly for data applications, whereas a single voice call uses a static amount of bandwidth. Delay for interactive data can be relatively longer than for voice, but the key measurement for data is application response time, which includes round-trip packet delays. Finally, data applications are much more tolerant of packet loss, because either the application will resend the data, or rely on TCP to resend the data, or just not care whether some data is lost.

29. What are the three steps suggested in this chapter for planning QoS policy implementation?

    Answer:

    Step 1 Identify traffic and its requirements

    Step 2 Divide traffic into classes

    Step 3 Define QoS policies for each class.

30. The chapter provides a suggested process for planning and implementing QoS policies. The first step involves identifying traffic classes and requirements. That step lists two specific types of audits that should be performed in this step. List and give a brief description of the two audit steps.

    Answer: The two steps are a network audit and a business audit. The network audit identifies the applications and prototocols that are used in the network, using tools like Sniffers and NBAR. The business audit examines compares the business needs for these applications, compared to the protocols found in the network audit, in order to decide of the importance of each applicataion.

31. Early in the chapter, a couple of different definitions of QoS were supplied. Paraphrase your own general definition of the term QoS.

    Answer: QoS stands for quality of service. In one sense, it is "managed fairness," and at the same time it is "managed unfairness"—you purposefully choose to favor one packet over another. To quote the Cisco QoS course: "The ability of the network to provide better or "special" service to a set of users/applications to the detriment of other users/ applications." In either case, the goal is to improve the behavior of one class of traffic, knowing that it will most likely degrade another type of traffic.

32. What is the purpose of service classes when implementing a QoS policy?

    Answer: To align business priorities with network resrouces.

Chapter 2

"Do I Know This Already" Quiz

QoS Tools Questions

1. Which of the following are not Queuing tools?

Answer: B

2. Which of the following tools monitors the rate at which bits are sent out an interface?

Answer: B, D

3. Which of the following tools can mark IP packet's DSCP field?

Answer: A, D

NBAR cannot actually mark packets, although it can be used to classify packets in conjunction with CB Marking. CB Policing can re-mark a packet's DSCP value.

4. Which of the following tools chooses to discard packets even though the router either has memory to queue the packets, or available physical bandwidth to send the packets?

Answer: B, C

WRED discards packets in order to get TCP senders to slow down, and CB Policing discards packets when overall defined bit rates are exceeded. ECN does not actually discard packets, but instead signals the TCP sender to slow down in a different way than just discarding packets.

Classifying Using Flows or Service Classes Questions

5. Which of the following are not used to identify a flow?

Answer: A, E

6. Which of the following are likely places at which to mark packets in a network using good QoS design practices?

Answer: B, C

The Differentiated Services QoS Model Questions

7. What does DSCP stand for?

Answer: C

8. According to the DiffServ, which PHB defines a set of three DSCPs in each service class, with different drop characteristics for each of the three DSCP values?

Answer: C

9. Which of the following is true about the location of DSCP?

Answer: A

10. Imagine a packet is marked with DSCP CS3. Later, a QoS tool classifies the packet. Which of the following classification criteria would match the packet, assuming the marking had not been changed from the original CS3 marking?

Answer: A, B, E

11. Imagine a packet is marked with AF31. Later, a QoS tool classifies the packet. Which of the following classification criteria would match the packet, assuming the marking had not been changed from the original AF31 marking?

Answer: B, D

The Integrated Services QoS Model Questions

12. Which of the following are reasons why IntServ does not scale as well as DiffServ?

Answer: A, B, D

Q&A

1. List the two classification and marking tools mentioned in this chapter, including the full names and popular acronyms.

Answer: Class-Based Marking (CB Marking), Network-Based Application Recognition (NBAR).

2. List four queuing tools, including the full names and popular acronyms.

Answer: Priority Queuing (PQ), Custom Queuing (CQ), Weighted Fair Queuing (WFQ), IP RTP Priority, Class-Based WFQ (CBWFQ), Low Latency Queuing (LLQ), Modified Deficit Round-Robin (MDRR).

3. List the two shaping tools mentioned in this chapter, including the full names and popular acronyms.

Answer: Frame Relay traffic shaping (FRTS) and Class-Based shaping (CB shaping).

4. List three Congestion Avoidance tools, including the full names and popular acronyms.

Answer: Random Early Detection (RED), Weighted RED (WRED), Explict Congestion Notification (ECN).

5. List four link efficiency tools, including the full names and popular acronyms.

Answer: Payload compression, RTP header compression (cRTP), TCP header compression, Multilink PPP fragmentation and interleaving (MLPPP LFI), Frame Relay fragmentation (FRF), link fragmentation and interleaving for Frame Relay and ATM VCs.

6. List the QoS tools that perform some classification function.

Answer: This is a bit of a trick question. Almost all IOS QoS tools perform classification—for instance, to place two different types of packets into two different queues, the queue tool performs classification.

7. Which of the following tools can be used for classification and marking? CB marking, PQ, CB shaping, WFQ, WRED, FRTS, LLQ, MLPPP LFI, NBAR, QPM, cRTP

Answer: CB marking. NBAR can be used for classification in conjunction with CB Marking.

8. Which of the following tools can be used for queuing? CB marking, PQ, CB shaping, WFQ, WRED, FRTS, LLQ, MLPPP LFI, NBAR, QPM, cRTP

Answer: WFQ, LLQ, PQ.

9. Which of the following tools can be used for shaping? CB marking, PQ, CB shaping, WFQ, WRED, FRTS, LLQ, MLPPP LFI, NBAR, QPM, cRTP

Answer: CB shaping and FRTS

10. Which of the following tools can be used for link efficiency? CB marking, PQ, CB shaping, WFQ, WRED, FRTS, LLQ, MLPPP LFI, NBAR, QPM, cRTP

Answer: cRTP, MLPPP LFI

11. Define the DiffServ term behavior aggregate.

Answer: According to RFC 2475, a behavior aggregate is "a collection of packets with the same DS code point crossing a link in a particular direction." The key points are that the DSCP has been set; the packets all move the same direction; and the packets collectively make up a class.

12. Define the DiffServ term DSCP, including what the acronym stands for.

Answer: According to RFC 2475, DSCP refers to "a specific value of the DSCP portion of the DS field, used to select a PHB." The acronym stands for differentiated services code point. It is the 6-bit filed in the redefined ToS byte in the IP header used for marking packets for DiffServ.

13. Define the DiffServ term PHB, including what the acronym stands for.

Answer: According to RFC 2475, PHB refers to "the externally observable forwarding behavior applied at a DS-compliant node to a DS behavior aggregate." The acronym stands for per-hop behavior. It is the collection of QoS actions that occur at one router (hop) in a network for a particular BA.

14. Define the DiffServ term MF classifier, including what the acronym stands for.

Answer: According to RFC 2475, an MF classifier is "a multi-field (MF) classifier which selects packets based on the content of some arbitrary number of header fields; typically some combination of source address, destination address, DS field, protocol ID, source port and destination port." It is the classification function used to classify packets before the DSCP has been set.

15. Define the DiffServ term DS ingress node, including what the acronym stands for.

Answer: According to RFC 2475, a DS ingress node is "a DS boundary node in its role in handling traffic as it enters a DS domain." DS stands for differentiated services. The term defines a node at which packets enter the DiffServ domain.

16. Compare and contrast the terms BA classifier and MF classifier, according to DiffServ specifications. Suggest typical points in the network where each is used.

Answer: A classifier is a DiffServ function that classifies or categories packets based on the contents of fields in the packet headers. A BA classifier performs this function only based on the DSCP field. An MF classifier can look at many fields in the packet header. MF classifiers typically classify ingress traffic near the edge of a network, and work with markers to set the DSCP field. BA classifiers are used at points in the network after an MF classifier and marker have set the DSCP field values.

17. Compare and contrast the contents of the IP ToS byte before and after the advent of DiffServ.

Answer: Before DiffServ, the ToS byte contained a 3-bit Precedence field, 4 bits in a ToS field, and 1 reserved bit. DiffServ redefined the ToS byte to contain a 6-bit DSCP field, which contains the DSCP values, and 2 reserved bits.

18. Describe the QoS behavior at a single DS node when using the AF PHB. Also explain what the acronym AF PHB represents and identify the RFC that defines it.

Answer: The assured forwarding per-hop behavior, as defined in RFC 2597, defines a PHB with two components. The first part defines four BAs or classes, each which should be placed in a separate queue and given a configured guaranteed minimum amount of bandwidth. The second component provides three different drop probabilities for a Congestion Avoidance tool such as RED.

19. Explain (by comparing and contrasting) whether AF and CS PHB DSCPs conform to the concept that "bigger DSCP values are better than smaller values."

Answer: CS uses values that have three binary 0s at the end, and the eight IP precedence values for the first three bits. In other words, CS includes the eight binary values for a 6-bit number for which the last three digits are 0s. CS conforms to the idea that a bigger value is better, to be backward compatible with IP precedence. AF uses 12 different values. Of the three AF DSCPs in each class, the highest of the three values actually receives the worst drop preference.

20. Describe the QoS behavior at a single DS node when using the EF PHB. Also explain what the acronym EF PHB represents and identify the RFC that defines it.

Answer: The expedited forwarding per-hop behavior, as defined in RFC 2598, defines a PHB with two components. The first part defines queuing, with features that reserve bandwidth for a single BA, with the added feature on minimizing latency, delay, and loss. The other action of the PHB provides a policing/dropper function, disallowing traffic beyond a configured maximum bandwidth for the class.

21. Describe the process used by RSVP to reserve bandwidth in a network.

Answer: A host signals to the network using an RSVP reservation request using an RSVP path message. The request passes along the route to the destination host; at each intermediate router, if that router can guarantee the right bandwidth, the request is forwarded. When received by the destination host, it replies with an RSVP resv message. The process is reversed, with each router passing the reserve message if it can guarantee the bandwidth in the opposite direction. If the original host receives the reservation message, the bandwidth has been reserved.

22. Compare and contrast DiffServ and IntServ in terms of using classes, flows, and scalability.

    Answer: IntServ applies to individual flows, whereas DiffServ differentiates traffic into classes. With large networks and the Internet, the number of IntServ-managed flows does not scale, because information retained about each flow, and the RSVP signaling messages for each flow, continues throughout the life of each flow. DiffServ uses classes, and the number of classes does not increase when packet volumes increase, which allows better scalability.

23. List and describe the two key advantages of the Best Effort model for QoS.

    Answer: Best Effort (BE) scales well, because routers and switches do not have to perform any extra work for each packet or frame. And because Best Effort does no specific PHB, it also requires no specific QoS tools.

24. List and describe the two key advantages of the DiffServ model for QoS.

    Answer: DiffServ scales well mainly due to its Class-Based operation. Also, DiffServ provides a large number of different classes, ensuring that most networks will have plenty of different classes for their network traffic.

25. List and describe the two key disadvantages of the DiffServ model for QoS.

    Answer: DiffServ tools can be complicated, which requires more training and higher skill levels. Also, DiffServ does attempt to provide the appropriate bandwidth, delay, jitter, and loss characteristics, but it does not absolutely guarantee those characteristics.

26. List and describe the two key disadvantages of the IntServ model for QoS.

    Answer: The main problem is poor scalability. IntServ scales poorly because it is flow-based, it signals repetitively for each flow, and the nodes must keep flow state information for each flow.

Chapter 3

"Do I Know This Already" Quiz

Cisco Modular QoS CLI

1. What does MQC stand for?

    Answer: D

2. Which of the following MQC commands is most related to the process of classifying packets into service classes?

   Answer: F

3. Which of the following is not a benefit of MQC?

   Answer: B

4. Which of the following is not true about the mechanics of MQC?

   Answer: B, C, D

   PHBs are defined inside a policy-map command. You can match up to eight DSCP values in a single command. A separate service-policy command is required to enable a policy on an interface for each direction of packet flow (in and out).

5. Examine the configuration snippet that follows. Which of the following statements is true about the configuration?

   ```
   Router(config)#class-map fred
   Router(config-cmap)#match dscp EF
   Router(config-cmap)#match access-group 101
   ```

   Answer: A

   The class-map command defaults to use the match-all parameter, which means both conditions established by the match command must be true in order to match the class.

Cisco QoS Policy Manager

6. Which of the following is false about QPM?

   Answer: A

Cisco AutoQoS Feature

7. Which option on a 2950 switch **auto qos voip** command tells the switch to trust the CoS only if a Cisco IP Phone is attached to the port?

   Answer: C

8. Which option on a 6500 switch **set port qos** command tells the switch to trust the CoS only if a Cisco IP Phone is attached to the port?

   Answer: D

9. Which of the following PHBs cannot be enabled using the AutoQoS VoIP feature on a router?

   Answer: E

   Policing is enabled as a PHB for 6500 Cat-OS when using the ciscosoftphone option, but not at all on a router with AutoQoS.

10. Which of the following router commands displays the configuration that results from enabling AutoQoS VoIP on a router's S0/0 interface, including the details of any class maps or policy maps?

    Answer: B, D

    show autoqos is not the correct syntax; show auto qos interface s0/0 does not show the details about any class maps and policy maps.

11. Which of the following statements are true about requirements before AutoQoS can be enabled on a router interface?

    Answer: A, B, E

    Cisco Express Forwarding (CEF) is required when there is no trust.

Comparisons of CLI, MQC, and AutoQoS

12. Comparing CLI, MQC, and AutoQoS, which are considered to require the least amount of time to implement?

    Answer: C

Q&A

1. Configure two class maps, one that matches the packets permitted by ACL 101, and one that matches packets denied by ACL 101. Do not use class-default, and do not bother configuring a policy map.

   Answer:

   ```
   class-map match-all c1
    match access-group 101
   class-map match-all c2
    match not access-group 101
   ```

2. Configure a **policy-map** that refers to predefined classes c1, C2, and c3, with the action for each class map being setting the DSCP value to AF11, AF21, and AF22, respectively. Assume that the class maps are already defined.

    Answer:

    ```
    policy-map fred
     class c1
      set dscp AF11
     class C2
      set dscp AF21
     class c3
      set dscp AF31
    ```

3. List the three major configuration steps, and the main command used in each step, for the configuration of a QoS feature using MQC.

    Answer: First, classification is configured with class-map commands. Then, PHBs are configured using a policy-map. Finally, the policy map is enabled for input or output packets on an interface using the service-policy command.

4. Describe two different ways with which you could classify packets with DSCP AF31, AF32, and AF33 into a single class using MQC commands.

    Answer: Inside a class-map, the match dscp AF31 AF32 AF33 command would match packets that had any of the three DSCP values. Alternately, you could use a class-map with the match-any parameter, followed by three match dscp commands, one for each DSCP value.

5. List 3 benefits of MQC as compared with non-MQC-based QoS features.

    Answer: Reduces the effort taken to configure QoS. Configuration of classification and PHBs are separated from the interfaces, allowing more concise configuration and more flexibility. Uniform command syntax across multiple QoS features in a single device. Uniform command syntax across router and IOS-based switch platforms. Class maps are reusable for multiple QoS policy maps.

6. Consider the configuration snippet that follows. What commands would list statistics for the QoS policy implemented on Fastethernet 0/0?

    ```
    class-map fred
     match dscp ef
    policy-map barney
     class fred
      set dscp af11
     class class-default
      set dscp be
    interface fastethernet0/0
     service-policy input barney
    ```

    Answer: The show policy-map interface fastethernet0/0 command, and the show policy-map interface fastethernet0/0 input command.

7. List the two SNMP MIBs included in Cisco router IOS that can be used by QPM to improve the statistics presented to a QPM user. List the long version of the names and the acronyms.

   Answer: The Class-Based QoS MIB (CBQoSMIB) and the Cisco NBAR Protocol Discovery (CNPD) MIB.

8. What information can be seen using the CBQoSMIB that cannot be seen with show commands on the device being managed?

   Answer: The CBQoSMIB allows you to see statistics about packets before and after the application of a policy.

9. How many classes can be associated with a single policy map in Cisco IOS Software Release 12.2(15)T?

   Answer: 256

10. On a router using AutoQoS, what command enables the feature for Frame Relay VCs that use Frame Relay to ATM service interworking?

    Answer: auto qos voip fr-atm.

11. On a router using AutoQoS, what command enables the feature on a serial interface when the router can trust the DSCP settings of incoming packets?

    Answer: auto qos voip trust.

12. Describe the classification configuration created by a router when enabling AutoQoS on a serial interface, with all default values chosen on the **auto qos** command.

    Answer: The router classifies voice payload into one service class, voice signaling into another, and all other traffic into a third. It uses NBAR and ACL for matching the voice traffic.

13. Describe the marking actions created by a router when enabling AutoQoS on a serial interface, with all default values chosen on the auto qos command.

    Answer: The router marks voice payload with DSCP EF, voice signaling with DSCP AF31, and all other traffic as DSCP BE.

14. List three of the requirements on router AutoQoS that need to be true before actually configuring AutoQoS.

Answer: IP CEF must be enabled on each interface or ATM VC, unless the trust option will be used. The bandwidth command should be configured correctly on each interface or VC. Any existing service-policy commands should be removed from interfaces on which AutoQoS will be enabled. Frame Relay must also use only point-to-point subinterfaces.

15. List the data link protocols on a router that support AutoQoS.

Answer: ATM, Frame Relay, HDLC, and PPP.

16. List the PHBs created by a router when the **auto qos voip** command is used on a PPP serial interface with default bandwidth setting.

Answer: Classification and Marking, Queuing (LLQ)

17. List the PHBs created by a router when the **auto qos voip** command is used on a PPP serial interface with **bandwidth 768** is configured.

Answer: Classification and Marking, Queuing (LLQ), MLP LFI, and cRTP. All links at 768 kbps or less also have cRTP and LFI added as PHBs.

18. List the PHBs created by a router when the **auto qos voip** command is used on a Frame Relay PVC with **bandwidth 832** is configured.

Answer: Classification and Marking, Queuing (LLQ), plus Shaping with FRTS. Had bandwidth 768 been configured, Frame Relay fragmentation and cRTP would also have been configured.

19. When configuring AutoQoS on a router, with a Frame Relay interface, what configuration mode must you be in before using the **auto qos** command? What command gets you into that configuration mode?

Answer: You must have used the frame-relay interface-dlci command to get into DLCI configuration mode.

20. When configuring a 2950 switch with the **auto qos voip trust** command, what PHBs are configured on the interface?

Answer: Queuing with queue 4 as the low latency queue, CoS-to-DSCP maps that correlate AF31 to CoS 3 and EF to Cos 5, and the trusting of incoming CoS values.

21. When configuring a 2950 switch with the **auto qos voip cisco-phone** command, what PHBs are configured on the interface?

    Answer: Queuing with queue 4 as the low latency queue, CoS-to-DSCP maps that correlate AF31 to CoS 3 and EF to CoS 5, and the trusting of incoming CoS values. However, it also includes extending the trust boundary to the IP Phone, so if an IP Phone is not found, all frames are considered to be CoS 0.

22. When configuring a 2950 switch with the **auto qos voip cisco-phone** command, what version of CDP is required in order for AutoQoS to work at all?

    Answer: CDP Version 2.

23. When planning to use AutoQoS on a 2950 switch, what types of ports are generally configured with the trust option, and what type are generally configured with the cisco-phone option?

    Answer: Ports that are connected to end users are configured with cisco-phone. Ports connected via 802.1Q trunks to other switches (or to trusted servers), for which those switches or servers have already marked CoS correctly, are configured with the trust option.

24. When using AutoQoS on a 6500 running Cat-OS, describe the difference in using the ciscosoftphone setting and the **trust dscp** setting.

    Answer: Both cause a port to trust DSCP, but with ciscosoftphone, AutoQoS also configures policing, preventing the device on the port from sending more traffic as DSCP EF than the SoftPhone application can send.

25. When using AutoQoS on a 6500 running Cat-OS, describe when you might choose to use the ciscosoftphone option versus the **trust dscp** option.

    Answer: trust dscp is typically used when the the engineer knows that the DSCP of incoming frames should have already been set correctly based on QoS policies. ciscosoftphone is used when a PC with the Cisco soft phone application has been installed on the PC.

26. When using AutoQoS on a 6500 running Cat-OS, describe when you might choose to use the ciscoipphone setting versus the **trust cos** setting.

    Answer: trust cos is typically used when the the engineer knows that the CoS of incoming frames should have already been set correctly based on QoS policies. ciscoipphone is used on most ports connected to end users, if an IP Phone might be installed.

27. When using AutoQoS on a 6500 running Cat-OS, the **set port qos autoqos 3/1 voip ciscoipphone** command has been configured. Describe what else must be true before AutoQoS will trust incoming CoS values for frames on port 3/1.

Answer: CDP version 2 must be enabled on the port. Also, CDP must recognize the presence of a Cisco IP Phone on the port. At that point, the switch will trust the marked CoS of incoming frames.

28. Comparing the CLI of older QoS options in a Cisco router, MQC, and AutoQoS, which takes the least time to implement?

Answer: AutoQoS.

29. Comparing the CLI of older QoS options in a Cisco router, MQC, and AutoQoS, which is considered to be the most modular?

Answer: AutoQoS and MQC are both modular, whereas older QoS features that do not use MQC are not.

30. Comparing the CLI of older QoS options in a Cisco router, MQC, and AutoQoS, which is considered to be the most difficult to use?

Answer: CLI.

Chapter 4

"Do I Know This Already" Quiz

Classification and Marking Concepts Questions

1. Which of the following tools can be used to classify packets generated on behalf of an application that uses static well-known TCP port numbers?

Answer: A, C

CB Marking can match well known port numbers easily, using an IP ACL. NBAR can match well known ports directly.

2. Which of the following tools can be used to classify packets generated on behalf of an application that dynamically allocates the TCP ports numbers used by the application?

Answer: C

NBAR can look at the application layer messages, noting which TCP and UDP port numbers the application dynamically assigns in each case.

3. Which of the following header fields are part of the IEEE 802.1Q header?

    Answer: B

4. Imagine a PC, connected to an IP phone via an Ethernet cable, with the IP phone connected to a 2950 switch. The switch is cabled to an access router, which in turn has Frame Relay connectivity to the central site. Assuming trunking is used between the IP phone and the switch, where is the recommended trust boundary for data coming from the PC toward the central site?

    Answer: B

Classification and Marking Tools Questions

5. Imagine a router configuration with several class-map commands, with a policy map referring to the service classes defined in the class-map commands. The policy map has been enabled for incoming packets on interface Fa0/1. What command would you look for in order to tell if Class Based Marking was in use, as opposed to some other MQC command?

    Answer: E

6. Examine the following example of commands typed in configuration mode in order to create a class map. Assuming that the class fred command was used inside a policy map, and the policy map was enabled on an interface, which of the following would be true in regards to packets classified by the class map?

    ```
    Router(config)#class-map fred
    Router(config)#match ip dscp ef
    Router(config)#match ip dscp af31
    ```

    Answer: D

    Each class-map has an optional parameter of match-all (default) or match-any. With the default of match-all, both match commands in the class-map must match, and a packet can't have both DSCP EF and AF31.

7. Examine the following configuration snippet, and assume that all commands related to the **class-map** and all **interface** commands are shown. Which of the following answer best explains why the **show** command shows that class barney is not matching any packets?

    ```
    class-map dino
     match protocol rtp audio
     !
    policy-map barney
    ```

```
        class dino
         set ip dscp ef
        !
        interface fastethernet0/0
         ip address 1.1.1.1 255.255.255.0
         service-policy input barney
```

Answer: D

CEF is required before CB Marking may be configured; therefore, the service-policy command in the questions would actually be rejected.

8. Assume that a router is configured correctly so that voice payload packets are marked with DSCP value EF. Which of the following commands could have been used inside the policy-map to cause CB Marking to set that value?

Answer: E

The keyword ef can be used inside the set command, or the decimal value can be used— in this case, decimal 46. Also, the IP keyword is optional as of IOS 12.2T, so the first four answers are all syntactically correct and also mark the packet with DSCP EF.

Classification Issues when Using VPNs Questions

9. Router A is the endpoint of an IPSEC VPN tunnel. Packets entering router A before being encrypted into the tunnel have been marked with meaningful DSCP values. What causes Router A to copy the ToS byte from the original packet into the new VPN IP header?

Answer: A

10. Router A is the endpoint of an IPSEC VPN tunnel. Packets entering Router A on interface fa 0/0 will be encrypted and then forwarded to a central site out interface S0/0. You want to enable CB Marking on egress packets on the serial0/0 interface, but you want to look at the fields in the IP, TCP, and UDP headers of the original packet, before encryption. What must be done to allow your policy map to work?

Answer: E

Q&A

1. Describe the difference between classification and marking.

Answer: Classification processes packet headers, or possibly other information, to differentiate between multiple packets. Marking changes a field inside the frame or packet header.

2. Describe, in general, how a queuing feature could take advantage of the work performed by a classification and marking feature.

   Answer: Queuing features can perform their own classification function to place different packets into different queues. After a classification and marking tool has marked a packet, the queuing feature can look for the marked value when classifying packets.

3. Characterize what must be true before the CoS field may be useful for marking packets.

   Answer: CoS only exists in 802.1P/Q headers and ISL headers. In turn, these headers are used only on Ethernet links that use trunking. Therefore, the CoS field can only be marked or reacted to for Ethernet frames that cross an 802.1Q or ISL trunk.

4. Most other QoS tools, besides classification and marking tools, also have a classification feature. Describe the advantage of classification, in terms of overall QoS design and policies, and explain why classification and marking is useful, in spite of the fact that other tools also classify the traffic.

   Answer: Classification and marking, near the ingress edge of a network, can reduce the amount of work required for classification by other QoS tools. In particular, many QoS tools can classify based on marked fields without using an ACL, which reduces overhead for each QoS tool. By marking packets near the ingress edge, QoS policies can be more consistently applied. In addition, configurations for most other QoS tools become simpler, which can reduce configuration errors in the network.

5. Which of the following classification and marking tools can classify based on the contents of an HTTP URL: class-based marking (CB Marking), QoS Pre-classification, network-based application recognition (NBAR), or cos-to-dscp maps?

   Answer: NBAR actually performs the classification based on HTTP header contents. CB Marking is the only tool that marks based on NBAR's match of the URL string.

6. Describe the differences between IP extended ACLs as compared with NBAR for matching TCP and UDP port numbers.

   Answer: You can use both tools to match packet based on well-known port numbers. However, some higher-layer protocols allocate dynamic port numbers, making the use of extended ACLs difficult at best. NBAR can look further into the packet contents to identify what dynamic ports are currently in use by certain protocols, and match packets using those dynamic ports.

7. Which of the following QoS marking fields are carried inside an 802.1Q header: QoS, CoS, DE, ToS byte, User Priority, ToS bits, CLP, Precedence, QoS Group, DSCP, MPLS Experimental, or DS?

   Answer: CoS and User Priority. CoS is the more general name, with User Priority specifically referring to the 3-bit field in the 802.1P header.

8. Which of the following QoS marking fields are carried inside an IP header: QoS, CoS, DE, ToS byte, User Priority, ToS bits, CLP, Precedence, QoS Group, DSCP, or MPLS Experimental?

   Answer: ToS byte, ToS bits, Precedence, DSCP.

9. Which of the following QoS marking fields are never marked inside a frame that exits a router: QoS, CoS, DE, ToS byte, User Priority, ToS bits, CLP, Precedence, QoS Group, DSCP, MPLS Experimental, or DS?

   Answer: QoS Group is only used for internal purposes in GSR and 7500 series routers.

10. Describe the goal of marking near the edge of a network in light of the meaning of the term "trust boundary."

    Answer: Good QoS design calls for classification and marking, based on well-defined QoS policies, as near to the ingress edge of the network as possible. However, packets marked in devices near the edge of the network may be able to be re-marked by devices whose administrators cannot be trusted. A packet can be marked by the end-user PC, for instance, but the end user can configure the value to be marked. An IP Phone, however, can mark packets, and the marked values cannot be overridden by the user of the phone. Therefore, the goal of marking near the edge must be tempered against the fact that some devices can be reconfigured for QoS by those outside the group responsible for QoS.

11. What configuration command lists the classification details when configuring CB Marking? What configuration mode must you use to configure the command? What commands must you issue to place the configuration mode user into that mode?

    Answer: The match command defines the details of what must be matched to classify a packet. The command is a subcommand under the class-map global configuration command.

12. What configuration command lists the marking details when configuring CB Marking? What configuration mode must you use to configure the command? What commands must you issue to place the configuration mode user into that mode?

    Answer: The set command defines what value to mark in the frame or packet header once a packet is classified. The command is a subcommand under the class command, which is a subcommand under the policy-map global configuration command.

13. What configuration command enables CB Marking? What configuration mode must you use to configure the command? What commands must you issue to place the configuration mode user into that mode?

    Answer: The service-policy command enables CB Marking for either input or output packets on an interface. The command refers to the policy map, which in turn refers to the class maps. The command is a subcommand under the interface global configuration command.

14. Describe how you can match multiple DSCP values with a single class map. How many can you match with a single command?

    Answer: The match ip dscp command allows for up to 8 DSCP values to be listed, so a single command can match 8 values. If you want to match more in a single class map, you could use multiple match ip dscp commands, with the match-any option configured on the class-map command.

15. What configuration command lets you match RTP audio without also matching RTP video traffic?

    Answer: The match protocol rtp audio command.

16. Describe the process by which NBAR can be updated to support new protocols, without upgrading IOS.

    Answer: Cisco builds Packet Descriptor Language Modules (PDLMs). These PDLMs define new protocols to NBAR. By downloading a copy of these from Cisco, and putting the PDLM in Flash memory, and reloading the router, NBAR knows how to identify new protocols, without requiring an updated IOS image.

17. What CB Marking command implies that a policy map requires NBAR in order to match packets?

    Answer: The match protocol command means that the policy map will use NBAR for matching the packets.

18. What command enables NBAR on an interface for incoming packets? For outgoing packets?

    Answer: The ip nbar protocol-discovery command enables NBAR for packets in each direction.

19. Describe the reason why you might see multiple **set** commands inside a single service class in a policy map, and give one example.

Answer: Multiple set commands means that the CB Marking policy is marking more than one header field. That may be useful when later devices might look at different marked fields. For example, a router fastethernet interface might have a policy-map that marks DSCP EF in the IP header, while marking CoS 5 in the Ethernet 802.1p header.

20. Imagine you are supposed to update a router configuration. The current configuration includes a class-map that refers to ACL 101, which has 23 ACL clauses (separate access-list commands). How could you easily create a new class map that matches the traffic denied by the ACL?

Answer: You could create a class map, with a match not access-group 101 command in it. This command matches all packets not permitted by ACL 101—in other words, packets denied by the ACL.

21. A router is configred to create a VPN tunnel. Explain the required steps you must take to cause a router to copy the ToS byte of the original packet into the ToS byte of the new IP header used to encapsulate the packet.

Answer: No additional overt action is required—Cisco IOS automatically copies the ToS byte into the newly-created IP header.

22. A router is configured to create a VPN tunnel, with unencrypted packets entering interface Fa0/0, and the encrypted packets going over a link to the internet (S0/0). Assuming as many defaults as possible were taken, could a policy map for packets entering the router's FA0/0 interface examine the packet headers as originally created by the end user device? Why?

Answer: The packet will not have been processed by the VPN feature of the router yet, so all the original packet headers will be available for matching.

23. A router is configred to create a VPN tunnel, with unencrypted packets entering interface Fa0/0, and the encrypted packets going over a link to the internet (S0/0). Assuming as many defaults as possible were taken, could a policy map for packets exiting the router's S0/0 interface examine the packet headers as originally created by the end user device? Why or why not?

Answer: The original packet headers will not be available for matching, because the router will have already encapsulated, and probably encrypted, those headers.

24. A router is configred to create a VPN tunnel, with unencrypted packets entering interface Fa0/0, and the encrypted packets going over a link to the Internet (S0/0). Assuming the qos pre-classify command was configured correctly, could a policy map for packets entering the router's FA0/0 interface examine the packet headers as originally created by the end user device? Why or why not?

   Answer: The packet headers will be available for matching, because the qos pre-classify command tells the router to keep a copy of the headers available for the purpose of performing QoS features.

25. Name the three configuration areas in which you might use the qos pre-classify command in order to enable pre-classification.

   Answer: Under a tunnel interface, under a crypto map, and under a virtual-template interface.

Chapter 5

"Do I Know This Already" Quiz

Cisco Router Queuing Concepts Questions

1. What is the main benefit of the hardware queue on a Cisco router interface?

   Answer: C

2. A set of queues associated with a physical interface, for the purpose of prioritizing packets exiting the interface, are called which of the following?

   Answer: B

3. Which of the following commands could change the length of a hardware queue?

   Answer: D

Scheduling Concepts: FIFO, PQ, CQ, and MDRR Questions

4. What is the main benefit of having FIFO queuing enabled on a Cisco router interface?

   Answer: C

5.   What are the main benefits of CQ being enabled on a Cisco router interface?

Answer: B, C

6.   What is the main benefit of enabling PQ on a Cisco router interface?

Answer: A

Concepts and Configuration: WFQ, CBWFQ, and LLQ Questions

7.   Which of the following are reasons why WFQ might discard a packet instead of putting it into the correct queue?

Answer: A, C

WFQ may discard the newly arriving packet, or it may discard a previously-enqueued packet in another queue, depending on sequence numbers.

8.   Which of the following settings cannot be configured for WFQ on the **fair-queue** interface subcommand?

Answer: D, E

9.   Examine the following configuration snippet. If a new class, called class3, was added to the policy-map, which of the following commands could be used to reserve 25 kbps of bandwidth for the class?

```
policy-map fred
 class class1
  priority 20
 class class2
  bandwidth 30
!
interface serial 0/0
 bandwidth 100
 service-policy output fred
```

Answer: A, B

Multiple classes can be configured as LLQs with the priority command. Also, only one style of bandwidth command is allowed in a single policy map, making the last two answers incorrect in this case.

10.   Examine the following configuration snippet. How much bandwidth does IOS assign to class2?

```
policy-map fred
 class class1
  priority percent 20
 class class2
  bandwidth remaining percent 20
```

```
interface serial 0/0
 bandwidth 100
 service-policy output fred
```

Answer: B

To find the answer, take interface bandwidth (100 kbps), subtract 25 percent of the bandwidth for the class-default bandwidth (based on max-reserved-bandwidth of 75 percent). That leaves 75 kbps. Then subtract 20 percent of the interface bandwidth (20 percent of 100 kbps) for the LLQ, leaving 55 kbps. Bandwidth remaining percent allocates percentages of the 55 kbps.

11. What is the largest number of classes inside a single policy map that can be configured as an LLQ?

    Answer: D

    A policy map allows 256 classes, with a maximum of 64 classes defined for CBWFQ. Multiple LLQ classes are allowed.

12. To prevent non-LLQ queues from being starved, LLQ can police the low-latency queue. Looking at the configuration snippet below, what must be changed or added to cause this policy-map to police traffic in class1?

    ```
    policy-map fred
     class class1
      priority 20
     class class2
      bandwidth remaining percent 20
     interface serial 0/0
      bandwidth 100
      service-policy output fred
    ```

    Answer: C

Q&A

1. Describe the benefits of having a single FIFO output queue.

   Answer: The most basic benefit of queuing is to provide a means to hold a packet while the interface is busy. Without at least a single FIFO queue, routers would have to discard packets if the outgoing interface were busy.

2. Explain the effects of changing a single FIFO queue's length to twice its original value. Include comments about how the change affects bandwidth, delay, jitter, and loss.

   Answer: With a longer queue, more packets can be enqueued before the queue fills. Therefore, the tail-drop process drops packets less often. However, with more packets in the queue, the average delay increases, which also can increase jitter. There is no impact on bandwidth.

3. Explain the purpose of a TX Ring and TX Queue in a Cisco router.

   Answer: By design, routers want to be able to begin immediately sending the next packet when the preceding packet's last bit is sent. To do this, the interface hardware must have access to a queue structure with the next packet, and not be impeded by waiting on service from other processes. On Cisco routers, the TX Ring and TX Queue provide queue structures that are available to the interface directly, without relying on the main processor.

4. Explain how a long TX Ring might affect the behavior of a queuing tool.

   Answer: Output queuing does not occur until the TX Ring is full. If the TX Ring is long, the Queuing tool might not be enabled. Because the TX Ring always uses FIFO logic, packets will not be reordered. With a short TX Ring, output queuing may be queuing the packets, and have an opportunity to reorder the packet exit sequence based on the queuing scheduling algorithm.

5. Describe the command output that identifies the length of the TX Ring or TX Queue, and whether the length was automatically lowered by IOS.

   Answer: The show controllers command lists output that includes the output line that reads something like "tx_limited=0(16)." The first number is 0 or 1, with 0 meaning that the statically-configured value is being used, and the number in parenthesis representing the length of the TX Ring/TX Queue. If the first number is 1, the TX Ring/ TX Queue has been automatically shortened by the IOS as a result of having a queuing tool enabled on the interface.

6. Explain under what circumstances the TX Ring, interface output queues, and subinterface output queues both fill and drain, and to where they drain.

   Answer: The TX Ring fills when the packets needing to exit an interface exceed the line (clock) rate of the interface. When the TX Ring fills, the interface output queues begin to fill. The subinterface output queues only fill if traffic shaping is enabled on the subinterfaces or individual VCs, and if the offered traffic on a subinterface or VC exceeds the shaped rate. The VC or subinterface queues drain into the interface queues, the interface queues into the TX Ring, and the TX Ring onto the physical interface.

7. Assume a queuing tool has been enabled on interface S0/0. Describe the circumstances under which the queuing tool would actually be used.

   Answer: Congestion must occur on the interface first, which causes packets to be held in the TX Ring/TX Queue. When the TX Ring/TX Queue fills, IOS enables the queuing function on the interface.

8. Explain the circumstances under which it would be useful to enable a queuing tool on a subinterface.

   Answer: Queues only form on subinterfaces when traffic shaping is enabled on the subinterface.

Scheduling Concepts: FIFO, PQ, CQ, and MDRR

9. Describe the process and end result of the scheduling feature of Priority Queuing.

   Answer: Always service higher-priority queues first; the result is great service for the High queue, with the potential for 100 percent of link bandwidth. Service degrades quickly for lower-priority queues, with possile total starvation of the lower queues.

10. Describe the process and end result of the scheduling feature of Custom Queuing.

    Answer: Scheduler services packets from a queue until a byte count is reached; round-robins through the queues, servicing the different byte counts for each queue. The effect is to reserve a percentage of link bandwidth for each queue.

11. Describe how the Modified Deficit Round-Robin scheduler works, and specifically why the word "deficit" refers to part of the scheduler logic.

    Answer: DRR schedules some number of bytes per pass through the queues. MDRR takes packets from the queue, which means it may take more than the allotted number of bytes; this excess is called the deficit. The deficit is subtracted from the number of bytes taken from that queue in the next round. As a result, MDRR can accurately predict the percentage bandwidth assigned to a queue.

Concepts and Configuration: WFQ, CBWFQ, and LLQ

12. WFQ classifies packets based on their flow. Other than a typical flow from an end user device, identify the other two types of flows recognized by WFQ.

    Answer: WFQ reserves 8 flow queues for system overhead traffic. It also adds flows in conjunction with RSVP, helping to reserve bandwidth for those flows.

13. Characterize the effect the WFQ scheduler has on different types of flows.

    Answer: Lower-volume flows get relatively better service, and higher-volume flows get worse service. Higher-precedence flows get better service than lower-precedence flows. If lower-volume flows are given higher precedence values, the bandwidth, delay, jitter, and loss characteristics improve even more.

14. Describe the WFQ scheduler process. Include at least the concept behind any formulas, if not the specific formula.

    Answer: Each new packet is assigned a sequence number, which is based on the previous packet's SN, the length of the new packet, and the IP precedence of the packet. The formula is as follows:

    Previous SN + (weight * New packet length)

    The scheduler just takes the lowest SN packet when it needs to de-queue a packet.

15. You previously disabled WFQ on interface S0/0. List the minimum number of commands required to enable WFQ on S0/0.

    Answer: Use the fair-queue interface subcommand.

16. What commands list statistical information about the performance of WFQ?

    Answer: The show interfaces and the show queueing fair commands list statistics about WFQ.

17. Define what comprises a flow in relation to WFQ.

    Answer: A flow consists of all packets with the same source and destination IP address, transport layer protocol, and transport layer source and destination port. Some references also claim that WFQ includes the ToS byte in the definition of a flow.

18. You just bought and installed a new 3600 series router. Before adding any configuration to the router, you go ahead and plug in the new T1 Frame Relay access link to interface S0/0. List the minimum number of commands required to enable WFQ on S0/0.

    Answer: No commands are required. WFQ is the default on E/1 and slower interfaces in a Cisco router.

19. Describe the CBWFQ scheduler process, both inside a single queue and among all queues.

    Answer: The scheduler provides a guaranteed amount of bandwidth to each class. Inside a single queue, processing is FIFO, except for the class-default queue. In class-default, Flow-Based WFQ can be used, or FIFO, inside the queue.

20. Describe how LLQ allows for low latency while still giving good service to other queues.

    Answer: LLQ is actually a variation of CBWFQ, in which the LLQ classes are always serviced first—in other words, the low-latency queues are a strict-priority queues. To prevent the low-latency queues from dominating the link, and to continue to guarantee bandwidth amounts to other queues, the LLQ classes are policed.

21. Compare and contrast the CBWFQ command that configures the guaranteed bandwidth for a class with the command that enables LLQ for a class.

Answer: The bandwidth command enables you to define a specific bandwidth, or a percentage bandwidth. The priority command, which enables LLQ in a class, appears to reserve an amount or percentage of bandwidth as well. However, it actually defines the policing rate, to prevent the LLQ from dominating the link. The priority command enables you to set the policing burst size as well.

22. Describe the CBWFQ classification options. List at least five fields that can be matched without using an ACL.

Answer: CBWFQ uses the Modular QoS CLI, and therefore can match on any fields that can be matched with other MQC tools, like CB marking. Other than referring to an ACL, CBWFQ can classify based on incoming interface, source/destination MAC, IP Precedence, IP DSCP, LAN CoS, QoS group, MPLS Experimental bits, and anything recognizable by NBAR.

23. Name the two CBWFQ global configuration commands that define classification options, and then the per-hop behaviors, respectively. Also list the command that enables CBWFQ on an interface.

Answer: The class-map command names a class map and places the user into class map configuration mode. Classification parameters can be entered at that point. The policy-map command names a policy and enables you to refer to class maps and then define actions. The service-policy command enables the policy map for packets either entering or exiting the interface.

24. Examine the following configuration (Example 5-10). Which of the five policy maps would certainly enable LLQ for voice payload traffic, based only of the information in the configuration?

Example 5-10 *Exhibit for CBWFQ Configuration Questions*

```
!
class-map match-all class1
  match ip rtp 16384 16383
class-map match-all class2
  match access-group 101
class-map match-all class3
  match ip rtp 16384 32767
class-map match-all class4
  match ip dscp ef
class-map match-all class5
  match access-group 102
!
```

Example 5-10 *Exhibit for CBWFQ Configuration Questions (Continued)*

```
policy-map pmap1
 class class1
  priority 60
policy-map pmap2
 class class2
  priority 60
policy-map pmap3
 class class3
  priority 60
policy-map pmap4
 class class4
  priority 60
policy-map pmap5
 class class5
  priority 60
!
interface Serial0/0
 service-policy output ?????
!
access-list 101 permit udp any gt 16383 any gt 16383
access-list 102 permit udp any range 16383 32767 any range 16383 32767
!
```

Answer: **All the policy maps except pmap4 would perform LLQ on voice payload. In some cases, the policy map would match more than just voice payload. Only pmap1 would match just RTP voice payload traffic.**

25. Using the same exhibit as in the preceding example, describe what must also be true for pmap4 to queue voice payload traffic successfully, and only voice payload traffic, in a low-latency queue.

Answer: **If some other classification and marking tool were configured, and it marked all voice payload traffic as DSCP EF, pmap4 would match all voice packets in the low-latency queue.**

26. Which of the following queuing tools can always service a particular queue first, even when other queues have packets waiting? First-In, First-Out Queuing (FIFO); Priority Queuing (PQ); Custom Queuing (CQ); Weighted Fair Queuing (WFQ); Class-Based WFQ (CBWFQ); Low Latency Queuing (LLQ).

Answer: **PQ and LLQ.**

27. Which of the following queuing tools allows for a percentage bandwidth to be assigned to each queue? First-In, First-Out Queuing (FIFO); Priority Queuing (PQ); Custom Queuing (CQ); Weighted Fair Queuing (WFQ); Class-Based WFQ (CBWFQ); Low Latency Queuing (LLQ).

Answer: CBWFQ and LLQ. CQ effectively does this as well, but you cannot specify the exact percentage.

28. Which queuing tools could be configured to provide the lowest possible latency for voice traffic? Of these, which does Cisco recommend as the best option for voice queuing today?

Answer: PQ and LLQ. PQ would probably not be a good option in many networks today, but it could provide the lowest possible latency for voice. Cisco currently recommends LLQ.

29. Which of the following queuing tools can use flow-based classification? First-In, First-Out Queuing (FIFO); Priority Queuing (PQ); Custom Queuing (CQ); Weighted Fair Queuing (WFQ); Class-Based WFQ (CBWFQ); Low Latency Queuing (LLQ).

Answer: WFQ and CBWFQ in the class-default queue.

30. Which of the following queuing tools uses the Modular QoS CLI? First-In, First-Out Queuing (FIFO); Priority Queuing (PQ); Custom Queuing (CQ); Weighted Fair Queuing (WFQ); Class-Based WFQ (CBWFQ); Low Latency Queuing (LLQ).

Answer: CBWFQ, LLQ.

31. Which of the following queuing tools allows for a value to be configured, which then results in a specific number of bytes being taken from each queue during a round-robin pass through the queues? First-In, First-Out Queuing (FIFO); Priority Queuing (PQ); Custom Queuing (CQ); Weighted Fair Queuing (WFQ); Class-Based WFQ (CBWFQ); Low Latency Queuing (LLQ).

Answer: CQ.

32. What model of Cisco router supports WFQ inside CBWFQ classes other than class-default?

Answer: 7500 series routers.

33. Give an explanation for the following comment: "WFQ can become too fair when it has a large number of active flows"?

Answer: With many flows, WFQ will give some bandwidth to every flow. In an effort to give each flow some of the link bandwidth, WFQ may actually not give some or most of the flows enough bandwidth for them to survive.

34. Imagine the following commands in Example 5-11 were typed in configuration mode, in order. Also assume that class maps **class1**, **class2**, and **class3** have already been correctly defined. How much bandwidth will class **class3** be assigned on interface S0/0?

Example 5-11 *Exhibit for CBWFQ Configuration Questions*

```
!
policy-map pmap1
 class class1
  priority 60
class class2
  bandwidth percent 30
class class3
  bandwidth percent 45
!
policy-map pmap2
 class class1
  priority percent 20
class class2
  bandwidth remaining percent 30
class class3
  bandwidth remaining percent 70
!
policy-map pmap3
class class1
  priority percent 20
class class2
  bandwidth 30
class class3
  bandwidth percent 30
!
interface Serial0/0
 service-policy output pmap1
!
interface Serial0/1
bandwidth 512
 service-policy output pmap2
!
interface Serial0/2
bandwidth 256
 service-policy output pmap3
!
```

Answer: Actually, none. The service-policy command would be rejected, because the 60 kbps in class1, plus the 75 percent total bandwidth in class2 and class3 would exceed the maximum bandwidth allowed in the policy map.

35. In the same example, what could be done so that the **service-policy output pmap1** command would be accepted under interface serial0/0—without changing the policy map? Assuming that was done, what actual bandwidth could be assigned to class3?

Answer: The 60 kbps for class1 is 4 percent of the configured interface bandwidth. So, the max-reserved-bandwidth 79 interface subcommand could be used on interface s0/0, and then the service-policy output pmap1 would be accepted. Then, class3 would get 45 percent of 1544 kbps, or 695 kbps.

36. In the same example, how much bandwidth would **class1** be assigned on interface serial 0/1?

Answer: class1, the LLQ, would get 20 percent of interface bandwidth, which is defined as 512 kbps. So, class1 would get 102 kbps.

37. In the same example, how much bandwidth would **class2** and **class3** be assigned on interface serial 0/1?

Answer: class2 and class3 use the bandwidth remaining percent command. So, you would subtract 25 percent of the link bandwidth from the configured 512 kbps interface bandwidth, as well as the 102 kbps reserved for class1. That leaves 280 kbps total remaining bandwidth. class2 gets 30 percent of the remainder, or 84 kbps, and class3 gets 70 percent of the remainder, or 196 kbps.

38. In the same example, how much bandwidth would **class2** and **class3** be assigned on interface serial 0/2?

Answer: Actually, class2 would get 30 kbps, and class3 would get none. When policy map pmap3 is configured as shown—recall, the example shows the commands as typed, not the output of a show running-config command—the bandwidth percent 30 class subcommand would be rejected, because you cannot mix different styles of bandwidth class subcommands inside a single policy map. In effect, you would not have a bandwidth class subcommand configured for class3 at this point.

Chapter 6

"Do I Know This Already" Quiz

1. How big is the token bucket used by CB Shaping when no excess bursting is configured?

Answer: C

2. Which of the following are true about Policers in general, but not true about Shapers?

Answer: B, D

3. If shaping was configured with a rate of 128Kbps, and a Bc of 3200, what value would be calculated for Tc?

Answer: C

The formula is Tc = Bc/CIR

4. With dual-rate policing, upon what value does the policer base the size of the token bucket associated with the second, higher policing rate?

Answer: B

The size of the bucket = Be (in bytes).

5. With single-rate policing, with three possible actions configured, how does the policer replenish tokens into the excess token bucket?

Answer: B

The size of the bucket = Be (in bytes).

Configuring Class-Based Shaping

6. Which of the following commands, when typed in the correct configuration mode, enables shaping at 128 kbps, with no excess burst?

Answer: A

shape peak actually shapes at a higher rate. Also, Be defaults to be equal to Bc, so to make it 0, you must set it directly. Also, the shaping rate is configured in bits/second.

7. Examine the following configuration, noting the locations of the comments lines labeled "point 1", point 2", and so on. Assume that a correctly-configured policy map that implements CBWFQ, called queue-it, is also configured but not shown. In order to enable CBWFQ for the packets queued by CB Shaping, what command is required, and at what point in the configuration would the command be required?

```
policy-map shape-question
! point 1
 class class-default
! point 2
  shape average 256000 5120
! point 3
interface serial 0/0
! point 4
  service-policy output shape-question
! point 5
interface s0/0.1 point-to-point
! point 6
```

```
     ip address 1.1.1.1
   ! point 7
     frame-relay interface-dlci 101
   ! point 8
```

Answer: B

The command could also have been used a point 2 in the configuration snippet.

8. Using the same configuration snippet as in the previous question, what command would list the calculated Tc value, and what would that value be?

Answer: E

Configuring Class-Based Policing

9. Which of the following commands, when typed in the correct configuration mode, enables CB policing at 128 kbps, with no excess burst?

Answer: C

The rate is configured in bits/second, and the omission of the violate-action keyword implies that the policer has no excess burst capability.

10. Examine the following configuration. Which of the following commands would be required to change this configuration so that the policing function would be a dual-rate policer, with CIR of 256 kbps and double that for the peak rate?

```
policy-map police-question
 class class-default
  police 256000 conform-action transmit exceed-action set-dscp-transmit af11
violate-action discard
interface serial 0/0
  service-policy input police-question
interface s0/0.1 point-to-point
  ip address 1.1.1.1
  frame-relay interface-dlci 101
```

Answer: B

11. In the previous question, none of the answers specified the settings for Bc and Be. What would CB policing calculate for Bc and Be when policing at rates of 256 kbps and 512 kbps with a dual-rate policing configuration?

Answer: C

Bc and Be are in bytes, with the formula to calculate each being Bc = CIR/32, and Be = PIR/32.

12.   Examine the following configuration, which shows all commands pertinent to this question. Which of the following **police** commands would be required to enable single-rate policing at approximately 128 kbps, with the Bc set to cause Tc = 10ms? (Note that a comment line shows where the **police** command would be added to the configuration.)

```
policy-map police-question2
 class class-default
! police command goes here
interface serial 0/0
  service-policy input police-question2
interface s0/0.1 point-to-point
  ip address 1.1.1.1
  frame-relay interface-dlci 101
```

Answer: D

CB Policing does not use a concept of a time interval (Tc) internally, but you can use the Tc concept when configured policing use the percent keyword. With the police percent command, the Bc parameter actually represents the same concept as Tc, because the actual Bc (in bytes) can be derived by multiplying the policing rate (calculated as a percent of the inerface bandwith) times the number of milliseconds configured for Bc in the police percent command. The math is a simple derivation of the Tc = Bc/CIR formula used with CB Shaping.

Q&A

1.   Explain the points during the process of a single router receiving and forwarding traffic at which shaping and policing can be enabled on a router.

   Answer: Shaping can be enabled for packets exiting an interface, subinterface, or individual VC. Policing can be performed both on packets entering an interface or exiting an interface.

2.   Compare and contrast the actions that shaping and policing take when a packet exceeds a traffic contract.

   Answer: Shaping queues packets when the shaping rate is exceeded. Policing either discards the packet, just transmits the packet, or it re-marks a QoS field before transmitting the packet.

3.   Compare and contrast the effects that shaping and policing have on bandwidth, delay, jitter, and loss.

   Answer: Shaping places packets into queues when the actual traffic rate exceeds the traffic contract, which causes more delay, and more jitter. Policing when making a simple decision to either discard or forward each packet causes more packet loss, but less delay and jitter for the packets that do make it through the network. Shaping and Policing both limit the amount of bandwidth allowed for a particuilar class of traffic.

4. Describe the typical locations to enable shaping and policing in an internetwork.

Answer: Shaping is typically performed before sending packets into a network that is under some other administrative control. For instance, shaping is typically performed before sending packets from an enterprise into a service provider's Frame Relay network. Policing, although supported as both an input and output function, is typically performed at ingress points, once again at the edge between two administrative domains.

5. Describe the reasons behind egress blocking in a Frame Relay network with a T1 access link at the main site, 128-kbps access links at each of 20 remote sites, with 64-kbps CIR VCs from the main site to each remote site.

Answer: Egress blocking can occur for frames leaving the Frame Relay network going to the main site, because the sum of the access rates of the 20 sites exceeds the access rate at the main site. Egress blocking occurs for packets leaving the Frame Relay network going to an individual remote site, because the access rate at the main site exceeds the access rate at each remote site.

6. If a router has CB Shaping configured, with a shaping rate of 256 kbps, and a Bc of 16,000 bits, what Tc value does the shaping tool use?

Answer: Because Tc = Bc/CIR, the answer is 16,000/256,000, or 62.5 ms.

7. If a router has CB Shaping configured, with a shaping rate of 512 kbps, and a Be of 16,000 bits, what Tc value does the shaping tool use?

Answer: Tc is not calculated based on Be. However, at rates higher than 320 kbps, CB Shaping uses a set 25 ms Tc.

8. Define the terms Tc, Bc, Be, and CIR.

Answer:
Tc: Time interval, measured in milliseconds, over which the committed burst (Bc) can be sent.

Bc: committed burst size, measured in bits. This is the amount of traffic that can be sent during every interval Tc. Typically also defined in the traffic contract.

Be: Excess burst size, in bits. This is the number of bits beyond Bc that can be sent in the first Tc after a period of inactivity.

CIR: committed information rate, in bits per second, defines the amount of bandwidth that the provider has agree to provide as defined in the traffic contract.

9. Describe the concept of traffic-shaping adaption.

Answer: Adaption causes the shaper to reduce the shaping rate during congestion. Shapingreacts to frames with the BECN bit set, or to Foresight congestion messages.

10. Describe the difference between interface output queues and shaping queues, and explain where the queues could exist on a router with 1 physical interface and 20 subinterfaces.

    Answer: Output queues exist on the physical interface, and can be controlled with queuing tools such as CBWFQ andWFQ. Shaping queues exist when traffic shaping is enabled; the shaping queue is associated with the particular instance of shaping. If shaping has been enabled on 20 subinterfaces on a single physical interface, for instance, 20 sets of shaping queues exist, all feeding into the single set of physical interface software queues.

11. How many token buckets are used by the CB Shaping internal processes with Be = 0? How big are the buckets?

    Answer: Only 1 token bucket is used. The size is equal to Bc bits.

12. How many token buckets are used by the CB Shaping internal processes with Be = 8000? How big are the buckets?

    Answer: Only 1 token bucket is used, but the size is Bc + Be bits.

13. How many token buckets are used by the CB Policing internal processes with Be = 0? How big are the buckets?

    Answer: Only 1 token bucket is used. The size is equal to Bc bytes.

14. How many token buckets are used by CB Policing internal processes, configured for single-rate policing, with Be = 8000? How big are the buckets?

    Answer: Two token buckets are used, with Bc bytes in one bucket, and Be bytes in the other.

15. How many token buckets are used by CB Policing internal processes, configured for dual-rate policing, with Be = 8000? How big are the buckets?

    Answer: Two token buckets are used, with Bc bytes in one bucket, and Be bytes in the other.

16. Imagine a CB Shaping configuration with a rate of 128000, Bc = 8000, and Be = 16000. What is the Tc value, and how many tokens are refilled into the first bucket during each Tc?

    Answer: Tc = Bc/CIR, or in this case, 8000/128000, or 62.5ms. Each Tc (62.5ms), 8000 tokens (Bc tokens) are refilled into the bucket. CB Shaping only uses one bucket. (Author's note: IOS actually rounds these numbers so there are no fractions in use.)

17. Imagine a CB Shaping configuration with a rate of 128000, Bc = 8000, and Be = 16000. At the beginning of the next time interval, the token bucket is full. If the physical clock rate of the interface on which shaping is enabled is 256 kbps, describe how much traffic that will be sent in this next Tc, and why.

    Answer: At a physical link speed of 256 kbps, with a calculated Tc of 62.5 ms (see previous question's answer for that math), the maximum number of bits that can be sent in 62.5 seconds at that rate is 256000 * .0625 = 16000. The bucket has a size of Bc + Be, or 24,000; because there are 24,000 bits worth of tokens are in the bucket at the beginning of the interval, all packets totalling 16,000 bits can be sent in this first interval, with the bucket containing 8000 more tokens.

18. If a policer is called a "two color" policer, what does that mean?

    Answer: It means that the policer designates each policed packet as either conforming to the traffic contract, or exceeding the contract. The numer of colors is the number of categories, in terms of meeting the traffic contract, into which the policer can place a packet.

19. If a policer is called a "three color" policer, what does that mean?

    Answer: It means the same general thing as a "two color" policer, but with three categories – conform, exceed, and violate.

20. With CB Policing, how are tokens refilled into the bucket associated with the CIR policing rate?

    Answer: Unlike CB Shaping, CB policing replenishes tokens in the bucket in response to policing a packet, as opposed to every Tc seconds. Every time a packet is policed, CB policing puts some tokens back into the bucket. The number of tokens placed into a bucket is calculated as follows:

    Answer: $$\frac{(Current\_packet\_arrival\_time - Previous\_packet\_arrival\_time) \times CIR}{8}$$

21. With a dual-rate policer, how are tokens refilled into the token bucket associated with PIR?

    Answer: It fills the PIR bucket in the same general method as filling the CIR bucket, but with the formula using the PIR, as follows:

    Answer: $$\frac{(Current\_packet\_arrival\_time - Previous\_packet\_arrival\_time) \times PIR}{8}$$

22. With a single-rate policer, with Be > 0, how are tokens refilled into the excess token bucket?

    Answer: The tokens are filled into the first token bucket. Any that spill due to that bucket already being full of tokens spill into the excess token bucket.

23. With a single-rate policer, with Be = 0, what must be true for the policer to decide that a packet exceeds the traffic contract?

    Answer: If there are fewer tokens in the single token bucket than the number of bytes in the packet, the packet is considered to exceed the contract.

24. With a single-rate policer, with Be > 0, what must be true for the policer to decide that a packet exceeds the traffic contract?

    Answer: If there are fewer tokens in the first token bucket than the number of bytes in the packet, but at least that many tokens in the second bucket, the packet is considered to exceed the contract.

25. With a single-rate policer, with Be > 0 what must be true for the policer to decide that a packet violates the traffic contract?

    Answer: If there are fewer tokens in the first token bucket than the number of bytes in the packet, plus fewer than that many tokens in the second bucket, the packet is considered to violate the contract.

26. With a single-rate policer, regardless of Be setting, what must be true for the policer to decide that a packet conforms to the traffic contract?

    Answer: If there are at least as many tokens in the first token bucket than the number of bytes in the packet, the packet is considered to conform to the contract.

27. For policing configurations that use two buckets, a packet is classified as conforming, exceeding, or violating the traffic contract. When processing a new packet, in which of these three cases does the policer then also remove or spend the tokens?

    Answer: When the packet either conforms to or exceeds the traffic contract. In order to conform or exceed, one or the other bucket must have had enough tokens to allow the policer to consider the packet either as conforming or exceeding. For packets that violate, the buckets are not decremented.

28. Comparing the logic used for a single-rate and dual-rate policer, when both use two token buckets, their logic differs slightly in terms of how the tokens are removed from the buckets when policing a packet. Explain that difference.

    Answer: For a single-rate, two bucket policer, for packets that conform to the contract, the policer removes tokens from the first bucket only. With a dual-rate policer, for packets that conform to the contract, it removes tokens from both buckets.

29. Comparing the logic used for a single-rate and dual-rate policer, when both use two token buckets, their logic differs slightly in terms of how the tokens are added to the buckets before policing a newly-arrived packet. Explain that difference.

    Answer: For a single-rate, two bucket policer, Bc bytes of tokens are added to the first bucket; spillage falls into the second bucket; and any spillage from the second bucket is wasted. For a dual-rate policer with two buckets, each pucket is replenished directly, based on the CIR and PIR, respectively. Tokens spilled from either bucket are wasted.

Class-Based Shaping Configuration

30. Along with the **class-map**, **policy-map**, and **service-policy** commands, CB shaping requires one specific command that actually sets values used for the shaping function. List the command, with the correct syntax, that sets a shaped rate of 128 kbps, a Bc of 8000, and a Be of 8000, when using CB shaping. Do not assume any defaults; explicitly set the values in the command.

    Answer: shape average 128000 8000 8000

31. Explain the context inside the configuration mode under which the **service-policy** command can be used to enable LLQ on a CB shaping queue. ("Context" means what part of configuration mode—for instance, global-configuration mode, interface configuration mode, and so on.)

    Answer: CB shaping requires a policy map, with class commands inside the policy map. Inside class configuration mode inside the CB shaping policy map, the service-policy command can refer to another policy map, which could enable LLQ for the class.

32. CB shaping has been configured under subinterface s0/0.1. What **show** command lists statistics for CB shaping behavior just for that subinterface?

    Answer: show policy-map interface s0/0.1

33. Which of the traffic-shaping tools can be enabled on each VC on a Frame Relay multipoint subinterface?

    Answer: FRTS.

34. At what rate would CB Shaping actually shape traffic when using the command **shape peak 64000 8000 16000**?

Answer: **The formula to figure out the peak rate is Actual_rate = configured_rate (1 + Be/ Bc). In this case, the formula is 64000 (1 + 16000/8000), or 192,000 bits/second.**

35. Assume that two class maps have already been defined, called C1 and C2. You decide to add a **policy map**, and enable it on **interface serial 0/1**, so that the policy map has both classes C1 and C2 in it. For class C1, you do not use any shaping, but for class C2, you will shape with a rate of 128 kbps. Create the rest of the syntactically correct configuration commands to meet this requirement.

Answer:

```
policy-map fred
 class C1
 class C2
   shape average 128000
interface serial 0/1
 service-policy output fred
```

The command "Class C1" is shown, with no action, just to point out that traffic matched in class C1 wouldn't be shaped.

36. Assume the same general requirements as the previous question. Create the configuration, defining the shaping rate as a percentage, assuming the interface already has a **bandwidth 256** command under it.

Answer:

```
policy-map fred
 class C1
 class C2
   shape average percent 50
interface serial 0/1
 bandwidth 256
 service-policy output fred
```

37. Assume the same general requirements as the previous question, except now you want to tune the Tc down to 10ms, and not have any excess burst capability. Create the configuration.

Answer:

```
policy-map fred
 class C1
 class C2
   shape average 128000 1280 0
interface serial 0/1
 bandwidth 256
 service-policy output fred
```

38. Assume the same general requirements as the previous question, except now you want to keep the default Bc, but make Be equal to twice Bc. Create the configuration.

Answer:

```
policy-map fred
 class C1
 class C2
   shape average 128000 8000 16000
 interface serial 0/1
 bandwidth 256
 service-policy output fred
```

Answer: At rates lower than 320 kbps, CB Shaping uses a default of Bc = 8000 = Be. At higher speeds, Bc = Be if not specified, with Bc calculated as Tc * CIR, with Tc defaulted to .025 seconds.

39. Assume the same general requirements as the previous question, except now you want to adapt the shaping rate to 50 percent of the originally configured rate upon the receipt of Frame Relay BECNs. Create the configuration.

Answer:

```
policy-map fred
 class C1
 class C2
   shape average 128000 8000 16000
   shape adaptive 64000
 interface serial 0/1
 bandwidth 256
 service-policy output fred
```

Class-Based Policing Configuration

40. Assume that two class maps have already been defined, called C1 and C2. You decide to add a **policy-map**, and enable it on **interface serial 0/1**, so that the policy-map has both classes C1 and C2 in it. For class C1, will configure policing at a rate of 128 kbps, and for class C2, you will police at a rate of 256 kbps. You want to transmit packets that conform to the contract, and re-mark to DSCP AF13 for those that exceed the contract. Create the rest of the syntactically-correct configuration commands to meet this requirement.

Answer:

```
policy-map fred
 class C1
   police 128000 conform-action transmit exceed-action set-dscp-transmit af13
 class C2
   police 256000 conform-action transmit exceed-action set-dscp-transmit af13
 interface serial 0/1
 service-policy output fred
```

41. Assume the same general requirements as the previous question, but in this case, you want to create a two-bucket/three-color policer, and drop packets that violate the traffic contract. Create the configuration commands.

    Answer:

    ```
    policy-map fred
     class C1
       police 128000 conform-action transmit exceed-action set-dscp-transmit af13 violate-
    action drop
     class C2
       police 256000 conform-action transmit exceed-action set-dscp-transmit af13 violate-
    action drop
    interface serial 0/1
     service-policy output fred
    ```

42. Assume that two class maps have already been defined, called C1 and C2. You decide to add a **policy map**, and enable it on **interface serial 0/1**, so that the policy map has both classes C1 and C2 in it. For class C1, will configure policing at a rate of 128 kbps, and for class C2, you will police at a rate of 256 kbps. You can configure any actions you like for the three categories. However, you need to change the Bc setting such that the first token bucket's size is equal to 1/2 second's worth of data. Create the configuration commands.

    Answer:

    ```
    policy-map fred
     class C1
       police 128000 8000 conform-action transmit exceed-action set-dscp-transmit af13
    violate-action drop
     class C2
       police 256000 16000 conform-action transmit exceed-action set-dscp-transmit af13
    violate-action drop
    interface serial 0/1
     service-policy output fred
    ```

    Remember, the Bc value is set in bytes, and the rate in bits. At 128,000 bits per second, 64,000 bits can be sent in 1/2 second, which equals 8000 bytes.

43. Assume the same general requirements as the previous question, but now you decide to create a dual-rate policer for class C2, with the PIR set at double the CIR of 256 kbps. Create the configuration commands. Assuming you didn't configure Be, what would CB Policing calculate for the Be setting?

    Answer:

    ```
    policy-map fred
     class C1
       police 128000 8000 conform-action transmit exceed-action set-dscp-transmit af13
    violate-action drop
     class C2
       police cir 256000 bc 16000 pir  512000 conform-action transmit exceed-action set-
    dscp-transmit af13 violate-action drop
    interface serial 0/1
     service-policy output fred
    ```

    Be = PIR/32, or in this case, 16,000 bytes.

44. Assume the same general requirements as the previous question, but now configure the **police** commands assuming that **interface serial 0/1** has a **bandwidth 512** command configured, and you have to use the percent option in both police commands.

Answer:

```
policy-map fred
 class C1
   police cir percent 25  bc 500 ms conform-action transmit exceed-action set-dscp-
transmit af13 violate-action drop
 class C2
   police cir percent 50 bc 500 ms pir percent 100 conform-action transmit exceed-action
set-dscp-transmit af13 violate-action drop
interface serial 0/1
 service-policy output fred
```

With an interface bandwidth of 512000, class C1 needs 25 percent of that value to continue to police at 128 kbps. Also note that the original requirement for setting Bc in each command was for Bc to be equal to 1/2 second's worth of data. With the percent option used for the rate, Bc is set as a number of milliseconds, which would be 500 ms, or .5 seconds.

45. CB Policing has been configured under subinterface s0/0.1. What **show** command would list statistics for CB Policing behavior just for that subinterface?

Answer: show policy-map interface s0/0.1

46. List the command, with the correct syntax, that sets a Policed rate of 512 kbps, a Bc of 1 second's worth of traffic, and a Be of an additional .5 seconds worth of traffic, when using CB Policer. Do not assume any defaults; explicitly set the values in the command. You can choose any other settings needed for the command.

Answer: police 512000 64000 32000 conform-action transmit exceed-action drop violate-action drop

47. Explain the concept behind re-marking policed packets versus discarding the packets.

Answer: By re-marking the packets, you can increase the packet's likelihood of being dropped later. For instance, WRED reacts to the precedence or DSCP value, discarding certain marked values more aggressively. By re-marking, if no congestion occurs, the packet may still get through the network. If congestion does occur, the packet that the policer marked down has a greater chance of being dropped.

Chapter 7

"Do I Know This Already" Quiz

Congestion-Avoidance Concepts and RED Questions

1. TCP Slow Start controls the rate a TCP sender sends data by controlling:

Answer: B

2. For which of the following WRED categories will WRED discard all packets?

Answer: B

Answer: While "Tail Drop" may be considered to be the same thing as "Full Drop" by many people, the important distinction is that WRED acts based on the average queue depth, whereas Tail Drop acts on the actual queue depth.

3. For which of the following WRED categories will WRED discard a subset of the packets?

Answer: C

WRED Questions

4. On which of the following types of queues can you enable WRED on routers that are not part of the 7500-series router line?

Answer: A, B

WRED can be enabled on a physical interface, but it creates a single FIFO queue, and can't be used with another queuing tool (like WFQ) at the same time. It can also be enabled in a CBWFQ, but it cannot be enabled in an LLQ.

The next three questions refer to the following configuration snippet:

```
ip cef
!
! The following classes are used in the LLQ configuration applied to S0/0
!
class-map match-all class1
  match protocol http url "*important*"
class-map match-all class2
  match protocol http url "*not-so*"
class-map match-all class3
  match protocol http
!
policy-map wred-q
  class class1
    bandwidth percent 25
    random-detect dscp-based
    random-detect dscp af22 25 35 50
  class class2
    bandwidth percent 20
    random-detect
```

```
            random-detect precedence 2 25 35 50
          class class3
            bandwidth percent 15
            random-detect dscp-based
            random-detect dscp af22 50 25 35
          class class-default
            random-detect dscp-based
            random-detect dscp af22 2 25 50
        !
       interface s0/0
        ip address 1.1.1.1 255.255.255.0
        random-detect dscp-based
        random-detect dscp af22 50 25 35
        !
       interface s0/1
        ip address 2.2.2.2 255.255.255.0
        service-policy output wred-q
```

5. For which of the following will WRED discard 2 percent of packets of some precedence or DSCP value, when the average queue depth approaches the maximum threshold?

   Answer: B, C, E

   Please refer to the answer to the next question for some background information.

6. Imagine a packet marked as AF22. Out which interface or class must the packet be forwarded in order to have a 35 percent chance of being discarded, assuming that WRED's average queue depth calculation was approaching the maximum threshold?

   Answer: F

   The last of the parameters on the random-detect dscp and random-detect precedence commands set the mark probability denominator (MPD). MPD is not set as a percentage, but the percentage is 1/MPD. None of the settings give a percentage of 35. Note that on the previous question, with a setting of 50 in some cases for MPD, that 2 percent of the packets would be dropped (1/50 = 2 percent).

7. Assuming the commands in the configuration snippet were typed into configuration mode in a router, one of the **random-detect** commands would be rejected. Under which configuration mode can that erroneous command be found?

   Answer: D

   The random-detect dscp AF22 50 25 35 command attempts to set the minimum threshold to 50, and the maximum to 25, which is not allowed.

ECN Questions

8. Imagine that WRED with ECN has been configured for a CBWFQ class. Under which of the following cases could WRED randomly choose to discard a packet, but instead, mark the ECN bits inside the packet header and allowing the packet to pass?

   Answer: B

9. Referring to the configuration snippet before question 5, what command would be required to enable ECN for class2 in **policy-map wred-q**?

Answer: C

Q&A

Congestion-Avoidance Concepts and Random Early Detection (RED)

1. Describe the function of the congestion window in TCP, and how it is changed as a result of packet loss.

Answer: The TCP congestion window, or CWND, is one of two windowing mechanisms that limit TCP senders. CWND can be split in half as a result of packet loss, slowing the sending rate. CWND can also be slammed shut to the size of a single segment in some cases.

2. Identify the two TCP windowing mechanisms, and describe when each is used.

Answer: The TCP congestion window, or CWND, and the TCP receiver window, are the two windowing mechanisms. The lower of the two values is used at all times.

3. Describe the process of TCP slow start, and when it occurs.

Answer: TCP slow start governs the growth of the TCP congestion window after the window has been lowered in reaction to a packet drop. Slow start increases the window by one segment size for each positively acknowledged packet received.

4. Describe the meaning of the term "global synchronization," and discuss what causes it.

Answer: Global synchronization describes a condition in which many TCP connections have their congestion windows lowered due to unacknowledged or lost segments at around the same instant in time. The connections all grow CWND at about the same rate, re-creating the same congestion levels again, causing more drops, which in turn reduces again the TCP congestion windows. Global synchronization is caused by a large number of packet drops in a very short period, typically the result of tail drops.

5. Define the meaning of the term "tail drop."

Answer: When a queue fills, and a new packet must be placed into the queue, the packet is dropped. Because the packet would be placed into the end, or tail, of the queue, it is called tail drop.

6. Define the meaning of the term "TCP starvation."

Answer: When packets are dropped, TCP connections slow down, but UDP flows do not slow down. UDP packets can consume a disproportionate amount of queue space as a result, which could get to the point that the TCP connections simply get little or no queue space; this is called TCP starvation.

7. Does RED compare the actual queue depth or the average queue depth to queue thresholds when deciding whether it should discard a packet? Why this one, and not the other?

Answer: RED uses average queue depth. By using the average, rather than the actual queue depth, RED behaves more consistently, rather than more erratically, which helps prevent synchronization of TCP flows.

8. Describe how RED uses actual queue depth to calculate average queue depth. Do not list the formula, but just describe the general idea.

Answer: RED calculates the average by adjusting the previously calculated average a small amount based on the current actual queue depth. By default, the current queue depth is weighted at about .2 percent in the formula.

9. Assume the RED minimum threshold is 20, the maximum threshold is 40, and the mark probability denominator is 10. What must be true for RED to discard all new packets?

Answer: The average queue depth must be above 40.

10. Assume the RED minimum threshold is 20, the maximum threshold is 40, and the mark probability denominator is 10. What must be true for RED to discard 5 percent of all new packets?

Answer: The average queue depth must be at 30. Because the discard percentage grows linearly from 0 percent to 10 percent (in this case), between average queue depth of 20 through 40, average queue depth of 30 would mean that the discard percentage had grown to 5 percent.

11. Define how RED uses the mark probability denominator. Give one example.

Answer: RED calculates the discard percentage based on the formula 1/MPD. For instance, with an MPD of 20, the discard percentage is 1/20, or 5 percent.

12. Define the term "exponential weighting constant." If the value is lowered compared to the default setting of 9, how does RED behave differently?

Answer: The exponential weighting constant defines how quickly the average queue depth changes, by determining how much the actual queue depth affects the rolling average queue depth. If EWC is lowered, the average changes more quickly, because the formula weights the current actual queue depth more than before. Therefore, a larger constant provides more handling of bursty traffic, but too large and congestion avoidance will be ineffective.

13. Define the term "WRED Profile."

Answer: A WRED profile is a collection of WRED parameters applied to a single IP Precedence or DSCP value. The parameters include the minimum threshold, the maximum threshold, and the Mark Probability Denominator (MPD).

14. Explain how you can tune how fast or slow that WRED changes the calculated average queue depth over time.

Answer: WRED calculates a new average based on the old average and the current queue depth. You can tell WRED to count the current queue depth as a larger or smaller part of the calculation by tuning the exponential weighting constant. The formula is:

New average = $(Old\_average * (1 - 2^{-n})) + (Current\_Q\_depth * 2^{-n})$

Where "n" is the exponential weighting constant.

Weighted RED (WRED)

15. Spell out the words represented by the initials RED, WRED, and FRED.

Answer: Random Early Detection (RED), Weighted Random Early Detection (WRED), Flow-Based Weighted Random Early Detection (FRED).

16. List the three WRED terms that name the separate states in which WRED discards no packets, a percentage of packets, and all packets.

Answer: No Discard, Random Discard, and Full Discard, respectively.

17. List the queuing tools that can be concurrently supported on an interface when WRED has been enabled directly on a serial interface, assuming no retrictions on the particular model of router.

Answer: FIFO Queuing only.

18. Identify the most important difference between RED operation and WRED operation.

Answer: WRED weights its discard decisions based on precedence or DSCP, whereas RED ignores precedence and DSCP.

19. Describe how WRED "weights" packets.

Answer: WRED weights packets based on precedence or DSCP by assigning different minimum threshold, maximum threshold, and mark probability denominator values for each precedence or DSCP.

20. List the queuing tools that can enable WRED for use with some or all of their queues, effectively enabling WRED concurrently with the queuing tool, assuming no retrictions on the particular model of router.

Answer: CBWFQ and LLQ.

21. What command enables you to look at WRED drop statistics when WRED is configured inside an MQC class?

Answer:

```
show policy-map interface
```

22. Taking as many defaults as possible, list the configuration commands needed to configure precedence-based WRED on interface S1/1.

Answer:

```
interface serial 1/1
      random-detect
```

23. Taking as many defaults as possible, list the configuration commands needed to configure DSCP-based WRED on interface S1/1.

Answer:

```
interface serial 1/1
      random-detect dscp-based
```

24. Taking as many defaults as possible, list the configuration commands needed to configure DSCP-based WRED inside class class1, inside policy map my-policy. (You can assume that the CBWFQ configuration has already been completed, and you just entered global configuration mode. Assume that you need just to enable WRED in class class1.)

Answer:

```
policy-map my-policy
      class class1
         random-detect dscp-based
```

25. List the command needed to set the minimum threshold to 25, the maximum threshold to 50, and the mark probability denominator to 4, for precedence 2.

Answer:

```
random-detect precedence 2 25 50 4
```

26. What show command lists detailed statistics about random drops on interface S1/1?

Answer:

```
show queueing interface s1/1
```

Explicit Congestion Notification

27. For a single WRED profile, WRED can be either dropping no packets, randomly choosing packets to discard, or dropping all packets. For which of these three states does ECN impact WRED's discard actions? How does it change what WRED does to the packets?

Answer: For Random Discard only. WRED forwards the packets instead of discarding them, but only after setting the ECN bits to "11".

28. Identify the bits in the IP header used with ECN, by name and location.

Answer: The low-order 2 bits of the DSCP byte are called the ECN field. The first bit is called the ECN Capable Transport (ECT) bit, and the second one is the Congestion Experienced (CE) bit.

29. Imagine a router on which WRED and ECN are enabled, and WRED decides to randomly discard a packet. What must be true in order for WRED to discard the packet, instead of using ECN logic to mark and forward the packet? Explain the role of any other devices besides the router.

Answer: With ECN enabled, it would set the ECN bits to "11", unless the ECN field was set to 00. An ECN field of 00 means that the sender did not support ECN for that TCP connection.

30. Imagine a router on which WRED and ECN are enabled, and WRED decides to randomly discard a packet. What must be true in order for WRED to use ECN logic to mark and forward the packet, instead of discarding the packet? Explain the role of any other devices besides the router.

Answer: The ECN field must be set to something besides 00. The sender of the packet would choose to set ECN to one of those two values if it did support ECN for that TCP connection.

31. Imagine a policy map with WRED already configured for class class-web. What additional command is required to also enable ECN for the packets in that class?

Answer: The random-detect ecn command.

Chapter 8

"Do I Know This Already" Quiz

Compression Questions

1. With CB RTP header compression, which of the following are compressed?

    Answer: A, C, D

2. With CB TCP header compression, which of the following are compressed?

    Answer: B, C

3. With Layer 2 payload compression, which of the following could be compressed?

    Answer: A, B, C, D, E

    Payload compression compresses everything inside the layer 3 packet.

4. Which of the following Modular QoS Command-Line Interface (MQC) class subcommands enables CB RTP header compression?

    Answer: B, E

    the compress header ip command enables both RTP and TCP header compression.

5. In the **show policy-map interface** command output, with TCP or RTP header compression enabled, what does "efficiency improvement factor" mean?

    Answer: C, D

Link Fragmentation and Interleave Questions

6. What fragment size, in bytes, should be used on a 256-Kbps link in order to ensure each fragment has less than or equal to 10 ms of serialization delay?

    Answer: D

    The answer is derived by multiplying the speed times the delay, and converting to bytes: 256,000 bits/second * .01 seconds / 8 bits/byte = 320 bytes.

7. What serialization delay, in milliseconds, would be experienced by a 160 byte fragment on a 64-kbps link?

    Answer: D

    The answer is derived by dividing the number of bits in the fragment by the link speed, and converting to milliseconds: 160 bytes * 8 bits/byte / 64,000 bits/second = .02 seconds = 20ms.

8. A router has MLP LFI configured on **interface s0/0**. The **bandwidth 128** command is already configured on the multilink interface. Which of the following commands is used under a multilink interface in order to set the fragment size to 160 bytes?

    Answer: A

    The command ppp multilink interleave is required for LFI to work, but the ppp multilink fragment-delay 10 command sets the fragment delay. The fragment size is then calculated using the formula size = delay * bandwidth. In this case, it would be .01 seconds * 128,000 bits/second = 1280 bits = 160 bytes.

9. A router has FRF.12 configured for all VC's on **interface s0/0**. The **bandwidth 128** command is already configured on the interface. Which of the following commands is used under the **map-class frame-relay** command in order to set the fragment size to 160 bytes?

    Answer: B

10. Which of the following commands list statistics about the number of fragments created with FRF.12?

    Answer: D

Q&A

Compression Tools

1. Describe what is compressed, and what is not compressed, when using payload compression. Be as specific as possible regarding headers and data.

    Answer: Payload compression does not compress the data-link header and trailer, but it does compress all the higher-layer headers and data between the two. Specifically, the IP, TCP, UDP, RTP headers as appropriate, and the user data, are compressed.

2. Describe what is compressed, and what is not compressed, when using TCP header compression. Be as specific as possible regarding headers and data.

Answer: IP packets that also have TCP headers are compressed. The compression algorithm does not compress the data link header or trailer. It does compress both the IP and TCP headers. It does not compress any user data that follows the TCP header.

3. Describe what is compressed, and what is not compressed, when using RTP header compression. Be as specific as possible regarding headers and data.

Answer: IP packets that also have RTP headers are compressed. The compression algorithm does not compress the data-link header or trailer. It does compress the IP, UDP, and RTP headers. It does not compress any user data that follows the RTP header.

4. Suppose a packet is sent across a network with no compression. Later, a packet of the exact same size and contents crosses the network, but payload compression is used on the one serial link in the network. Describe the difference in bandwidth and delay in the network between these two packets.

Answer: The packet experiences longer processing delay as a result of the compression algorithm. However, the packet requires less time to be serialized onto the link, resulting in less serialization delay. Overall queuing delay should be decreased, because the shorter compressed packets take less time to serialize, thereby causing packets to exit the queues more quickly. The overall reduction in queue sizes can reduce delay and jitter.

5. How much bandwidth should a G.729 call require over Frame Relay, and how much should be required with cRTP?

Answer: A single G.729 call requires 28 kbps over Frame Relay, but it only needs 12.8 kbps using cRTP.

6. When TCP header compression is used, what is the range of sizes of the part of the frame that can be compressed, and what is the range of sizes for this field of the frame after compression?

Answer: TCP header compression compresses the 20-byte IP header and 20-byte TCP header, with the combined field size of 40 bytes. The compressed field will be between 3 and 5 bytes.

7. When RTP header compression is used, what is the range of sizes of the part of the frame that can be compressed, and what is the range of sizes for this field of the frame after compression?

Answer: RTP header compression compresses the 20-byte IP header, 8-byte UDP header, and 12-byte RTP header, with the combined field size of 40 bytes. The compressed field will be between 2 and 4 bytes.

The next several questions refer to the following configuration snippet.

```
!
hostname R1
!
ip cef
!
 class-map match-all class1
   match protocol telnet
 class-map match-all class2
   match protocol rtp audio
!
!
 policy-map test-compress
   class class2
     compression header ip
   class class1
     compression header ip tcp
     bandwidth 20
!
!
interface Serial0/1
 ip address 10.1.1.1 255.255.255.0
 service-policy output test-compress
 load-interval 30
 clockrate 64000
!
```

```
!
hostname R2
!
ip cef
!
 policy-map catch-all
   class class-default
     compression header ip
!
!
interface Serial0/1
 ip address 10.1.1.1 255.255.255.0
 service-policy output catch-all
 load-interval 30
```

8. The configuration snippet shows the configuration on two routers, R1 and R2, on the serial interfaces attached to a common serial link. Will VoIP RTP sessions be compressed, or even work at all? Explain why or why not in relation to what has been configured on the two routers.

   Answer: CB RTP Compression will occur. On R1, all RTP audio sessions match class class2, inside which both RTP and TCP header compression has been enabled. CB RTP must be enabled on R2 as well, and it is, because all packets fall into the class-default class, and RTP header compression is enabled in that class.

9. The configuration snippet shows the configuration on two routers, R1 and R2, on the serial interfaces attached to a common serial link. Will telnet connections be compressed, or even work at all? Explain why or why not in relation to what has been configured on the two routers.

   Answer: CB TCP Compression will occur. On R1, all Telnet connections match class class 2, inside which TCP header compression has been enabled. CB TCP Compression must be enabled on R2 as well, and it is, because all packets fall into the class-default class, and TCP header compression is enabled in that class.

10. The configuration snippet shows the configuration on two routers, R1 and R2, on the serial interfaces attached to a common serial link. Will web TCP connections be compressed, or even work at all? Explain why or why not in relation to what has been configured on the two routers.

    Answer: The web TCP connections will fail. On R1, all web TCP connections match class-default, inside which TCP header compression has NOT been enabled. CB TCP Compression is enabled on R2, because all packets fall into the class-default class, and TCP header compression is enabled in that class. Because compression has been enabled on only one side, the TCP connection will fail.

11. Without creating all the exact configuration commands, generally describe the types of changes to the configuration on R2 that would be required in order to ensure that none of the flows would fail due to one router wanting to compress, and the other one not wanting to compress.

    Answer: R2's policy map would need classes that match on exactly the same criteria as those on R1. In each class, the same compression command would be used on both routers, either enabling RTP, TCP, or both. The class map names and policy map names would not have to match, but by matching the exact same types of packets, both routers would treat the packets in a single flow equally—either compressing or not compressing.

LFI Tools

12. List the words represented by the abbreviation LFI.

Answer: Link fragmentation and interleaving.

13. Describe the main motivation for LFI tools in relation to the support of data, voice, and video traffic.

Answer: LFI tools interleave some packets between the fragments of other packets. Voice and two-way video traffic are particularly sensitive to delay. LFI reduces the delay for voice and video packets by interleaving voice and video packets between fragments of the data packets.

14. To achieve a 20-ms serialization delay on a 128-kbps link, how long can the fragments be?

Answer: The formula is max-delay * bandwidth, which is .02 * 128,000 = 2560 bits, or 320 bytes.

15. To achieve a 10-ms serialization delay on a 64-kbps link, how long can the fragments be?

Answer: The formula is max-delay * bandwidth, which is .01 * 64,000 = 640 bits, or 80 bytes.

16. To achieve a 10-ms serialization delay on a 56-kbps link, how long can the fragments be?

Answer: The formula is max-delay * bandwidth, which is .01 * 56,000 = 560 bits, or 70 bytes.

17. To achieve a 30-ms serialization delay on a 128-kbps link, how long can the fragments be?

Answer: The formula is max-delay * bandwidth, which is .03 * 128,000 = 3840 bits, or 480 bytes.

18. Suppose that a 1500-byte packet exits a 56-kbps serial interface, and LFI is not used. How long is the serialization delay?

Answer: The formula is packet length/link speed, which is 1500 * 8/56,000, or .214 seconds. The units used in the formula are bits, bits per second, and seconds, respectively.

19. Which queuing tools can you enable directly on a serial interface when using multilink Point-to-Point Protocol with link fragmentation and interleaving (MLP LFI), in order to interleave packets?

    Answer: PQ, LLQ and IP RTP Priority. CBWFQ can be configured, but because it does not have a PQ-like function, it does not interleave packets.

20. Which queuing tools can you enable with FRTS in order to actually interleave the traffic?

    Answer: LLQ and IP RTP Priority actually interleave packets.

21. Explain the scheduling logic used by MLP LFI to determine which packets can be interleaved in front of fragments of other packets.

    Answer: MLP LFI does not define scheduling logic. Instead, it relies on the scheduler of the queuing tool enabled on the interface to decide which packets to send next. If LLQ were used, for instance, packets from the low-latency queue would be interleaved in front of packets from other queues.

22. Suppose a 1500-byte packet arrives and needs to be sent over an MLP bundle that has two active links. LFI has not been configured. Which link does the packet flow across to achieve MLP load balancing?

    Answer: MLP fragments the packet into two equal-sized fragments, and sends one over one link, and one over the other.

23. What command can you use to determine the fragment size used for MLP LFI? What is the only parameter of the command?

    Answer: The ppp multilink fragment-delay command sets the maximum serialization delay in milliseconds. IOS calculates the fragment size using the formula max-delay * bandwidth.

24. What command enables the interleaving feature of MLP LFI?

    Answer: The ppp multilink interleave command.

25. What commands list counters for the number of interleaved packets using MLP LFI?

    Answer: The show queue and show interfaces commands.

26. What other QoS feature for Frame Relay must you enable when you also configure FRF.12?

    Answer: Frame Relay Traffic Shaping (FRTS).

27. What command enables FRF and sets the fragment size?

    Answer: The frame-relay fragment *fragment_size* command.

28. What command lists counters for the numbers of packets and bytes that were fragmented and unfragmented by FRF.12?

    Answer: The show frame-relay fragment interface subcommand.

29. What command lists counters for the numbers of packets and bytes that would have been sent if FRF.12 fragmentation had not been performed?

    Answer: The show frame-relay fragment interface subcommand.

30. What command lists counters for the number of packets that end up in the High and Normal Dual-FIFO siftware queues, when using FRF.12?

    Answer: The show queueing interface *x/y* command.

Chapter 9

"Do I Know This Already" Quiz

Classification and Marking

1. What methods does a Catalyst 2950 current use to classify traffic?

    Answer: C

2. What QoS map needs to be modified on the Catalyst 2950 to allow the switch to match the layer 2 and layer 3 currently marked by Cisco IP Phones?

    Answer: B

3. By default, what values will the Catalyst 2950 trust?

    Answer: D

4. Which of the following is NOT a trust option on the Catalyst 2950?

    Answer: B

5. What does the command **mls qos trust cos pass-through dscp** do?

Answer: B

This command forces the Catalyst 2950 to pass through the original DSCP value on a received packet rather than use the CoS to DSCP map to determine the value.

Congestion Management

6. How many egress queues are present on each Ethernet interface of the Catalyst 2950?

Answer: C

7. Which three scheduling methods are supported on the Catalyst 2950?

Answer: A, C, E

Answer: Strict priority scheduling, WRR scheduling and strict priority scheduling with WRR scheduling.

8. Which scheduling method is configured by default on a Catalyst 2950?

Answer: A

9. Which scheduling method is recommended for networks that transport IP Telephony traffic?

Answer: C

10. Which command is used to assign CoS value of 5 to queue 4?

Answer: C

11. Which of the following commands is used to enable strict priority with WRR scheduling on the Catalyst 2950?

Answer: C

wrr-queue bandwidth 20 1 80 0 where 20 1 and 80 are the values used by the WRR scheduler and the 0 indicates that queue 4 will use the priority scheduler.

Policing

12. What is a policer?

Answer: A

A policer measures the available bandwidth of an interface, identifies the traffic peaks and takes action on peak traffic based upon the traffic

13. What is out of profile or nonconforming traffic?

Answer: B

14. What can a policer do with nonconforming traffic on a Catalyst 2950?

Answer: D

AutoQoS

15. Which of the following commands enables Auto QoS on the Catalyst 2950?

Answer: B

16. What does the command auto qos voip trust do?

Answer: G

17. What does the command auto qos voip cisco-phone do?

Answer: G

18. What command can you use to verify Auto QoS on a Catalyst 2950?

Answer: B

Q&A

1. Why do you need QoS in the LAN?

Answer: Buffer Management as well as Classification and Marking as close to the sources as possible are the reasons you need QoS is the LAN.

2. What is buffer overflow and when does it occur?

Answer: The term buffer overflow indicates that a buffer on and interface has received more traffic that it can transmit. It occurs when an interface is oversubscribed.

3. What IOS types are available for the Catalyst 2950 and which one is preferred for QoS?

Answer: Standard and Enhanced. Enhanced is preferred for QoS

4. You have a Catalyst 2950 running the standard IOS image and need to migrate to a Catalyst 2950 running the enhanced IOS image. What are your options to migrate to a 2950 running the enhanced IOS image?

   Answer: The Catalyst 2950 IOS version is hardware dependent. This means that you cannot upgrade a standard IOS image to an enhanced IOS image. You must order a new switch.

5. What methods can a Catalyst 2950 current use to classify traffic?

   Answer: Trust, Port-based, CoS, DSCP and access lists

6. What map needs to be changed on the Catalyst 2950 to reflect the current markings of Cisco IP Phones?

   Answer: CoS-to-DSCP Map

7. What command is used to verify the CoS-to-DSCP map?

   Answer: mls qos map cos-dscp

8. By default a Catalyst 2950 will map voice-media traffic and voice-signaling traffic to which DSCP values?

   Answer: Voice-Media CS5 (decimal 40) and voice-signaling CS3 (decimal 24)

9. To keep the DSCP values of the voice-media traffic and the voice-signaling traffic consistent between the IP Phones and the Catalyst 2950, which DSCP values need to be configured on the Catalyst 2950?

   Answer: Voice-Media EF (decimal 46) and voice-signaling AF31 (decimal 26)

10. By default, what values will the Catalyst 2950 trust?

    Answer: None

11. Name two of the three markings and / or devices that the Catalyst 2950 can use to extend a trust boundary.

    Answer: Trust of CoS, trust of DSCP or trust of Cisco IP Phone

12. Where is the trust command configured on a Catalyst 2950?

    Answer: On an Ethernet interface

13. What does the **switchport priority extend cos 0** command do?

    Answer: This command causes any CoS value received from a PC attached to an IP phone to be overwritten with a CoS value of 0.

14. What does the mls qos trust cos pass-through dscp command do?

    Answer: This command forces the Catalyst 2950 to trust the received CoS value and pass through the original DSCP value on a received packet rather than use the CoS to DSCP map to determine the DSCP value.

15. What command is used to enable the trust of a Cisco IP Phone on a Catalyst 2950?

    Answer: mls qos trust device cisco-phone

16. How does the Catalyst 2950 determine if a Cisco IP Phone is connected to a port configured to trust device cisco-phone?

    Answer: The switch will used CDP version 2 to discover the phone and apply the trust.

17. What happens if an interface is configured to trust device cisco-phone and a PC is connected to the interface?

    Answer: If CDP version 2 does not detect a Cisco IP Phone, the interface will remain untrusted.

18. Which command is used to set the default CoS value of an interface to 2 for all untagged frames received?

    Answer: mls qos cos 2

19. What does the command **mls qos cos override** do?

    Answer: This command overrides the CoS values of packets received on an interface causing all tagged and untagged frames to use the default CoS value configured on that interface.

20. What command is used to view the current trust state of interface Fast Ethernet 0/1?

    Answer: show mls qos interface fastethernet 0/1

21. A router that is not configured for 802.1Q is connected to interface 0/1 of the Catalyst 2950. The router interface forwards a voice-media packet to the switch. What CoS value will the switch receive?

    Answer: None. If there is no 802.1Q trunk there is no CoS value.

22. A router that is not configured for 802.1Q is connected to interface 0/1 of the Catalyst 2950. The switch is configured to trust CoS on this interface. The router interface forwards a voice-media packet to the switch. What DSPC value will the switch use for this packet by default?

    Answer: DSCP 0. Because the switch is configured to trust CoS and there is no 802.1Q trunk, the switch will use the default CoS for that interface. By default, this value is CoS 0 which will be mapped to DSCP 0. To allow the DSCP value to pass, enable trust of DSCP on interface 0/1.

23. What can MQC be used for on the Catalyst 2950?

    Answer: Classification, Policing, and Marking.

24. What is a class map used for?

    Answer: To identify or classify traffic.

25. What is a policy map used for?

    Answer: To apply actions to the classified traffic.

26. How is a policy map applied to an interface?

    Answer: Using the service-policy command

27. In which direction can a service policy be applied on a Catalyst 2950?

    Answer: Inbound only

28. How many ingress queues are present on each Ethernet interface of the Catalyst 2950?

    Answer: 1

29. How many egress queues are present on each Ethernet interface of the Catalyst 2950?

    Answer: 4

30. What scheduling methods are supported on the Catalyst 2950?

    Answer: Strict priority scheduling, WRR scheduling and strict priority scheduling with WRR scheduling, also known as strict priority queuing.

31. What mark does the Catalyst 2950 use to determine the proper queue for a packet?

    Answer: CoS value

32. Which scheduling method is configured by default on a Catalyst 2950?

    Answer: Strict priority scheduling

33. Which scheduling method is recommended for networks that transport IP Telephony traffic?

    Answer: Strict priority queuing

34. How does strict priority scheduling work?

    Answer: Each queue is services by order of priority with 4 being the highest and 1 being the lowest. A packet in a higher queue will always be transmitted before a packet in a lower queue.

35. What are the advantages and disadvantages of using strict priority scheduling?

    Answer: Strict priority scheduling offers the ability to guarantee minimum delay to applications in the highest priority queue, but lower priority queues have the potential for queue starvation.

36. How does Weighted Round Robin scheduling work?

    Answer: Each queue is allocated a minimum amount of bandwidth to be serviced in a weighted round robin fashion.

37. What are the advantages and disadvantages of WRR scheduling?

    Answer: WRR scheduling offers each queue the capability to transmit packets eliminating queue starvation, but lacks a strict priority queue, which may cause voice quality issues with voice-media traffic due to added delay.

38. How does strict priority queuing work?

    Answer: Strict priority queuing combines the benefits of strict priority scheduling and WRR scheduling by offering a single strict priority queue and 3 WRR serviced queues. Packets are transmitted from the strict priority queue if present. If no packets are in the priority queue, the WRR scheduler will divide that available bandwidth between the remaining 3 queues.

39. What queue is configured for the strict priority queue when using strict priority queuing?

Answer: 4

40. What command is used to assign CoS value of 5 to queue 4?

Answer: wrr-queue cos-map 4 5

41. What command is used to assign WRR scheduling with queue 1 servicing 5 packets, queue 2 serviceing 10 packets, queue 3 servicing 25 packets and queue 4 servicing 50 packets?

Answer: wrr-queue bandwidth 5 10 25 50

42. What command is used to enable the strict priority queue when using strict priority queuing?

Answer: wrr-queue bandwidth x x x 0 where x is the value of the WRR scheduler and the 0 indicates that queue 4 will be the priority queue.

43. What command is used to verify that queue 4 has been configured for the priority queue?

Answer: show wrr-queue bandwidth

44. What is a policer?

Answer: A policer defines the amount of acceptable traffic in a class and specifies what to do with traffic that exceeded the acceptable rate.

45. What is out of profile or nonconforming traffic?

Answer: Received traffic that exceeds the rate specified by the policer.

46. What can a policer do with nonconforming traffic on a Catalyst 2950?

Answer: Drop or remark the DSCP of the traffic.

47. How many policers can be applied to a single 10/100 Ethernet interface on a Catalyst 2950? How about a Gigabit interface on a Catalyst 2950?

Answer: 6. 60.

48. What is the maximum burst size that a policer can use for a 10/100 interface on a Catalyst 2950?

Answer: 64K.

49. What is the maximum burst size that a policer can use for a Gigabit interface interface on a Catalyst 2950?

    Answer: 512K.

50. What is the minimum traffic rate that a policer used for conforming traffic for a 10/100 interface on a Catalyst 2950?

    Answer: 1000000 (1 Meg).

51. What is the minimum traffic rate that a policer used for conforming traffic for a Gigabit interface on a Catalyst 2950?

    Answer: 8000000 (8 Meg).

52. What commands can be used to enable AutoQoS on the Catalyst 2950?

    Answer: auto qos voip trust and auto qos voip cisco-phone

53. Where are the **auto qos voip trust** and **auto qos voip cisco-phone** commands applied?

    Answer: On an Ethernet interface.

54. What does the command **auto qos voip trust** do?

    Answer: It enables trust of CoS for the interface it was applied to, changes the CoS to DSCP map and configures strict priority queuing.

55. What doe the command **auto qos voip cisco-phone** do?

    Answer: It enables trust of a Cisco IP Phone for the interface it was applied to, changes the CoS to DSCP map and configures strict priority queuing.

56. When is configuring trust manually preferred over Auto QoS?

    Answer: When trust is based upon DSCP.

57. When Auto QoS is enabled, what CoS values are mapped to queue 1? What percentage of the WRR scheduler does queue 1 receive?

    Answer: CoS values mapped to queue 1 include 0, 1, 2 and 4. Percentage of the WRR scheduler is 20 percent.

58. When Auto QoS is enabled, what CoS values are mapped to queue 2? What percentage of the WRR scheduler does queue 2 receive?

    Answer: No CoS values are mapped to queue 2; however, the percentage of the WRR scheduler is 1 percent. Because there will never be traffic in this queue, it will never use the 1 percent.

59. When Auto QoS is enabled, what CoS values are mapped to queue 3? What percentage of the WRR scheduler does queue 3 receive?

    Answer: CoS values mapped to queue 3 include 3, 6 and 7. Percentage of the WRR scheduler is 80 percent.

60. When Auto QoS is enabled, what CoS values are mapped to queue 4? What percentage of the WRR scheduler does queue 4 receive?

    Answer: CoS 5 is the only CoS value mapped to queue 4. Queue 4 becomes the priority queue and will not use the WRR scheduler.

61. What command can you use to verify Auto QoS?

    Answer: show auto qos

Chapter 10

"Do I Know This Already" Quiz

1. Which of the following traffic types provides a consistent packet exchange?

    Answer: B

2. Which of the following factures influence the bandwidth requirements of a VoIP call?

    Answer: B, C, D

3. The International Telecommunications Union (ITU) G.114 specification states that the one-way delay of a voice packet should not exceed how many milliseconds (ms)?

    Answer: B

4. How much bandwidth should be provisioned for a 384-kbps interactive video stream?

    Answer: B

5. How sensitive is mission-critical data to jitter?

   Answer: B

6. A converged network should be designed for less than what percentage of packet loss in the class that supports real-time applications?

   Answer: B

7. A converged network should be designed for less than how many milliseconds of jitter in the class that supports real-time applications?

   Answer: C

8. Where should traffic be classified?

   Answer: B

9. What is the recommended differentiated services code point (DSCP) value for scavenger traffic?

   Answer: C

10. What is the recommended DSCP class for bulk data applications?

    Answer: A

11. What are the preferred methods of queuing on Cisco routers?

    Answer: C

12. When using LFI, what is the recommended serialization delay of a voice packet?

    Answer: B

13. Where does WRED perform the most effectively?

    Answer: C

14. What QoS mechanism should never be used in the core of the campus LAN?

    Answer: A

15. If the service provider manages the CE router, what inbound policy is required on the PE router?

    Answer: E

Q&A

1. What is end-to-end QoS?

    Answer: End-to-end QoS is a means of offering the same treatment to a packet on each node it traverses.

2. What do service providers use to contractually guarantee specific delay, jitter, and packet loss to their customers?

    Answer: A service-level agreement (SLA)

3. When would an SLA be offered on a per PVC basis?

    Answer: When the physical interface services multiple customers.

4. In a Cisco IP Telephony environment, which codec is best suited for the LAN?

    Answer: G.711

5. In a Cisco IP Telephony environment, which codec is best suited for the WAN?

    Answer: G.729

6. By default, how many milliseconds of speech are placed into every packet in a voice media stream?

    Answer: 20 ms

7. How much bandwidth is required to transport a G.729 VoIP call @ 50 packets per second over a Frame Relay circuit? Assume that cRTP and VAD are not enabled.

    Answer: 28 kbps

8. Enabling cRTP can reduce the overhead of the IP/UDP/RTP header from 40 bytes to how many bytes?

    Answer: 2 or 4

9. Cisco DSPs have the capability to compensate for how many milliseconds of lost speech?

    Answer: 30 ms

10. A Cisco IP Phone can compensate for how much jitter?

    Answer: 20–50 ms

11. Data applications should be separated into no more than how many distinct classes?

Answer: Four or five

12. In a converged network supporting voice, interactive video, streaming video, mission-critical data, transactional data, and best-effort traffic, which class or classes should use the low latency queue?

Answer: Voice and interactive video

13. What tool is recommended to discover applications on your network?

Answer: NBAR

14. What DSCP value do Cisco IP Phones currently mark voice media traffic with?

Answer: EF

15. What CoS value do Cisco IP Phones currently mark voice media traffic with?

Answer: 5

16. What DSCP value do Cisco IP Phones currently mark voice signaling traffic with?

Answer: AF31

17. What CoS value do Cisco IP Phones currently mark voice media signaling with?

Answer: 3

18. What is the recommended CoS value for IP routing protocols?

Answer: 6

19. What is the recommended DSCP value for IP routing protocols?

Answer: CS6

20. What is the recommended DSCP class for transactional applications?

Answer: The AF2x class

21. Which type of queue should voice signaling traffic use in an enterprise network?

Answer: CBWFQ

22. Which command is used to allocate 100 percent of the link to MQC?

Answer: max-reserved-bandwidth 100

23. What value should the Tc be configured for on a Frame Relay circuit that will transport voice media traffic?

Answer: 10 ms

24. What is needed in a campus LAN before QoS is implemented?

Answer: A hierarchical and redundant campus design

25. Where in the campus LAN is policing typically configured?

Answer: The access and distribution layers

26. What is the recommended CoS value for IP routing protocols?

Answer: CoS value of 6

27. What QoS mechanism should never be implemented in the core of the campus LAN?

Answer: Classification and marking

28. If Cisco IP Phones have the capability to mark voice media and voice signaling traffic, why is it necessary to use access lists to classify these types of traffic?

Answer: Cisco Softphone and certain CTI applications might not have the capability to mark this traffic, yet they have the same QoS requirements.

29. When is a CoS-to-DSCP map used?

Answer: When a switch receives a trusted frame with a CoS value, it will assign a DSCP value to the packet based upon this map.

30. When should the CoS-to-DSCP map be modified?

Answer: When the CoS value does not match the desired DSCP value by default. For example, a received packet with a CoS value of 5 will be marked with a DSCP value of decimal 40, which is not the same as DSCP EF (decimal 46). The CoS-to-DSCP map must be modified to map a CoS value of 5 to a DSCP value of EF (decimal 46).

31. Which two queuing methods should be used in the service provider's backbone network?

Answer: LLQ/CBWFQ and MDRR

Index

C

F

G

H

I

W

SEARCH THOUSANDS OF BOOKS FROM LEADING PUBLISHERS

Safari® Bookshelf is a searchable electronic reference library for IT professionals that features more than 2,000 titles from technical publishers, including Cisco Press.

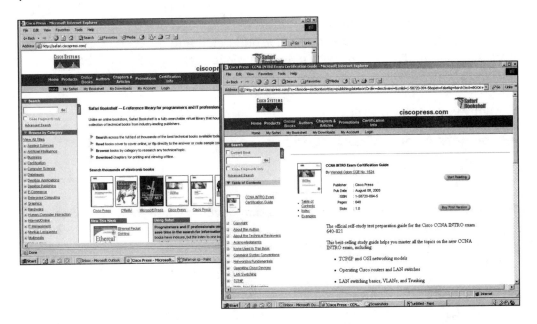

With Safari Bookshelf you can

- **Search** the full text of thousands of technical books, including more than 70 Cisco Press titles from authors such as Wendell Odom, Jeff Doyle, Bill Parkhurst, Sam Halabi, and Karl Solie.

- **Read** the books on My Bookshelf from cover to cover, or just flip to the information you need.

- **Browse** books by category to research any technical topic.

- **Download** chapters for printing and viewing offline.

With a customized library, you'll have access to your books when and where you need them—and all you need is a user name and password.

TRY SAFARI BOOKSHELF FREE FOR 14 DAYS!

You can sign up to get a 10-slot Bookshelf free for the first 14 days.
Visit **http://safari.ciscopress.com** to register.

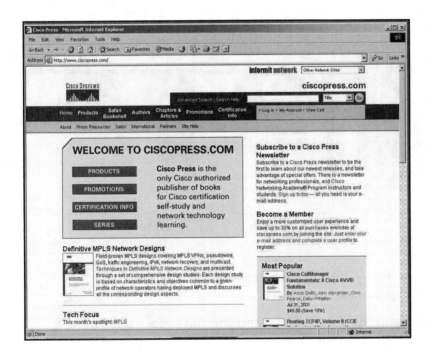
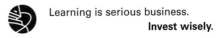

Cisco Press

3 STEPS TO LEARNING

STEP 1

First-Step

STEP 2

Fundamentals

STEP 3

**Networking
Technology Guides**

STEP 1   **First-Step**—Benefit from easy-to-grasp explanations.
No experience required!

STEP 2   **Fundamentals**—Understand the purpose, application,
and management of technology.

STEP 3   **Networking Technology Guides**—Gain the knowledge
to master the challenge of the network.

NETWORK BUSINESS SERIES

The Network Business series helps professionals tackle the
business issues surrounding the network. Whether you are a
seasoned IT professional or a business manager with minimal
technical expertise, this series will help you understand the
business case for technologies.

Justify Your Network Investment.

Look for Cisco Press titles at your favorite bookseller today.

Visit **www.ciscopress.com/series** for details on each of these book series.